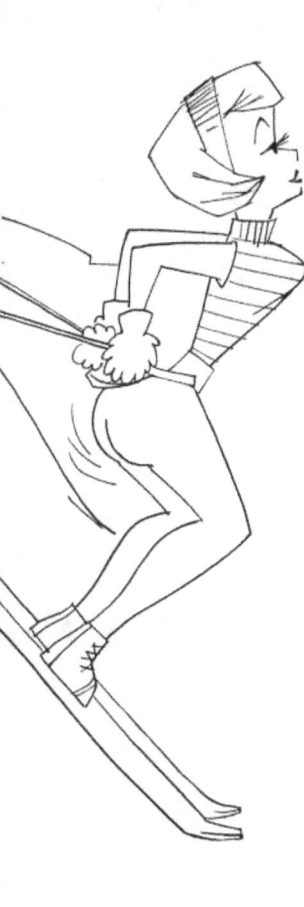

ADULT
COLORING
BOOKS
OF THE
1960s

COMPILED BY
ABOUT COMICS
CAMARILLO, CA

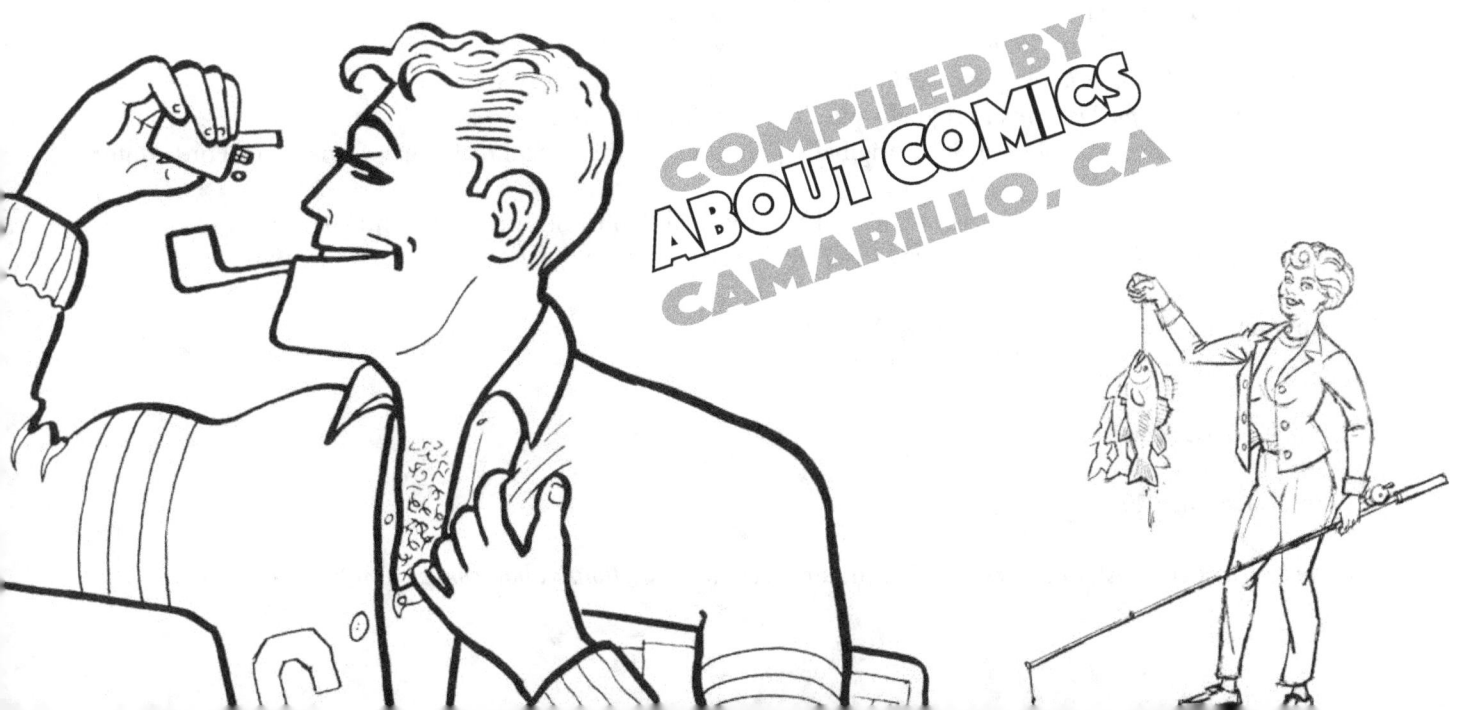

Adult Coloring Books of the 1960s

The Executive Coloring Book originally published by The Funny Products Company., 1961.
The Original Campus Coloring Book originally published by Magnum Publications, Inc., 1962.
Bridge Players' Coloring Book originally published by Heines Publishing, 1962.
The Saga of Dr. Anton Pazu originally published by Project D, 1962.
The Bureaucrat's Coloring Book originally published by Athene Press, 1962.
The Amazing Los Angeles Angels Coloring Book originally published in 1962.
A Coloring Book for Fishermen originally published by IMPKO, 1962.
The 1963 Car Buyer's Coloring Book originally published by the Lincoln-Mercury Division of Ford Motor Company, 1962.
The Skier's Coloring Book originally published by Universal Publishing and Distributing Corporation, 1962.
Mother Goose is Loose and *The Therapy Coloring Book* originally published by Kanrom Inc., 1962.

Annotations created for this edition by About Comics.
Compilation copyright 2016 About Comics.

ISBN: 978-1936404-57-5

Published June, 2016.

For bulk orders, custom covers, or other inquiries, contact *questions@aboutcomics.com*

CONTENTS

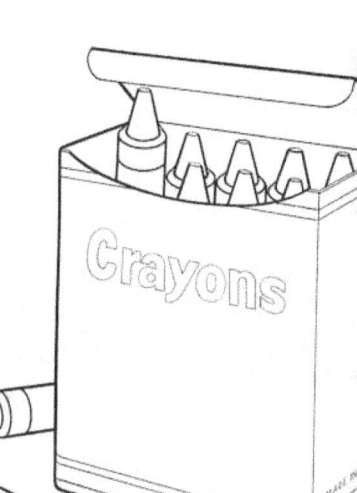

FOREWORD

With America in the throes of an adult coloring book craze, it's easy to overlook that we've had such a craze before, in the early 1960s. However, the adult coloring books of the time were very different. They were not meant to be colored for a pastime or as therapy. Indeed, they were not meant to be colored at all (although sometimes they got colored nonetheless.) Instead, these books used a parody of the coloring book form in order to cast comment on society, on politics, on careers, and on hobbies.

The very first adult coloring book was *The Executive Coloring Book*, a look at the New York men in their grey flannel suits and the numb lifestyles they lead, which you'll see in just a couple pages. When that book was released in December of 1961, it rushed onto the best seller lists – and it wasn't the only adult coloring book to do so, as *JFK Coloring Book* (which you can find reprint in Cold War Coloring: Political Adult Coloring Books of the Kennedy Era, a sister volume to this one) achieved even more success.

Success breeds imitation, in droves. Some of them kept up with the sort of snide social commentary of Executive, with coloring books supposedly aimed at bureaucrats or Senators. Others actuall were aimed at the folks they were making fun of, as you'll see in the coloring books for dentists, fishermen, skiers, and bridge players in this book. They were even used to exploit and to advertise products.

And as with anything that seems cool and fresh, it can be overused and become passé. Almost all the coloring books in this collection are from 1962. By the time 1963 rolled around, the craze had burned out. It didn't kill the satirical coloring book entirely; there continue to be occasional examples of new ones even to this day.

So here's a little piece of history for you. It's easy reading, with lots of pictures. And if you want to get out your crayons, that's up to you!

Nat Gertler
Publisher
About Comics
June, 2016

THE EXECUTIVE COLORING BOOK

A Coloring Book for Executives

Two of the three people who created this craze-launching book, Cohen and Altman, would team with Robert E. Nakin the next year to create *The John Birch Coloring Book*, taking on the ultraconsertive John Birch Society. (You can see it in this book's sister volume, *Cold War Coloring: Political Adult Coloring Books of the Kennedy Era*) Altman himself would return to the form yet again in 2014 to send up conservative political funders the Koch brothers with his *The Choke Brothers Coloring Book*, which you can learn more about at www.ChokeBrothers.com.

Published by
The Funny Products Company
1047 W. Albion Avenue
Chicago 26, Illinois

THIS IS MY COLORING BOOK

My name is _____

My company is _____

My title is _____

My next title will be _____

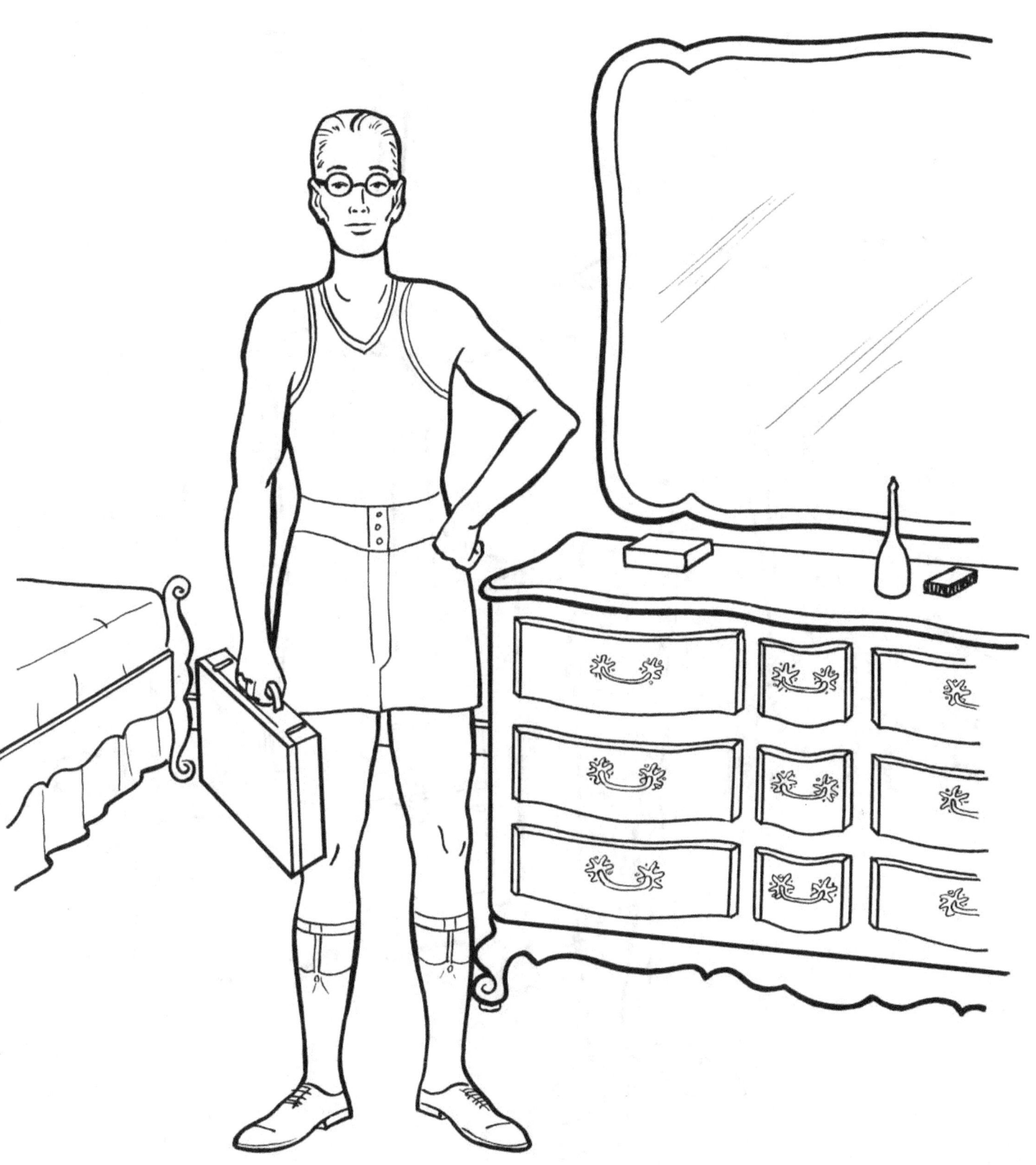

THIS IS ME. I am an executive. Executives are important. They go to important offices and do important things.
Color my underwear important.

11

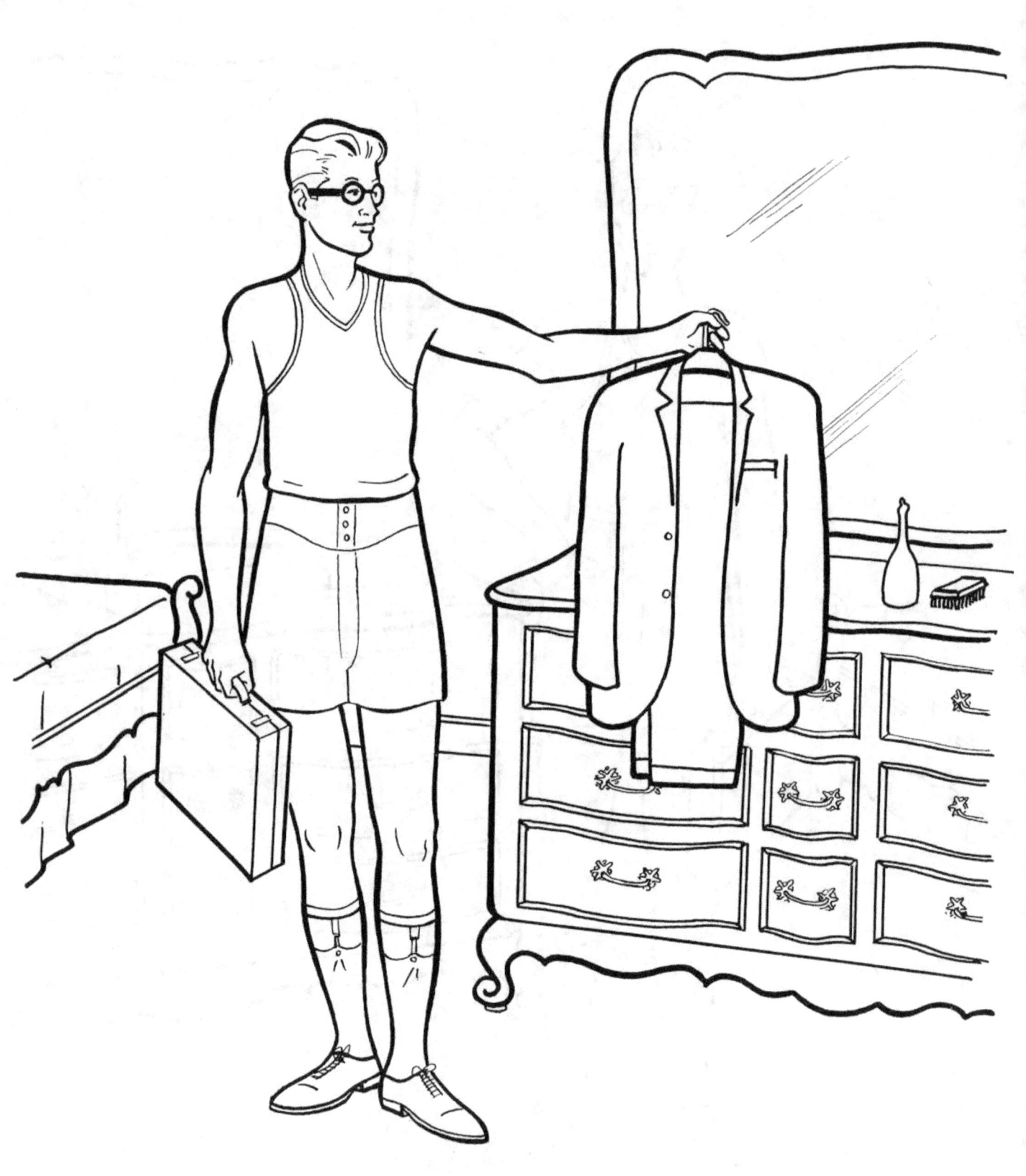

THIS IS MY SUIT. Color it gray or I will lose my job.

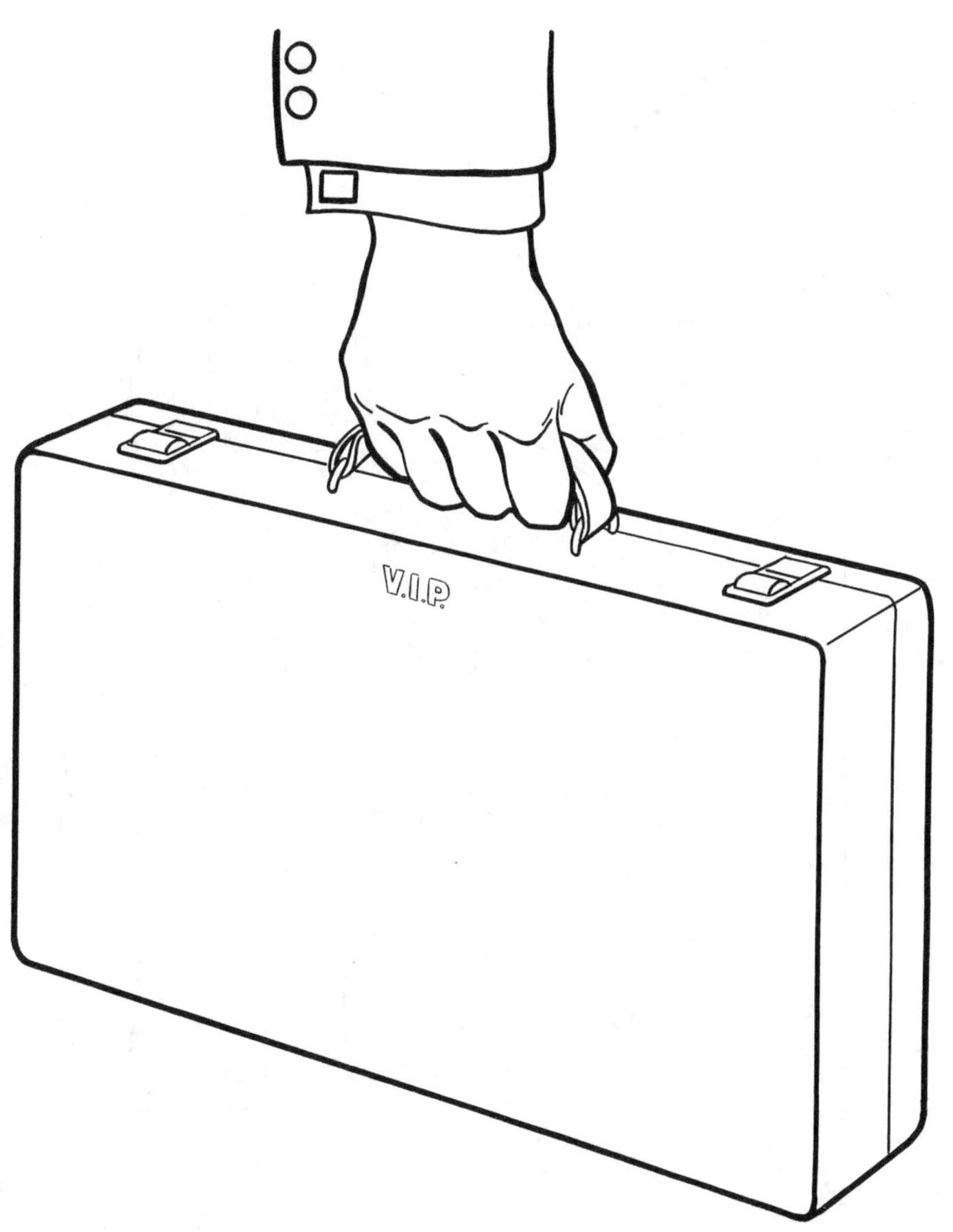

THIS IS MY ATTACHE' CASE. It helps people know I am an executive. It makes me look efficient. Organized. Competent. I wonder if it opens.

13

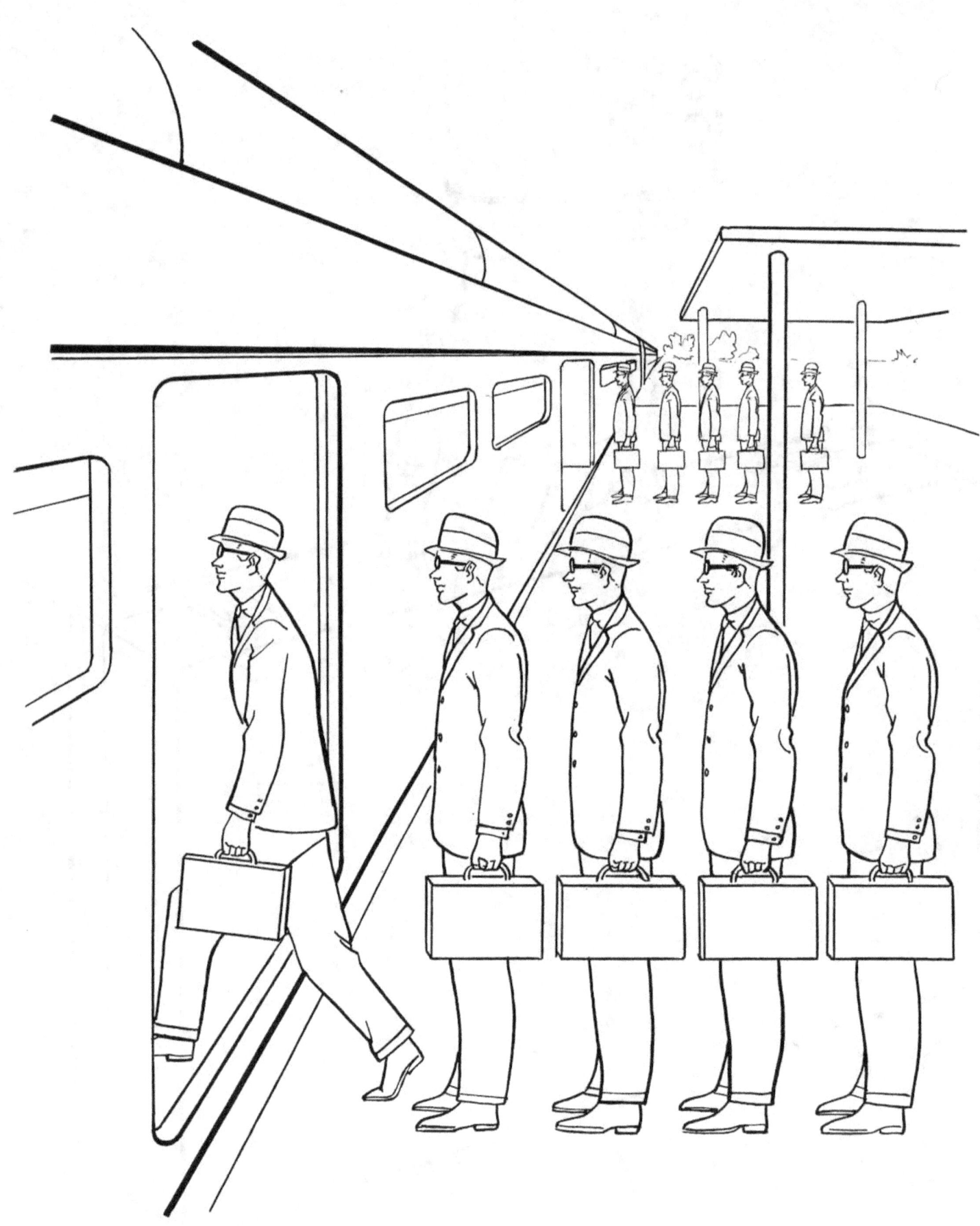

THIS IS MY TRAIN. It takes me to my office every day. You meet lots
of interesting people on the train. Color them all gray.

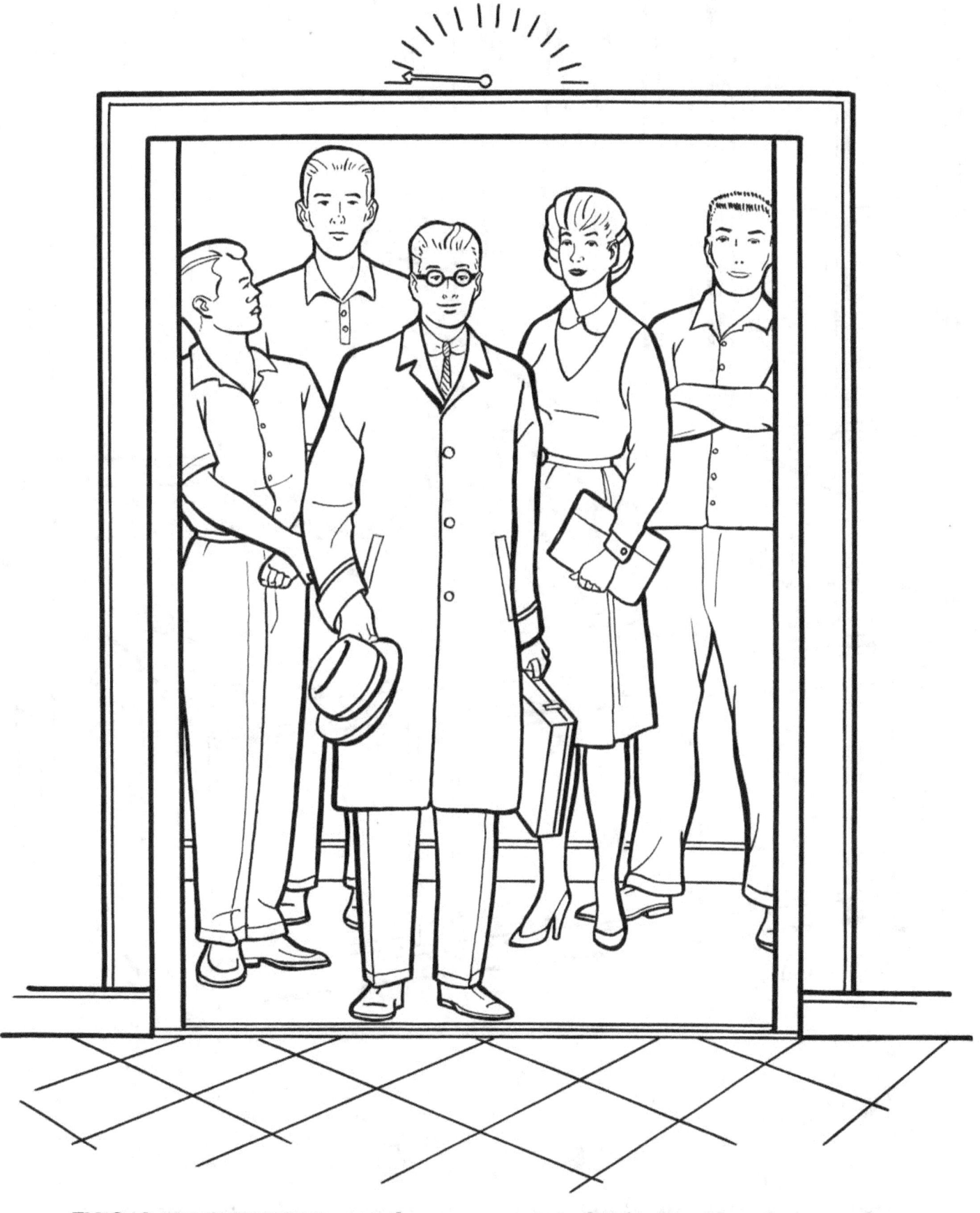

THIS IS MY ELEVATOR. It takes me way up high. People who are not executives stand right next to me in my elevator. They are all right, but I would not want my daughter to marry one of them.

15

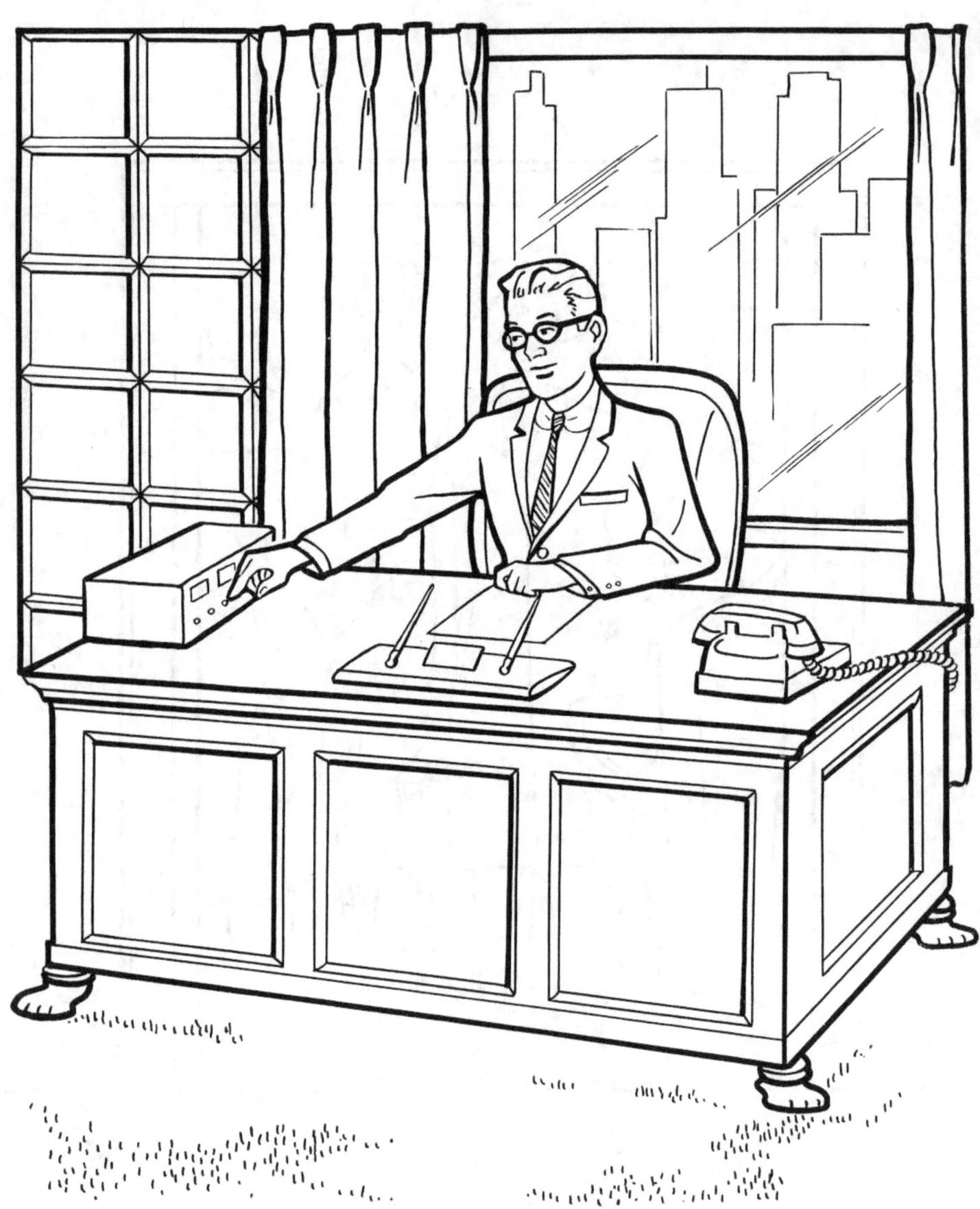

THIS IS MY DESK. It is mahogany. Important people have mahogany desks. My walls are mahogany, too. I wish I were mahogany.

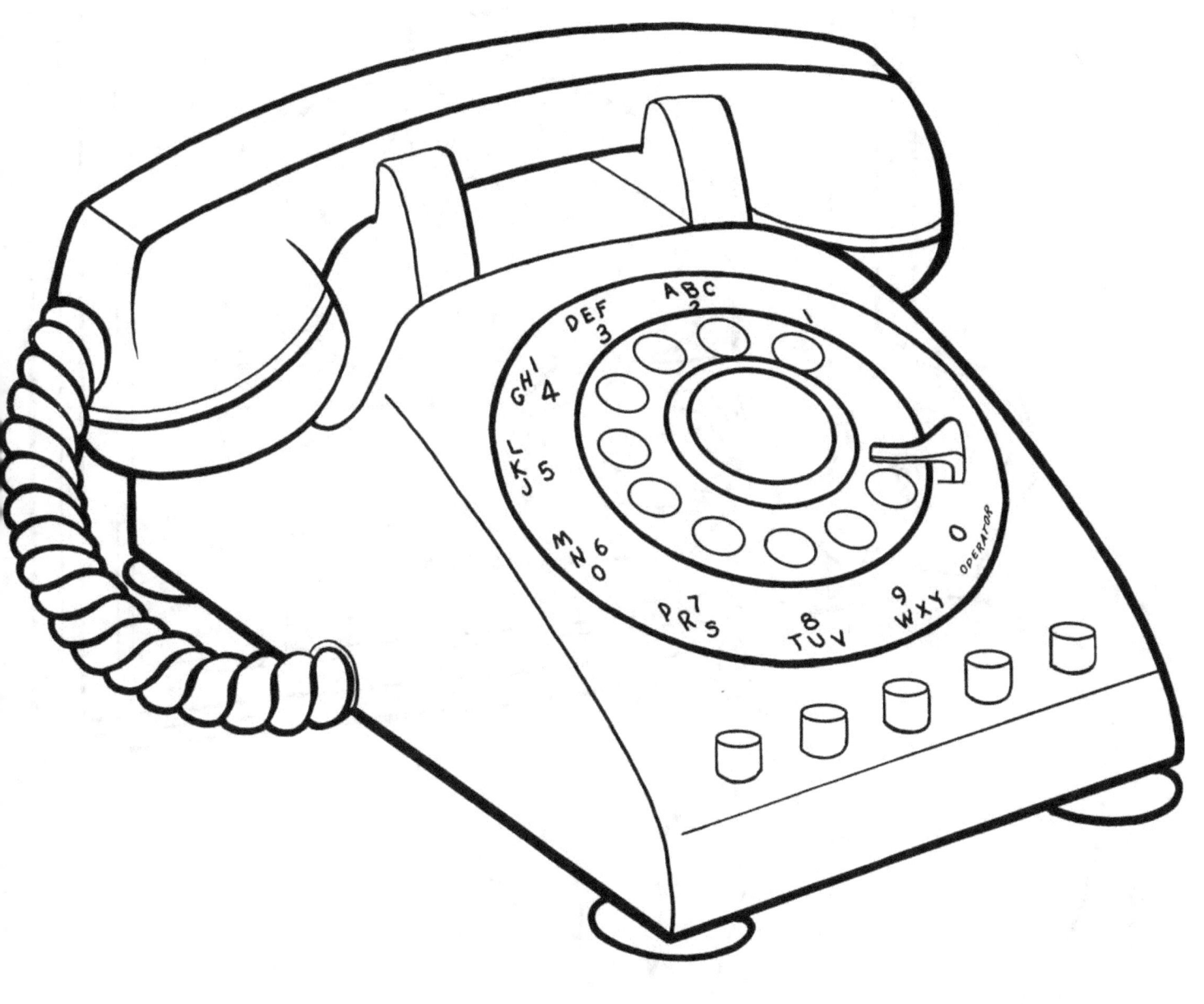

THIS IS MY TELEPHONE. It has five buttons. Count them. One, two, three, four, five. Five buttons. How many buttons does your telephone have? Mine has five.

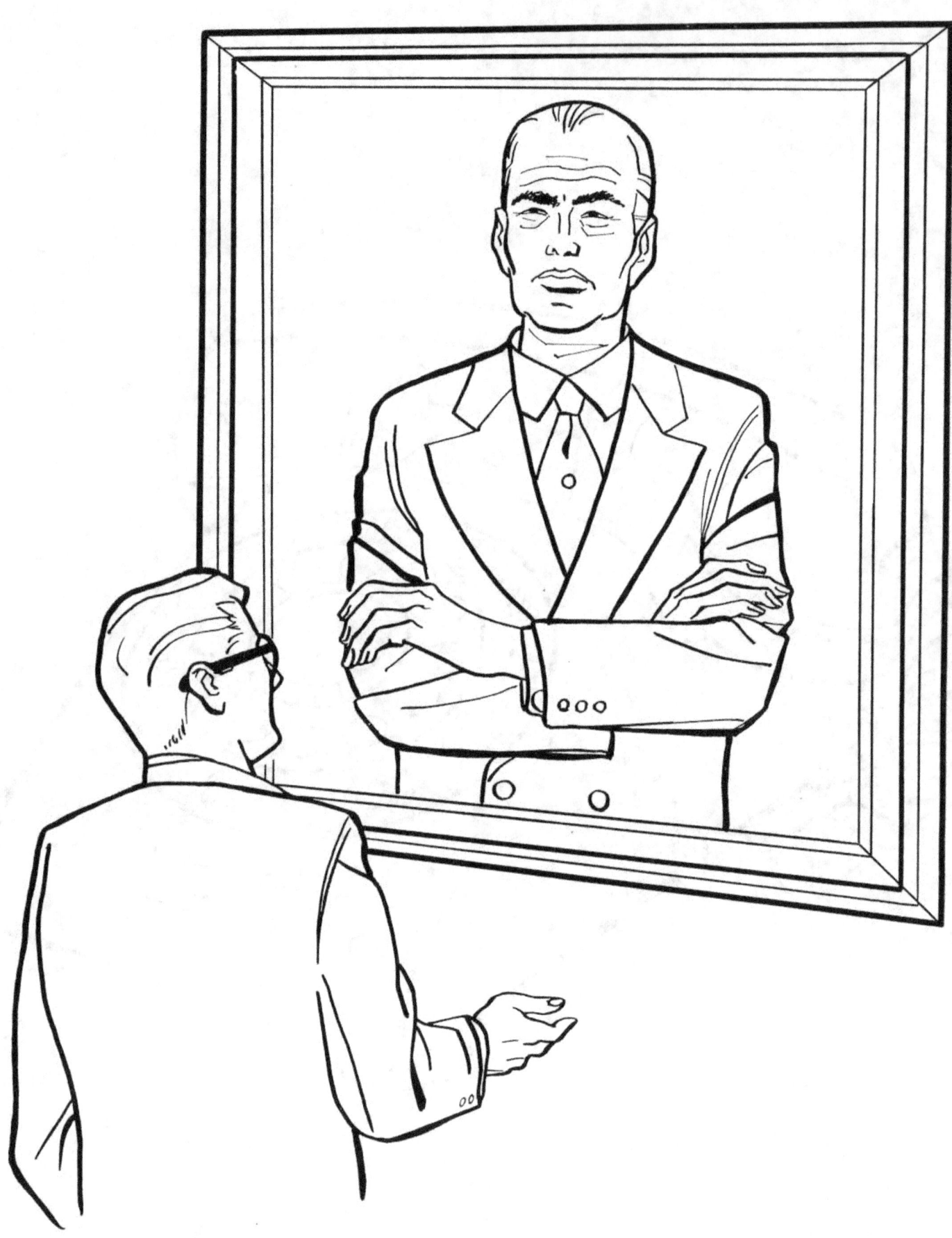

THIS IS MY COMPANY'S PRESIDENT. He hates me. He calls me bad names, but he gives me lots of raises. My wife calls him "papa".

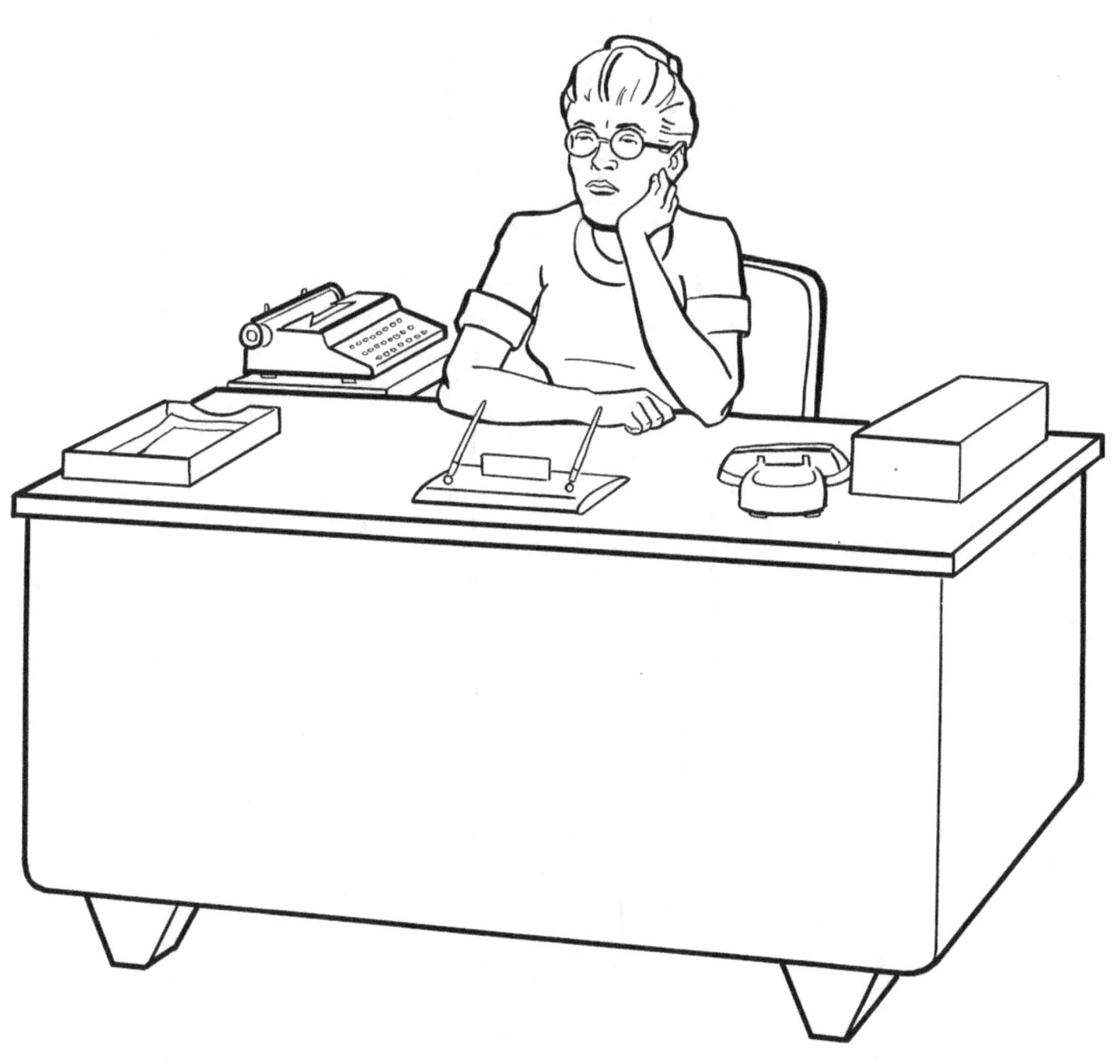

THIS IS MY SECRETARY. I hate her. She is mean. I used to have a soft, round lady. But my wife called her papa.

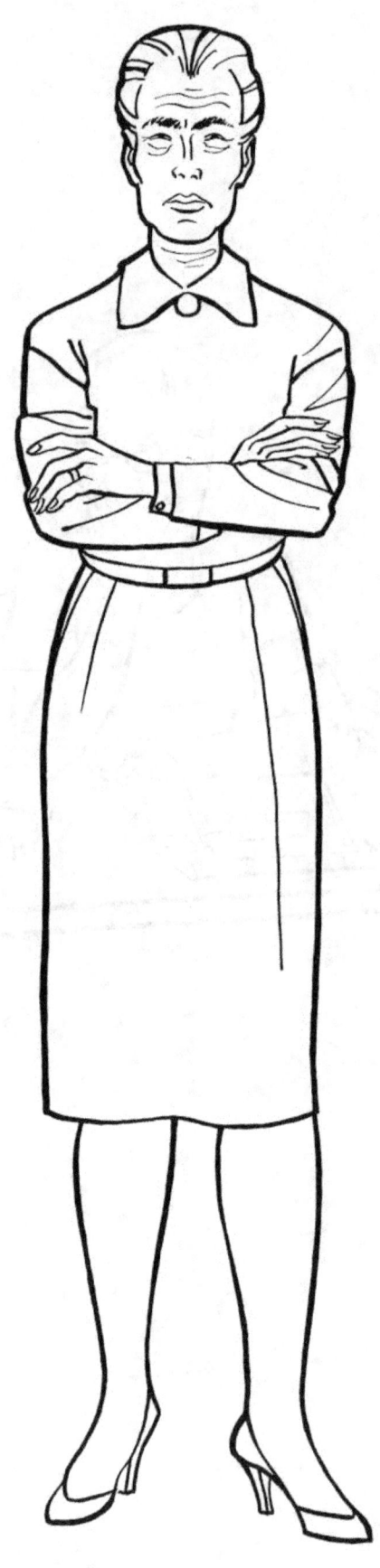

THIS IS MY WIFE.

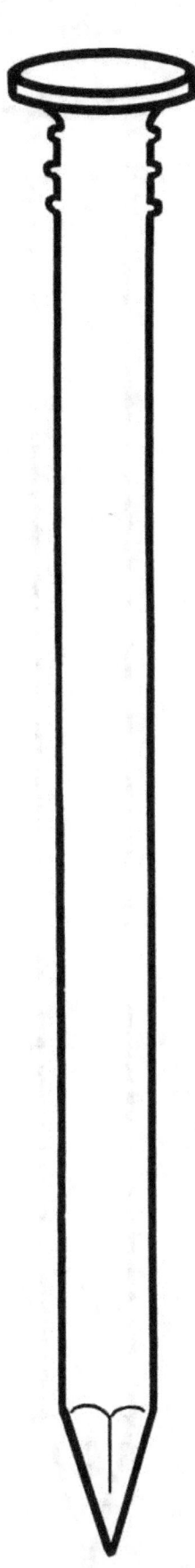

THIS IS THE PRODUCT MY COMPANY MAKES. It is an
inter-fibrous friction-fastener.

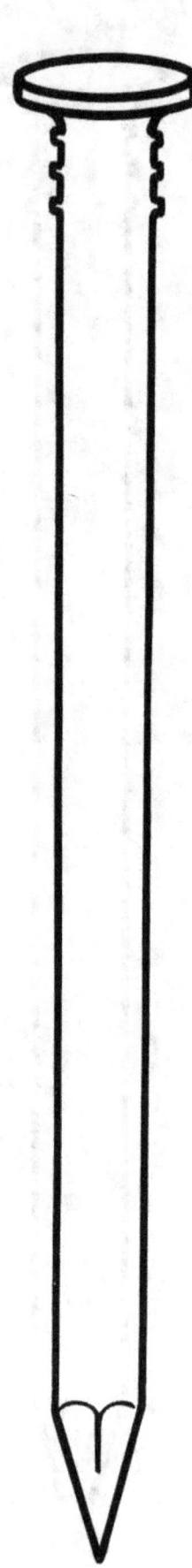

THIS IS OUR COMPETITOR'S PRODUCT. It is a nail.

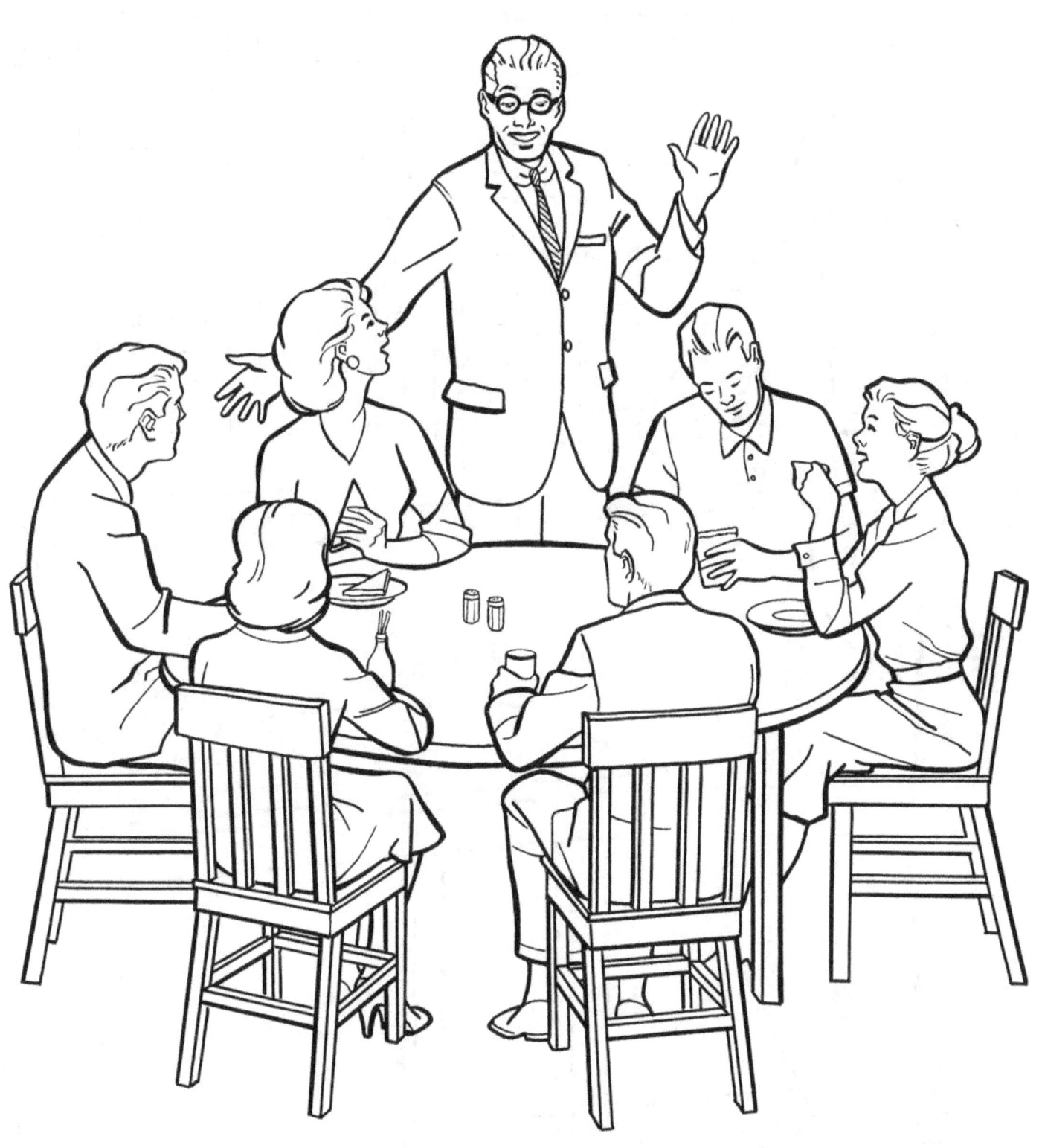

THIS IS MY COMPANY'S LUNCHROOM. Sometimes I walk through it and smile at the employees. "Hello, employees," my smile says, "I am one of you." I never eat there.

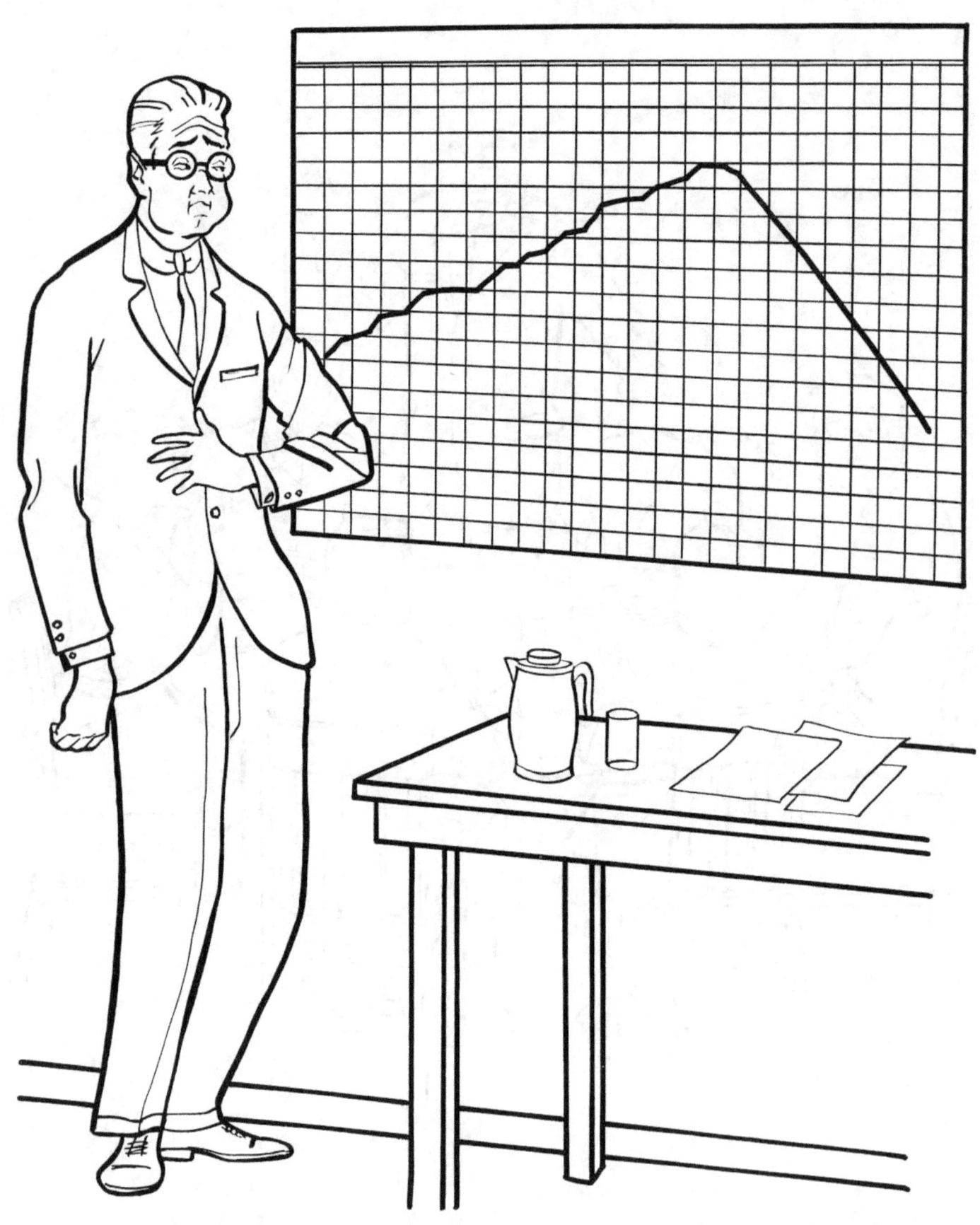

THIS IS MY SALES CHART. When the line goes up, I feel good. When the line goes down, I get gas. Color me green.

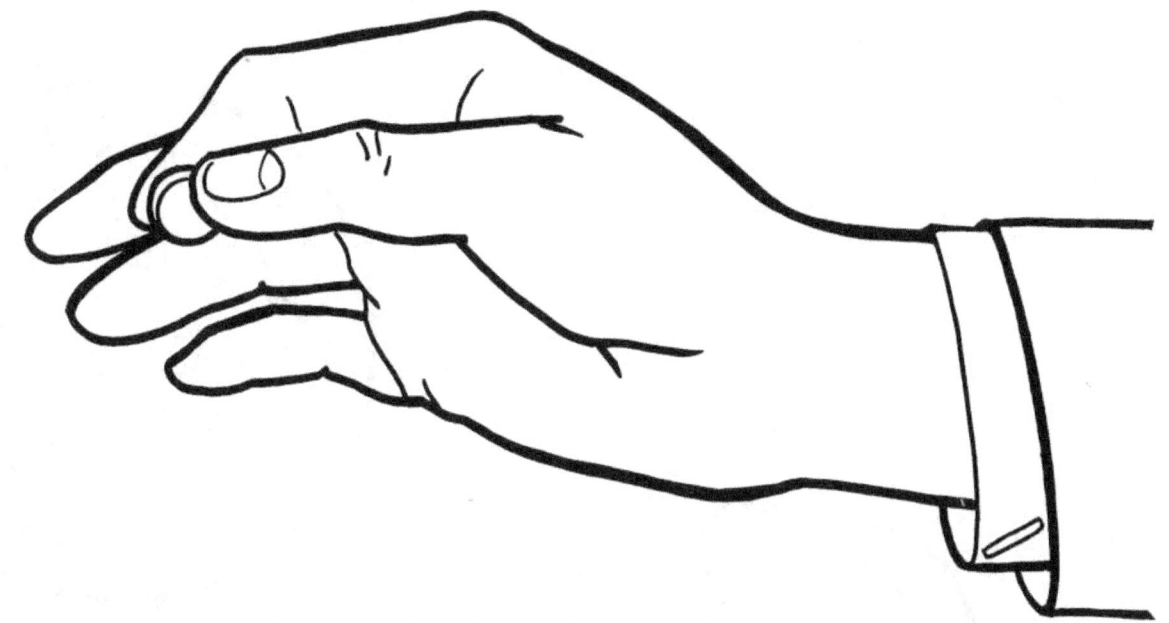

THIS IS MY PILL. It is round. It is pink. It makes me not care.

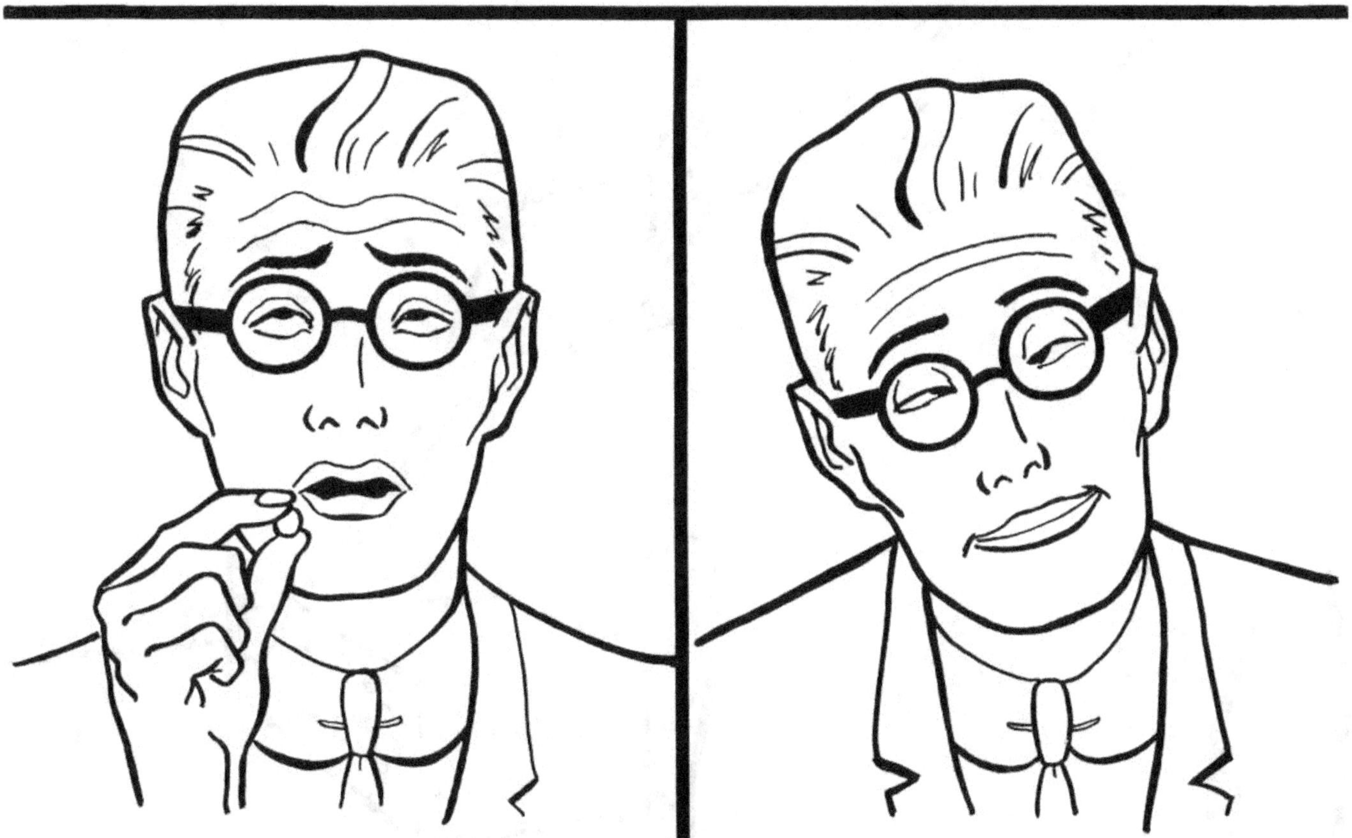

Watch me take my round, pink pill   . . . and not care.

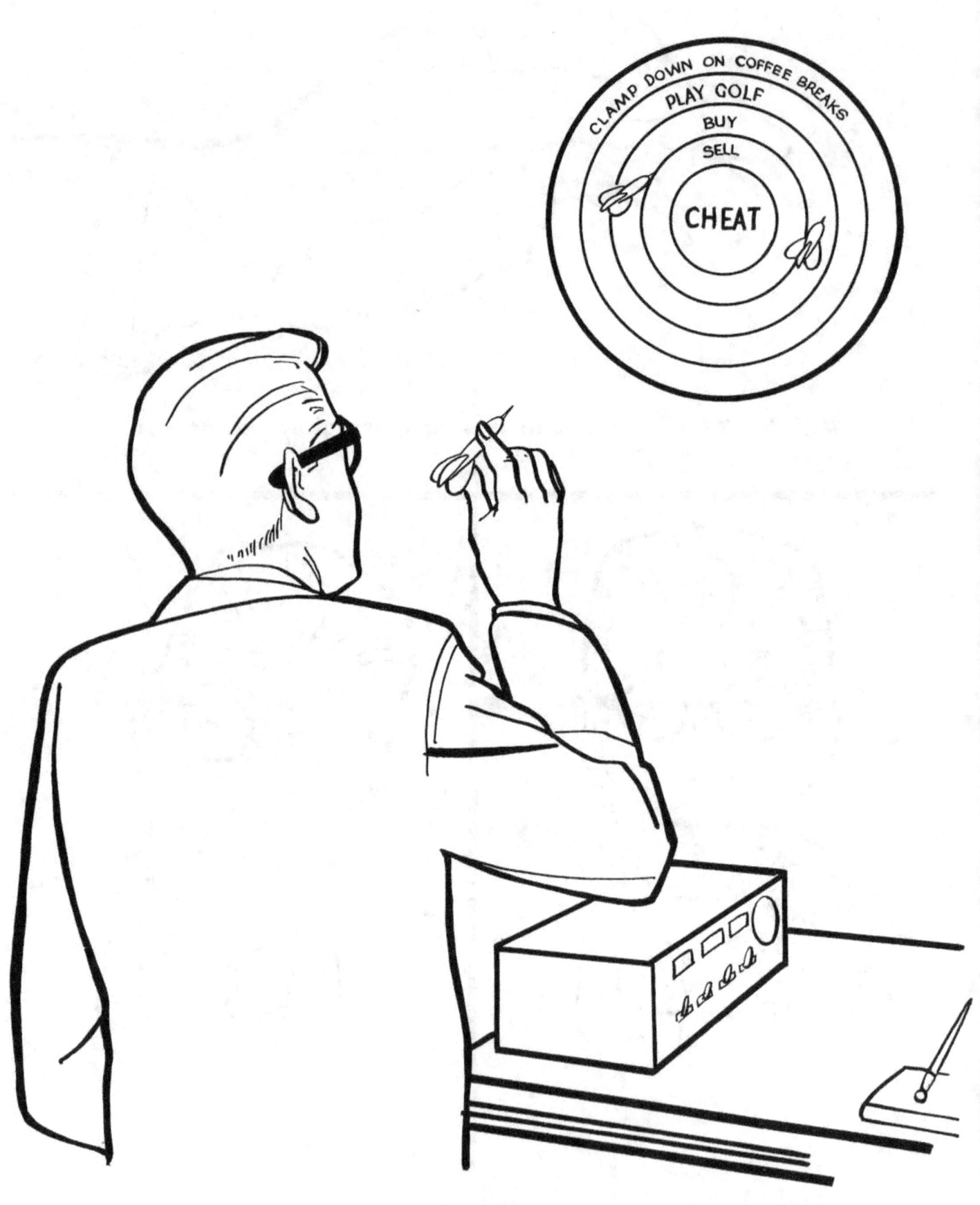

THIS IS MY SECRET.

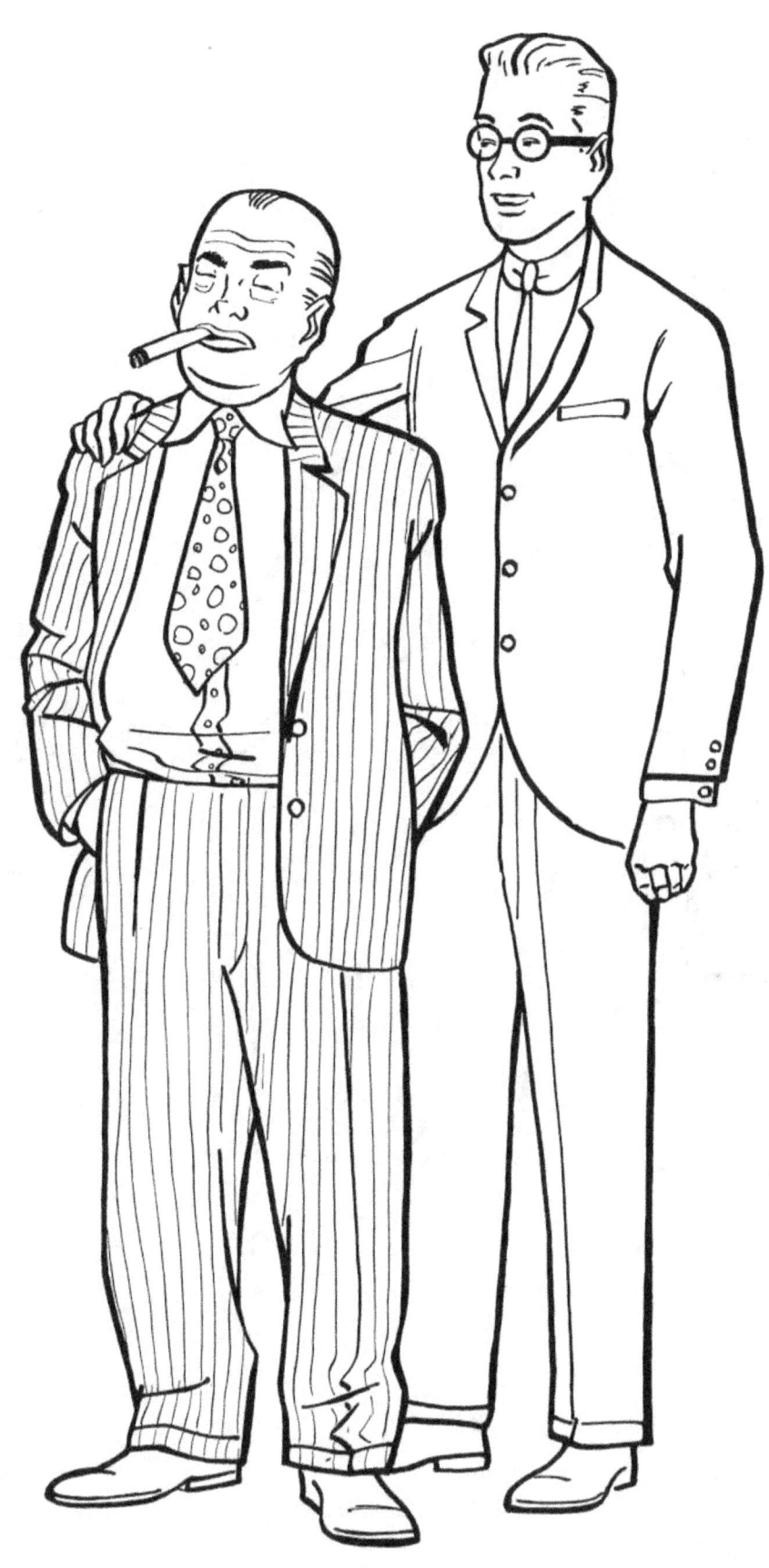

THIS IS A CUSTOMER. He smells bad. He has money to spend. I like him.

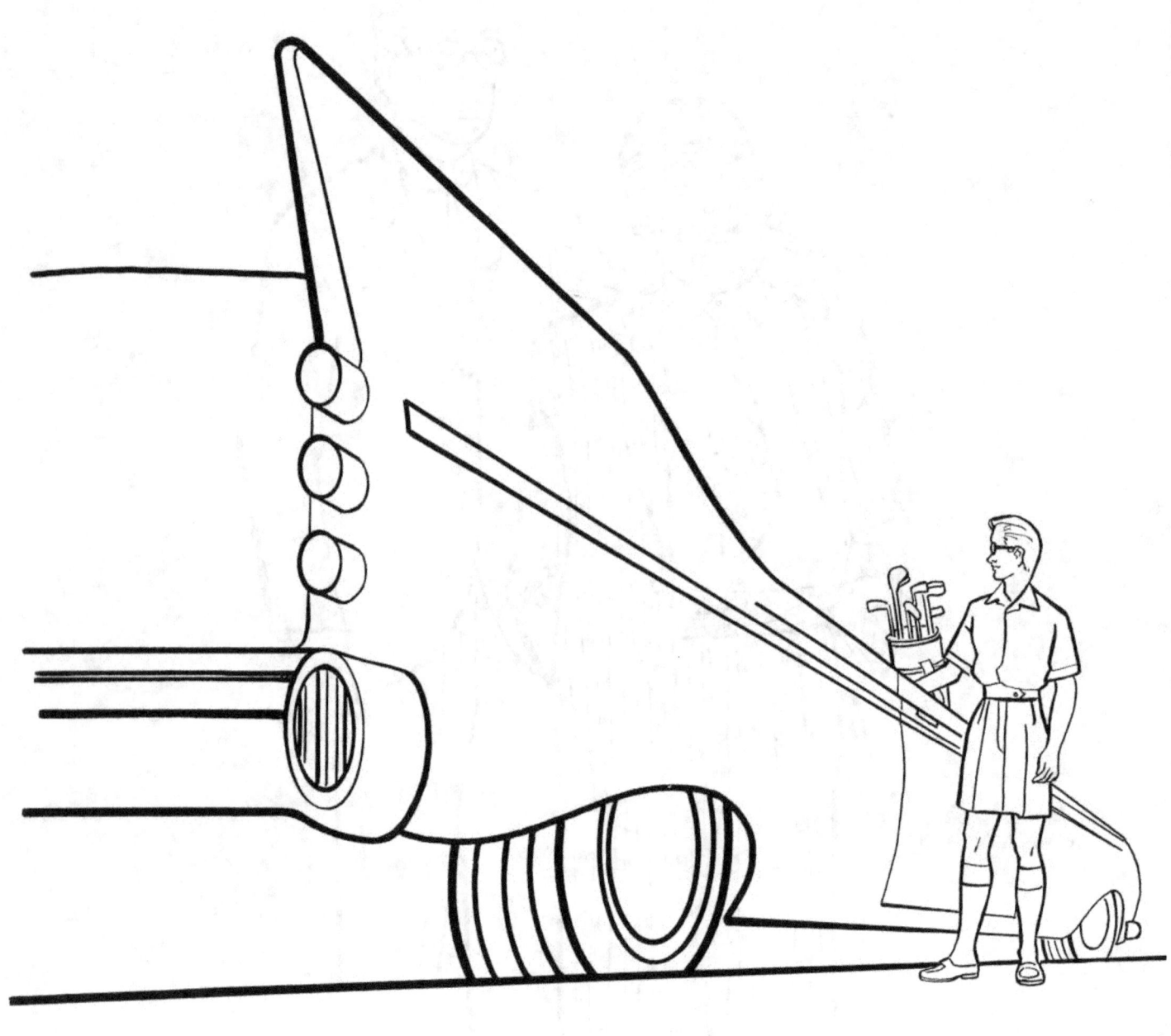

THIS IS MY CAR. It is a company car. It is used for deliveries only.

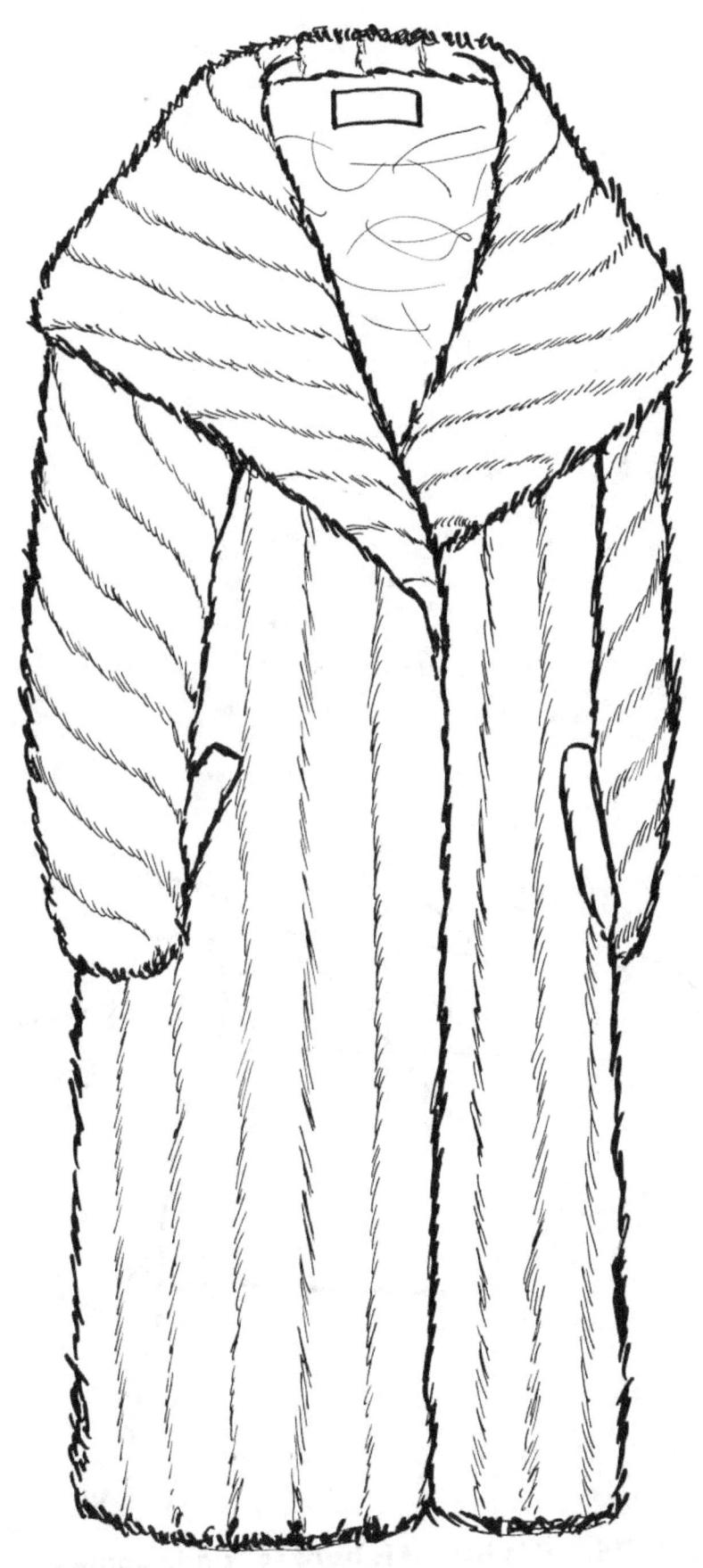

THIS IS MY MINK COAT.   I take it to my club. I take it to banquets.
It goes lots of places with me.   My wife comes, too.

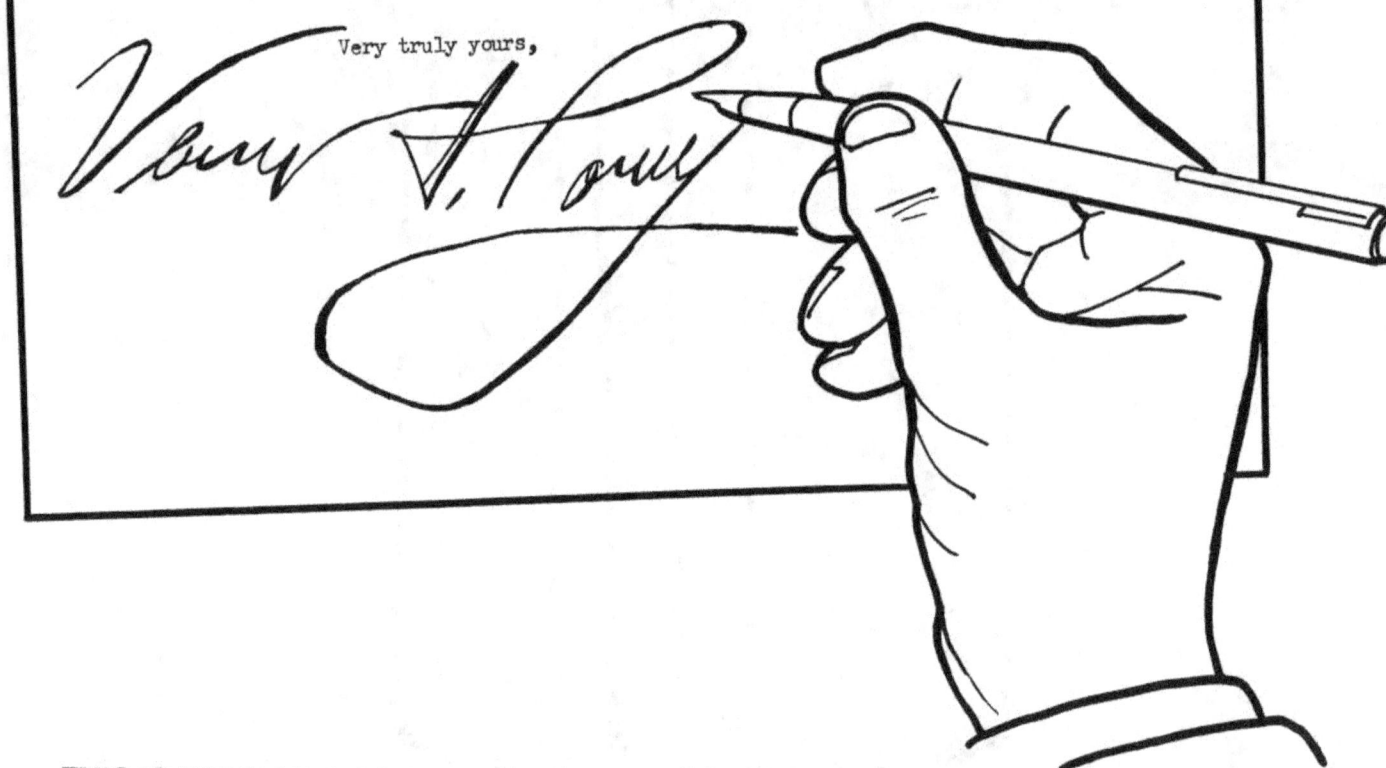

Furthermore notwithstanding heretofore consequently, stock option. Business-wise general picture debenture. Sales picture tax loss henceforth. Net worth.

Amortize co-operate firm up cost-plus employee relationship profit picture. Simultaneously depletion allowance company policy heretofore solidify. Corporate bond industrial outlook. Inventory profit straightforward profit margin complaint heretofore without prejudice.

Budget non-recurring phenomenon co-operate option. General picture labor problem annuity, inventory kickback subsequently nonetheless.

Fiscal year notwithstanding company policy gross mark up. Debenture solid front. Government percent draft re-order renewable. Contractually solid front.

With best personal regards to Mildred and the children.

Very truly yours,

THIS IS MY SIGNATURE. It is big. It is hard to read. Some people have little signatures that are easy to read. They never make over a hundred a week.

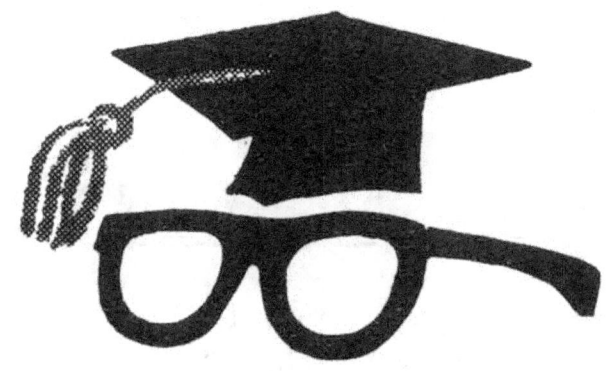

THE ORIGINAL CAMPUS COLORING BOOK

by **MORT GERBERG** AND THE **EDITORS OF SWANK**

MY NAME IS _____

MY COLLEGE IS _____

MY CLASS IS _____

MY FRATERNITY IS _____

WHEN I GRADUATE I WILL BE A _____

The Original Campus Coloring Book was a 1962 release by Magnum Publications, publishers of the skin magazine *Swank*. Artist Mort Gerberg is still a working cartoonist over half a century later, having racked up respectable credits at such key cartoon markets as *Playboy* and the *New Yorker*.

This volume was later reprinted under the title *The Campus Coloring Book*, no "Original."

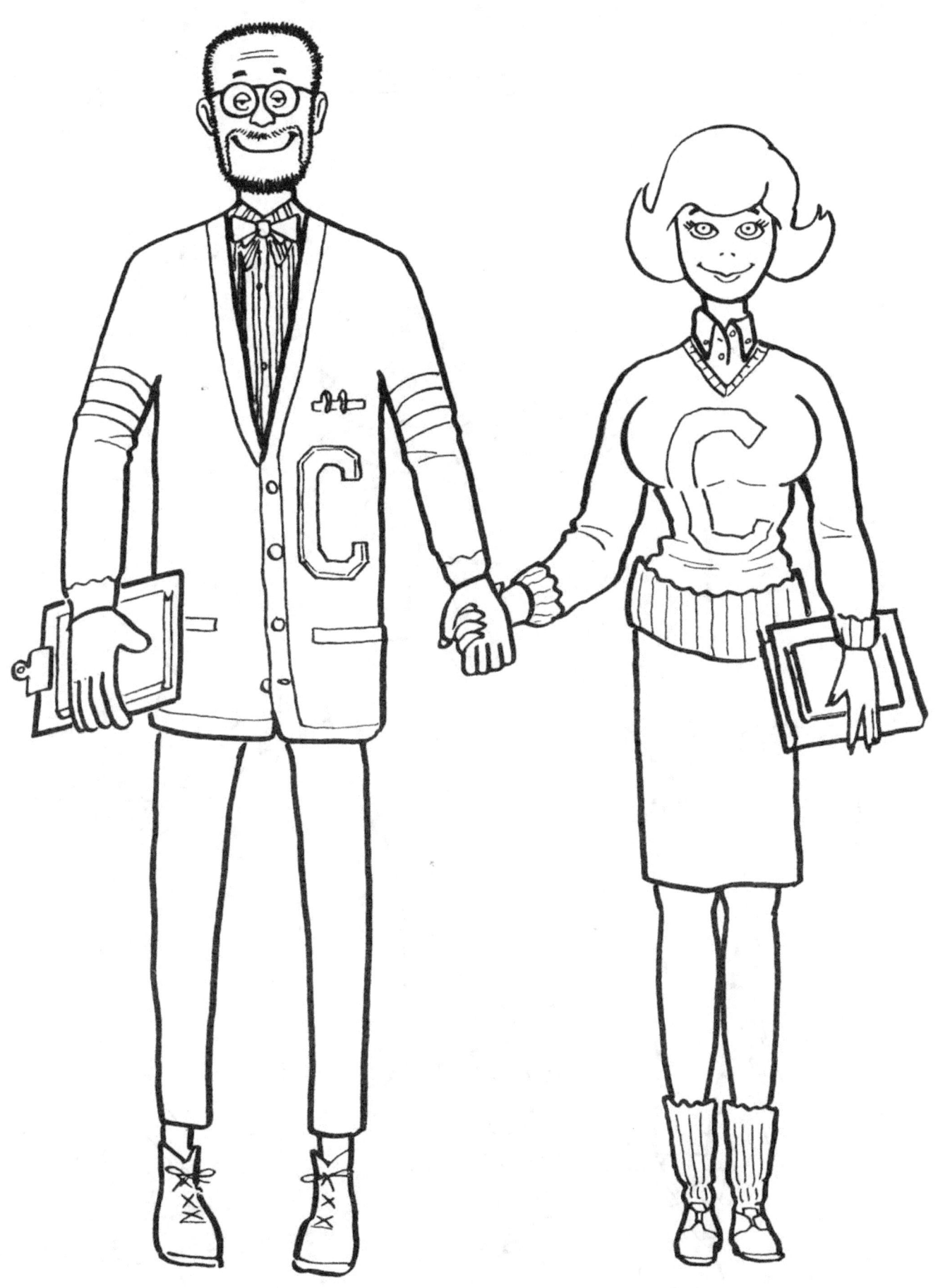

I am Ted. I am Pam. We go to college. We are smart. President Kennedy says we are the hope of America's future. Color us red, white and blue. Maybe you better leave out the red.

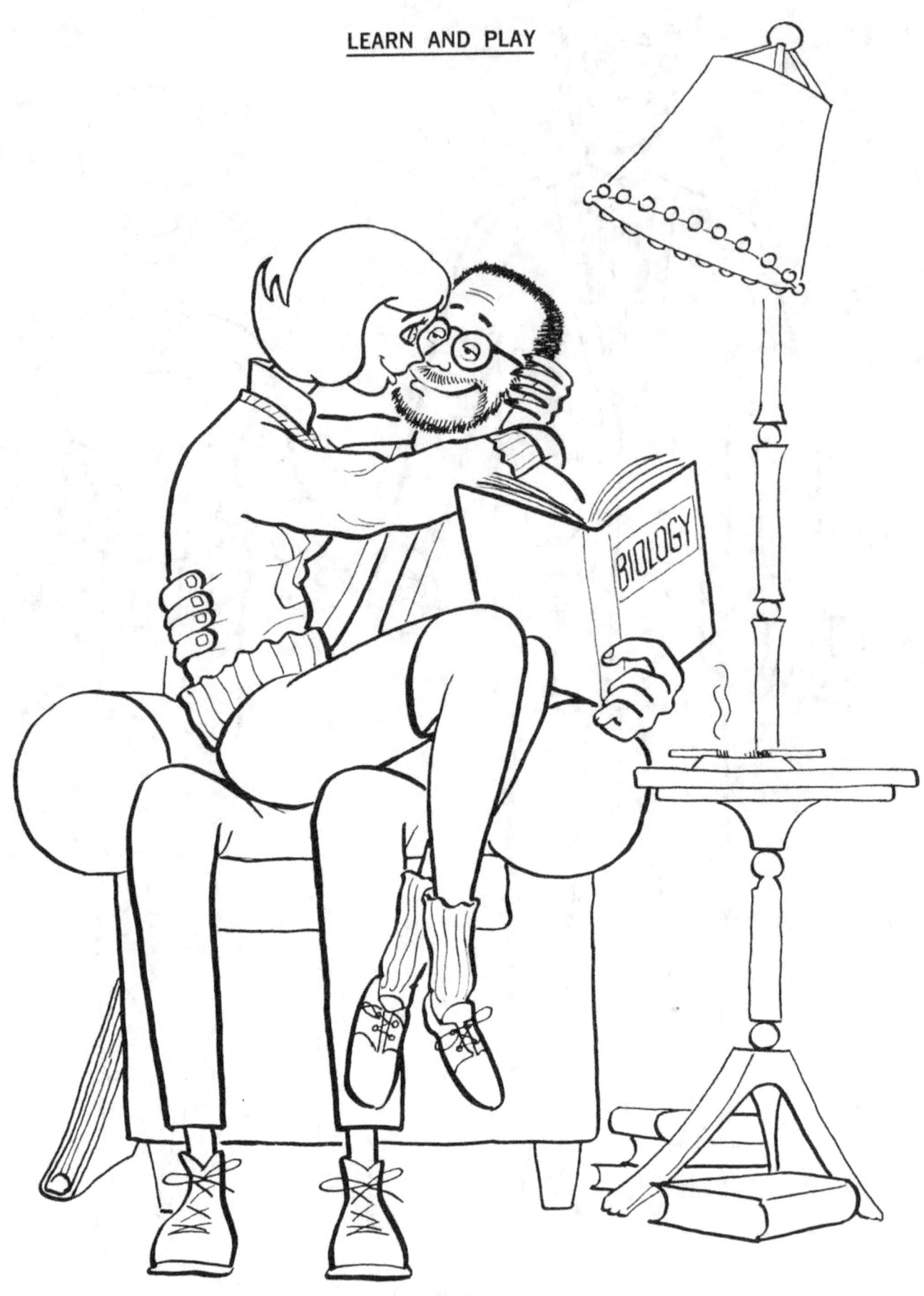

College is to learn and play. See us learn? You should see us play. Color us excited.

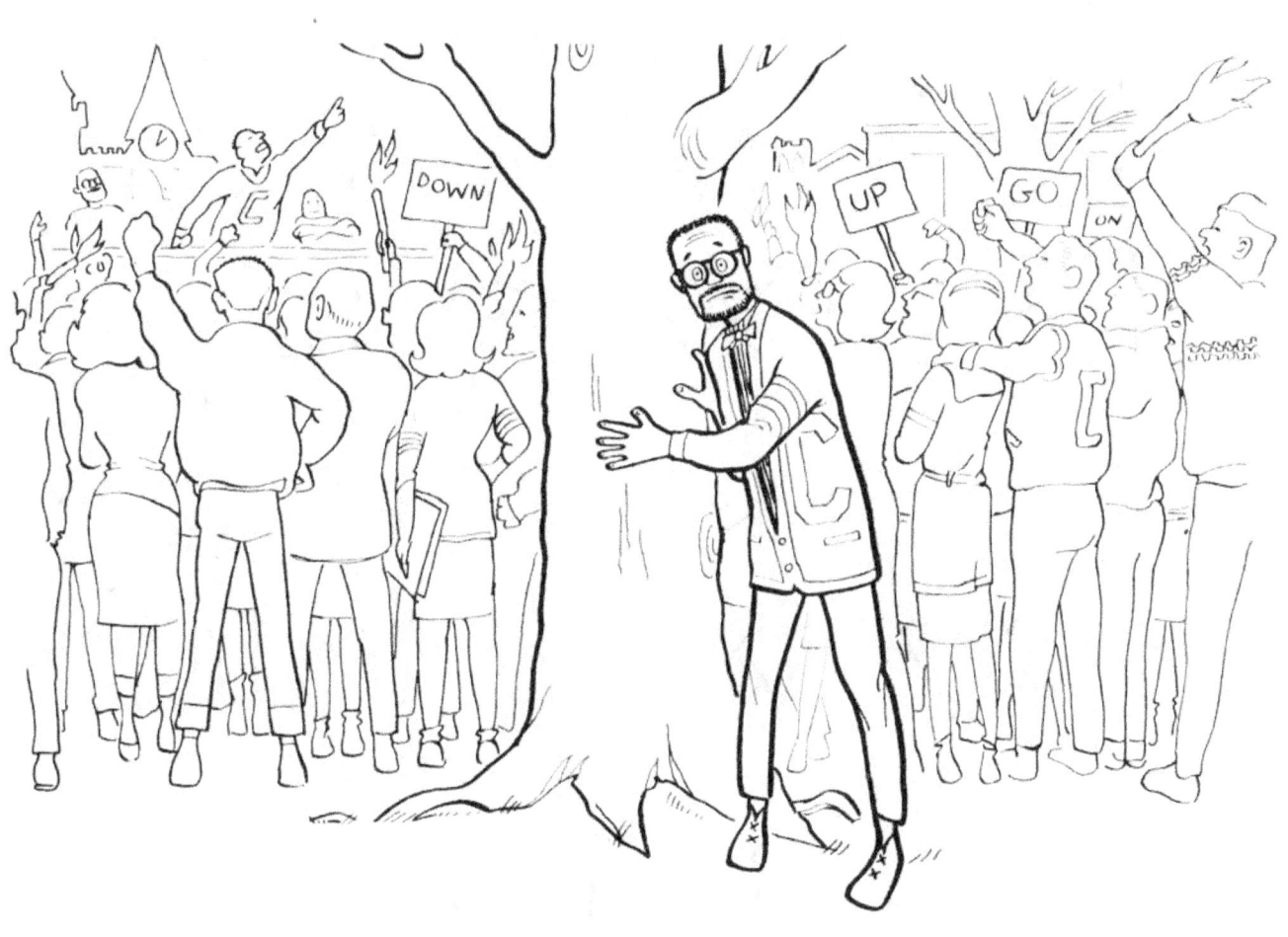

This is a campus political rally. Rallies are important.
Rallies make you have opinions. Rallies make you think. I don't
know what this rally is about but I don't think I should be
seen here. Color me yellow.

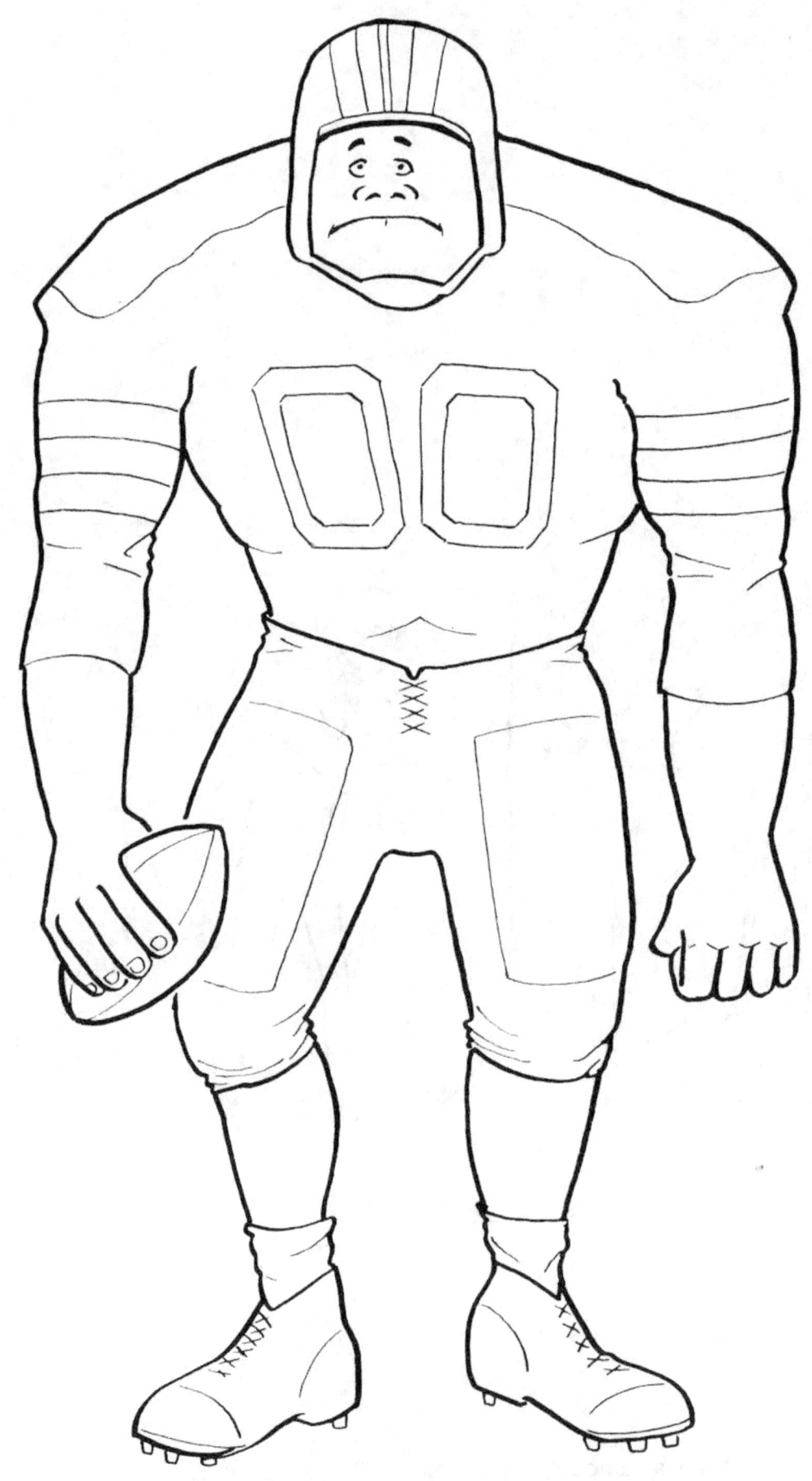

This is Bronco. Bronco is our fullback. Bronco runs fast.
See him run? The other way, Bronco! The other way!

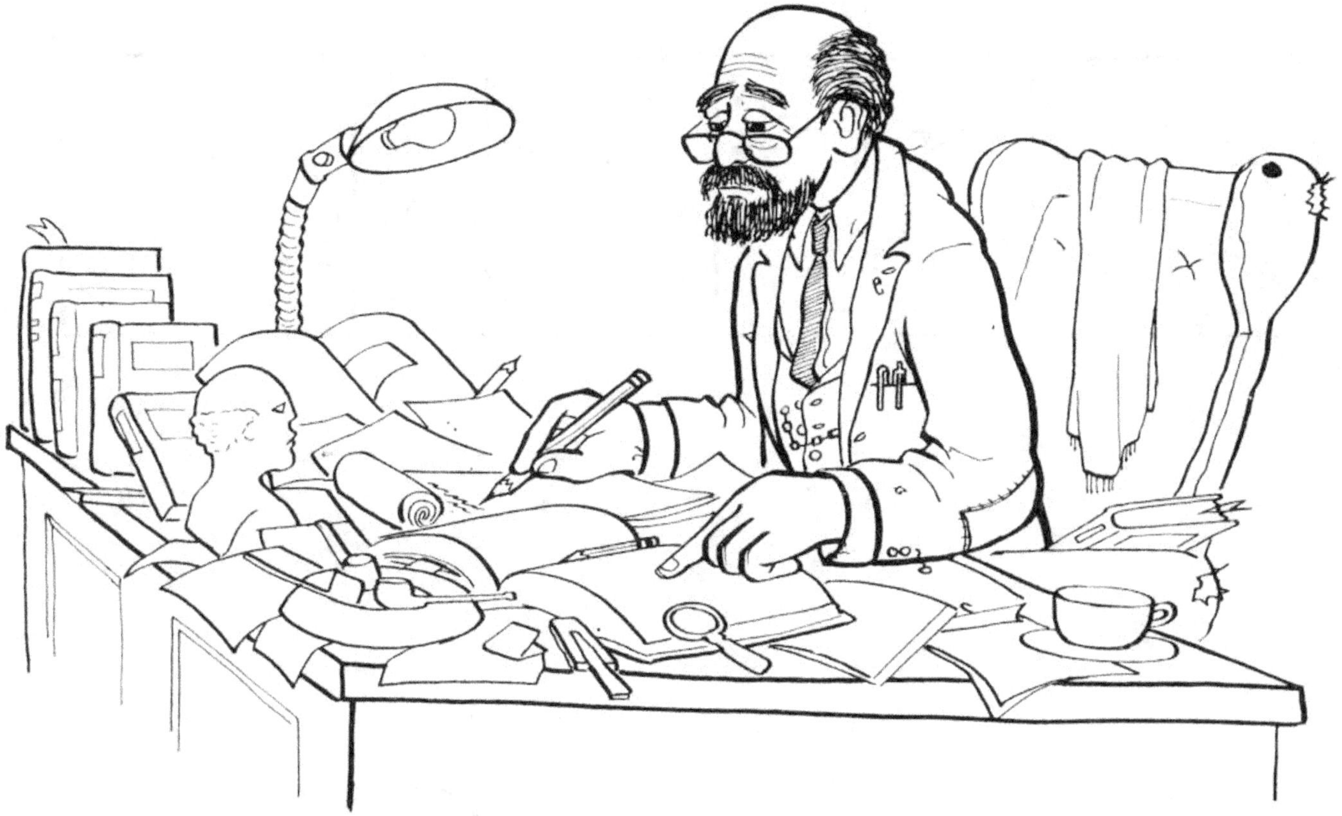

See Professor Eirkopf? He has nine degrees. He speaks twelve languages. He has written eighteen books. He makes less money than Bronco. Silly professor! Color him silly.

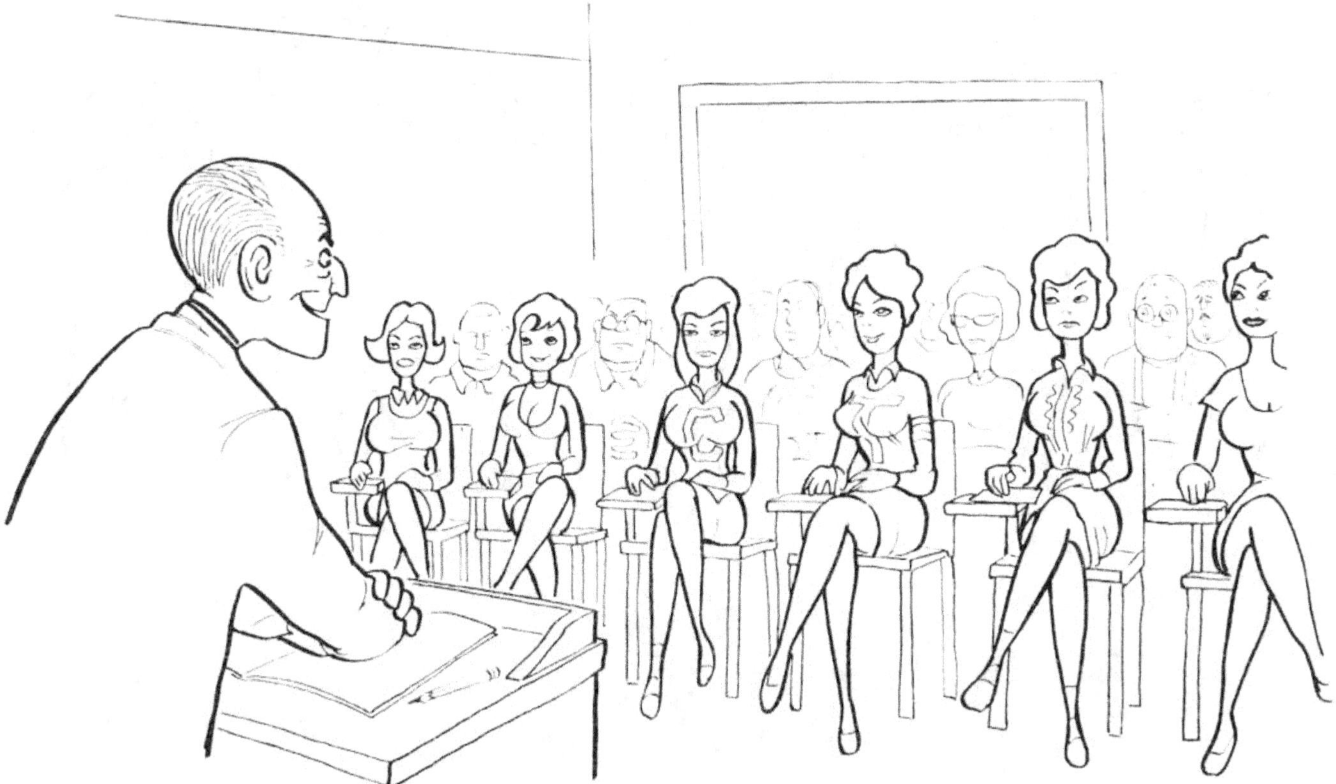

This is Professor Lecher. He's a tough marker. Color him purple. (But give all the girls in the front row an A)

THINGS TO MAKE AND COLOR

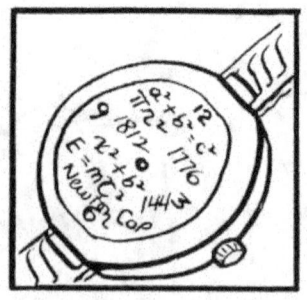 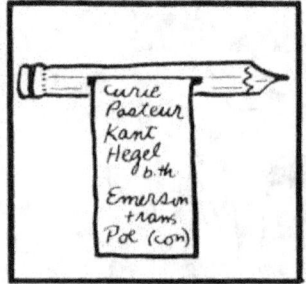 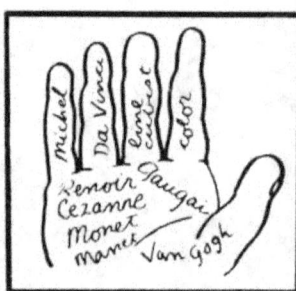 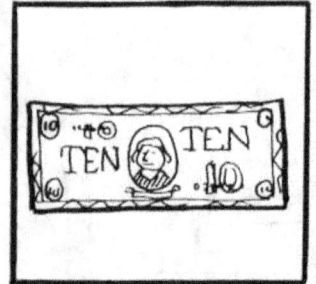

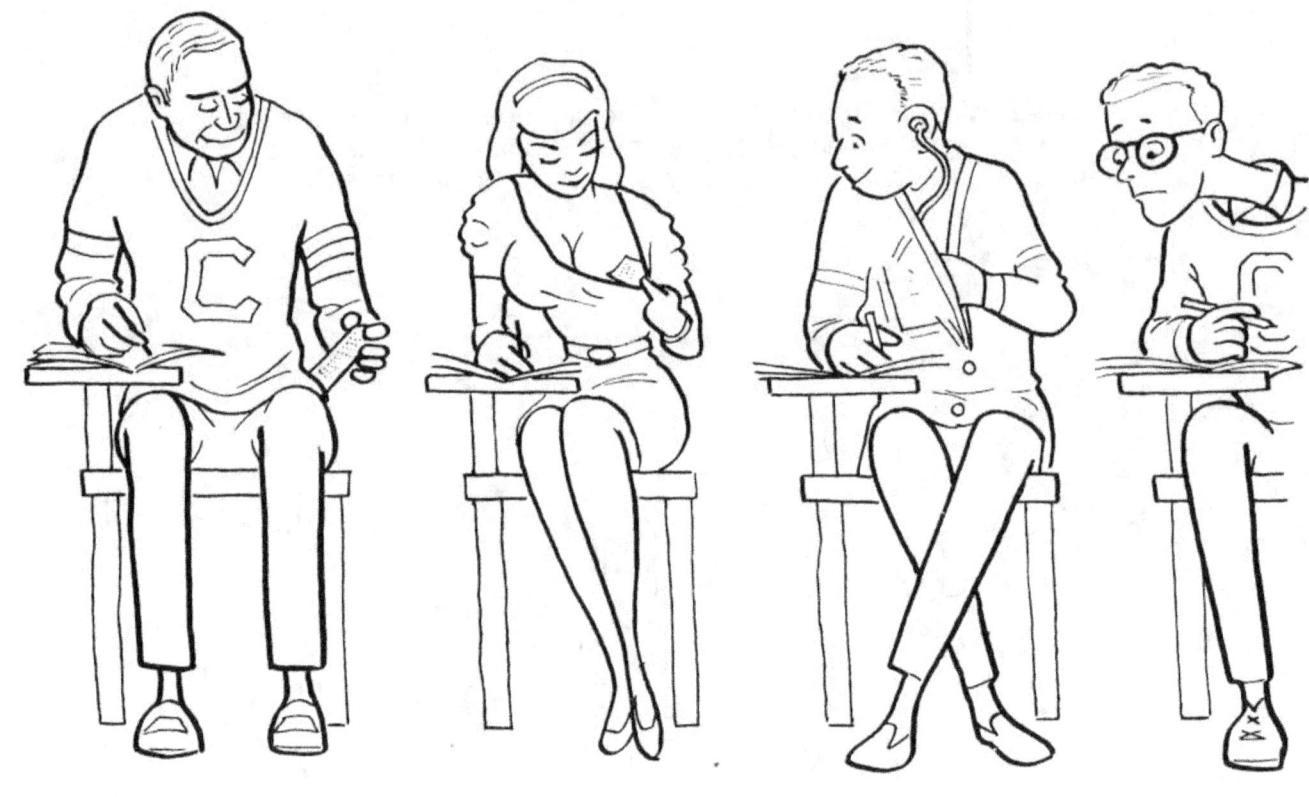

This is a test. Tests are good. They make you know things.
Important things. Like how to pass tests and cheat.

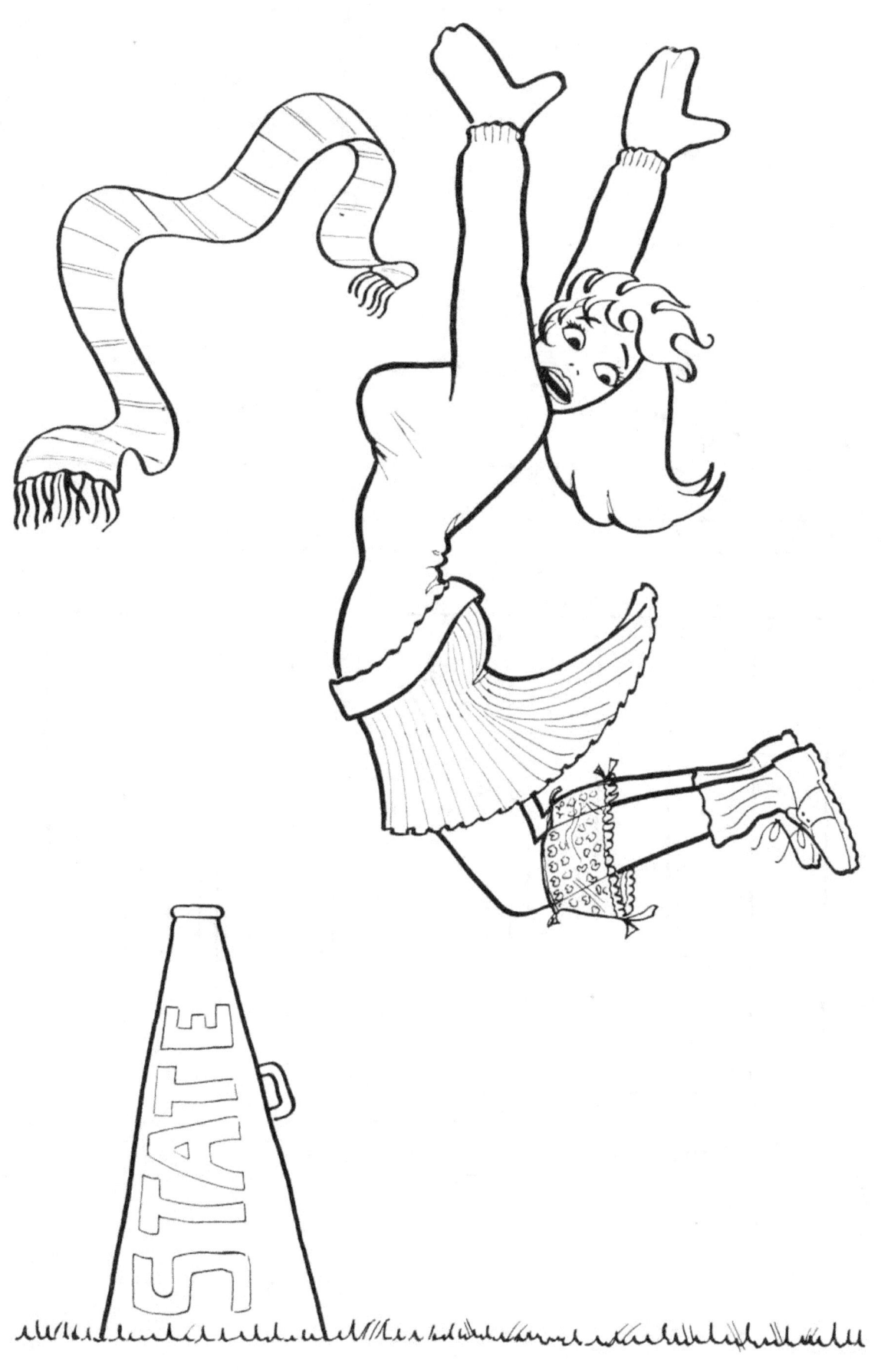

This is a cheerleader. She yells and jumps. She can jump high.
See how high she jumps? Everybody cheer. Color her face red.

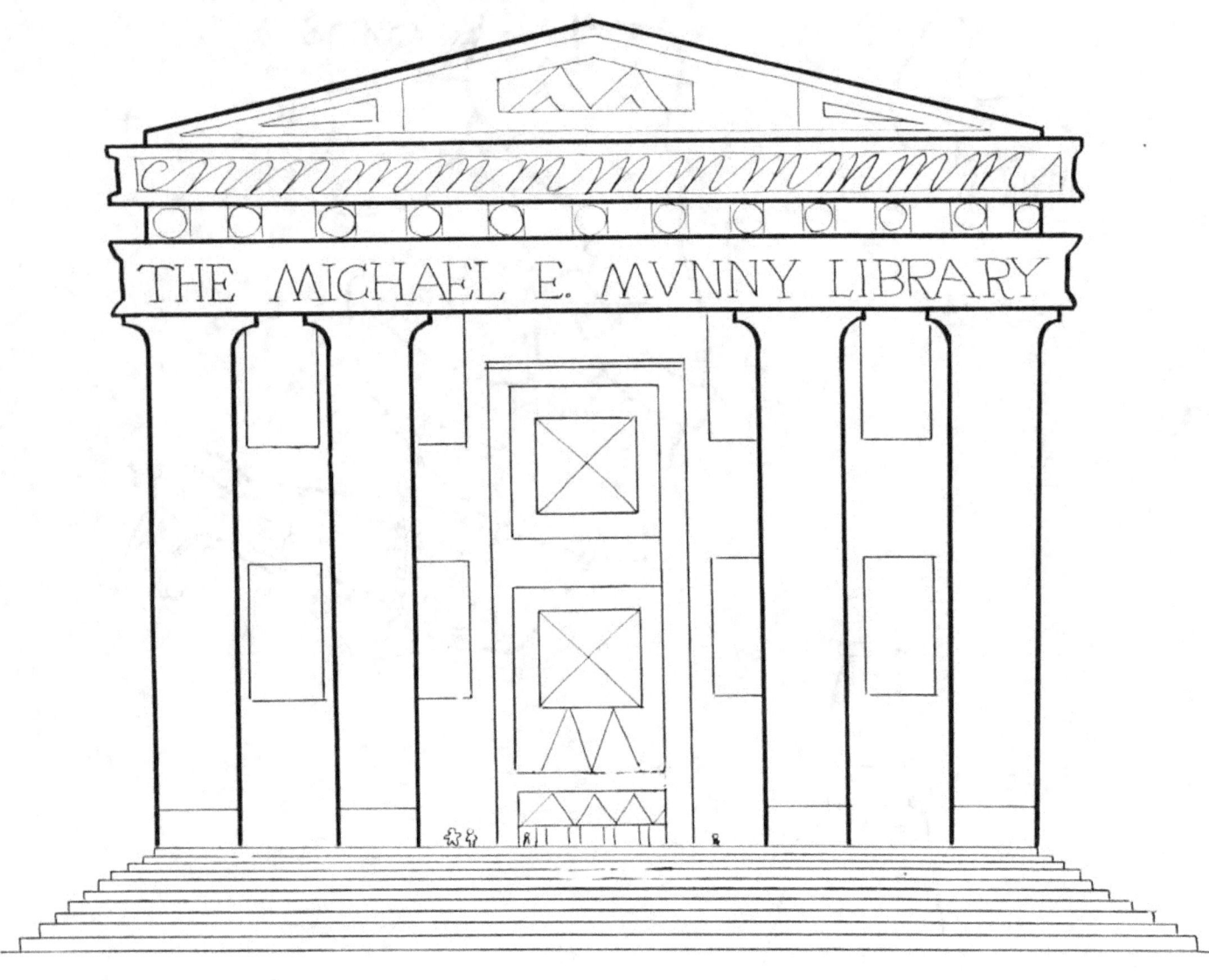

THE MICHAEL E. MVNNY LIBRARY

This is our library. It is gold. Isn't it beautiful? Color it beautiful.
It was even in LIFE once, it's so beautiful.
They say it's even more beautiful inside.

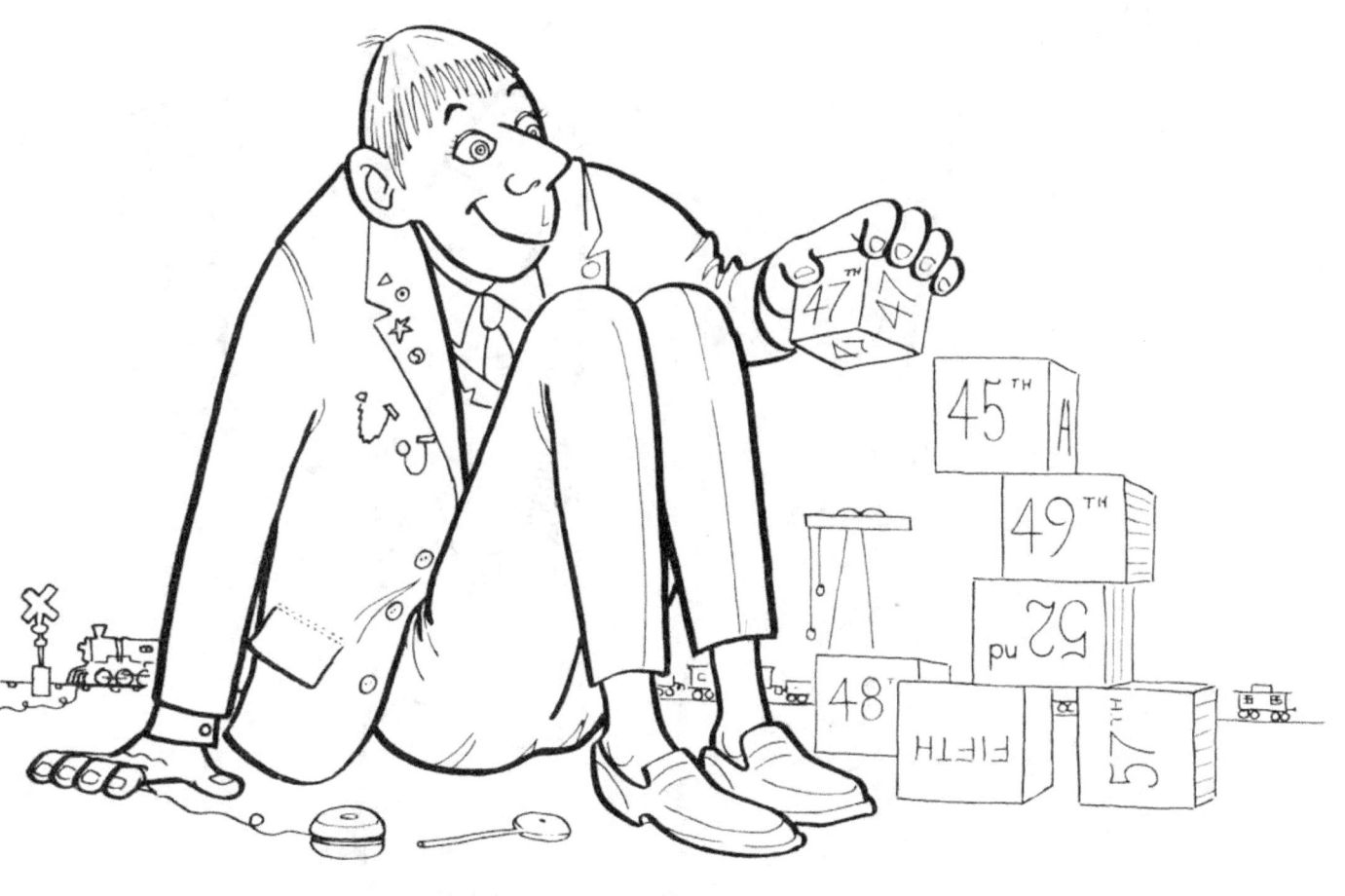

This fellow has an IQ of 37. He has an A average.
He belongs to 12 fraternities, including two honoraries.
Do you know him? He's Michael E. Munny II.

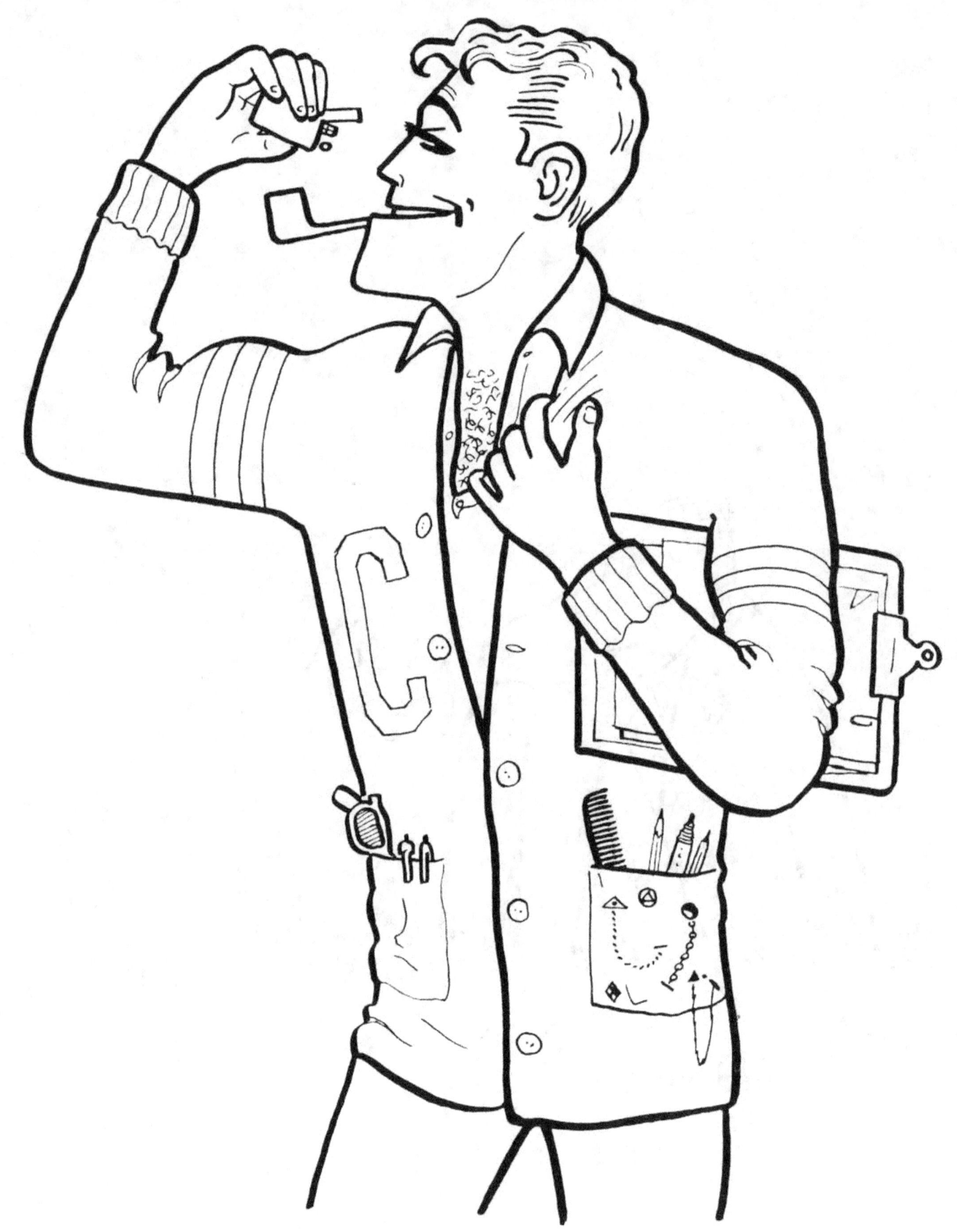

Hey, see Me? I'm the BMOC. Color me Royal Blue. I'm Handsome, Rich, Strong, Sexy, Brilliant, Charming, Honorable, Immensely Popular, Terrifically Talented and Utterly Irresistible. Also modest and Humble.

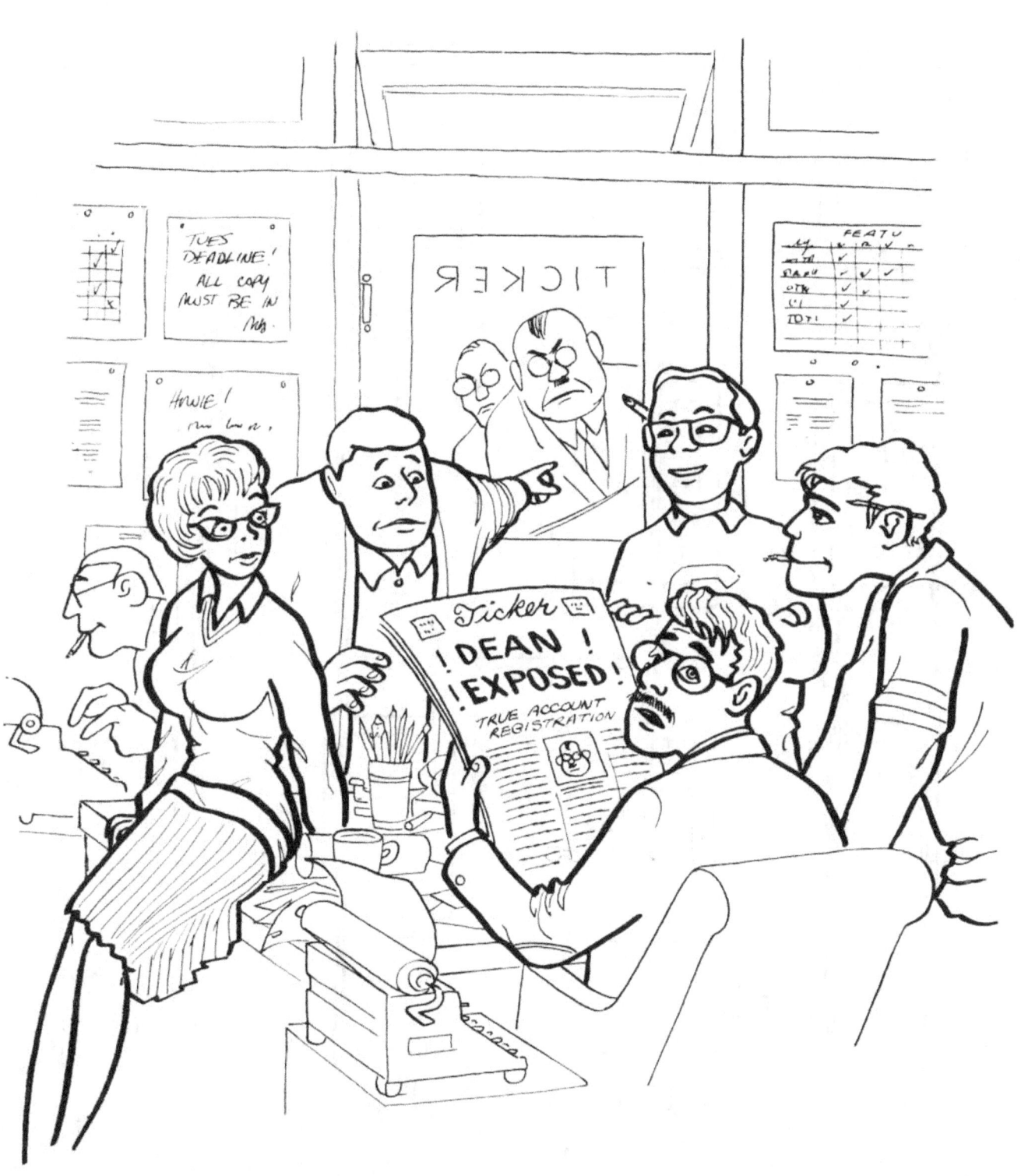

We are the newspaper editors. We are crusading, honest, objective and true. Color us fast before we're expelled.

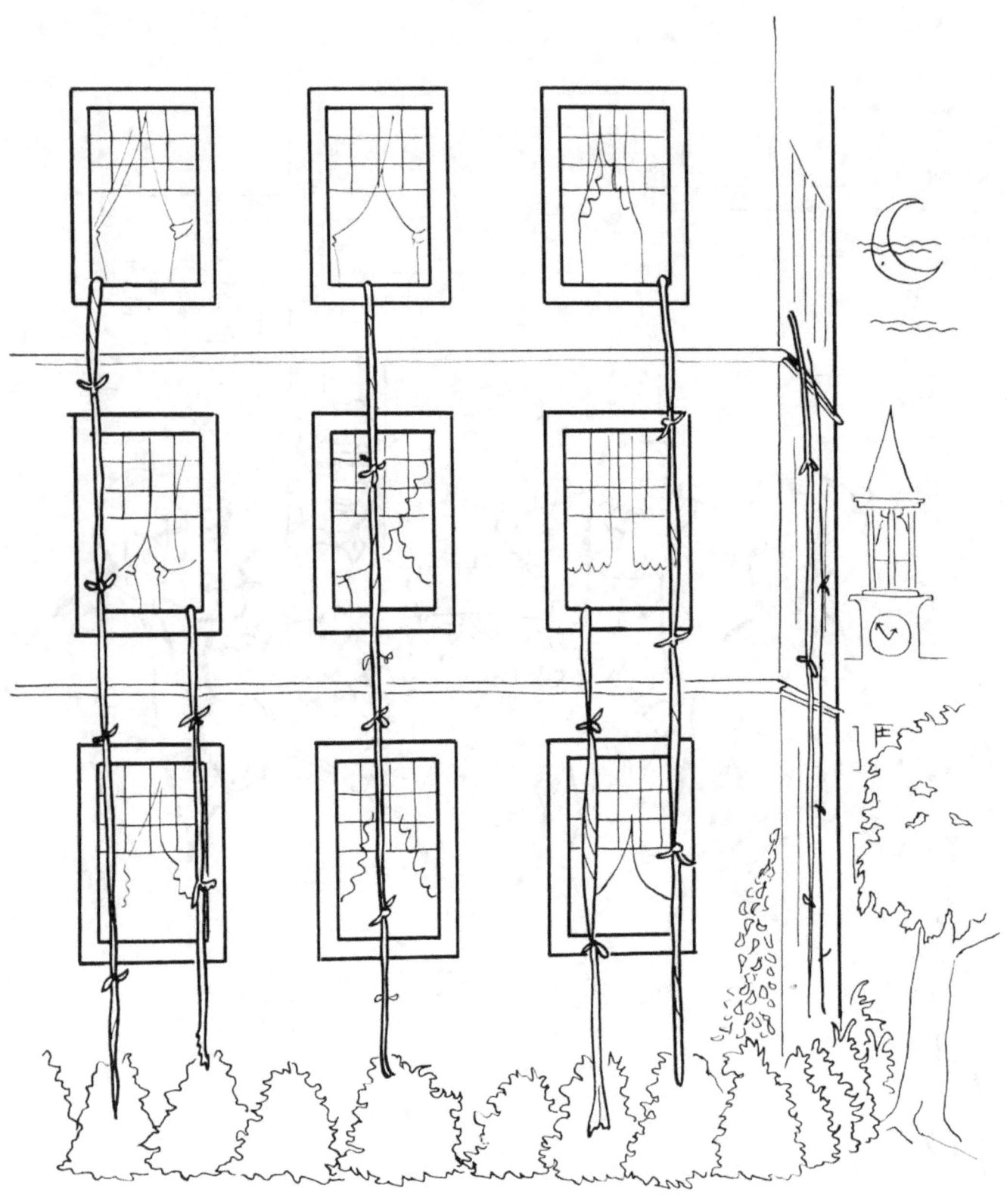

This is the girl's dorm. Boys are not allowed in here at night.

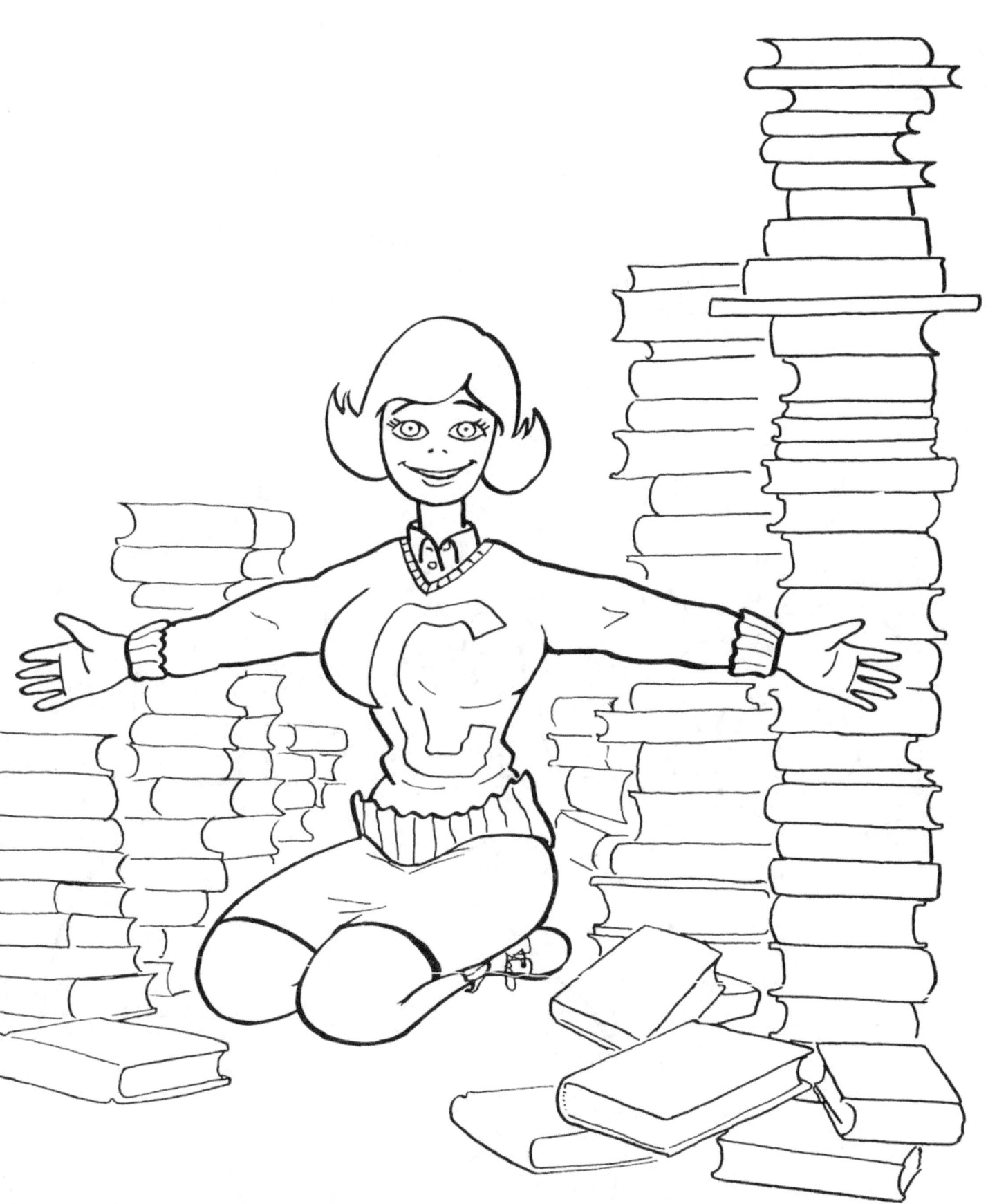

See my books. Aren't they pretty? I have 182 little ones
and 160 big ones. 246 books. Would you trade me a red one for
two greens? Color the books pretty.

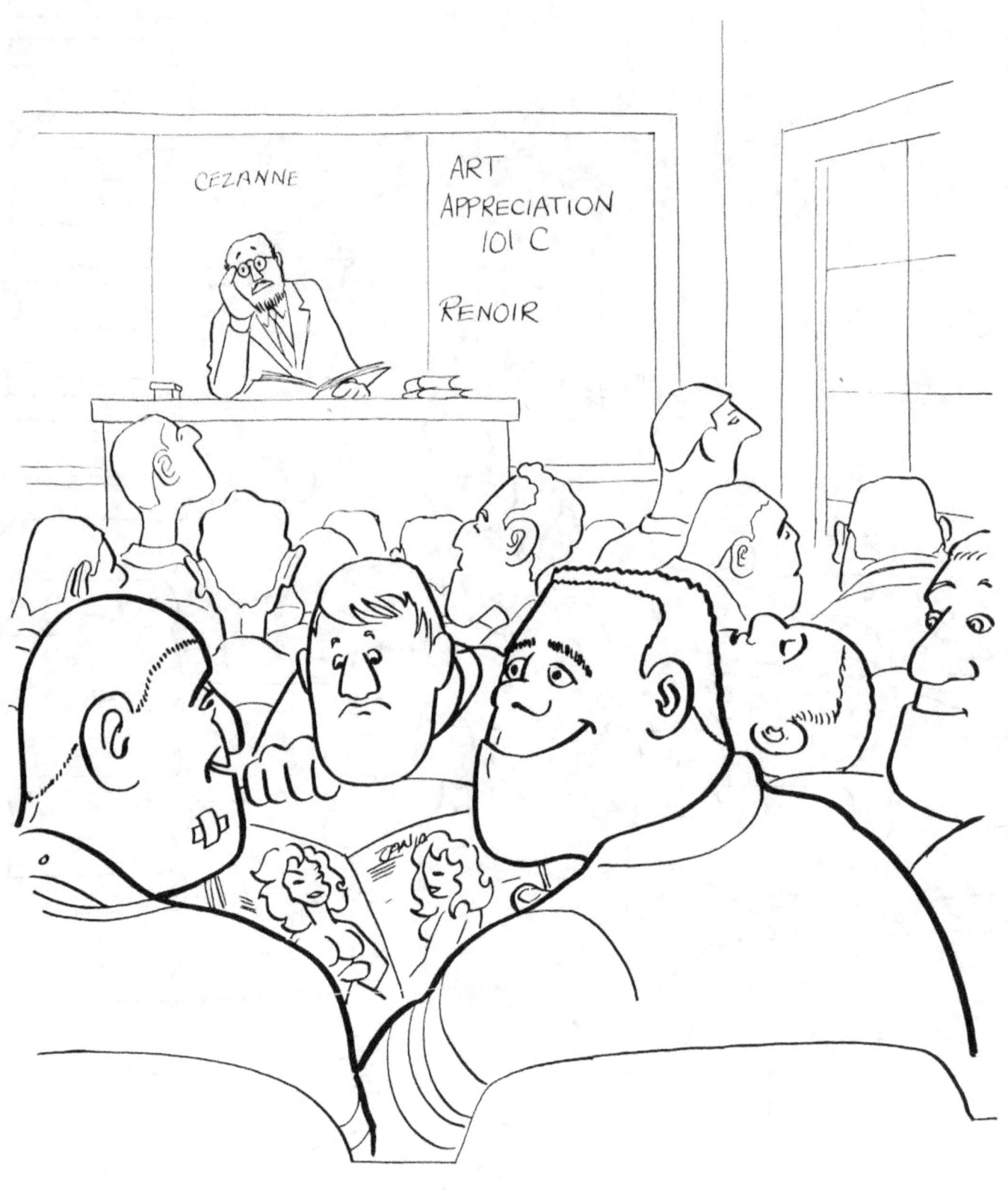

This is a crap course. Color it crappy. You'll get an A anyhow.

FIND IT AND DO IT.

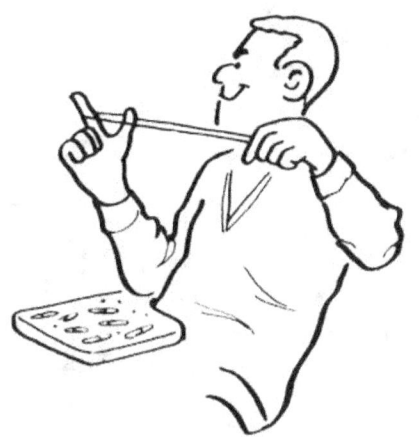

steal a mascot

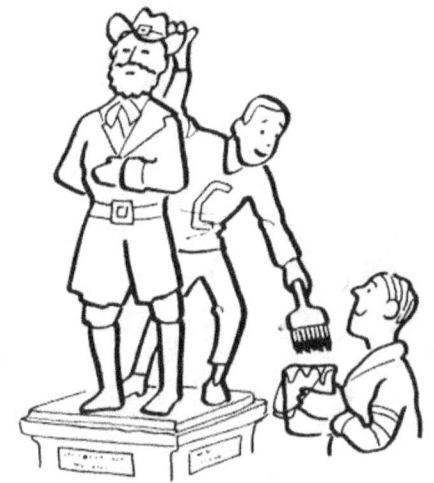

blow up a lab

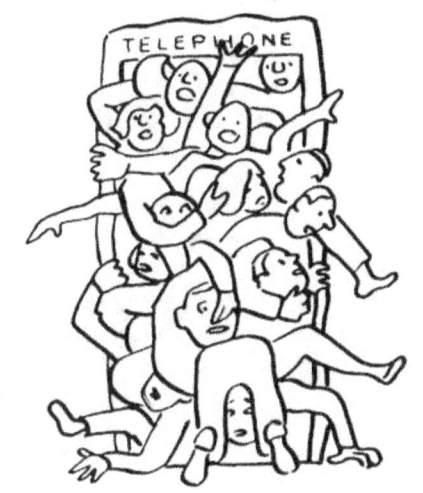

paint a statue

pay tuition

bug a professor

stuff a phone booth

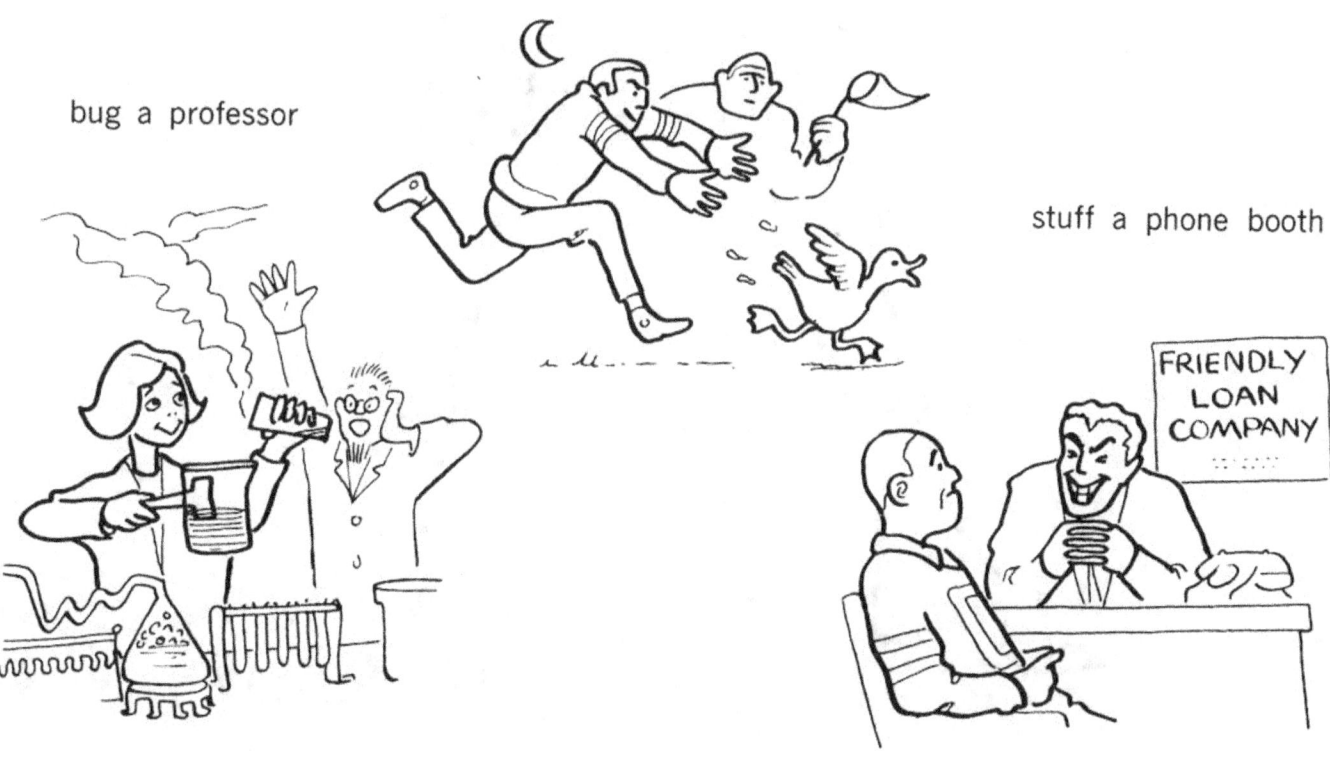

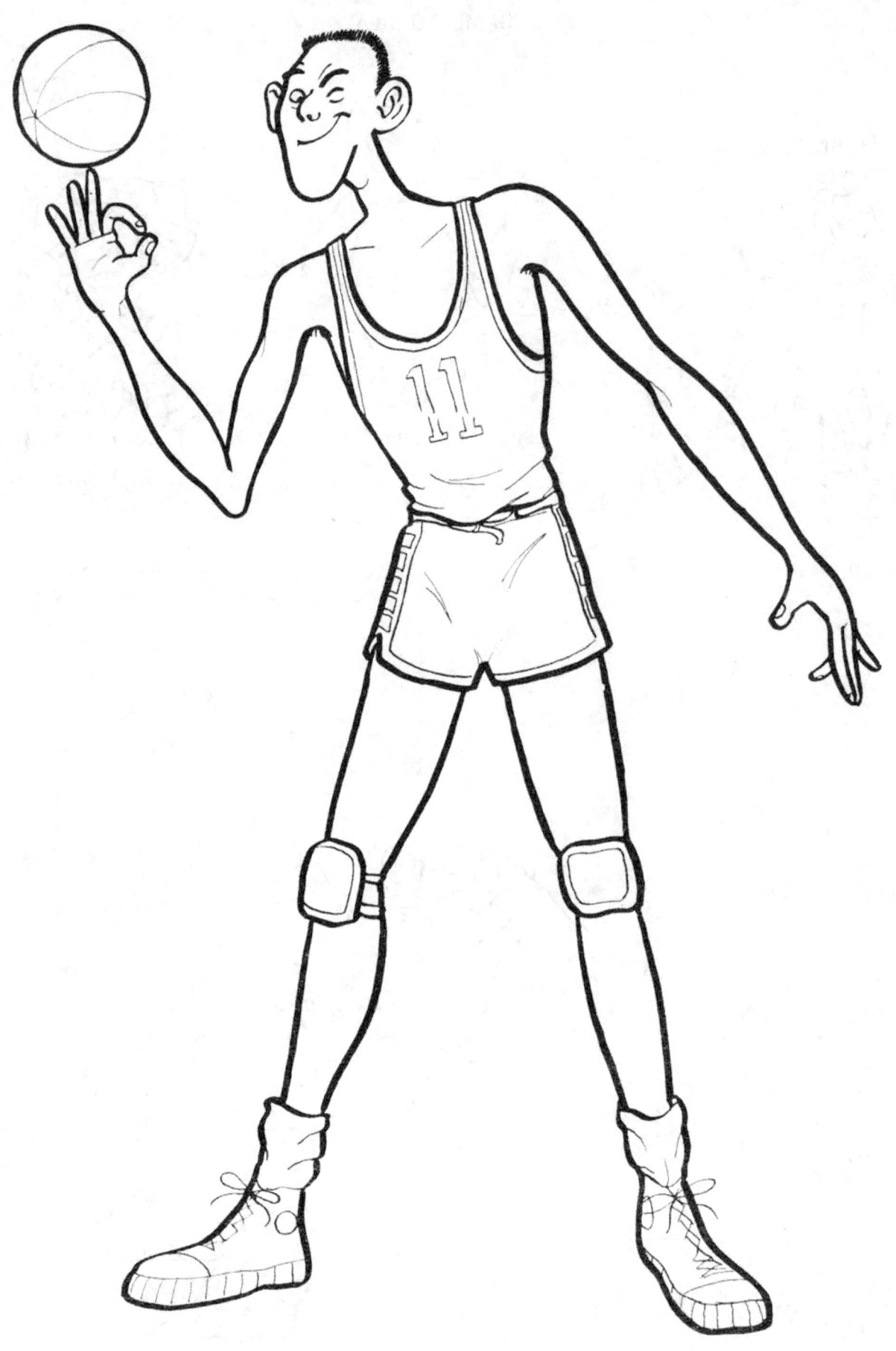

See Clever Leroy. He is our basketball star. He has a nice
apartment, a new car, good clothes and lots of cash.
Clever, Clever Leroy.

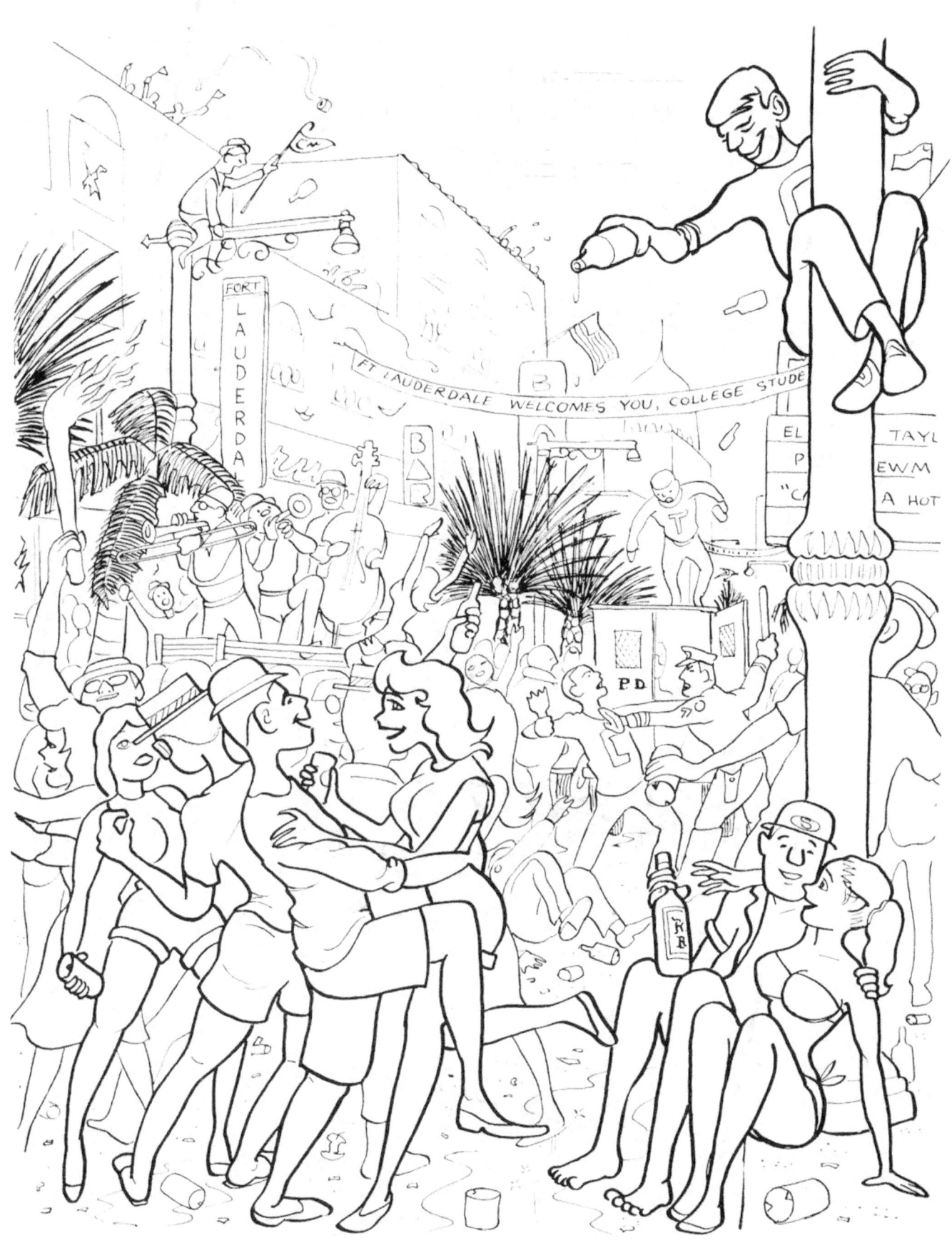

This is Intersession. This is how we behave at Intersession.
And at all public places.
Color us riotously.

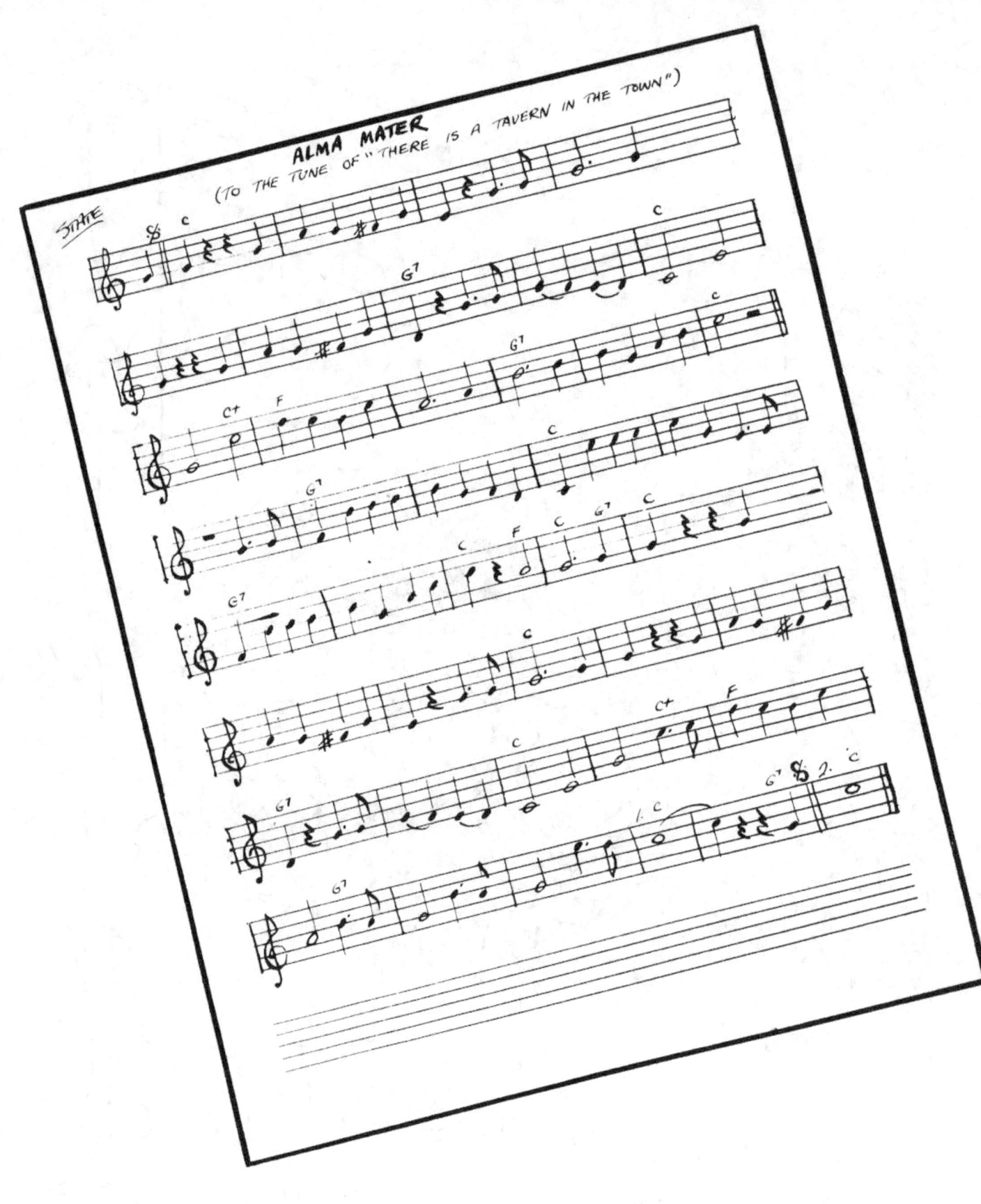

This is our school song. It's the living end. I only hum it, 'cause I
can't remember the words. I go to pieces when they sing it.
(Don't color it; fake it.)

50

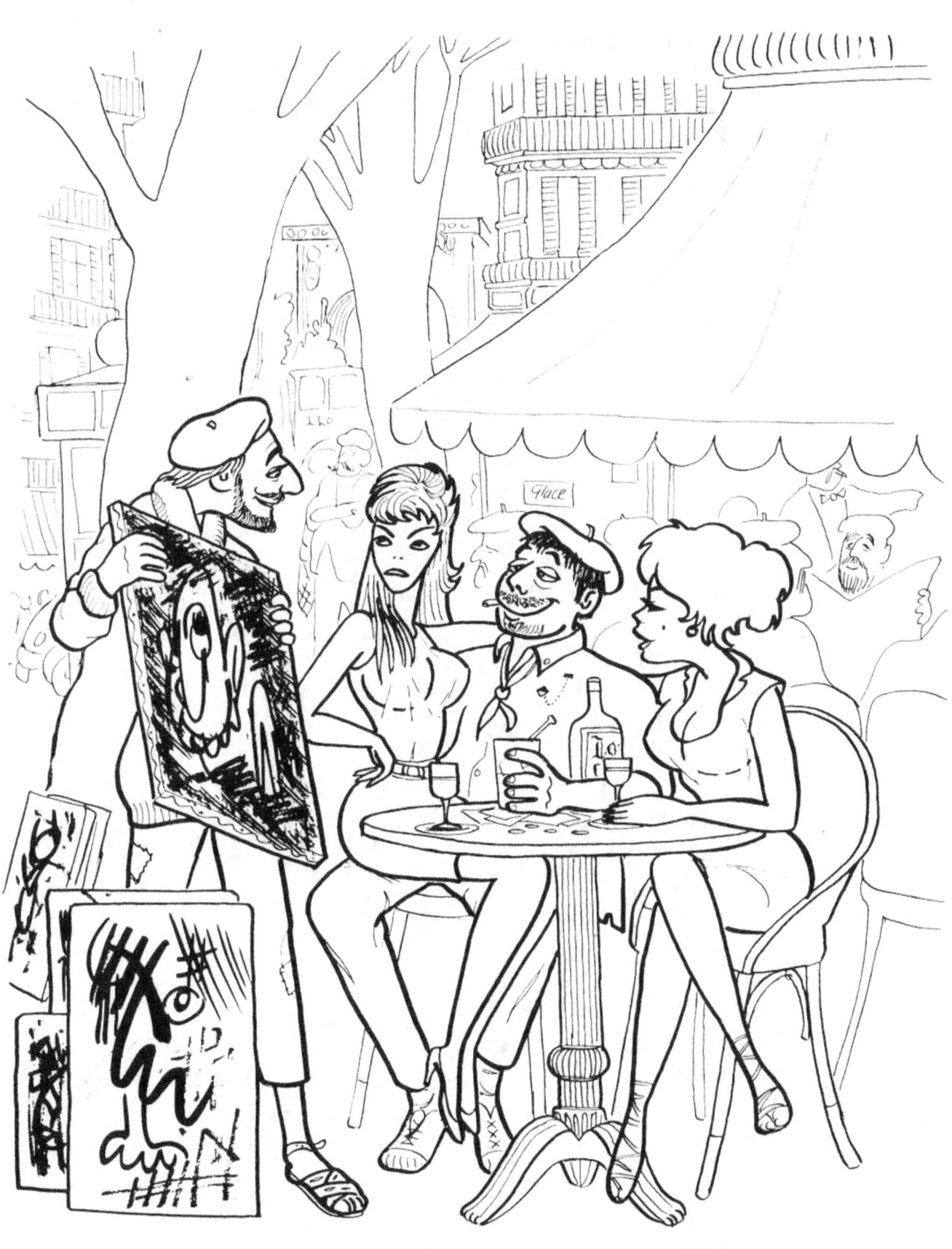

This is Irwin. He's taking his junior year abroad.
Irwin is studying contemporary French art.
Color him full-bright.

CUT OUT AND USE.

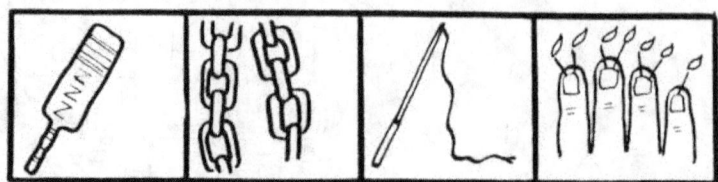

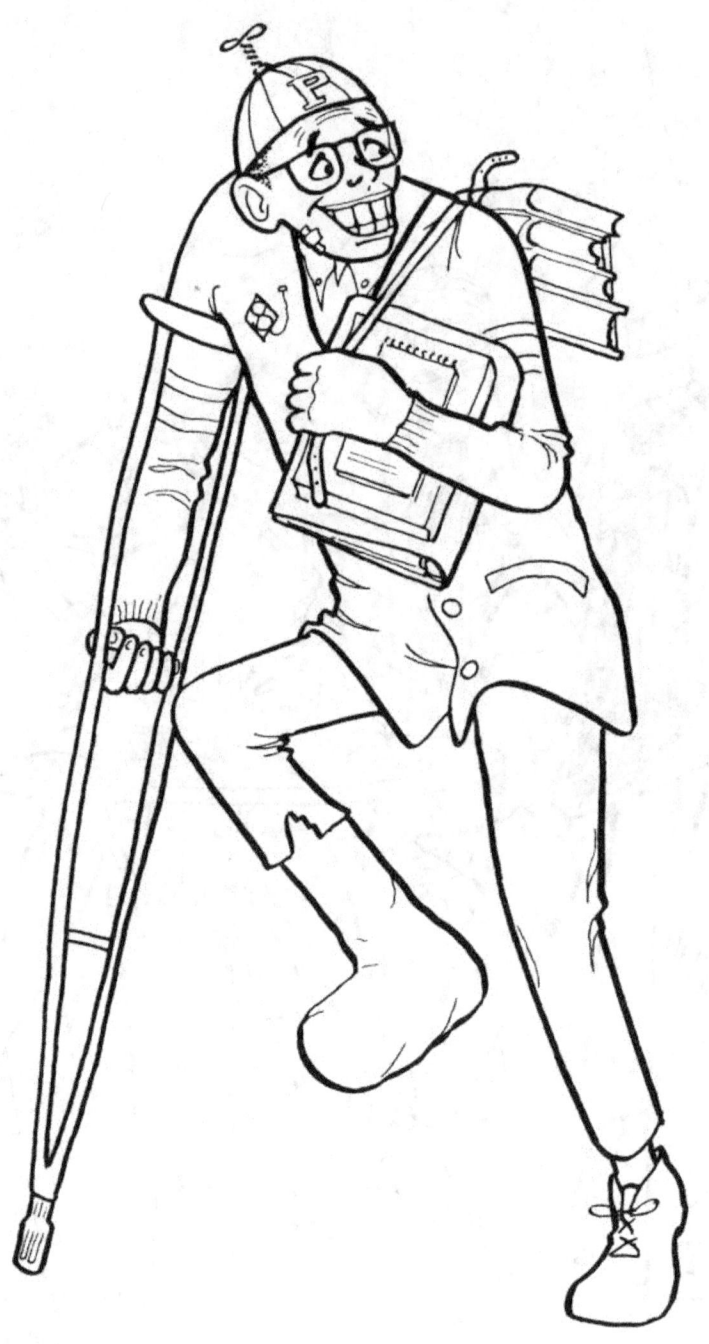

This is a happy pledgee. Hop and skip, pledgee! Laugh!
Sing! Play! RUN! Color him black and blue.

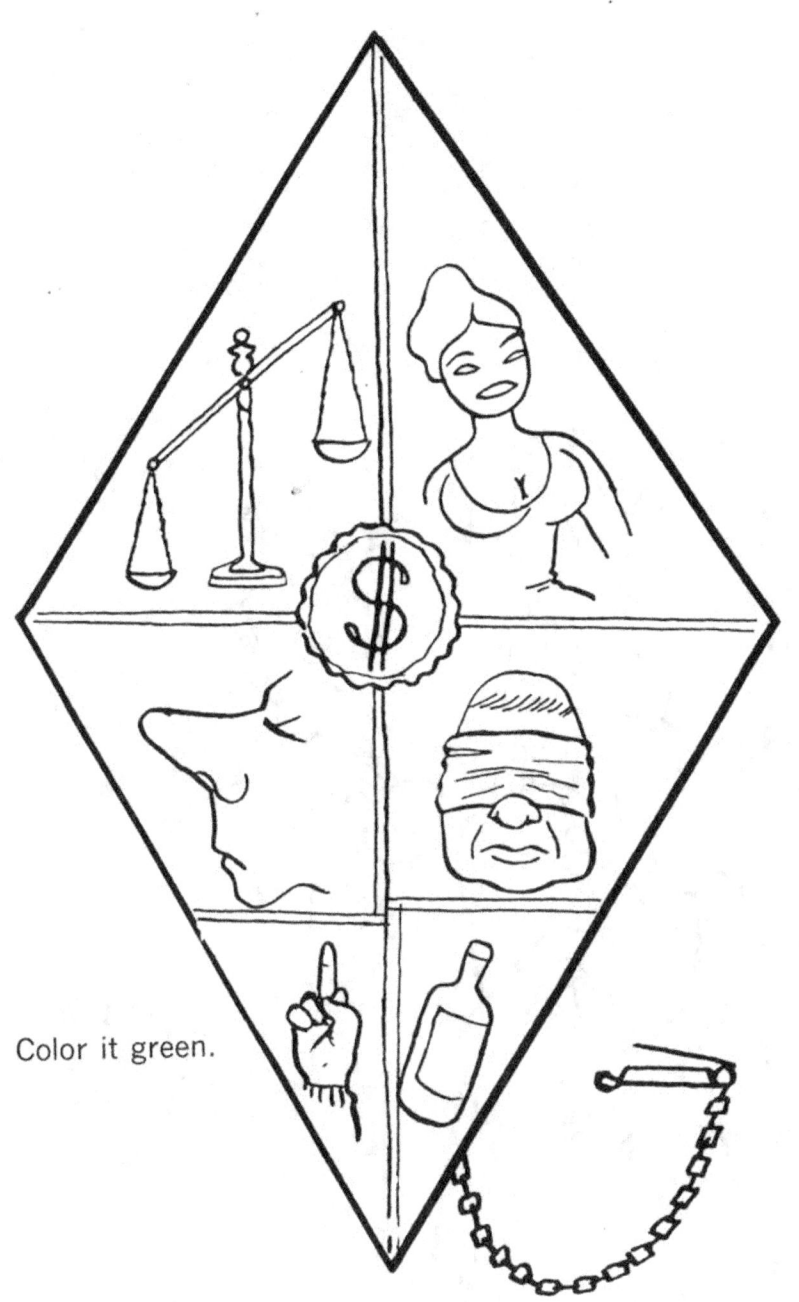

Color it green.

This is my fraternity pin. It is real gold. It stands for honor. Truth. Reverence. How much would you give me for it?

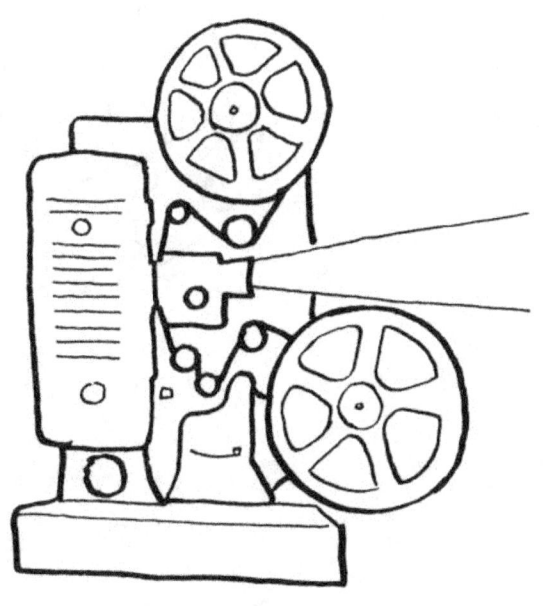

Let's all go to a fraternity party.

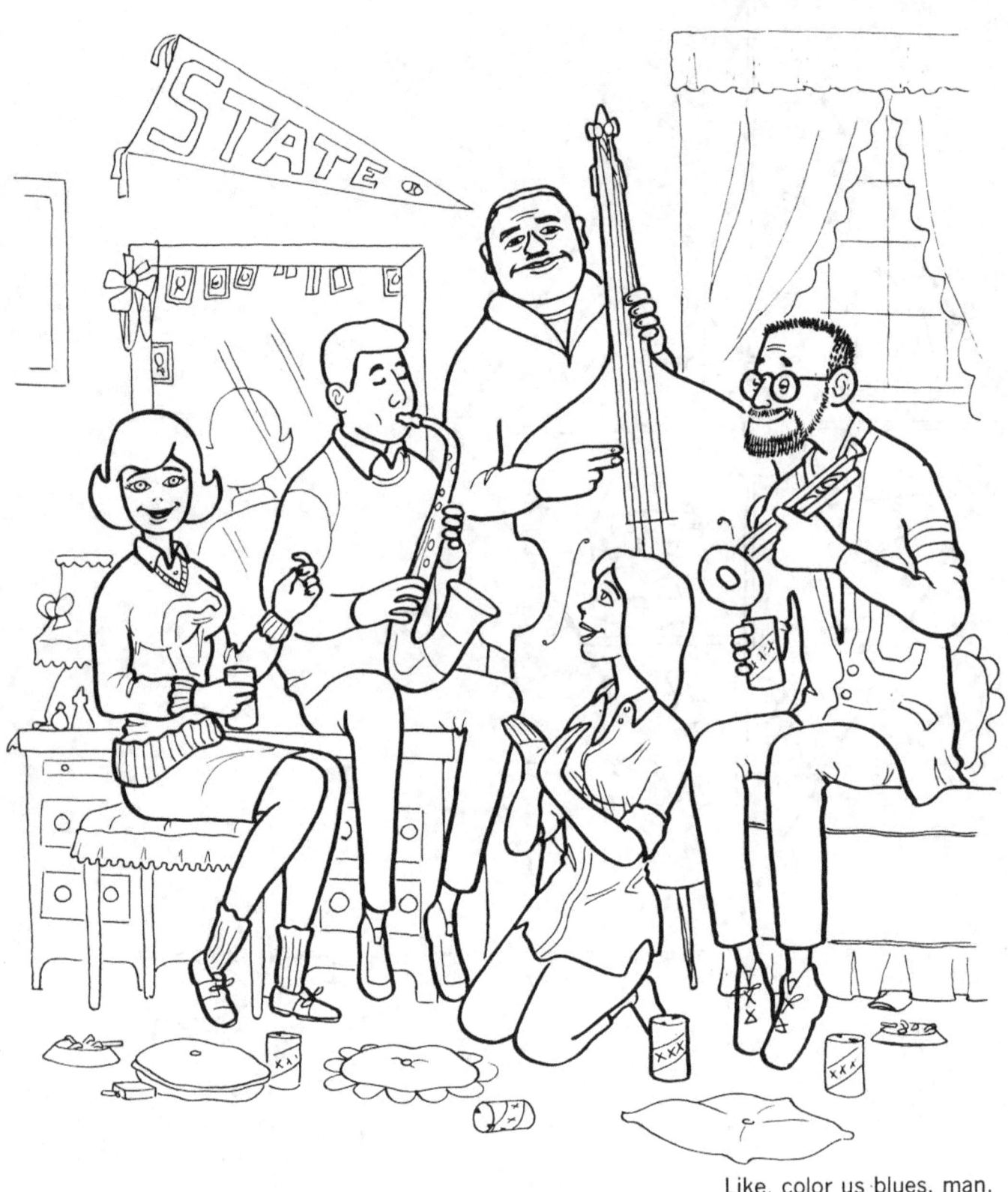

Like, color us blues, man.

This is our English class. We cut.

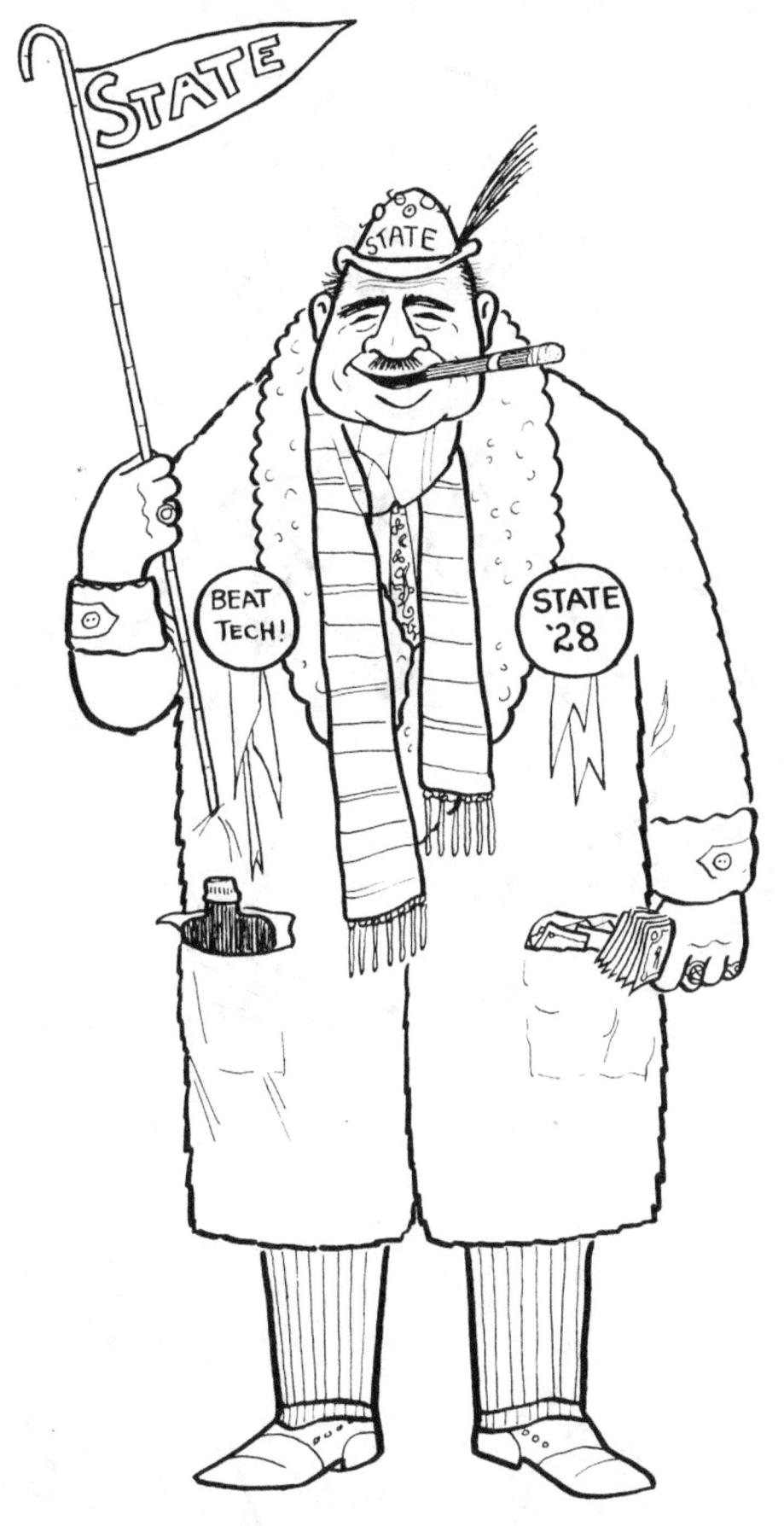

This is Faithful Old Grad. Color him true blue. He's here for the big game against Tech. He comes every year. He's got Tech and 13.

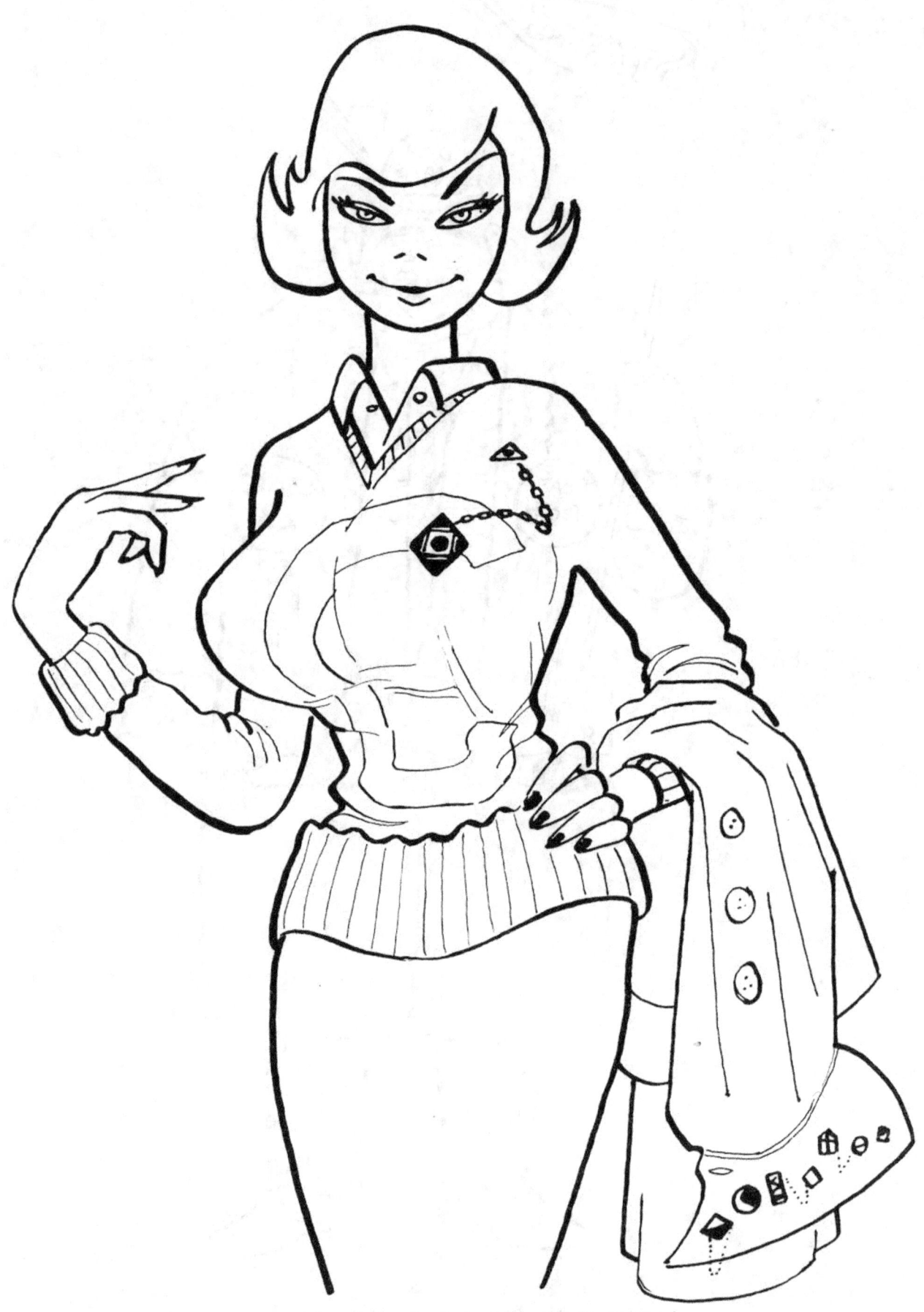

This is my new boy friend's fraternity pin. It means I
belong to him alone, forever and ever and maybe even after
he graduates. Isn't it a pretty pin? Would you like to
color it, big boy?

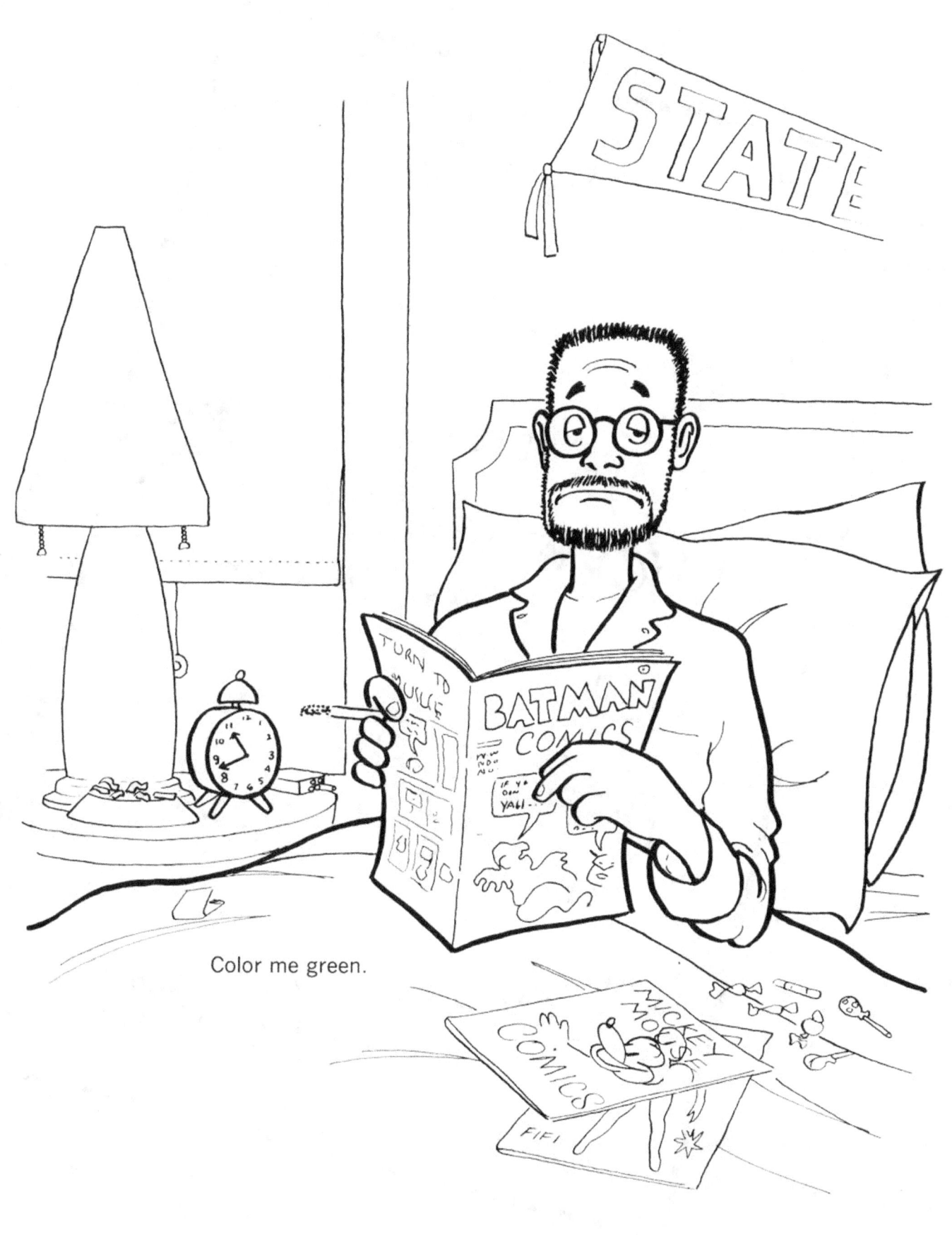

Color me green.

Tonight is the Junior Prom. I hate proms. They're boring. They're just for football players and show-offs. I wouldn't go even if I <u>had</u> a date.

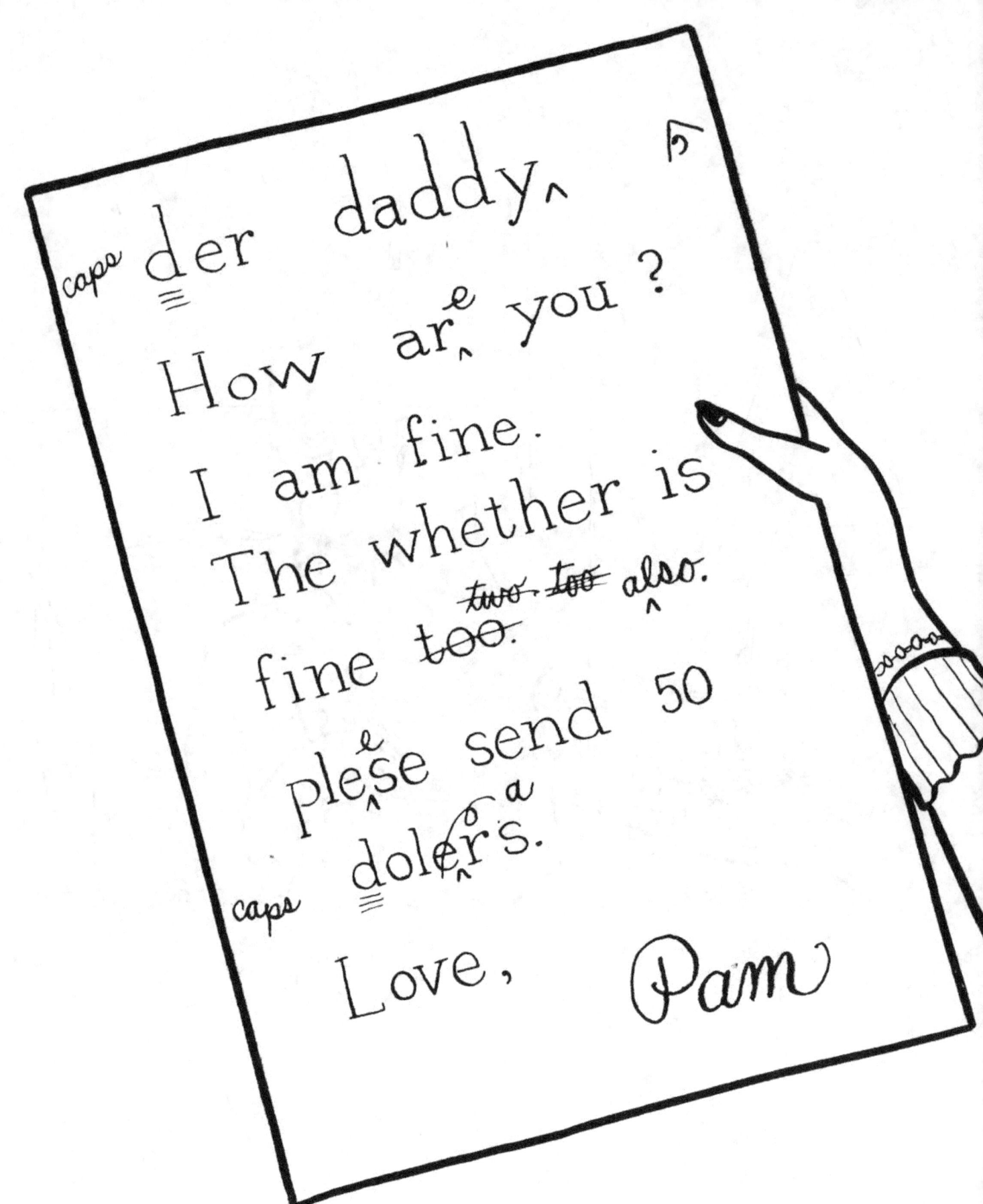

caps der daddy.

How are you?

I am fine.
The whether is
fine too. ~~two too~~ also.

plese send 50
dolers.
caps

Love, Pam

This is how I write. I am an English major. I am learning how to write for money. My Daddy says I know how already.

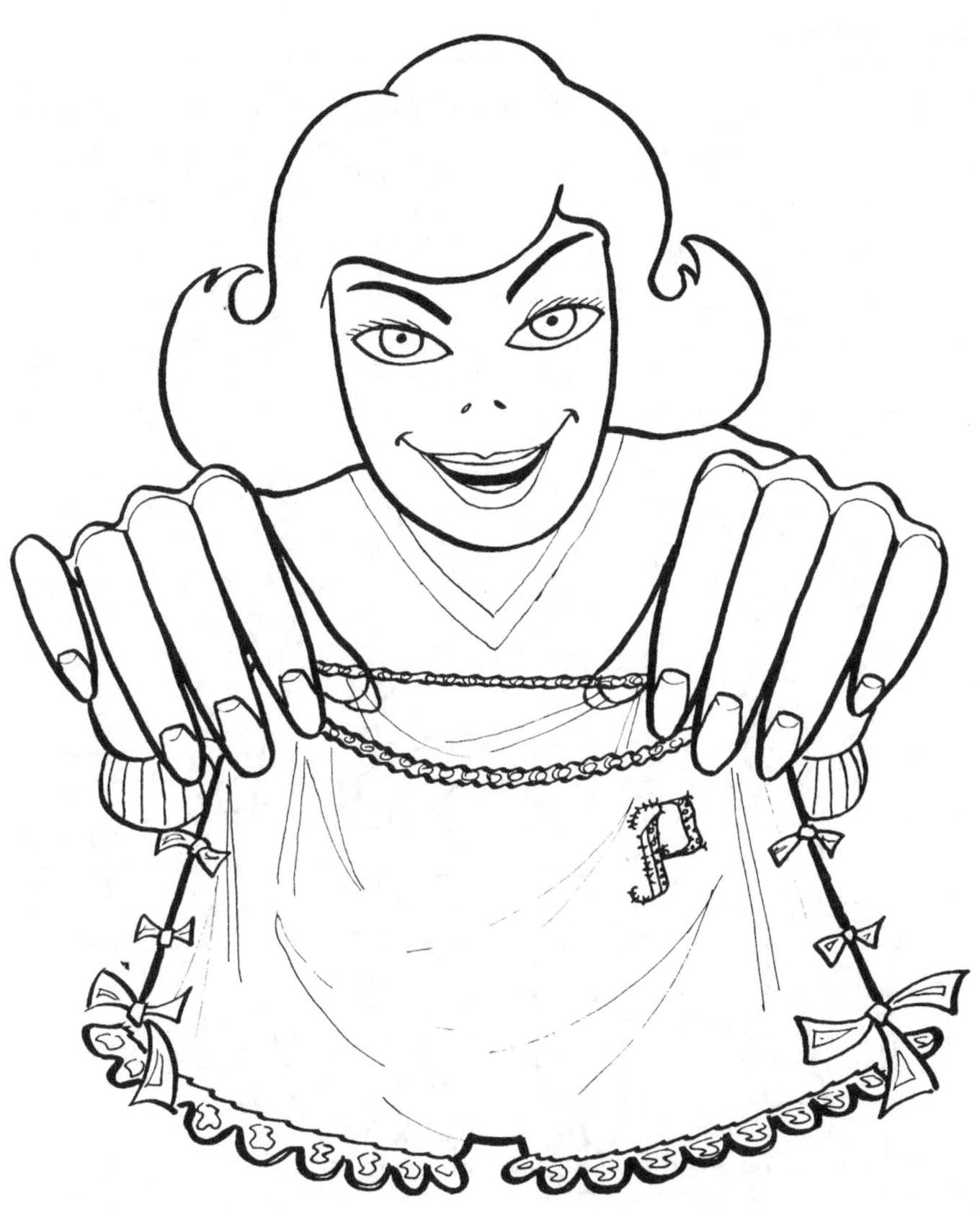

These are panties. You steal them.

COUNT YOUR BEERS.

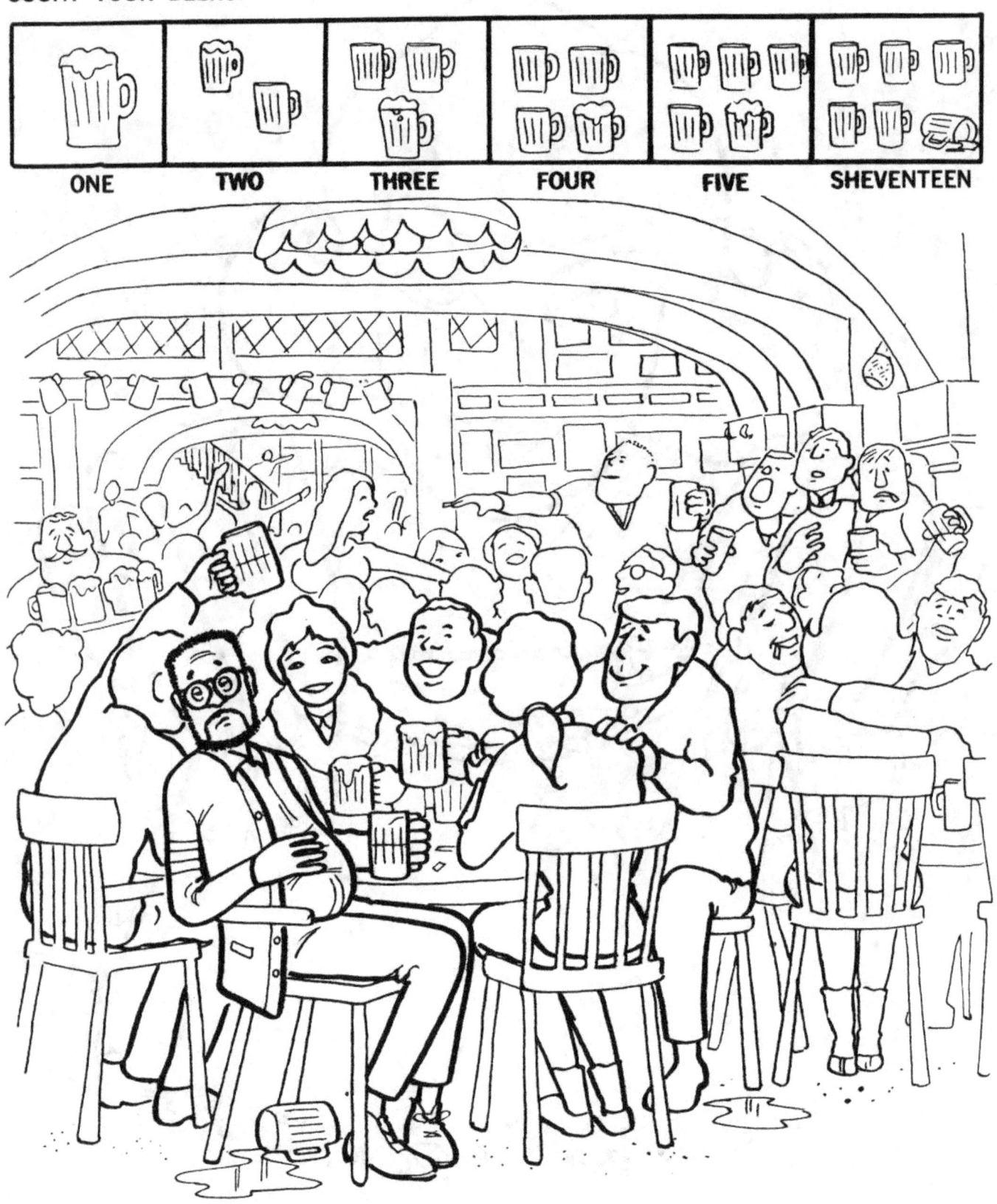

| ONE | TWO | THREE | FOUR | FIVE | SHEVENTEEN |

This is a beer party. See us drink? Drink, drink, drink!
Don't you love beer? I hate it. But I have to drink it to
be like the other guys. Color me . . . urp . . .

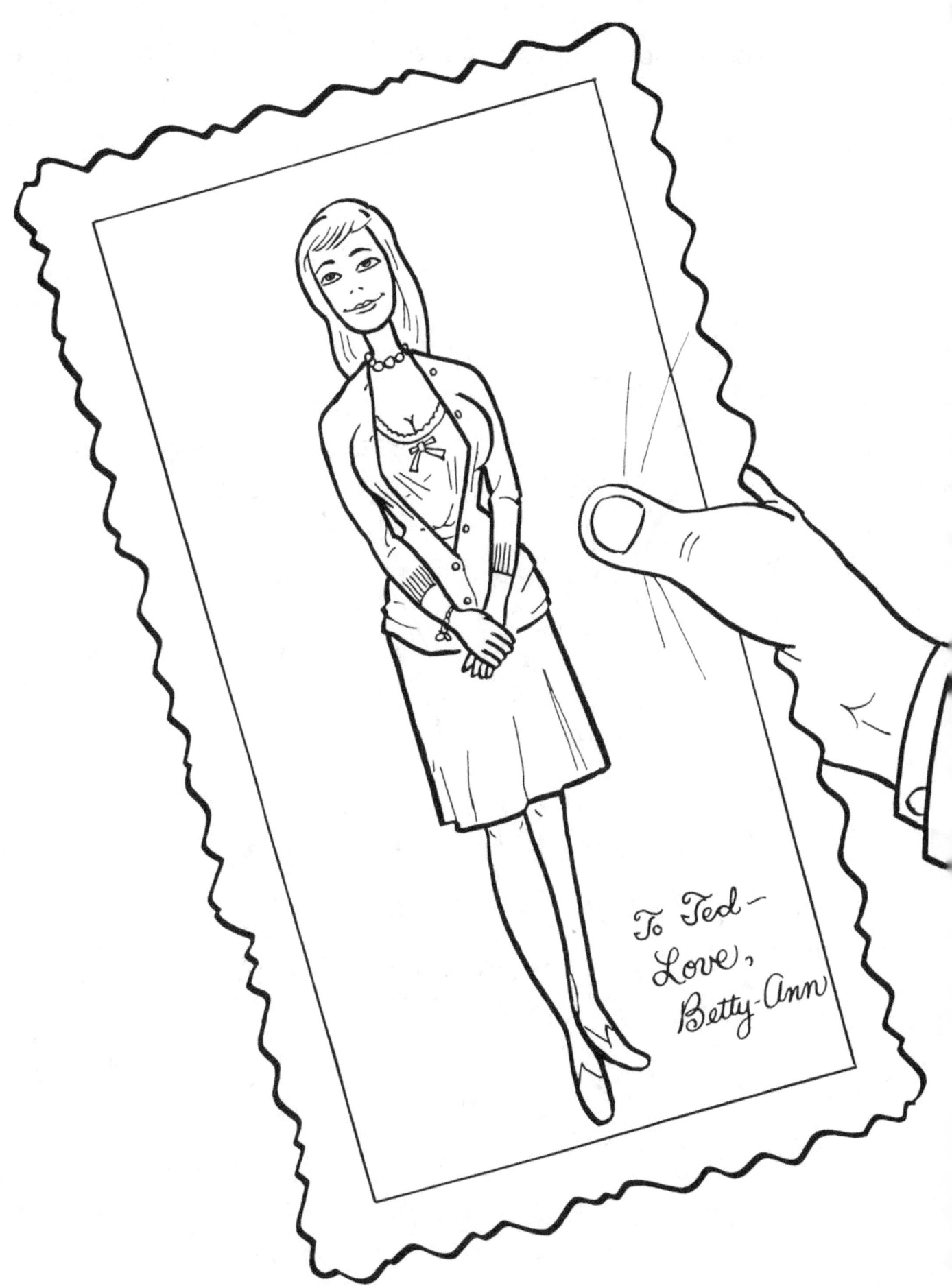

This is a girl. She lives and works in town. She does not go to college. She never went to college. She is not smart like Pam. I go out with her sometimes but I wouldn't want to marry her.

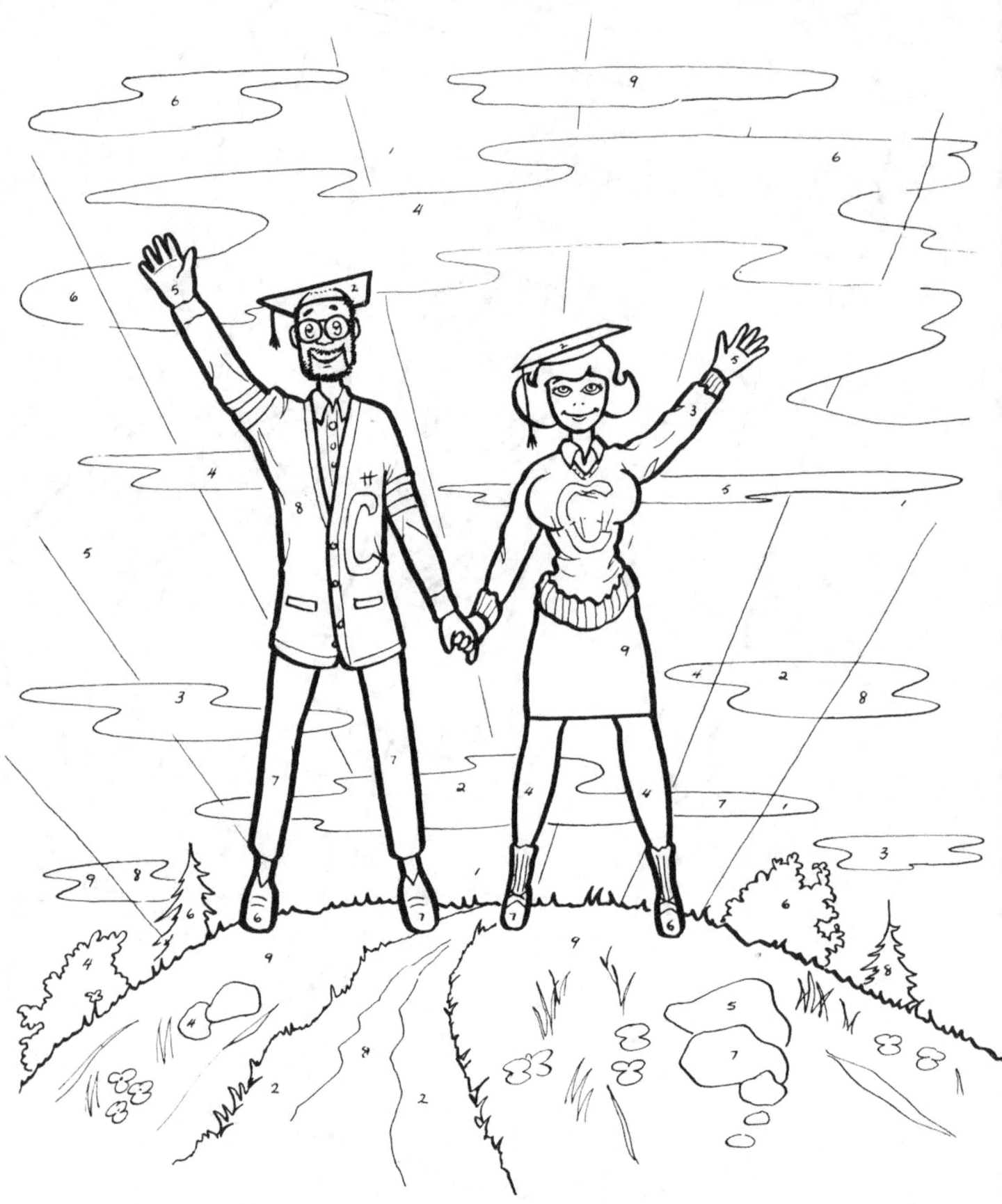

This is The End (in Technicolor). We have to go but you stay and color it. Obey the numbered color guide. Stay inside the lines. You should never go outside a line. Unless somebody tells you.

BRIDGE PLAYERS' COLORING BOOK

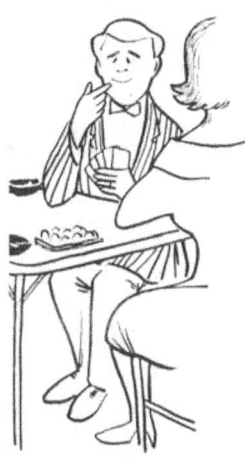

The card game Bridge was, while perhaps down from its peak, still a popular home pastime in the early 1960s. The Bridge culture was largely made of couples getting together with their friends for a foursome. *Bridge Players' Coloring Book* sent up the standard foibles of these gatherings. Created by Robert N. Wilson's company Swarthmore Press and published by Heines Publishing Company, this came out in 1962.

While most books collected here were originally printed at this size or a little larger, this was a smaller volume. The pages have been rotated so that they maintain their original scale while still appearing side-by-side with their original facing page.

See the table!
It is a bridge table—ready for a bridge game.
Color everything nice and bright.
Soon, Mr. and Mrs. Coles will be over to play a game
  with the Wilsons.
They play every Tuesday night, and sometimes
  on Saturdays.
That's how bridge is.

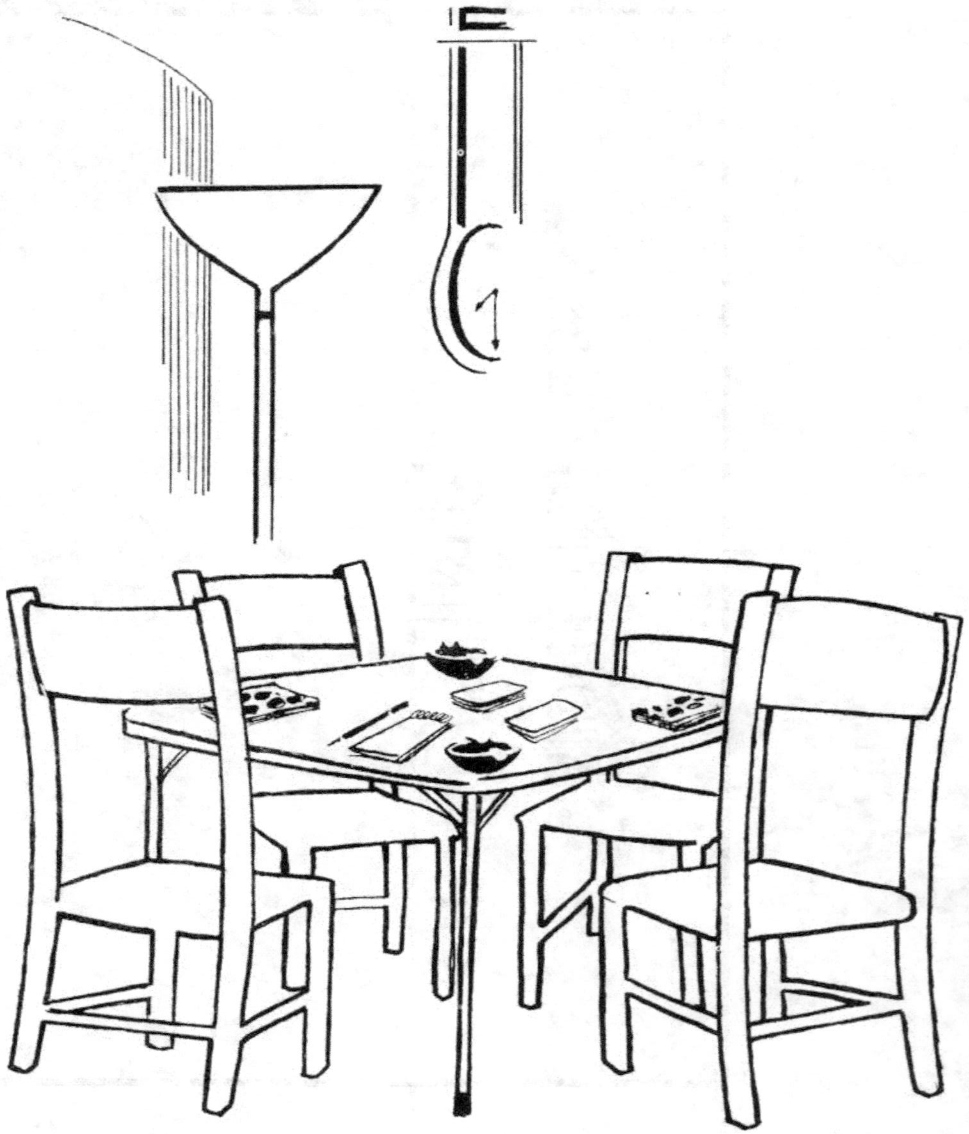

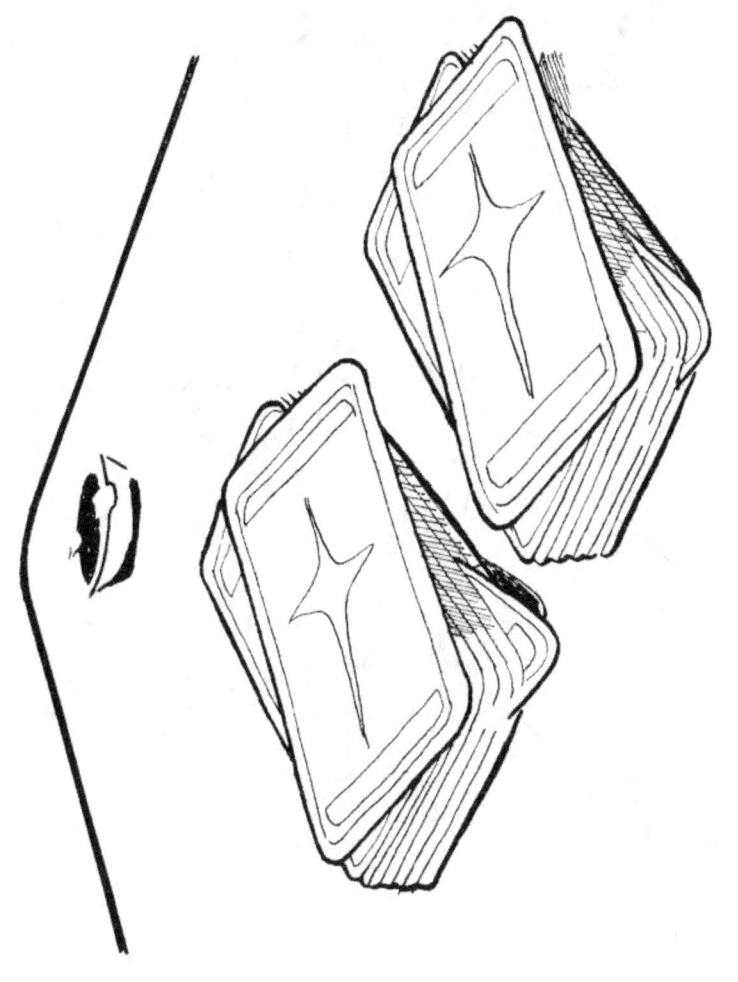

For a game of bridge there are two decks of cards.
Color them two different colors—
    like maybe lavendar and cerise.
It would never do to have both bridge decks
    the same color.
Why are there two decks?
That is a good question,
and someday we must ask Mr. Goren.

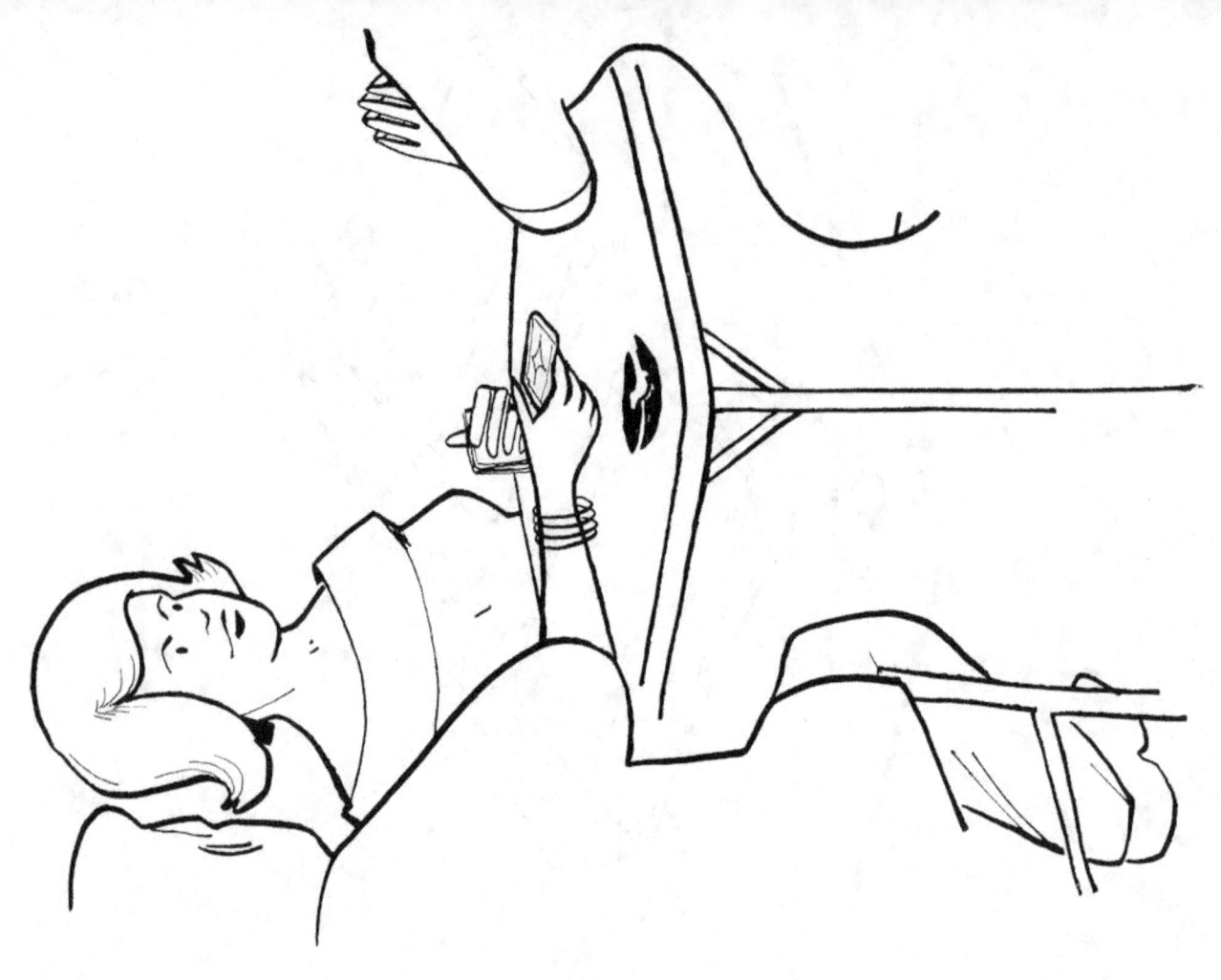

This is Mrs. Coles.

She is dealing the cards, because she is the Visiting Lady.

Color her dress light blue. Color her hair brown.

Isn't it nice that bridge players divide the cards evenly, and there is no quarreling about who gets the most?

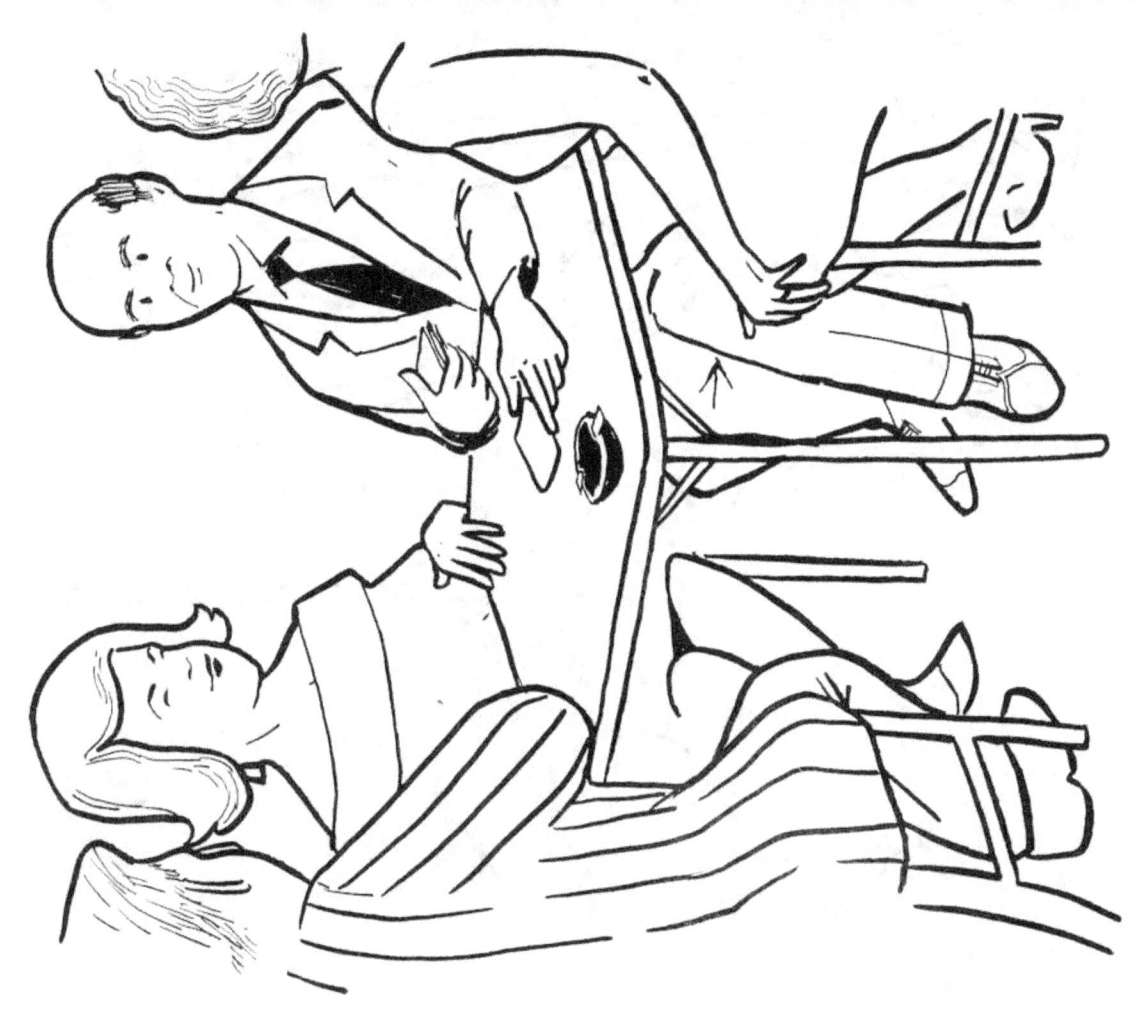

Now Mr. Wilson is dealing with the other cards.
Nobody wanted to play with those Mrs. Coles dealt.
Everybody passed.
No, they are not angry with Mrs. Coles.
They will let her deal some more after a while.
That's how bridge is.

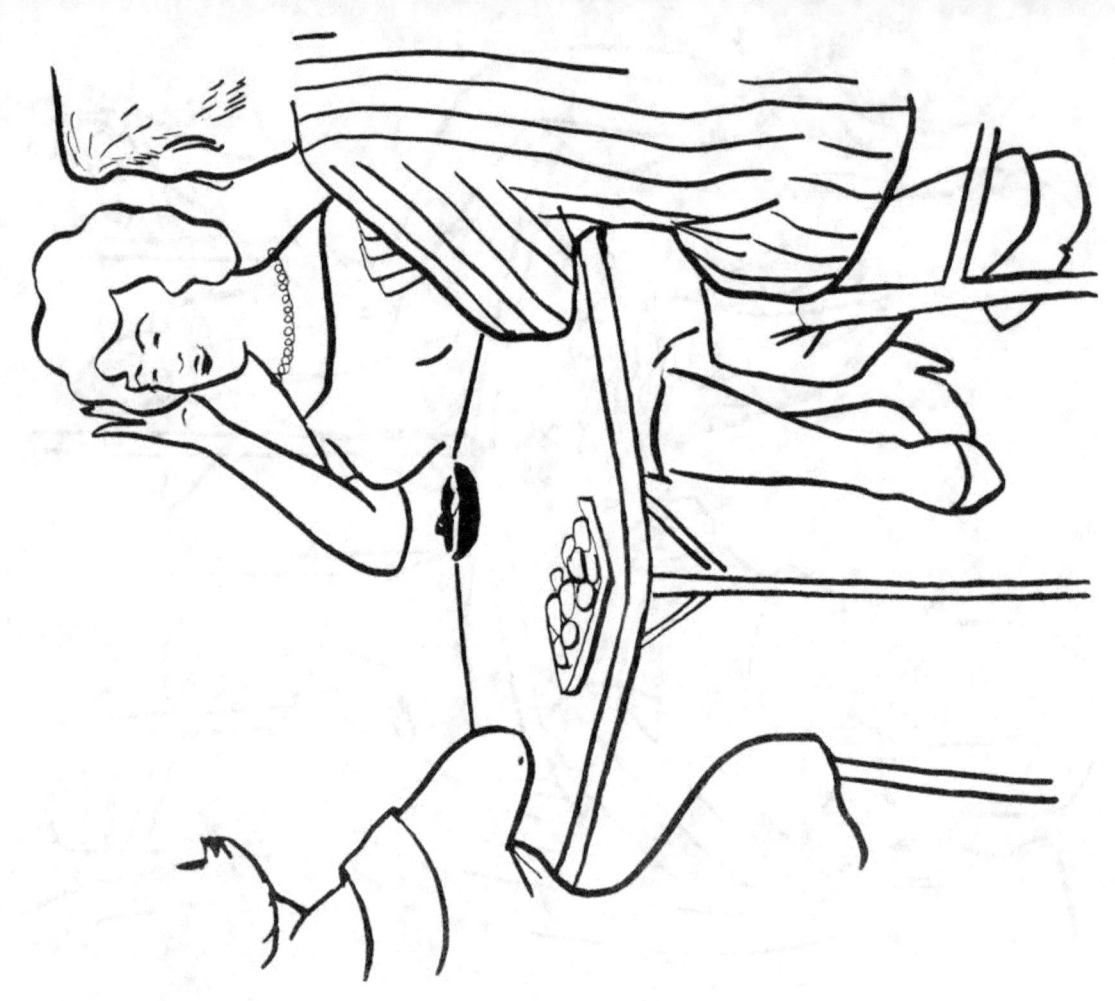

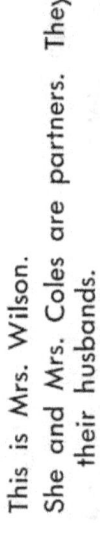

This is Mrs. Wilson.

She and Mrs. Coles are partners. They play against their husbands.

Color Mrs. Wilson's dress to go nicely with her red hair.

Yes, it was blonde last week; but this week it is red.

No, that is not part of the bridge game.

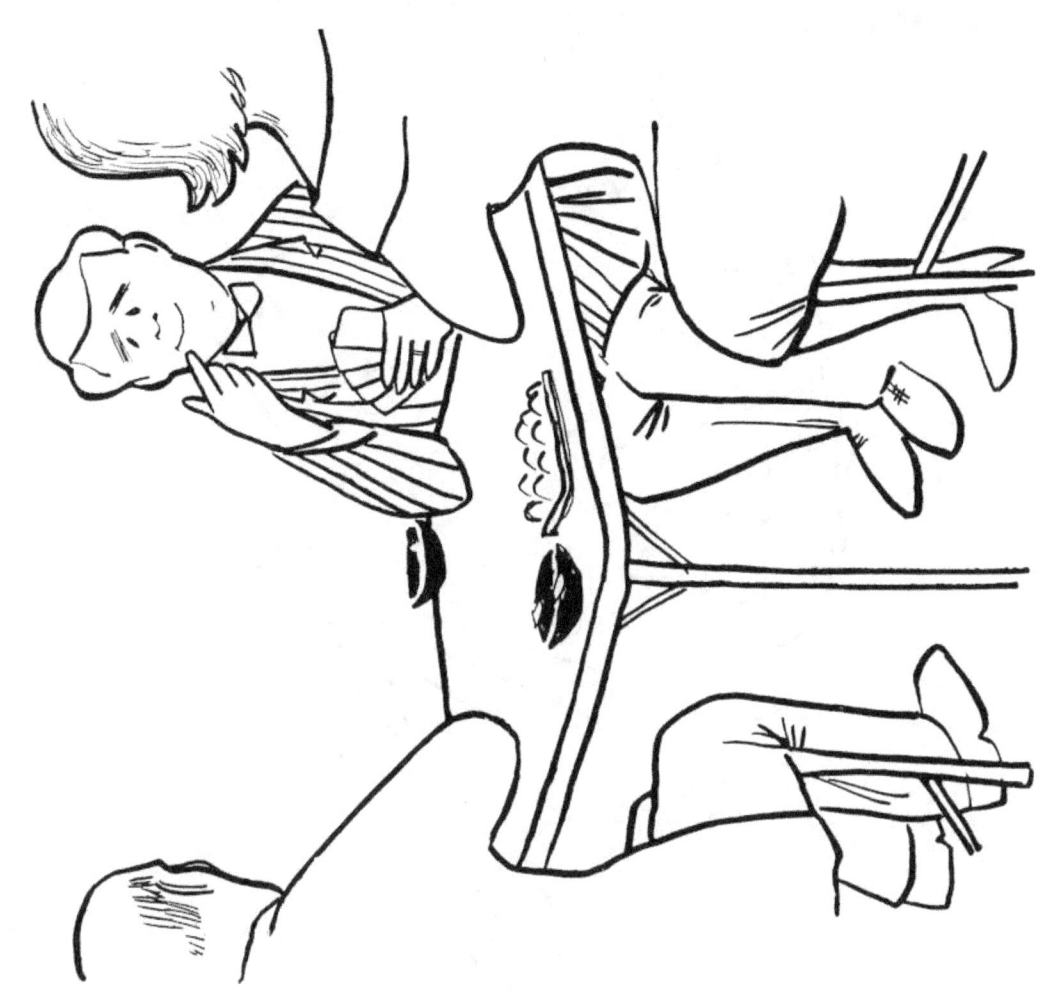

Here is Mr. Coles.
Color his hair black.
Color his suit gray with nice, snappy pink stripes.
Mr. Coles is the sporty type.
He is ready to make an opening bid of four no-trump.

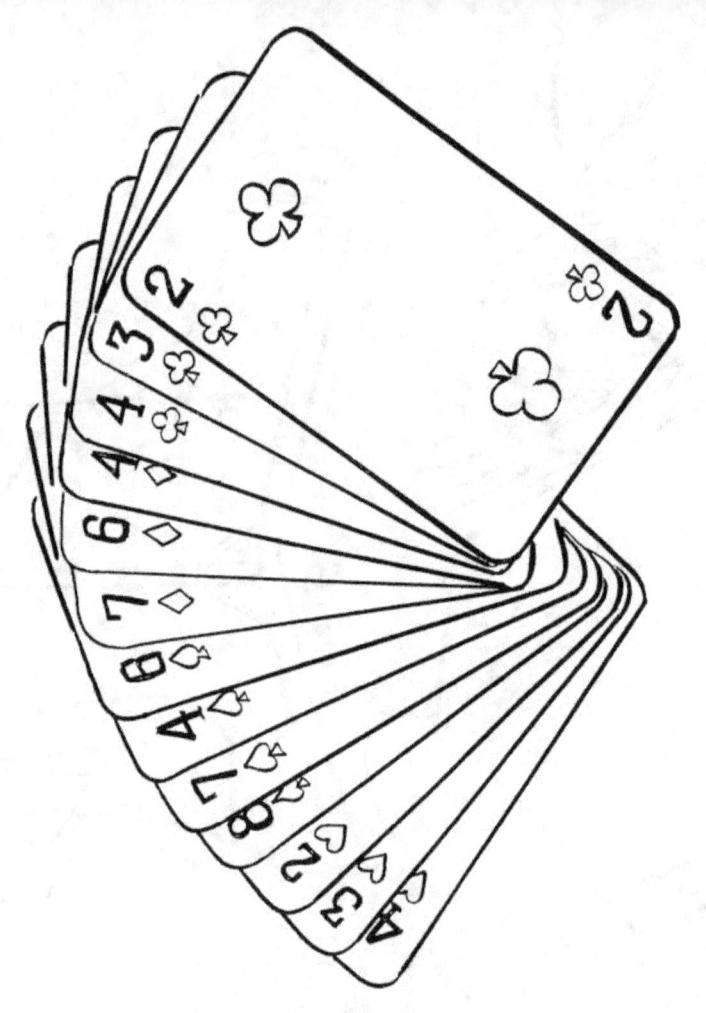

These are the cards Mr. Wilson is holding
   when Mr. Coles bids four no-trump.
Color some of the little spots black.
Color the others red.
It doesn't matter much about the colors;
Mr. Wilson and Mr. Coles are not going to have
too much use for these cards.

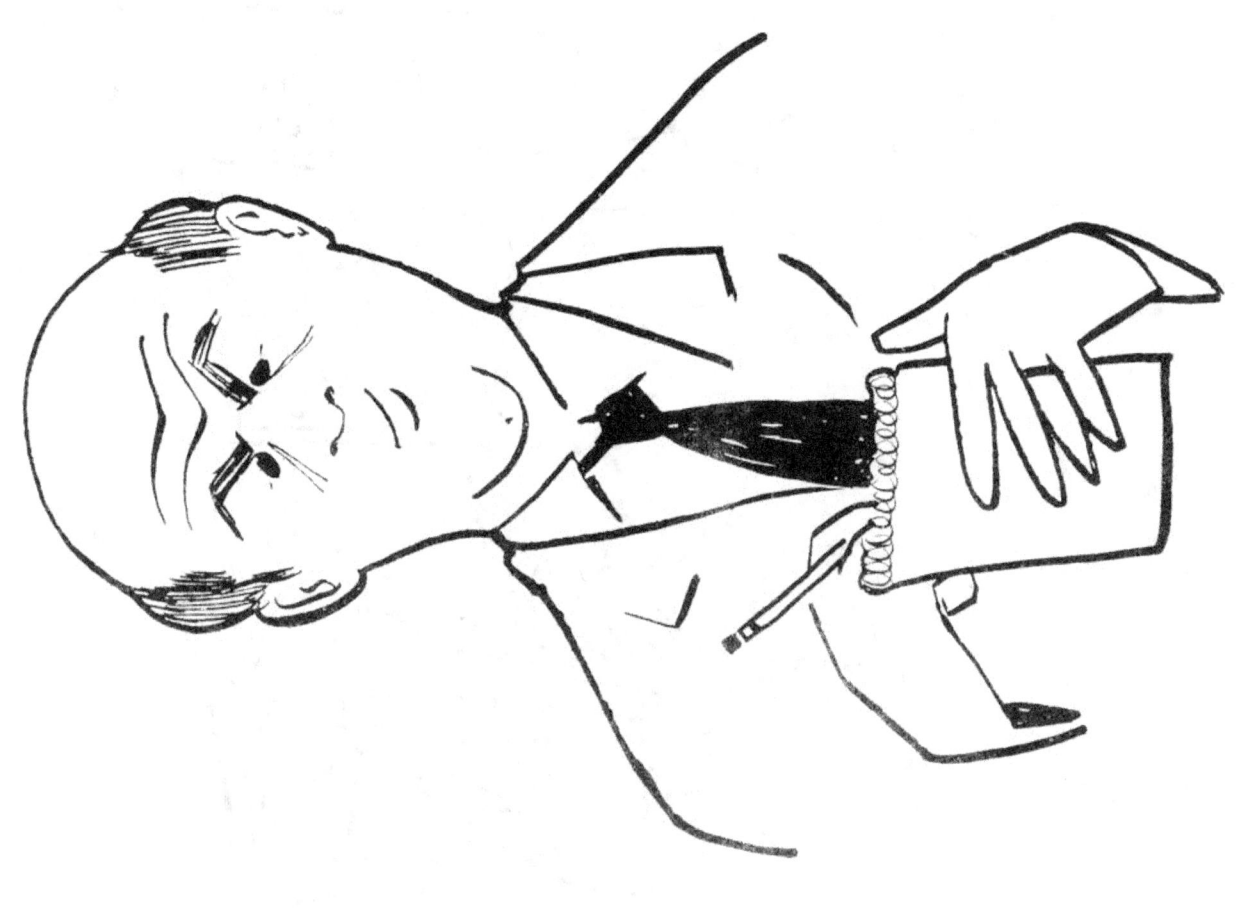

Mr. Wilson is putting down the score.
See the frown marks on his forehead!
Color them black.
Mr. Wilson is frowning because he can't remember
How much is down three, doubled.

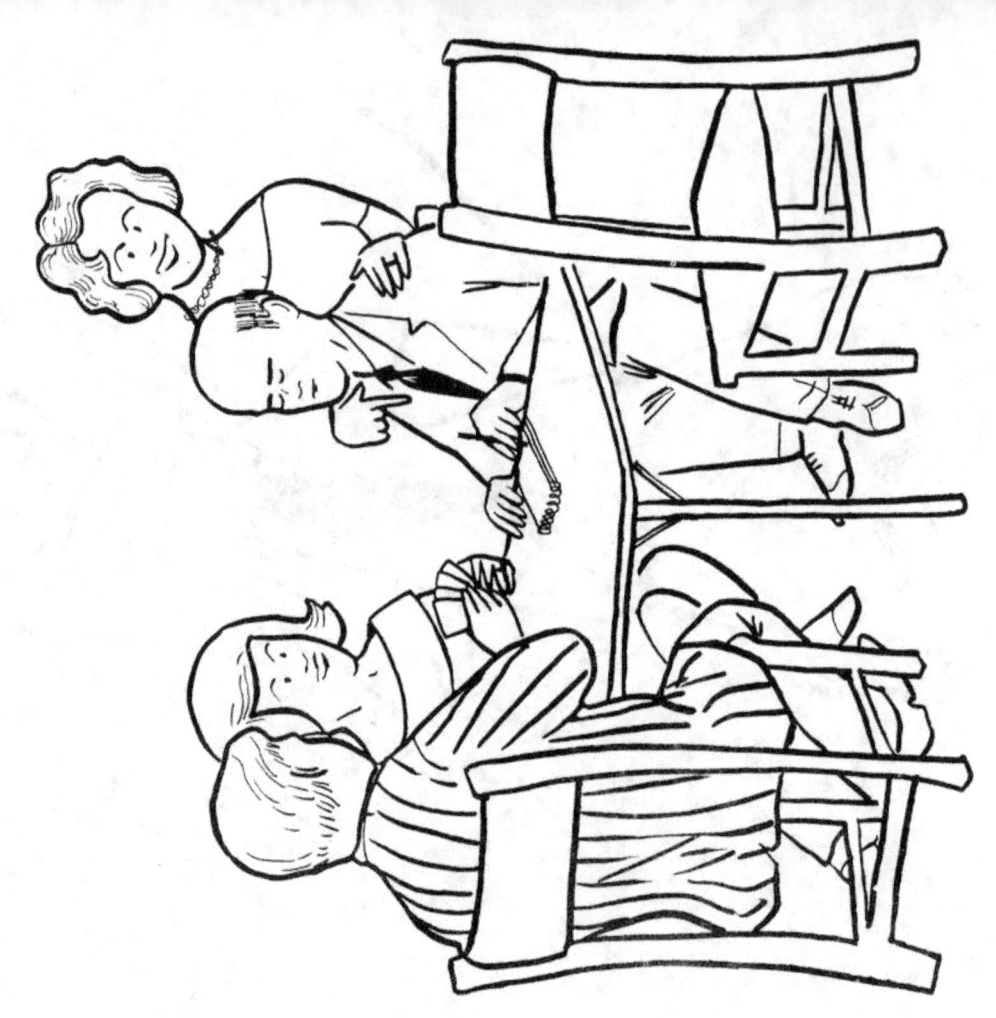

Mrs. Wilson is helping her husband keep score.
She says: "Don't forget you were vulnerable, too!"
This does not fill Mr. Wilson with joy.
But his wife looks pleased, doesn't she?
Color her pleased.

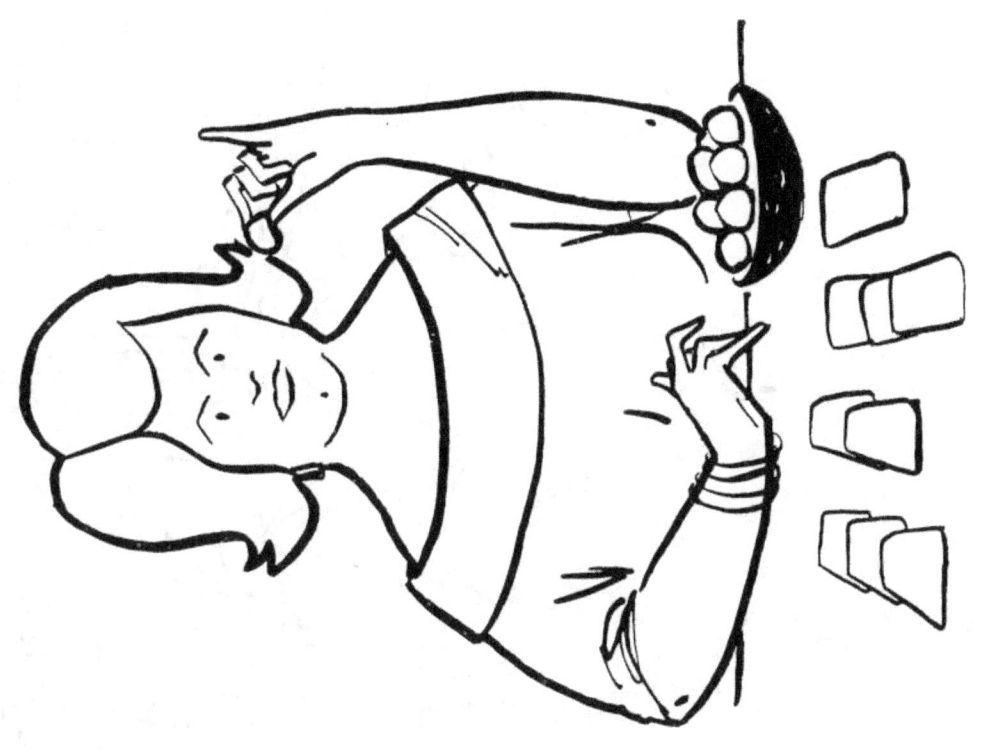

Mrs. Coles is not playing this hand; she is the dummy.
Color a little dark brown on her lips;
    also on her finger tips.
She is eating chocolate candy.
The dummy lady always eats chocolate candy . .
    or else salted peanuts.
That's how bridge is.

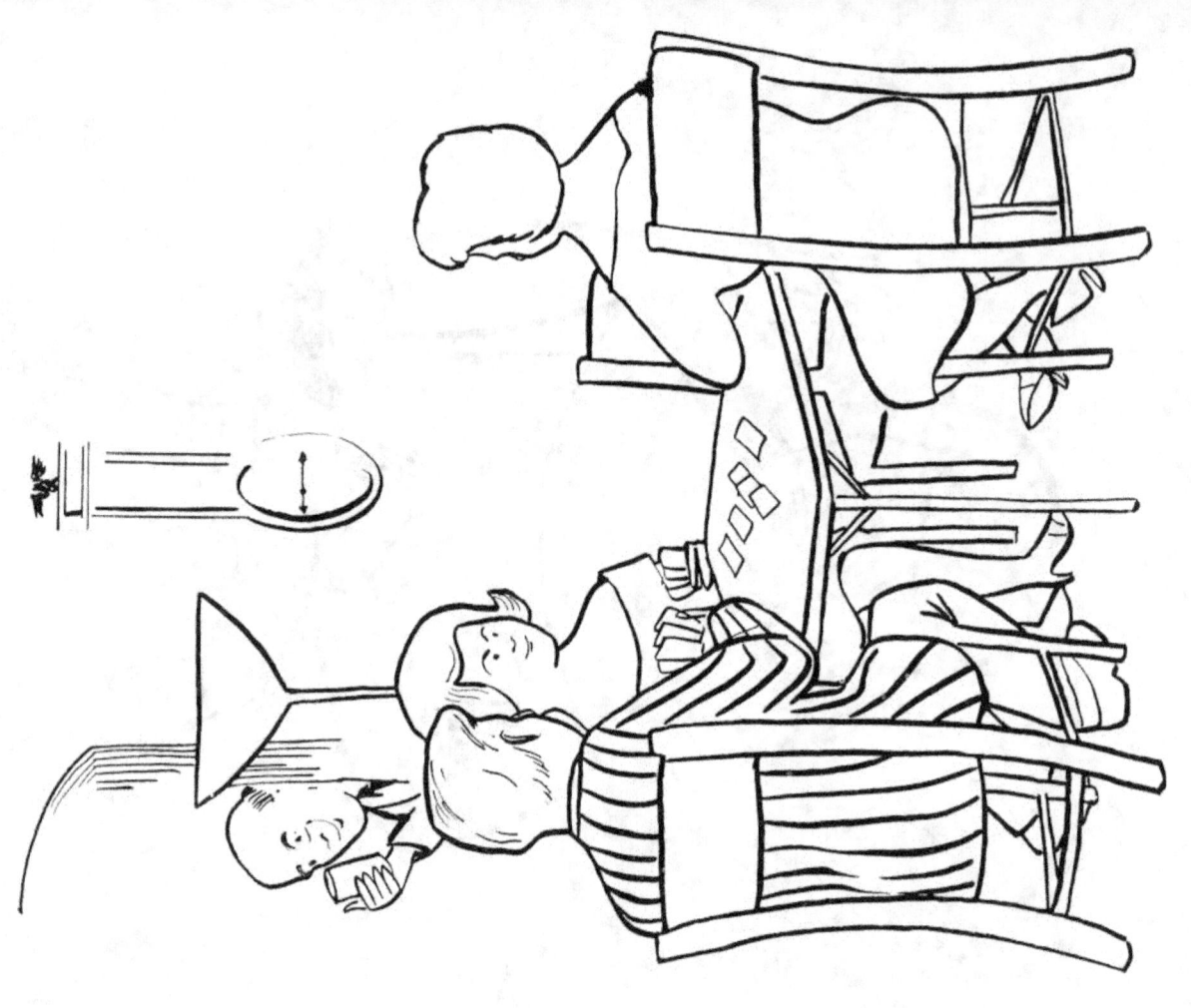

This time, Mr. Coles is playing the hand.

Mr. Wilson is the dummy.

There is not much of Mr. Wilson to color.

That's because he is out in the kitchen fixing a little something to drink.

That's how bridge is, too.

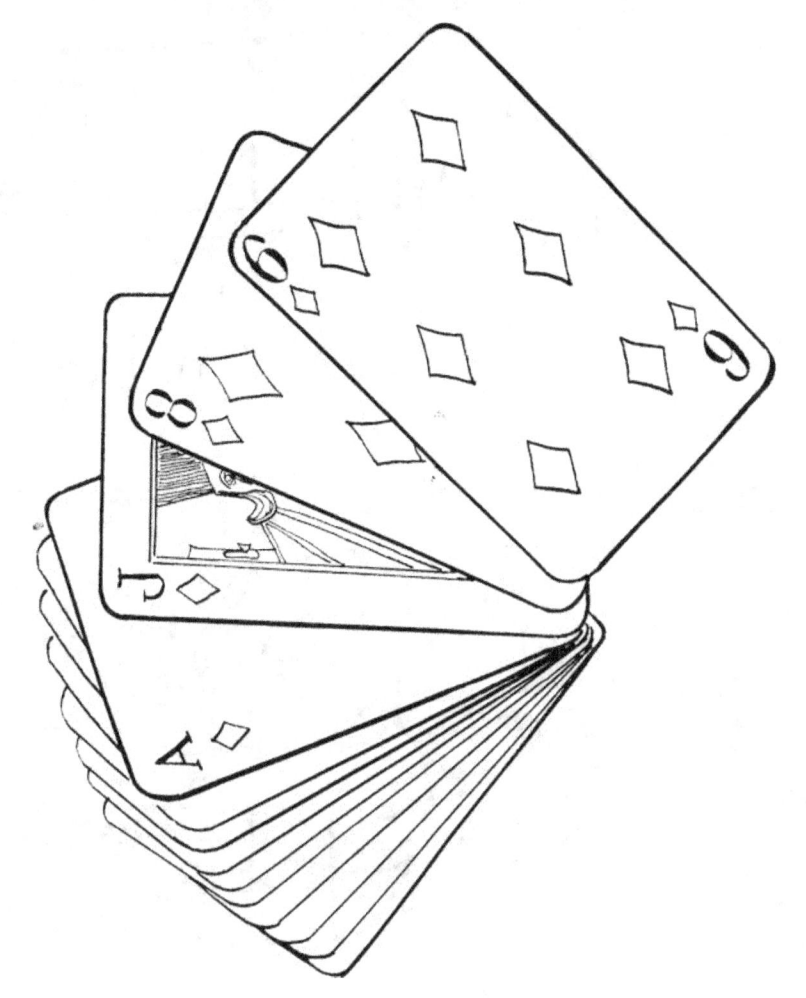

This is a four-card suit.
Color all four cards the same color—red.
Color them as much as you want.
You won't get into as much trouble coloring them
as Mr. Coles and Mr. Wilson do when they keep
bidding them.

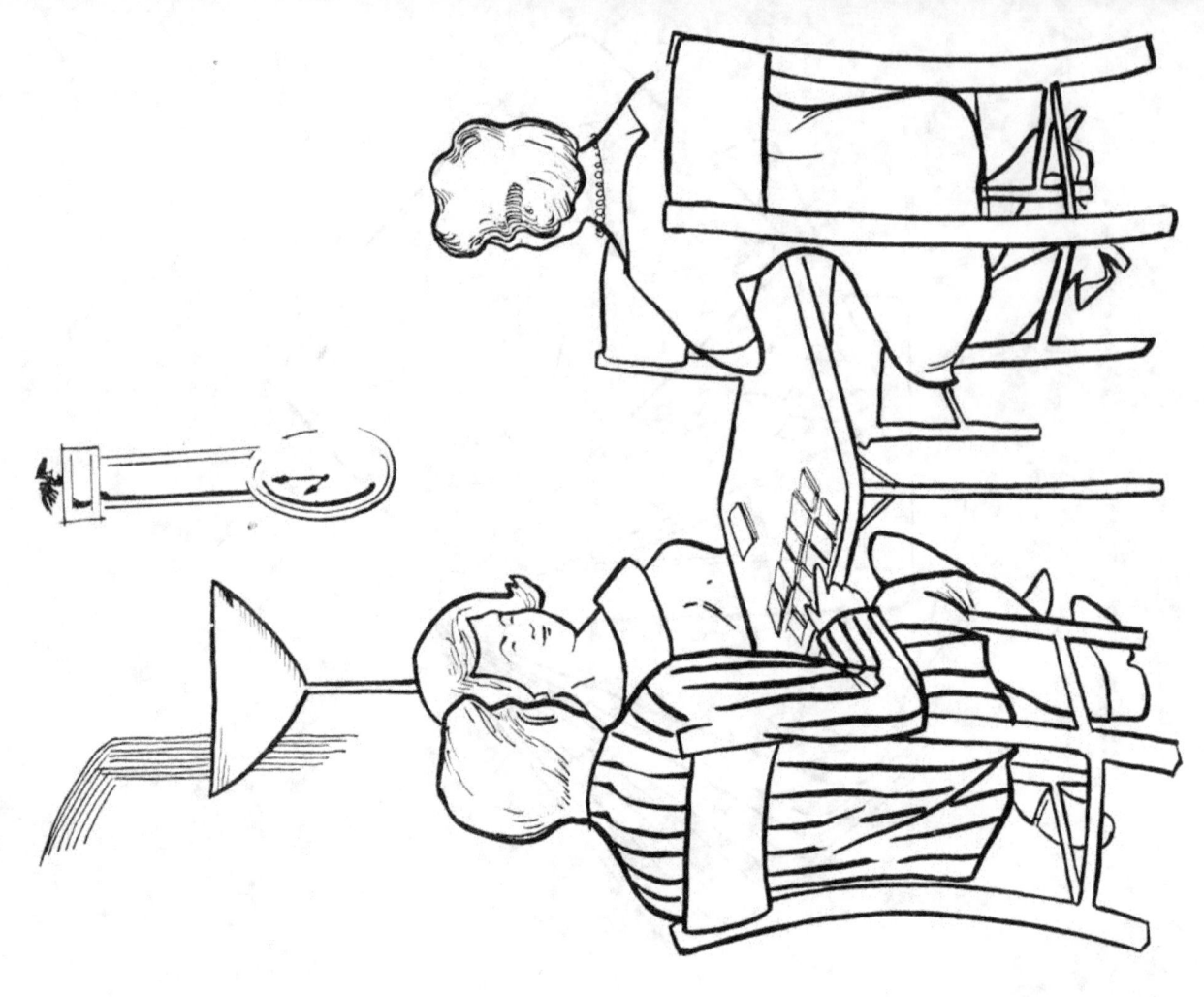

See all the tricks Mr. Coles has taken.
Twelve tricks—all except one.
This is a little slam; it is usually very good.
But not if your partner raised you to a grand slam—
which is what Mr. Wilson did.

He is out in the kitchen again,
and Mr. Coles is down one!

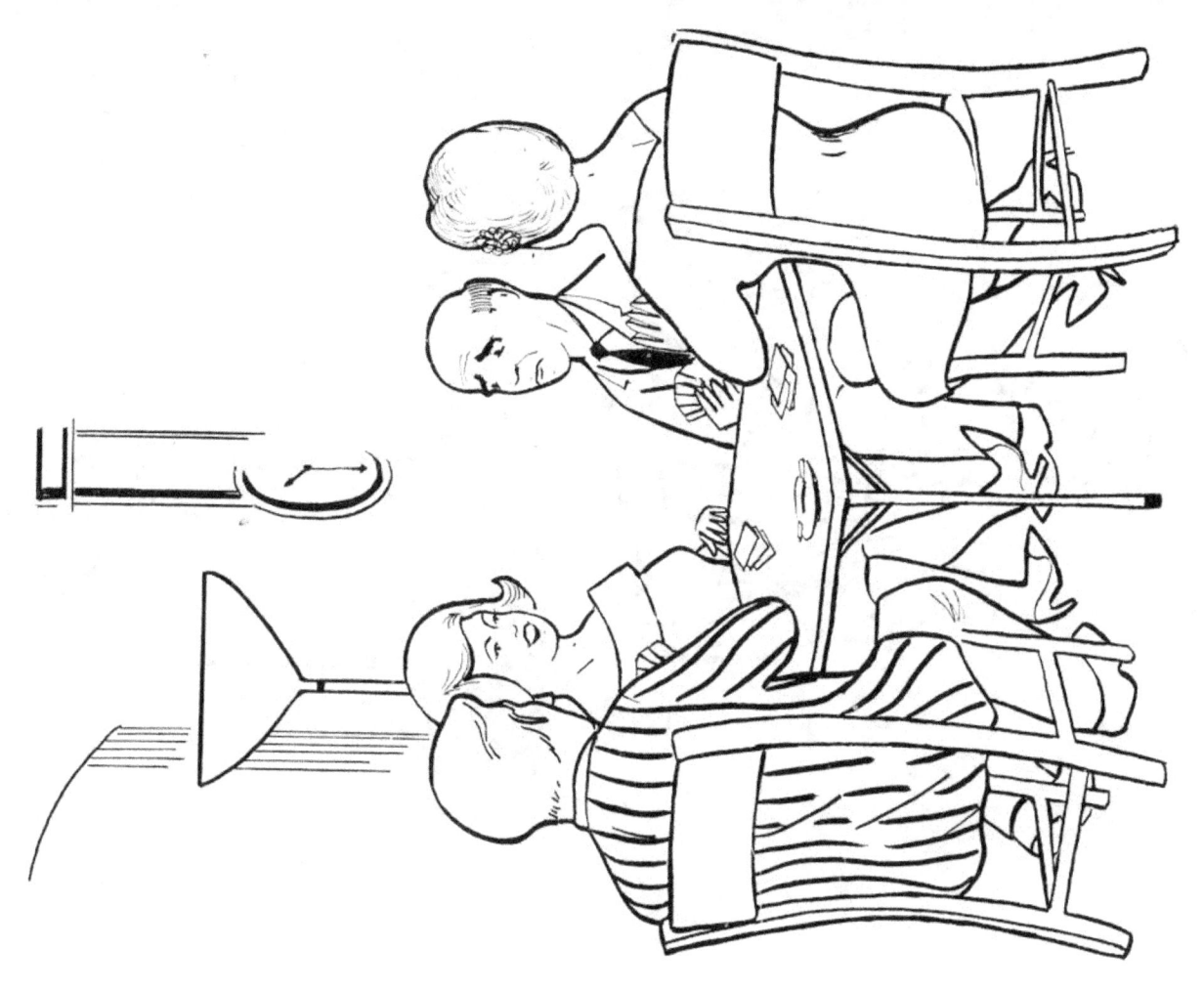

Mrs. Coles is telling Mrs. Wilson what a nice wedding
the Turners' daughter had the other day.
Next, they will talk about a what a fine boy
she married.
Color both ladies lively to match their conversation.
Color the men somewhat duller.

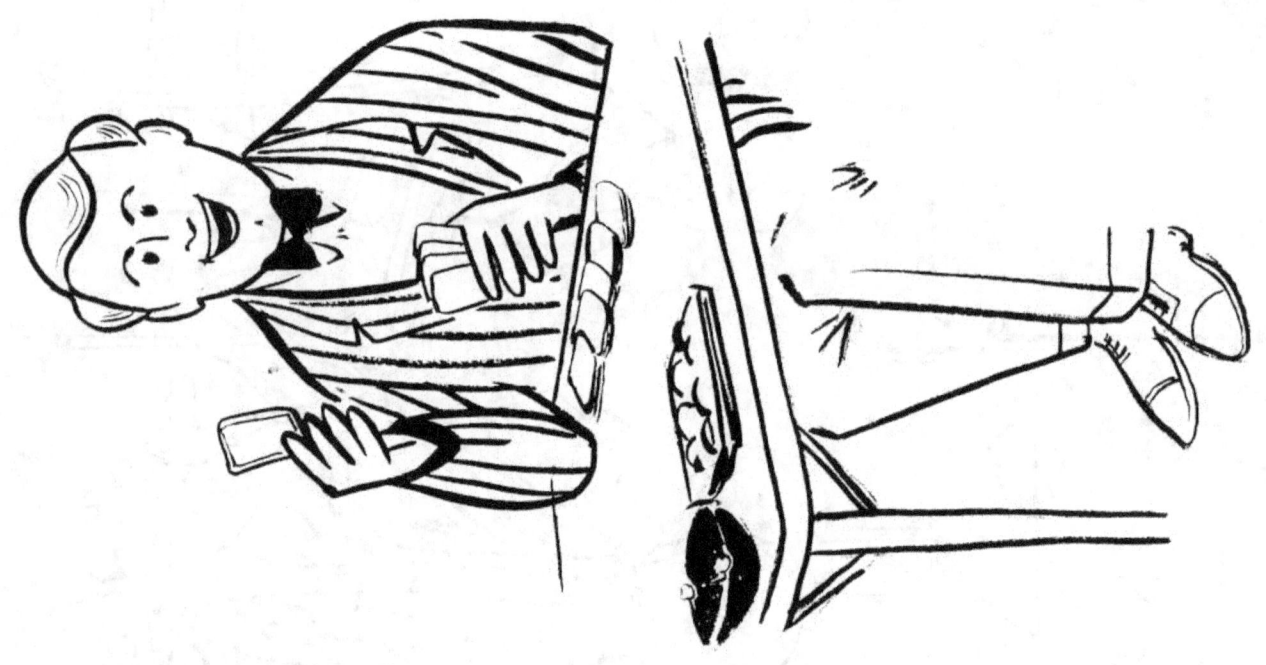

Look at Mr. Coles.

He is so happy you might think he is making a grand slam.

But it is even better than that.

His wife bid three no-trump without having the hearts stopped.

Mr. Coles has taken five heart tricks, and now he is playing his ace of clubs.

No wonder he is so happy. That's how bridge is.

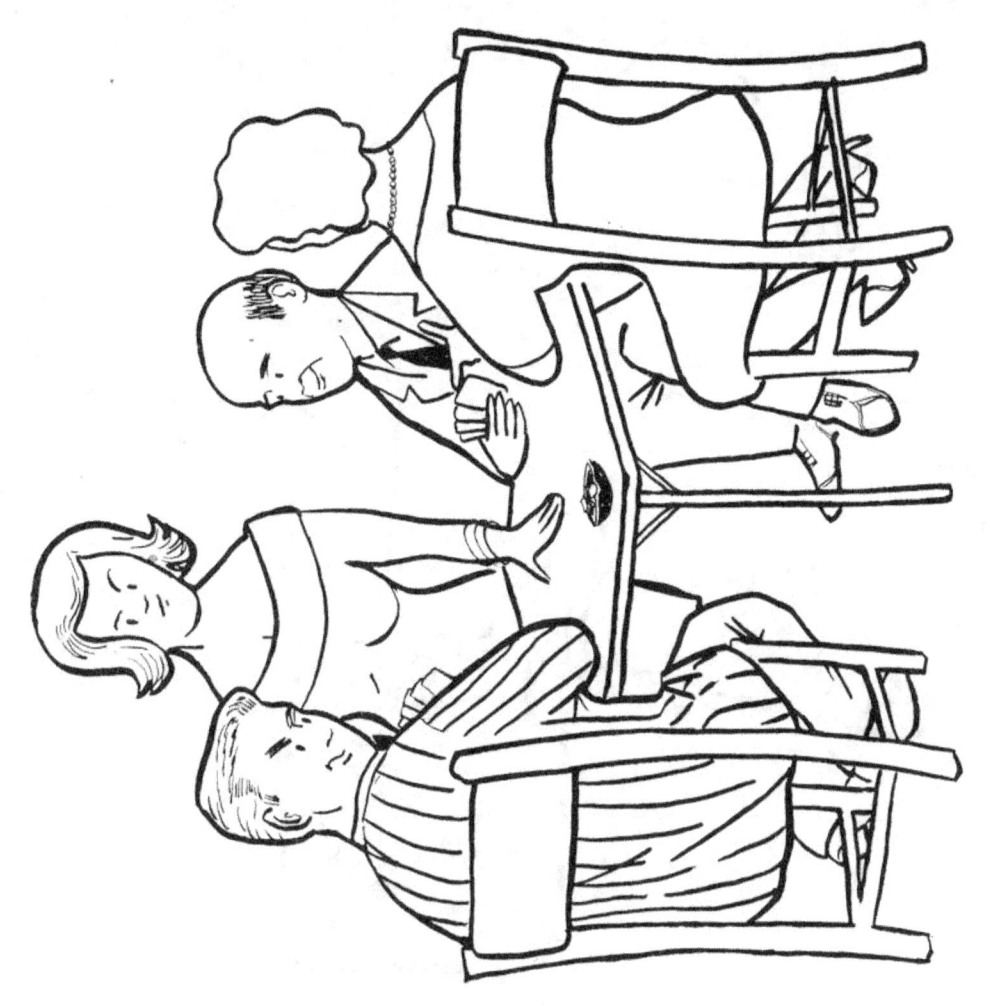

Mrs. Coles has a good hand.
But every time she bids, Mr. Coles bids higher.
Mrs. Coles wants to see what is in his hand;
    she bets he doesn't have anything at all.
Mr. Coles doesn't particularly want her to see.
Color this situation a little stormy.

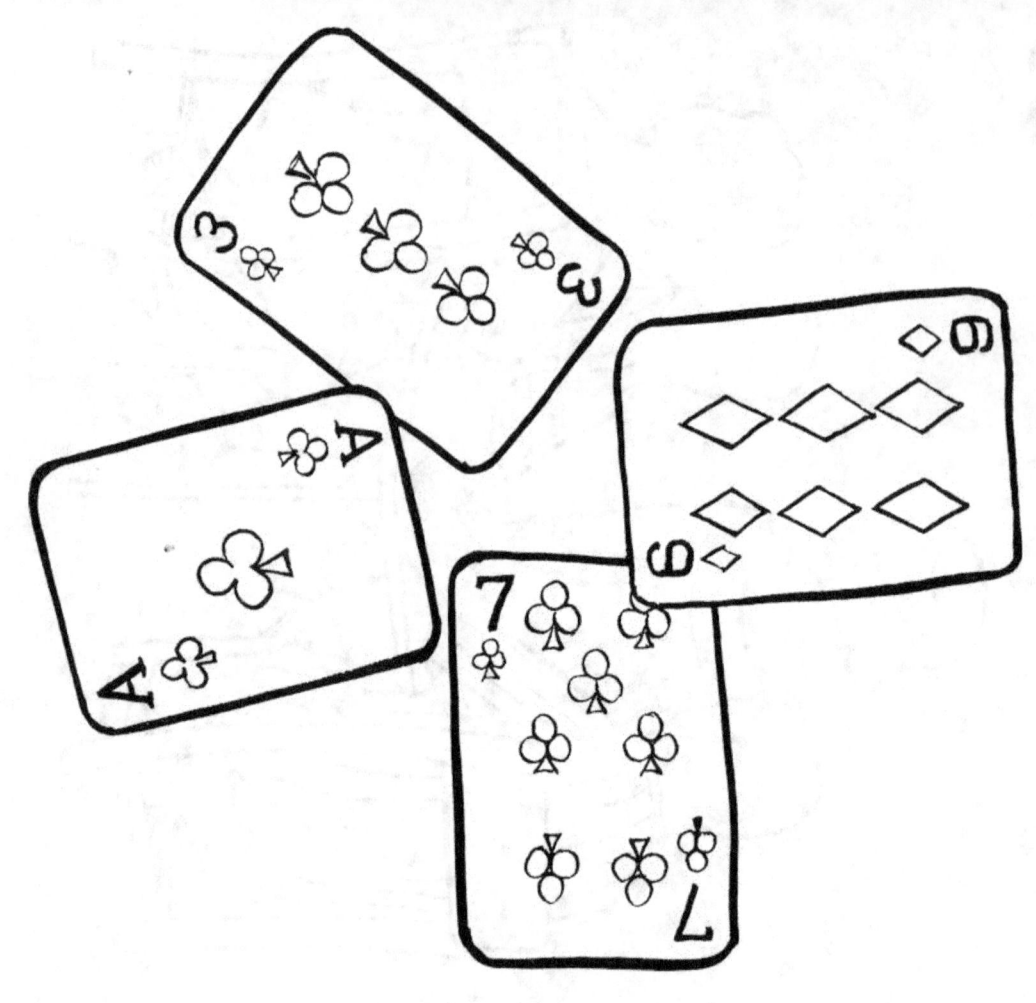

Here are four cards to color.
The Ace of Clubs belongs to Mr. Wilson; color it black.
The two other clubs should be black, too.
The other card is a diamond. Color it red.
Diamonds are trump; Mr. Coles didn't have any clubs,
so he put the trump on Mr. Wilson's ace.

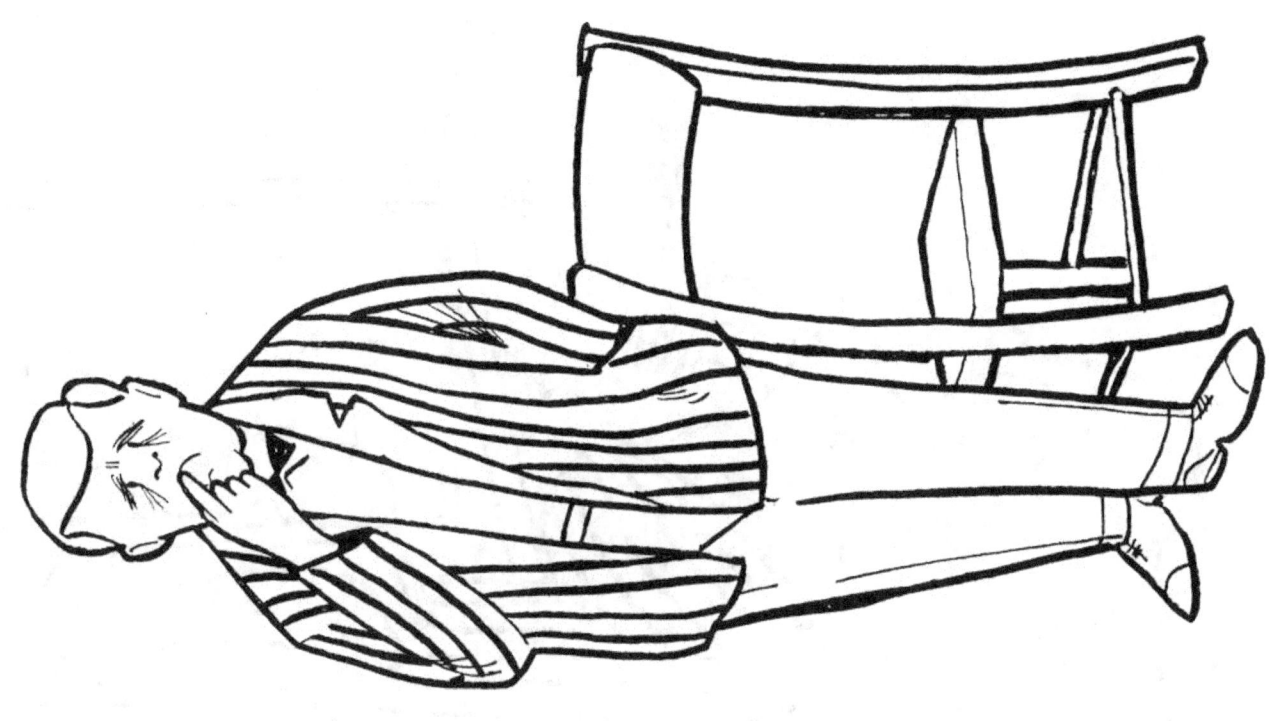

Mr. Coles is walking around his chair.
Why? Because he hopes it will change his luck.
Maybe it will; but not very much if he keeps on
trumping his partner's ace.
Better color this whole picture black.

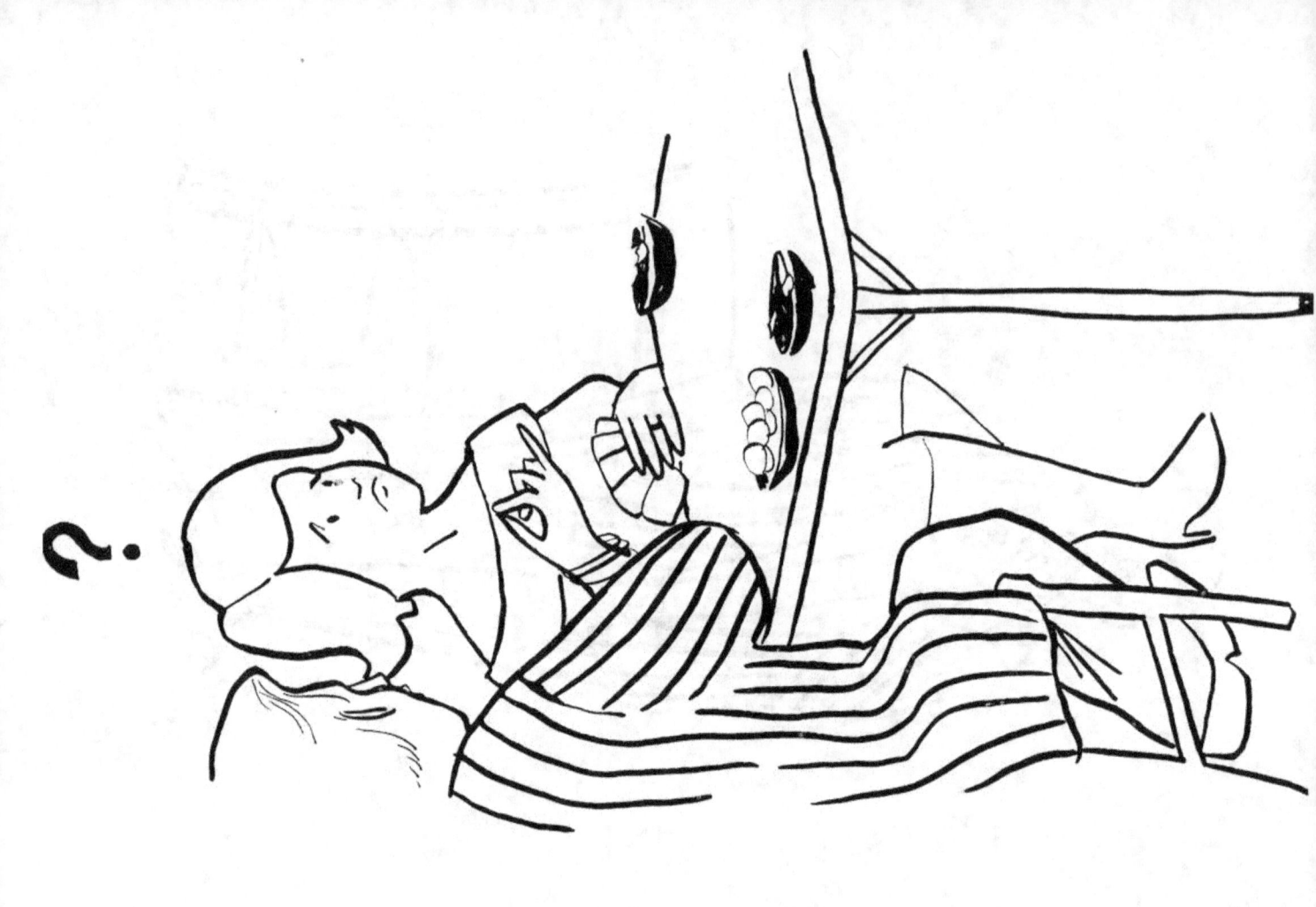

Mrs. Coles has a funny look on her face.
No, she is not ill.
She forgot to count trump.
Now she doesn't know whether there is any trump out
  against her, or not.
Color her face red.

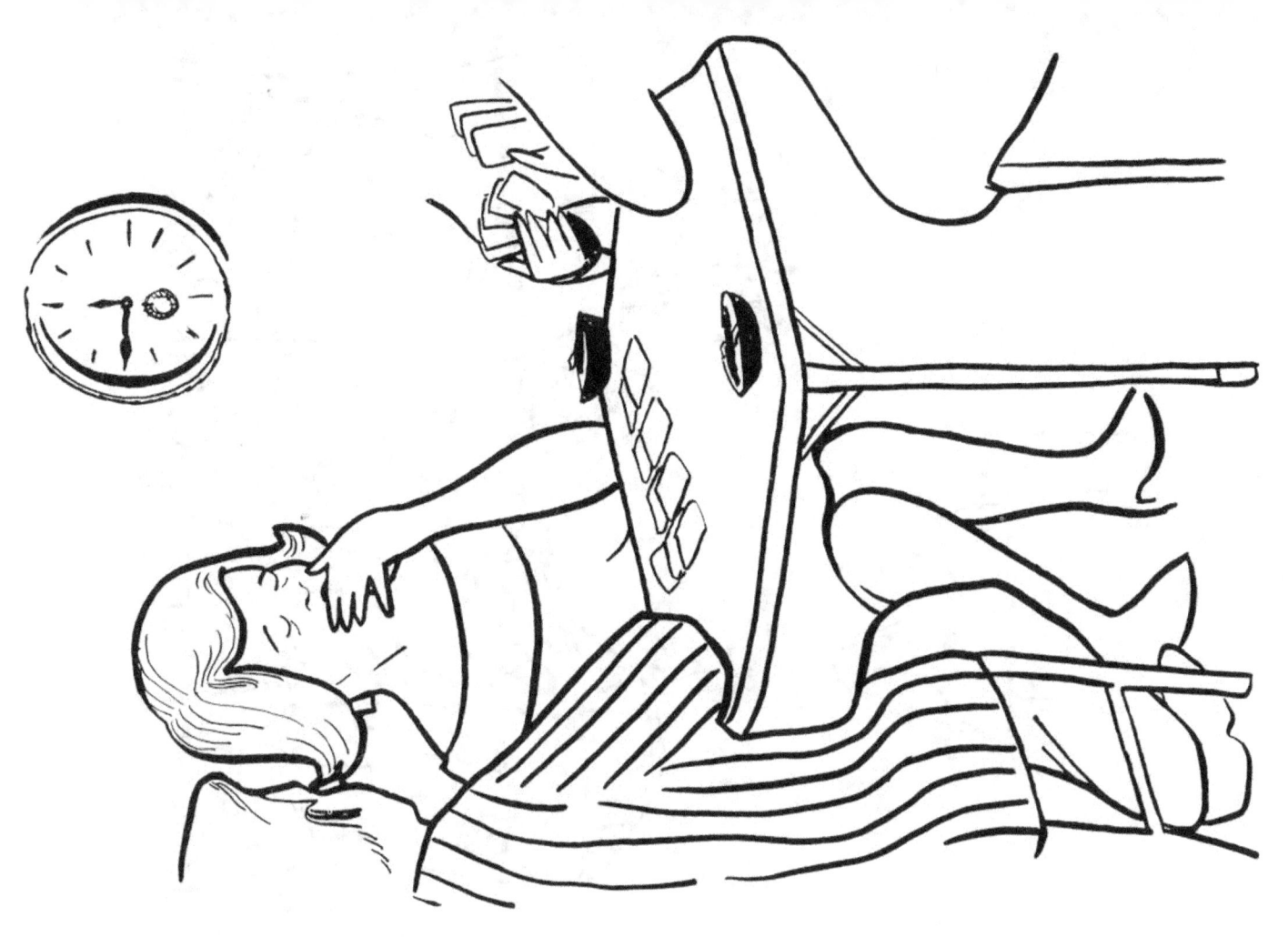

See the clock!
Paint the clock mahogany.
Mrs. Coles has been looking at the clock, too.
And it looks like this bridge game is about over.

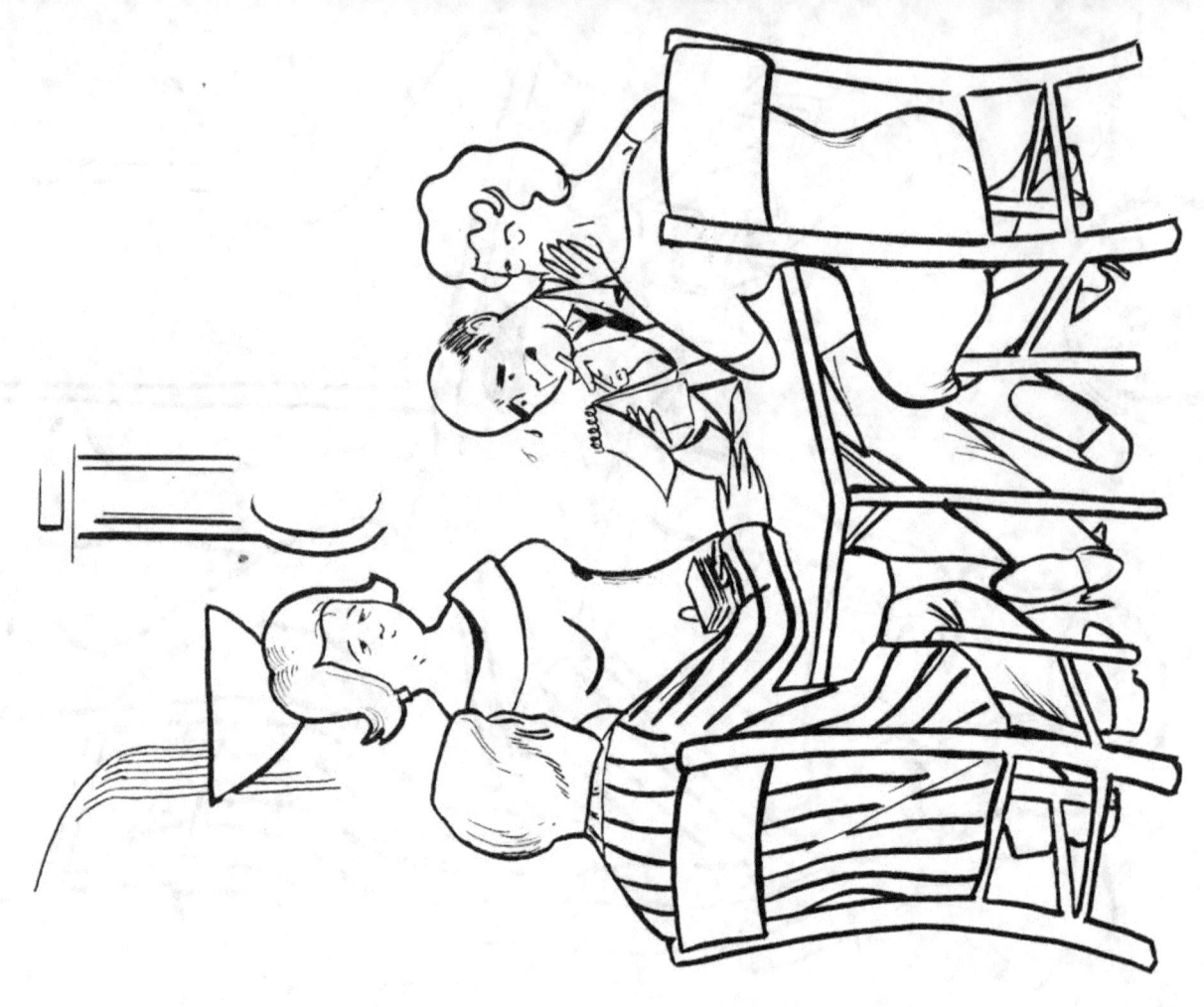

While Mr. Wilson puts down the score,
Mr. Coles wants to deal another hand.
He says: "C'mon, it's still early."
But the ladies seem to think the game is over.
Better color this picture quickly.

WE	THEY
	500
	750
	50
	50
	100
	20
	300
50	100
30	
60	180
140	2050

Here is the score.

"They" means Mrs. Coles and Mrs. Wilson.

"We" means the men.

After five rubbers, all the scores look about like this.

Which is why the men want to keep on playing.

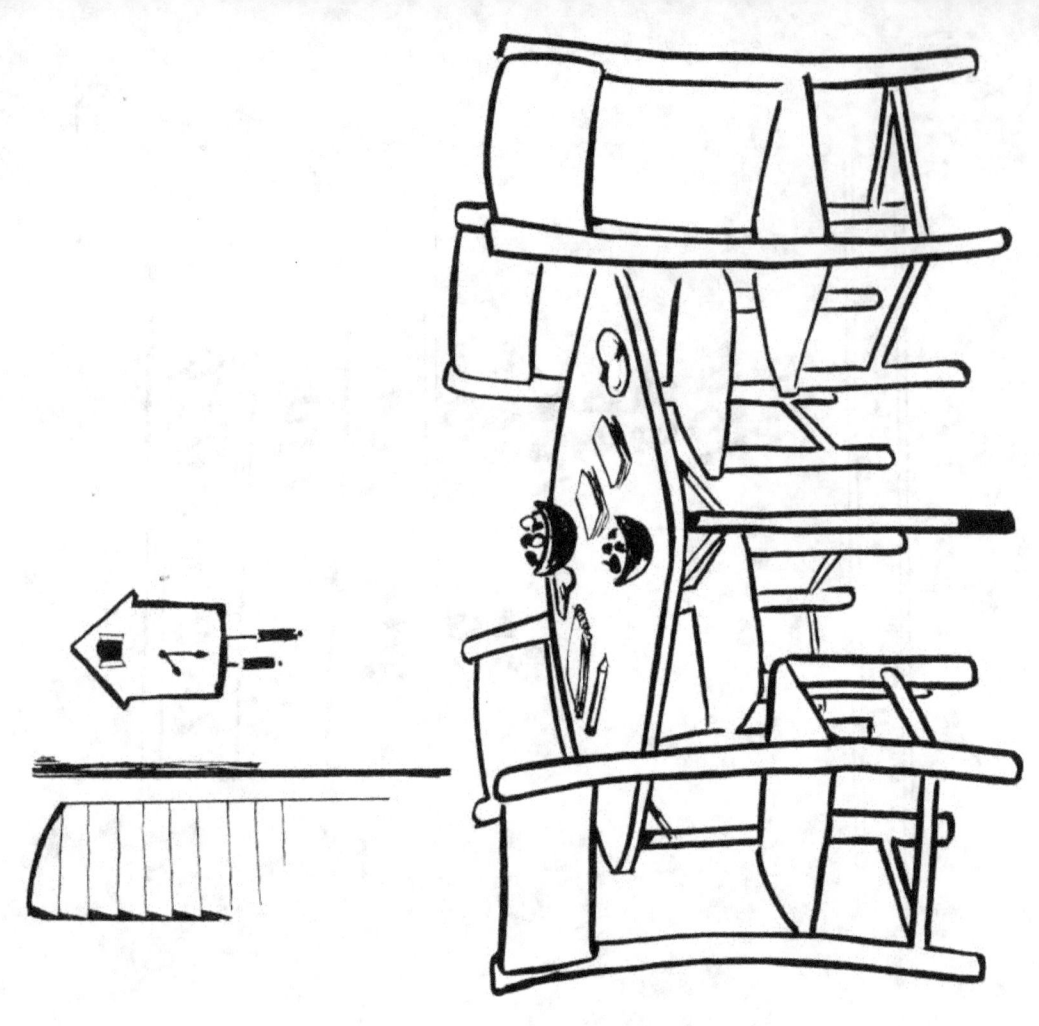

Color this bridge table like the first one.
It is ready for the game next Tuesday
    at the Coleses' house.
Surely the men will win next week, because, after all,
    they are the better players?
But isn't it remarkable how much luck
    the wives always have?

    —That's how bridge is.

THE SAGA OF
DR. ANTON PAZU

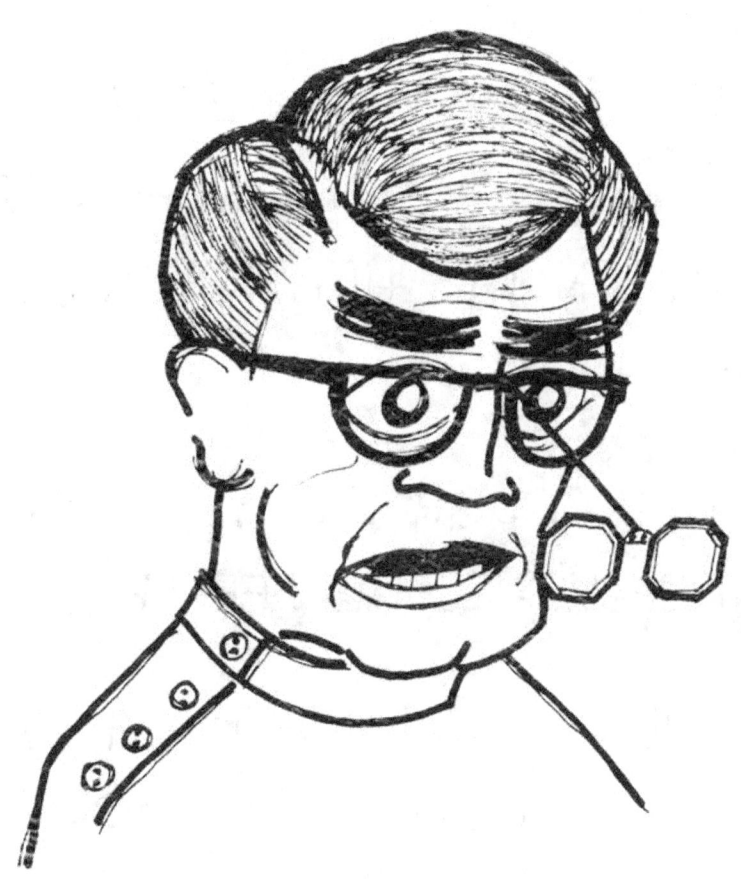

A COLORING BOOK
FOR DENTISTS

Originally published in 1962 and reprinted through the decade, *The Saga of Dr. Anton Pazu* is an inside look at dentistry, produced anonymously by Dr. Neil B. Brahe, DDS, an Appleton, Wisconsin dentist who produced a number of books on the business of dentistry. This saga even had a sequel, 1969's *The Incredible Story of Dr. Anton Pazu and the Internal Revenue Service: Another Coloring Book for Dentists.*

THE ONLY SERIOUS THOUGHT IN THIS BOOK:

THIS LITTLE GEM WAS PRODUCED WITH ONE THOUGHT IN MIND. THAT MY HARD WORKING COLLEAGUES MAY, IN THE HEAT OF A BUSY DAY, SIT BACK AND CHUCKLE..

I HAVE FOUND THROUGH THE YEARS THAT A LAUGH AT OURSELVES IS THE VERY BEST KIND..

IF IT WILL CUT THE CORONARY RATE BY ONE-MILLIONTH OF ONE PERCENT IT WILL HAVE BEEN WORTH WHILE..

ANY RESEMBLANCE TO ANYONE EXCEPT MYSELF IS AN ARTIFACT..

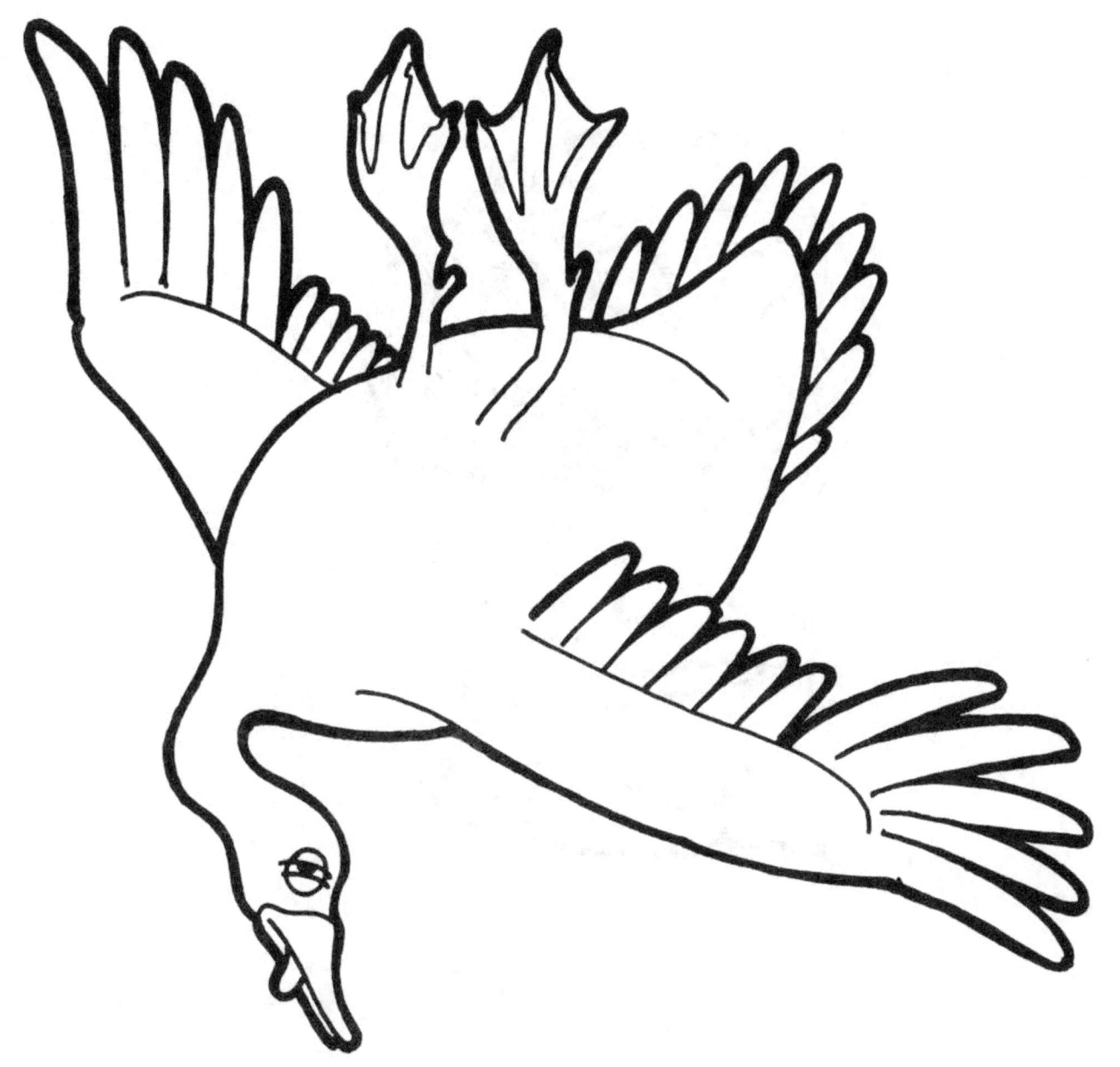

THIS IS A **DEAD DUCK** • AND IF THE DENTAL SOCIETY • ANY HYGENIST • SUPPLY MAN • OR ANY OF MY FORMER ASSISTANTS EVER FIND OUT WHO I AM • THAT'S EXACTLY WHAT I'LL BE • THEREFORE I PREFER ANONIMITY...

NO DEDICATIONS
NO ONE WANTS ANY PART OF IT!

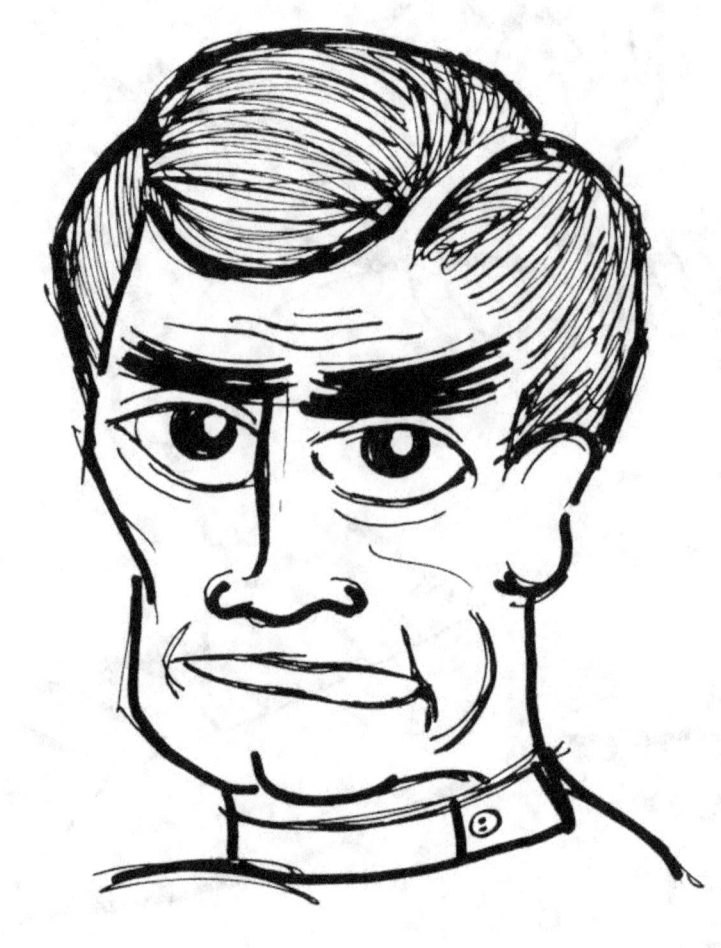

I AM THE GREAT **DR. ANTON PAZU** • THE OUT-
STANDING ORAL REHABILITATOR • I AM HAPPY!
I AM ENTHUSIASTIC • I AM A GREAT EXECUTIVE.
SOMETIMES I FEEL LIKE SAYING "THE HELL WITH IT"

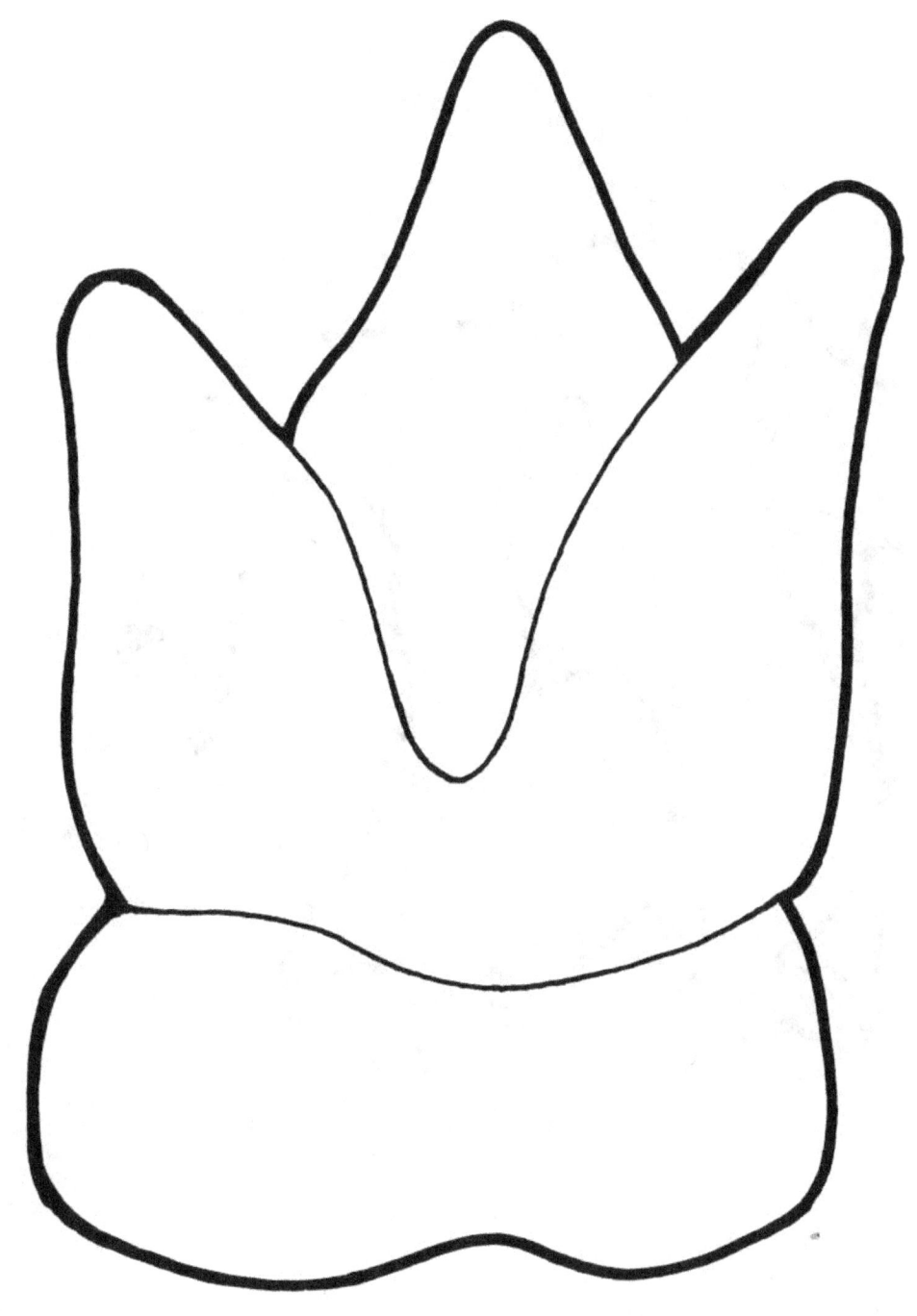

THIS IS A **TOOTH** • SOMETIMES I FIND IT DIFFICULT TO EXTRACT BECAUSE THE ROOTS ARE WRAPPED AROUND THE JAWBONE •••

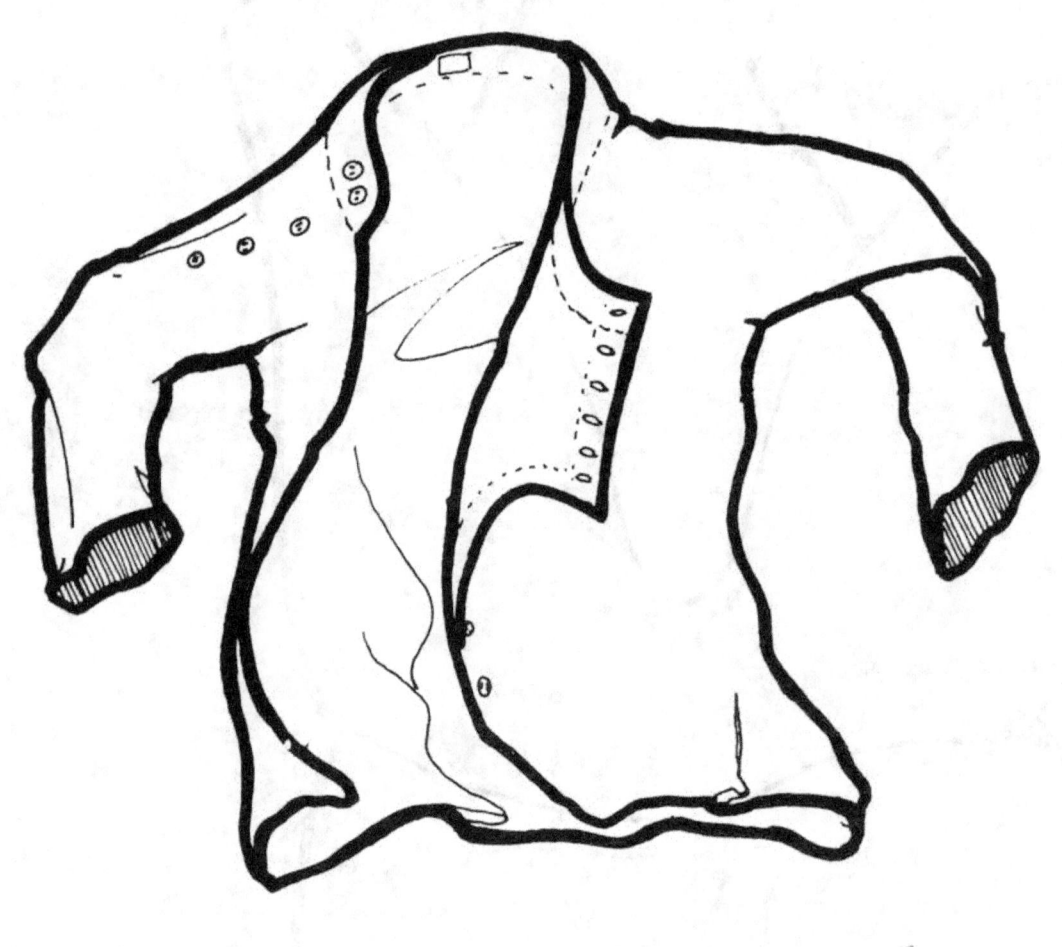

THIS IS MY SPARKLING WHITE **GOWN** · IT MAKES
ME STERILE...

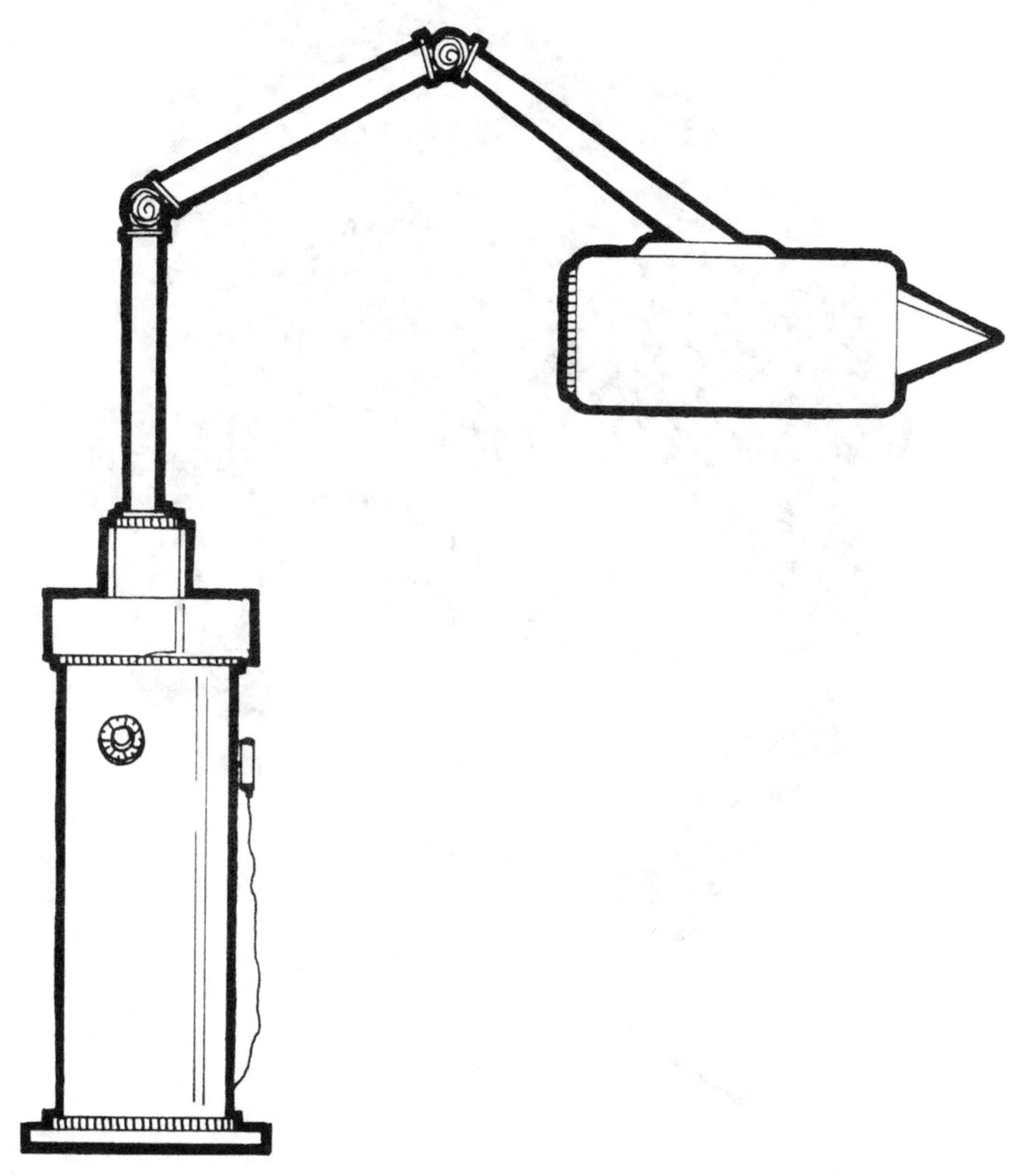

THIS DOES THE SAME THING !! ...

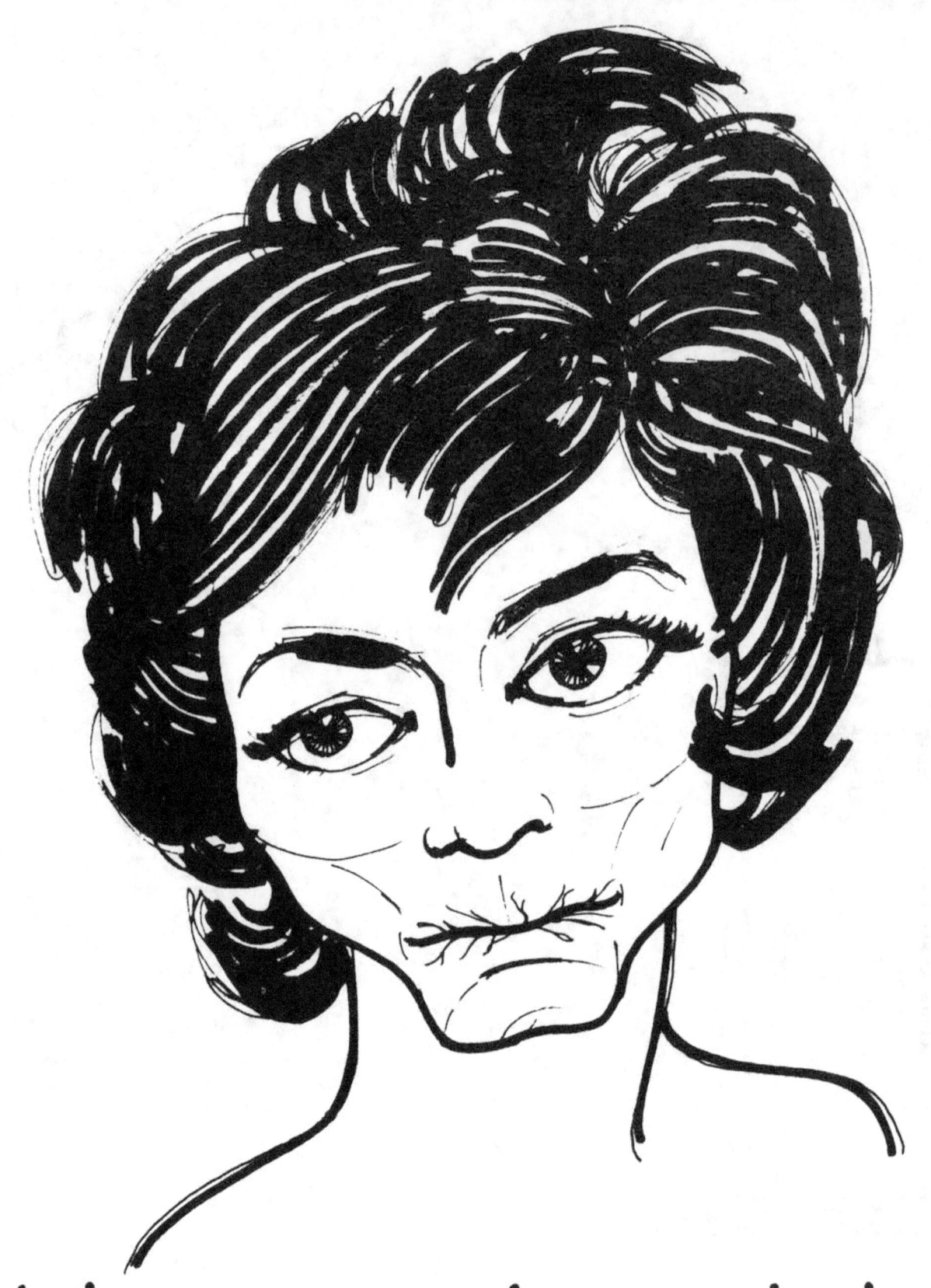

THIS IS A **DENTURE PATIENT** · SHE IS NINETEEN YEARS OLD · SHE IS HAPPY WHEN I TELL HER THAT NOW HER TROUBLES ARE OVER···

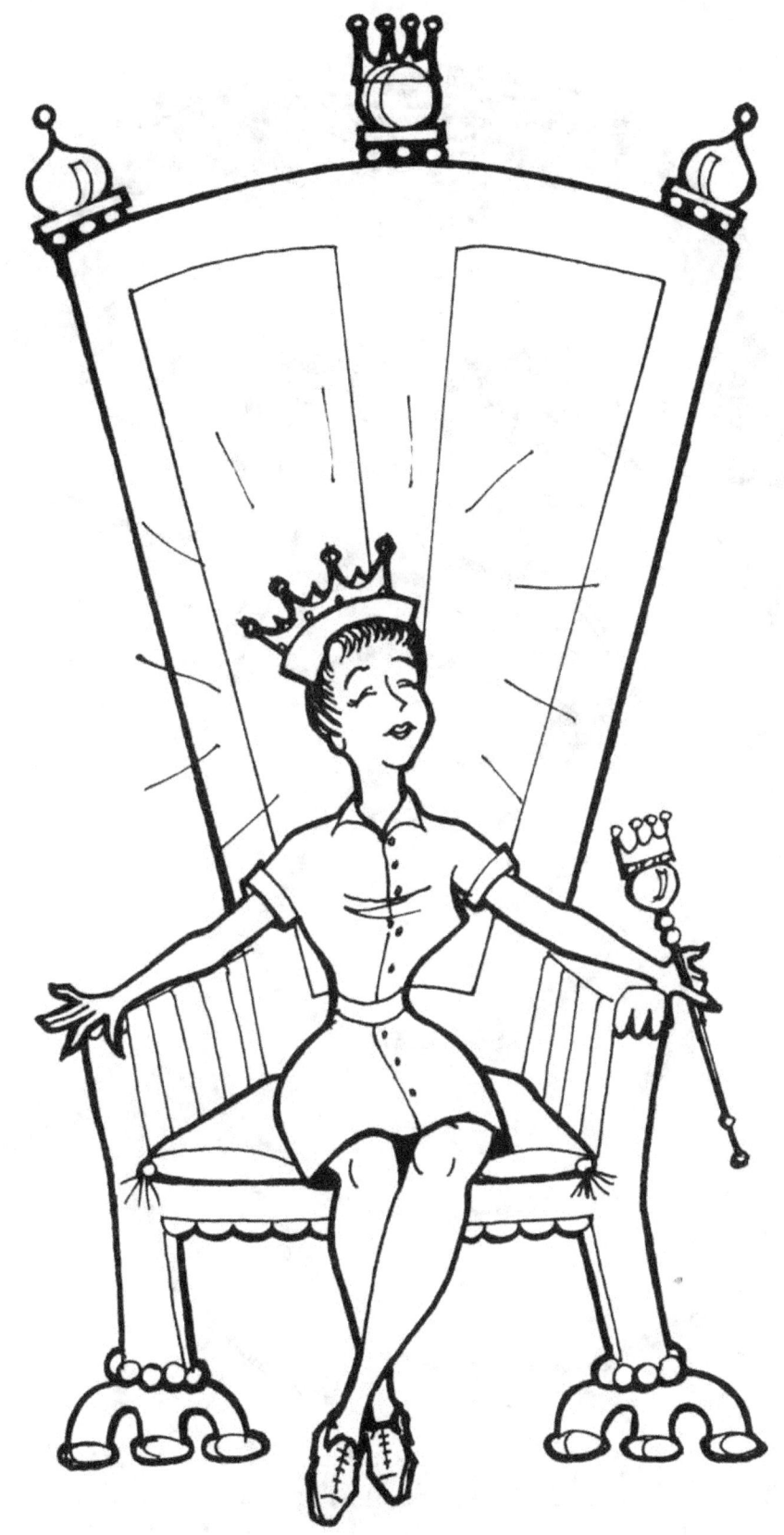

THIS IS MY **HYGIENIST** . SHE IS VERY INTELLIGENT . SOMETIMES I FEEL INADEQUATE! ...

COLOR HER REGAL ...

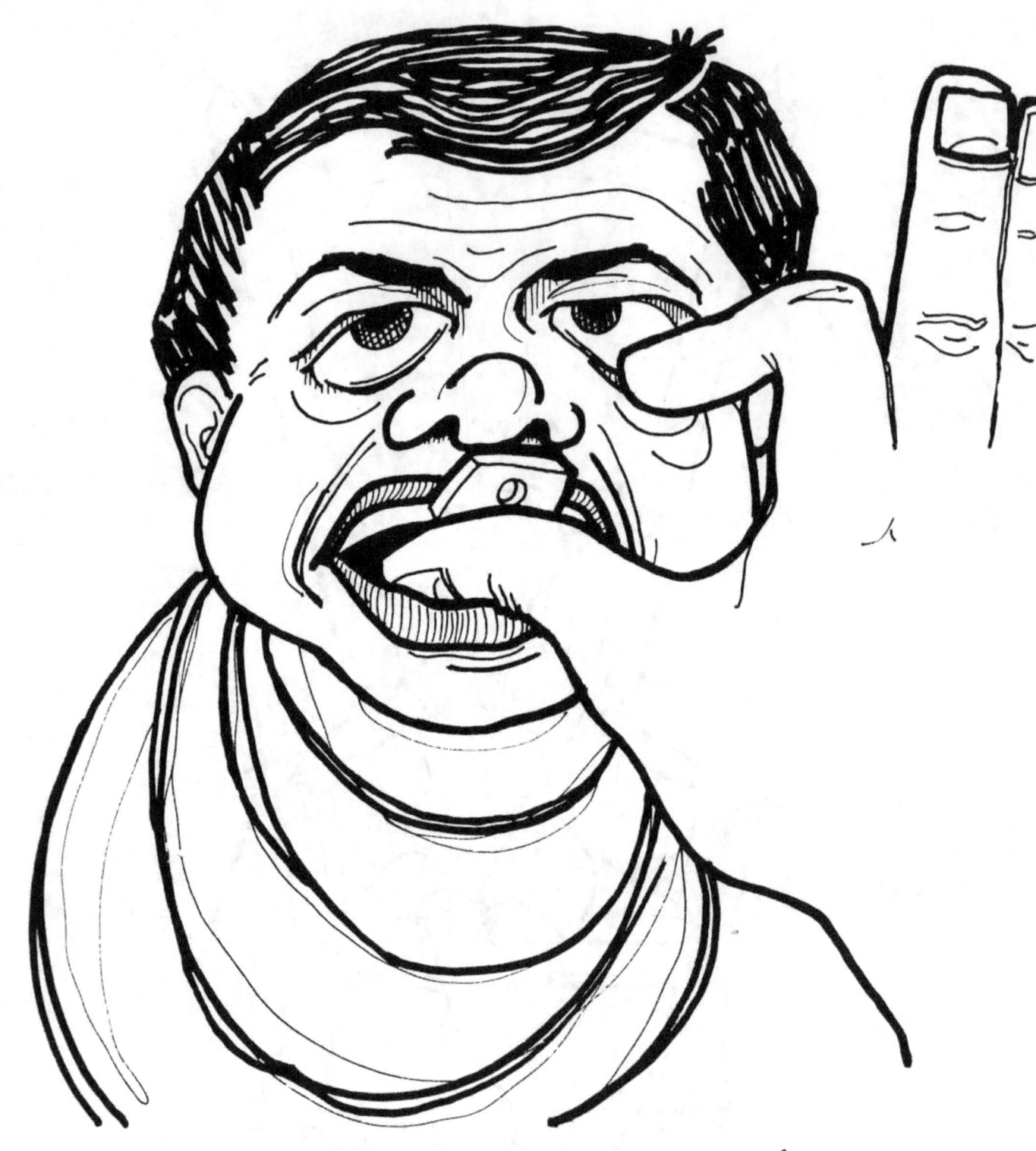

THIS IS MY **THUMB** • I AM TAKING AN IMPRESS-
ION • I FEEL IMPORTANT WHEN I AM TAKING
IMPRESSIONS •••

COLOR PATIENT GREEN •••

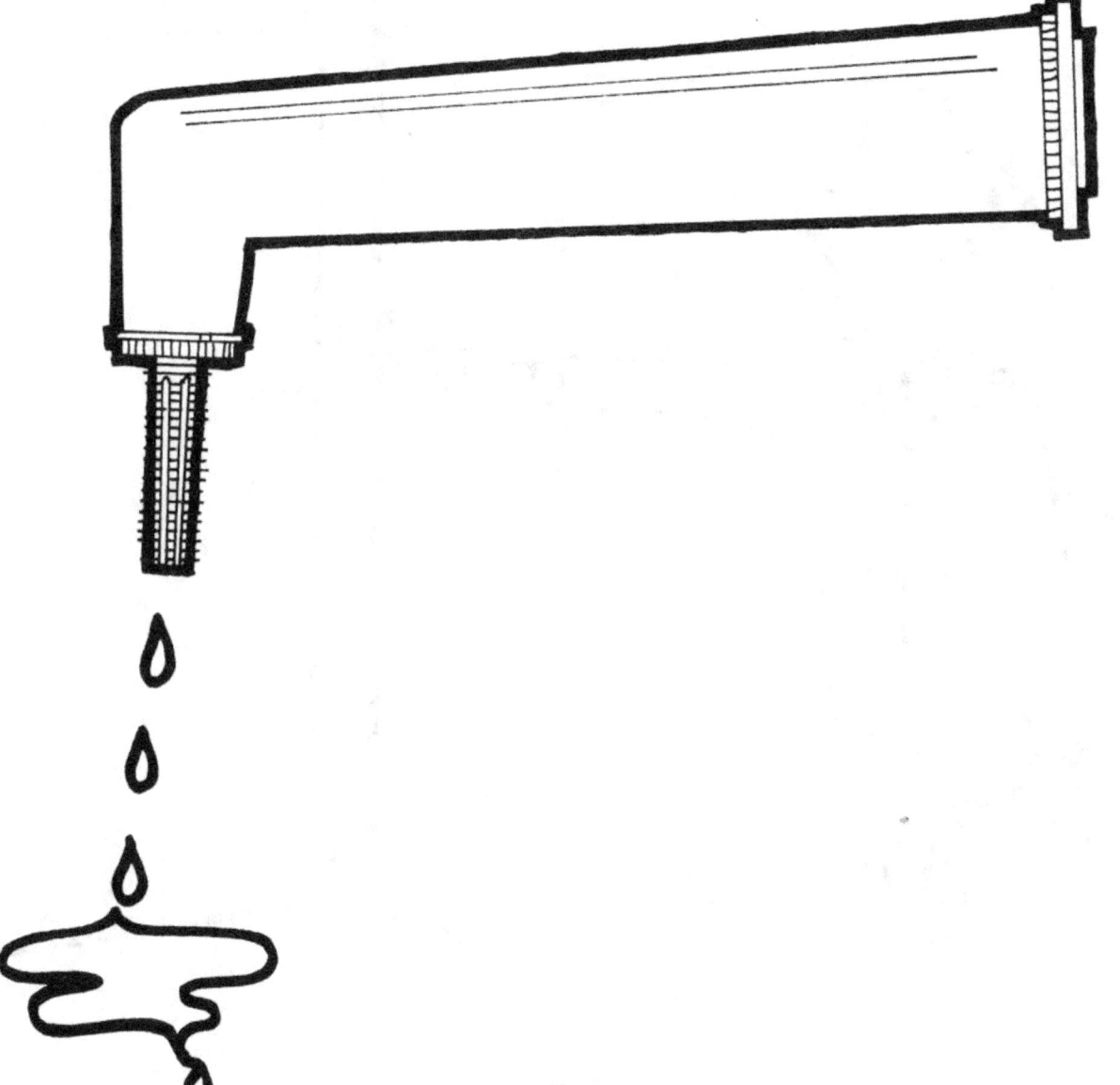

THIS IS MY **NEUTRON ROTOR** • IT REVOLVES AT 12 BILLION R.P.M. IT CUTS TEETH AND OTHER THINGS •••

COLOR DROPS RED•••

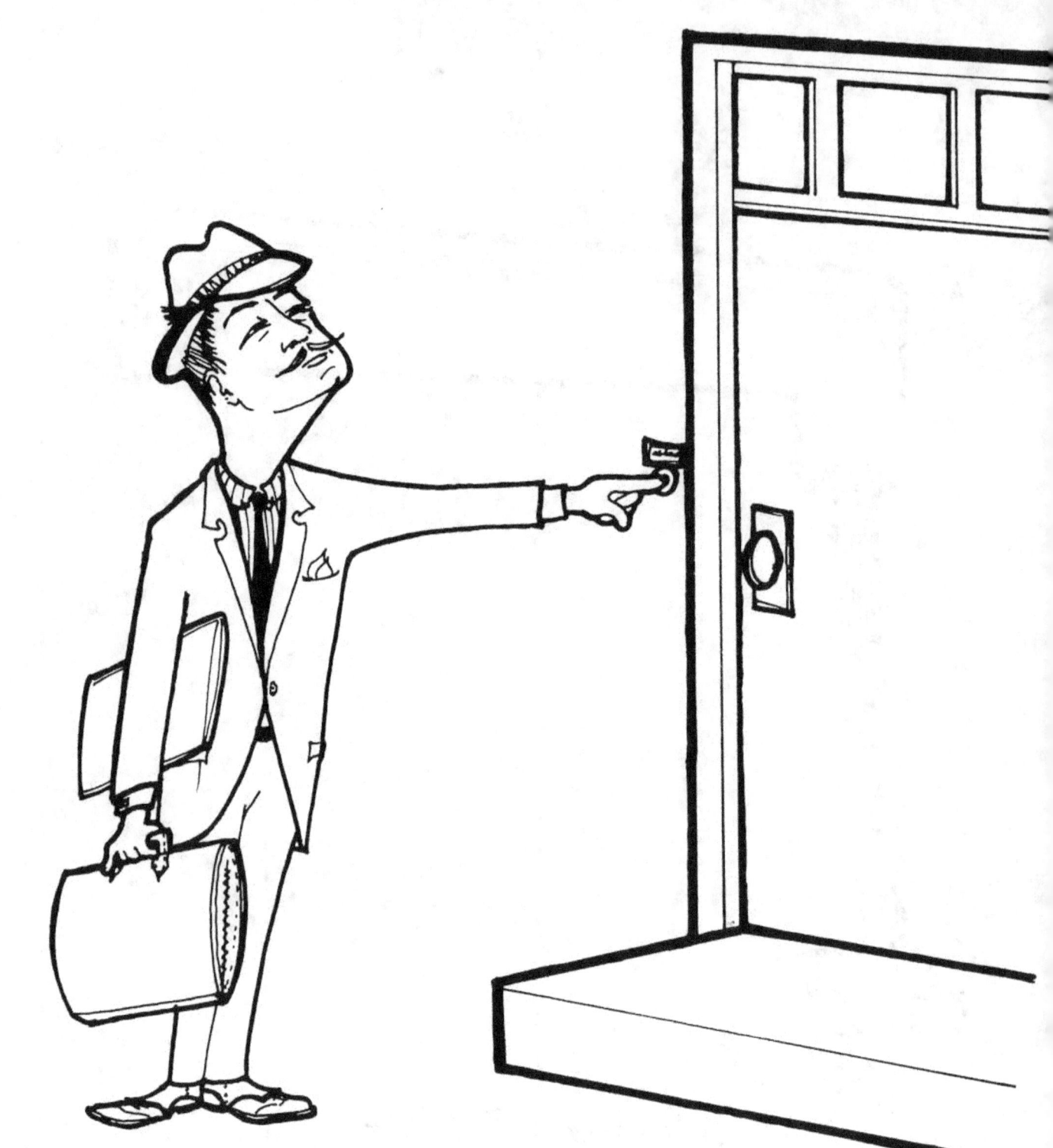

THIS IS MY **DENTAL SUPPLY SALESMAN** • HE BRINGS ME THINGS • SOMETIMES I PAY HIM • SOMETIMES I BUY THINGS I DON'T NEED •••
COLOR ME STUPID ON PAGE #4 ••

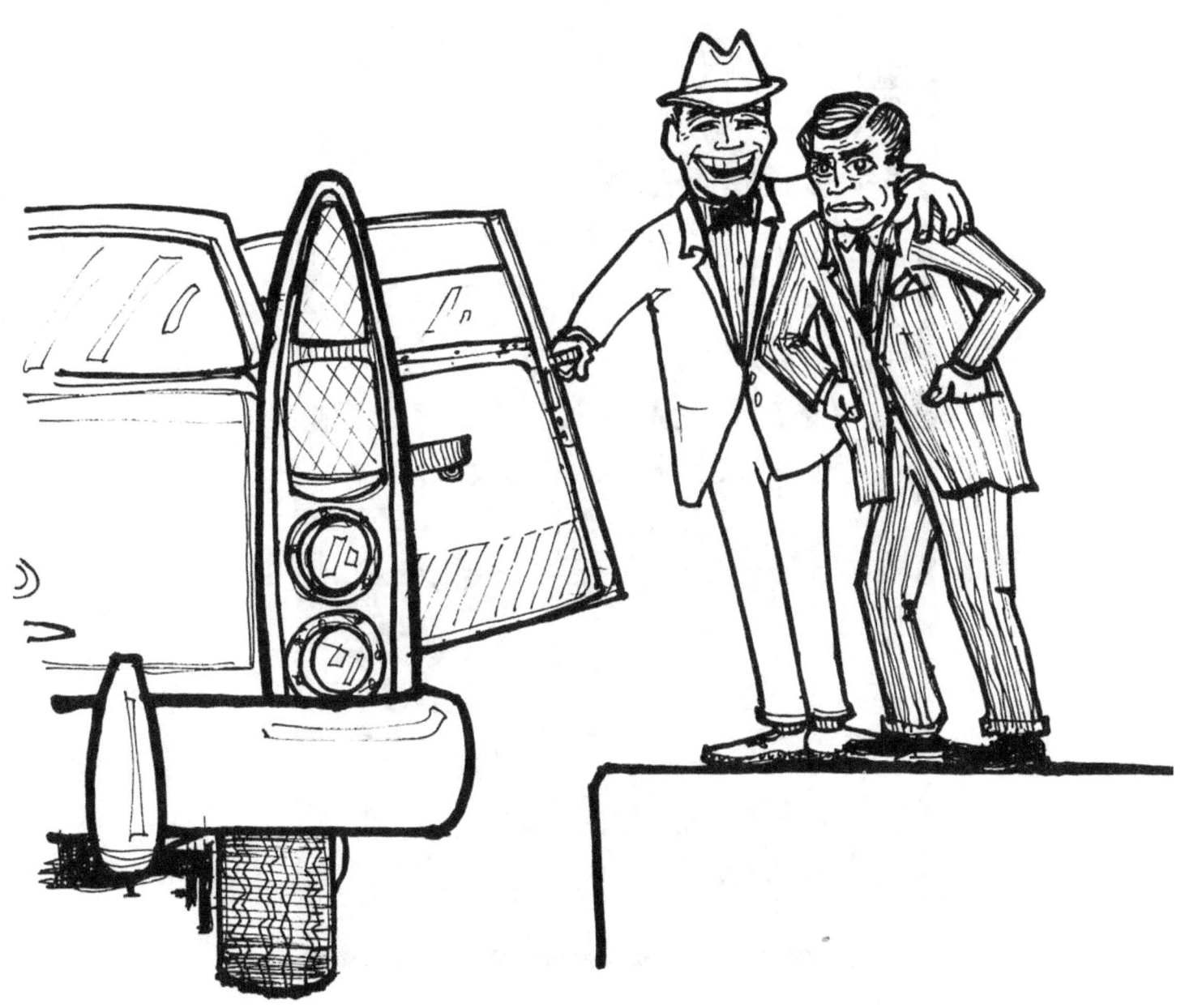

THIS IS AN **INSURANCE MAN** · TAKING ME TO LUNCH ·
WE TALK ABOUT MY FAMILY · HE TELLS ME THAT I
AM FAST BECOMING   KNOWN AS A VERY SUCCESSFUL
MAN · I LIKE HIM · I THINK HE LIKES ME · I AM
TAKING A PHYSICAL NEXT WEEK ···

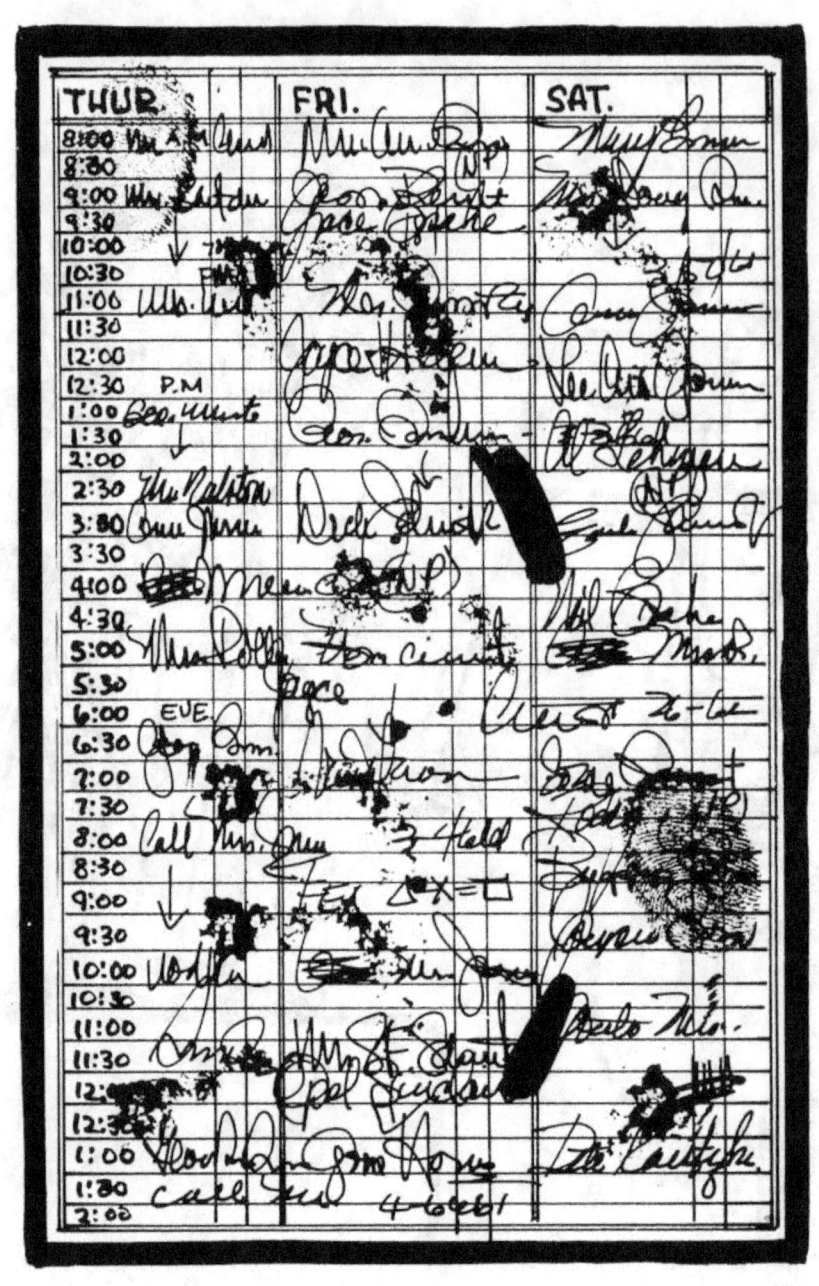

THIS IS MY **APPOINTMENT BOOK** · I MAKE ALL
APPOINTMENTS MYSELF · BECAUSE IT REQUIRES
AN ORGANIZED MIND····

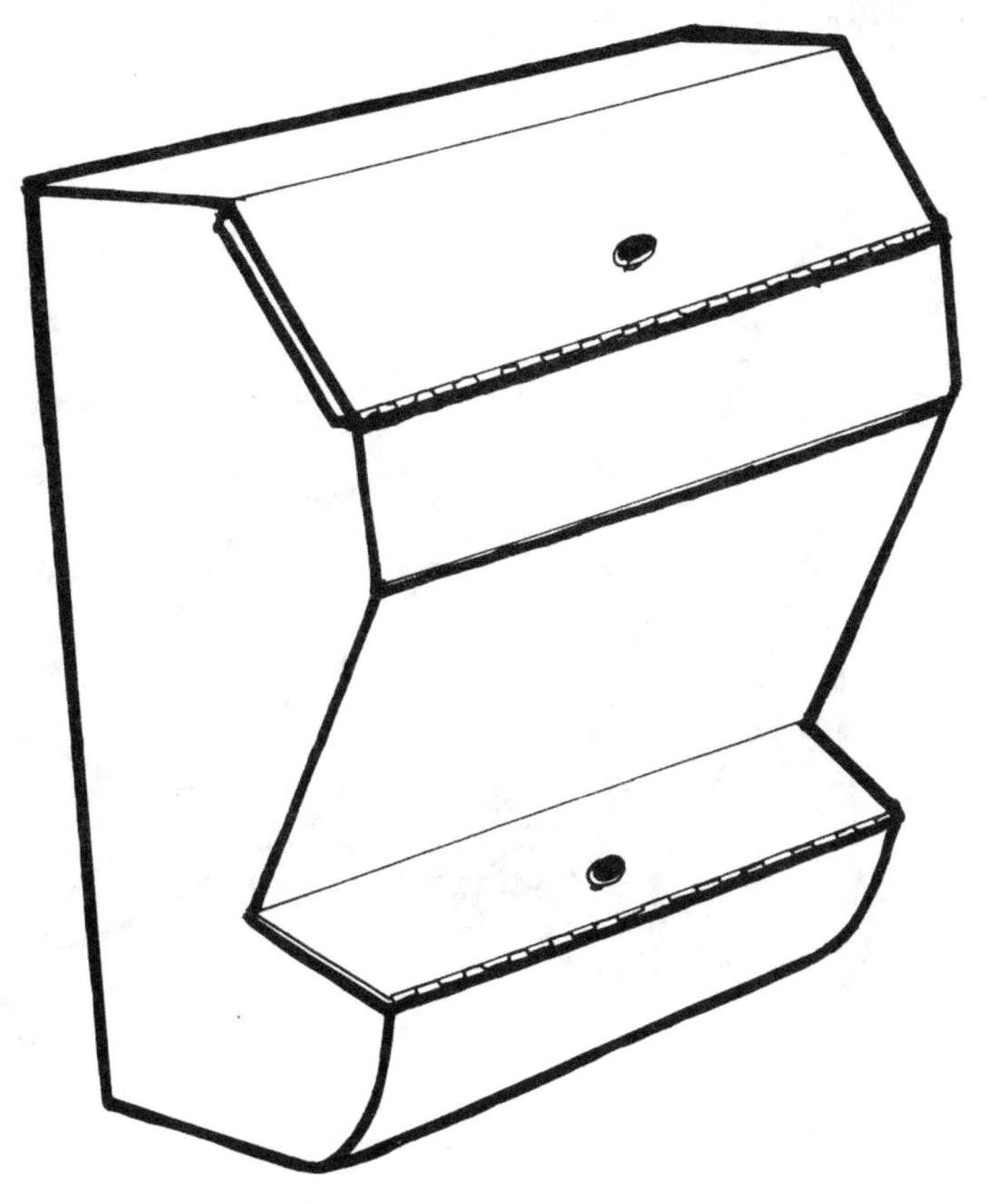

THIS IS MY SAFE. I KEEP MONEY AND OTHER
VALUABLES HERE. SOMETIMES PLASTER...

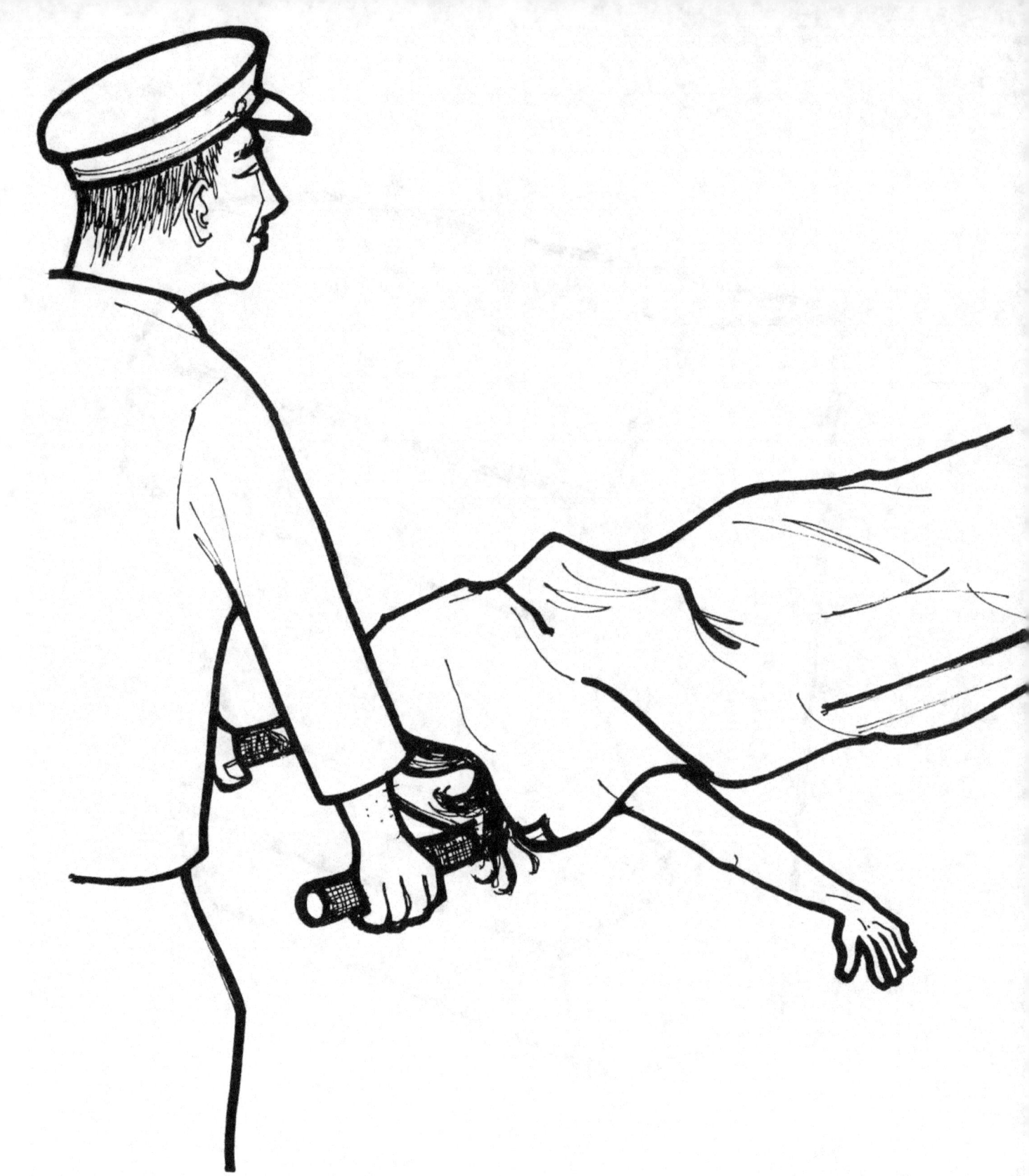

THIS IS MY FORMER ASSISTANT · I'LL NEVER
FORGET HOW WELL SHE FIRED THE FURNACE AND
SHOVELED THE WALK···

COLOR HER GRAY · VERY GRAY···

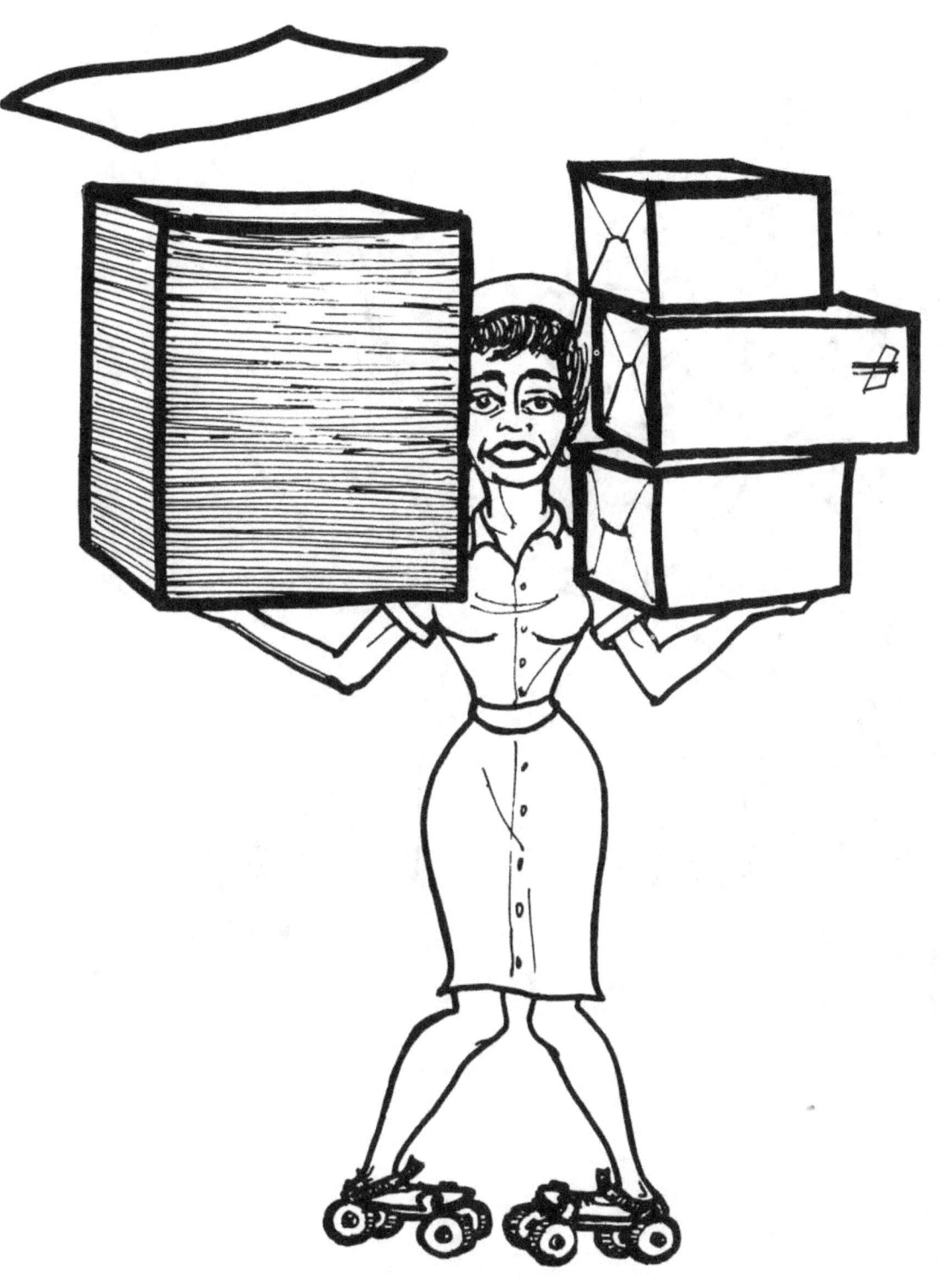

THIS IS MY PRESENT ASSISTANT. SHE WORKS
VERY HARD TOO. SOMEDAY I HOPE TO BE ABLE
TO PAY HER...

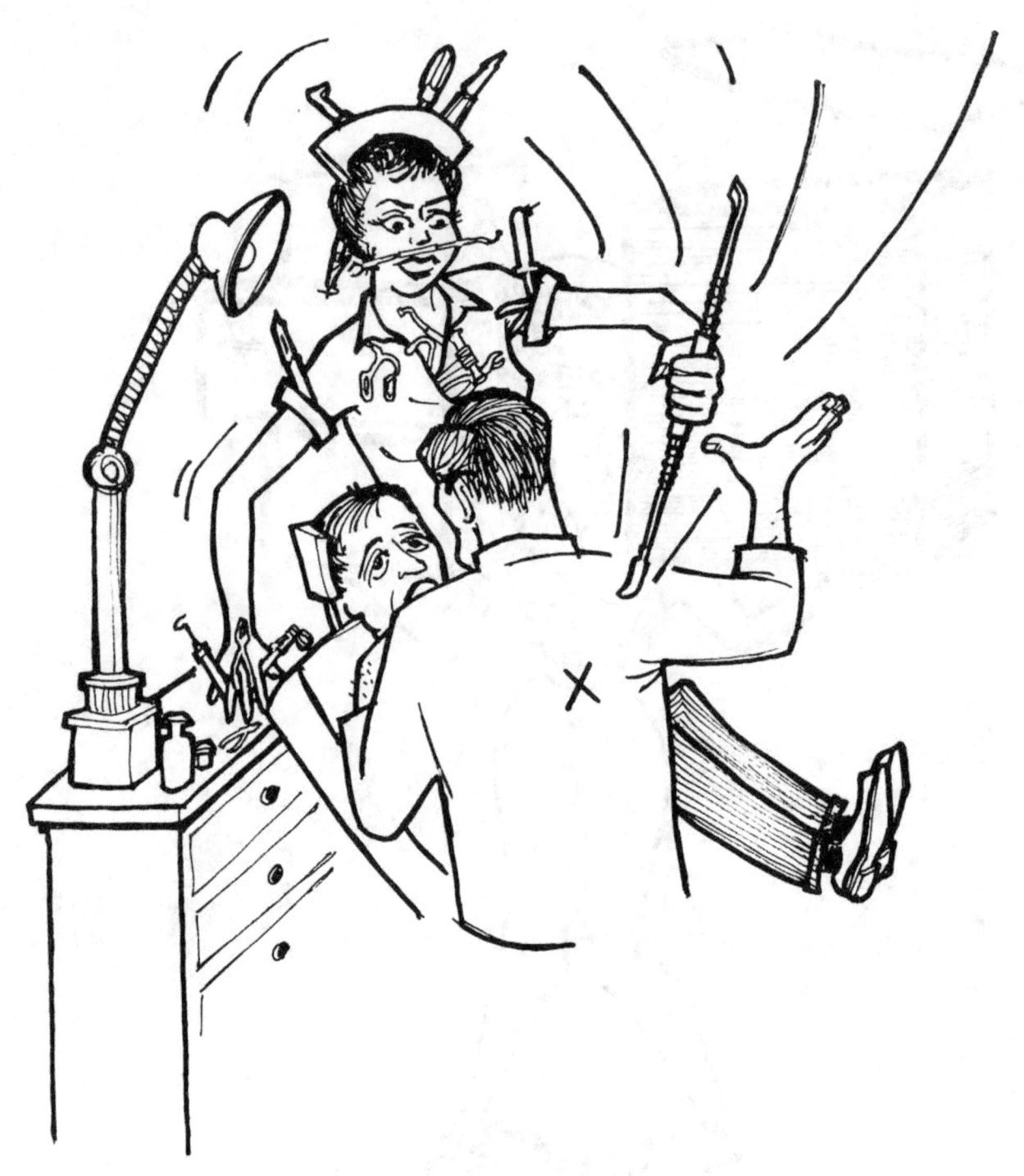

THIS IS MY **ASSISTANT** AT THE CHAIR · SOMETIMES
I THINK SHE GETS DISCOURGED ···
COLOR CARVER STAINLESS ···

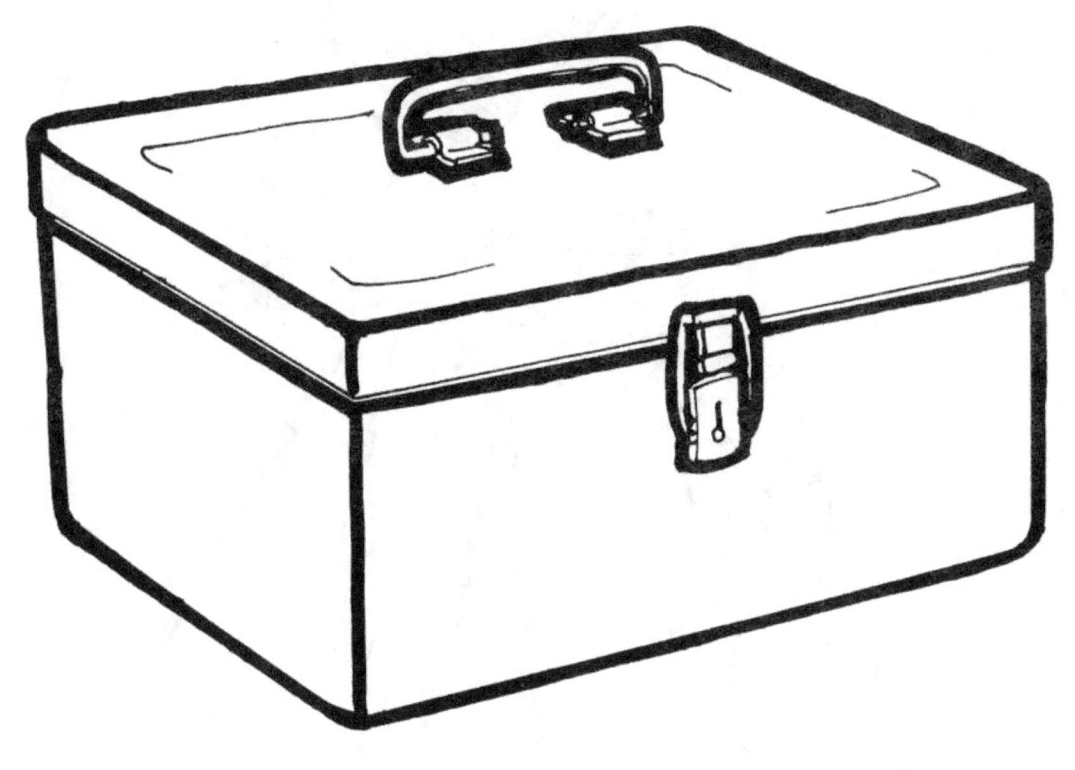

THIS IS MY **ASSISTANTS** PETTY CASH BOX • SOME-
TIMES IF I BORROW FROM IT – I GET MY
FINGERS SLAPPED •••

COLOR THEM RED •••

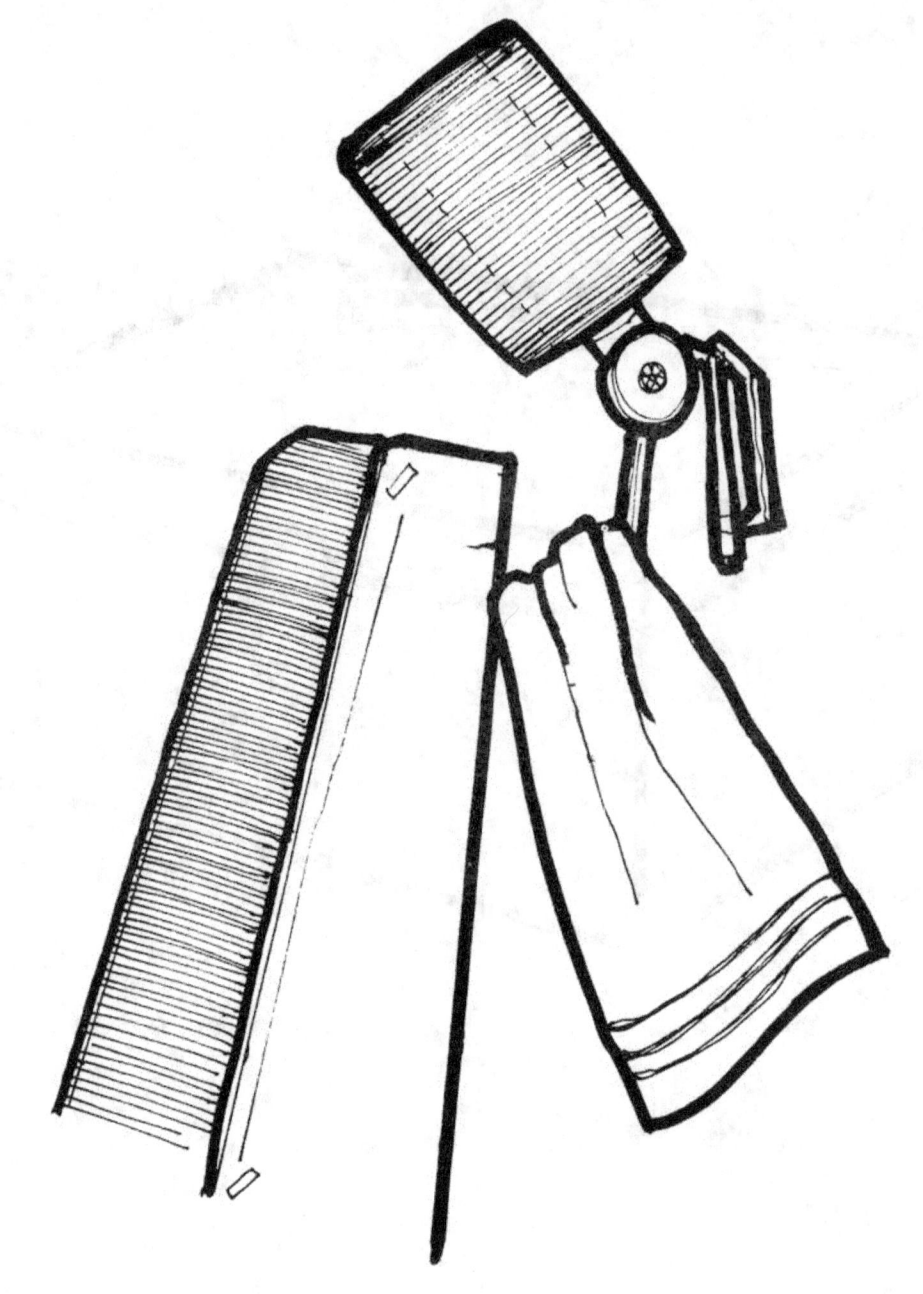

THIS IS A **TOWEL** • SOMETIMES I WIPE A CHILDS CHIN WITH IT • SOMETIMES I --- WELL NEVER MIND ...

COLOR CHILD DEEP·PURPLE·

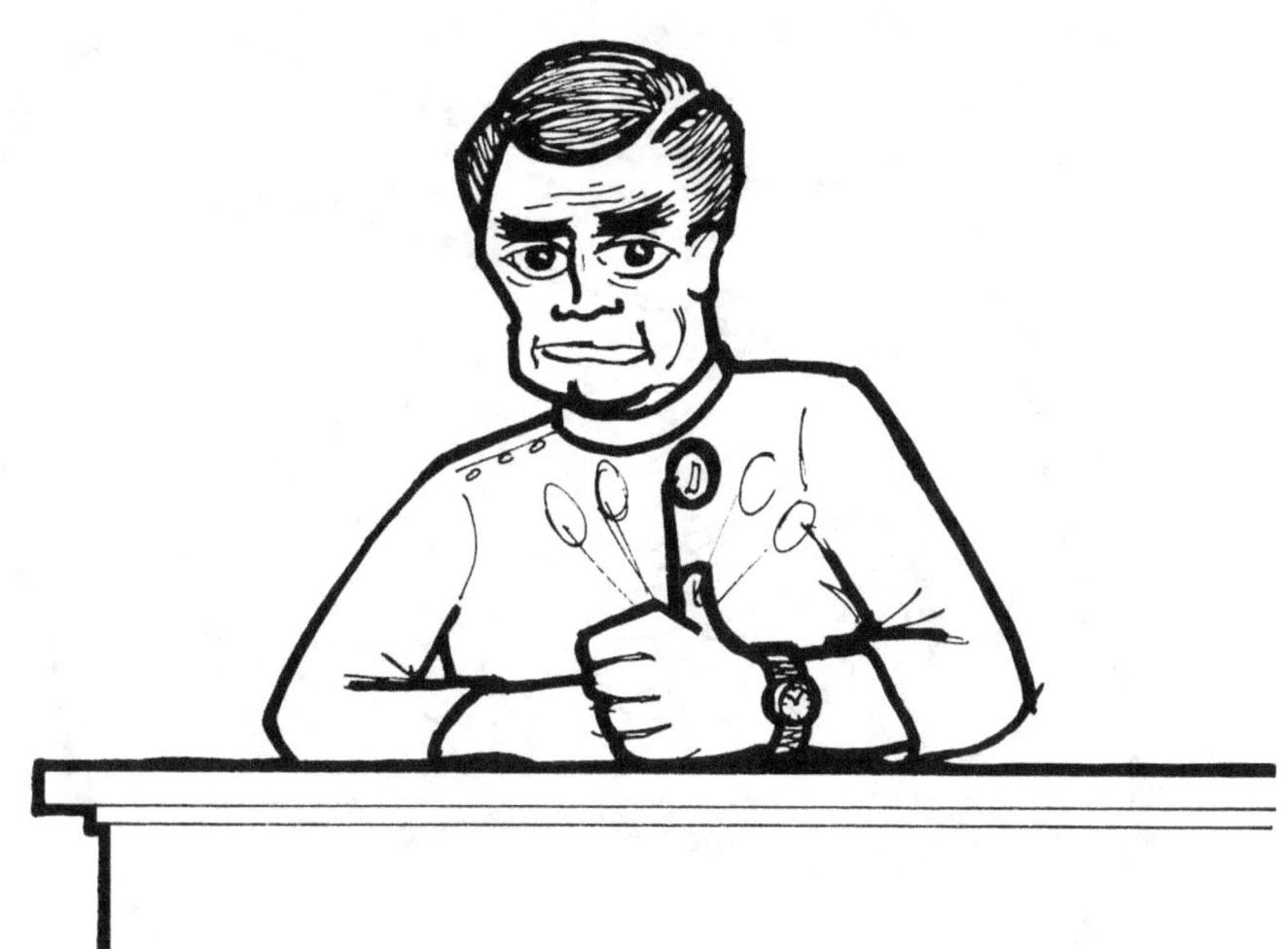

i HAVE A MASTERS DEGREE iN HUMAN RELATIONS.
i WiLL SHOW YOU HOW TO TAKE A DENTAL HiSTORY.
i AM SPEAKiNG TO THE PATiENT. i AM SAYiNG—
"i BELiEVE, MRS. JONES, THAT YOU ARE
JUSTiFiED iN PREFERRiNG CHiLDBiRTH*OVER
DENTiSTRY. THiNGS GET PRETTY ROUGH AROUND
HERE!"...

* IN THE FIELD OF SEMANTICS, IT IS MUCH MORE CULTURED TO SAY—
"CHILD BIRTH" RATHER THAN "HAVING A BABY"

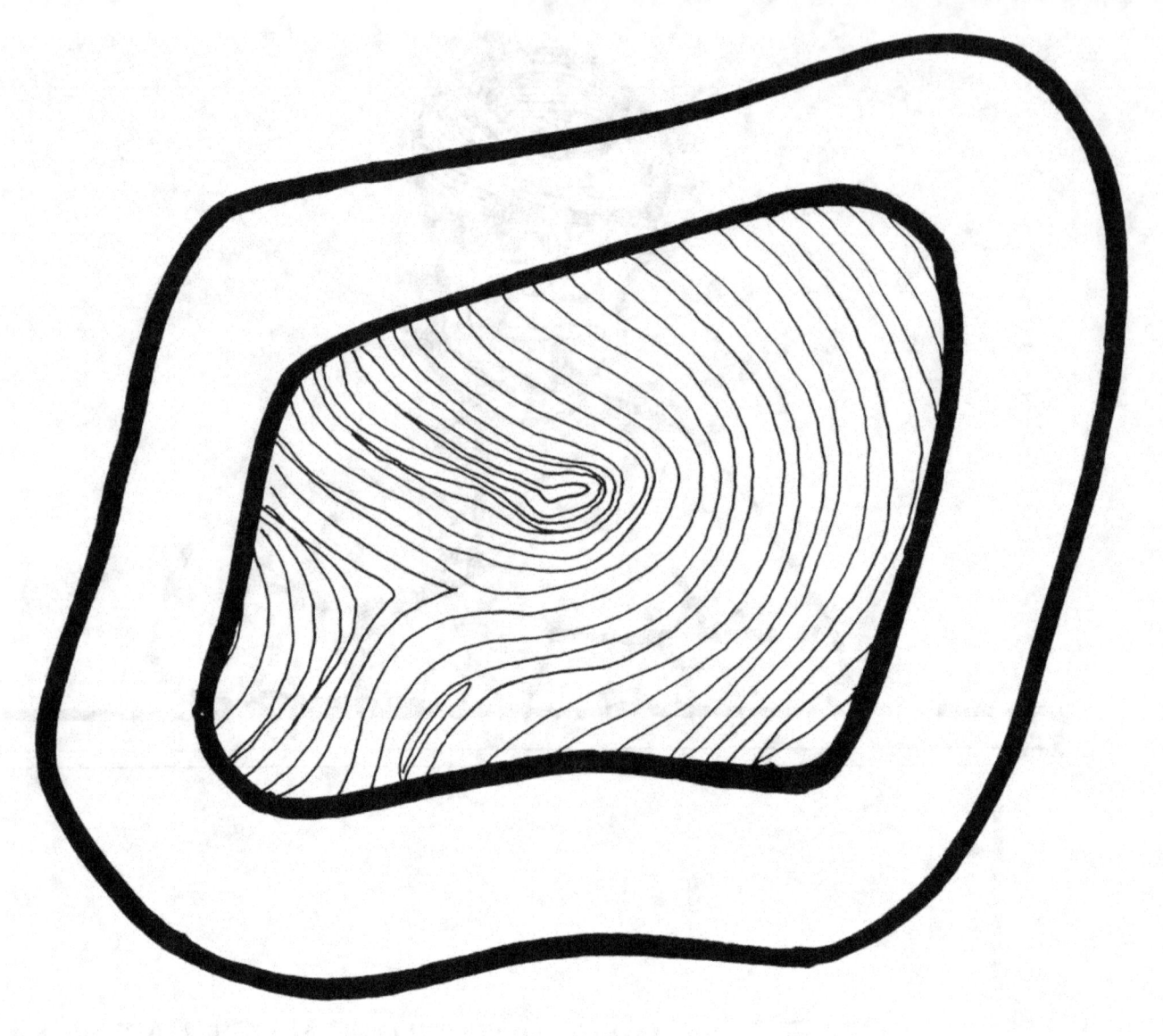

THIS IS SOME OF MY WORK · IT IS A PLATINUM
INLAY · WELL CONDENSED · AS YOU WILL NOTE I
AM A VERY PROUD OPERATOR···
COLOR INLAY SILVER····

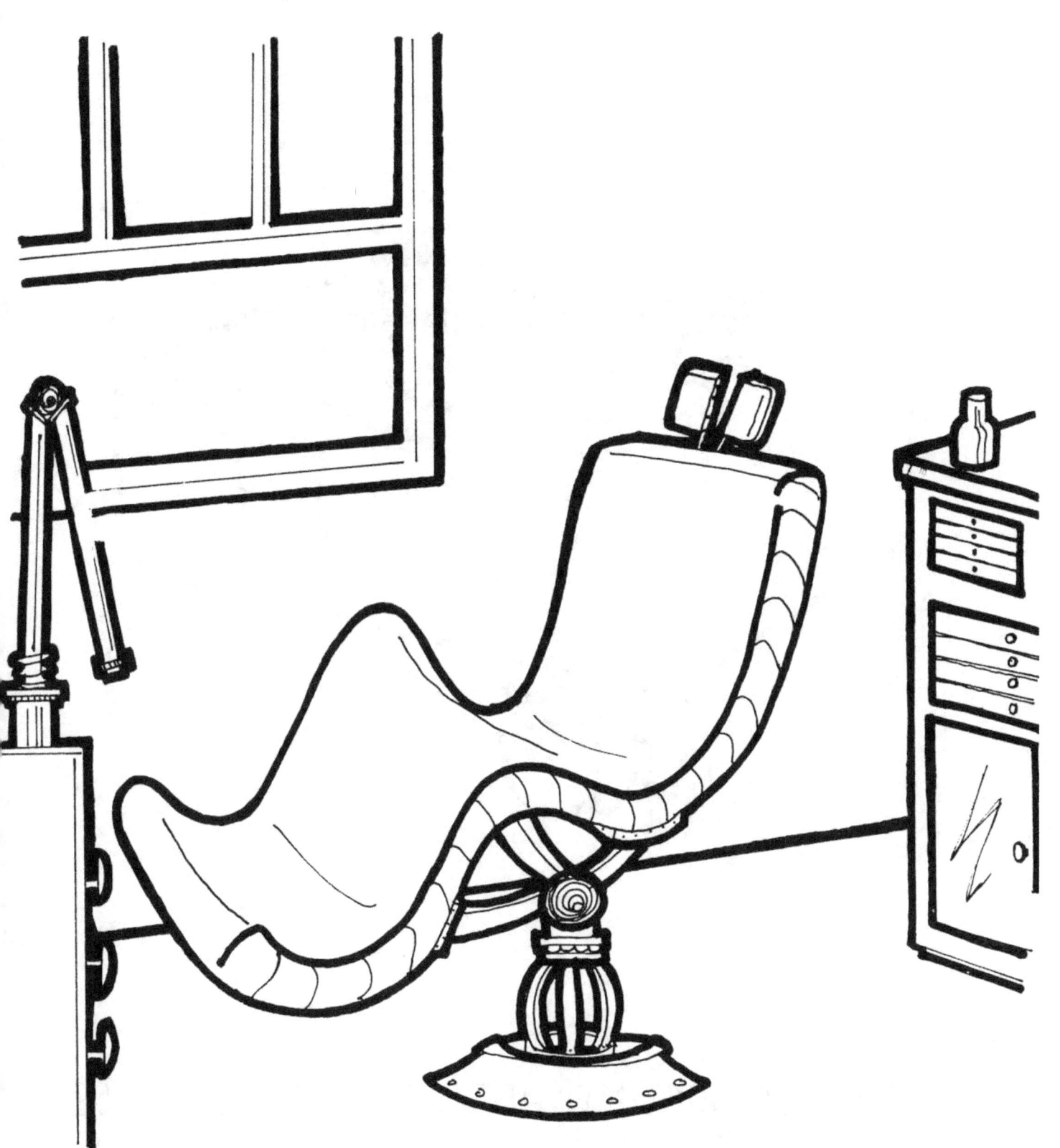

THIS IS MY NEW·CONTOUR CHAIR · SOME
PROCEDURES ARE VERY DIFFICULT WITH IT·
I DON'T THINK I LIKE IT · · ·

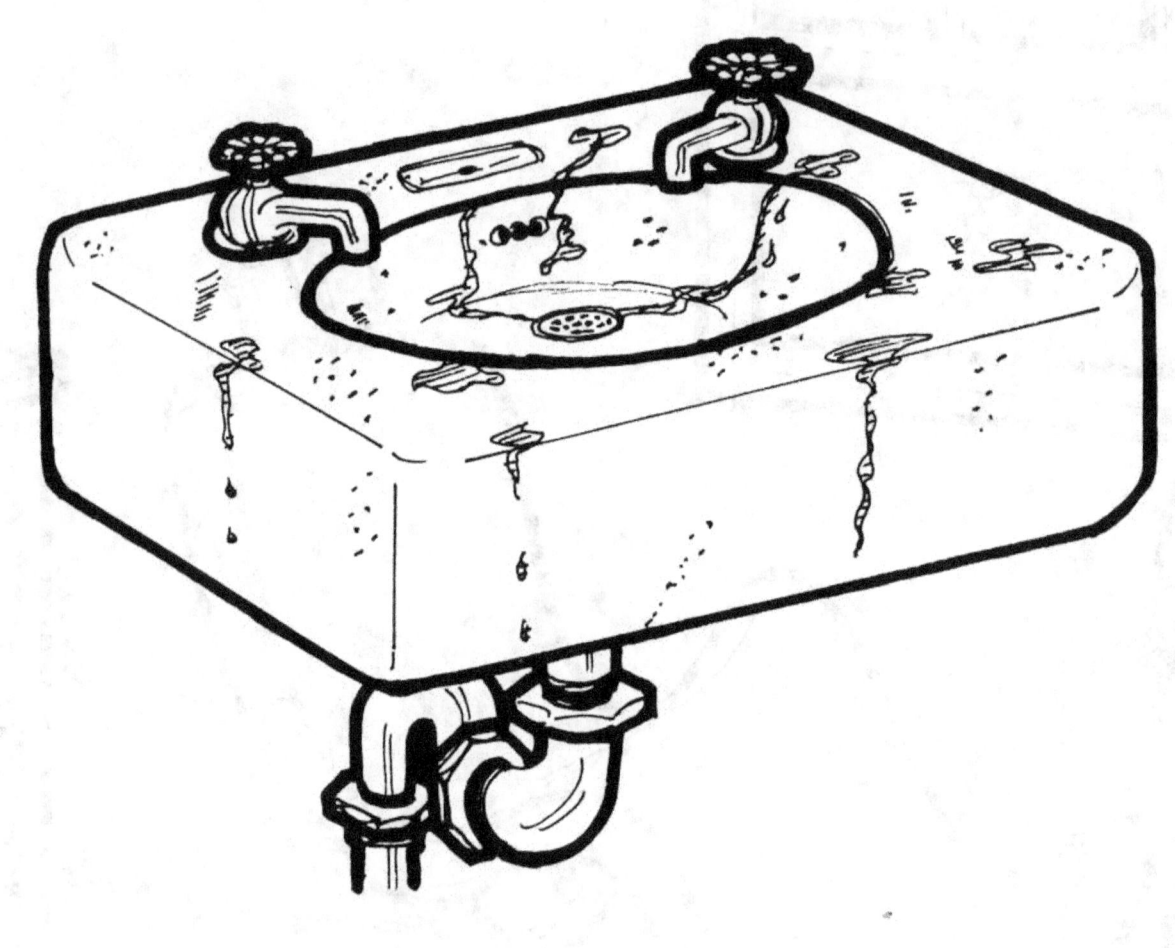

THIS IS MY **COMPOUND HEATER** · IT CAN BE USED
FOR OTHER THINGS TOO ···
          COLOR IT SPECKLED BROWNISH WHITE·

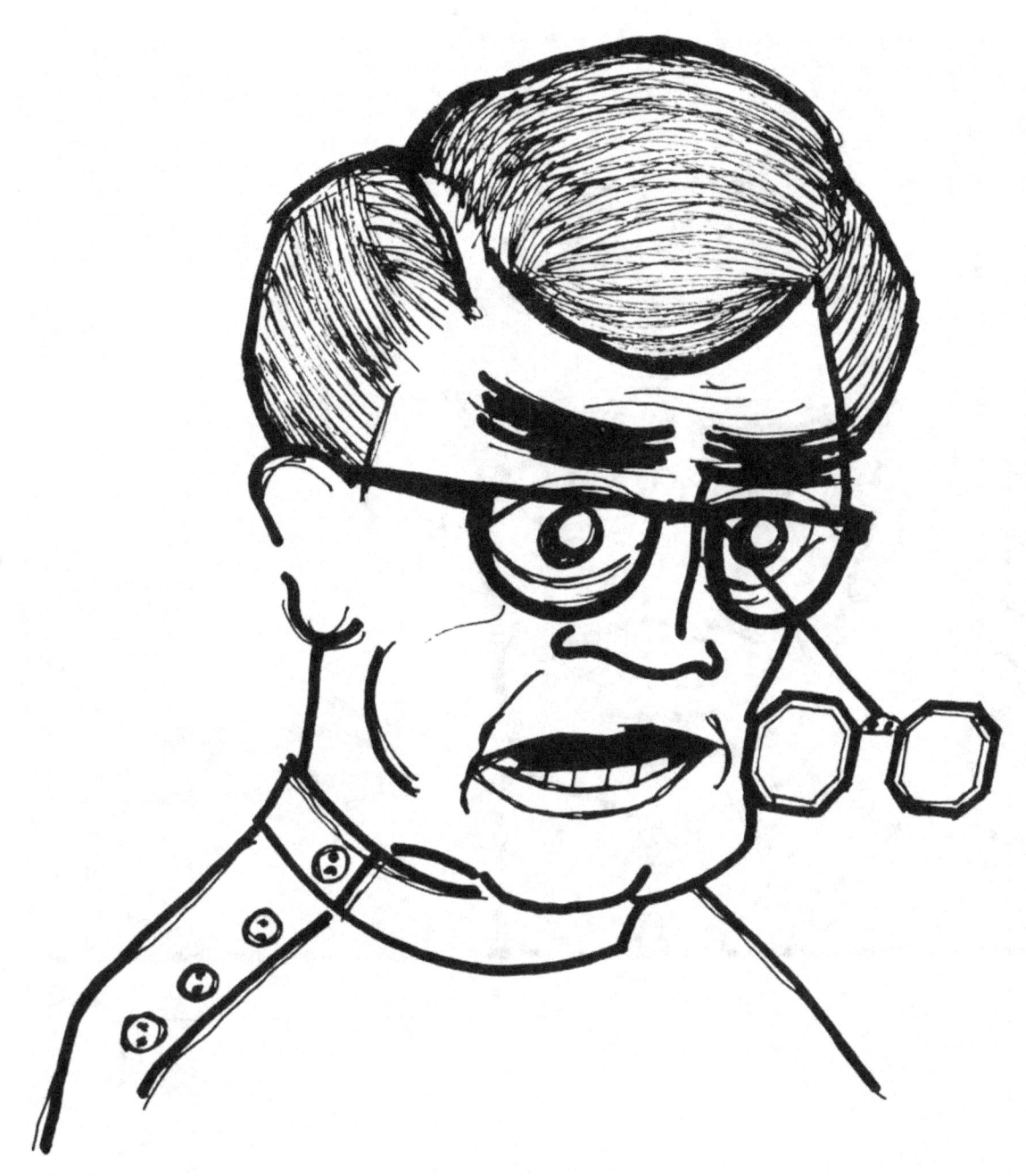

THIS IS **ME** AT THE CHAIR. I AM SAYING.
"MY GOD: MRS. BROWN, YOU'RE RIGHT!
THERE IS NOTHING LEFT!"

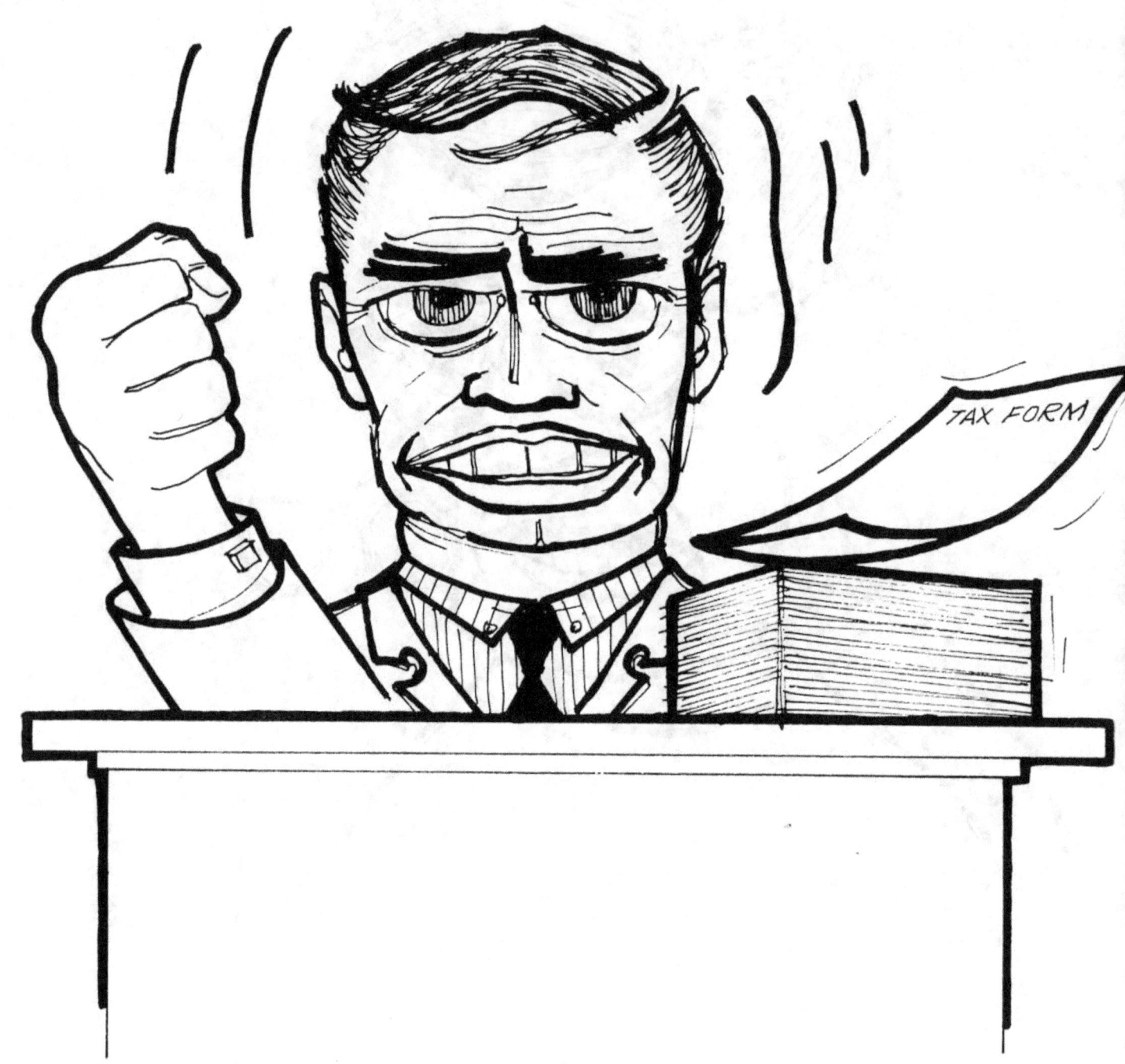

THIS IS MY **AUDITOR** • I HATE HIM • MY CAR
IS 100% **DEDUCTIBLE** • WHY DOES HE ALWAYS
ARGUE? ...

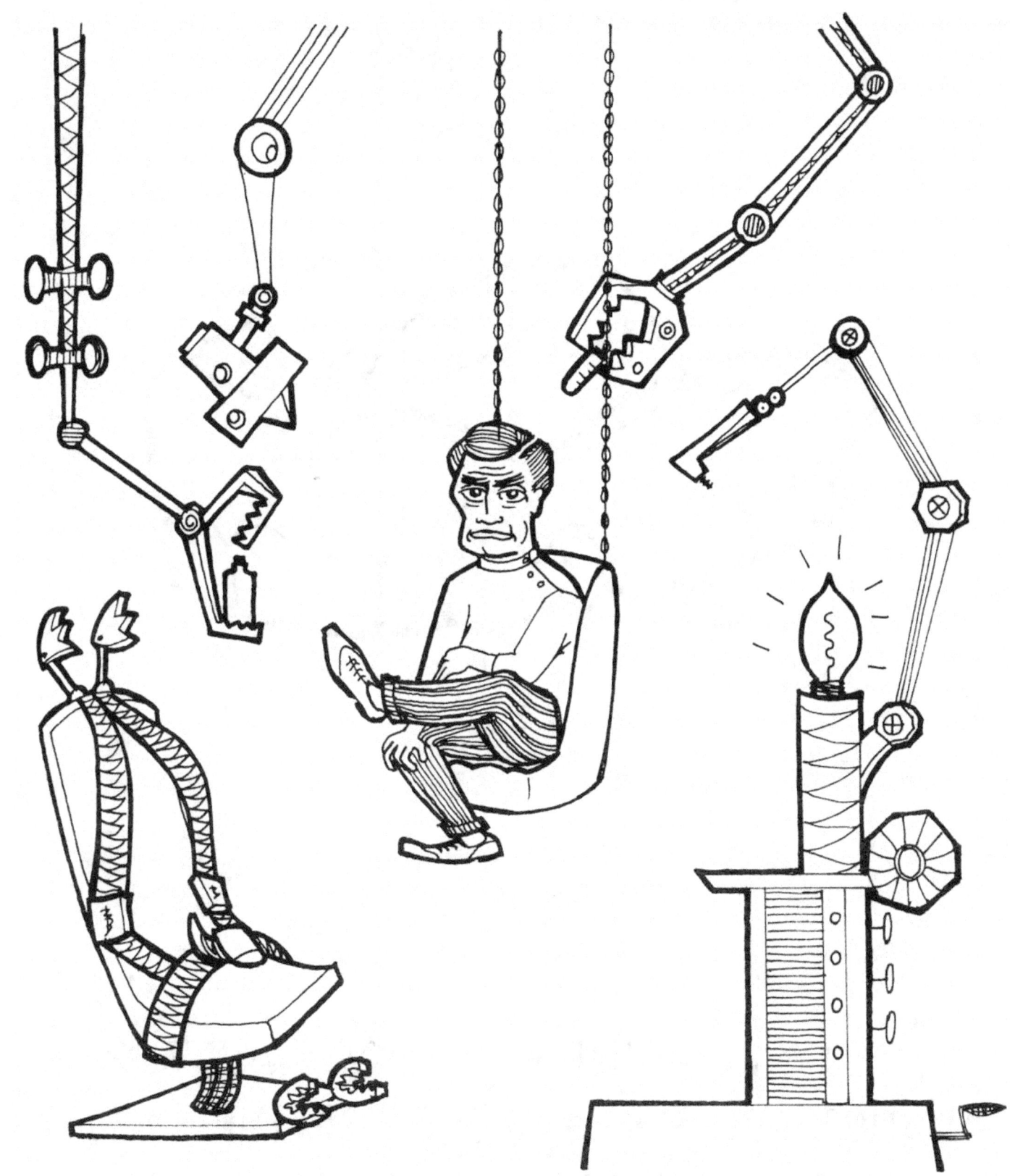

THIS IS ME LOOKING AT NEW EQUIPMENT · I GET
VERY EXCITED · I PREFER A BUCKET SEAT OVER
A STOOL BECAUSE YOU CAN HANG IT FROM THE
CEILING · COLOR ME CONFUSED ···

113

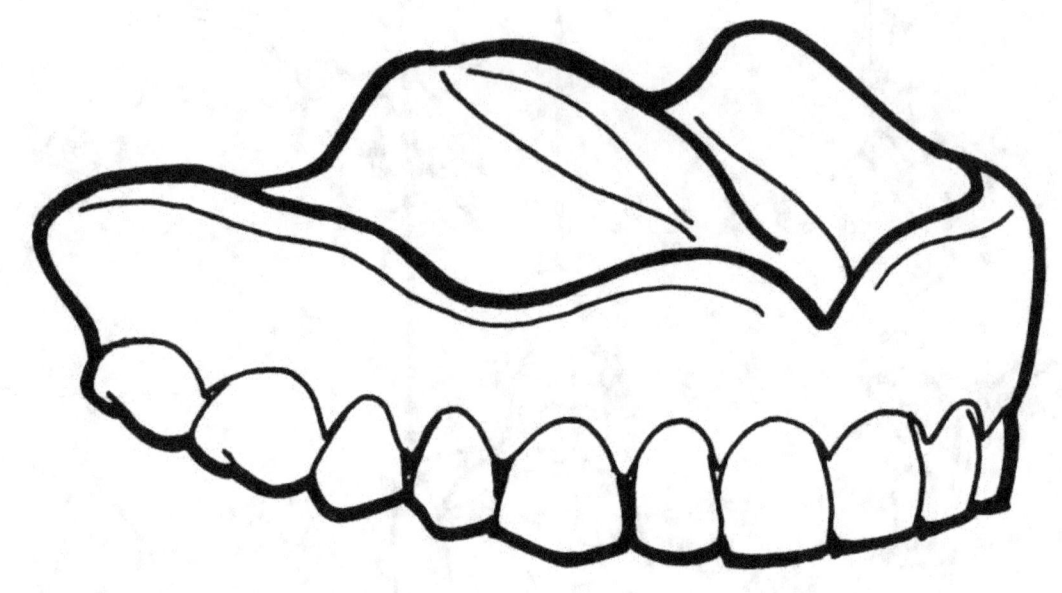

THIS IS A **DENTURE** • IT HAS HAD 732 ADJUSTMENTS • I WONDER IF THE PATIENT REALIZES HOW HAPPY I AM TO BE OF SUCH EXTREME SERVICE ···

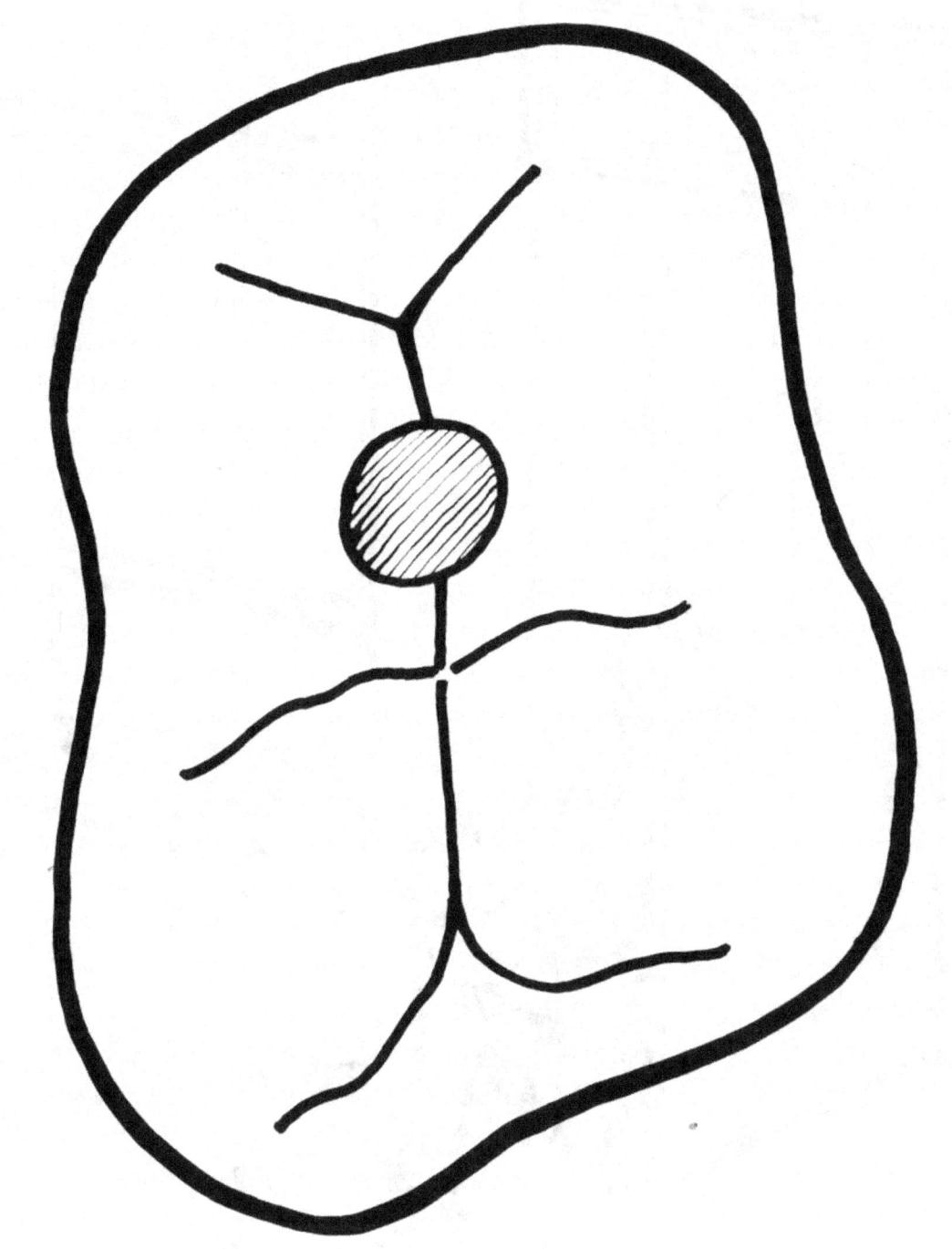

THIS IS A **PATIENT** WHOSE FILLING FELL OUT· I
EXPLAIN TO HER THAT SHE HAS A PROBLEM·
THAT HER TEETH ARE SOFT AND WILL NOT HOLD
FILLINGS· SHE UNDERSTANDS···

COLOR HOLE SOFT···

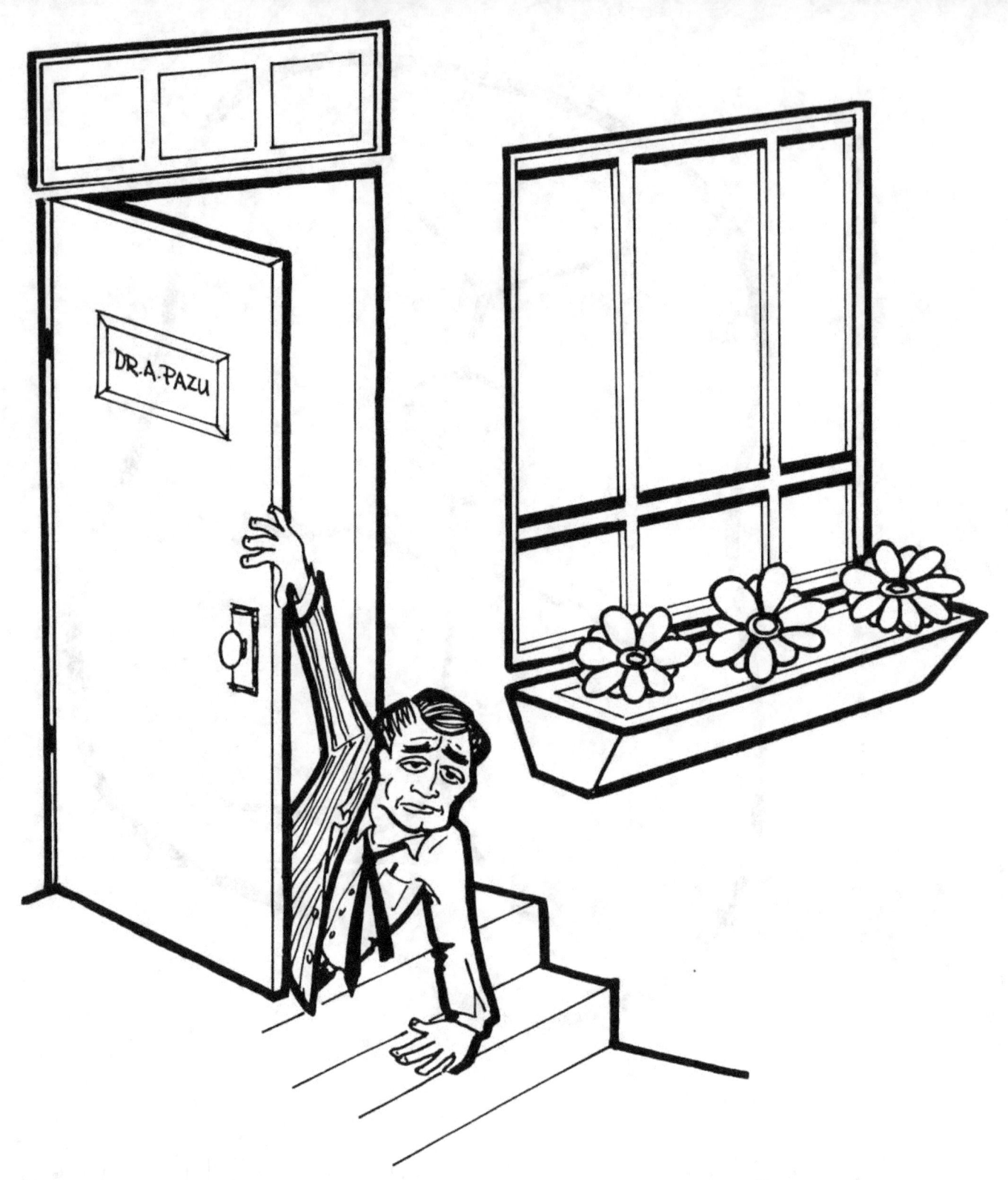

THIS IS ME • LEAVING THE OFFICE, PROMPTLY
AT 11 P.M. MY STAFF LEFT SIX HOURS AGO •
BUT THEY ARE NOT AS STRONG AS THE GREAT
ANTON PAZU • I UNDERSTAND •••

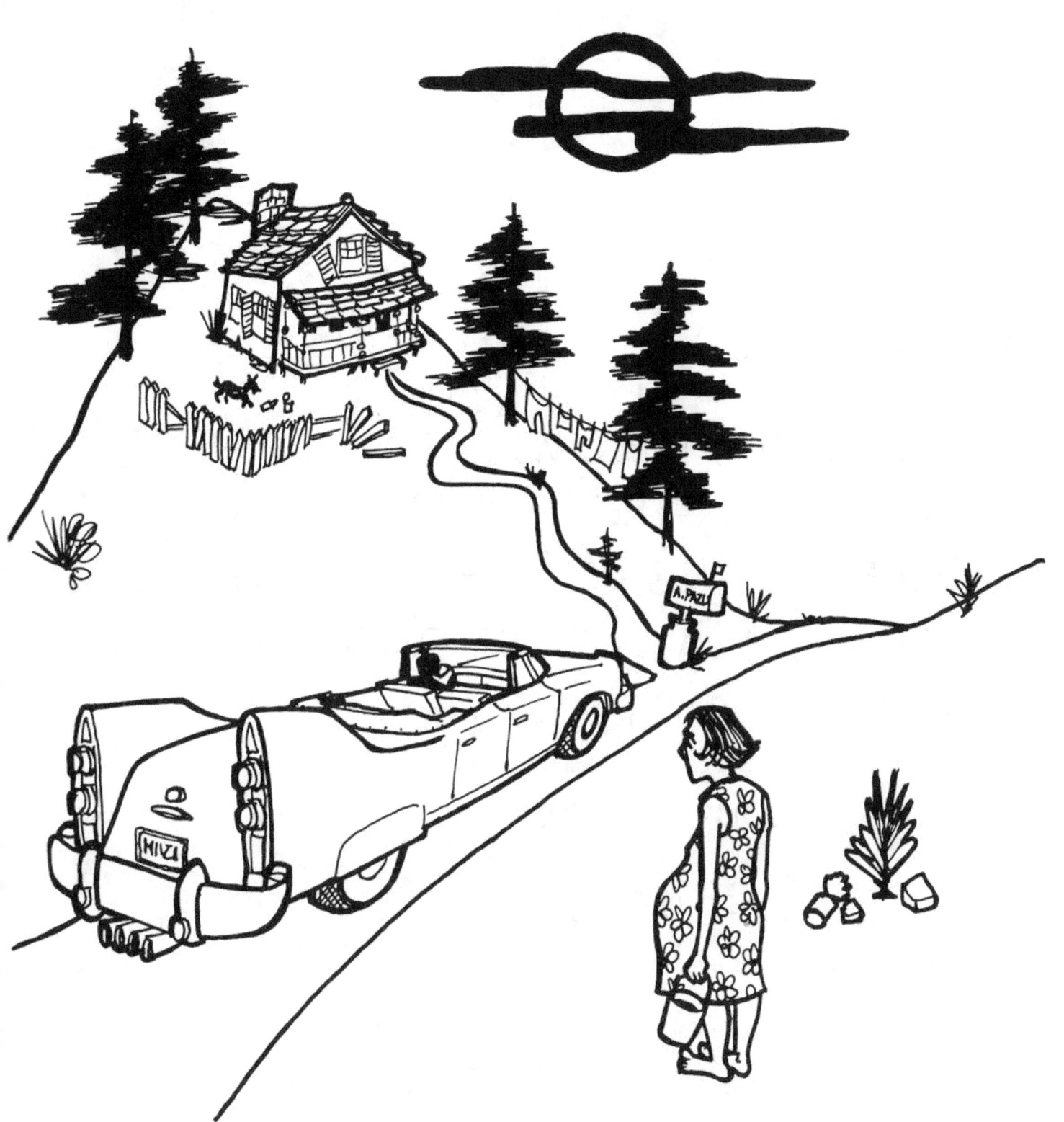

THIS IS ME• ARRIVING HOME • MY CHILDREN
ALWAYS WANTED A CONVERTIBLE • YOU WILL
NOTE • I TRY TO SATISFY MY FAMILY•••
          COLOR CONVERTIBLE EXPENSIVE•

AND FINALLY:

IF YOU SHOULD EVER WISH TO VISIT MY OFFICE.
PLEASE WRITE AHEAD. BECAUSE I AM
CONTEMPLATING A MOVE. THINGS ARE NOT
EXACTLY THE WAY I WANT THEM IN MY
PRESENT LOCATION.

THIS IS A LOUSY TOWN..

SINCERELY YOURS,

Dr. Anton Pazu

THE BUREAUCRAT'S COLORING BOOK

by Francesca Knight
and
Lois Roberts

THIS BOOK BELONGS TO_____

MY GS NUMBER_____

MY CODE NUMBER_____

MY PARKING LOT NUMBER_____

MY HEALTH PLAN NUMBER_____

MY RETIREMENT NUMBER_____

Jumping on board a fad does not always bring about the success one hopes. That would seem to be the case with *The Bureaucrat's Coloring Book*. Issued in 1962 by New York-based Athene Press, this appears to be the company's final publication; in prior years, it had issued a number of books about world affairs, such as *The Untold Story of Panama* and *The Continuing Struggle: Communist China and the Free World*.

While the other coloring books in here clearly followed in the wake of *The Executive Coloring Books*, this one shows its inspiration more than the rest. Compare the shot of the briefcase back on page 13 with its near-mirror image here on 129, or note how the dartboard shot on page 133 is not just conceptually similar but uses the same angles and the same caption as the one on page 26.

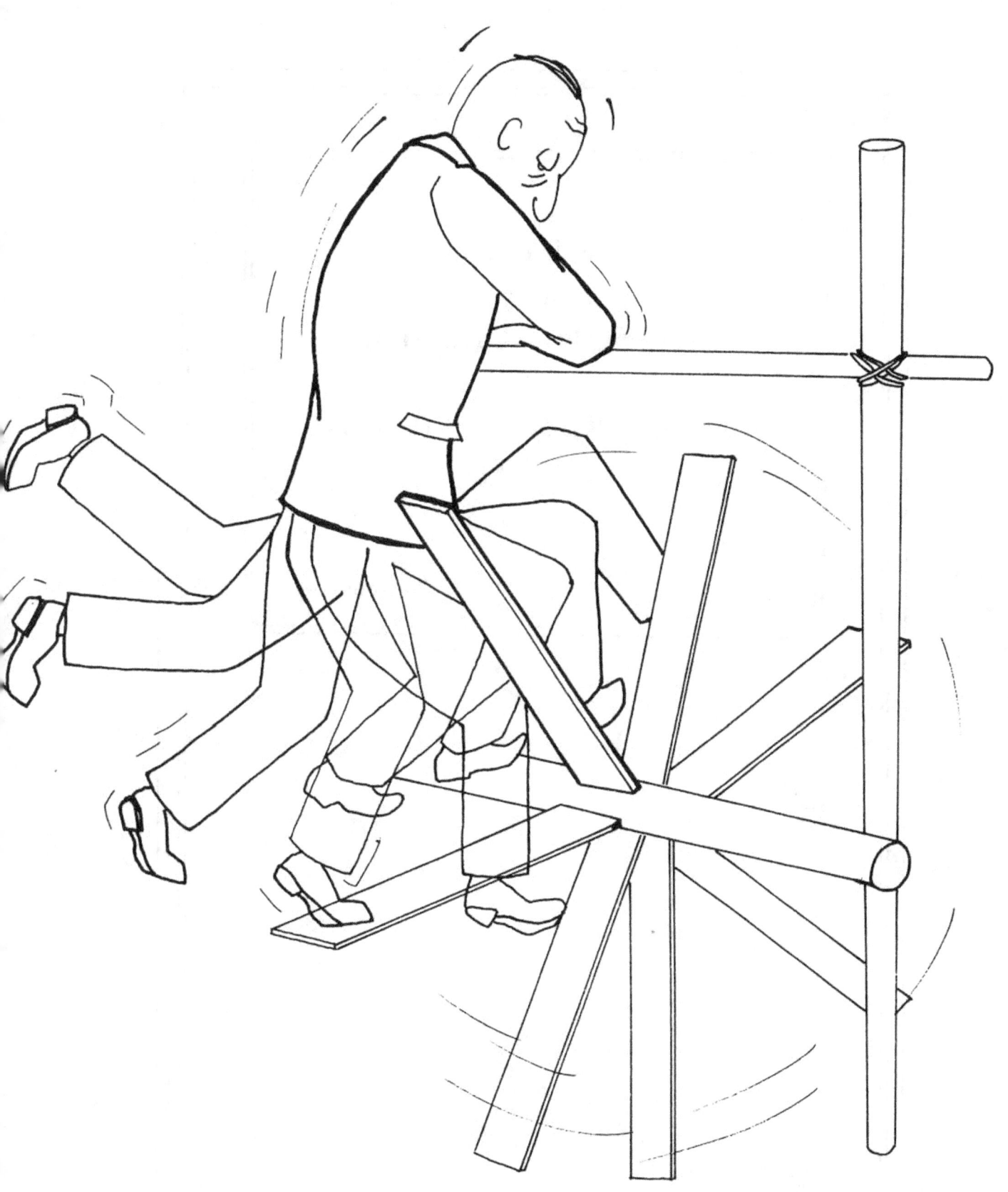

I AM A BUREAUCRAT. Bureaucrats are essential. They go to essential offices and do essential things. Without us, the country couldn't run.

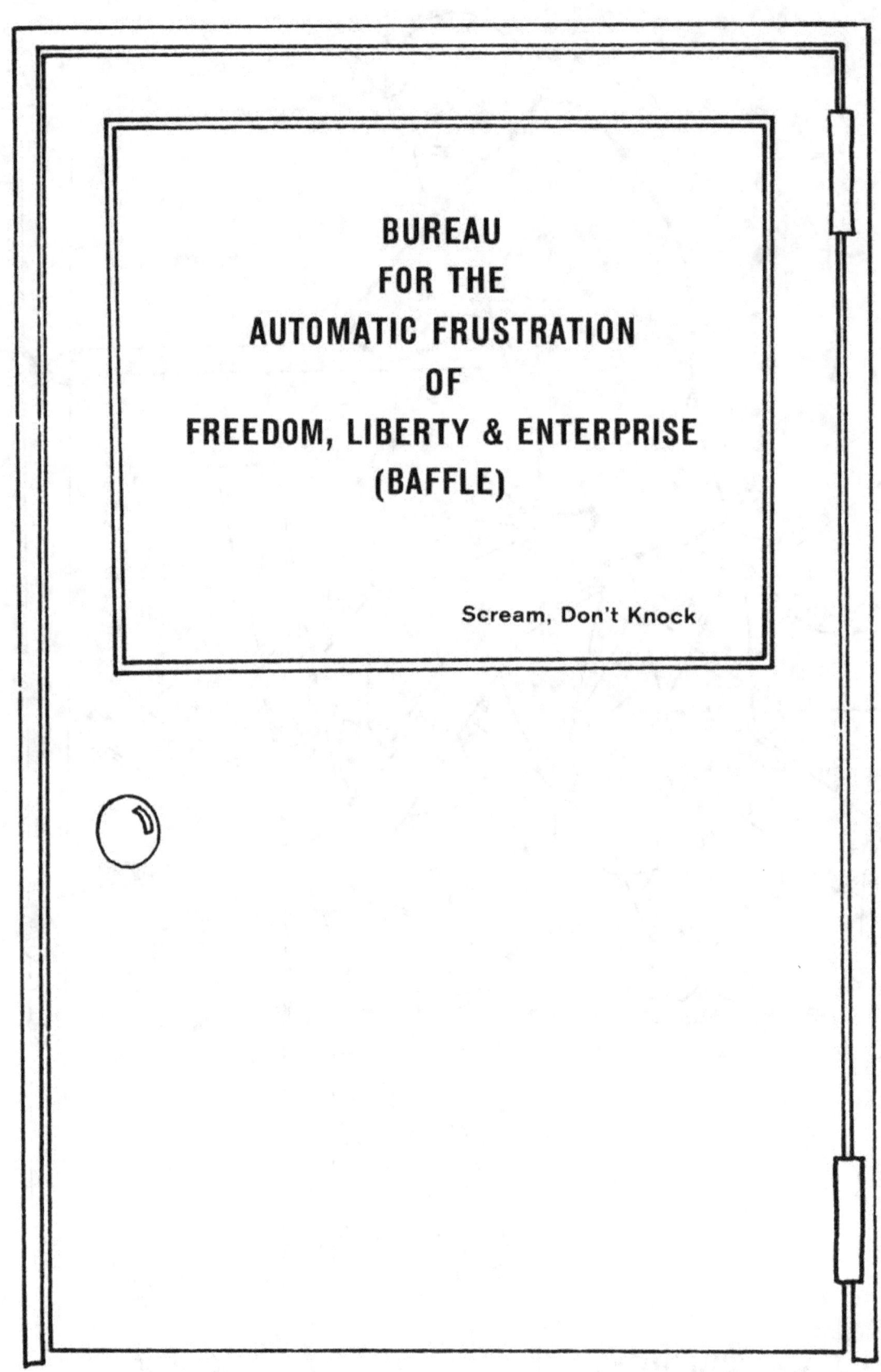

BUREAU
FOR THE
AUTOMATIC FRUSTRATION
OF
FREEDOM, LIBERTY & ENTERPRISE
(BAFFLE)

Scream, Don't Knock

THIS IS THE DOOR TO MY OFFICE. I enter it with a sensation of hope and purpose. Color the doorknob regimental red.

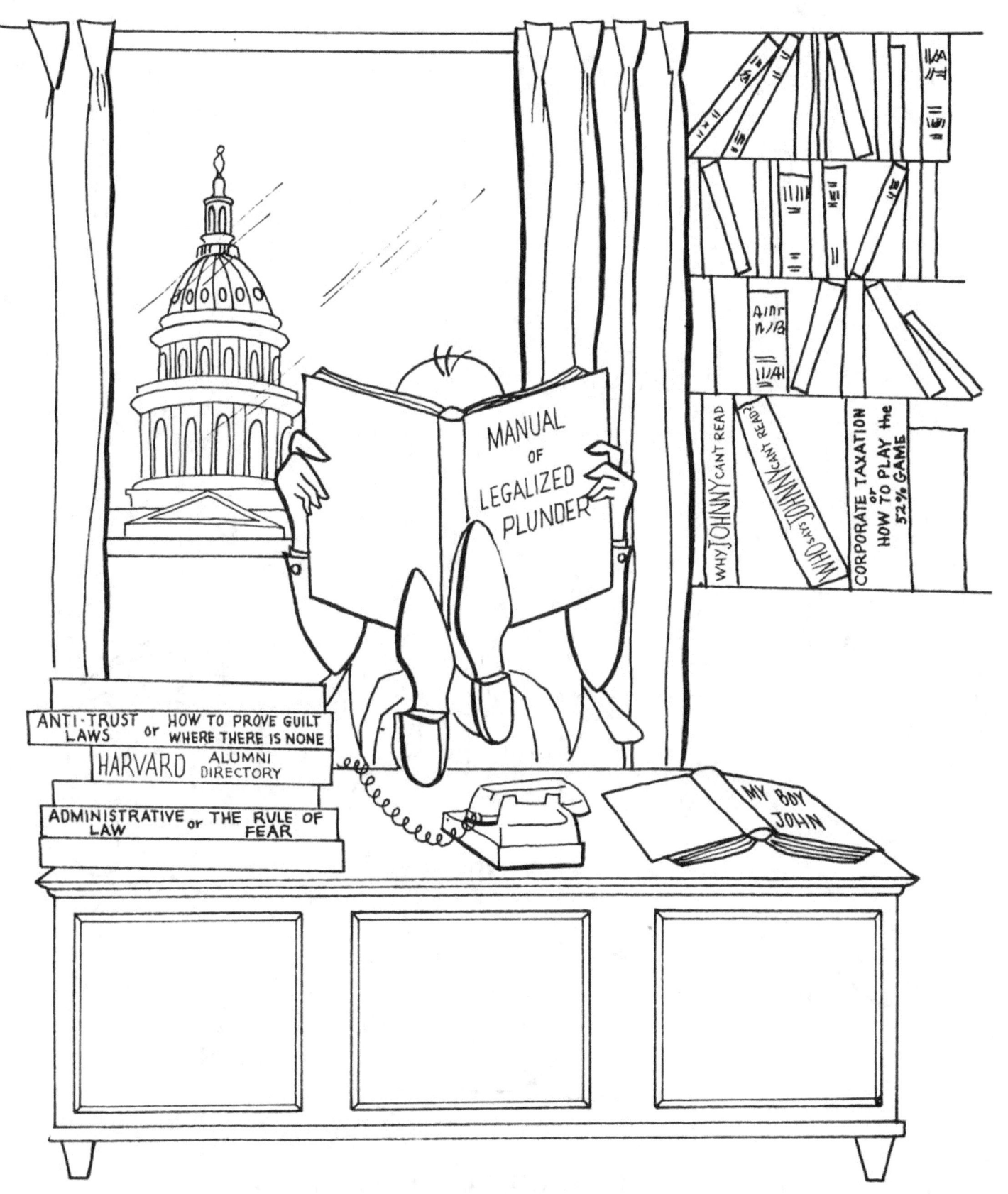

THIS IS MY DESK. It is where I make my plans.

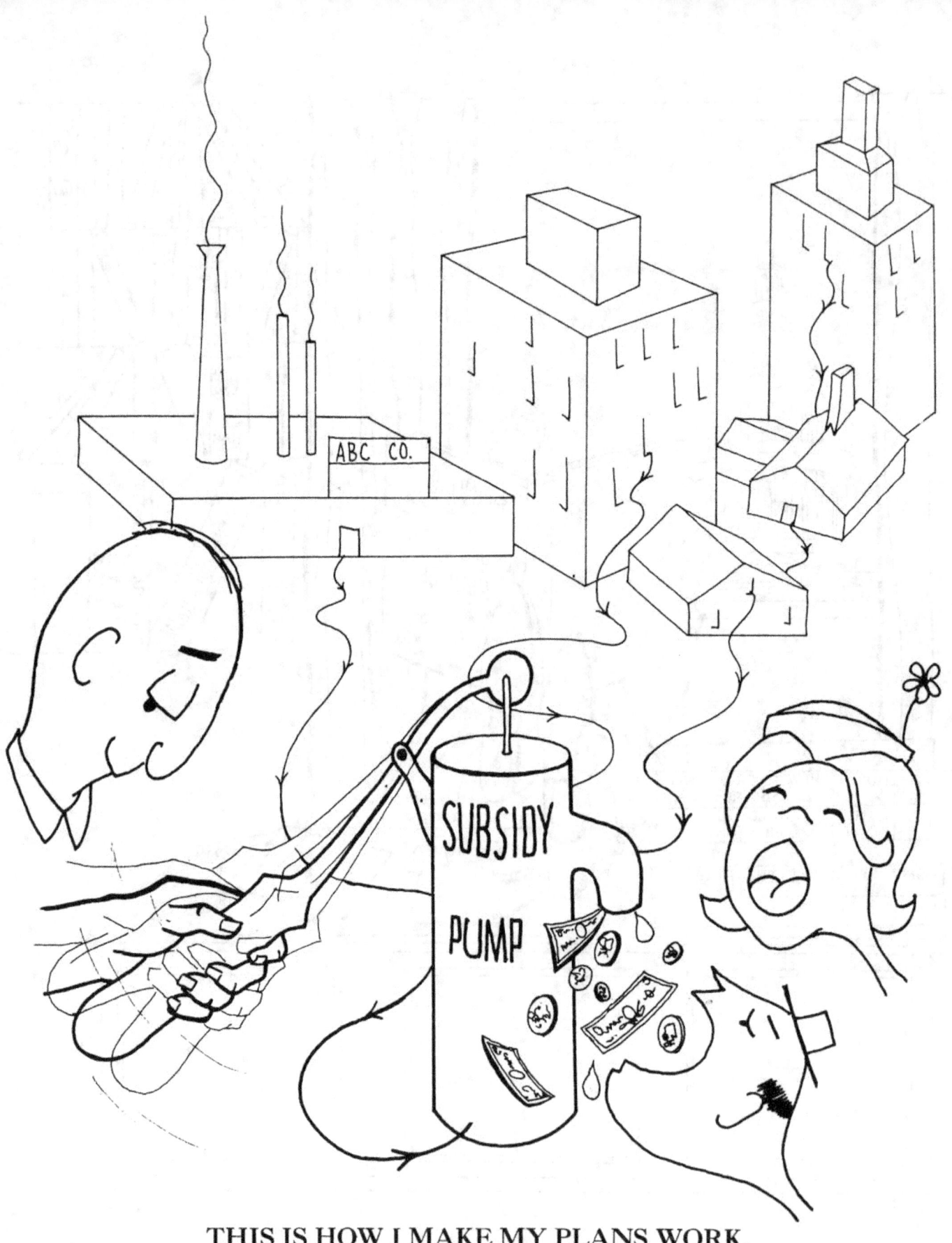

THIS IS HOW I MAKE MY PLANS WORK.

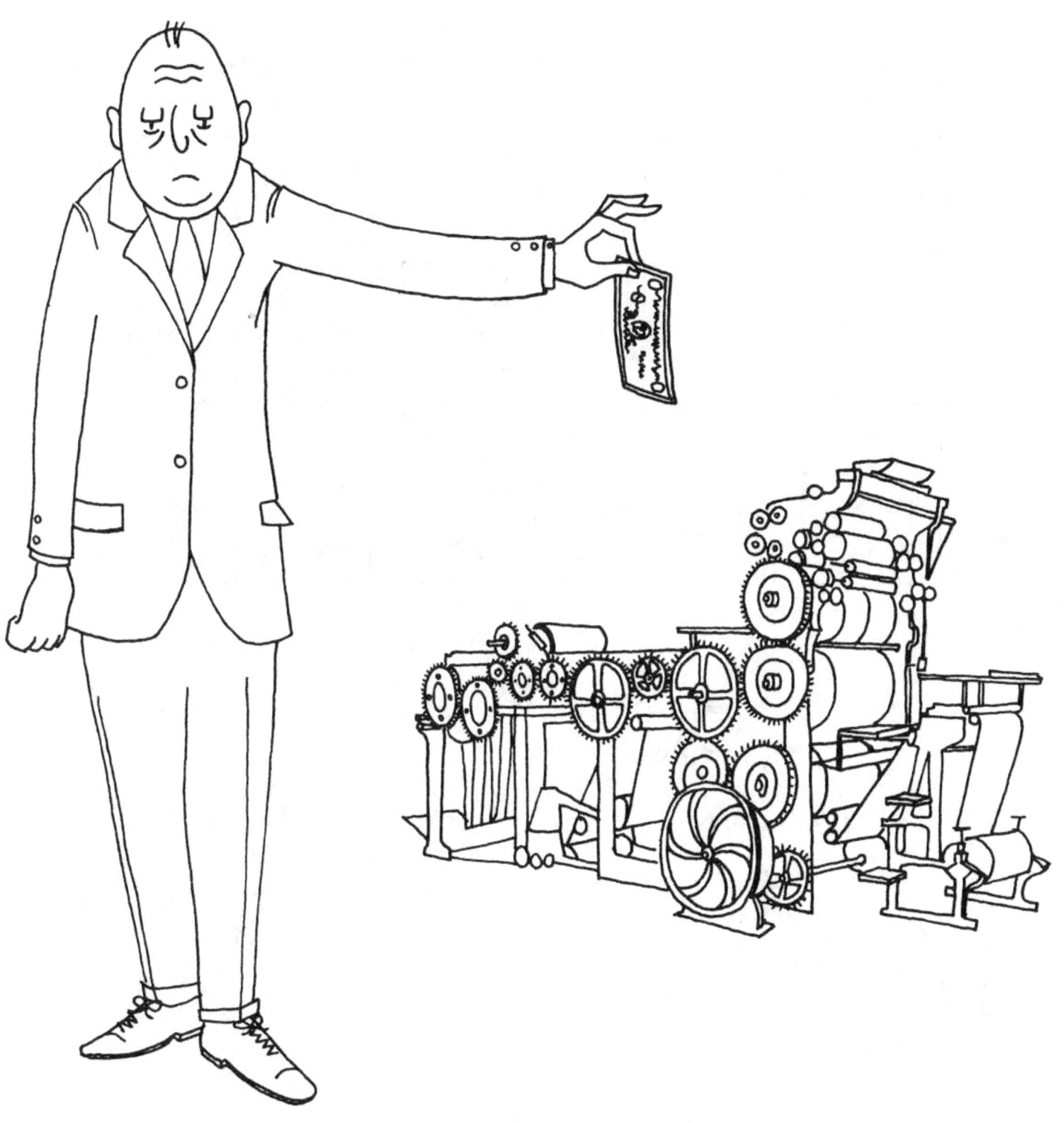

THIS IS MY PRINTING PRESS. No bureaucrat should be without one. Color what's in my hand green, not gold.

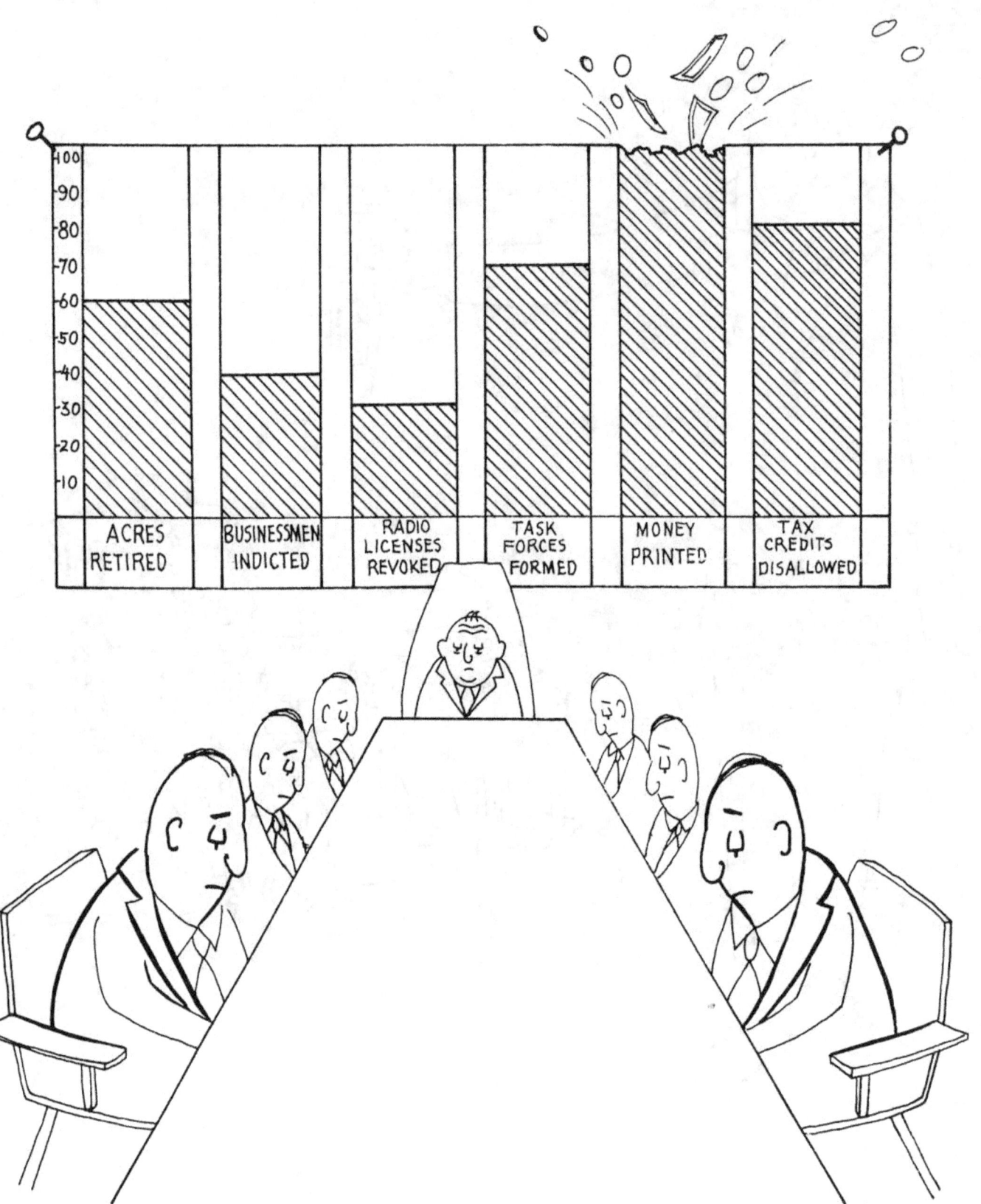

THIS IS MY COMMITTEE. We are very productive. Color us all grey.

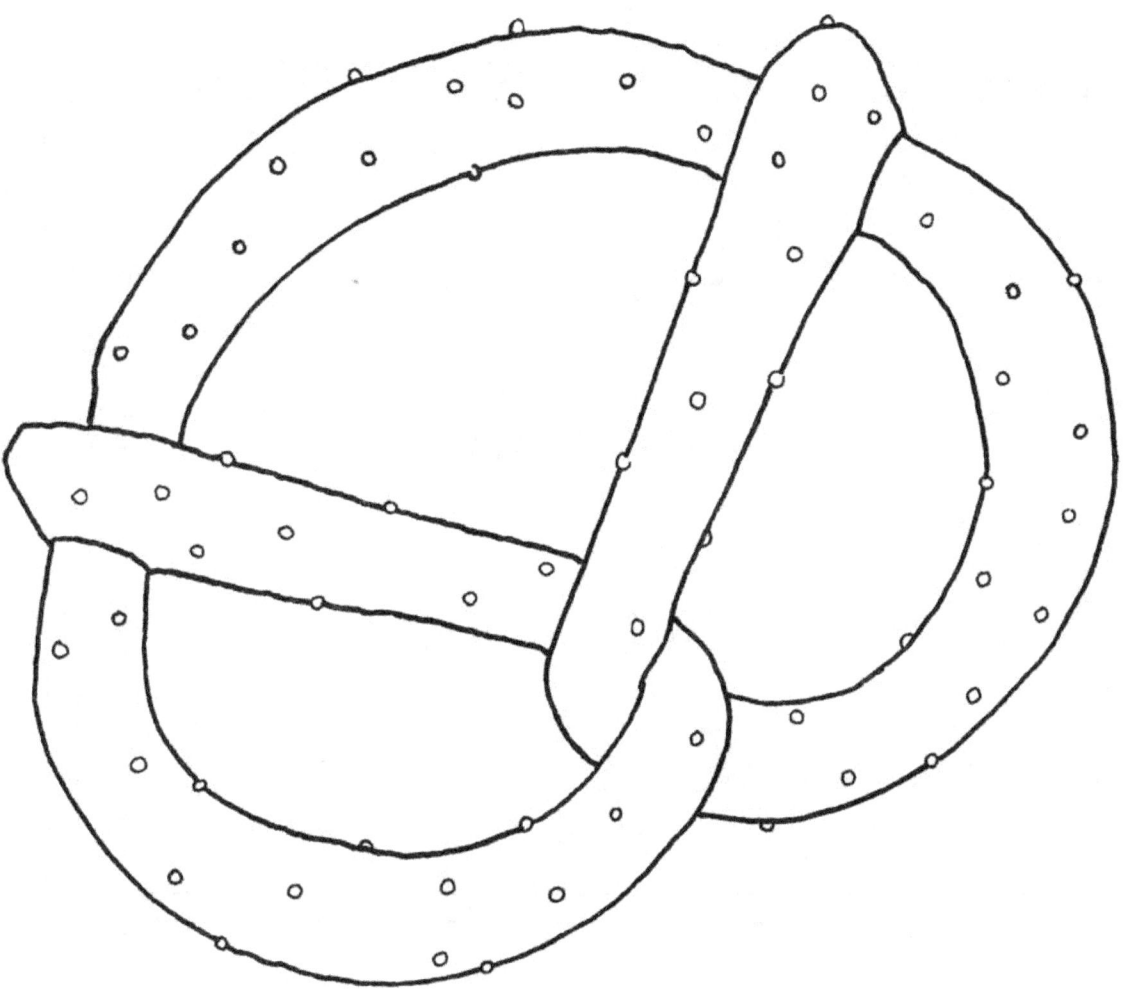

THIS IS MY MIND. Join the dots without crossing any lines.

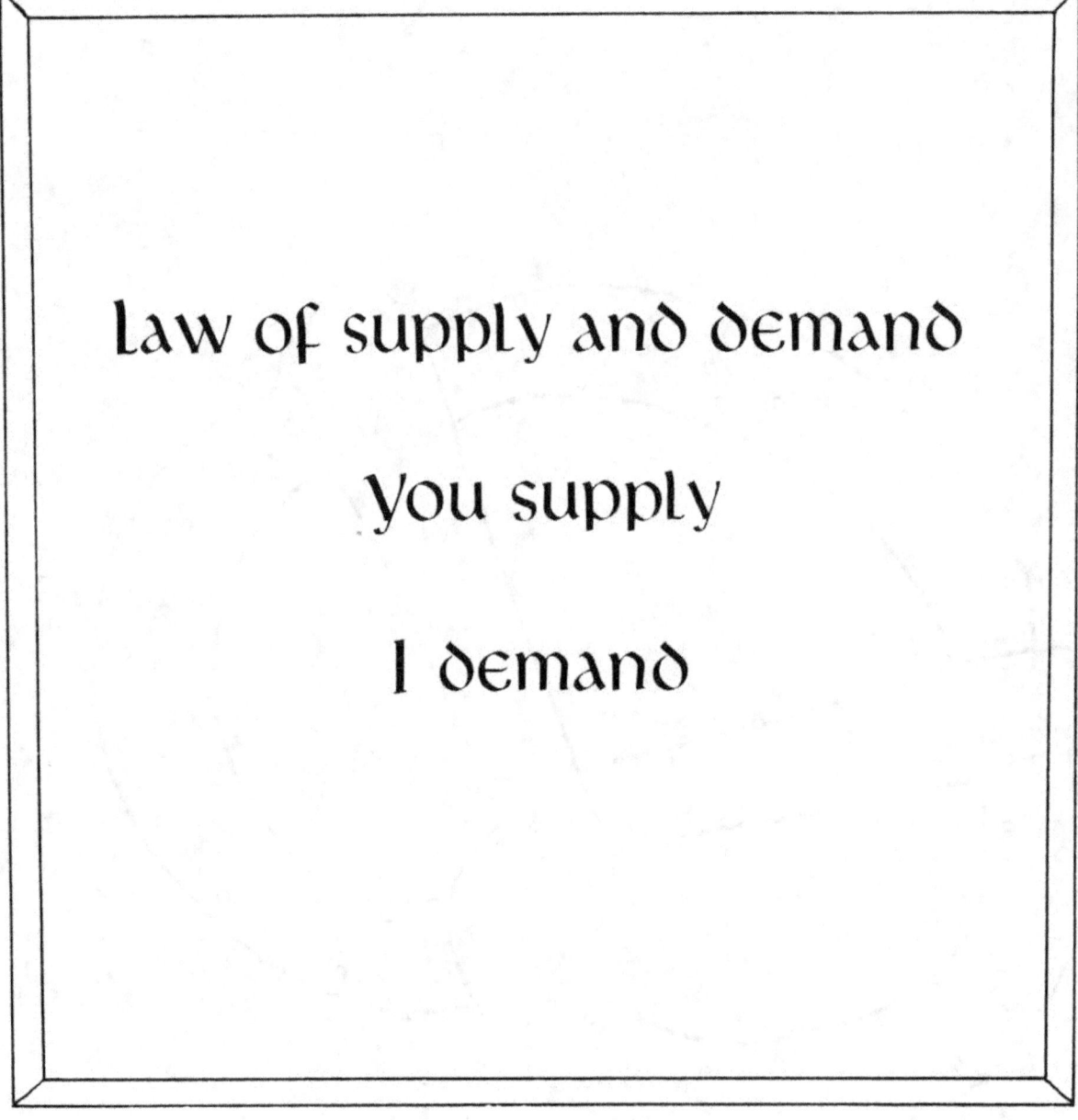

law of supply and demand

You supply

I demand

THIS IS MY CREDO. It comforts me in moments of need.

128

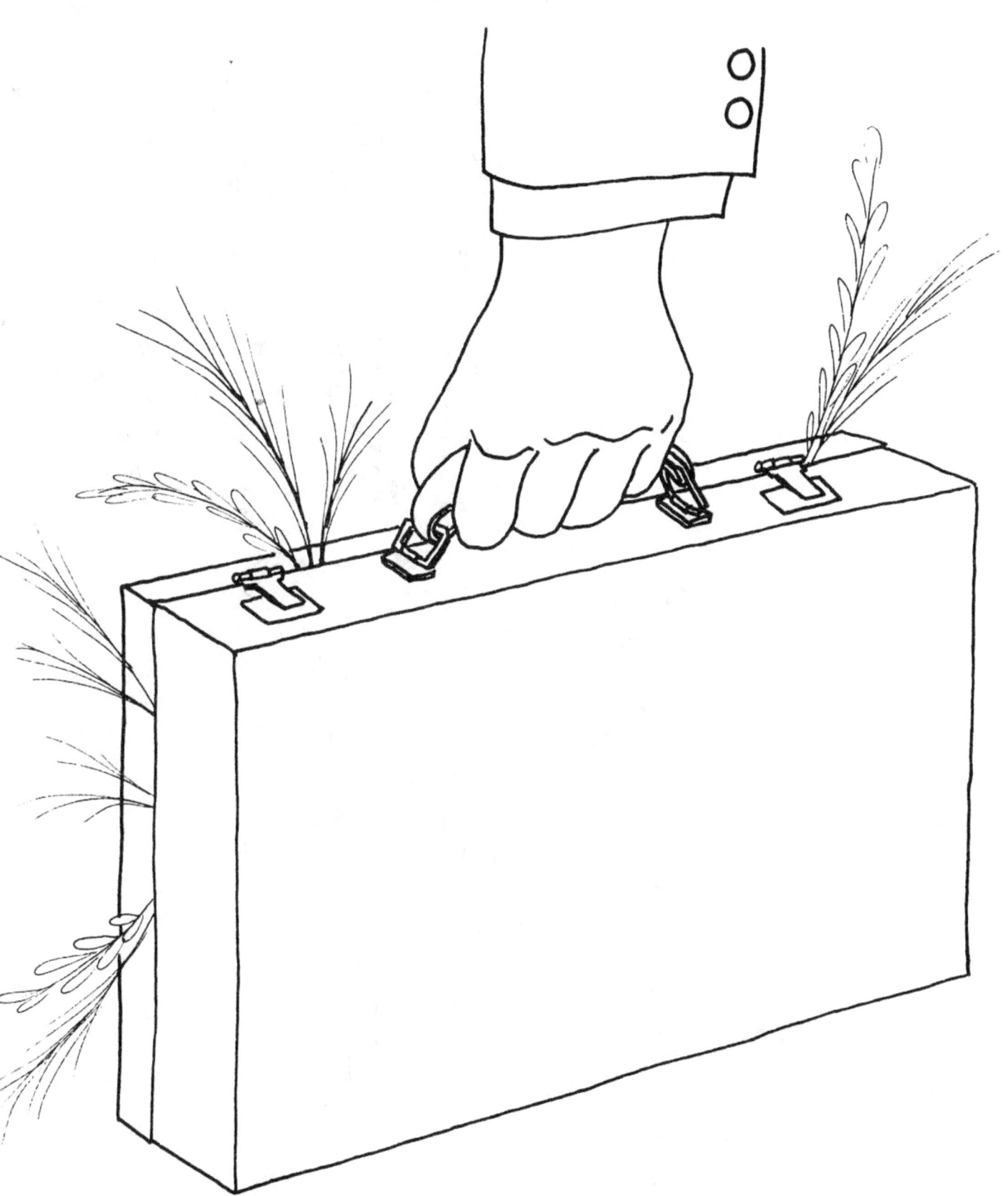

THIS IS MY ATTACHE CASE. It is full of surplus wheat. I carry it on peace missions to foreign countries. I keep a spare case in my fallout shelter.

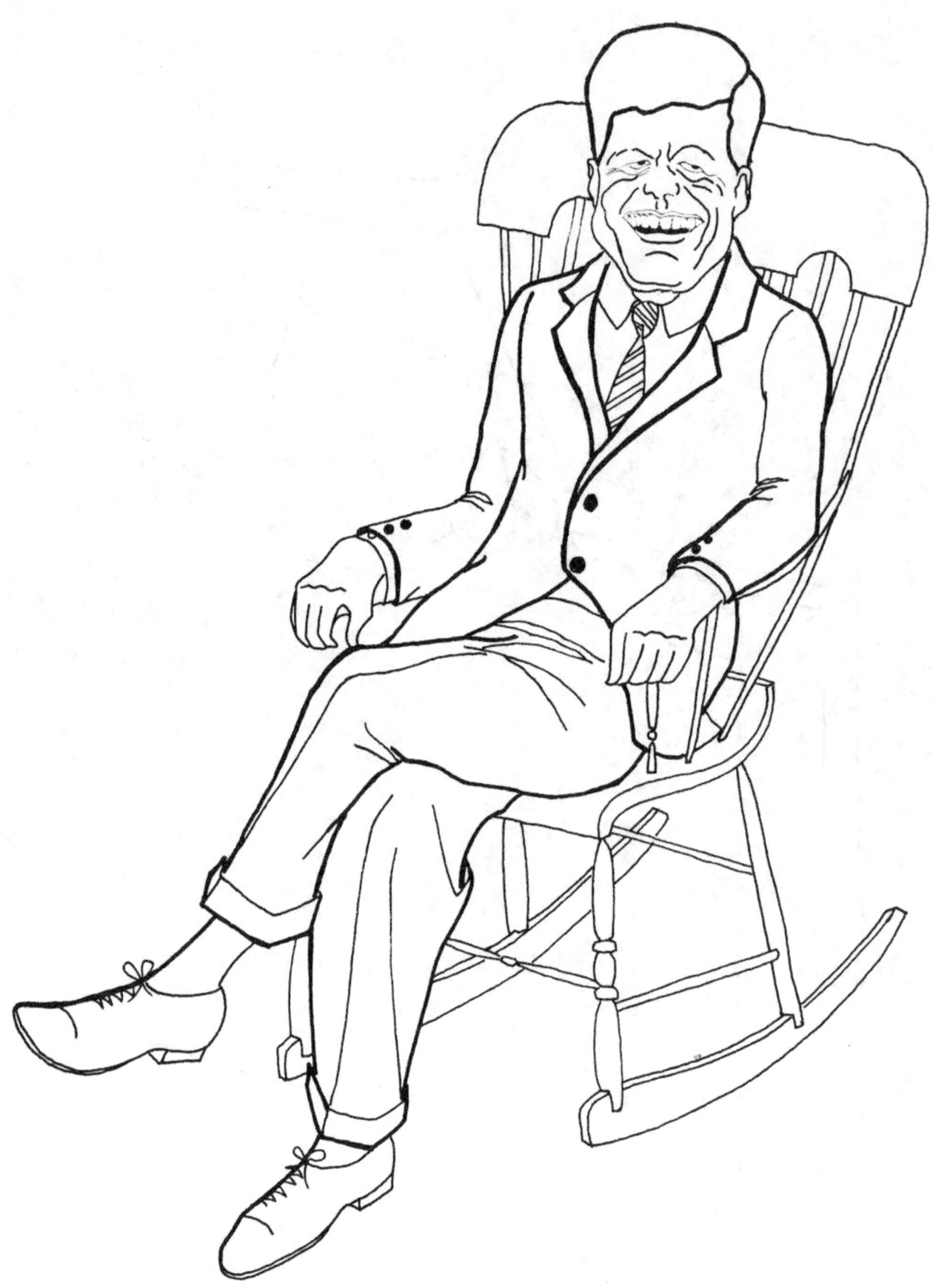

THIS IS MY BOSS. He is young. He moves fast. He hasn't told me where he's going.

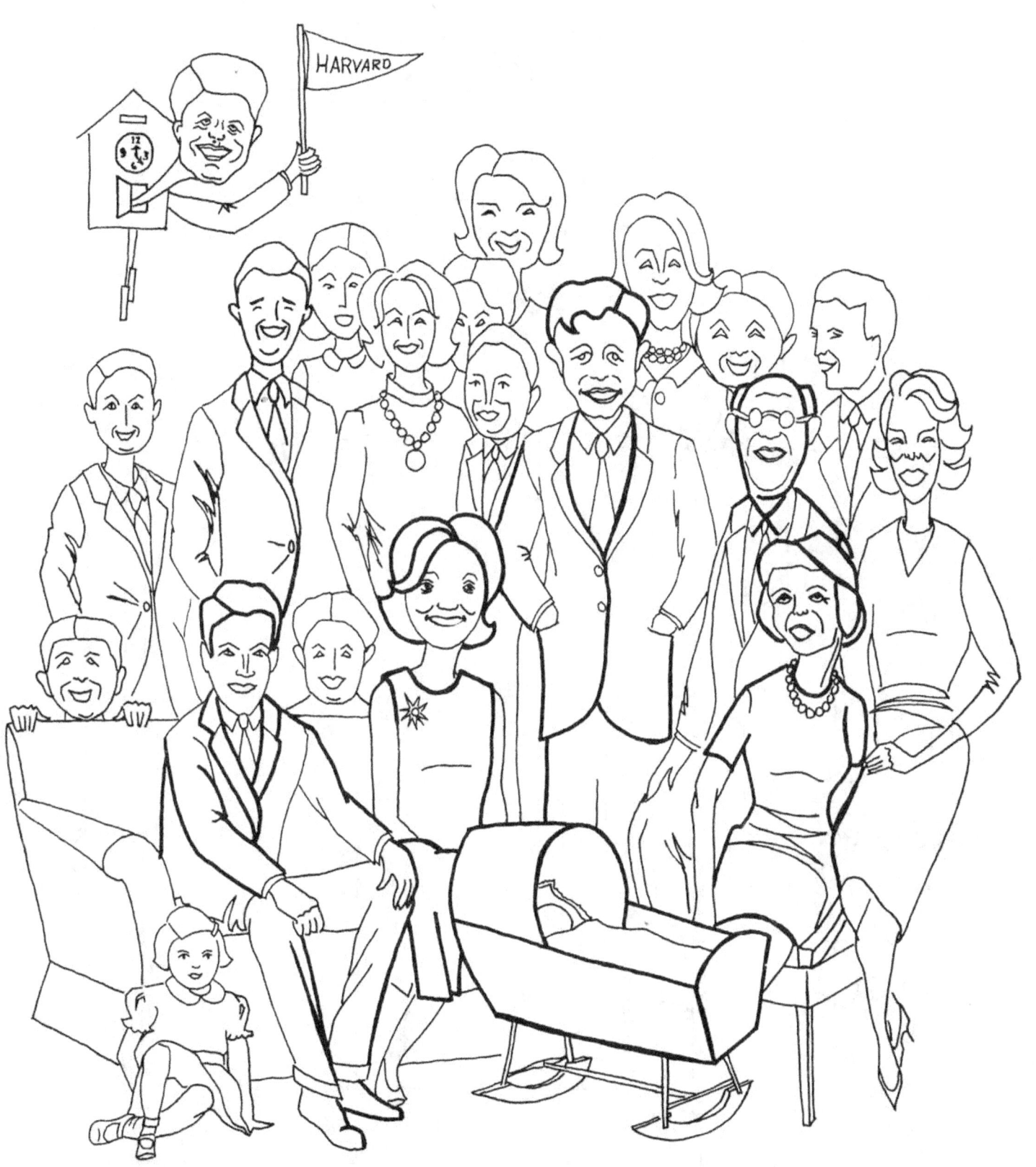

THIS IS MY BOSS'S FAMILY. They're going with him.

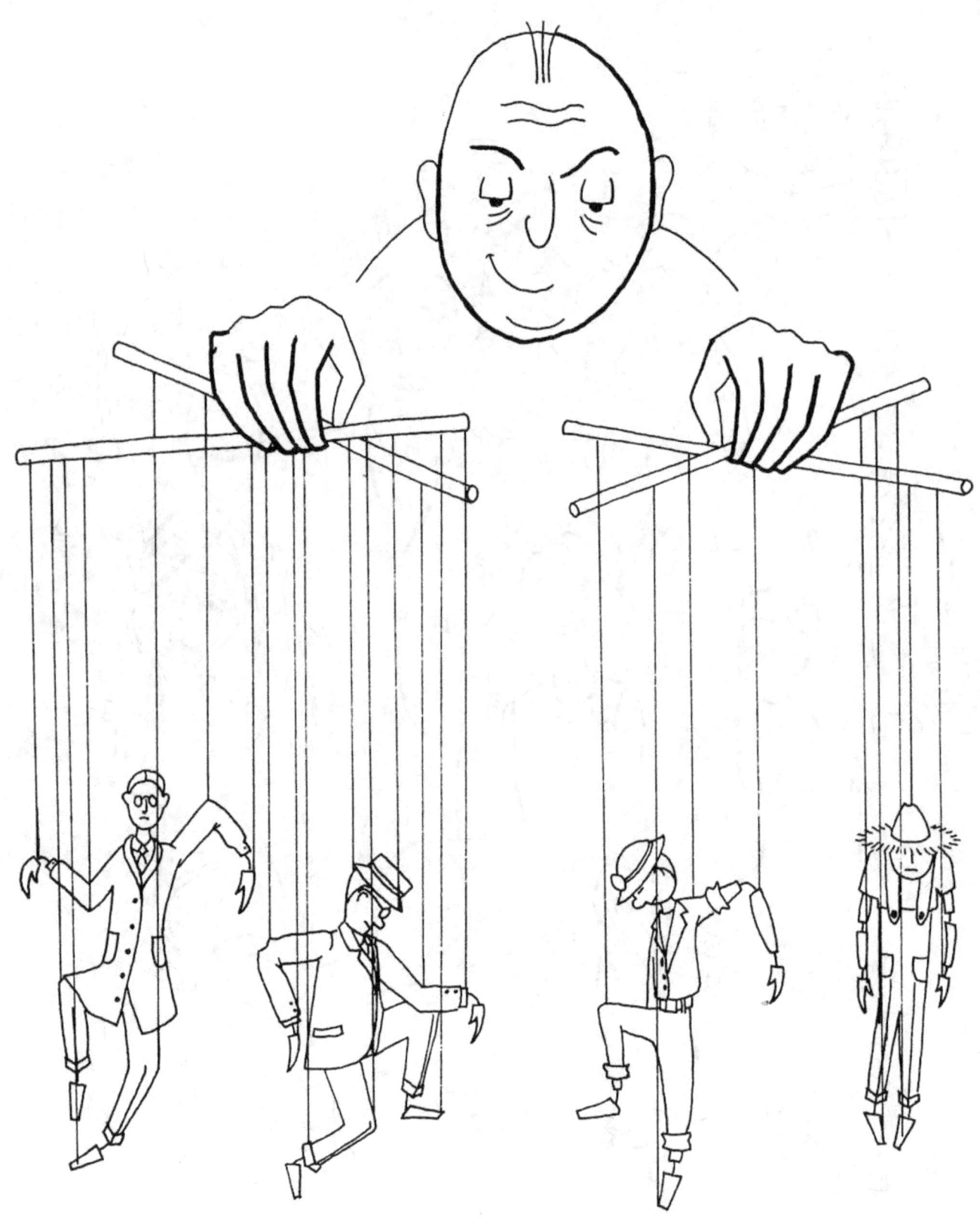

THESE ARE MY PEOPLE. I love people. I want them to be happy. People who dance are happy.

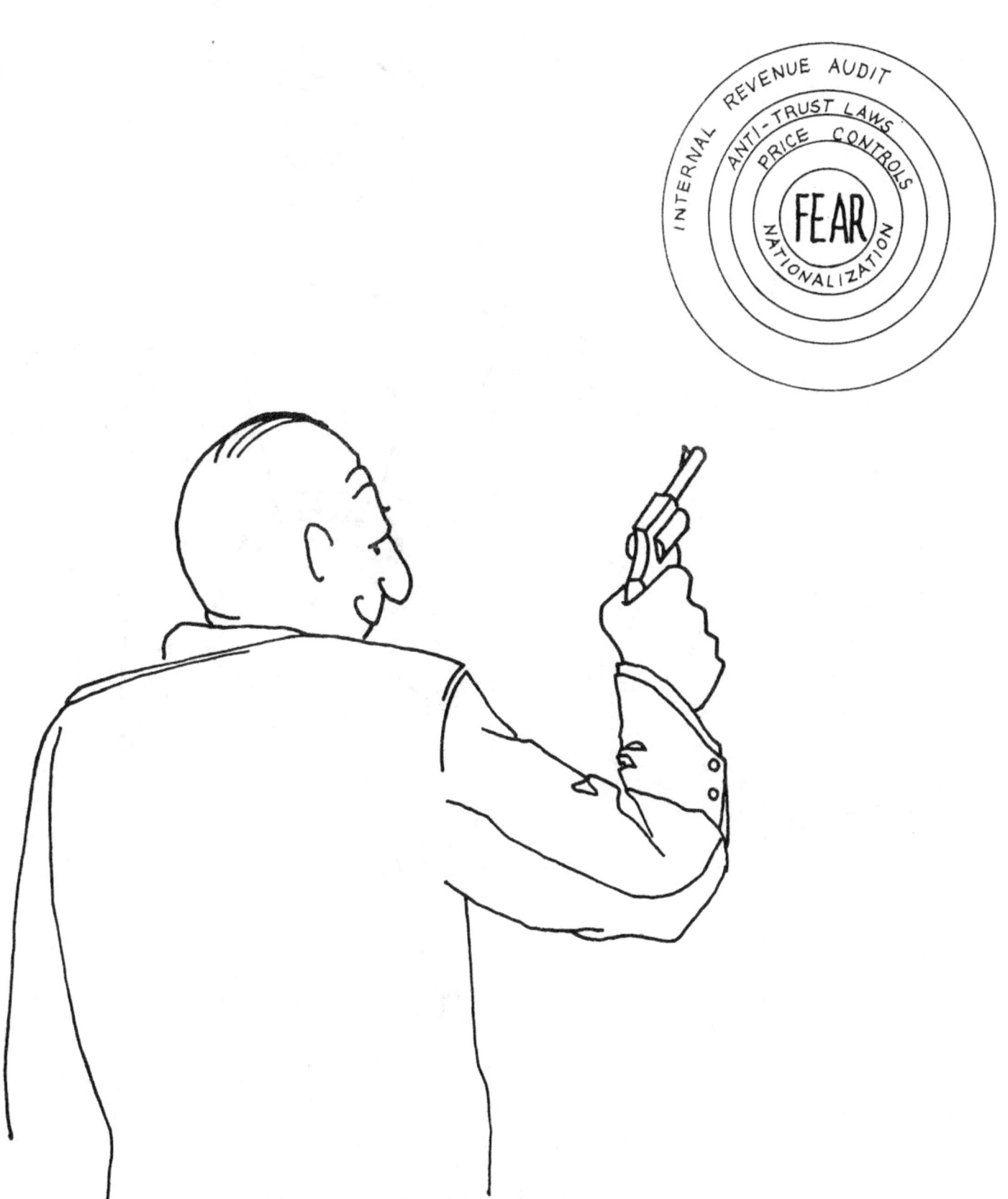

THIS IS MY SECRET.

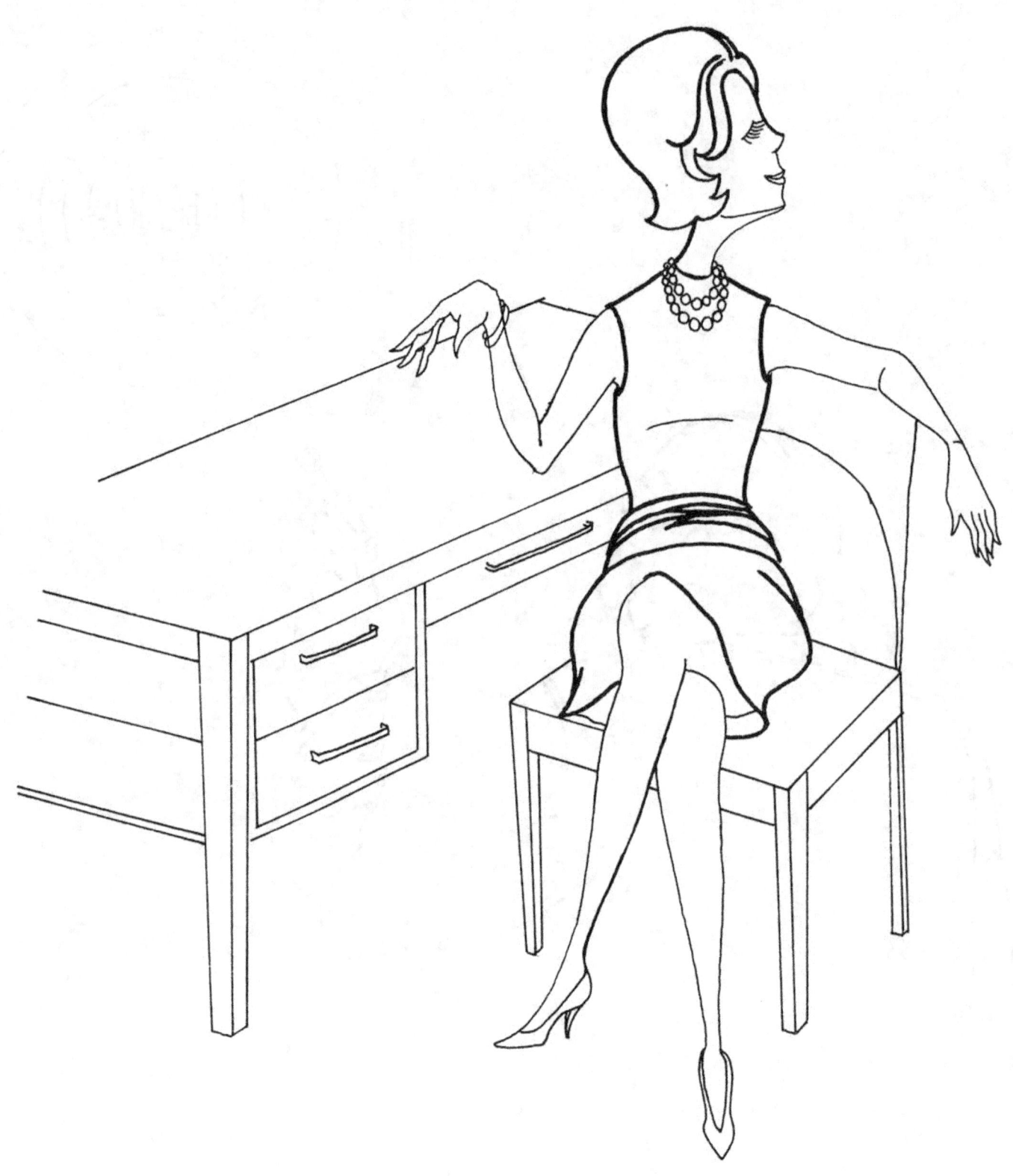

THIS IS MY SECRETARY. She speaks *le langage international*. She made many friends for America on our last trip abroad.

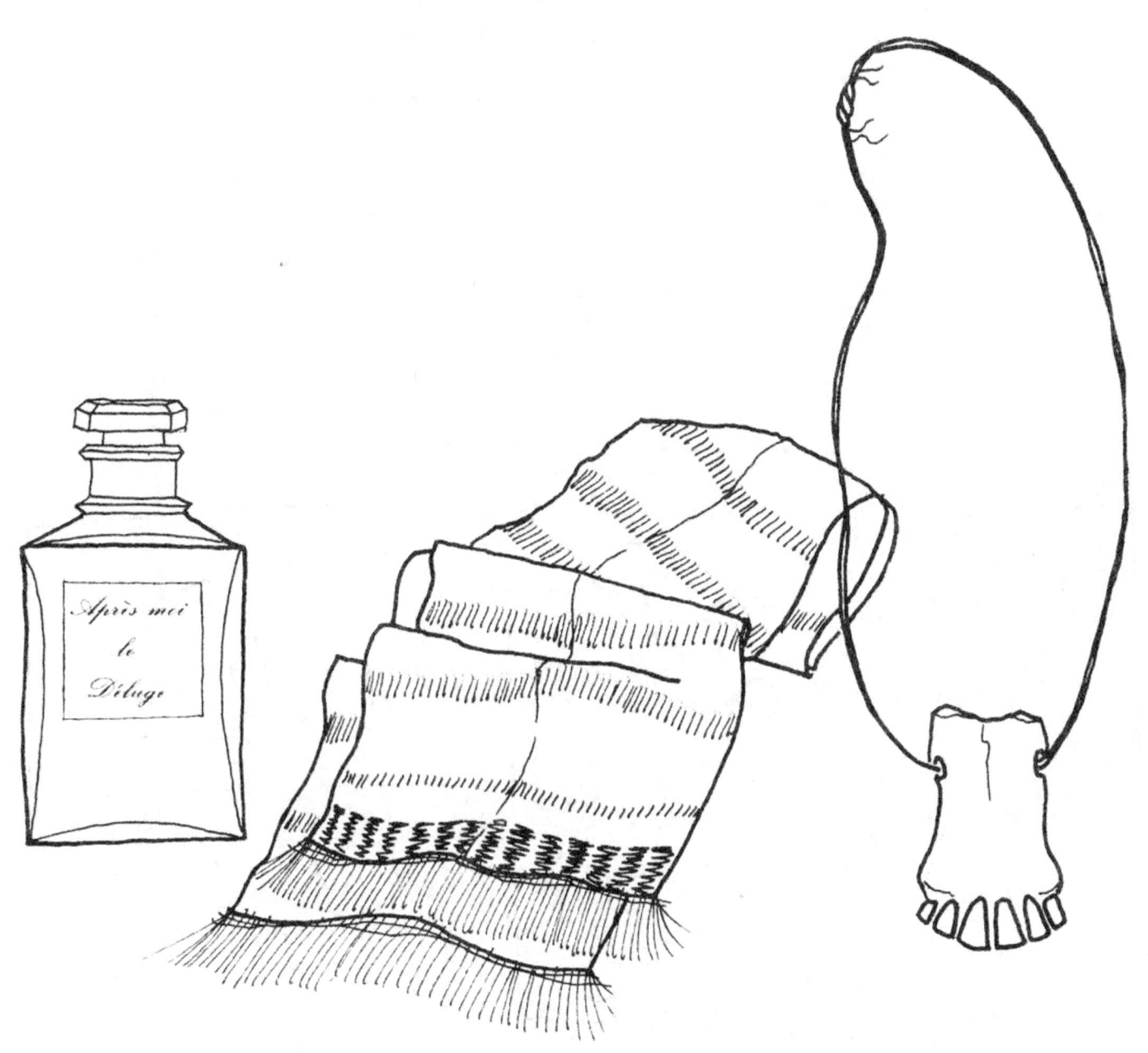

THESE ARE MY FRENCH PERFUME, MY CAMBODIAN
SILK STOLE AND MY AFRICAN NECKLACE. They go to
parties with me. My wife comes too.

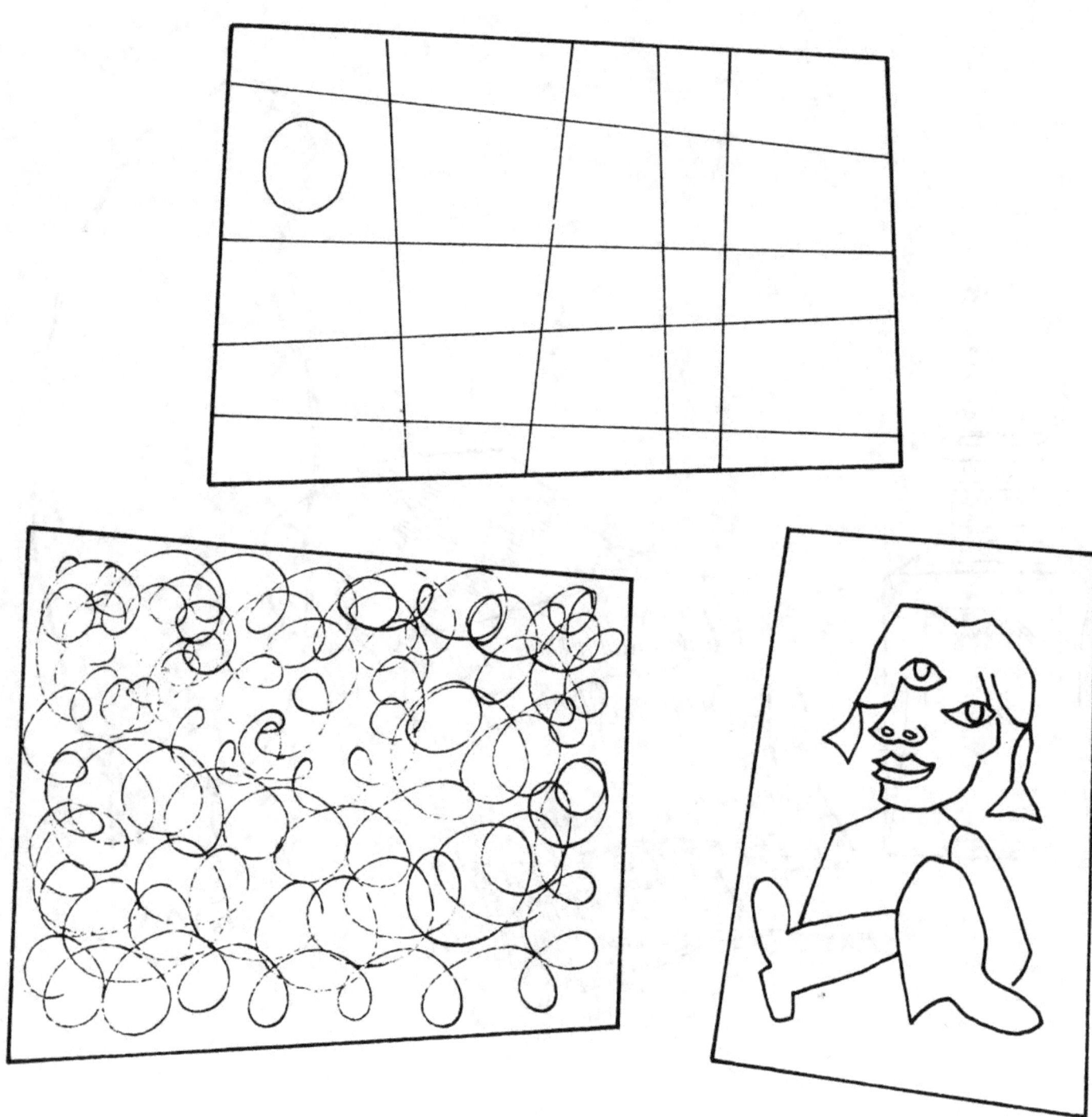

THIS IS MY ART COLLECTION. Bureaucrats like to encourage the creative mind. We will soon form a Commission to prove it.

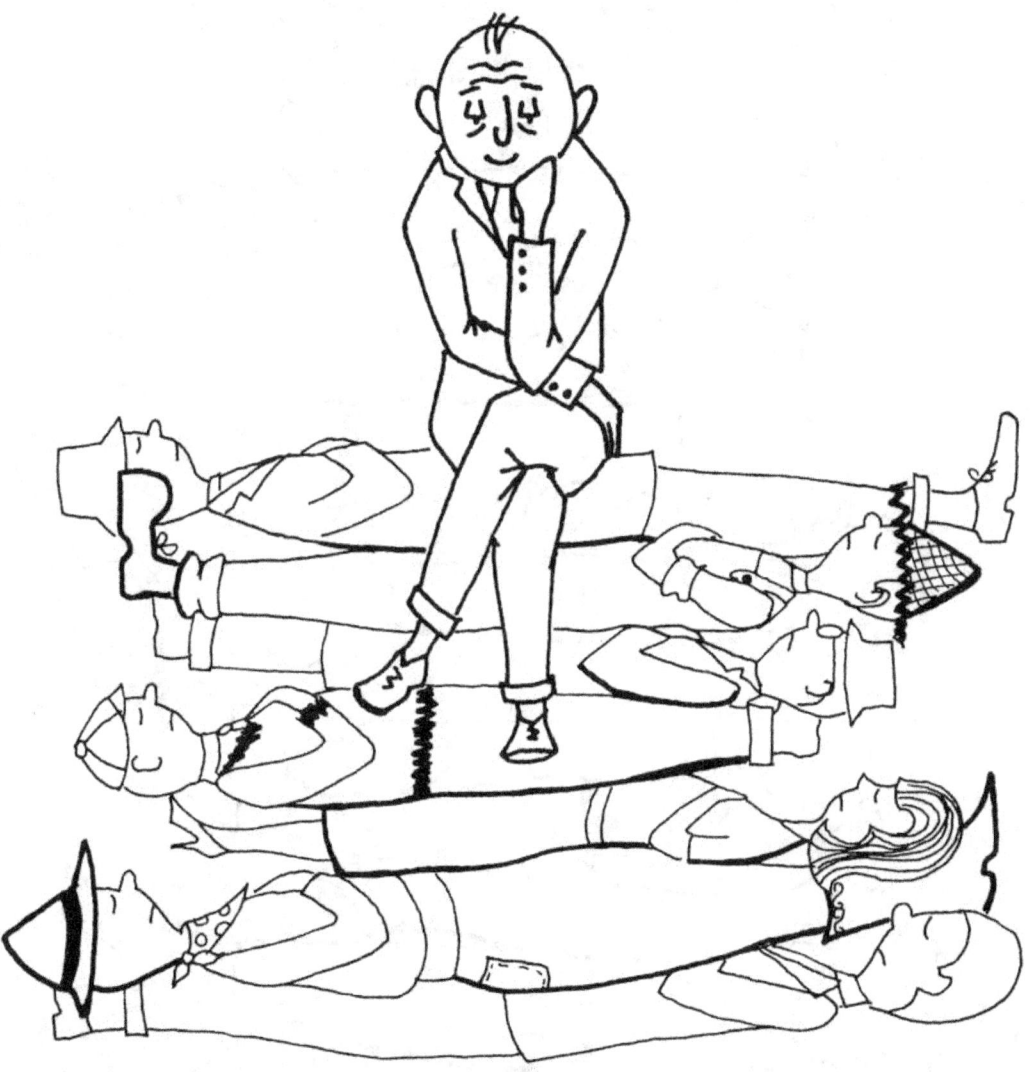

THIS IS OUR NATIONAL PURPOSE. It is socio-
political-democracy-based-on-brotherly-love-and-sacri-
fice-for-the-public-interest.

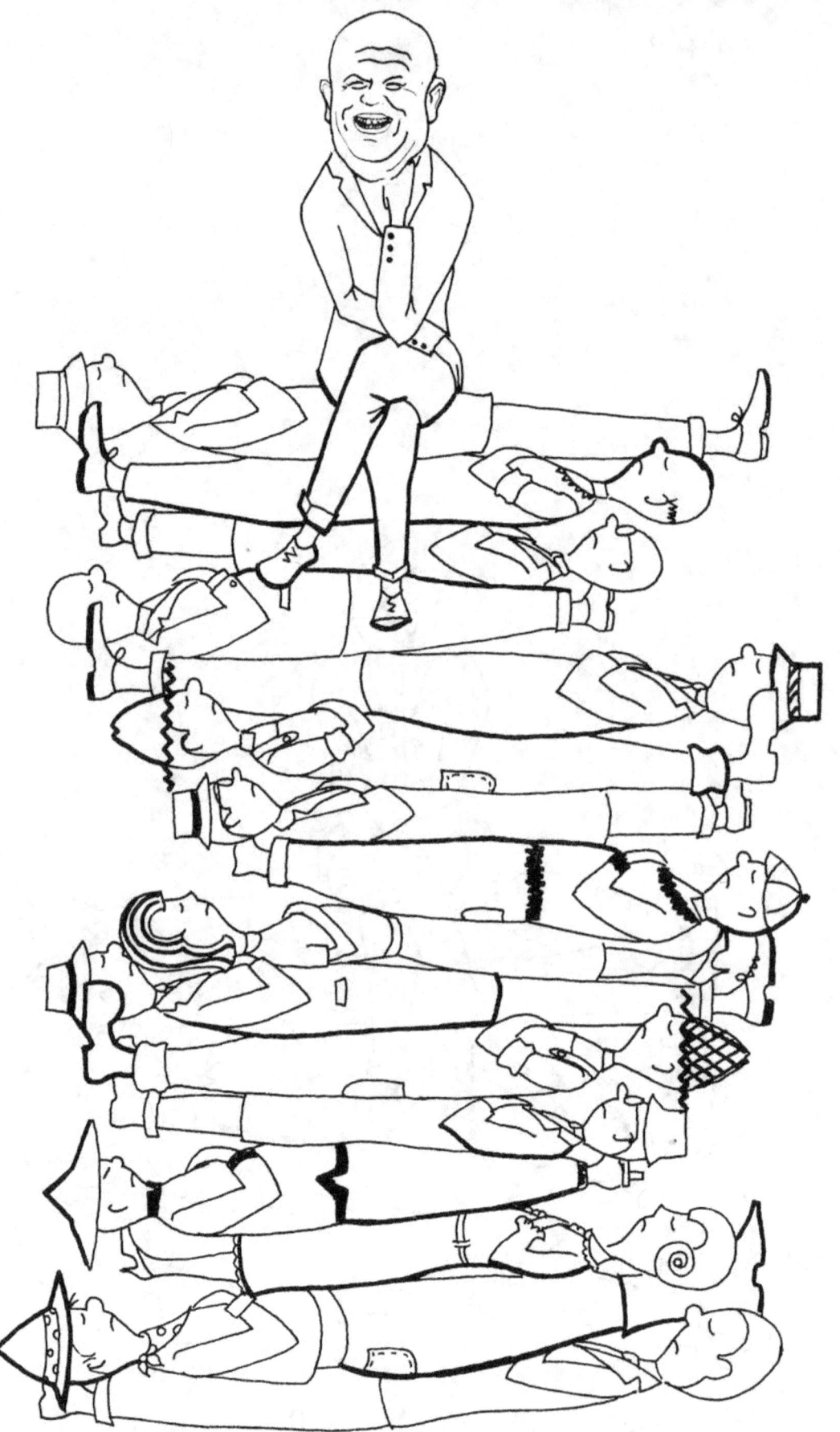

THIS IS OUR COMPETITOR'S PURPOSE. It is socialism.

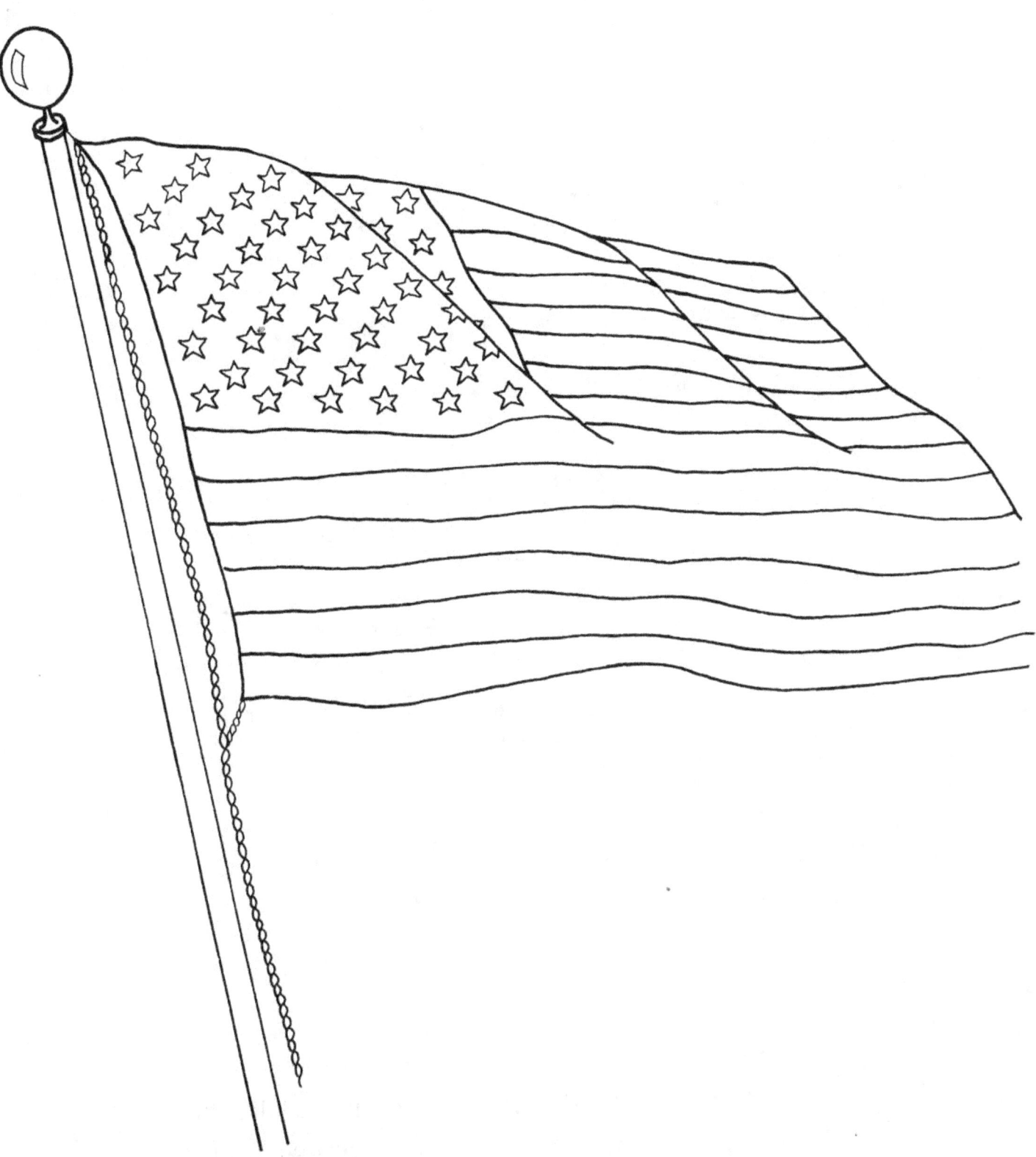

THIS IS MY FLAG. I like to see it wave. If there is no breeze, I blow hot air on it.

deem it necessary and desirable, therefore, to create the following offices:

Commission for the Obstinate Needs of Farmers Unsolved
by Subsidies, Intervention, Overproduction & Nationalization
(CONFUSION)

Jurisdiction for an Unlimited Moratorium on Bureaucrats'
Liabilities & Errors
(JUMBLE)

Temporary Headquarters of the World Authority for the
Restriction of Trade
(THWART)

Municipal Establishment for Sexual Security
(MESS)

Mutual Union of Democratic Demagogues & Lunatic Economists
(MUDDLE)

Bureau for Opportunism, Theatrics, Courtesy & Horticulture
(BOTCH)

Territorial Haven for Unsolicited Miscellaneous Problems
(THUMP)

THIS IS MY SIGNATURE. It is small and illegible. Small, illegible signatures are the sign of the humble and the self-effacing. I am, after all, just a servant of the omnipotent State.

The Amazing
LOS ANGELES ANGELS
COLORING BOOK

60¢
INC. TAX

In 1963, when this coloring book was published, the Los Angeles Angels were little more than rookies as a team, having only joined the Major League Baseball roster in 1961. At the time, they shared the stadium with the Los Angeles Dodgers, calling their home "Chavez Ravine" rather than using its proper name, Dodger Stadium, out of a sense of pride. This still placed them firmly within the city of Los Angeles, unlike the current iteration of the Los Angeles Angels.

Artist Jack Lane had been providing caricatures for the wall of Hollywood's famous Brown Derby restaurant for 15 years before creating this coloring book, and would continue drawing the famous customers of the hat-shaped eatery for more than 20 years, finishing his run in 1985.

The artist (and we use the word loosely) who wrote the copy and drew the caricatures is JACK LANE. Many of his caricatures are hung in the Hollywood Brown Derby and after this book is printed HE will probably be hung in Chavez Ravine.

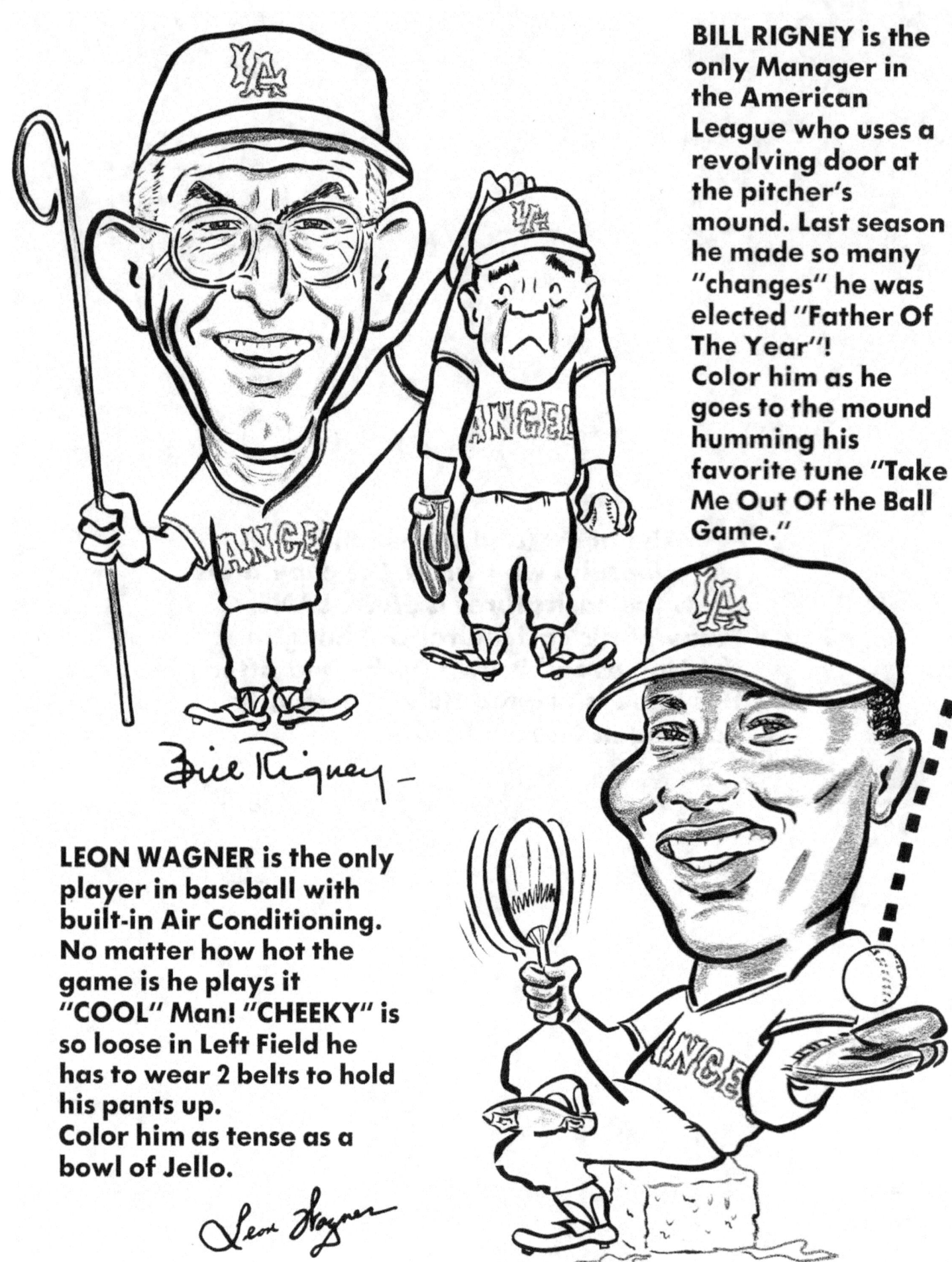

BILL RIGNEY is the only Manager in the American League who uses a revolving door at the pitcher's mound. Last season he made so many "changes" he was elected "Father Of The Year"! Color him as he goes to the mound humming his favorite tune "Take Me Out Of the Ball Game."

LEON WAGNER is the only player in baseball with built-in Air Conditioning. No matter how hot the game is he plays it "COOL" Man! "CHEEKY" is so loose in Left Field he has to wear 2 belts to hold his pants up.
Color him as tense as a bowl of Jello.

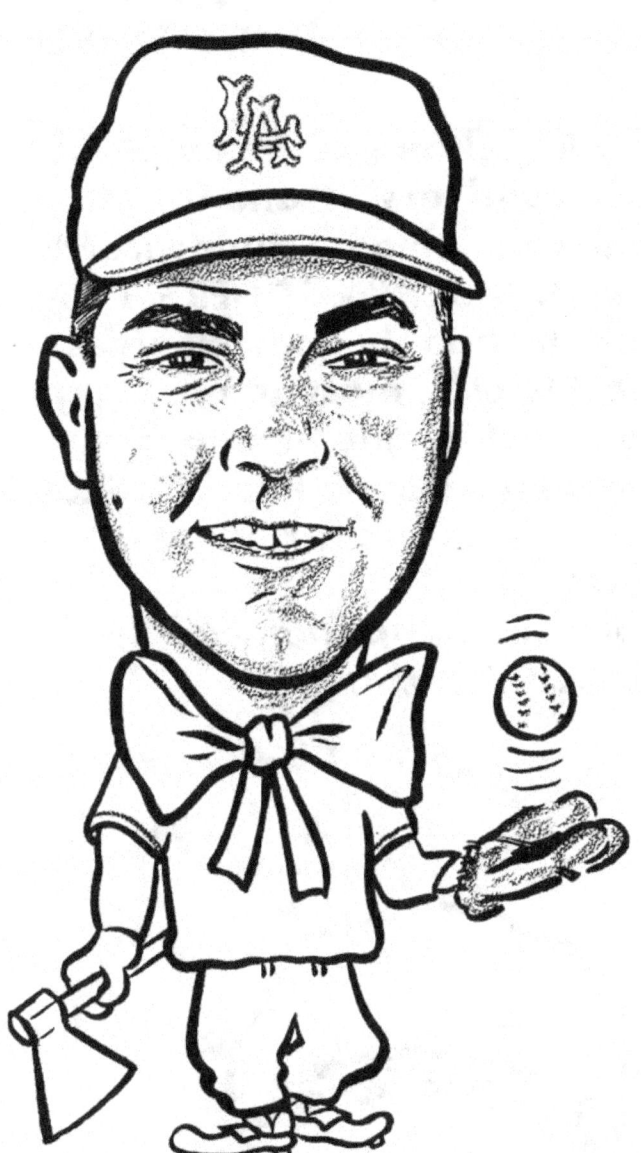

KEN McBRIDE is the strong silent type. He just goes quietly about his business of murdering the opposition, strangling the hitters, and slaughtering their batting averages. But he's a square shooter. He wouldn't throw a curve at anybody. Color him as innocent as a wink in the dark.

Ken McBride

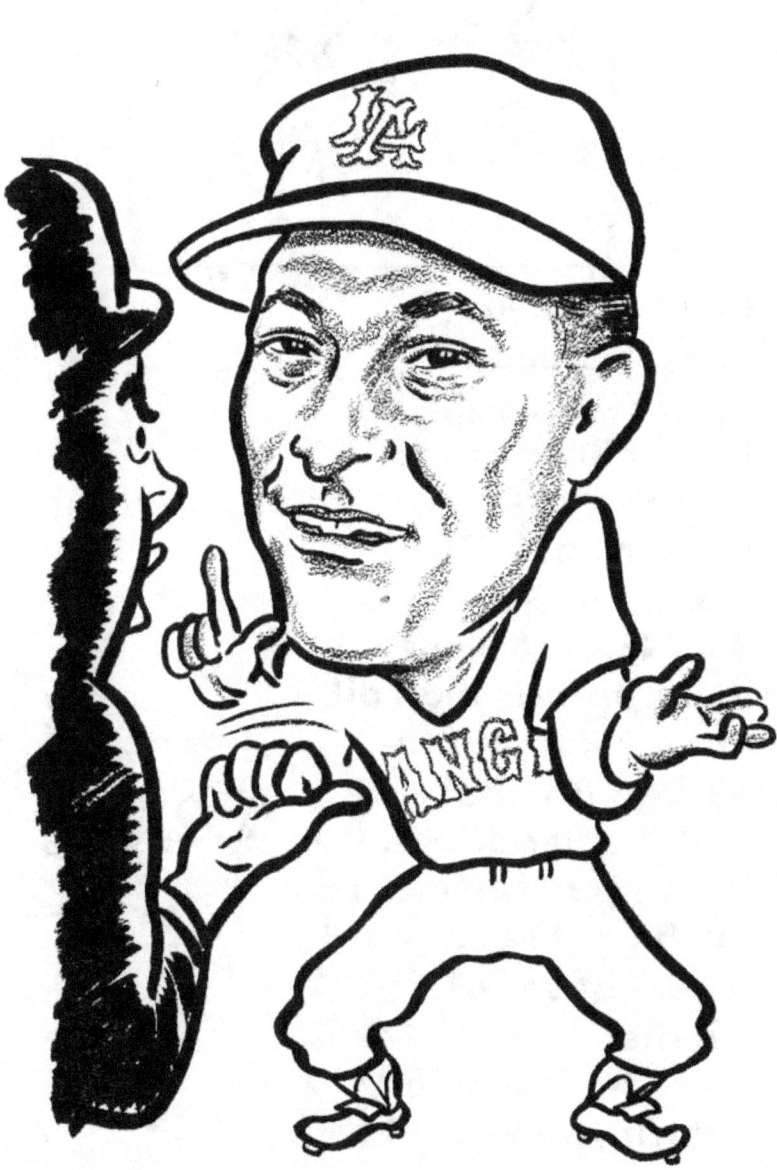

FELIX TORRES runs the bases like a man who is caught in quick sand and is wearing suction cups for shoes. He always wins arguments with umpires because the only two words he knows in English are "DROP DEAD"! As a result, color him the happiest man in baseball!

Felix Torres

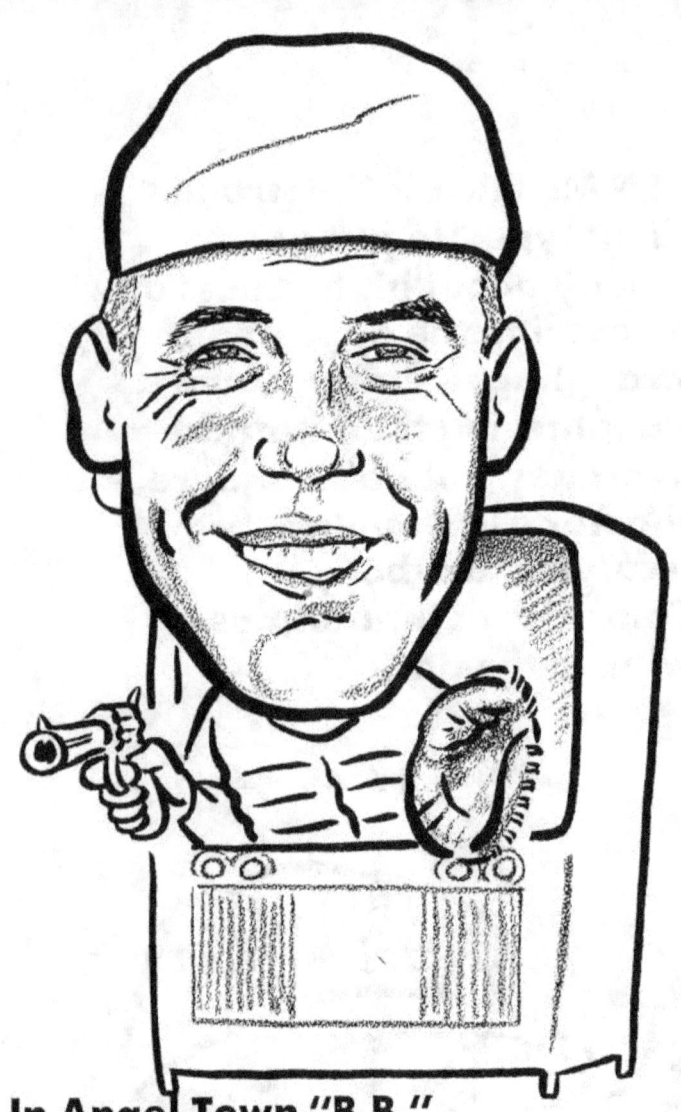

The Angels are in the hands of the "receivers"... and the No. 1 man collecting all their records is BOB "BUCK" RODGERS. Last year he had the most doubles, most triples, most games caught by a rookie, and after appearing on the Donna Reed TV Show, the most offers to get out of town.
Color his occupation like the flu... it's catching!

Bob Rodgers

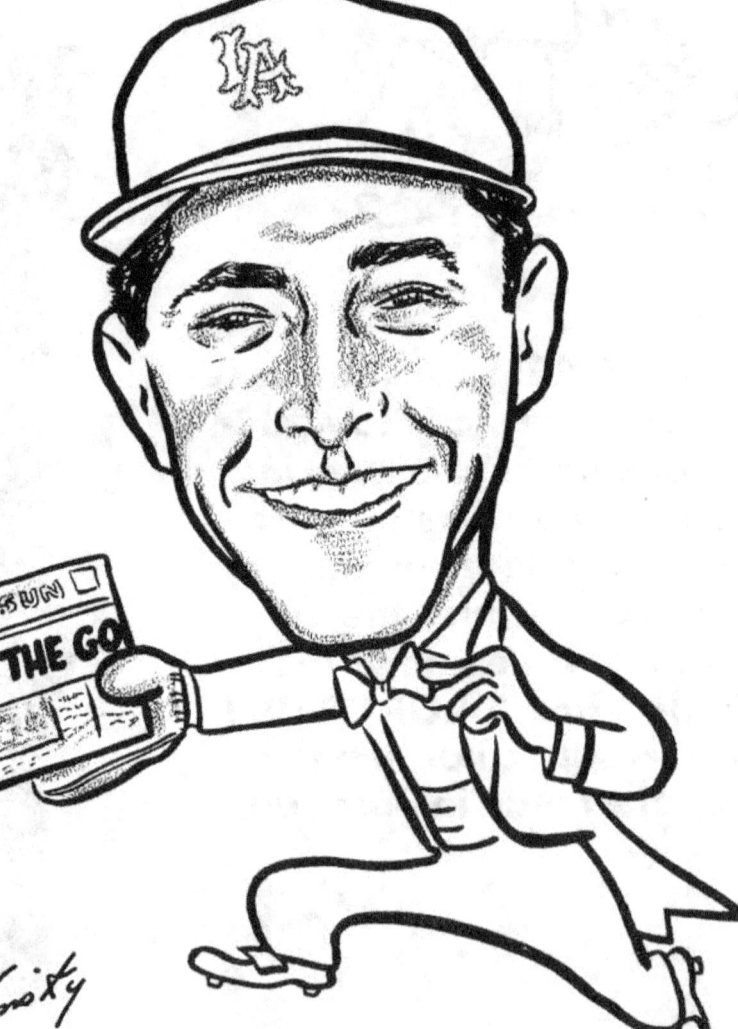

In Angel Town "B.B." doesn't stand for Brigitte Bardot, Baggy Britches, or Boston Blackie... altho what it DOES stand for, BO BELINSKY, causes more uproar than all other three put together. Bo's hobby is making headlines. If it isn't for "no hits" in pitching it's for "no show" at social events.
Color him colorful (which you've gotta admit).

Bo Belinsky

146

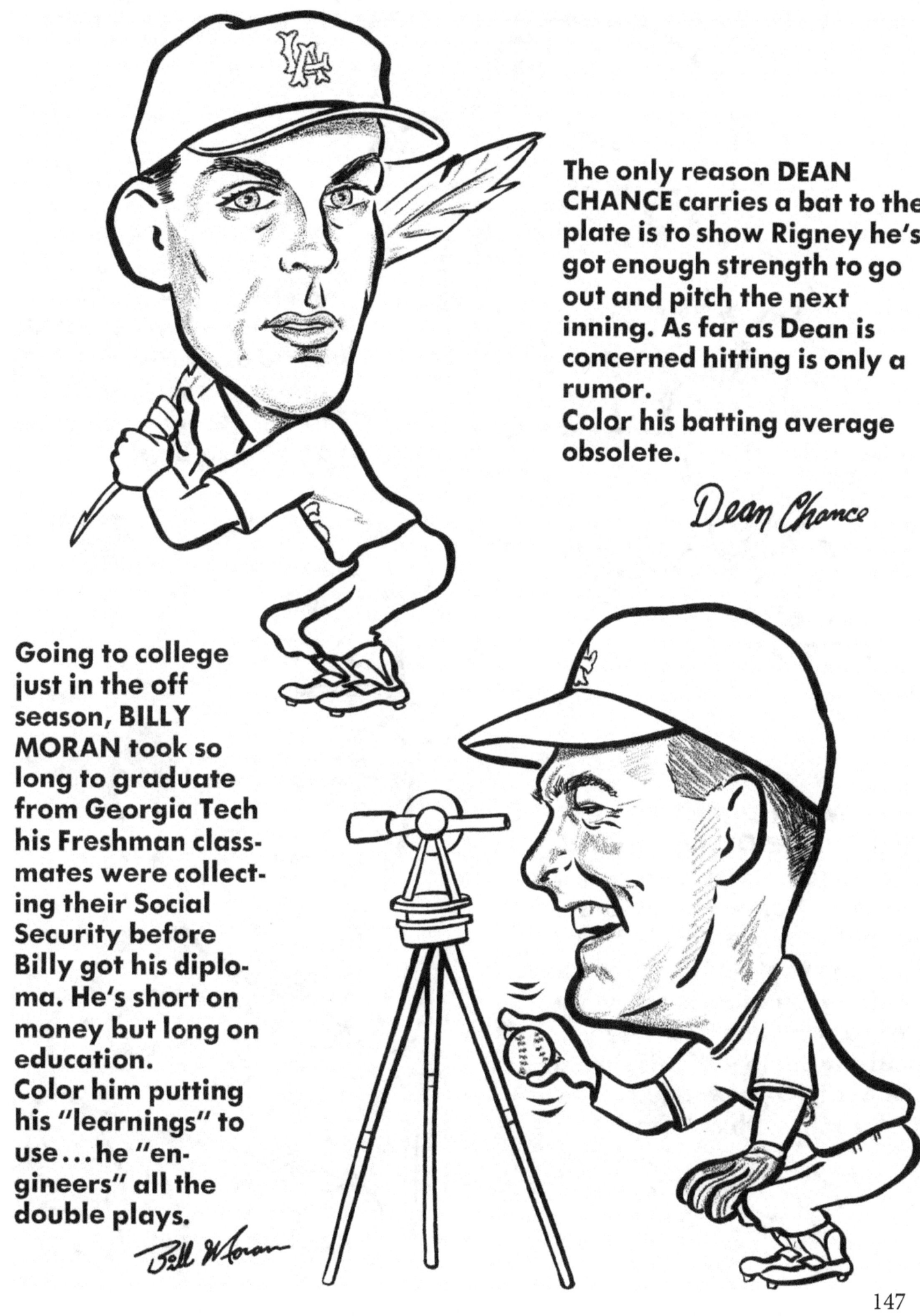

The only reason **DEAN CHANCE** carries a bat to the plate is to show Rigney he's got enough strength to go out and pitch the next inning. As far as Dean is concerned hitting is only a rumor.
Color his batting average obsolete.

Dean Chance

Going to college just in the off season, **BILLY MORAN** took so long to graduate from Georgia Tech his Freshman class-mates were collecting their Social Security before Billy got his diploma. He's short on money but long on education.
Color him putting his "learnings" to use...he "engineers" all the double plays.

Bill Moran

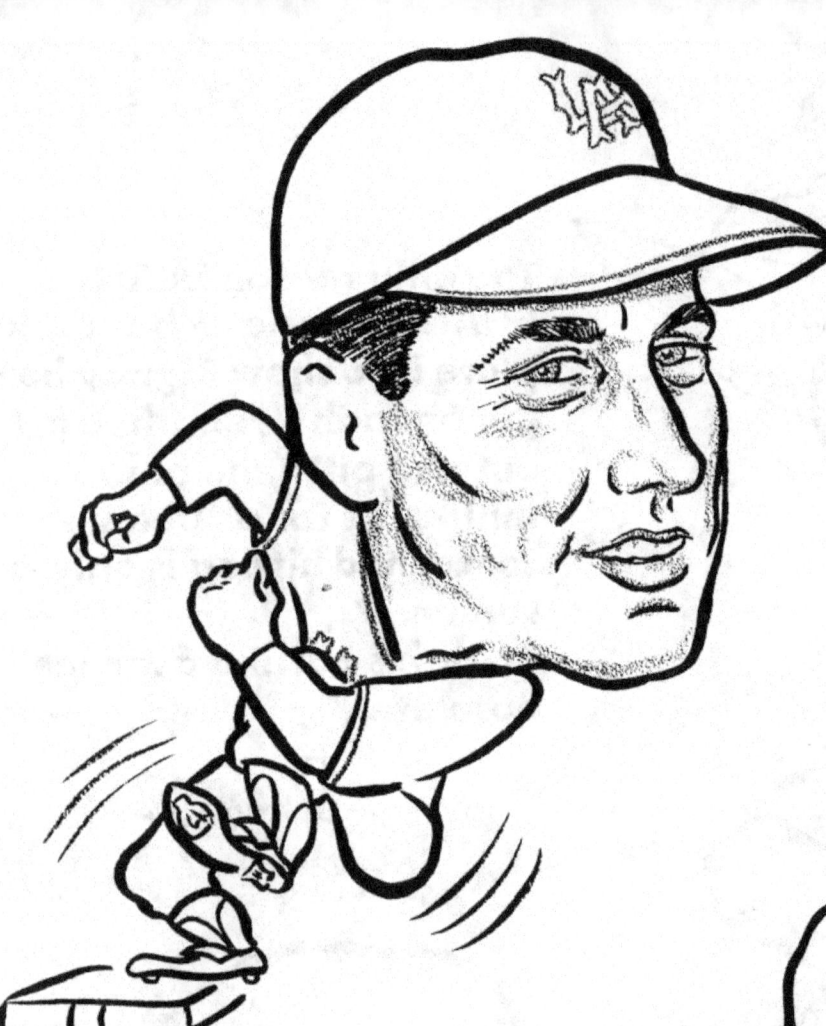

JIM FREGOSI is the fastest thing since Silky Sullivan (and HE does it on TWO legs!). He rounds third like he had just recognized the third base coach as a Process Server in disguise. Color him a blur!

James Fregosi

In his Major League career, **ALBIE PEARSON** has walked the 90 feet to 1st base so many times he has been claimed the inventor of the 50 mile hike. The fact that he is built so close to the ground he is out of the strike zone has absolutely nothing to do with his amazing **"WALKING"** average. Color him with calluses.

Al Chi Pearson

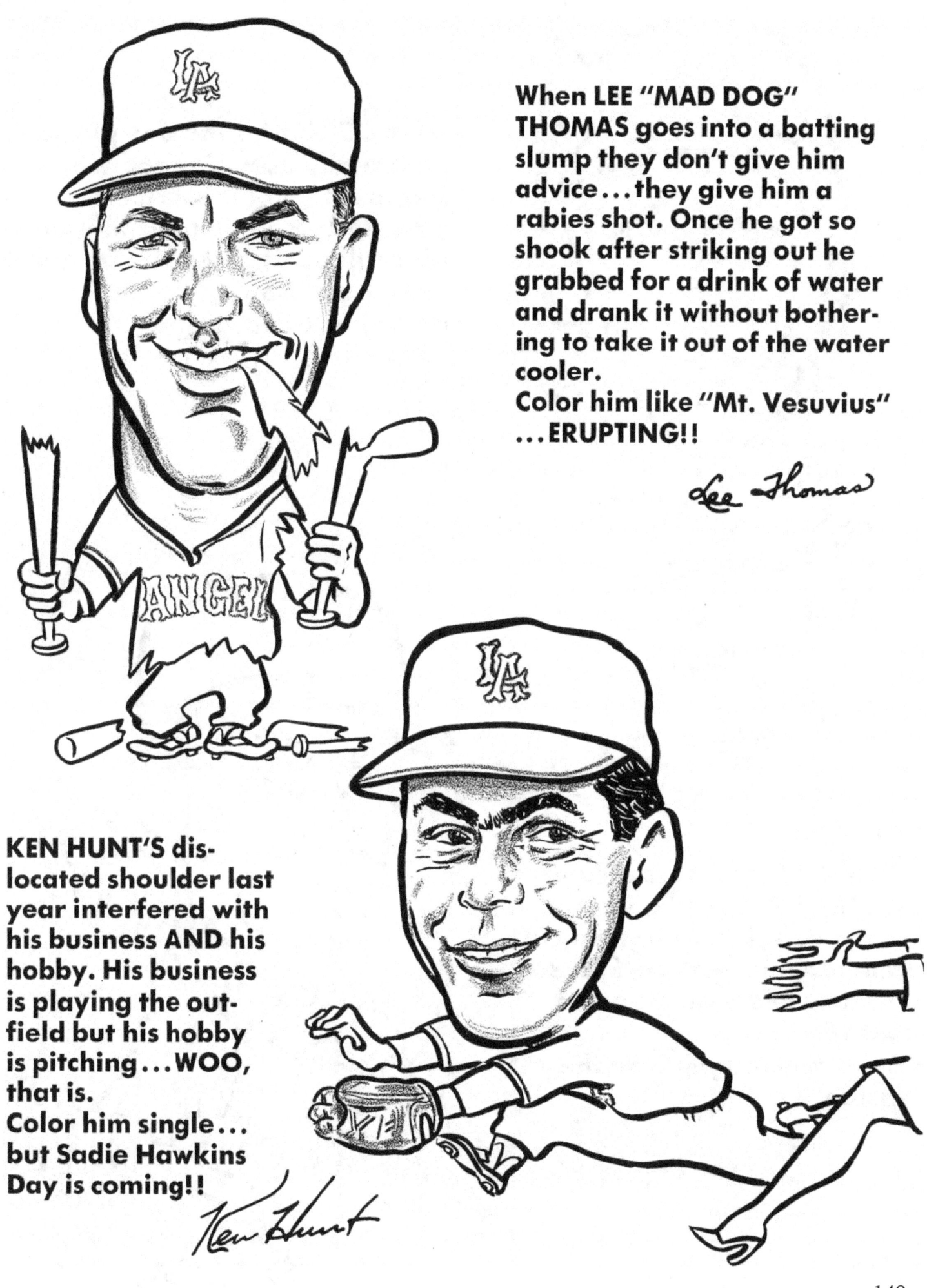

When LEE "MAD DOG" THOMAS goes into a batting slump they don't give him advice...they give him a rabies shot. Once he got so shook after striking out he grabbed for a drink of water and drank it without bothering to take it out of the water cooler.
Color him like "Mt. Vesuvius" ...ERUPTING!!

Lee Thomas

KEN HUNT'S dislocated shoulder last year interfered with his business AND his hobby. His business is playing the outfield but his hobby is pitching...WOO, that is.
Color him single... but Sadie Hawkins Day is coming!!

Ken Hunt

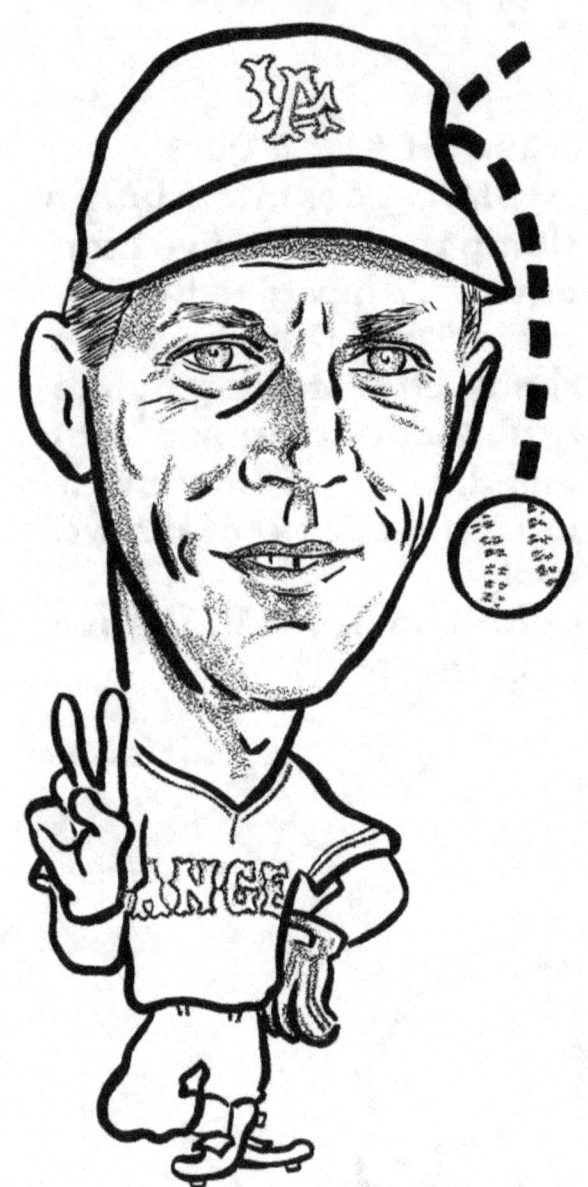

DAN OSINSKI is the one pitcher who really uses his head when it comes to making a double play. It doesn't do anything for his skull but it gives him an assist in the scorebook.
Color him head strong.

Dan Osinski

Pitchers cringe at the icy stare **GEORGE THOMAS** gives them when he's at bat but living in Minneapolis in the off season his face just hasn't thawed out yet.
Color him laughing on the inside.

George Thomas

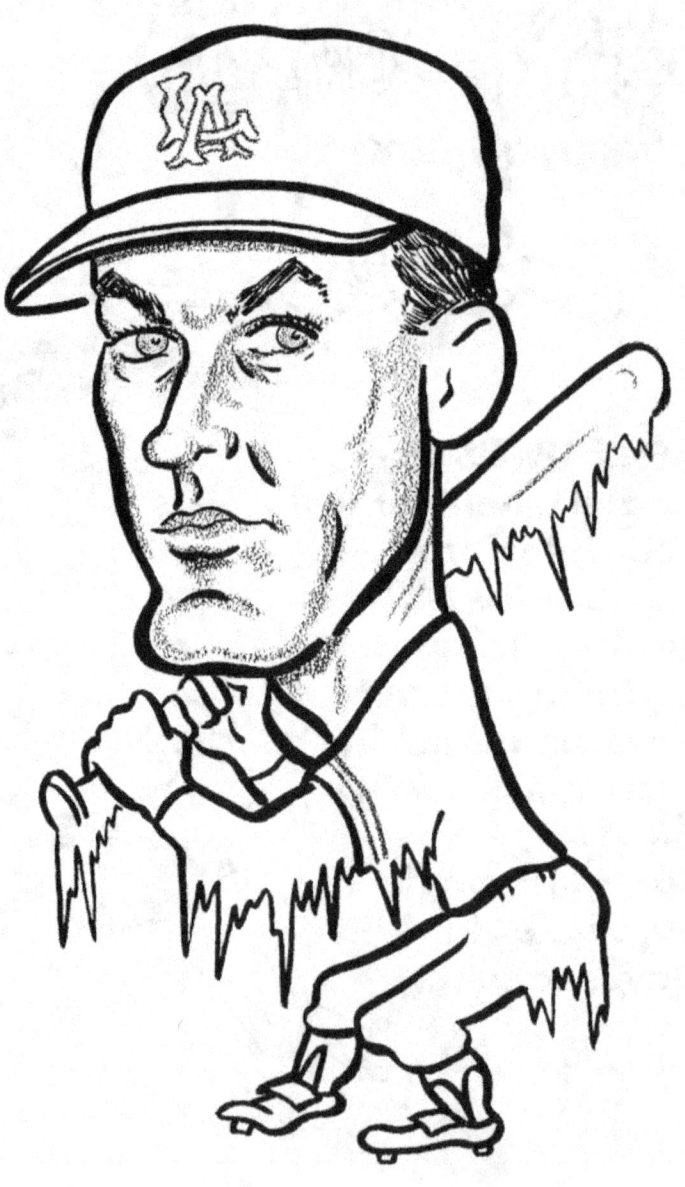

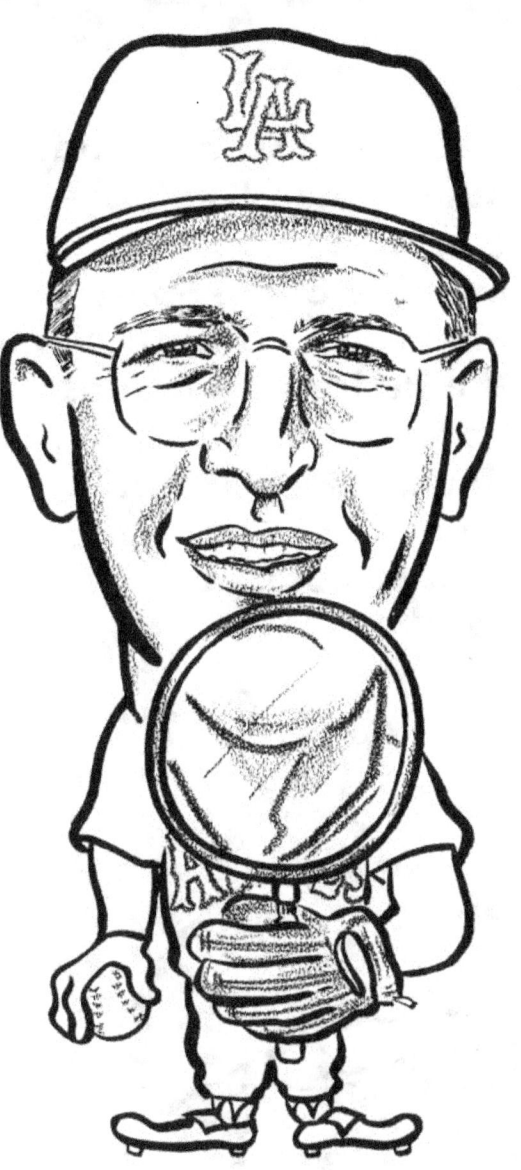

ELI GRBA has the distinction of being the first "Angel" drafted...and not by St. Peter! He wears glasses because of his 20-20 vision...20 inches out of each eye.
Color the batters out of focus.

Eli Grba

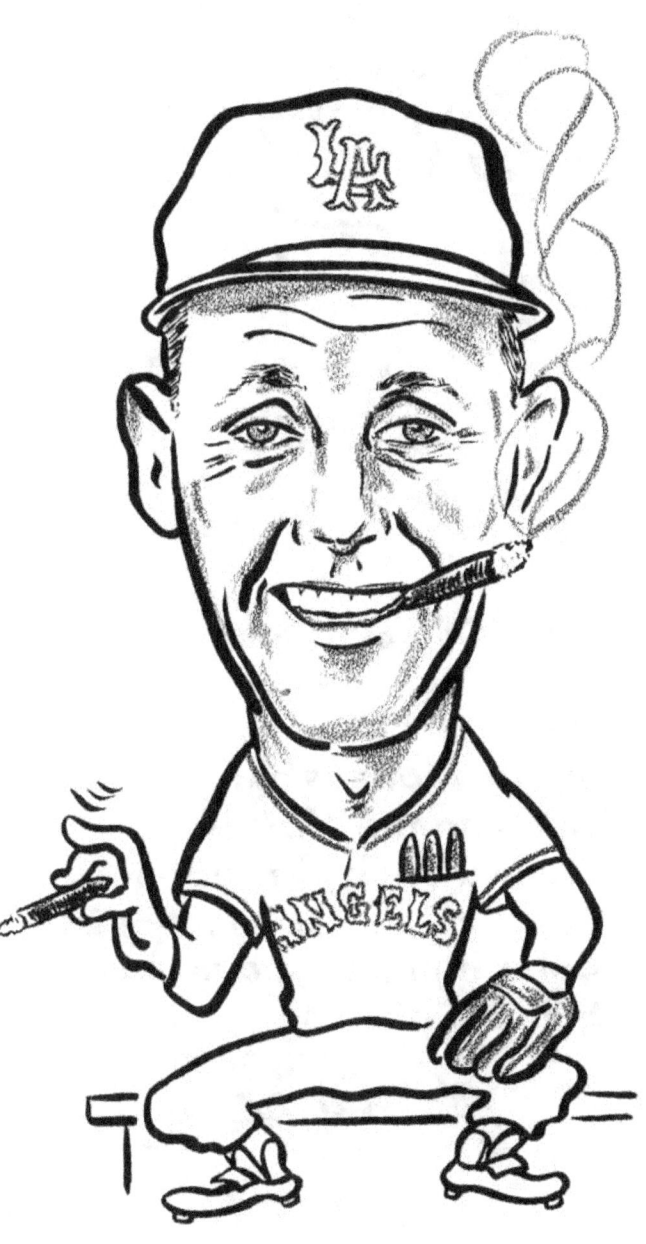

TOM MORGAN, lovingly called "PLOWBOY," is constantly trying to "cultivate" new friends on the team. He HAS to. Everytime he lights up one of his black stogies he loses his old ones.
Color him a Dale Carnegie reject.

Tom Morgan

151

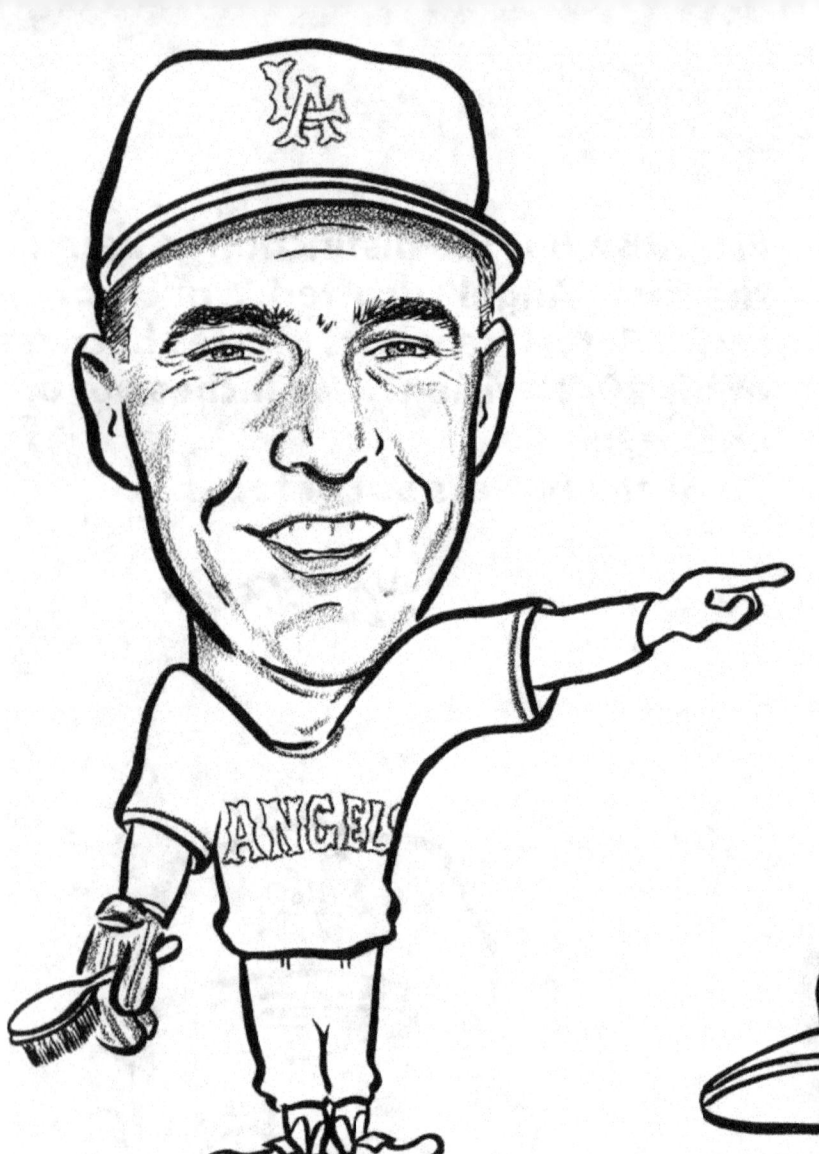

JACK SPRING has made so many "saves" he's been elected an honorary member of the Santa Monica Life Guards. Being the Daddy of 4 youngsters he knows all about putting down disturbances. Color him strict on the hitters (but a push-over for the kids).

Jack Spring

ART FOWLER is taking up where Satchel Paige left off. He won't tell anyone how old he really is but he admits catching the "first ball" thrown out by President Roosevelt...TEDDY, that is! Color him one of our oldest Senior Citizens.

Art Fowler

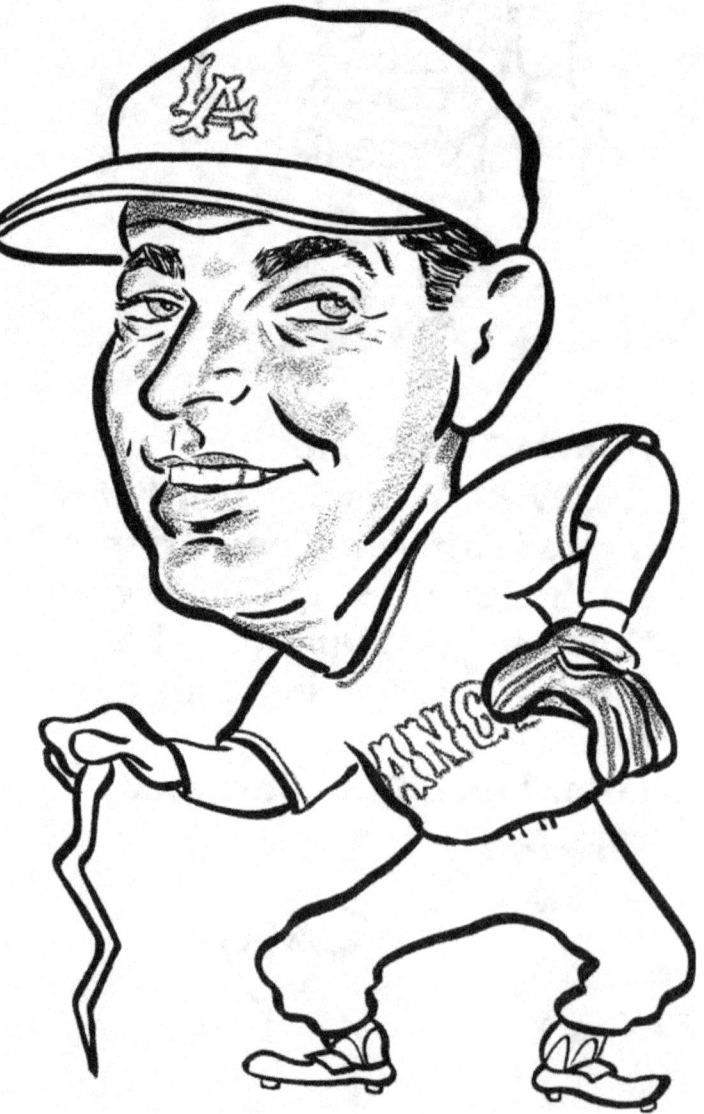

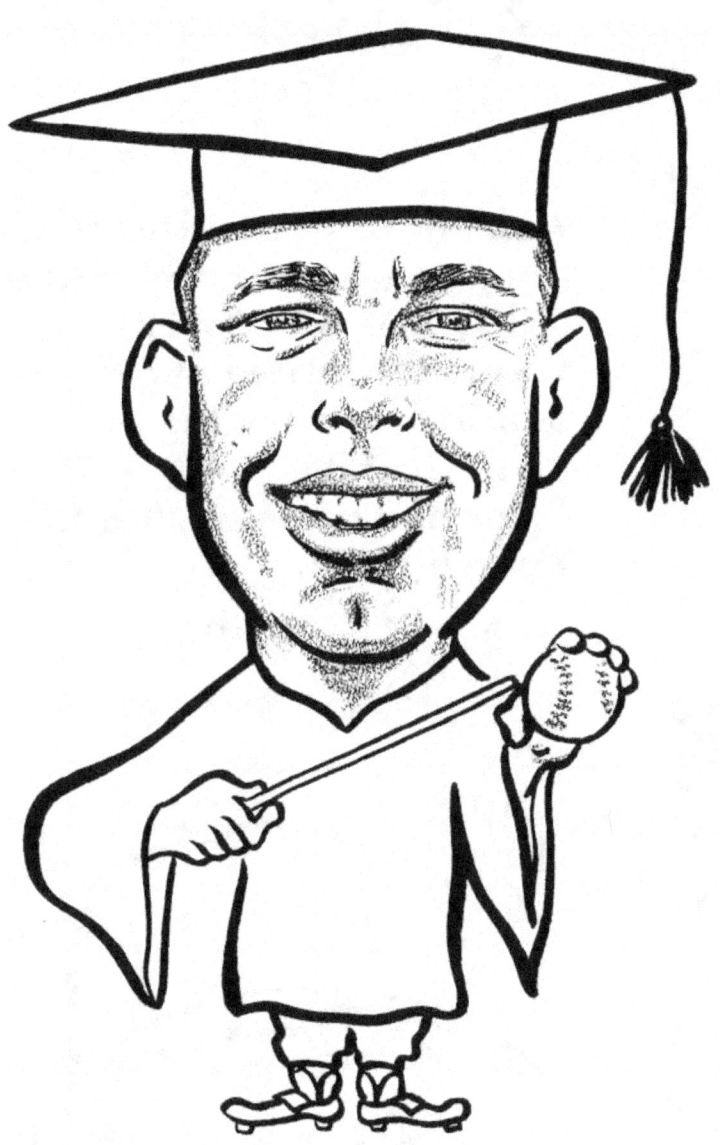

DON LEE is earning his Masters Degree in Education at the University of Arizona by teaching the batters a few manners at the plate. He has plenty of class and lots of principal.
Color him with a high I.Q.
(Thanks...high I.Q. TOO!)

Don Lee

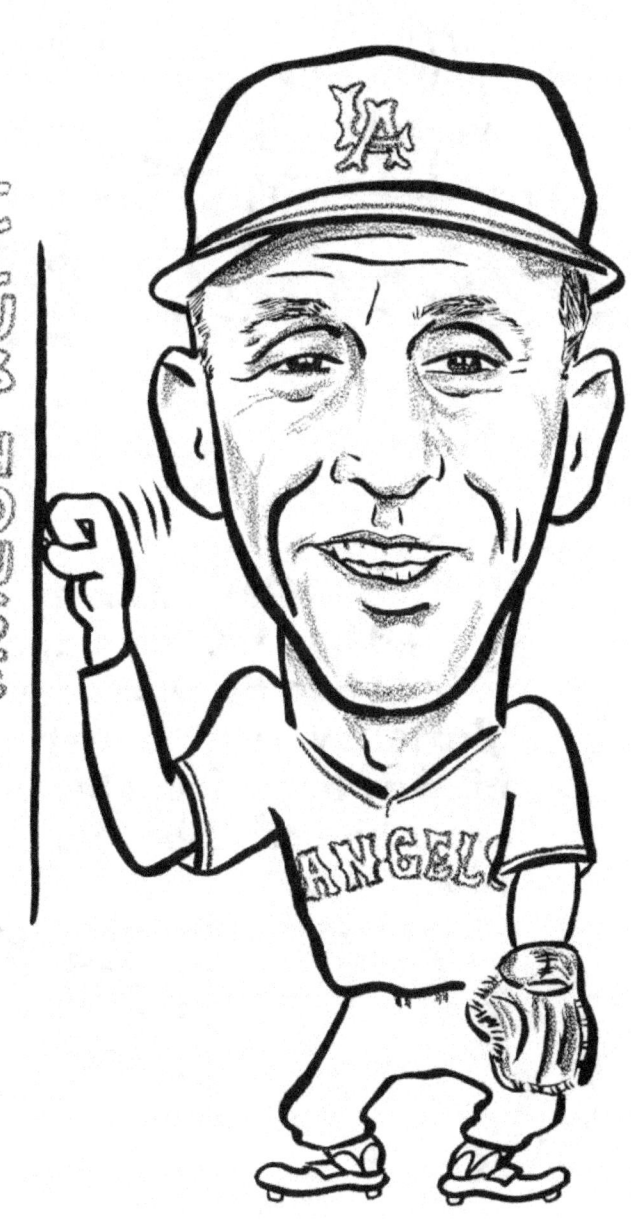

ED SADOWSKI (no relation to Bob...they just happen to have the same maiden name) is a carpenter thru-out the winter. He keeps his hand in during the season by "nailing" the runners at 2nd base.
Color him knocking on the wall.

Ed Sadowski

153

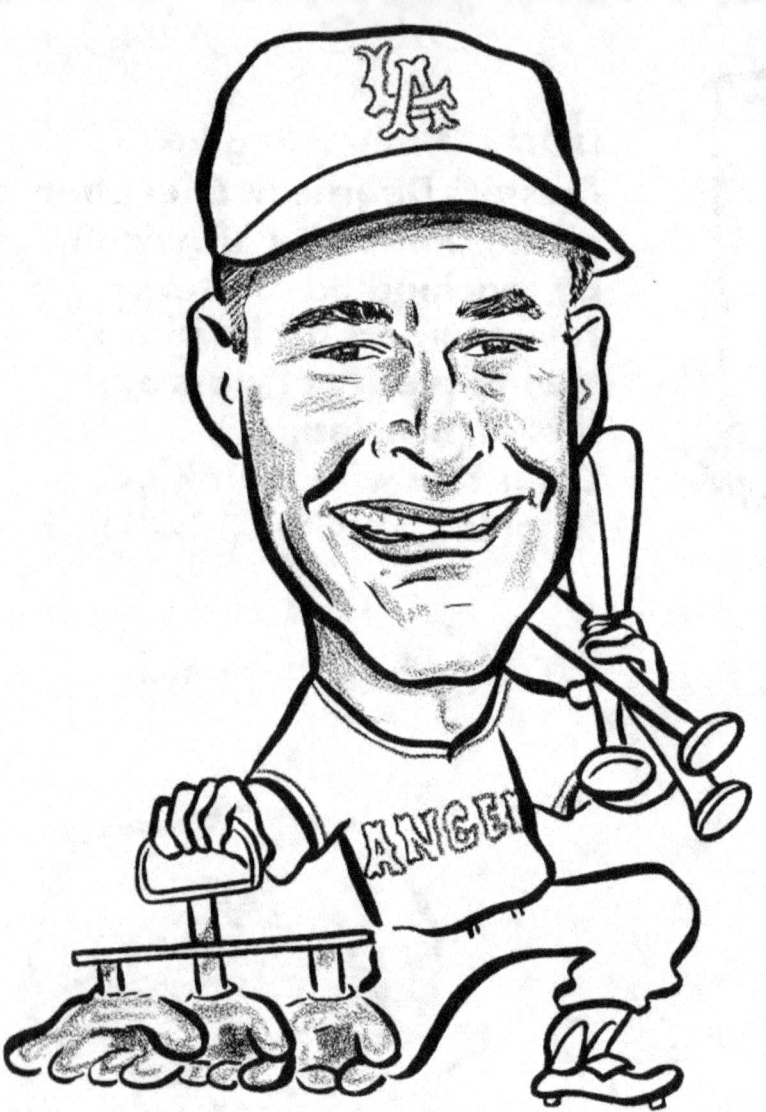

Webster calls a utility "something useful." Rigney calls a utility **BOB SADOWSKI.** He covers the infield like a tarpaulin and when Rig pinches him...he hits.
Color him a human "Do-It-Yourself" Kit.

Bob Sadowski

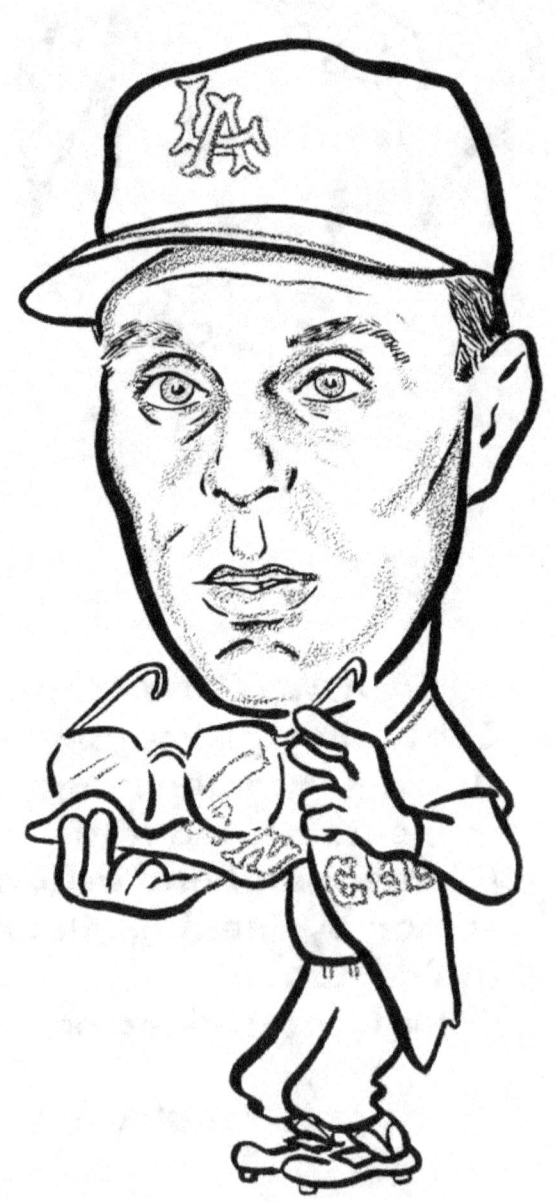

JOE KOPPE has so many mouths to feed he's taken on another job to help out. He wipes off Grba's glasses every night so he'll find his way home from the ball park. Color him contributing to "Visual Aids."

Joe Koppe

GAY   # HUMOROUS   WITTY

A COLORING BOOK

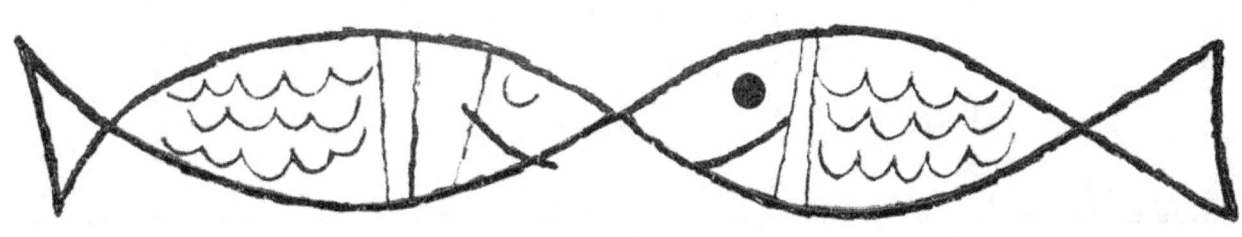

for Fishermen

Souvenir of CRYSTAL CAVE

A *Coloring Book for Fisherman* was published by New Jersey's Imprint Products Company, better known as IMPKO. The company is best remembered today for producing auto window decals sold commonly at souvenir shops, used by travelers to announce to the world what states and sites they had traveled to. as well as decals of monsters and way-out creatures.

A COLORING BOOK
FOR FISHERMEN

and other children

this coloring book belongs to:

_____

_____

_____

_____

Angler's Prayer

" Lord give me grace . . . to catch a fish
so big . . that even I . . when telling of
it afterward . . may never need to lie! "

humbly dedicated
to the piscatores
of america

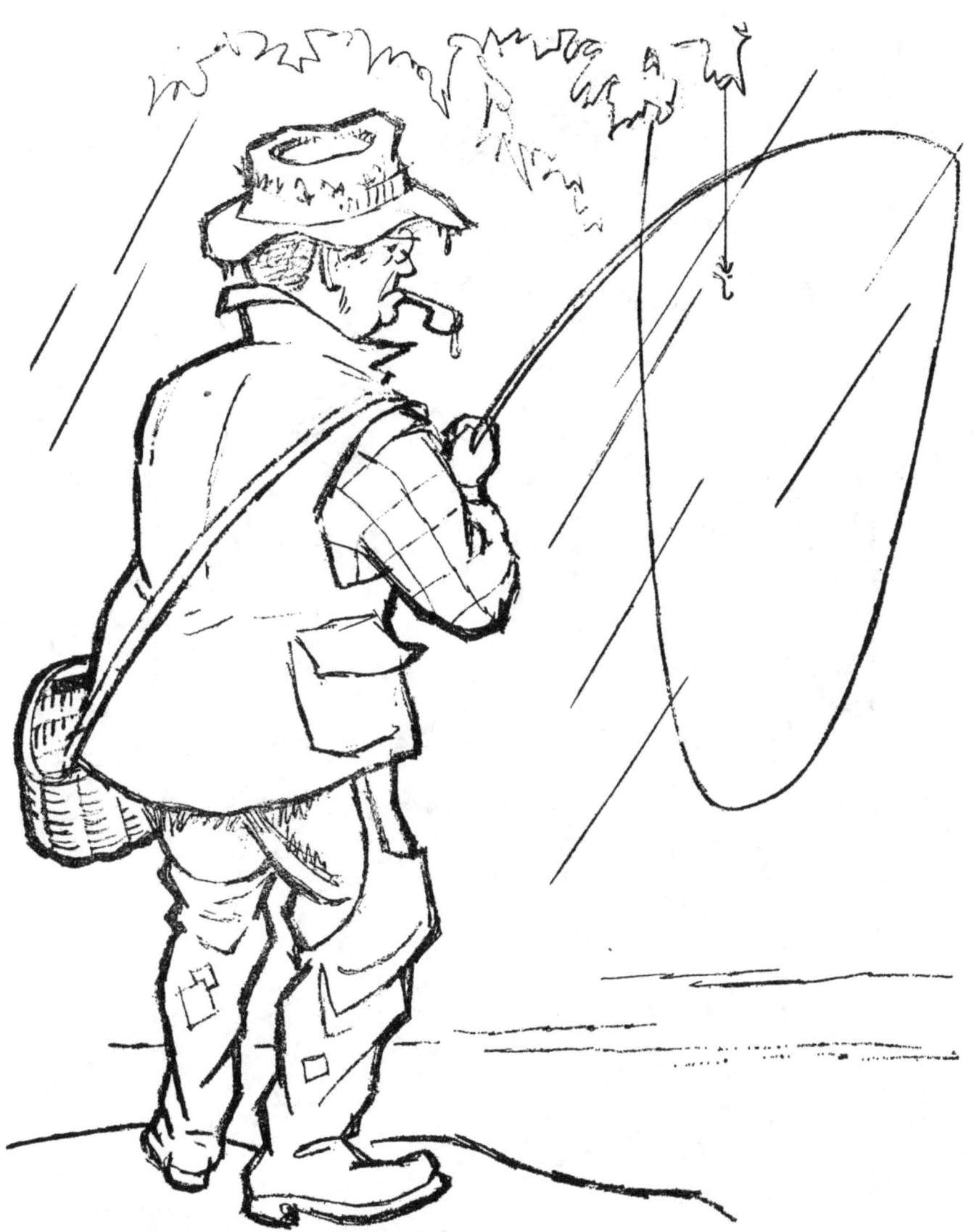

THIS IS A FISHERMAN – Color him blue as he is often that color from wading in cold water on rainy days. Color his fishing basket empty.

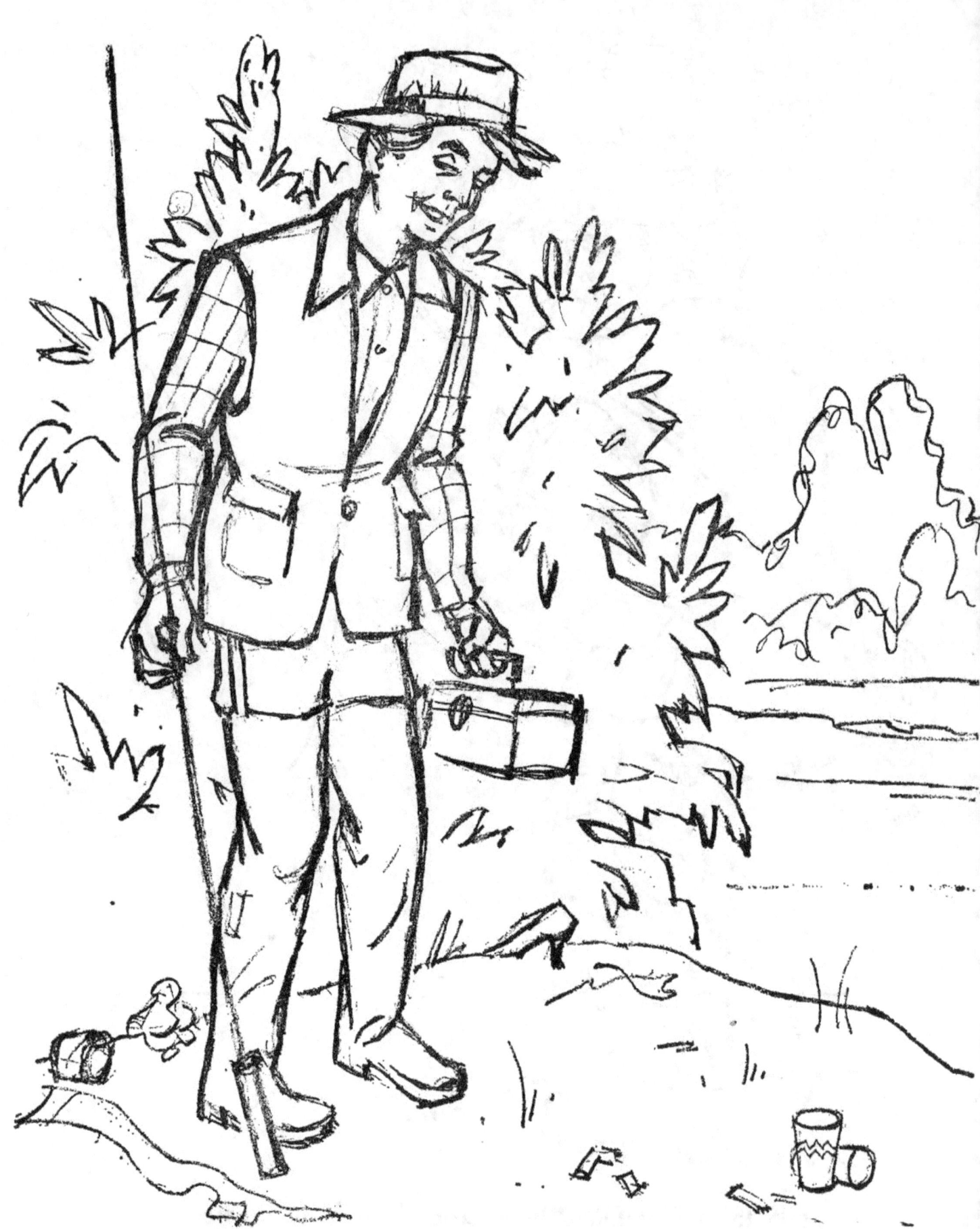

This is my secret fishing place. Sometimes I think
it is someone elses secret place too.

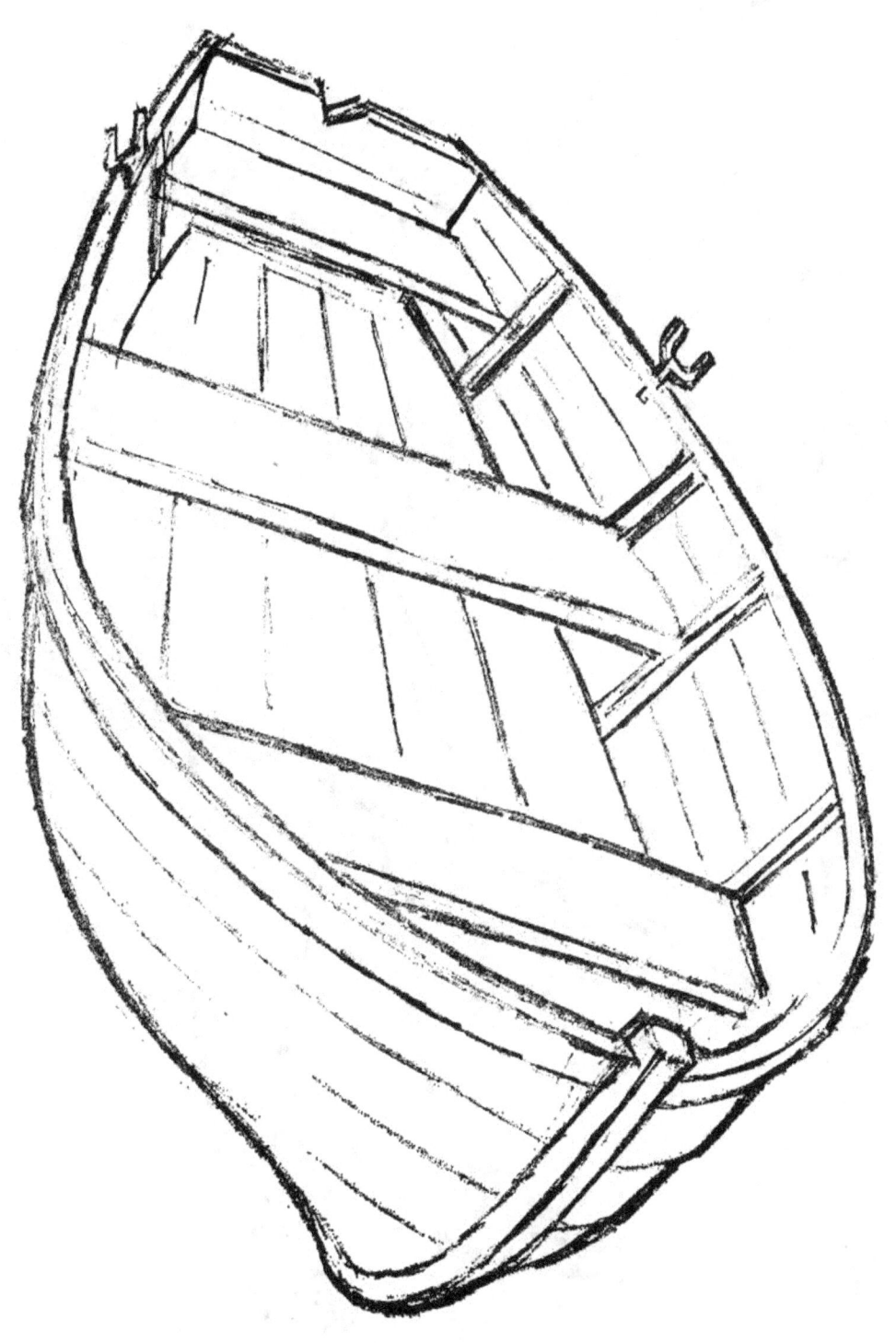

THIS IS MY BOAT. I take good care of it, and
paint it every year. Color it a nice color. It leaks.

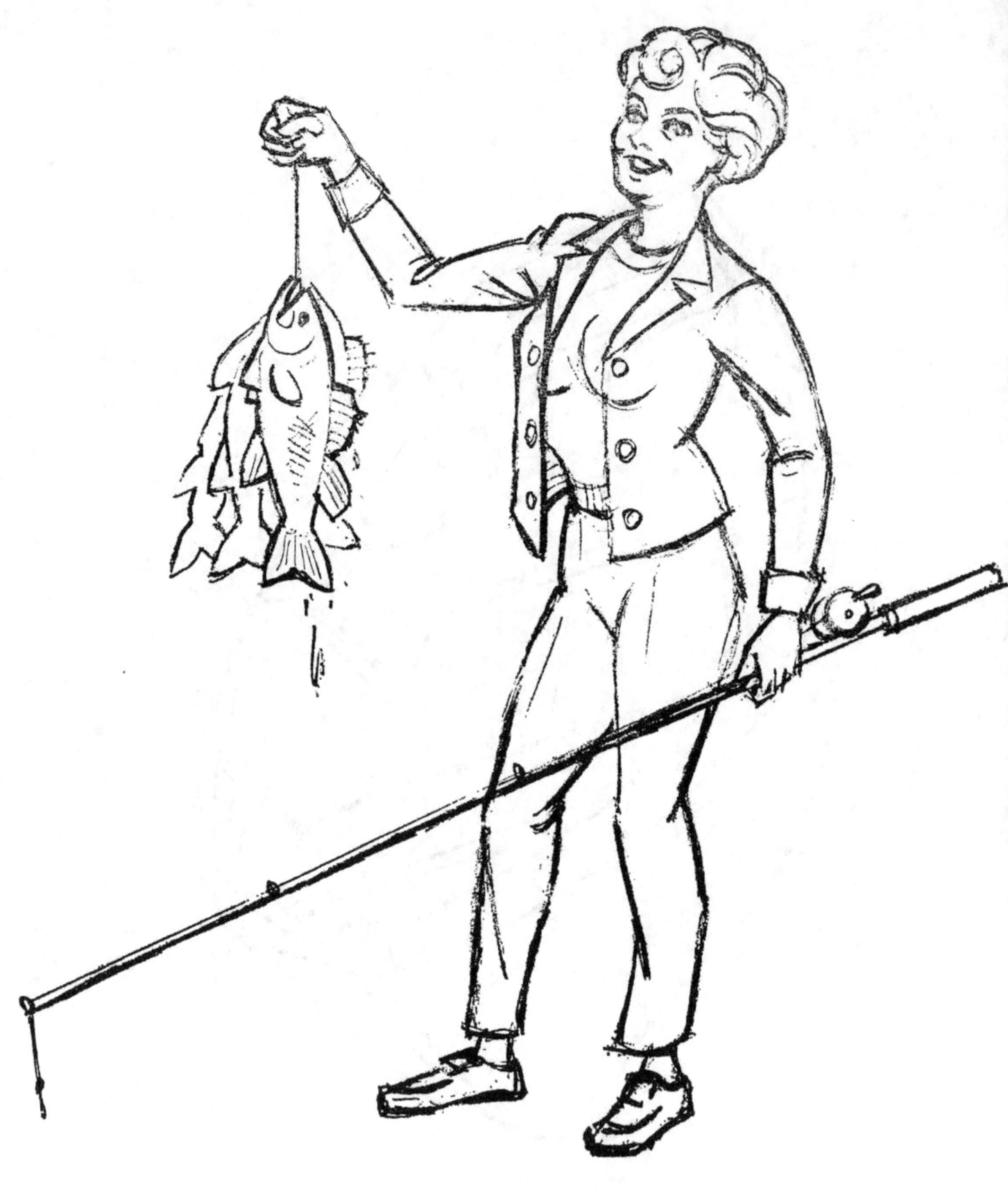

Sometimes I take my wife fishing, but not often.

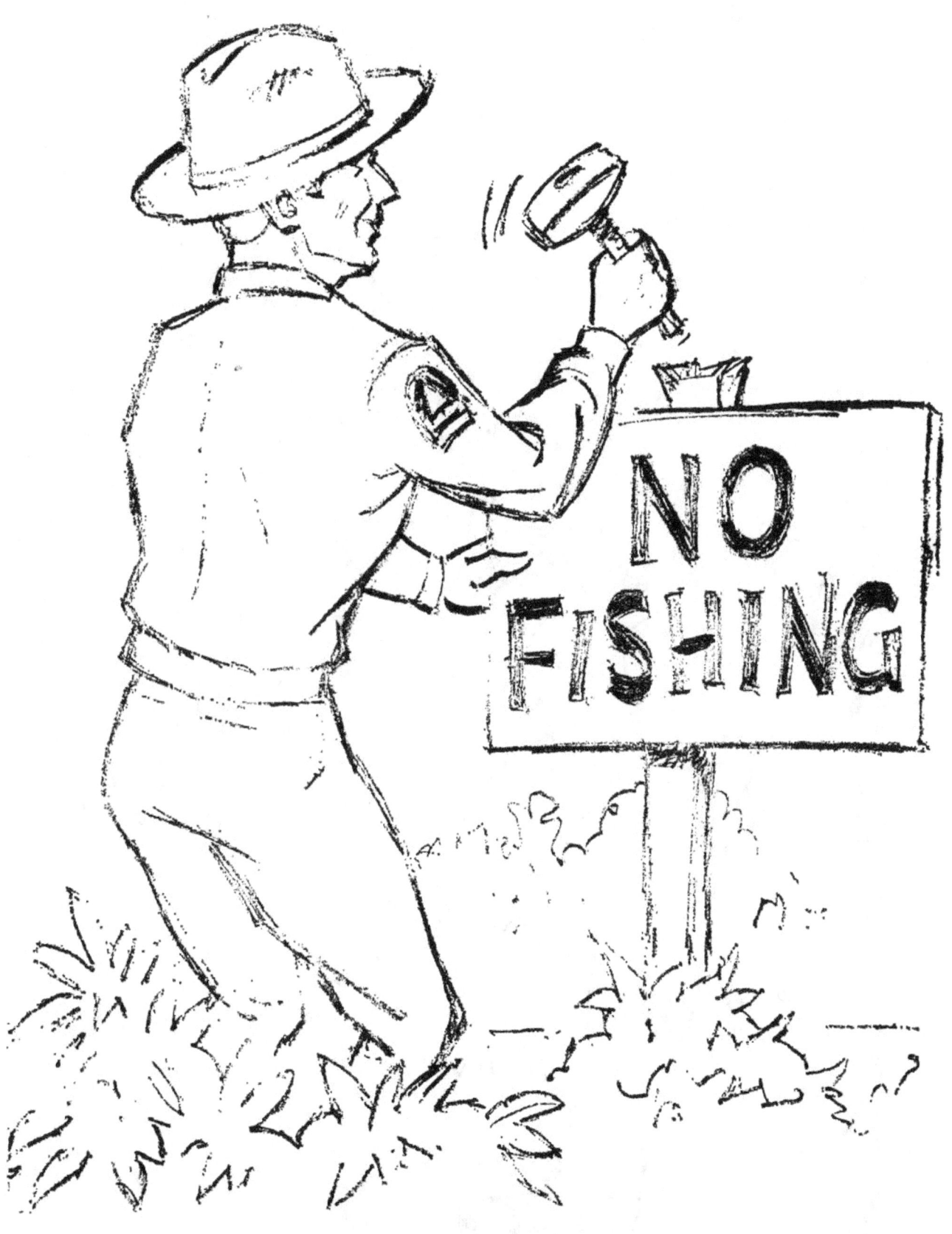

THIS IS A GAME WARDEN. He puts up signs like this one to hide behind. I obey the signs. I don't fish when he is there.

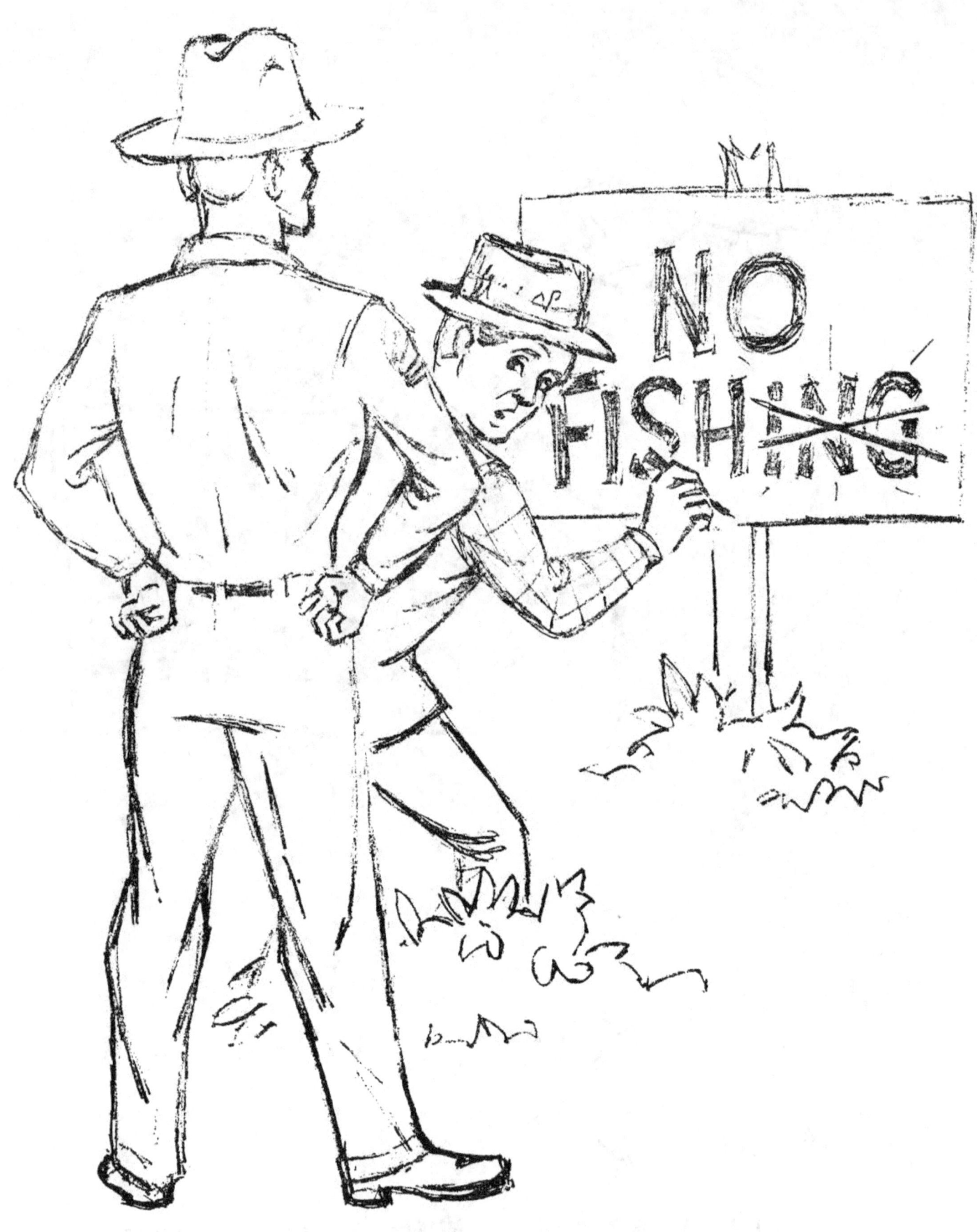

Sometimes the signs are wrong and I correct them. Sometimes the Game Warden corrects me.

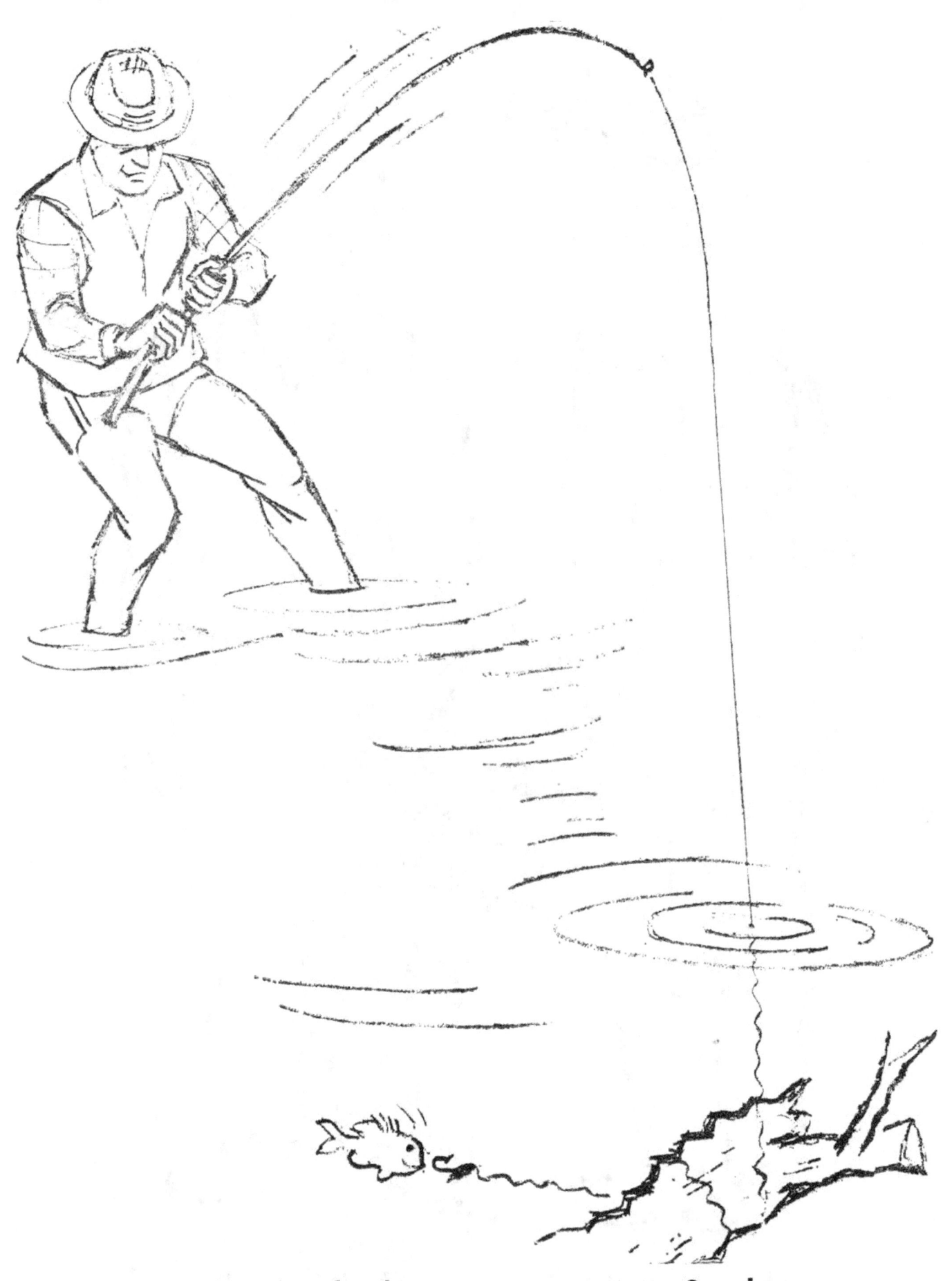

Sometimes the big ones get away. See how hard they pull.

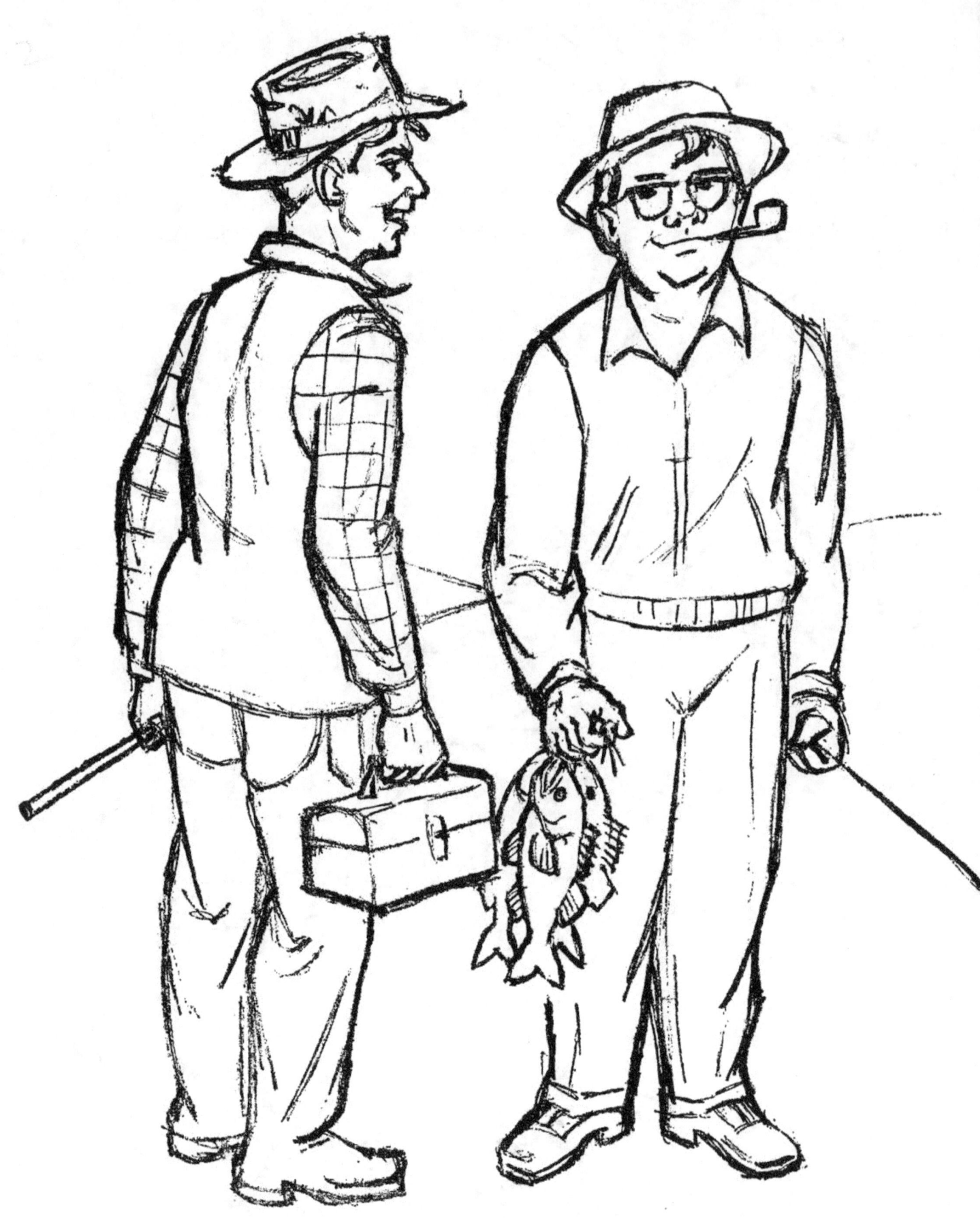

This man was lucky. He caught fish. I ask him where he caught them. He tells me where to go.

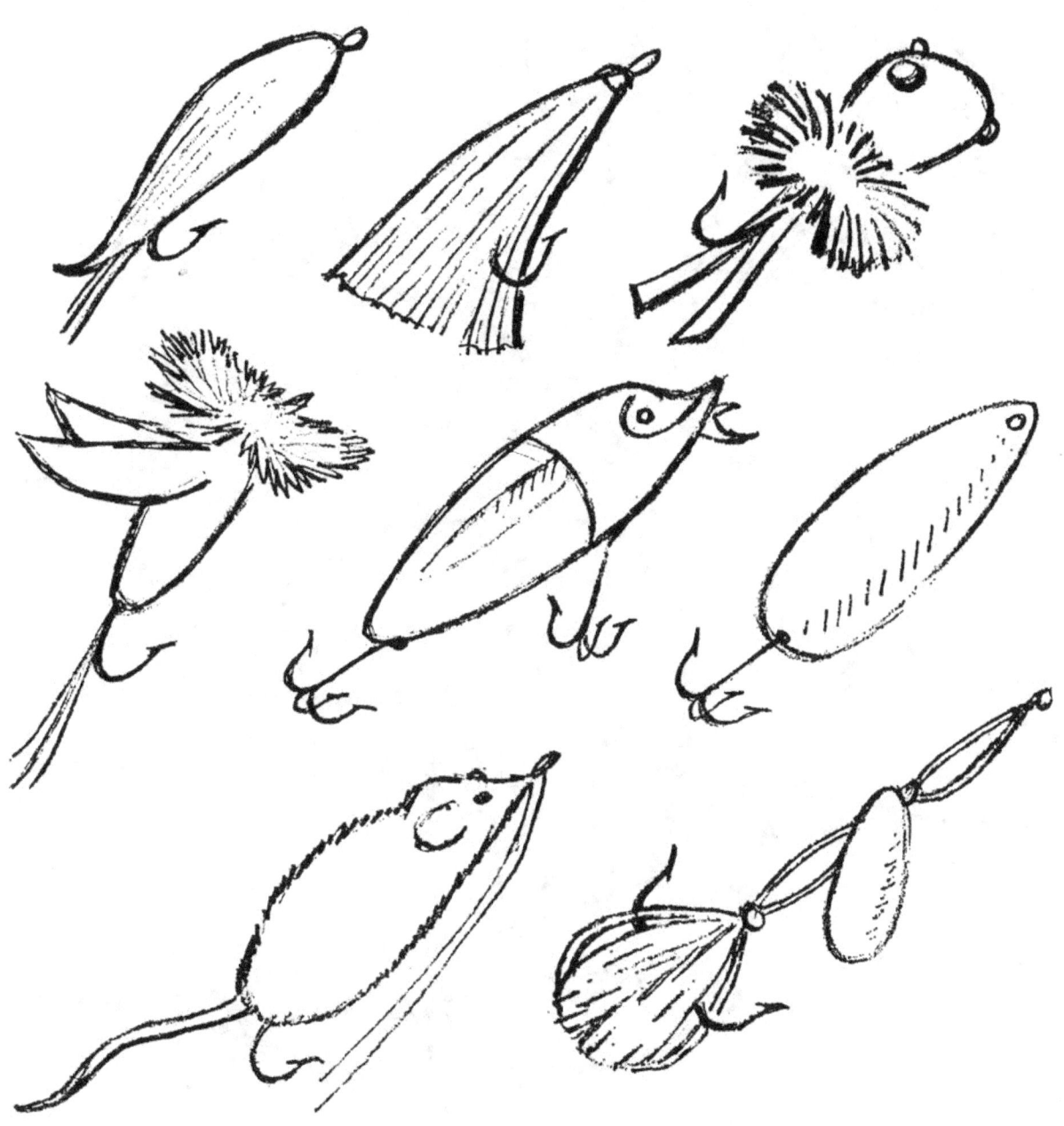

Here are some of my pretty lures. Make them nice colors. Do you like them? **THE FISH DO NOT LIKE THEM.**

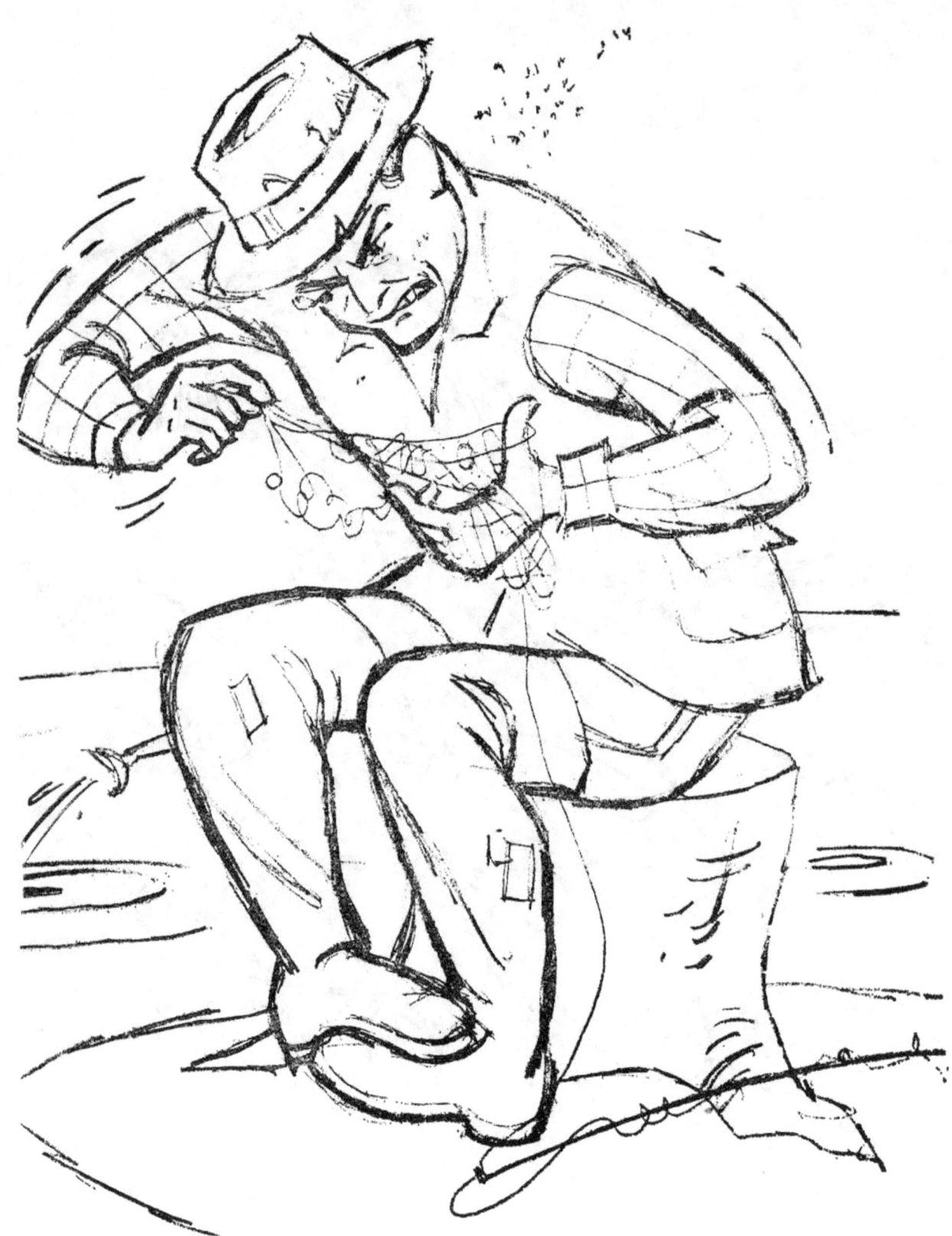

Can you make up a story about this picture?
What are some of the words you will use in
your story?

....
....

Color his face red.

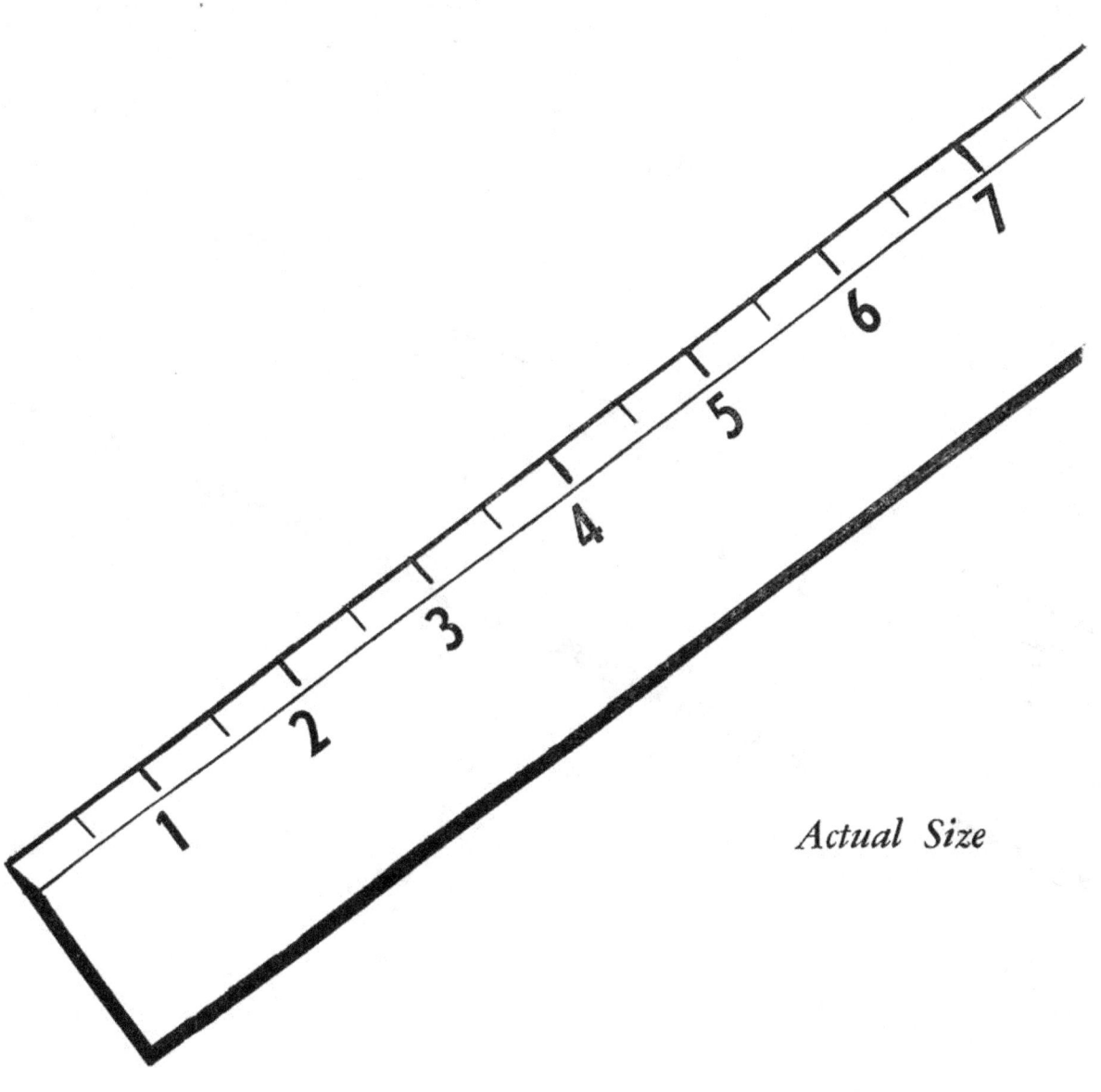

Actual Size

THIS IS A RULER. It is the honest kind of ruler
I use to measure the honest fish I catch . . .
Honestly.

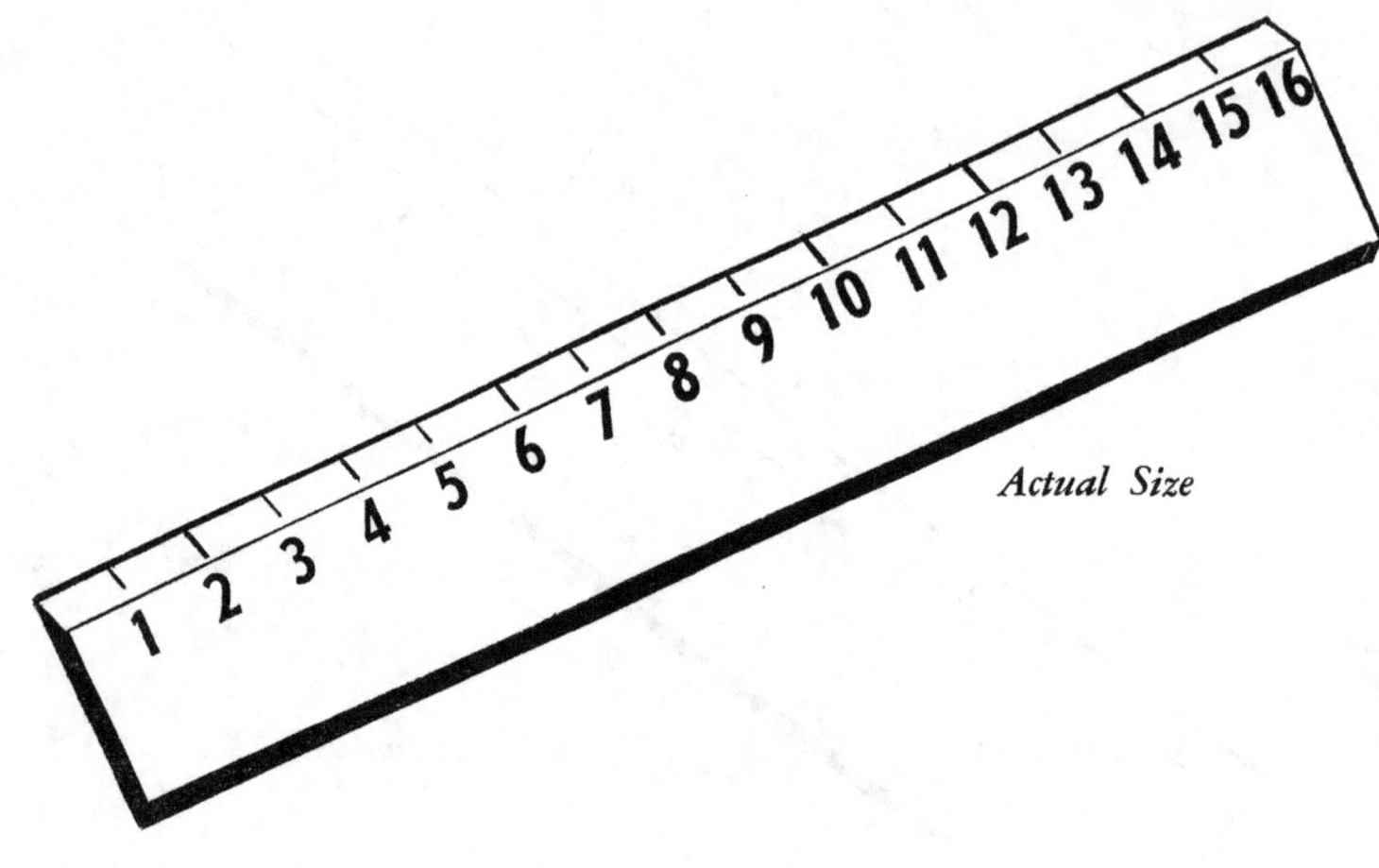

Actual Size

THIS IS ANOTHER RULER. It is the kind other fishermen use to measure the fish "they almost caught."

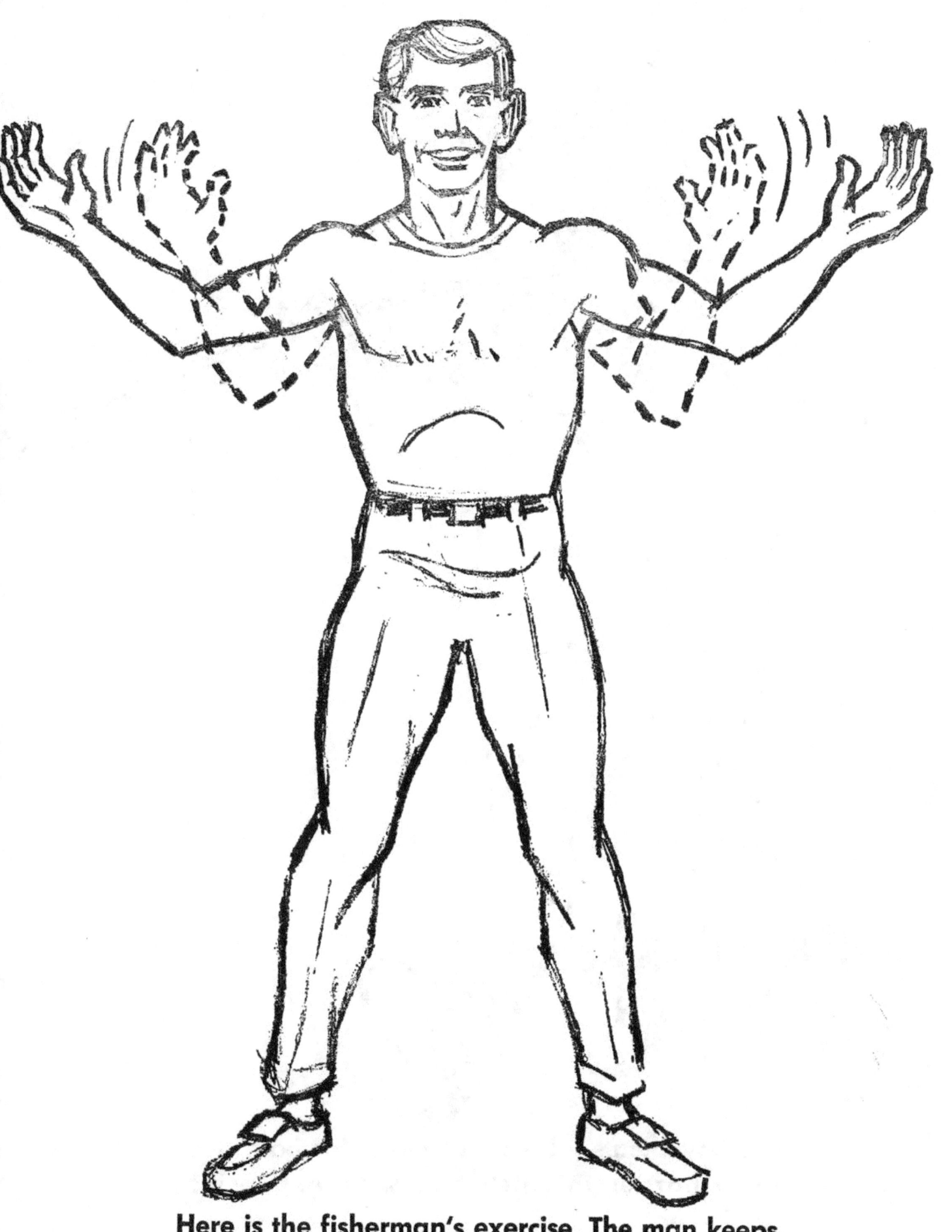

Here is the fisherman's exercise. The man keeps saying: "It was THISSS big."

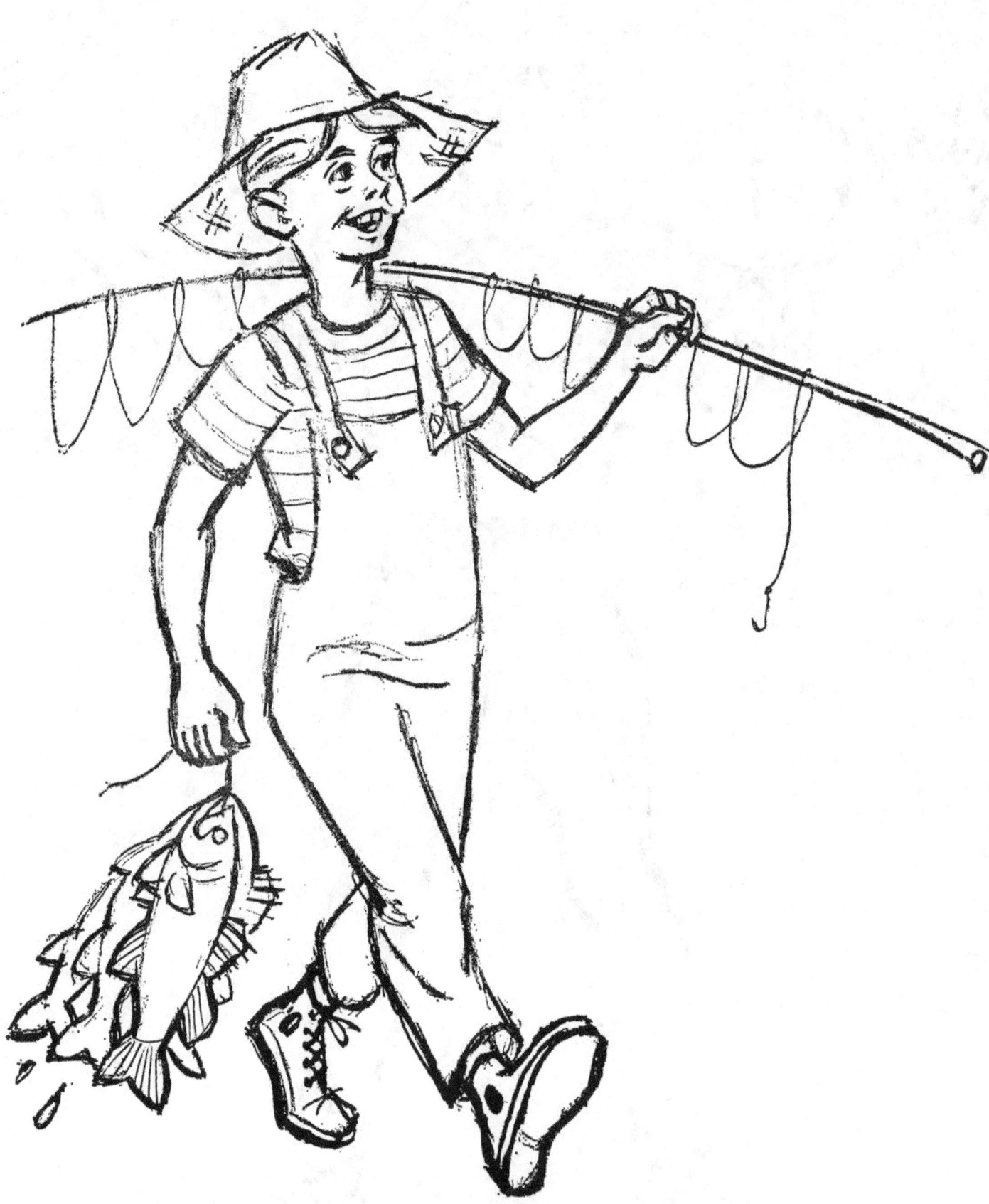

This boy cheats – He uses worms for bait. It is much harder to catch fish with expensive equipment.

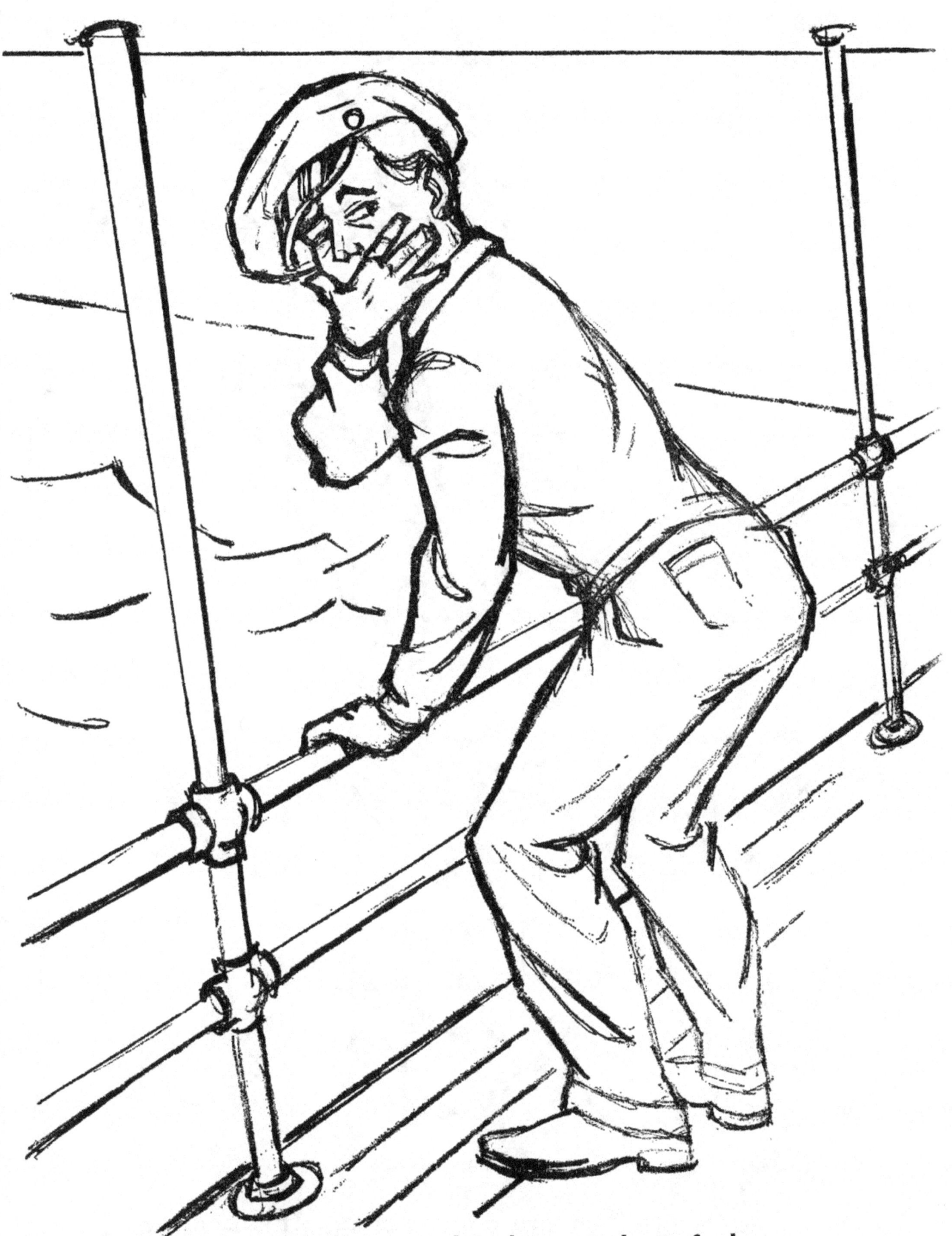

When I go fishing on a big boat, I don't feel good. Color me green.

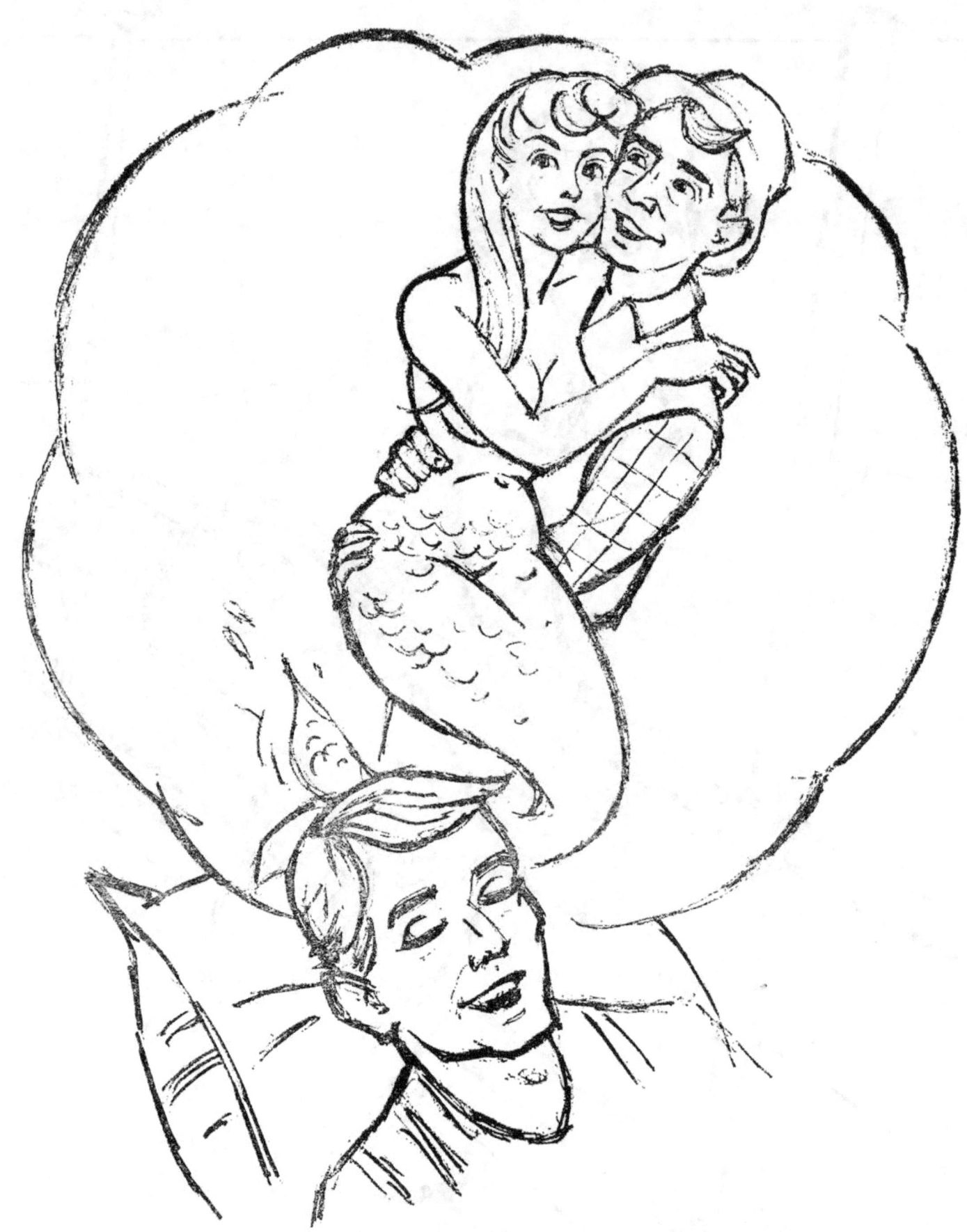

Sometimes I dream about fishing. This is more fun than reel fishing. That's a joke, HA, HA.

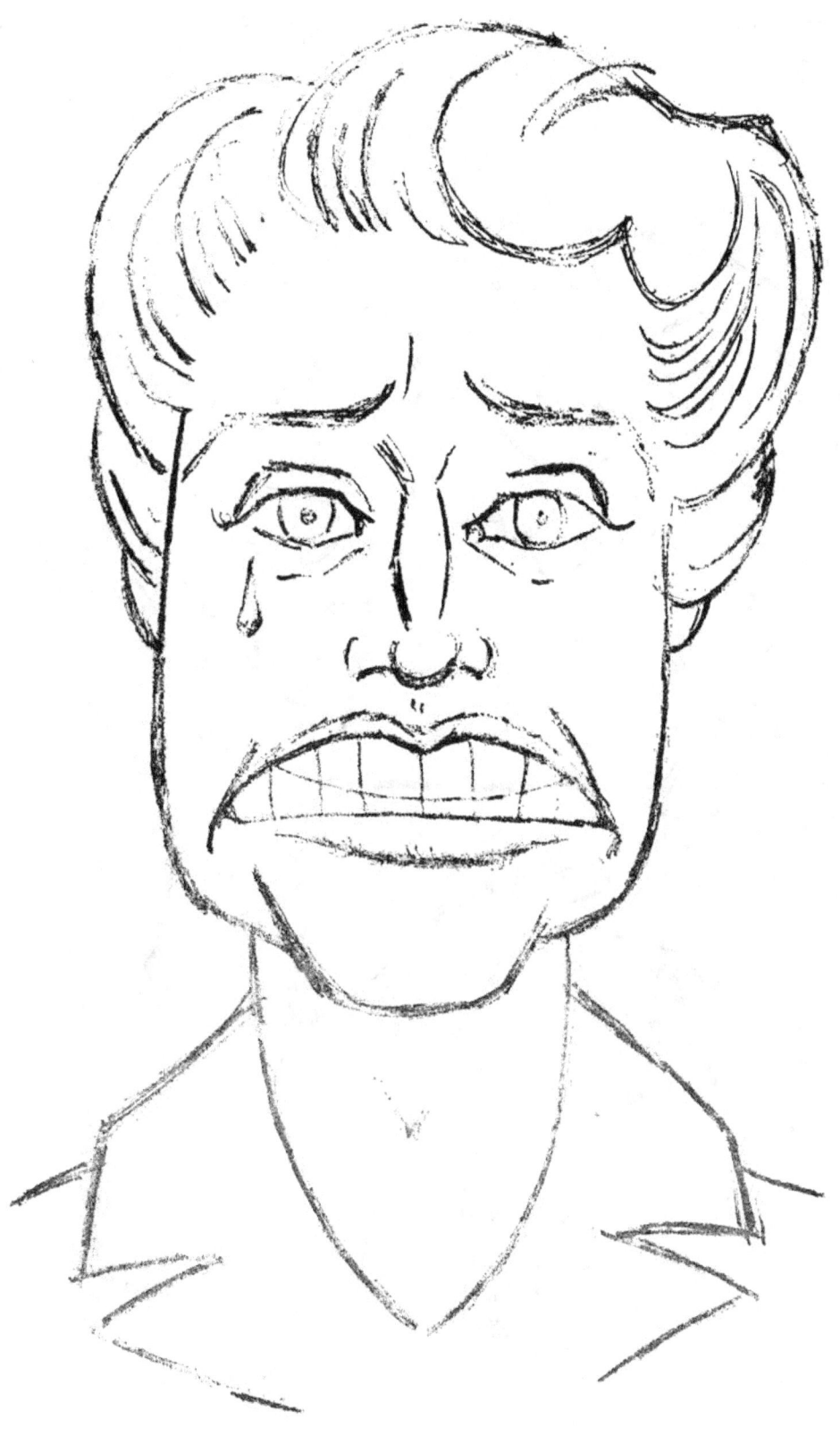

My wife is so happy when I bring home fish.
She smiles, and smiles and smiles.

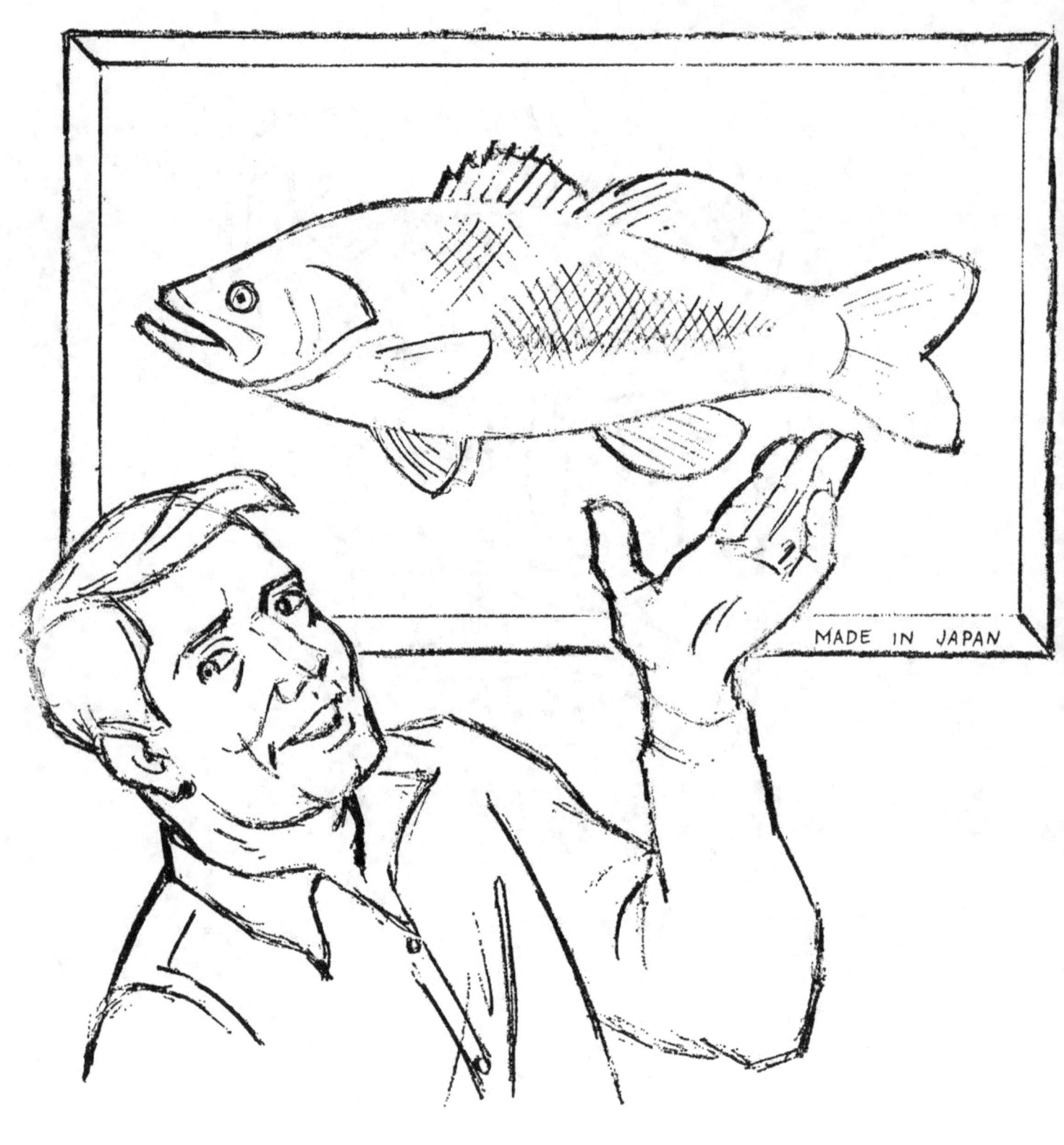

MADE IN JAPAN

Here's a fish I bought – er, caught – last summer.

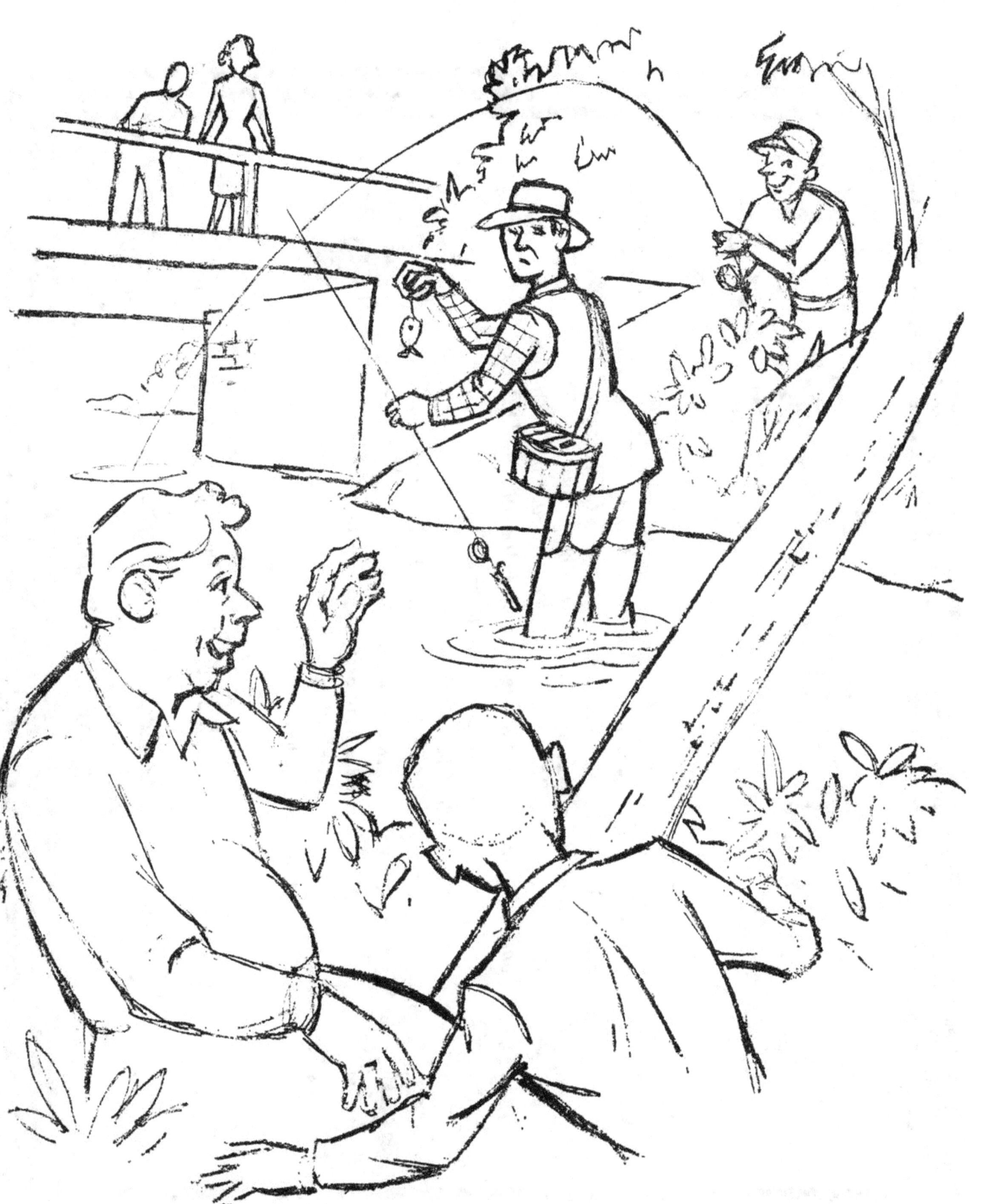

When I catch a little fish everyone looks. When
I catch a big fish no one is around.

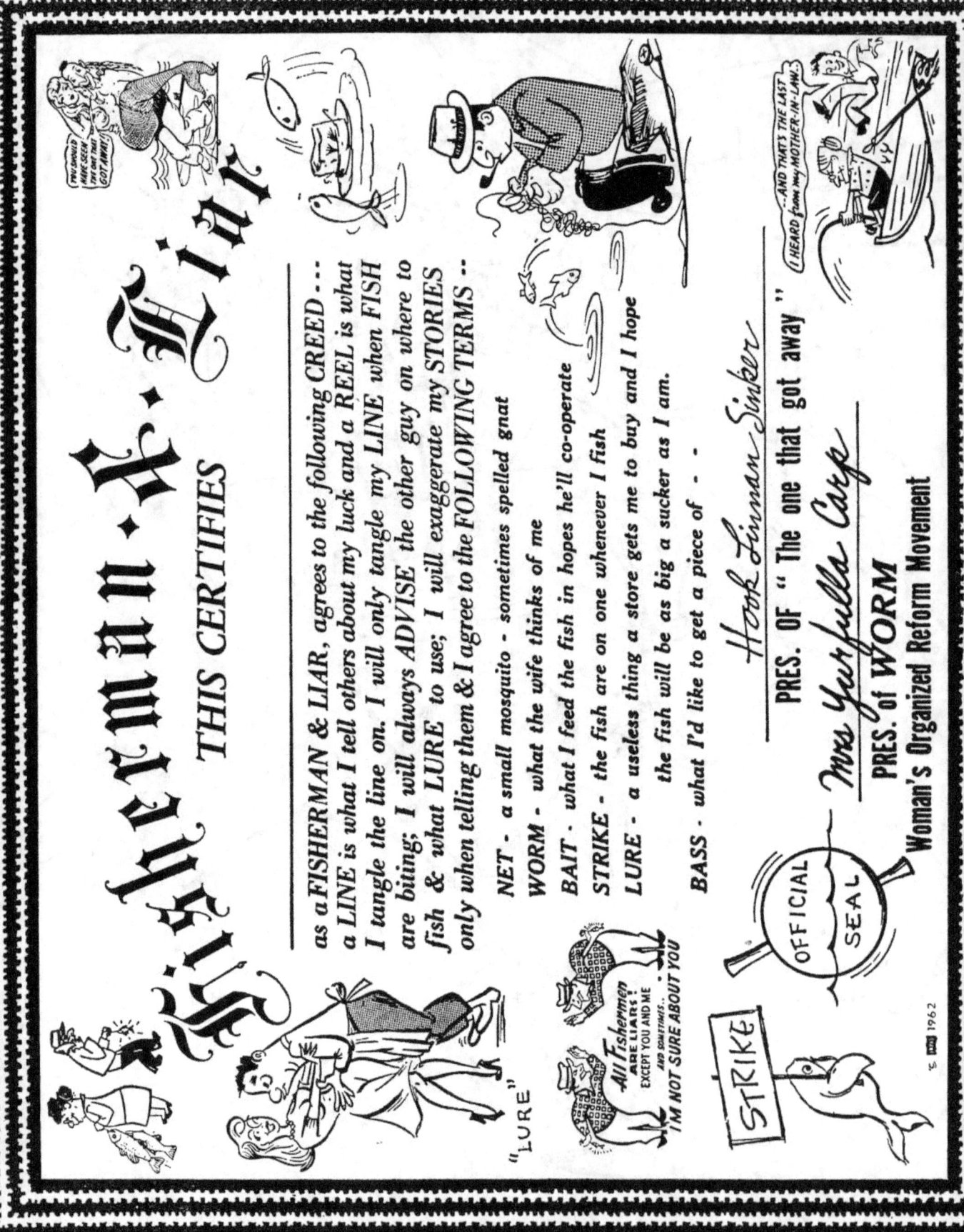

Fisherman & Liar

THIS CERTIFIES

as a FISHERMAN & LIAR, agrees to the following CREED —
a LINE is what I tell others about my luck and a REEL is what
I tangle the line on. I will only tangle my LINE when FISH
are biting; I will always ADVISE the other guy on where to
fish & what LURE to use; I will exaggerate my STORIES
only when telling them & I agree to the FOLLOWING TERMS —

NET - a small mosquito - sometimes spelled gnat
WORM - what the wife thinks of me
BAIT - what I feed the fish in hopes he'll co-operate
STRIKE - the fish are on one whenever I fish
LURE - a useless thing a store gets me to buy and I hope
the fish will be as big a sucker as I am.

BASS - what I'd like to get a piece of — -

Hook Linnan Sinker
PRES. OF " The one that got away "

Mrs. Yurfulla Carp
PRES. of WORM
Woman's Organized Reform Movement

"LURE"

All Fishermen ARE LIARS! EXCEPT YOU AND ME
AND SOMETIMES... I'M NOT SURE ABOUT YOU

OFFICIAL SEAL

STRIKE

1962

the 1963 car buyer's coloring Book

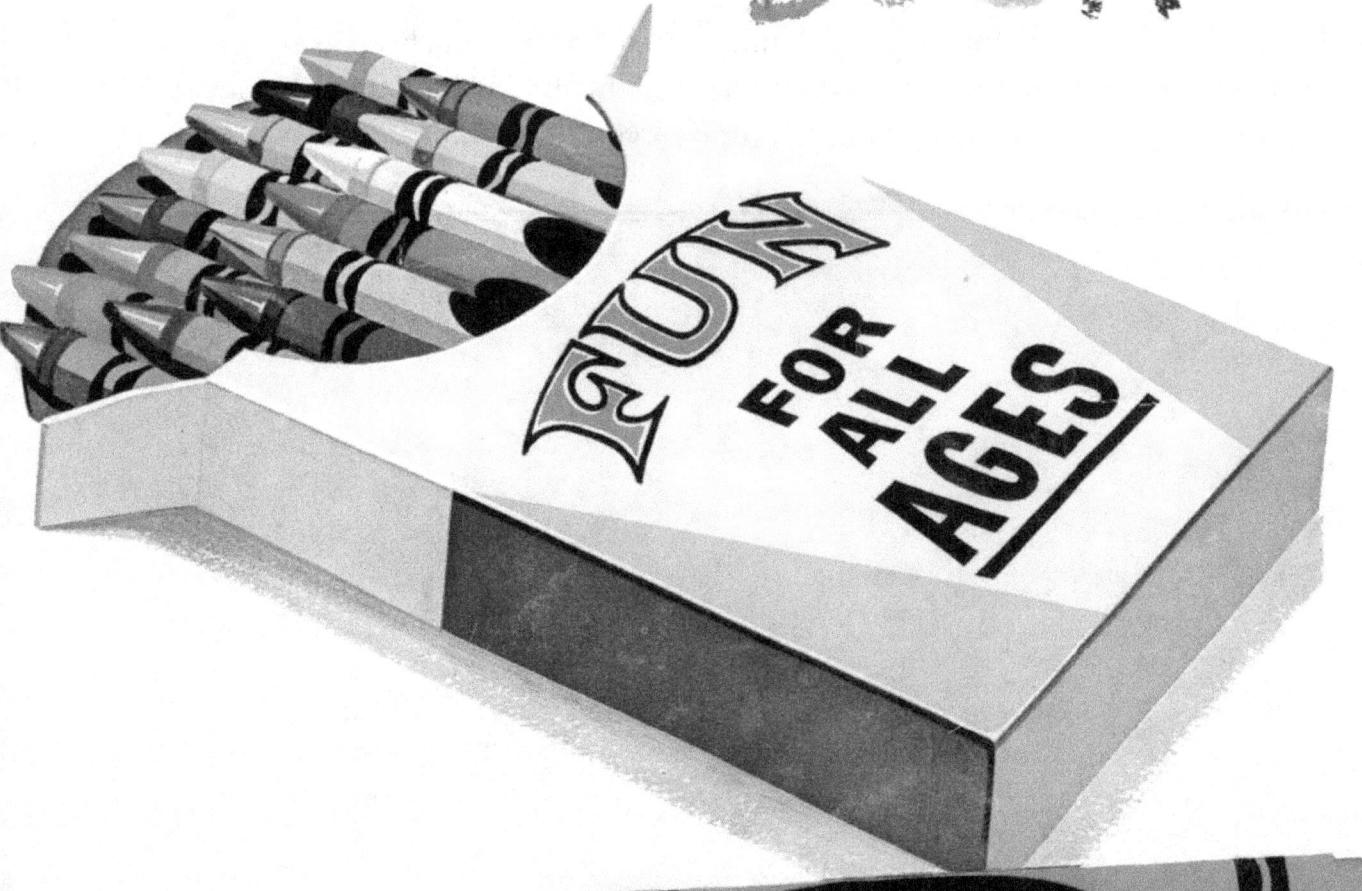

FUN FOR ALL AGES

FRIENDLY

Dedicated to artistic new-car buyers who want to

learn some colorful facts about the new

Mercurys for '63, but are too busy

to read boring statistics.

Mercury was Ford Motor Company's mid-priced line, not as cheap as the cars that bore the Ford label, but not as expensive as the Lincoln. Pushing the then-new 1963 models, this coloring book would've been released in the fall of 1962.

The Lincoln-Mercury Division of Ford Motor Company acknowledges its sincere appreciation to the originators of the Executive Coloring Book, Funny Products Company, without whose inspiration this offering probably would not have been created.

THIS IS MY CAR BUYER'S COLORING BOOK

My name is _____

My address is _____

My present car is _____

My next car will be a _____ 1963 Mercury _____

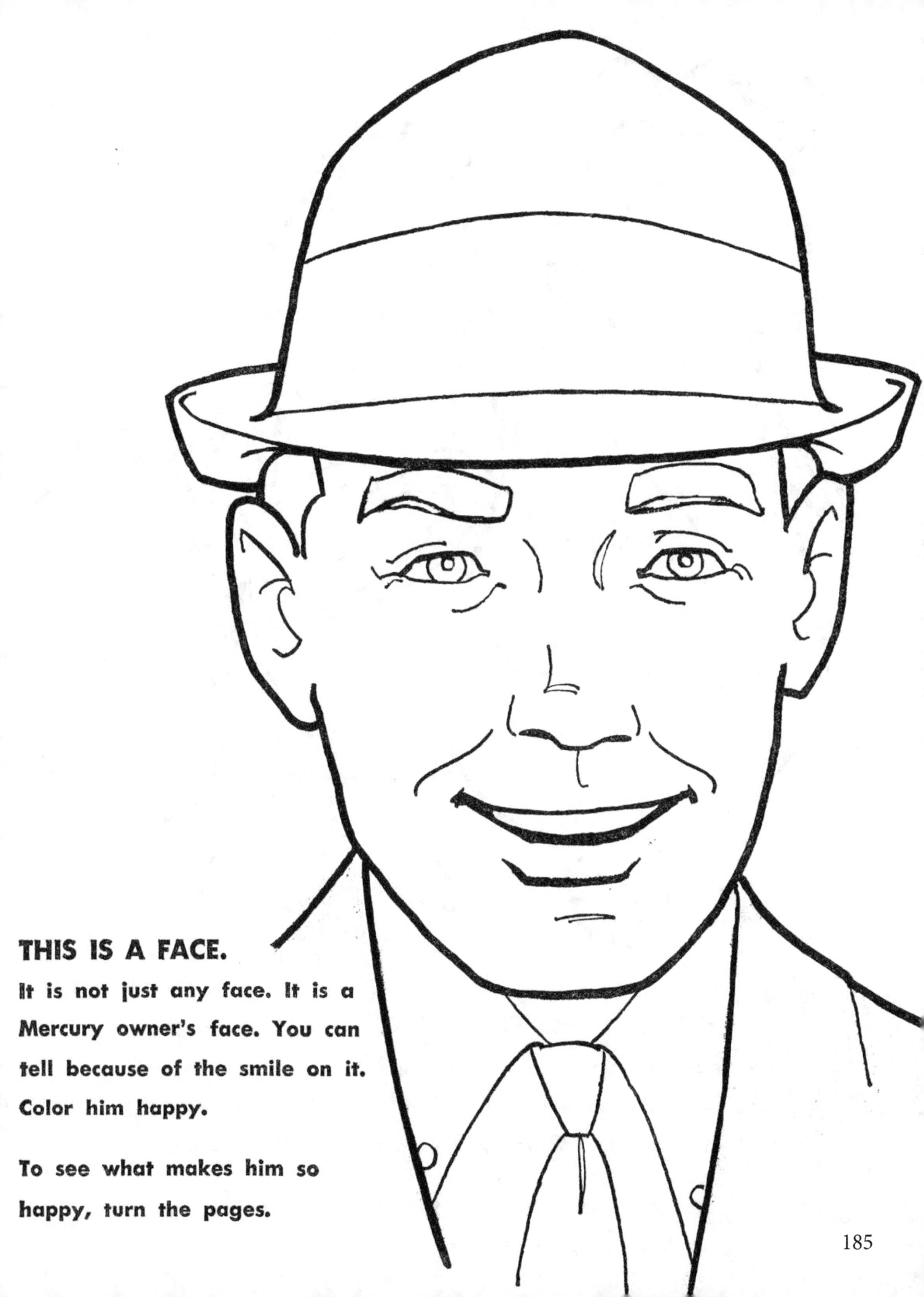

THIS IS A FACE.

It is not just any face. It is a
Mercury owner's face. You can
tell because of the smile on it.
Color him happy.

To see what makes him so
happy, turn the pages.

185

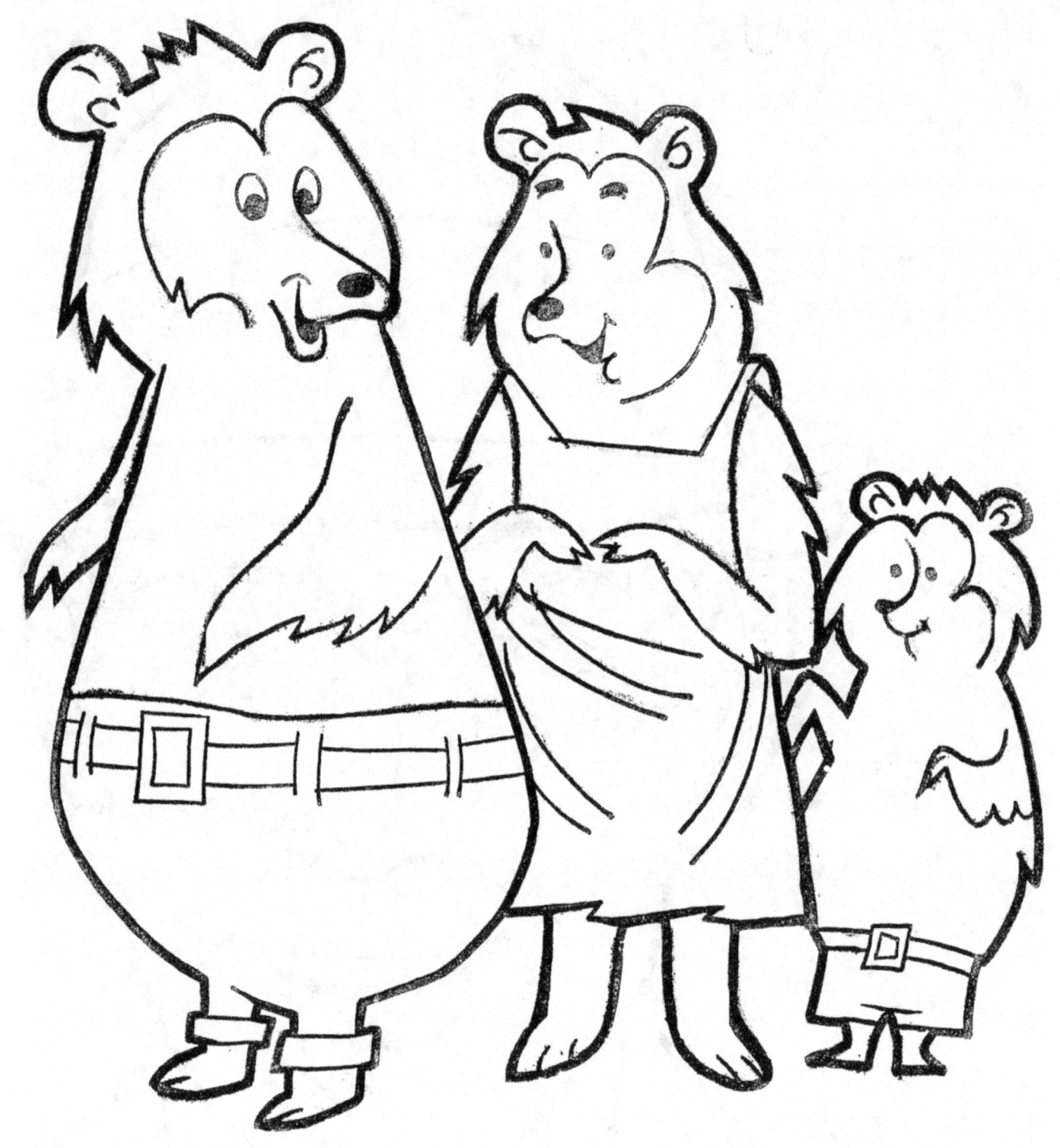

THESE ARE THE THREE BEARS: Papa Bear, Mama Bear, and Baby Bear. Papa Bear is big. Mama Bear is midsize. Baby Bear is smaller. Just like the three-sized Mercurys—the Monterey, the Meteor, and the Comet.

Better not color the bears, they bite. Instead get the bare facts at your Mercury dealer's.

THESE ARE THE THREE-SIZED MERCURYS

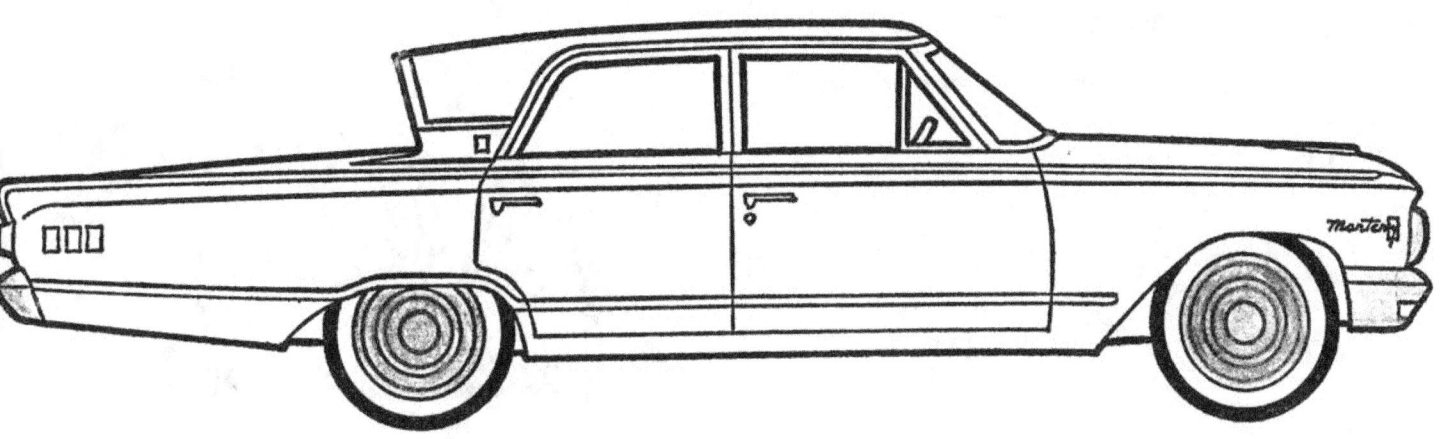

The Mercury Monterey

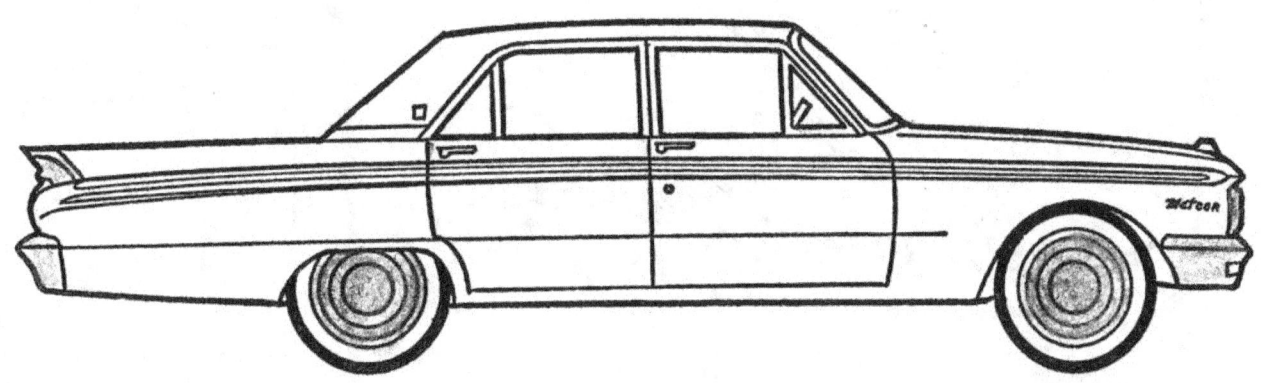

The Mercury Meteor

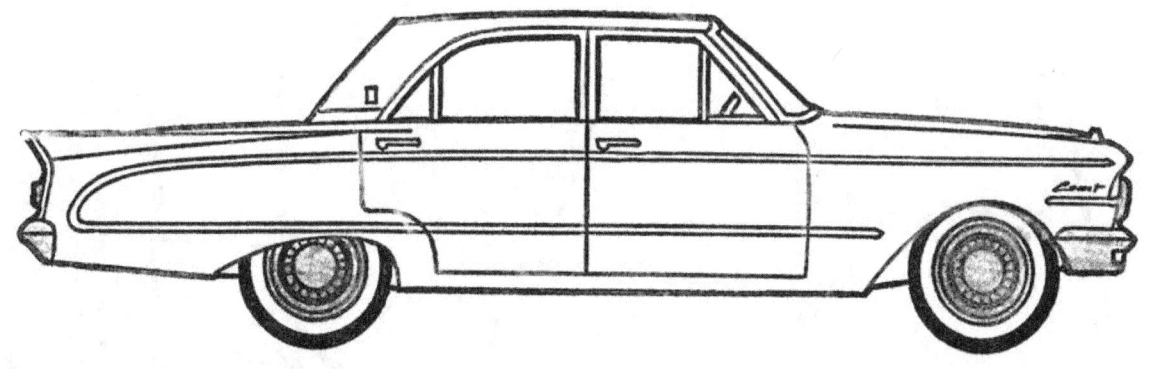

The Mercury Comet

Mercurys come in lots of colors but everything's rosy when you own one.

THIS IS A GRILLE. This is a hot grille. The new '63 Mercurys all have hot new grilles (front and rear). Color the grille "HOT." Better yet—see them on the new Mercurys.

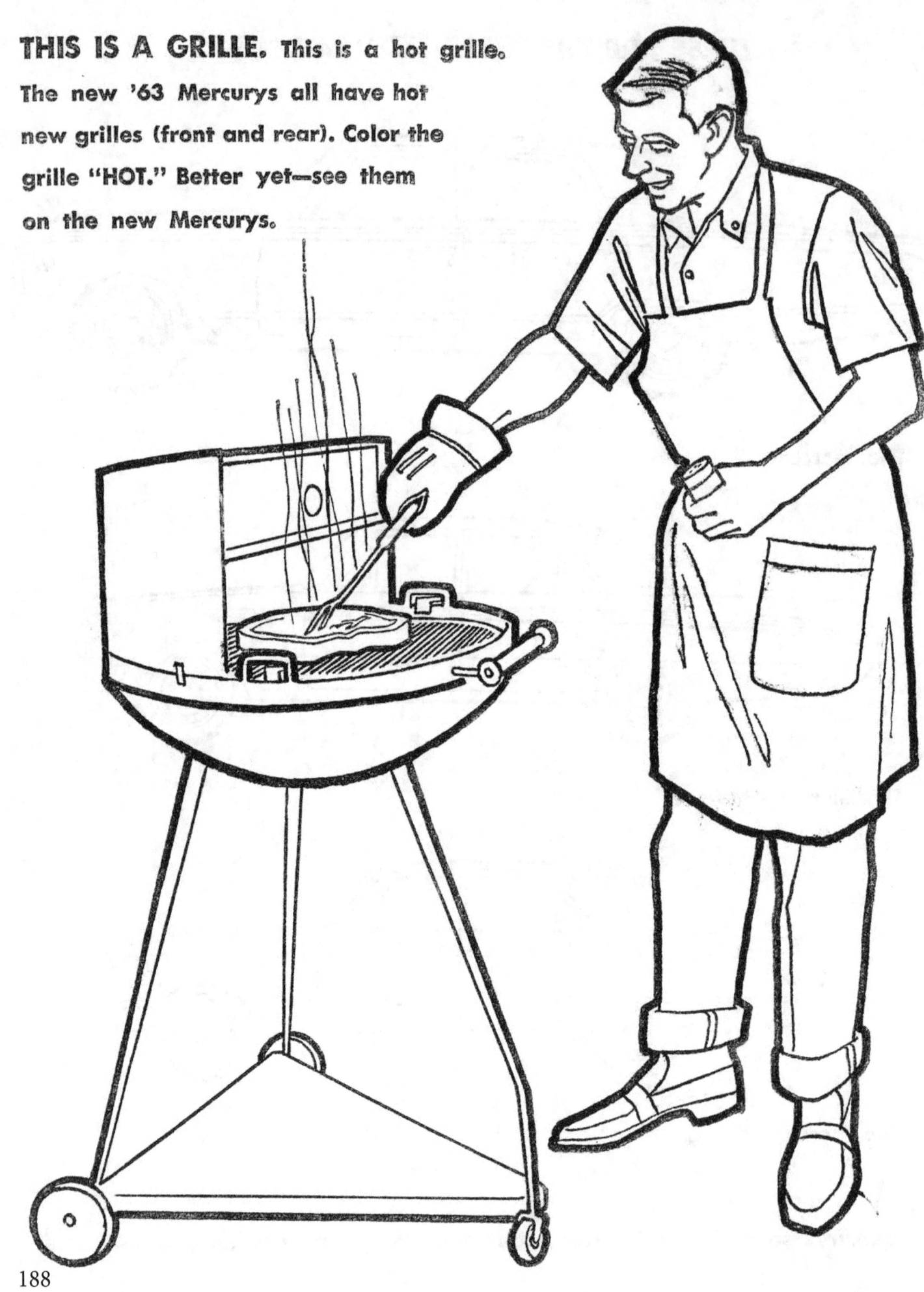

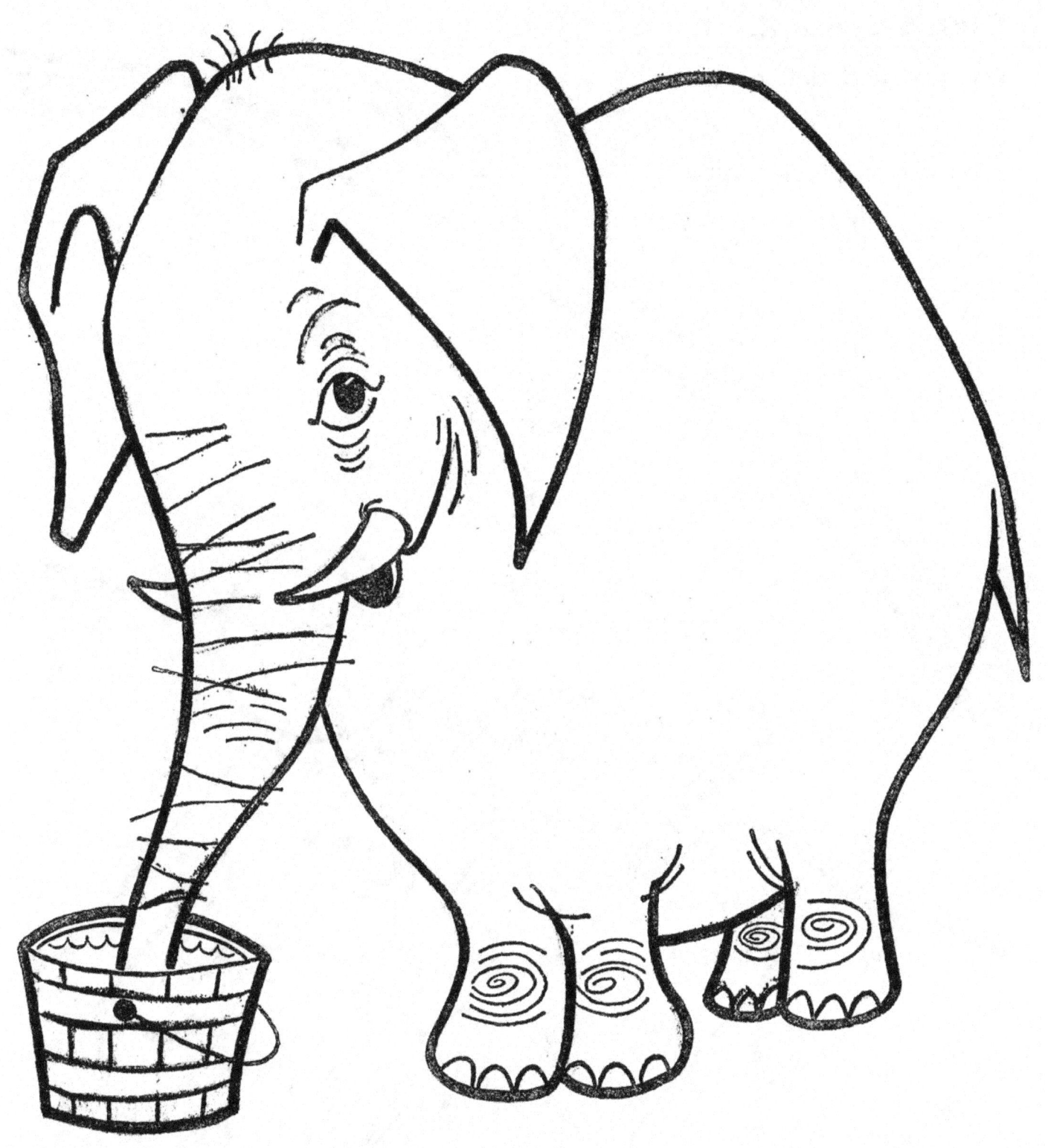

THIS IS AN ELEPHANT. The elephant is a big animal. It has a big trunk. Mercury cars have big trunks too. The elephant's trunk takes in water. Mercury trunks are not like elephant's trunks—they are sealed against water.

Color the elephant's trunk aqua.

189

THIS IS A STICK.

You can find one on the
floor of the forest.
It is used to make little
boys move faster.

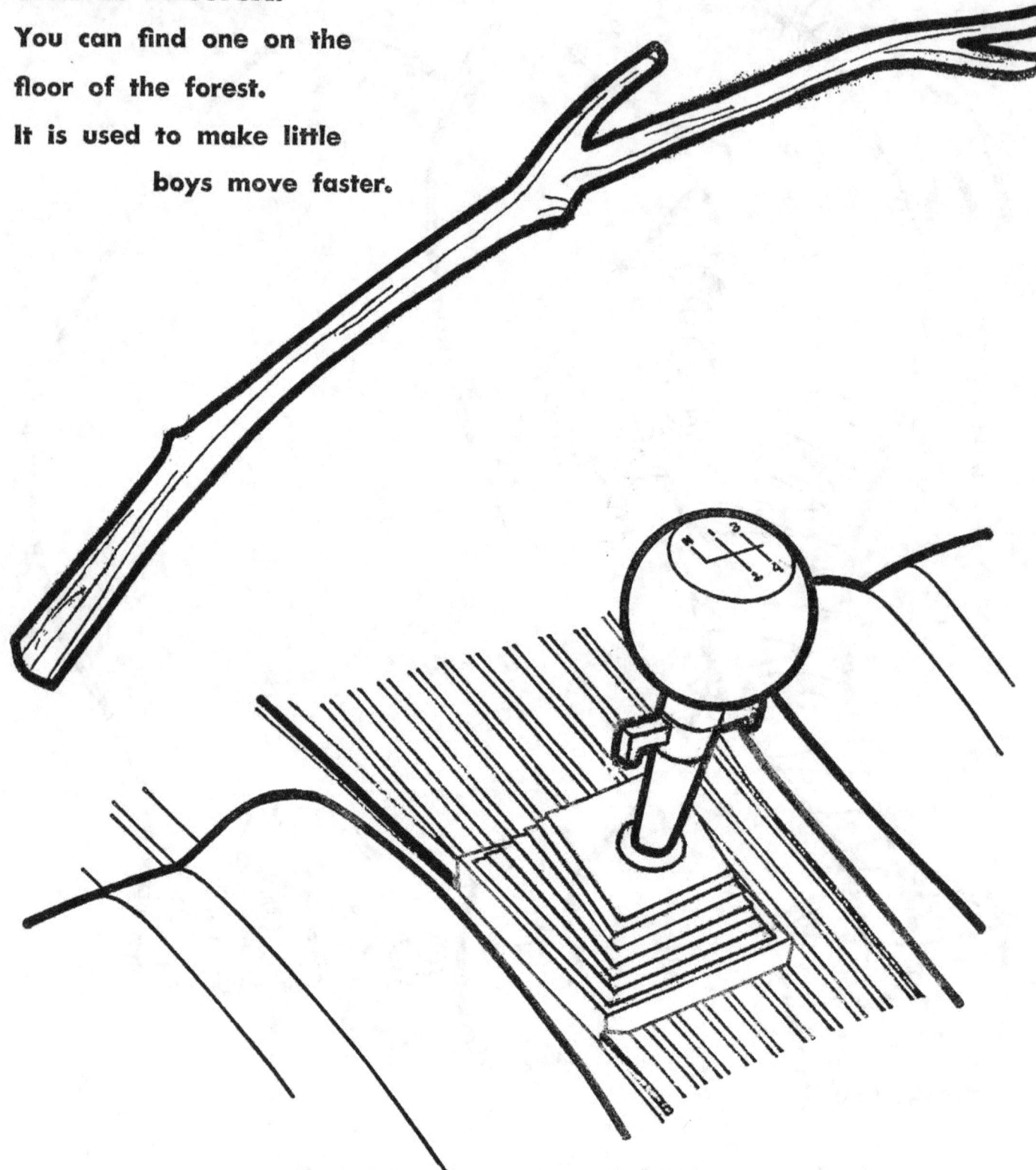

THIS IS A STICK, TOO.

It is a 4-speed stick. You can find one on the floor of a
Mercury Monterey. It is used to make big boys move faster.

Color it red hot!

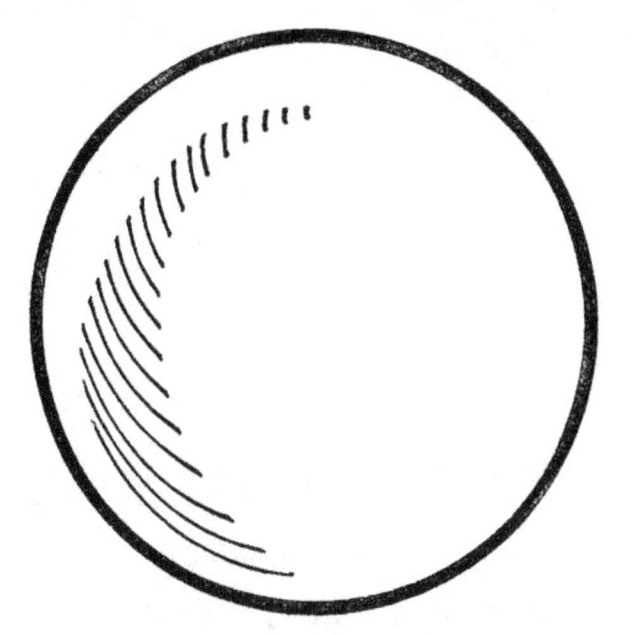

THIS IS A PLANET.

Its name is Mercury.

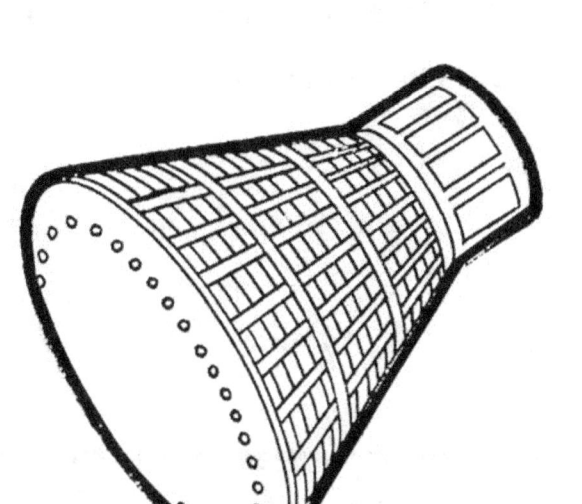

THIS IS A SPACE CAPSULE.

Its name is Mercury, too.

THIS IS A CAR.

Its name is Mercury, also.

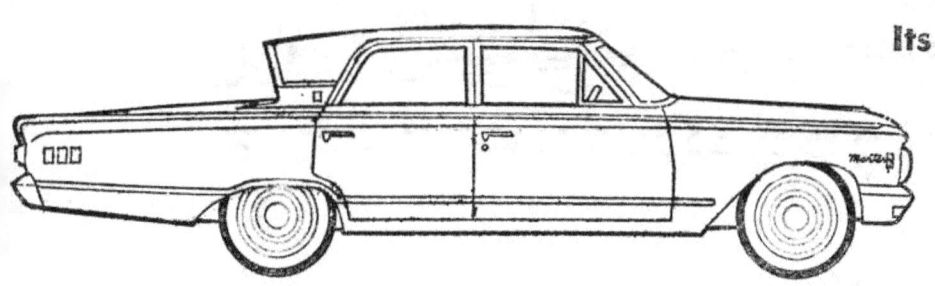

All Mercurys go through space very fast. Color the three Mercurys speedy.

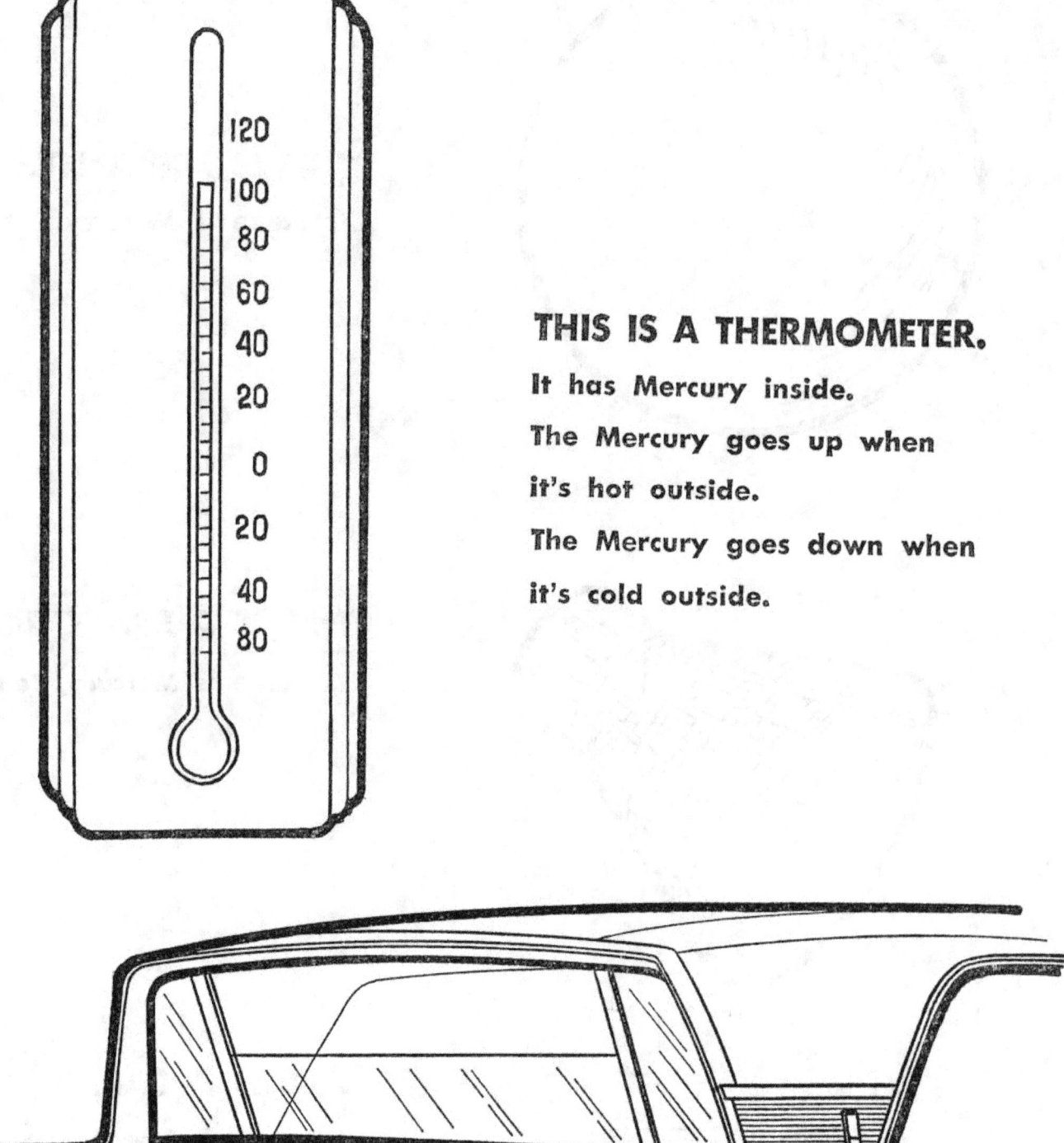

THIS IS A THERMOMETER.

It has Mercury inside.
The Mercury goes up when
it's hot outside.
The Mercury goes down when
it's cold outside.

THIS IS A RETRACTABLE REAR WINDOW. You can find one
on a Mercury Monterey. The window goes down when it's hot outside.
The window goes up when it's cold outside. Color the window "clean"
because it is always protected from dirt, snow and rain.

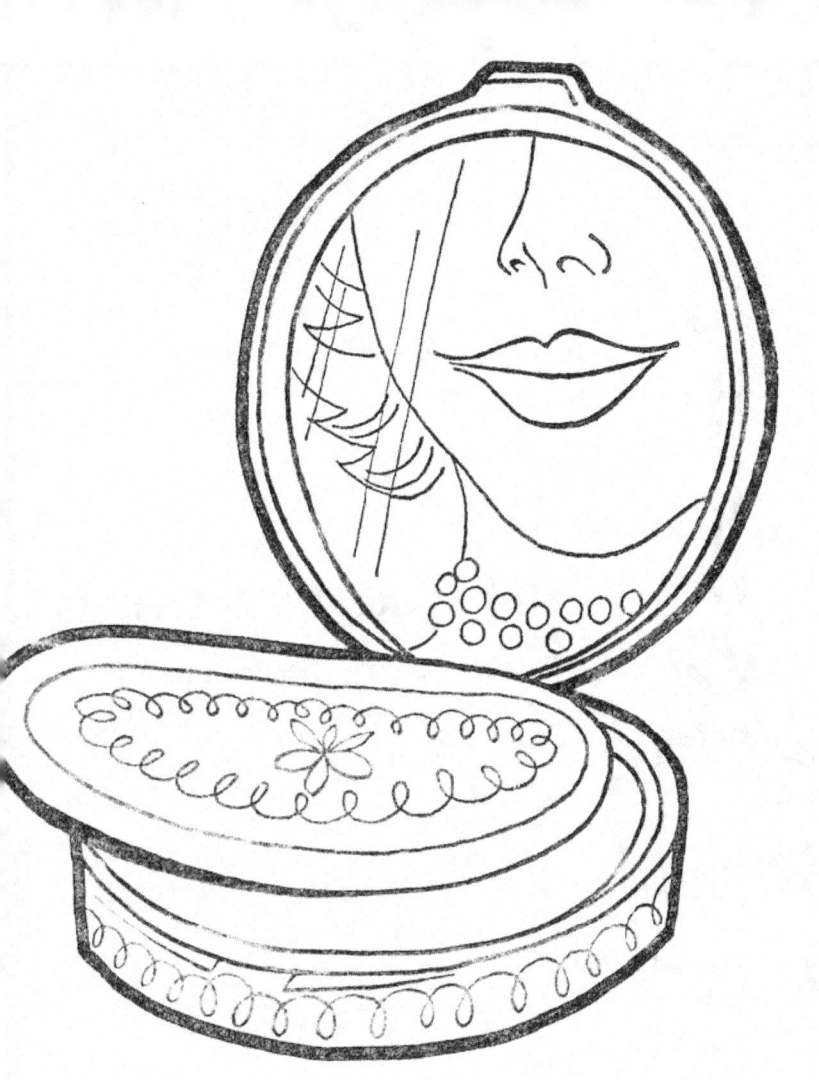

THIS IS A COMPACT. The top goes up and down and there is beauty inside.

The ladies love them because it makes them more attractive.

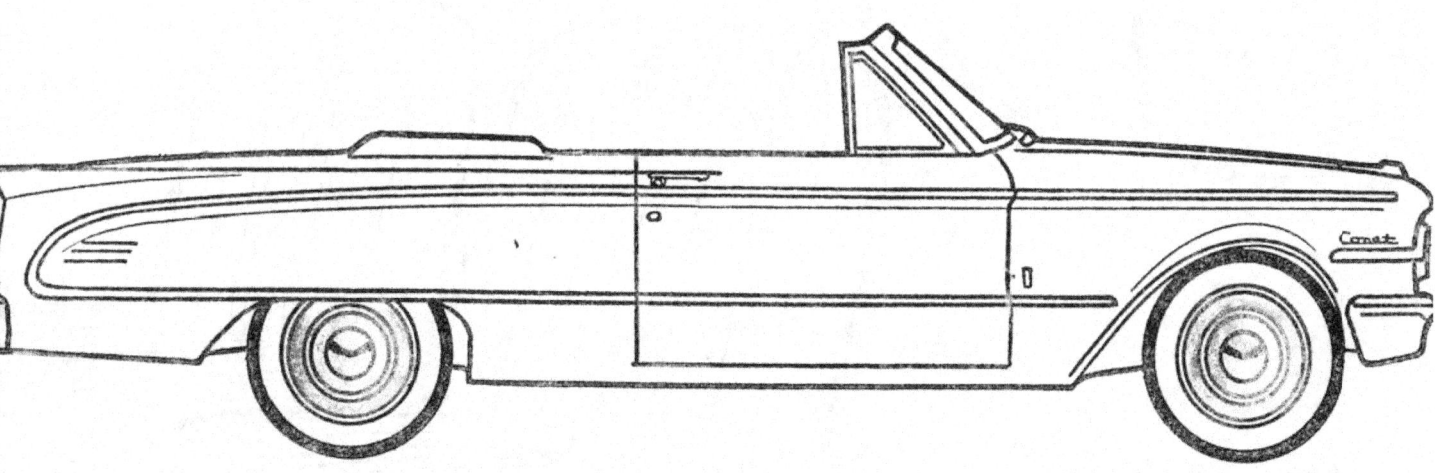

THIS IS A COMPACT, TOO. It is the <u>new</u> Mercury Comet Convertible. Its top goes up and down and there is beauty inside. The ladies love them because it makes them more attractive.

Color them attractive.

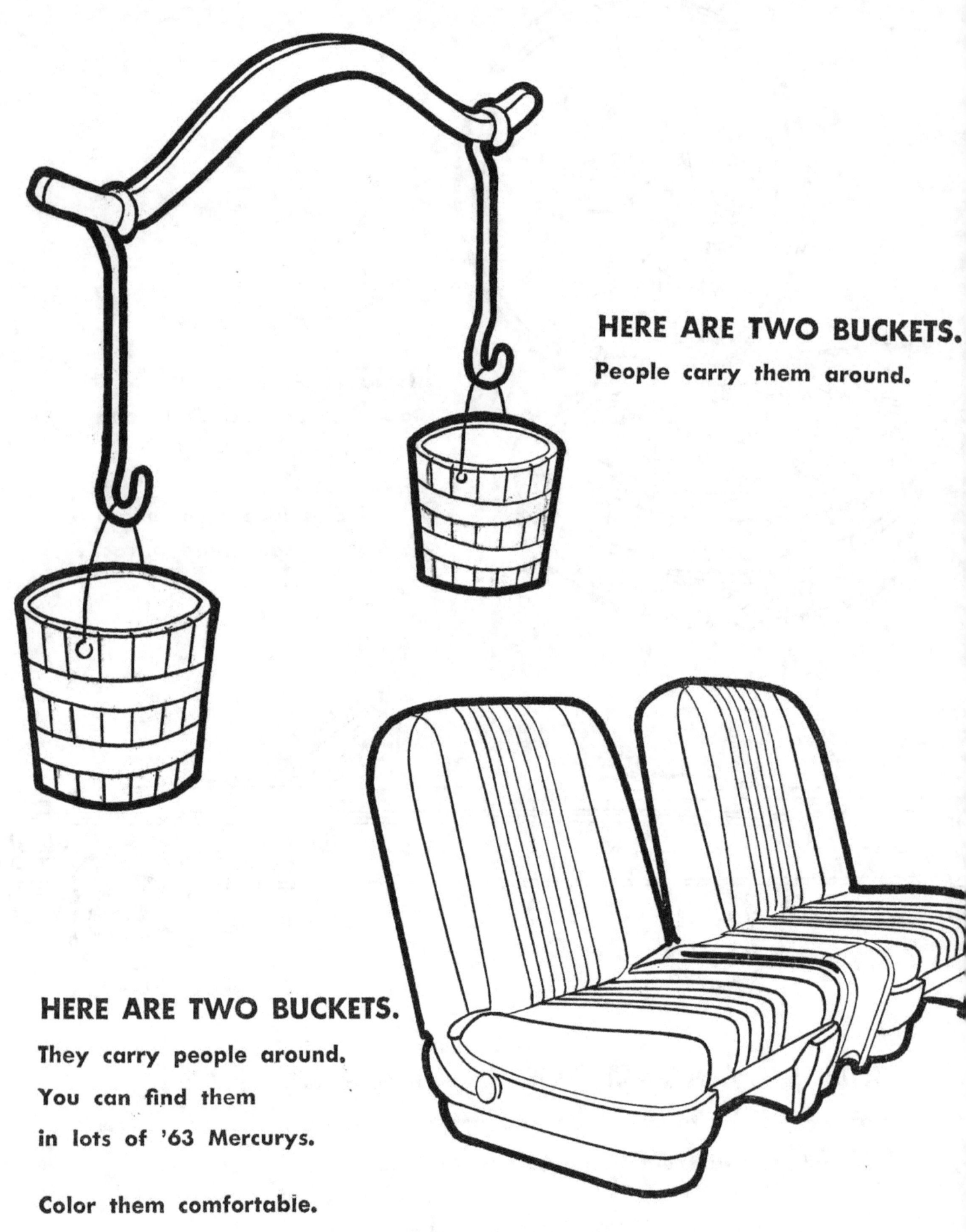

HERE ARE TWO BUCKETS.

People carry them around.

HERE ARE TWO BUCKETS.

They carry people around.

You can find them

in lots of '63 Mercurys.

Color them comfortable.

THIS IS A BIG MAN.

He is a big wheel.

He goes around in
big circles.

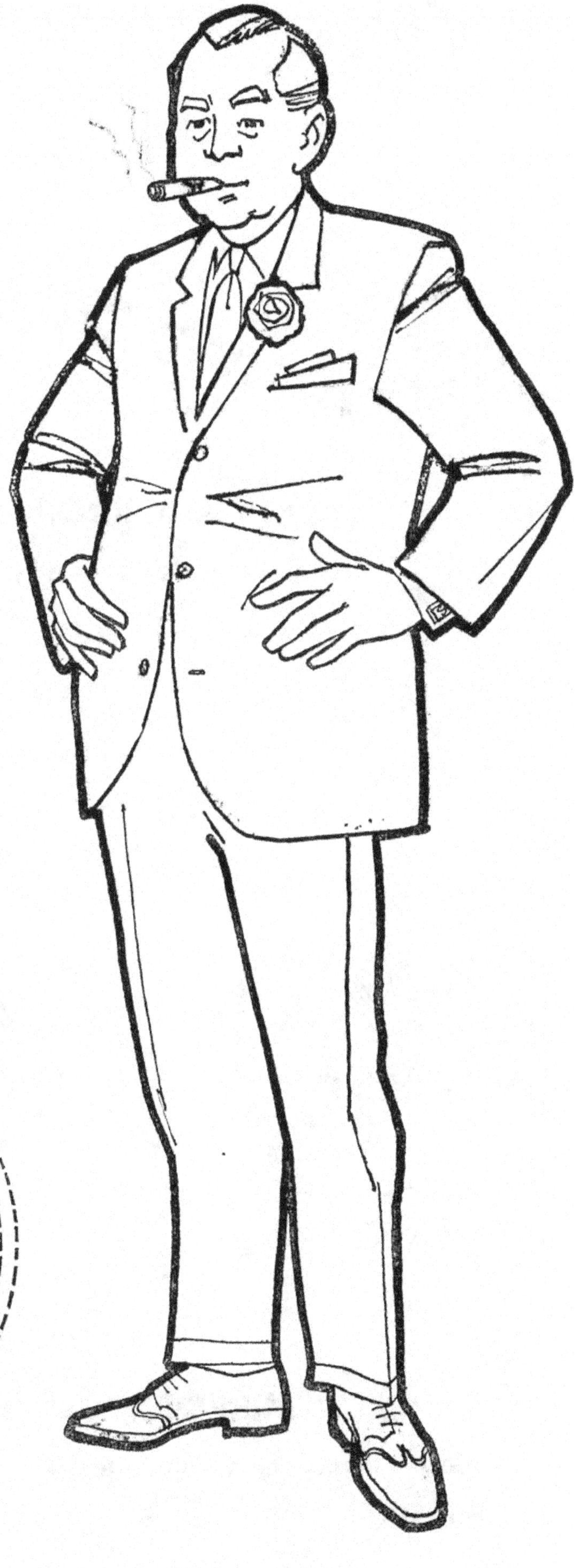

THIS IS A STEERING WHEEL.

It is a 1963 Mercury Monterey
"swing-away" steering wheel.

It goes around in little circles.

It can also be moved aside so
"big wheels" can get behind it easily.

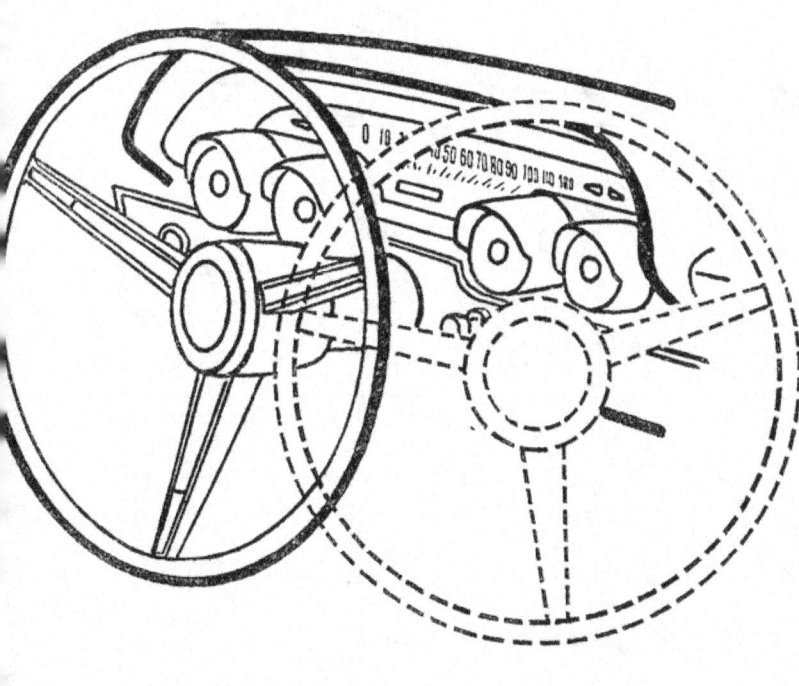

Color the steering wheel movable. (Put a smile on the "big wheel's" face.)

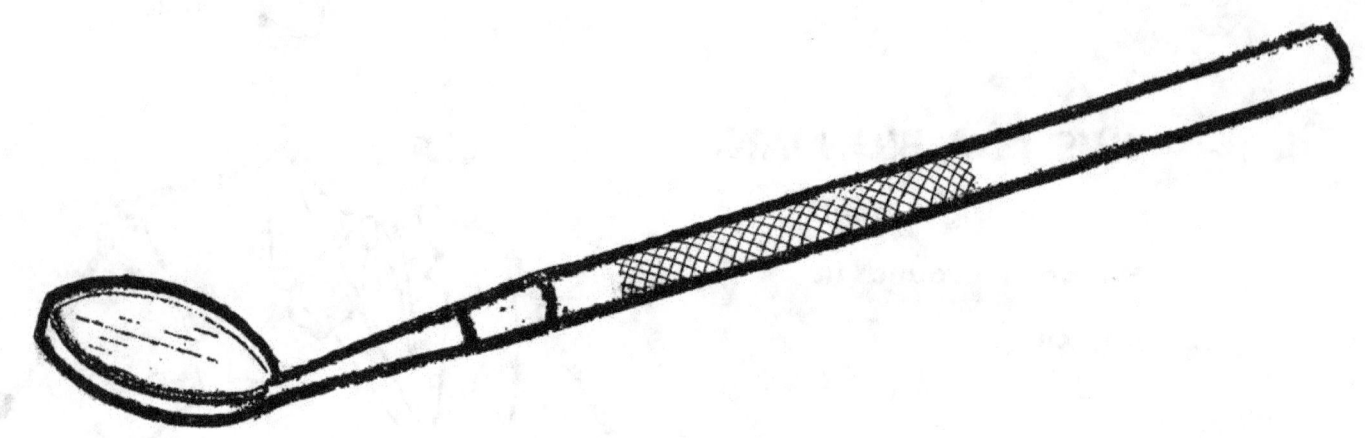

THIS IS A MIRROR. This is a dentist's mirror. It is controlled from the *outside* to see better *inside*.

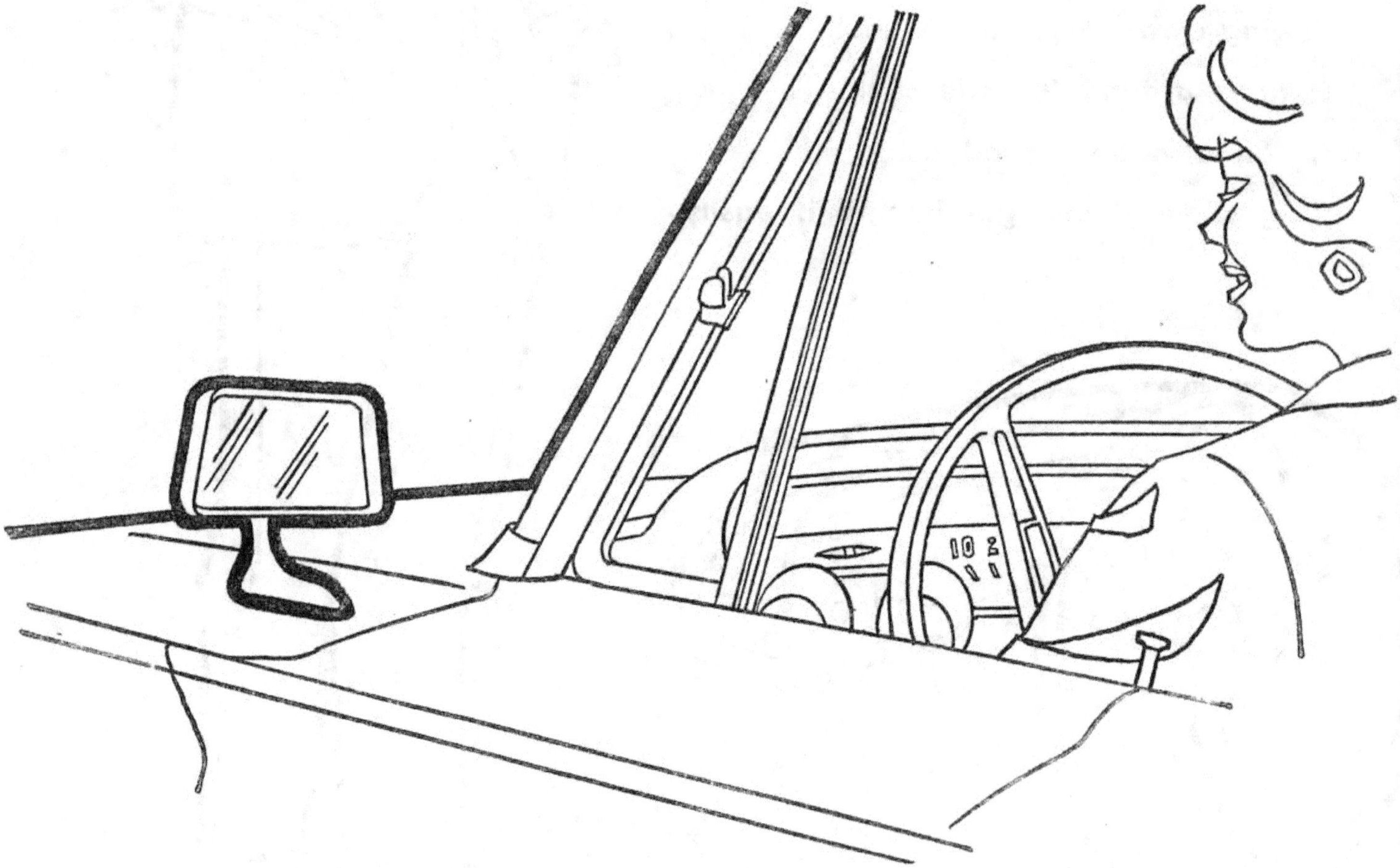

THIS IS A MIRROR, TOO. It is a Mercury remote control side-view mirror. It is controlled from the *inside* to see better *outside*.

Color the mirror convenient.

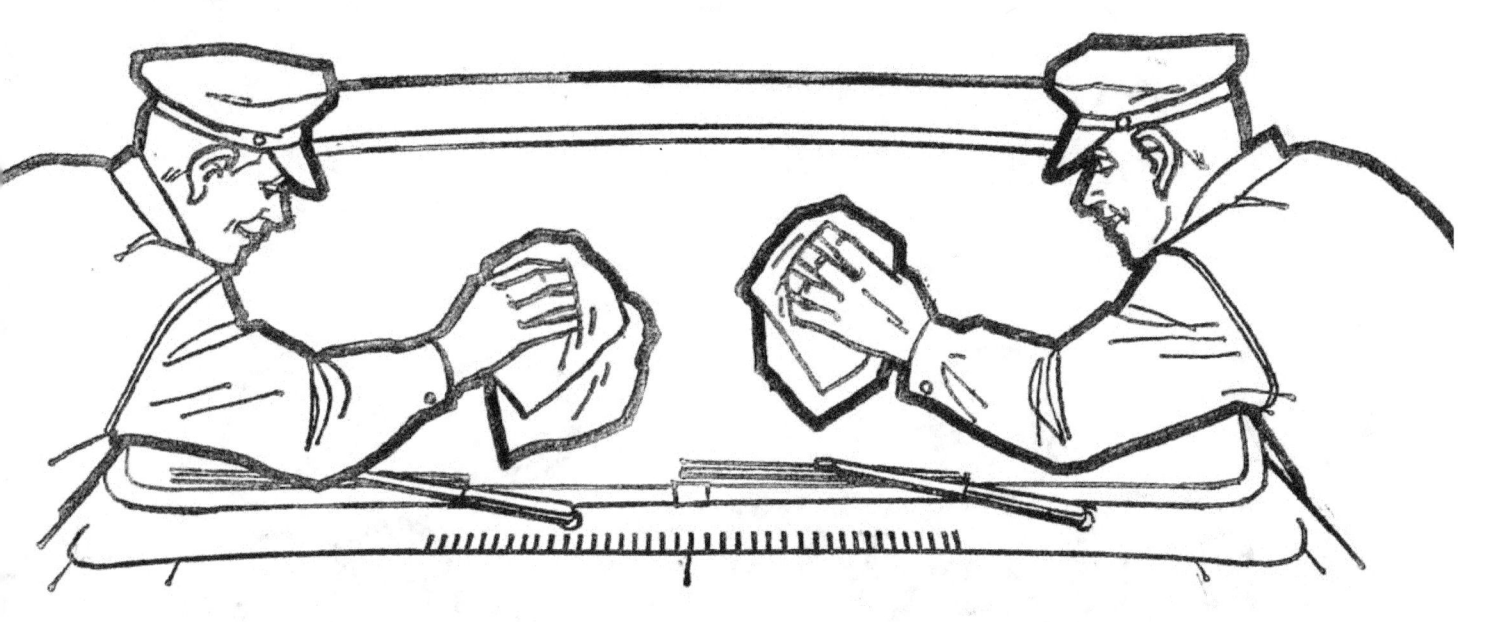

THESE ARE TWO WINDSHIELD WIPERS.

They clean a car's windshield all the way across. They leave no blind spots in the center. They are nice to have.

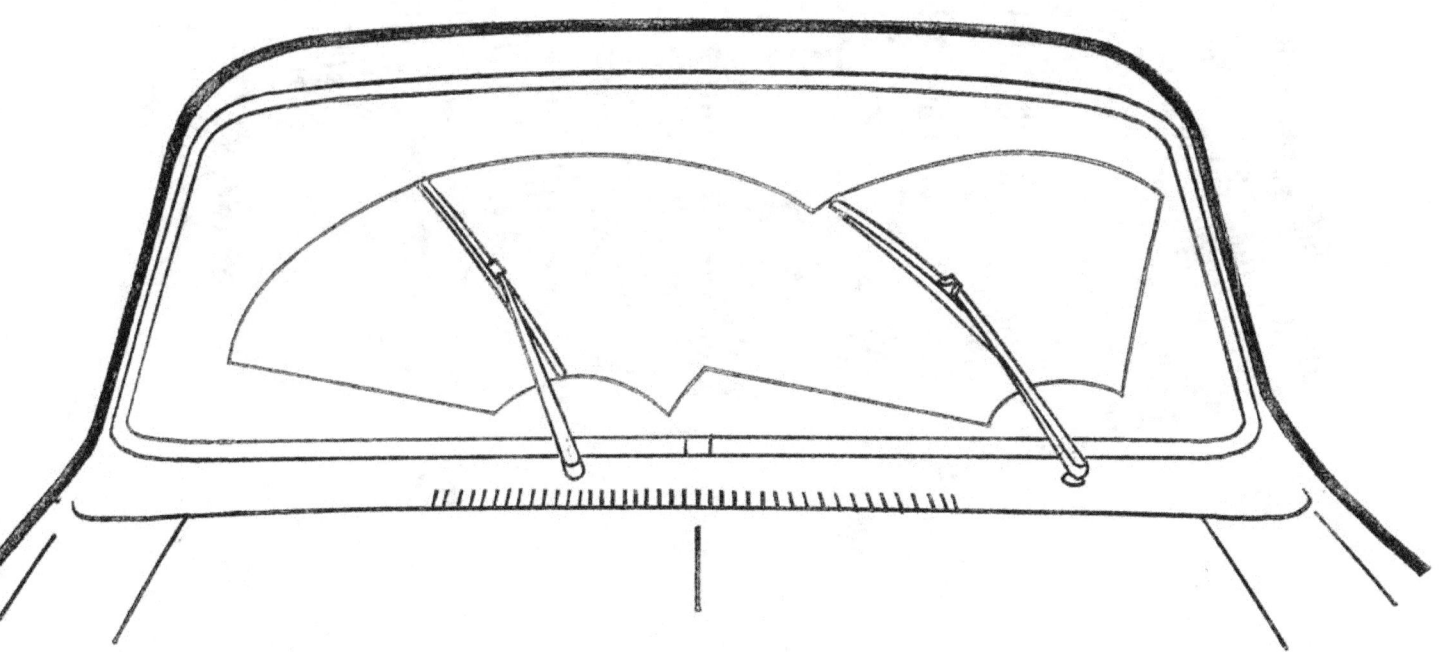

THESE ARE TWO WINDSHIELD WIPERS, TOO. They are Mercury tandem-action windshield wipers. They clean your Mercury's windshield all the way across. They leave no blind spots in the center. They are nice to have, too.

Don't color the windshield...keep it clean all the way across.

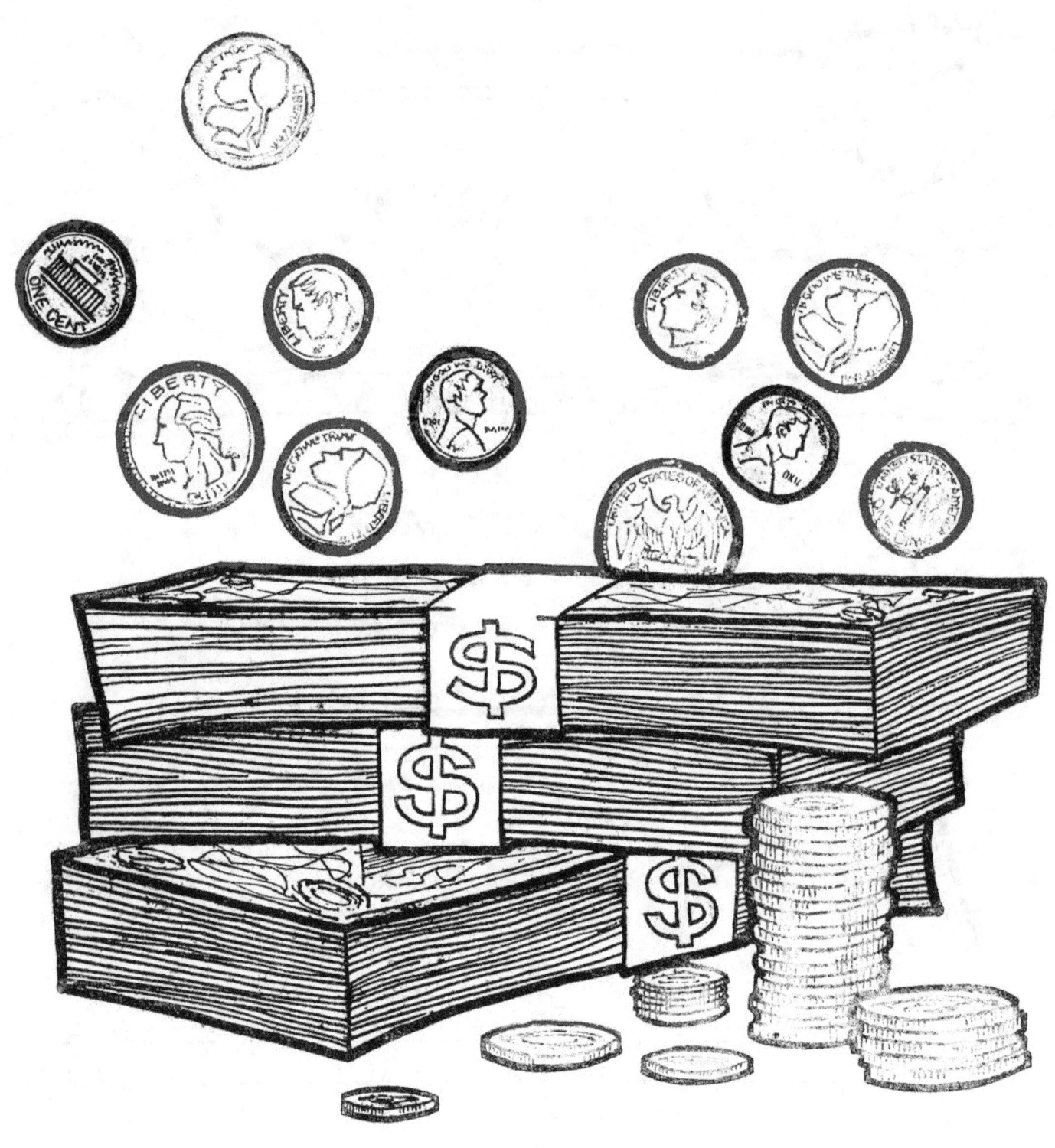

THIS IS MONEY. Some people save it. Mercury owners are big money-savers because their cars cost them less to buy, run and keep up. You should be a big money-saver too—are you?

Color the money silver, copper and green.

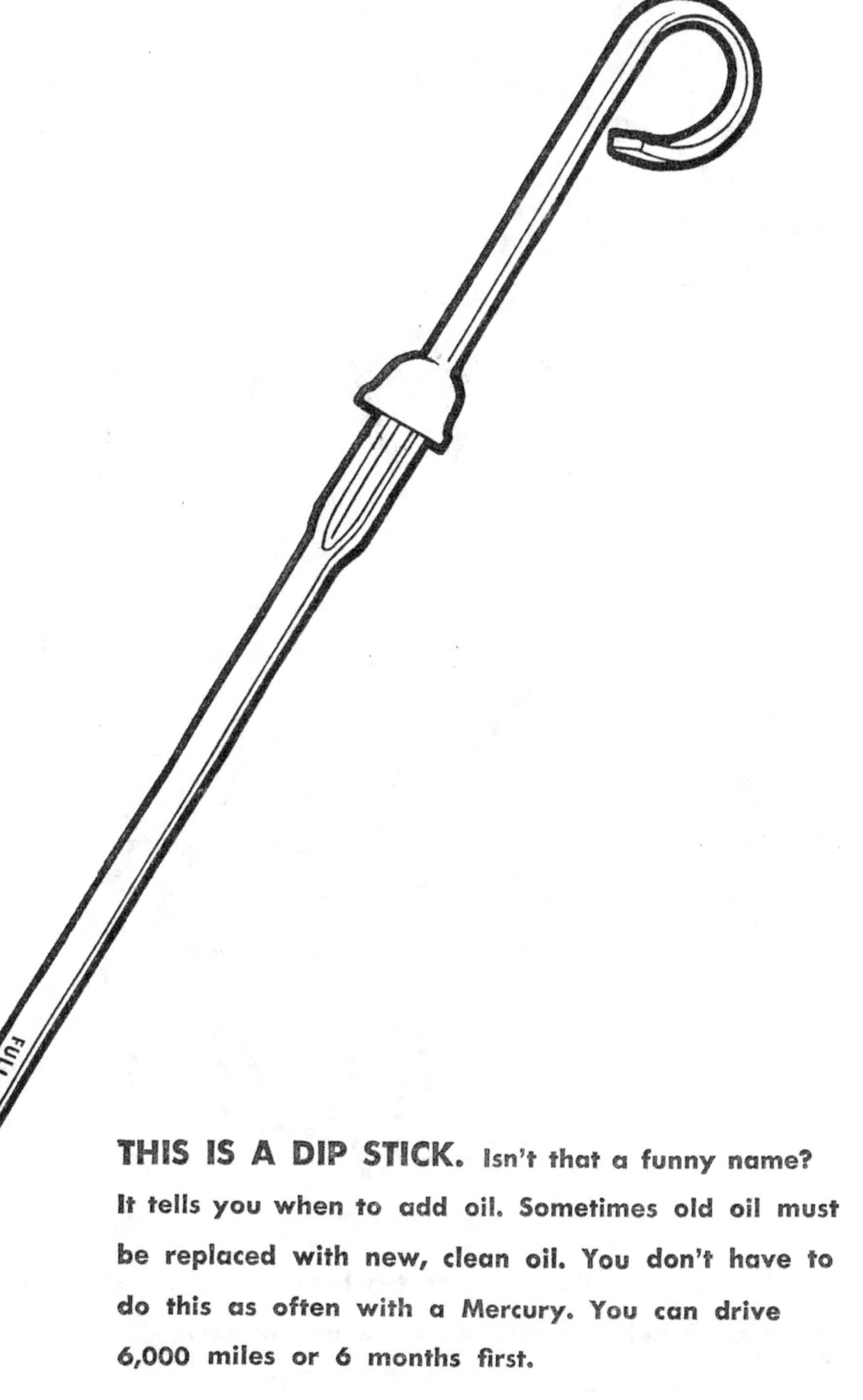

THIS IS A DIP STICK. Isn't that a funny name? It tells you when to add oil. Sometimes old oil must be replaced with new, clean oil. You don't have to do this as often with a Mercury. You can drive 6,000 miles or 6 months first.

Do not color this page. Squirt oil on it.

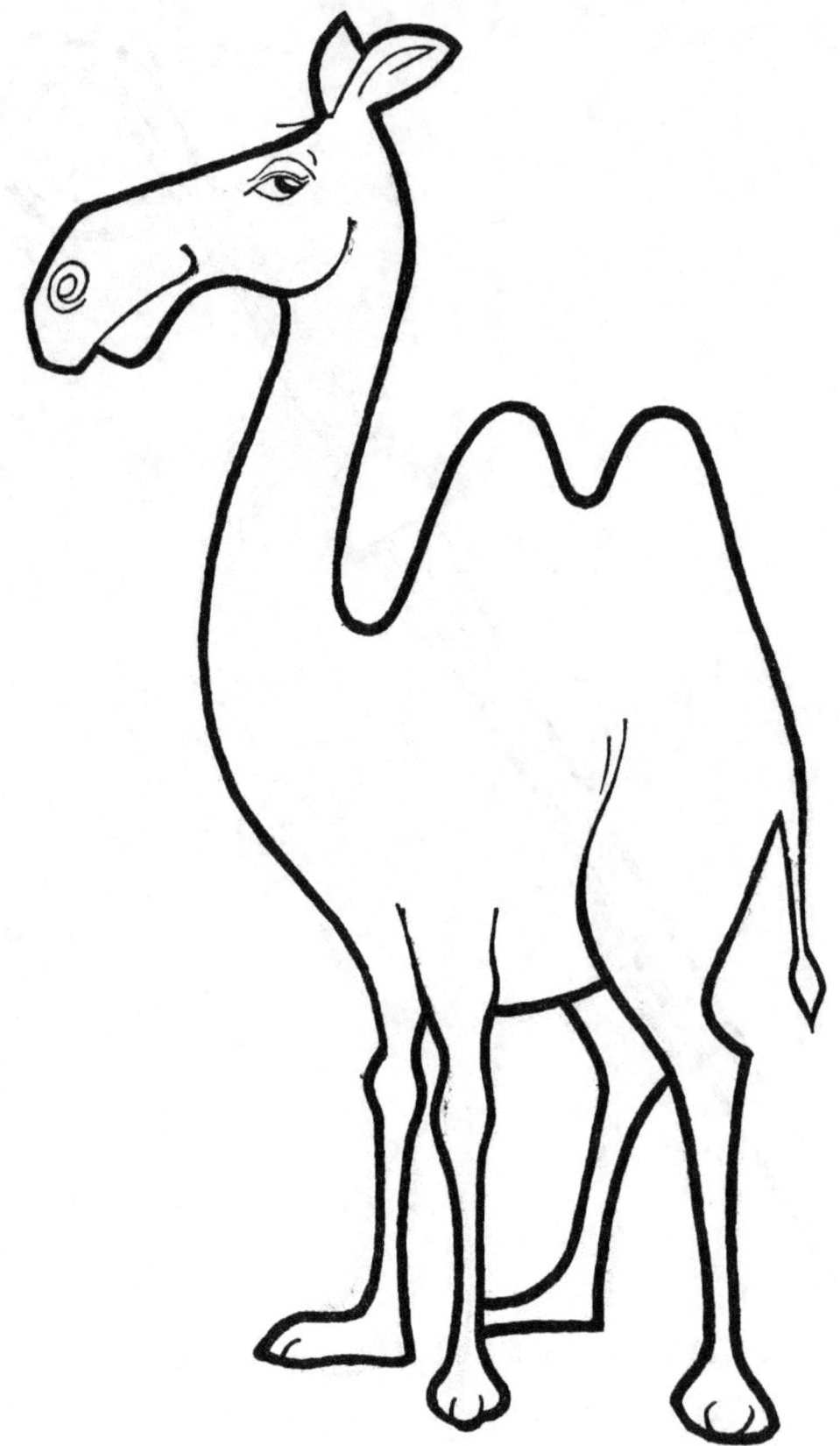

HERE IS A CAMEL. It has two humps. The camel can go two weeks without drinking water. Mercury's anti-freeze/anti-rust radiator coolant can go 2 years or 36,000 miles.

Color the camel green with envy.

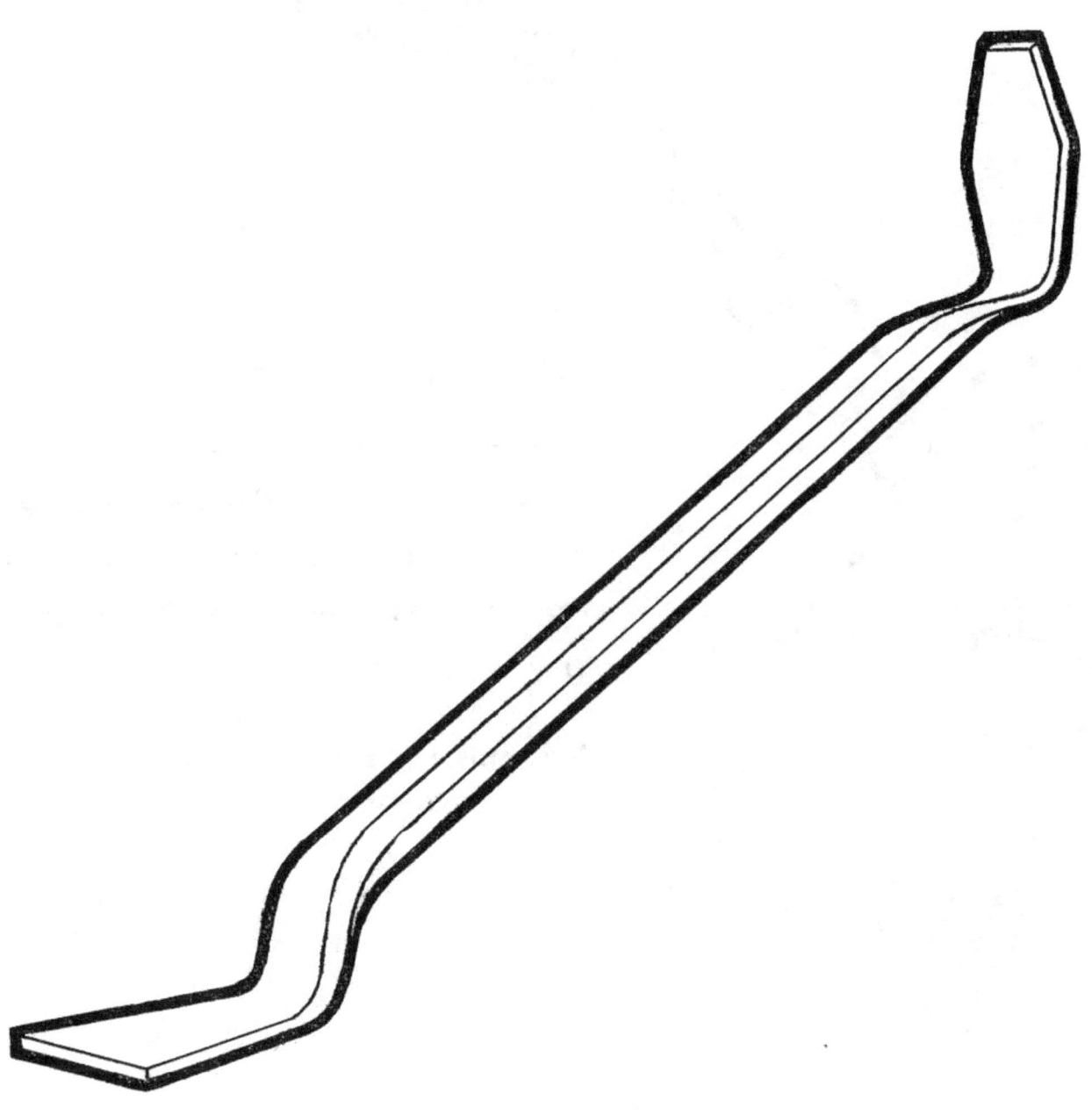

THIS IS A BRAKE ADJUSTING TOOL. Mercury mechanics seldom need this tool. Mercury's brakes adjust themselves.

Color this tool rusty.

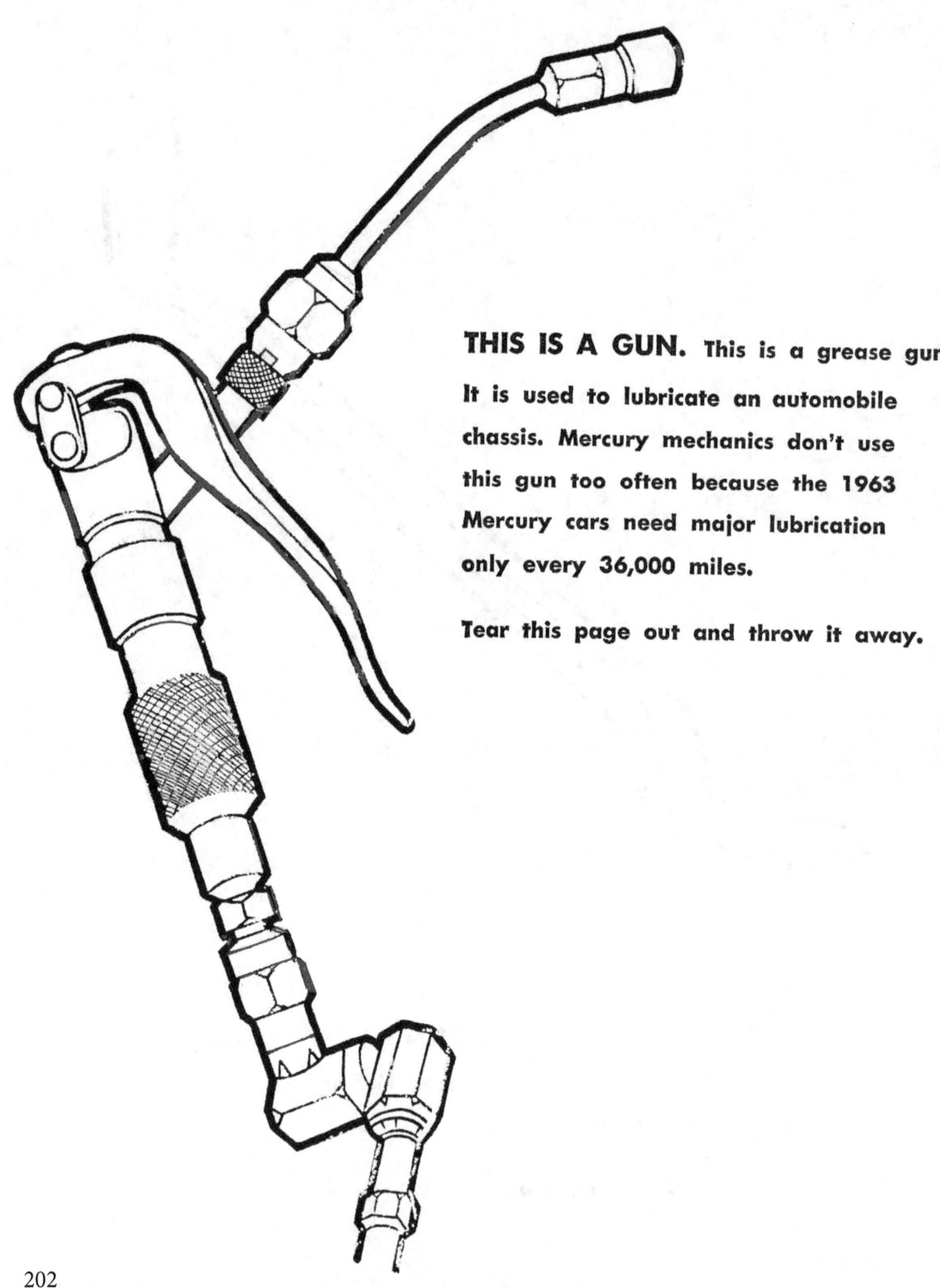

THIS IS A GUN. This is a grease gun. It is used to lubricate an automobile chassis. Mercury mechanics don't use this gun too often because the 1963 Mercury cars need major lubrication only every 36,000 miles.

Tear this page out and throw it away.

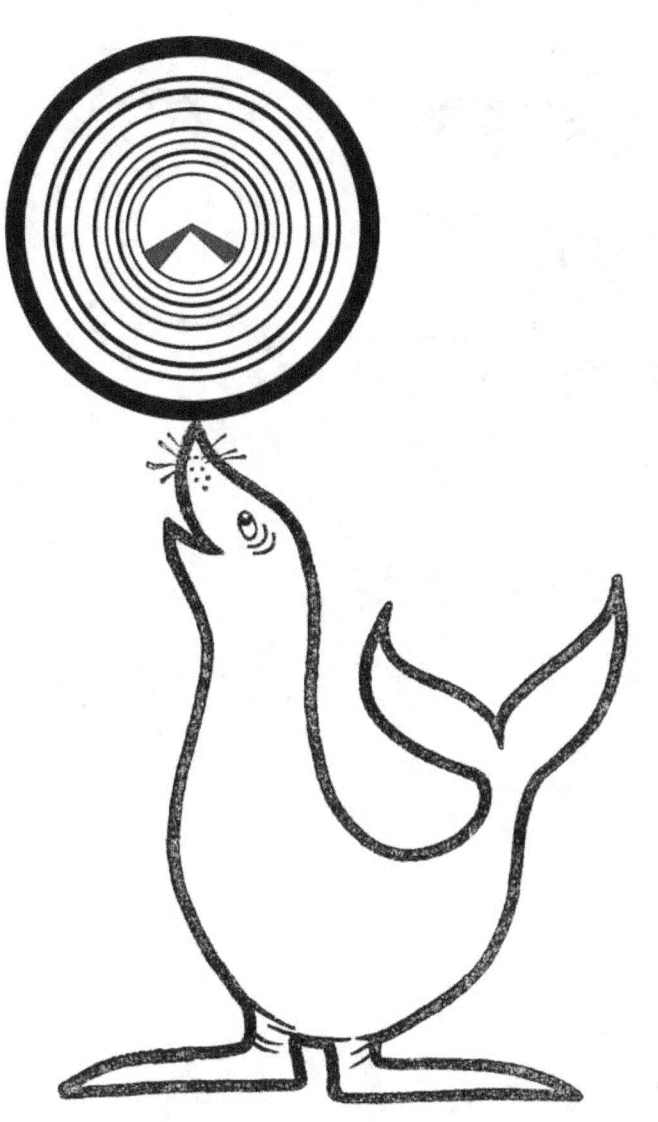

THIS IS A WHEEL BALANCER.

He can balance wheels perfectly because he went to a seal training school.

THIS IS A WHEEL BALANCER, TOO.

He is a Mercury mechanic. He can balance Mercury wheels perfectly because he went to a Mercury Service Training School.

Make sure the colors you use are balanced.

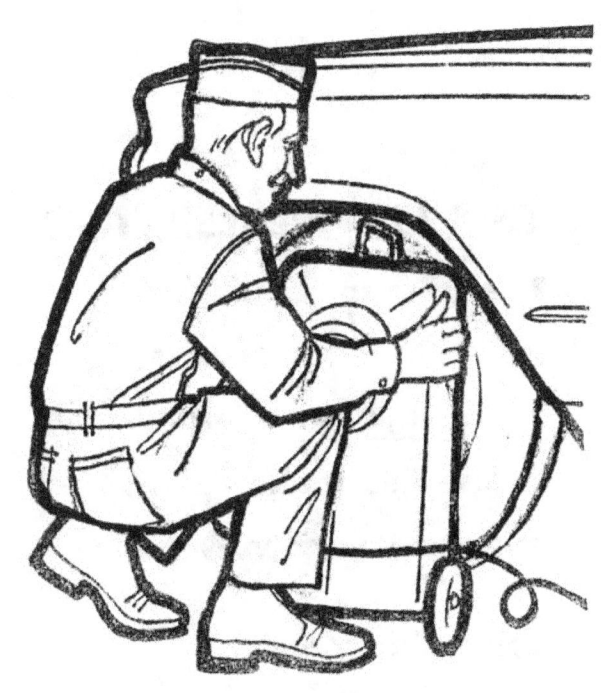

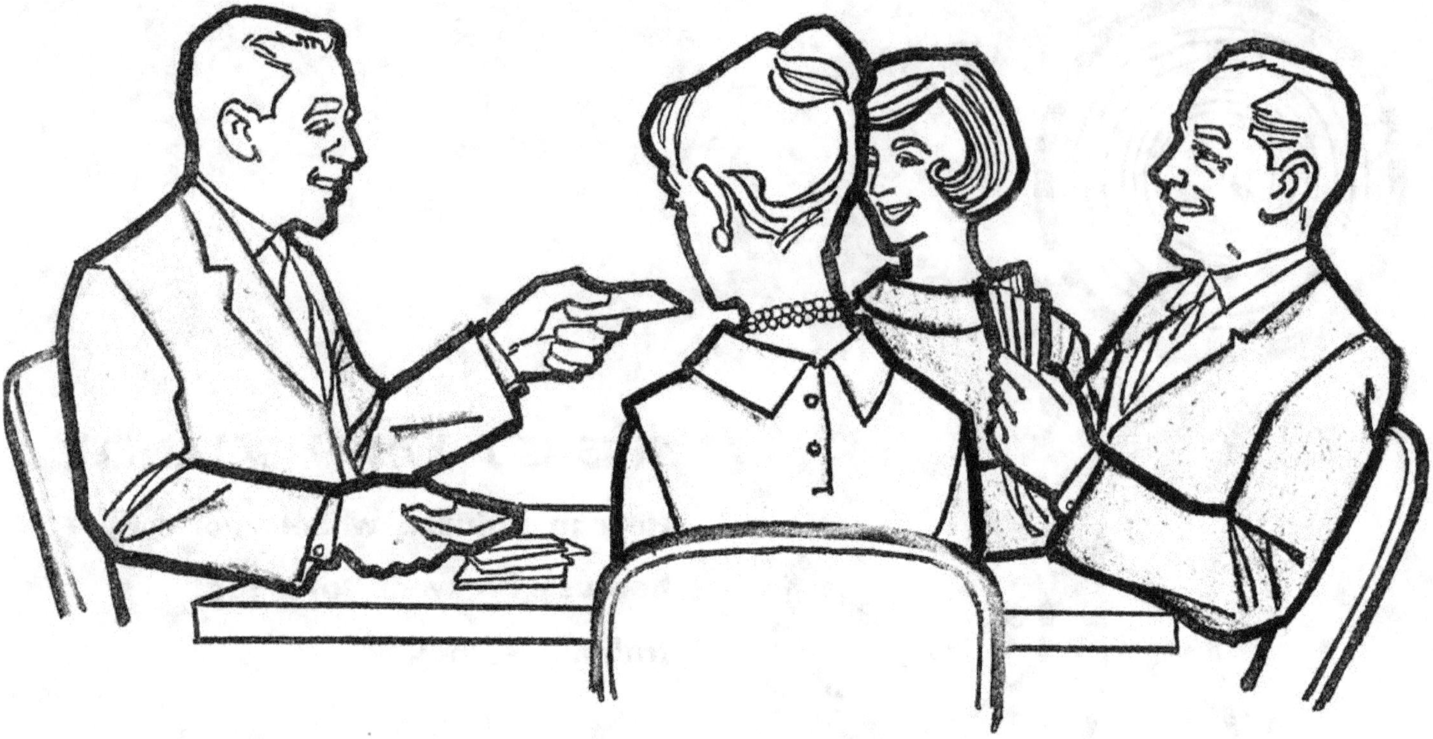

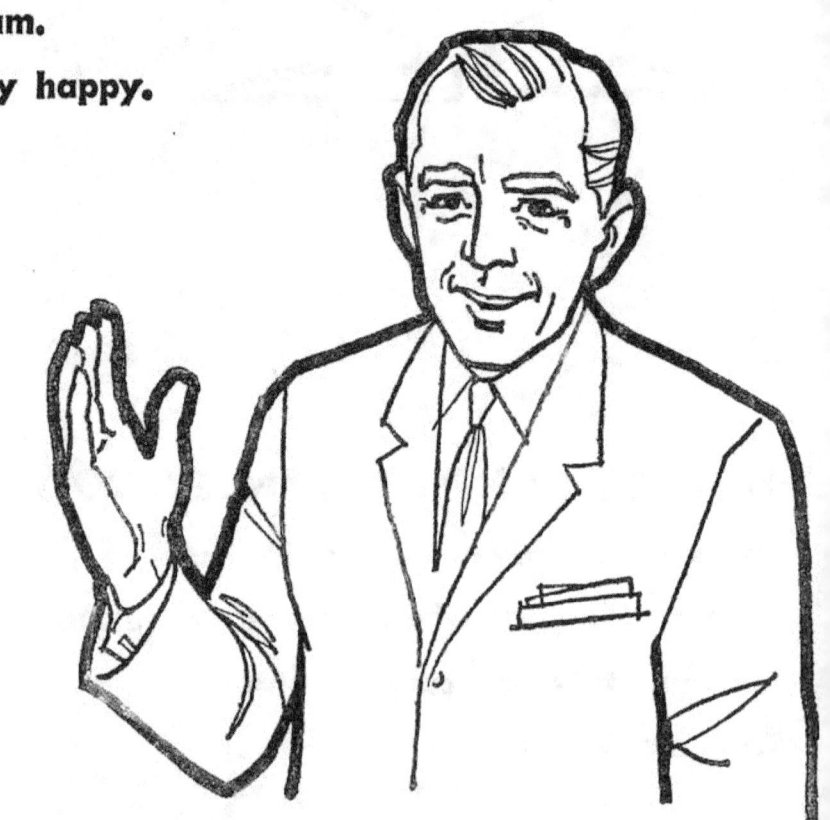

THIS IS A DEALER.

This is a card dealer.

Sometimes he deals a grand slam.

This makes the person very very happy.

THIS IS A DEALER, TOO.

This is a car dealer.

He sells new Mercurys.

He **always** gives grand-slam
deals. This makes
everyone very very happy.

Color him friendly.

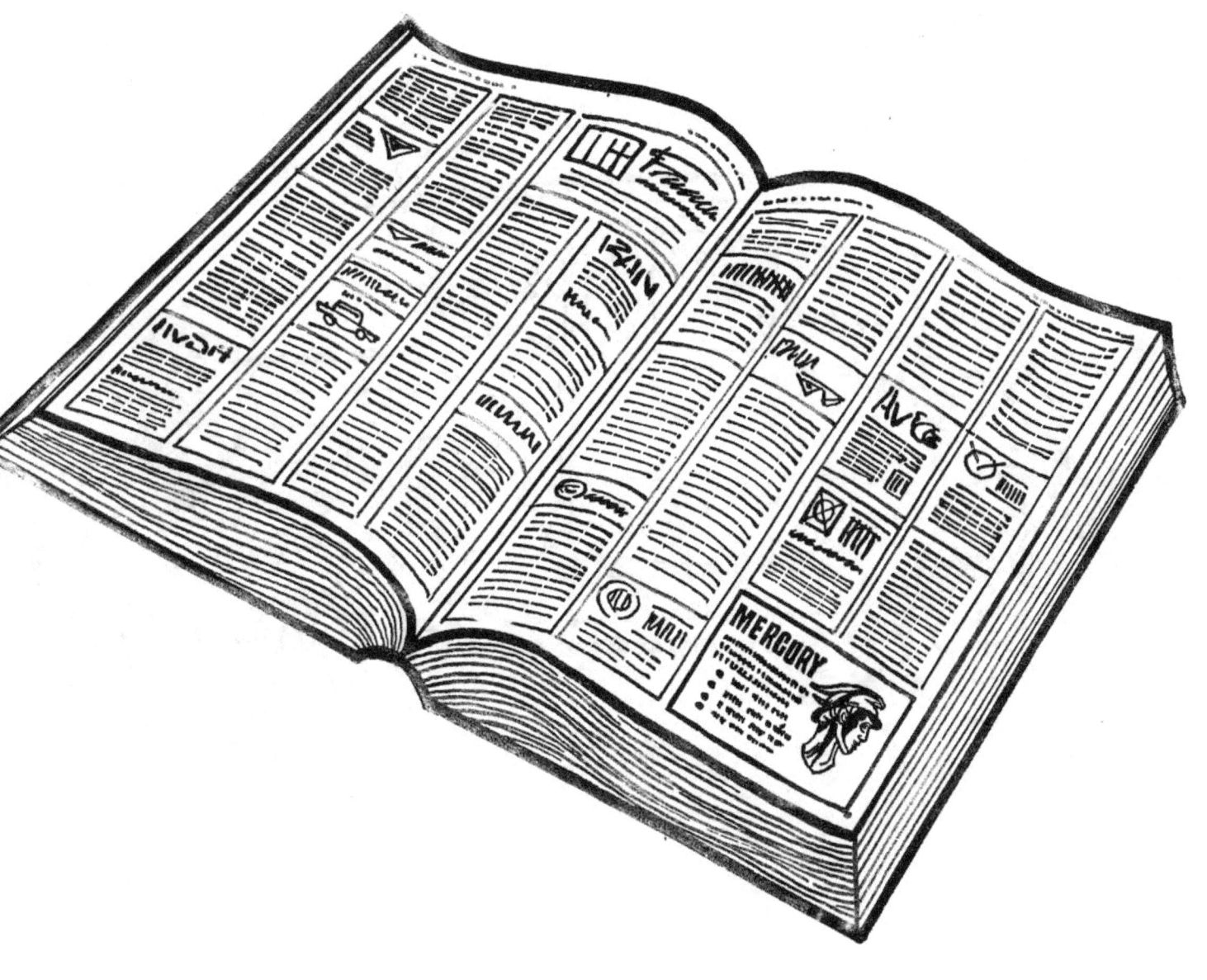

THIS IS A TELEPHONE BOOK. It is a classified telephone book.
It tells where your nearest Mercury dealer is located.

Color the pages yellow, then walk across them with your fingers.

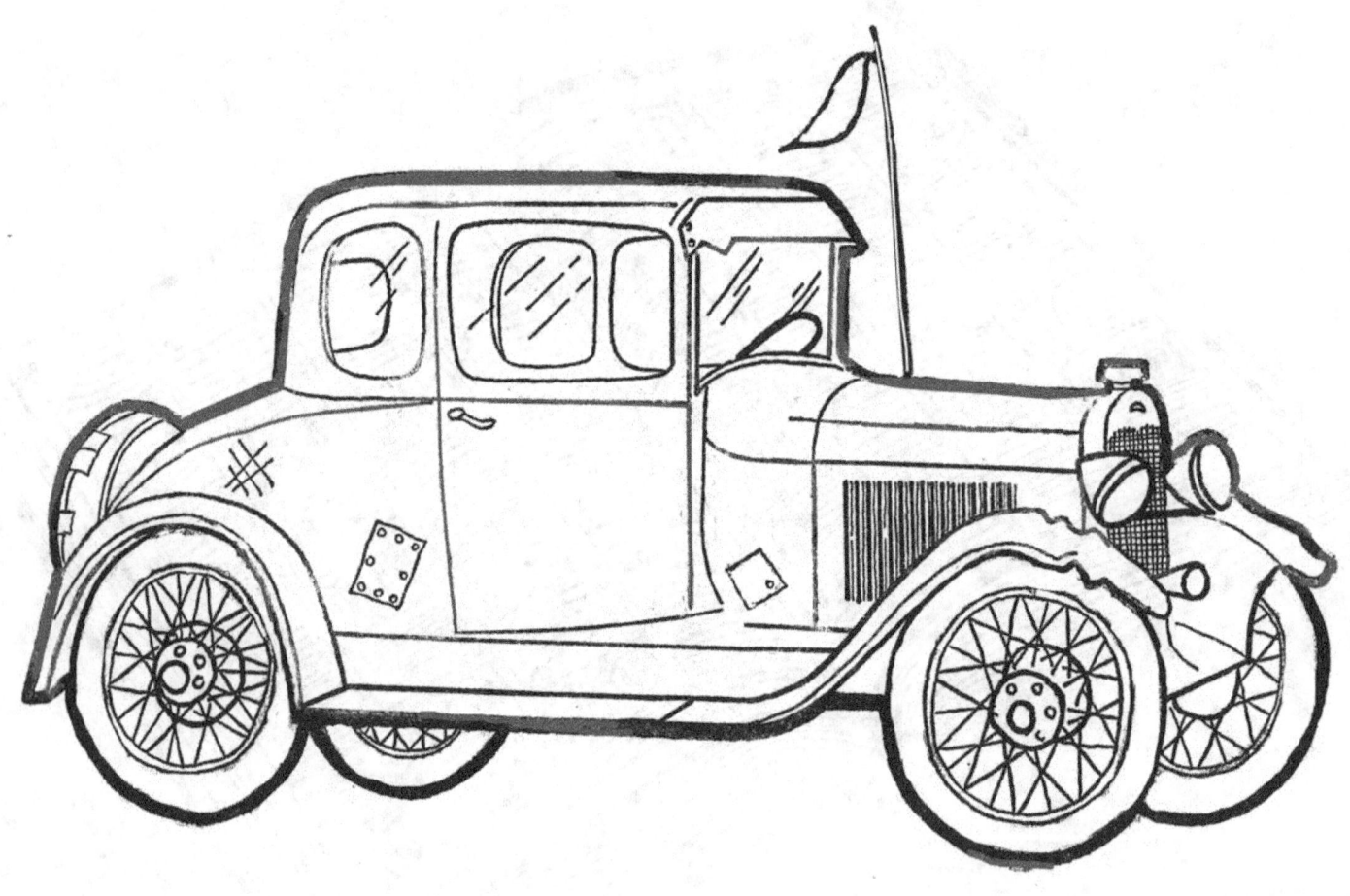

THIS IS A CAR.

This is a used car. Every car owner has one. Used cars
are worth a lot of money—especially at your Mercury dealer's.
He'll give you more for your used car in trade on a new Mercury.

Color the used car gray.

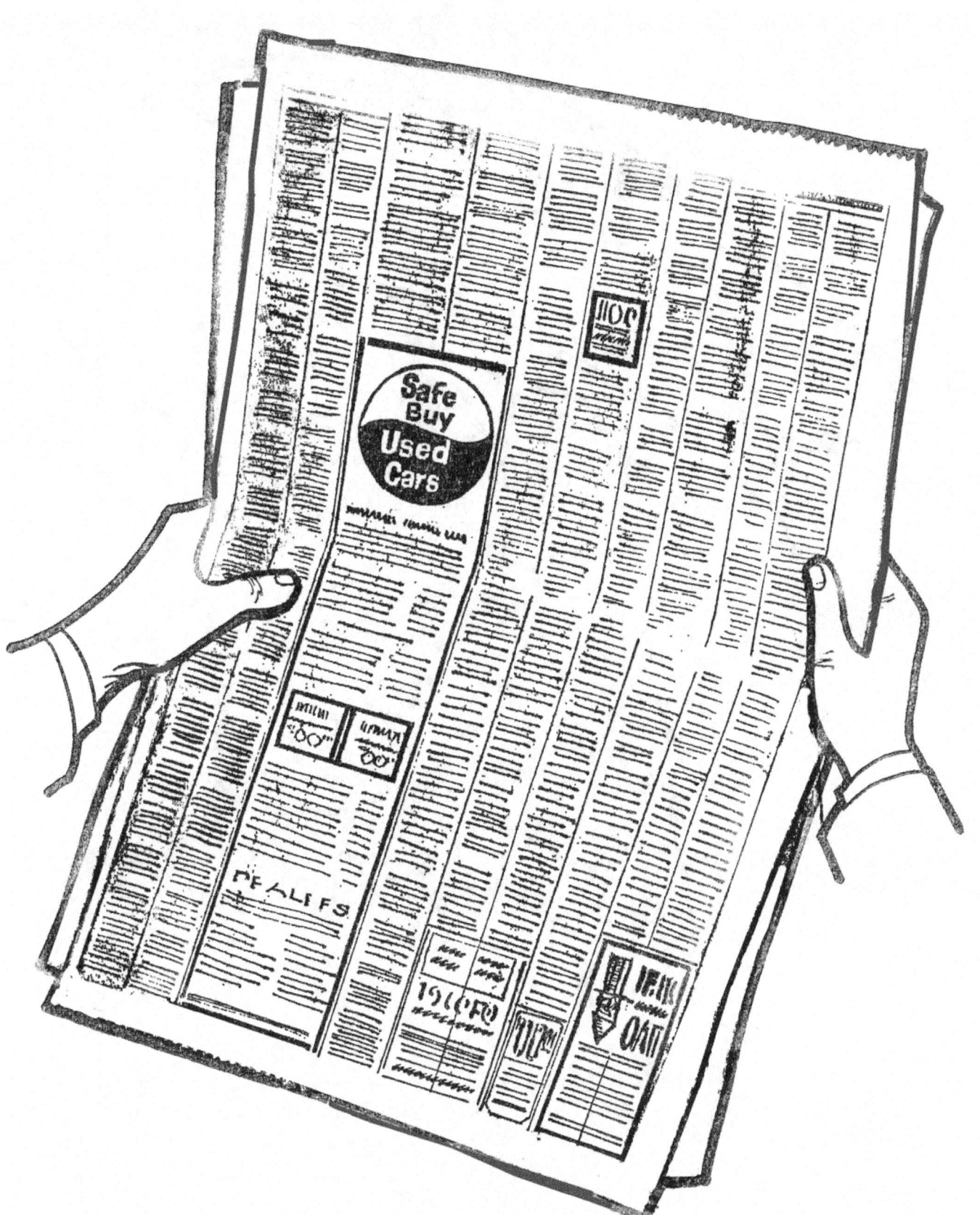

THIS IS A NEWSPAPER. It is black and white and read all over.

It's a good place to look for "Safe-Buy" used car bargains advertised by your local Mercury dealer.

Color it "read" ... every day.

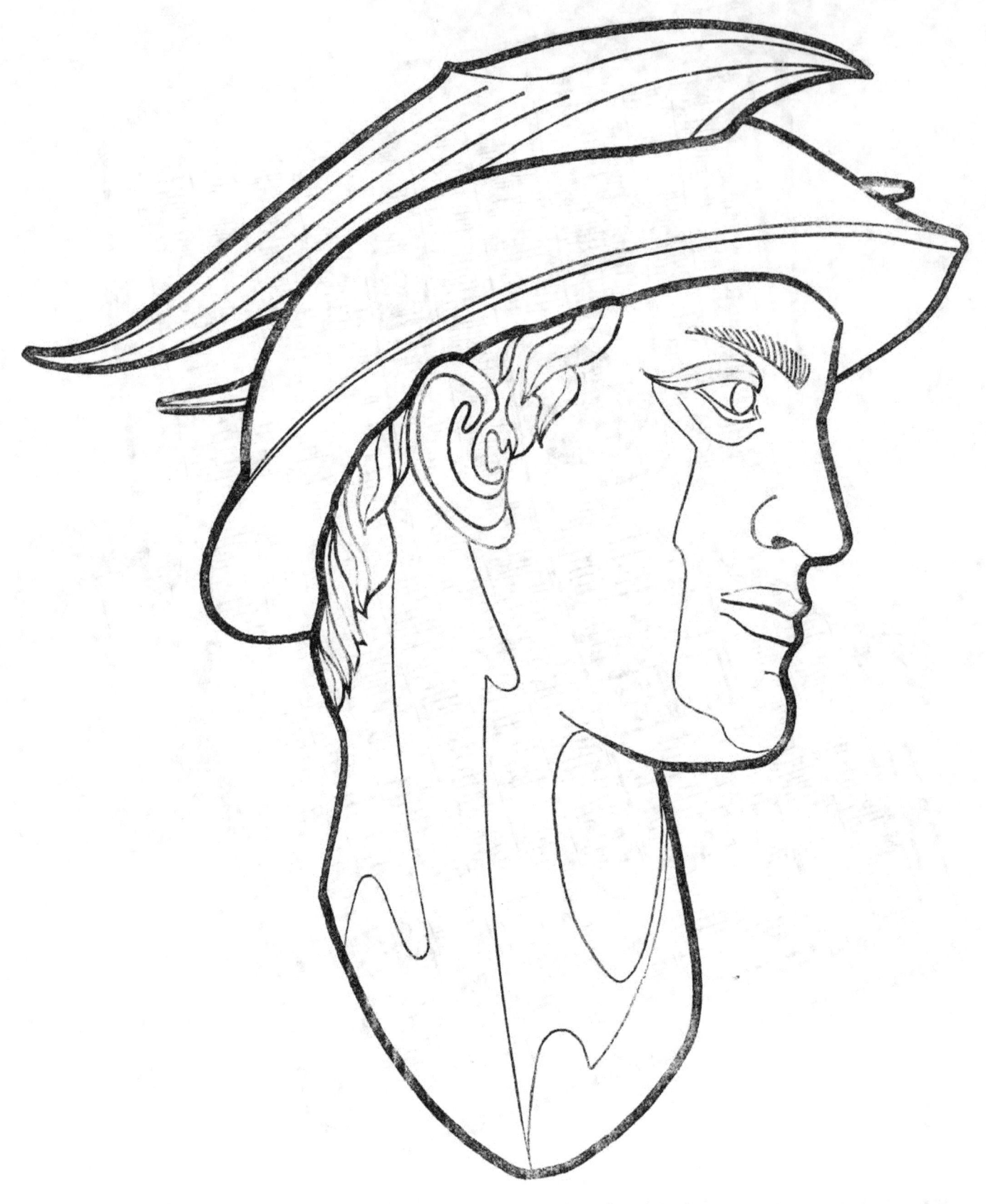

THIS IS A HEAD. It is the head of Mercury—the "fleet-footed" mythical god. It is the trademark of the fleet Mercury cars.

Color the Mercury head as it is on the back cover.

If your hand is tired from coloring, just slide it across this page. Pretty smooth, isn't it? Just like the ride in a 1963 Mercury.

The 1963 Mercurys look smooth, too. Just turn the page and see.

Here they are: The colorful Mercurys for 1963

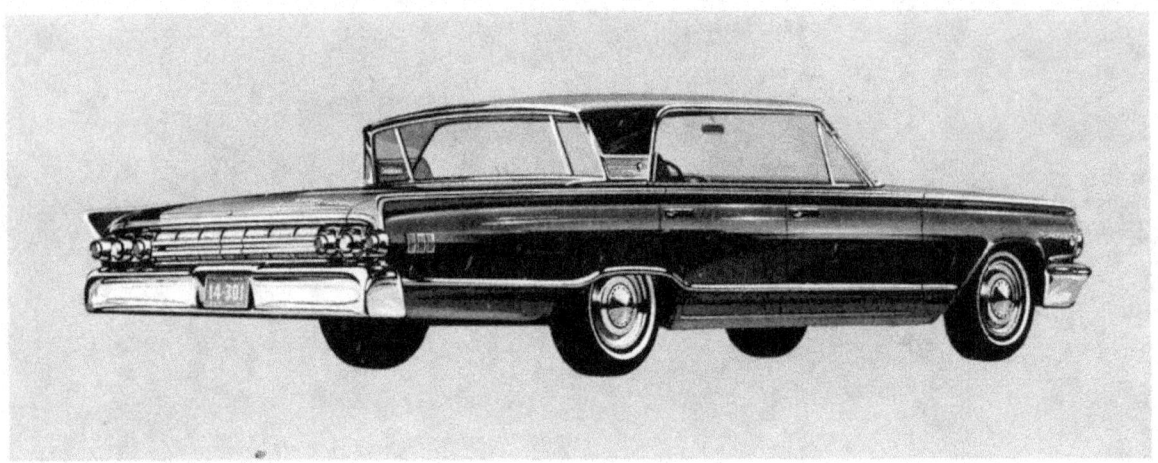

Mercury Monterey Custom four-door hardtop

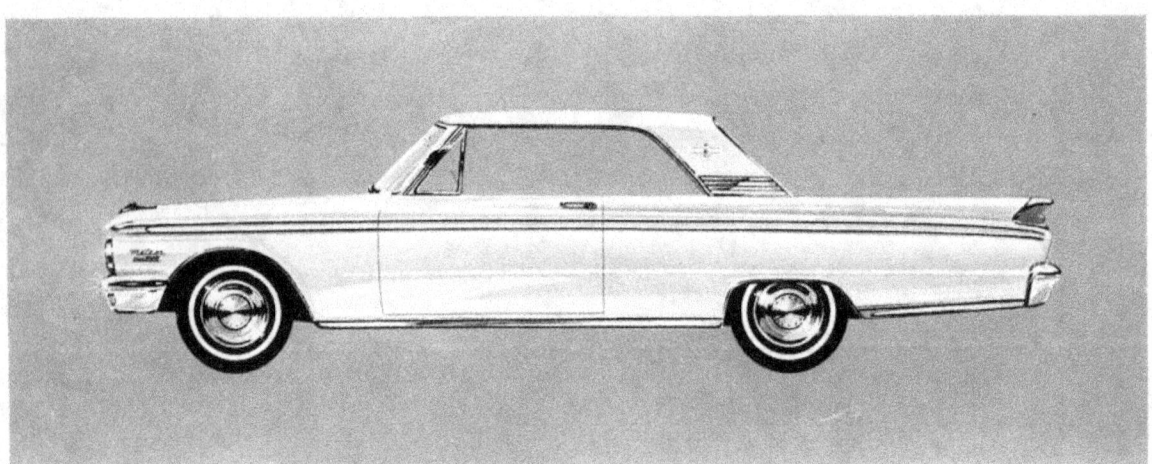

Mercury Meteor Custom two-door hardtop

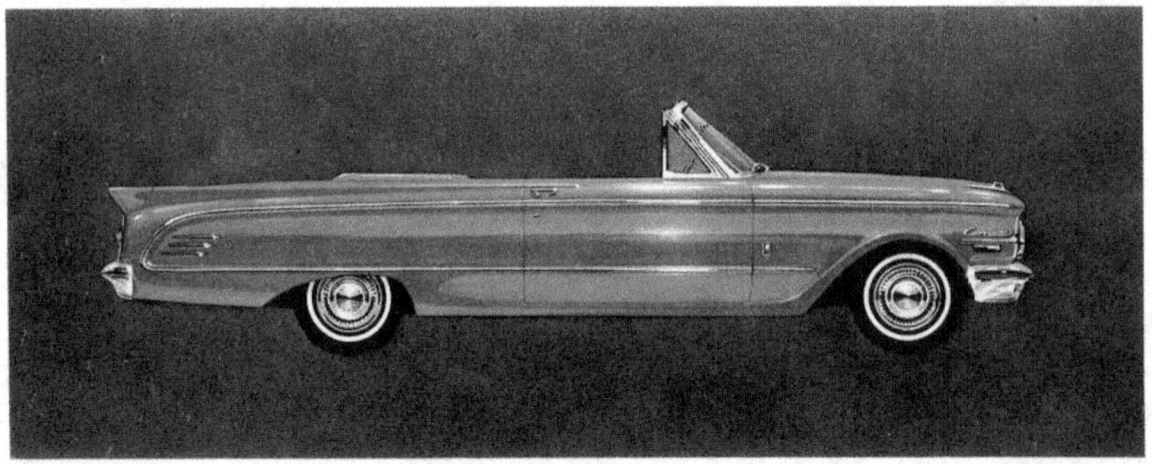

Mercury Comet Custom convertible

There are eleven Mercury Montereys

The S-55 convertible
The S-55 two-door hardtop
The Custom convertible
The Custom two-door hardtop
The Custom four-door hardtop
The Custom four-door sedan
The two-door hardtop
The four-door hardtop
The two-door sedan
The four-door sedan
The Colony Park station wagon*

*Available in six- or nine-passenger models.

There are nine Mercury Meteors

The S-33 two-door hardtop
The Custom two-door hardtop
The Custom two-door sedan
The Custom four-door sedan
The two-door sedan
The four-door sedan
The Custom Country Cruiser station wagon*
The Custom four-door station wagon*
The four-door station wagon*

*Available with optional foam 3rd-seat cushions.

There are twelve Mercury Comets

The S-22 convertible
The S-22 two-door
The Custom convertible
The Custom two-door sedan
The Custom four-door sedan
The two-door sedan
The four-door sedan
The Custom Villager station wagon
The Custom two-door station wagon
The Custom four-door station wagon
The two-door station wagon
The four-door station wagon

1963 MERCURY COLORS

The 1963 Mercurys are offered in a wide variety of solid and two-tone colors. They include:

Presidential Black
Sultana White
Carnival Red
Black Cherry*
Cascade Blue
Pacific Blue*
Blue Satin*
Scotch Green*
Castilian Gold*
Ocean Turquoise*
Jamaica Yellow**
Pink Frost*
Champagne
Desert Frost*
Peacock Turquoise

*Metallic color
**Available on Mercury Monterey only

Visit your nearby Mercury dealer soon and select the color you like best. He will arrange to have your new Mercury colored for you (using durable Super-Enamel paint).

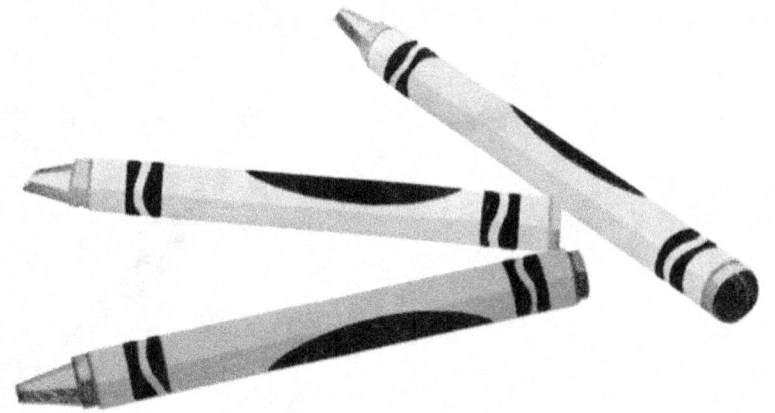

PRODUCTS OF 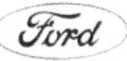 MOTOR COMPANY

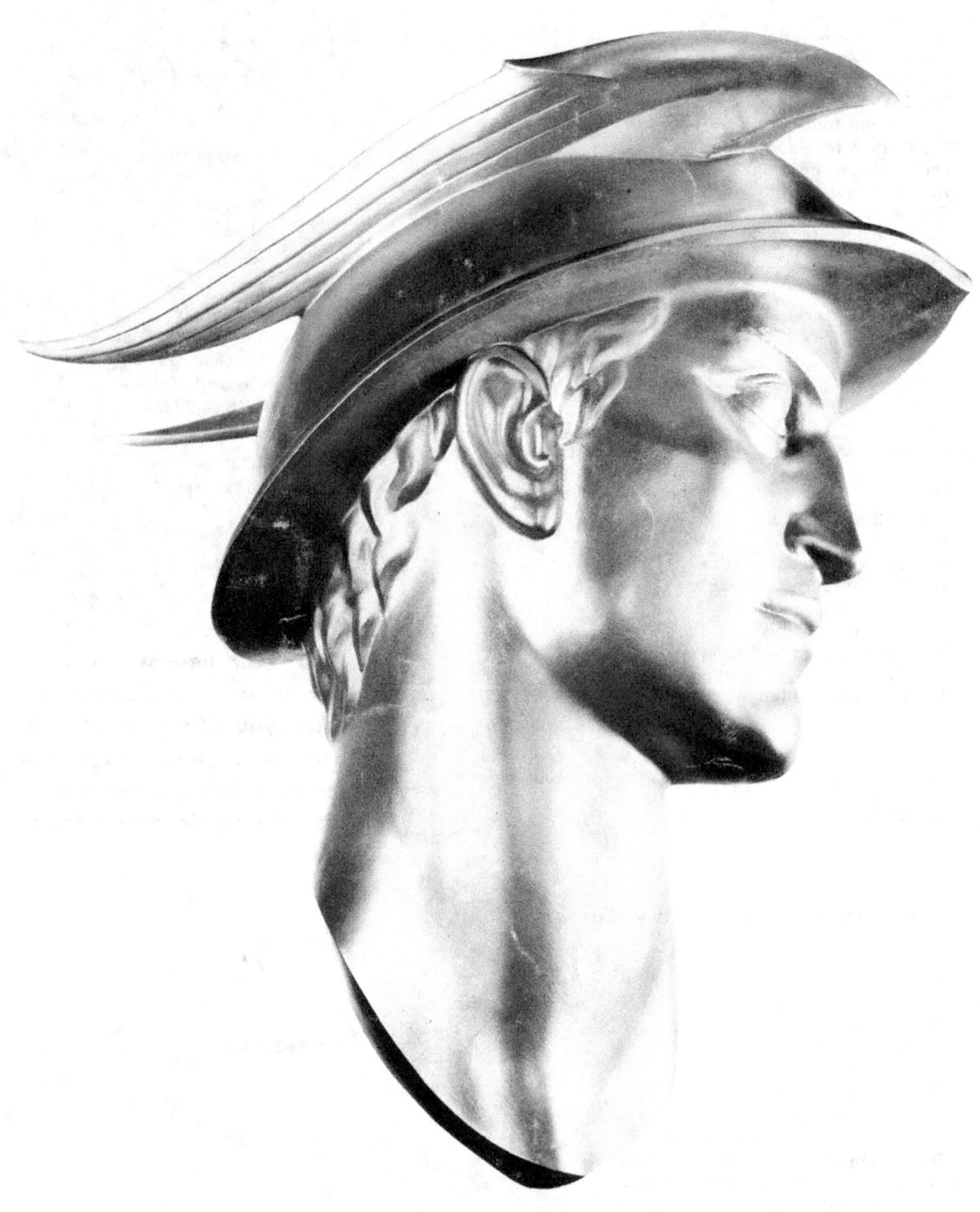

THE
SKIER'S
COLORING BOOK

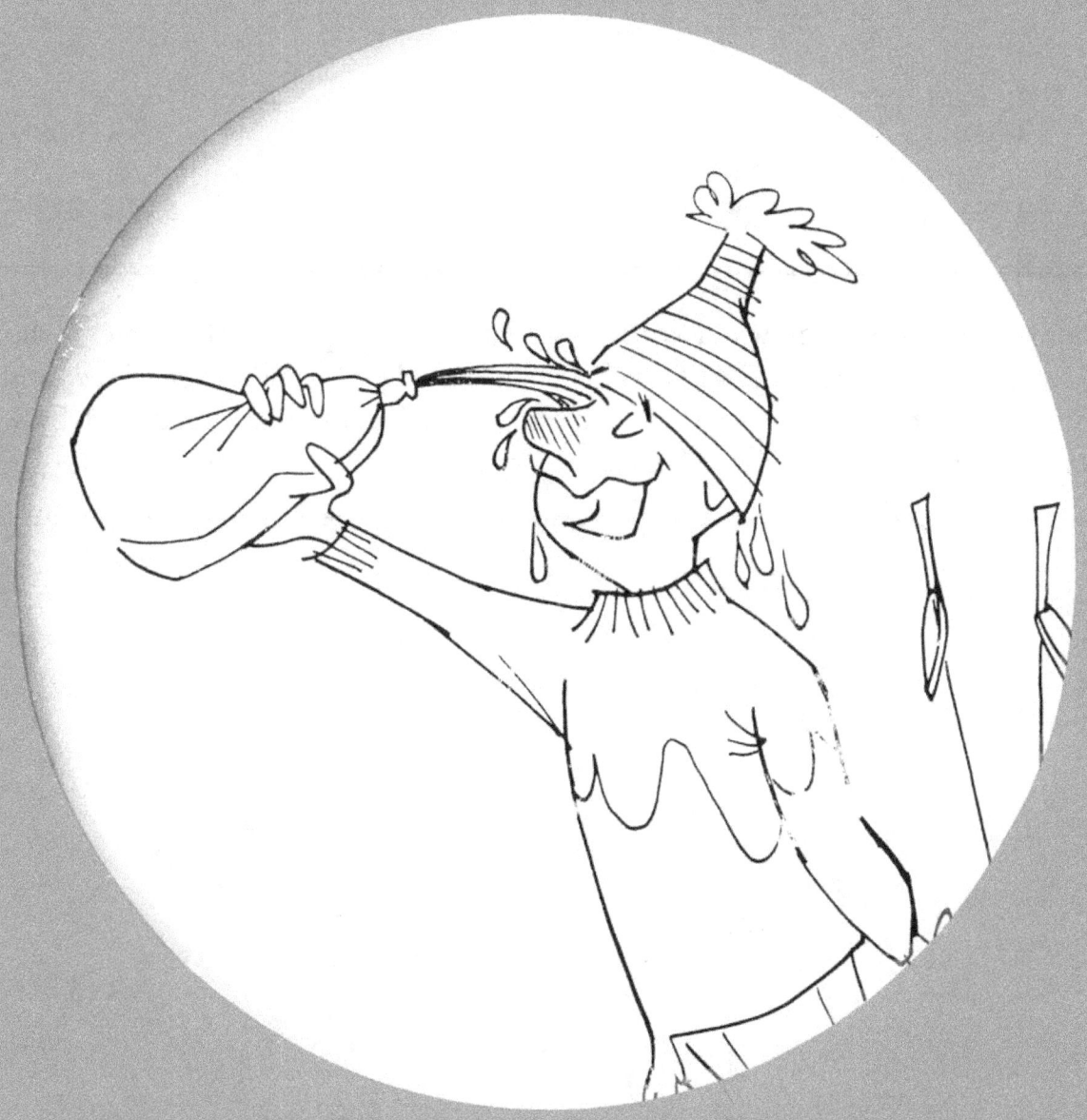

TWO USELESS FEATURES:

- **WAY OUT GLOSSARY OF SKI TERMS**
- **DO'S AND DON'TS FOR WOULD BE SKIERS**

213

Cartoonist Gabe Josephson was a World War II vet and Purple Heart recepient who fought at the Battle of the Bulge. His art clients included Disney and *Sesame Street*, and he provided illustrations and cartoons for everything from books aimed at Hebrew school students to the *New York Times Book Review*.

THE
SKIER'S
COLORING BOOK

Illustrated by GABE JOSEPHSON

SKIERS ARE WONDERFUL PEOPLE.
THEY ARE SO COURAGEOUS... SO WHOLESOME...
SO FANATICAL... SUCH SCREWBALLS.
TO BE A GOOD SKIER, YOU MUST DEDICATE YOURSELF.
INSTEAD, I AM DEDICATING THIS BOOK
TO EACH AND EVERY SKIER,
WHEREVER HE MAY BE.

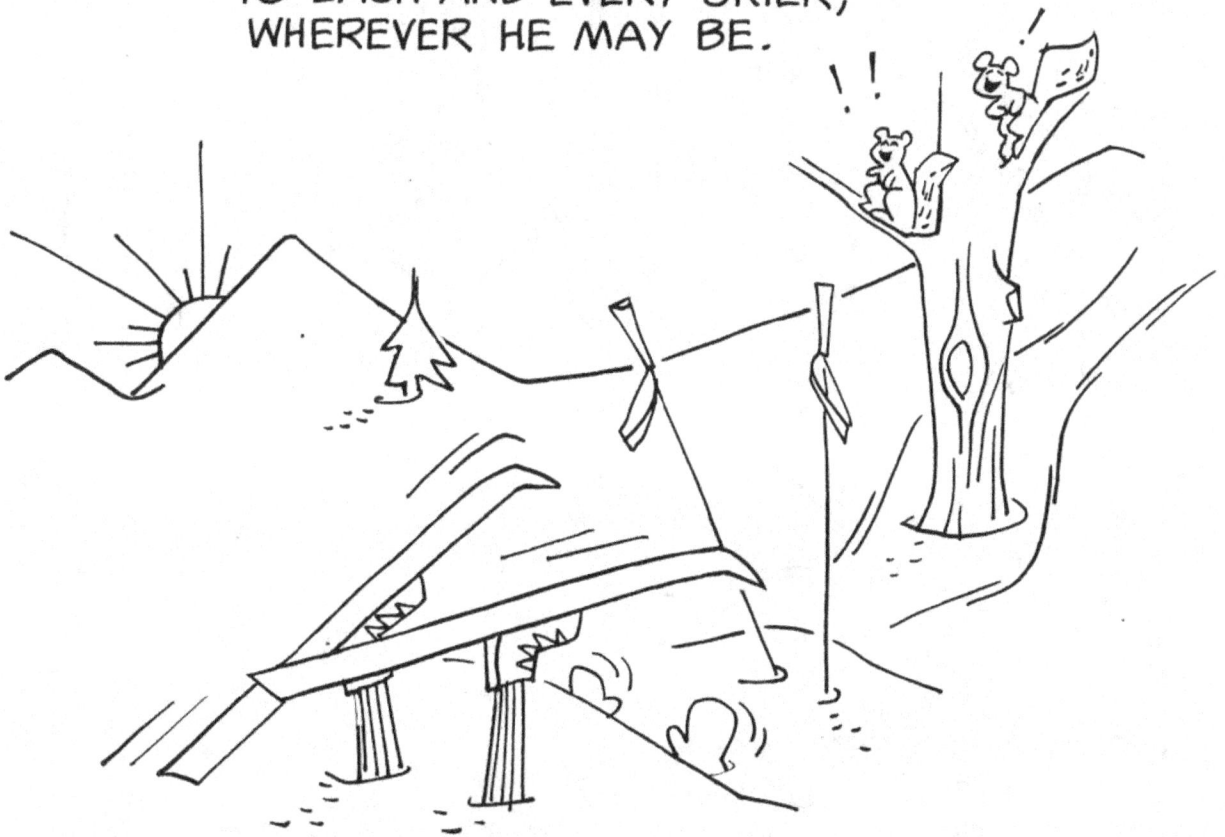

SKIING OFTEN GIVES ONE A NEW PERSPECTIVE OF THE WORLD.

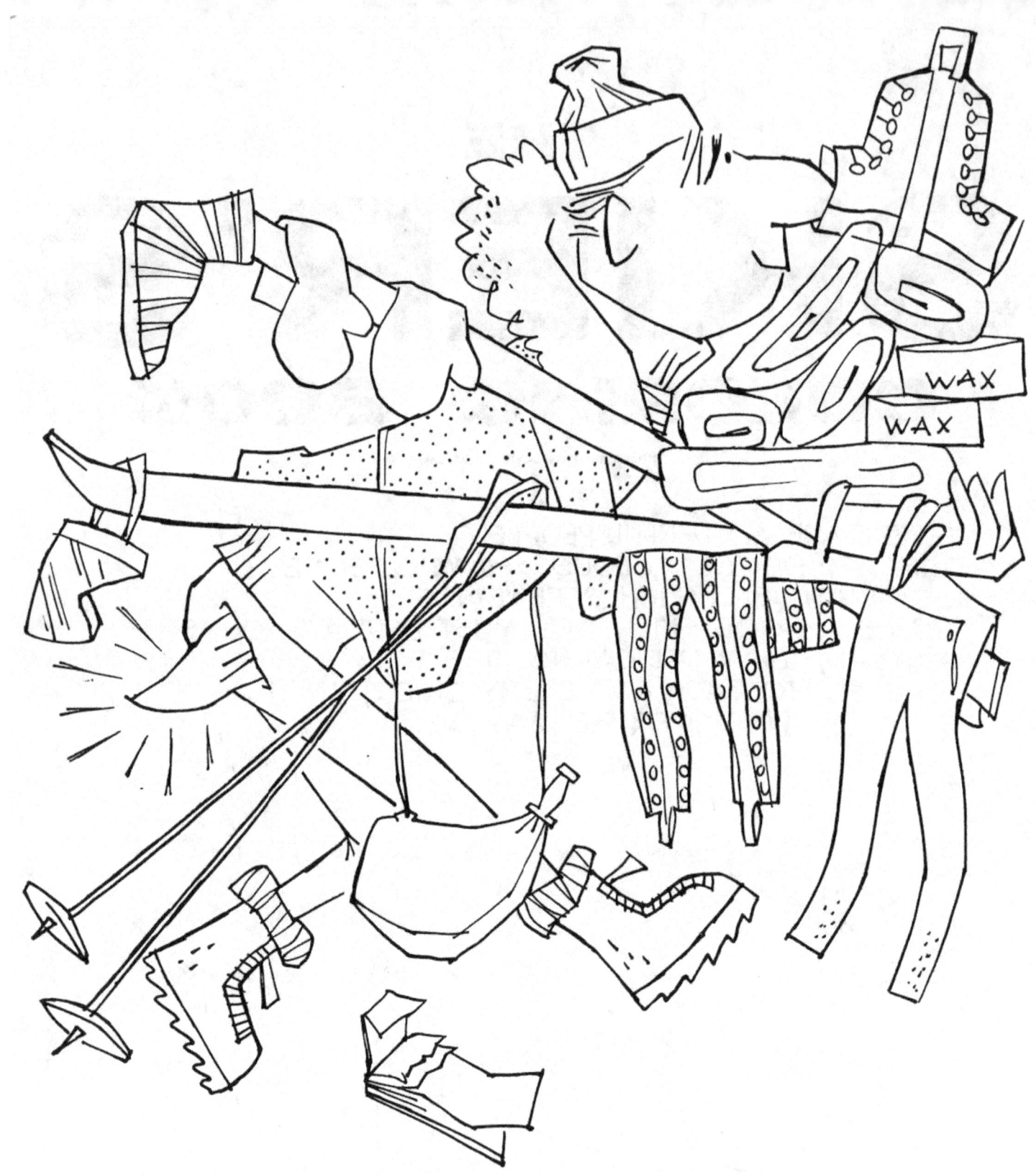

SKIING IS A MODEST SPORT.
THIS IS A SKIER'S EQUIPMENT.
SEE MY POLES... SEE MY SKIS... SEE MY SWEATER... AND
MY PARKAS... AND MY MITTS... AND MY BOOTS... AND MY
SOCKS... AND MY INSULATED UNDERWEAR... AND MY
GOGGLES... MY WAXES...
COLOR MY POCKETS EMPTY.

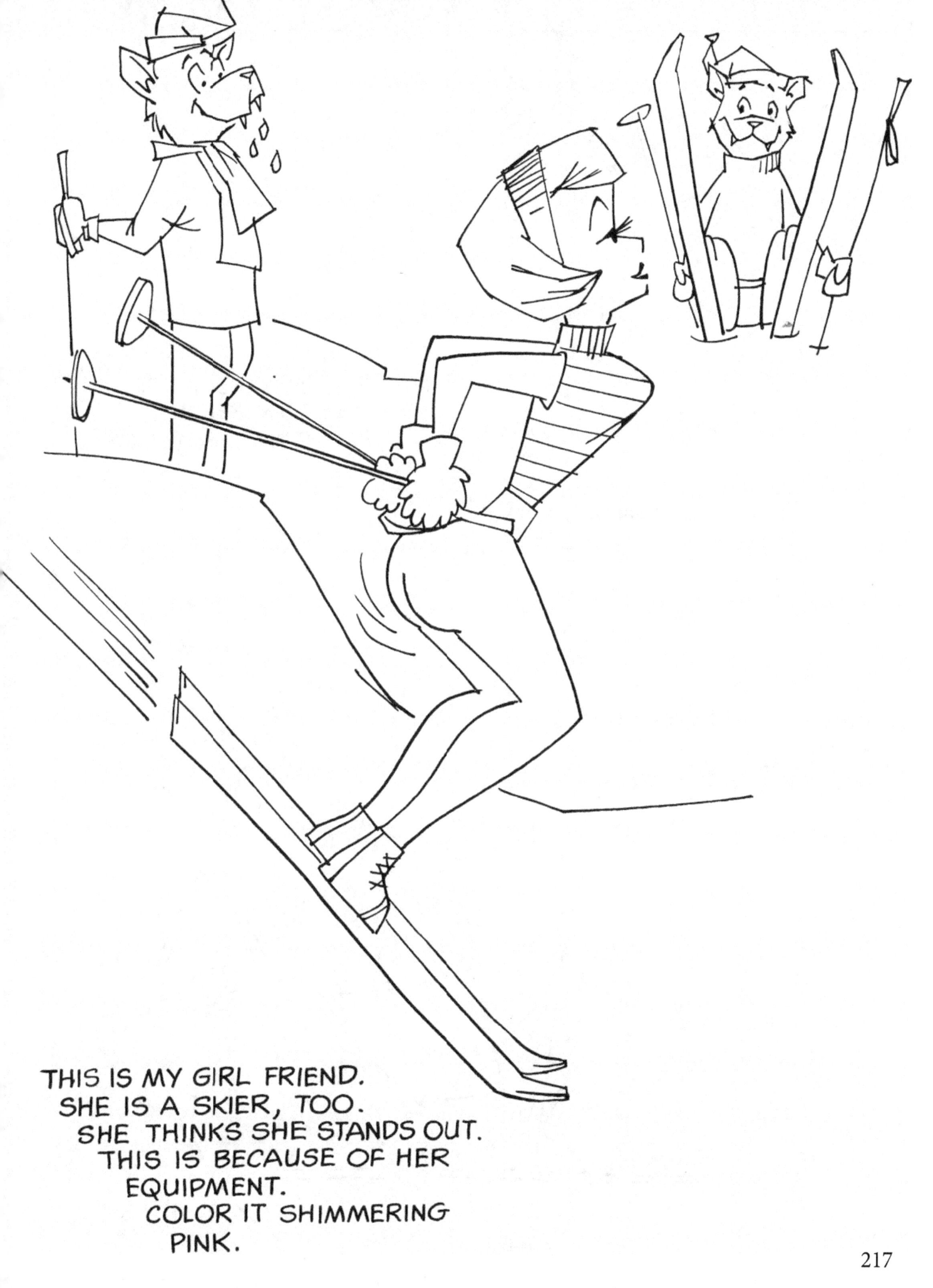

THIS IS MY GIRL FRIEND.
SHE IS A SKIER, TOO.
SHE THINKS SHE STANDS OUT.
THIS IS BECAUSE OF HER
EQUIPMENT.
COLOR IT SHIMMERING
PINK.

217

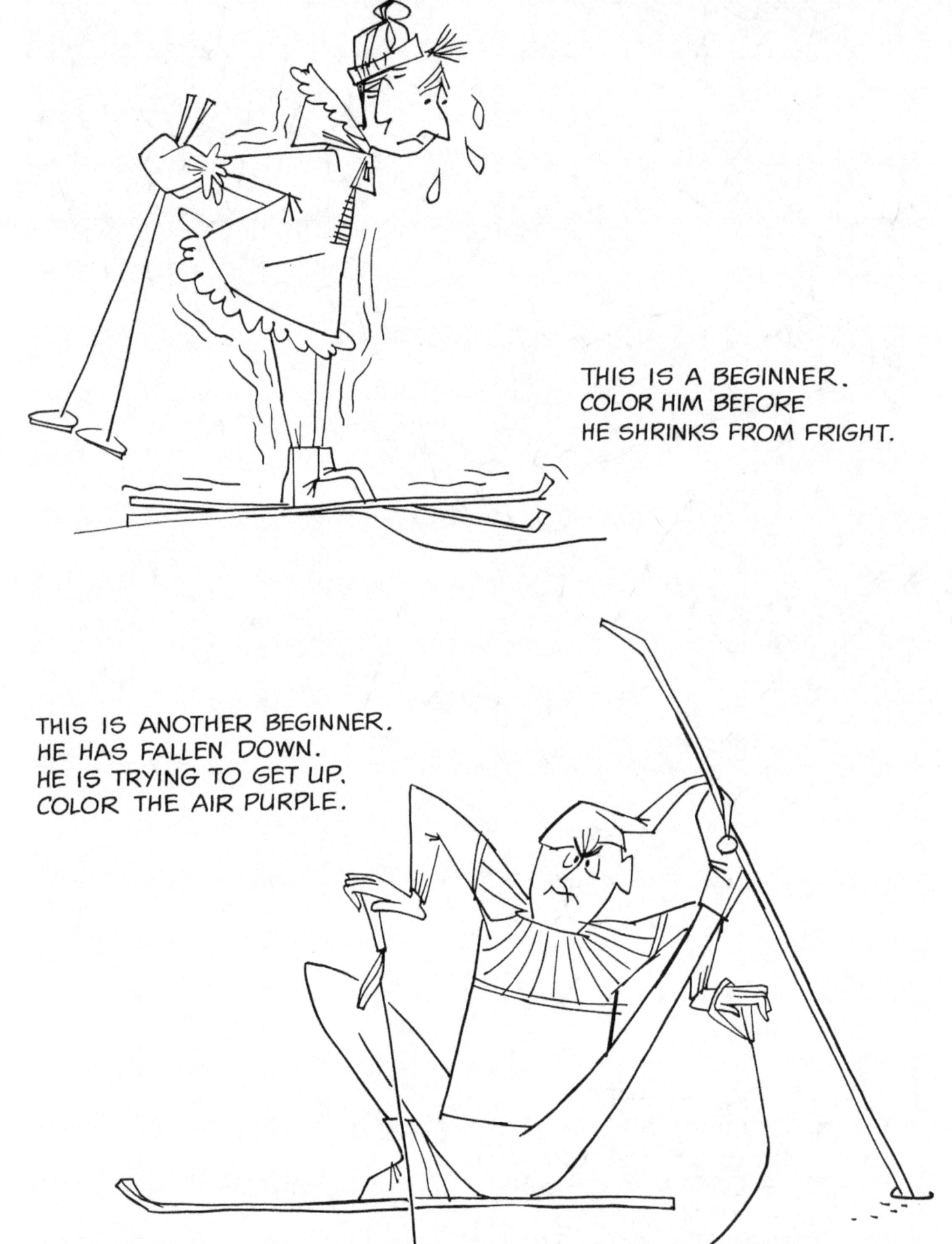

THIS IS A BEGINNER.
COLOR HIM BEFORE
HE SHRINKS FROM FRIGHT.

THIS IS ANOTHER BEGINNER.
HE HAS FALLEN DOWN.
HE IS TRYING TO GET UP.
COLOR THE AIR PURPLE.

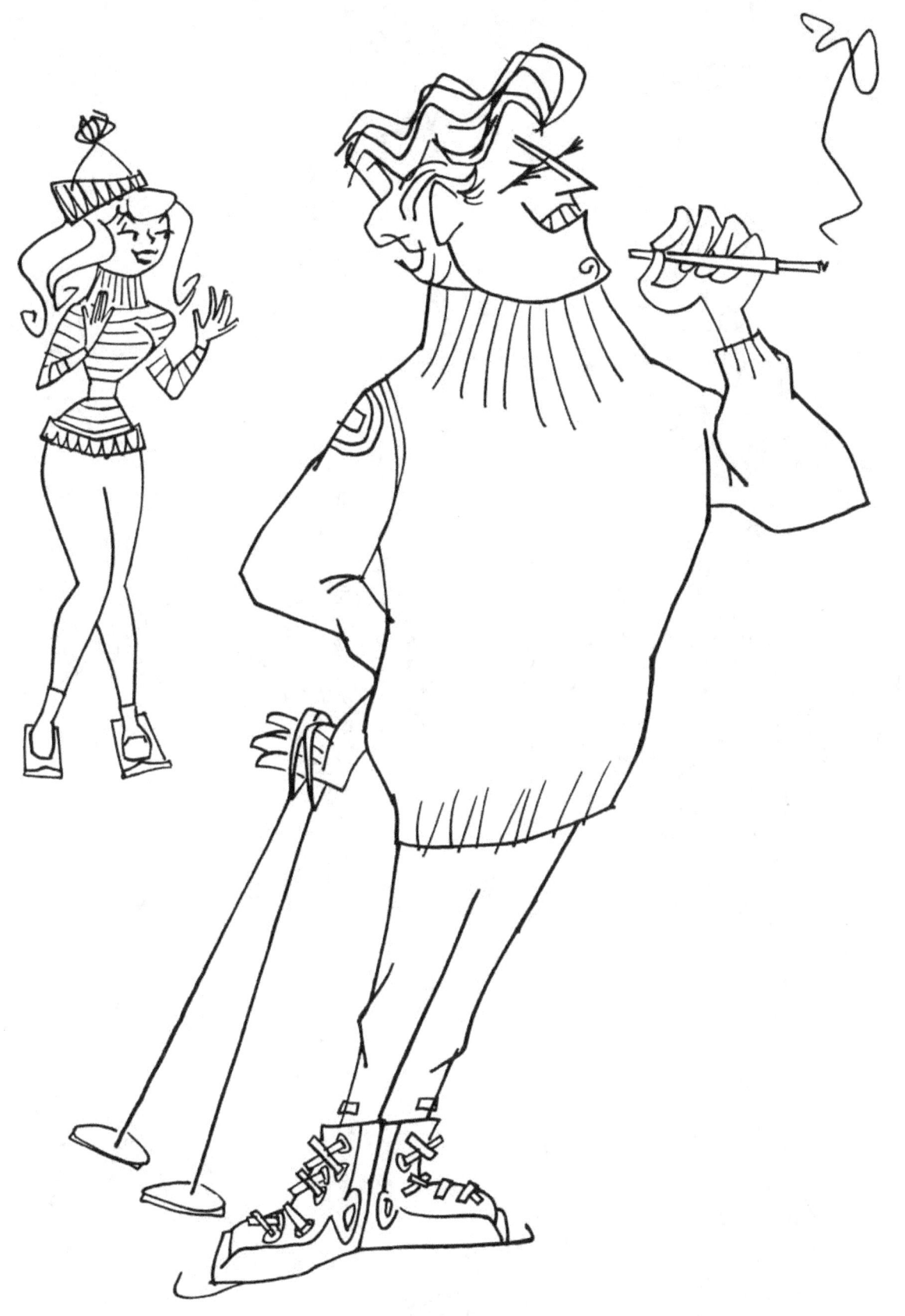

THIS IS A SKI INSTRUCTOR.
NOTICE HIS MODESTY.
DO YOU AGREE WITH HIM THAT HE IS HANDSOME?
MAYBE SOME RICH GIRL WILL AGREE WITH HIM.
HE WOULD LIKE THAT.
COLOR HIS POMPADOUR CAREFULLY.
COLOR HIS EGO ENORMOUS.

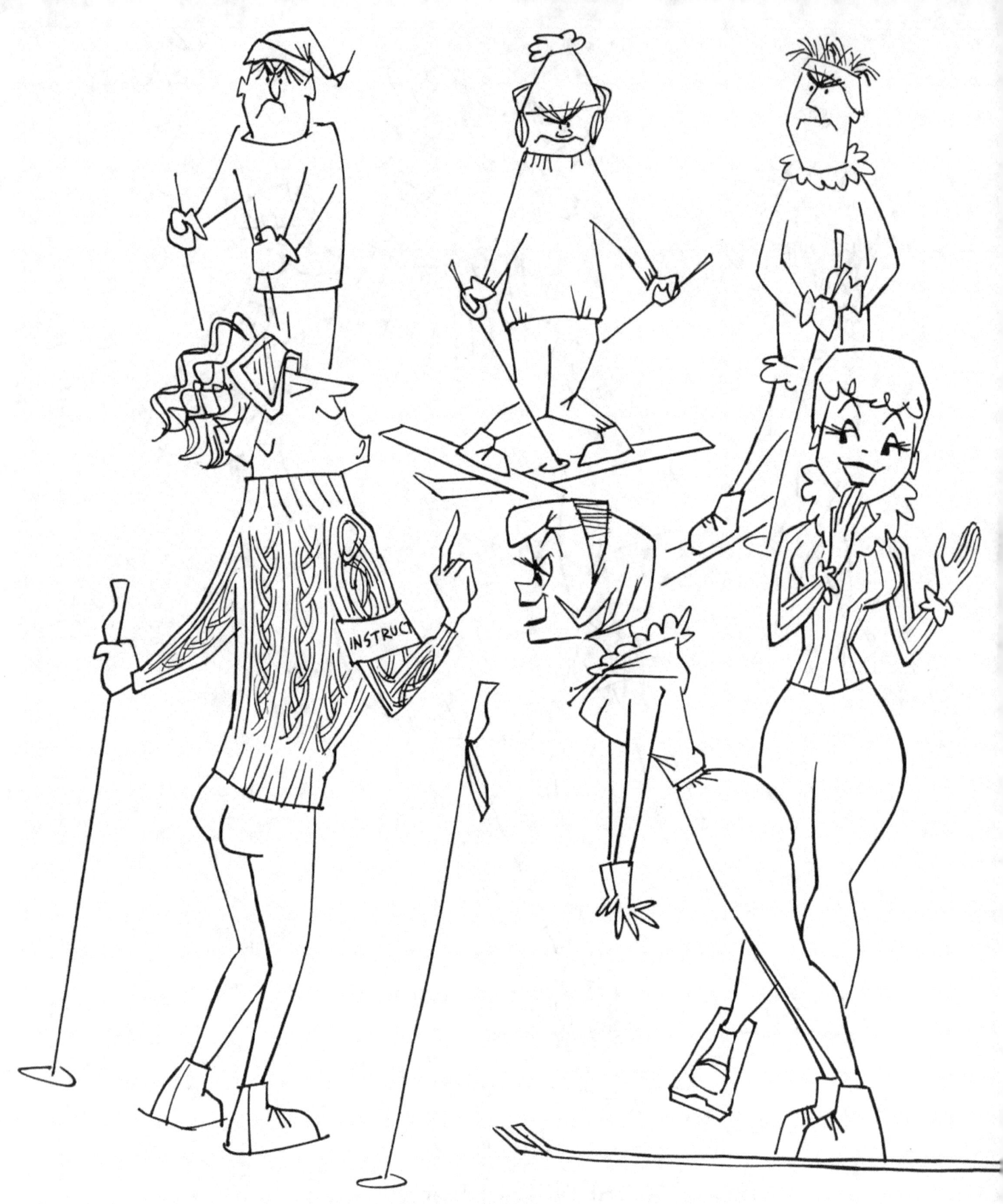

HERE IS A SKI CLASS INSTRUCTOR.
THE GIRLS THINK HE IS DREAMY.
COLOR THEIR EYES BEDROOM.
THE MEN THINK TO THEMSELVES.
COLOR THEIR HEARTS BLACK.

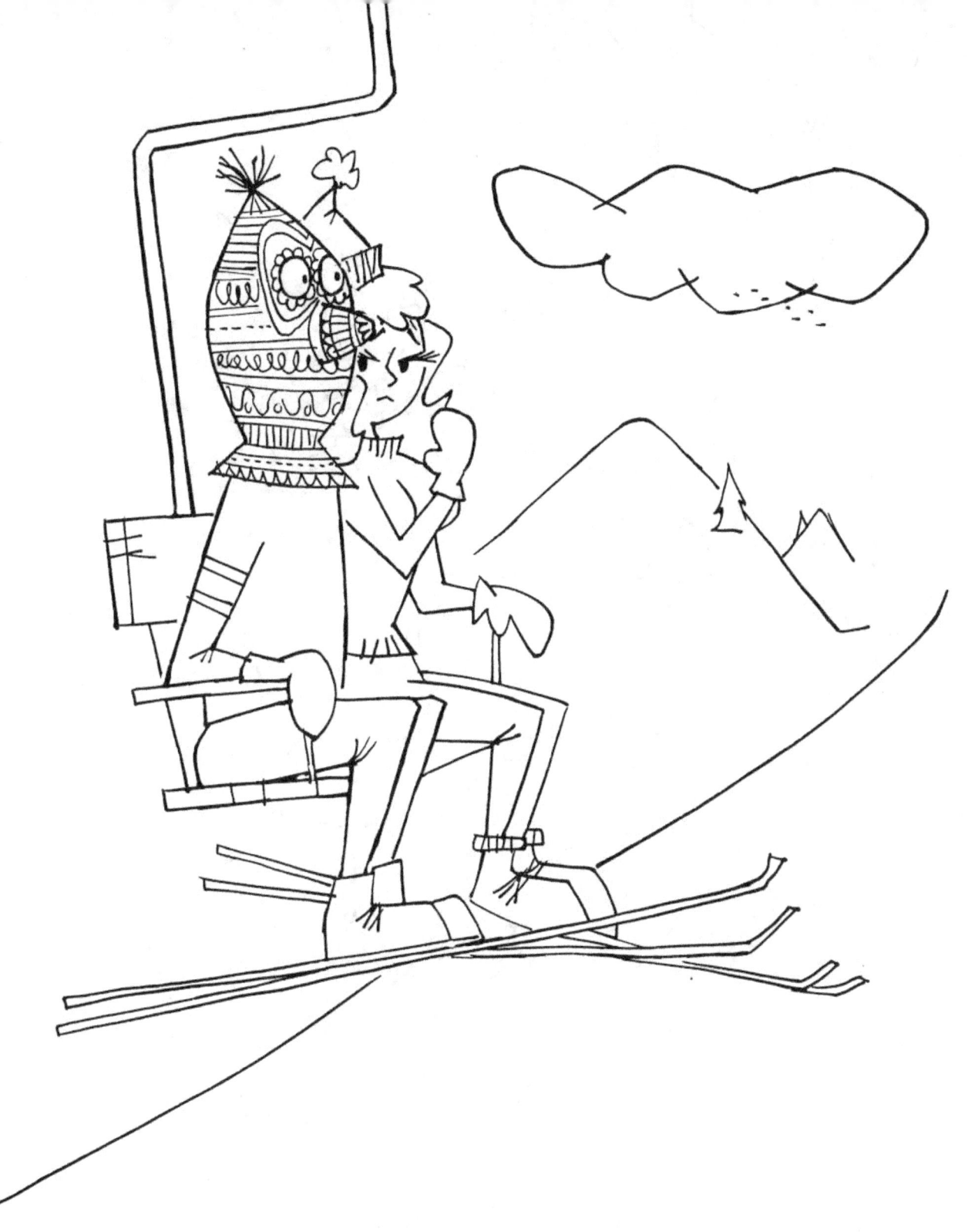

THIS CHARACTER IS WEARING A PERUVIAN SKIING MASK.
COLOR IT ANY COLOR YOU LIKE.
DO YOU THINK IT IS FUNNY LOOKING?
YOU SHOULD SEE WHAT'S INSIDE IT!

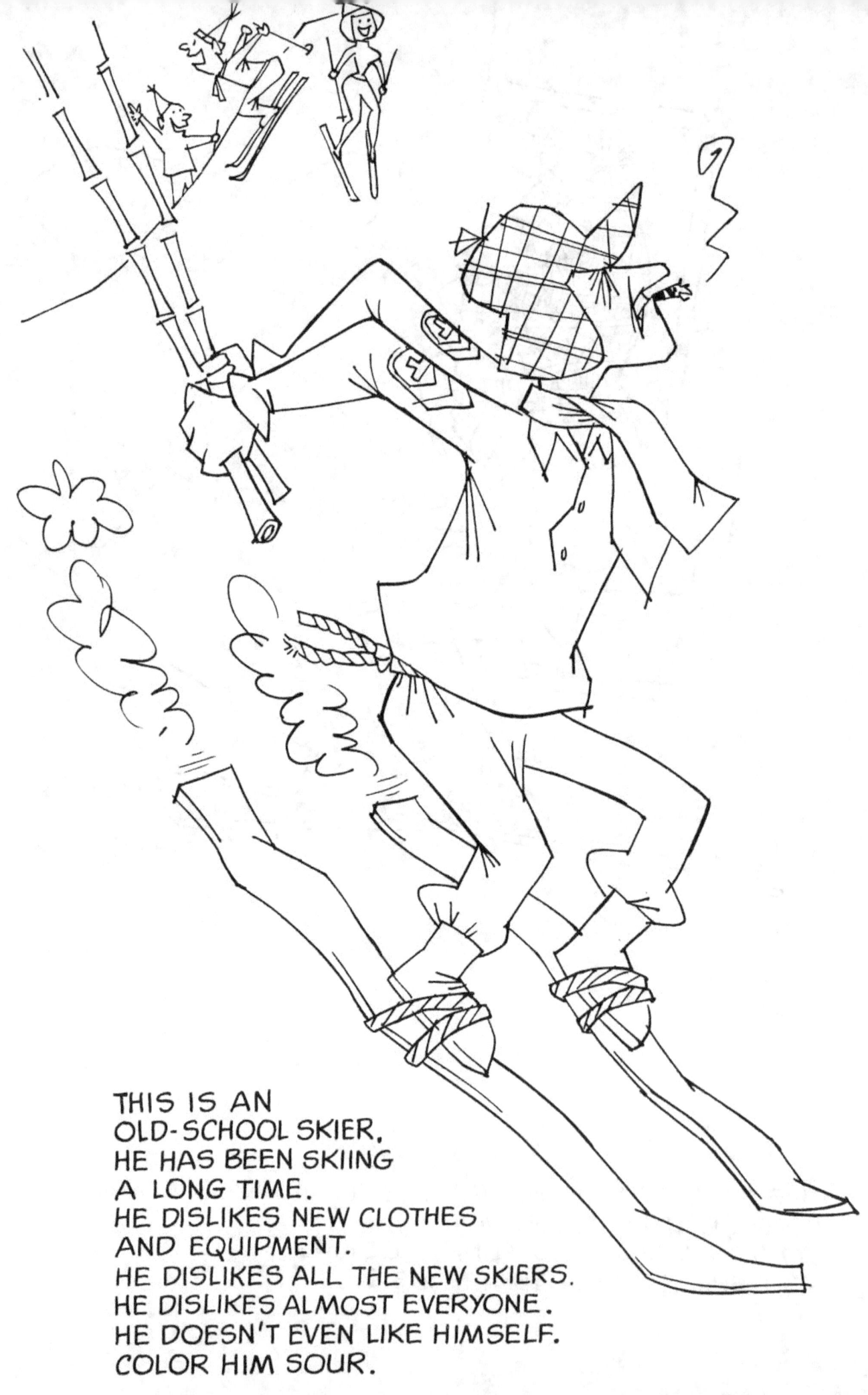

THIS IS AN
OLD-SCHOOL SKIER.
HE HAS BEEN SKIING
A LONG TIME.
HE DISLIKES NEW CLOTHES
AND EQUIPMENT.
HE DISLIKES ALL THE NEW SKIERS.
HE DISLIKES ALMOST EVERYONE.
HE DOESN'T EVEN LIKE HIMSELF.
COLOR HIM SOUR.

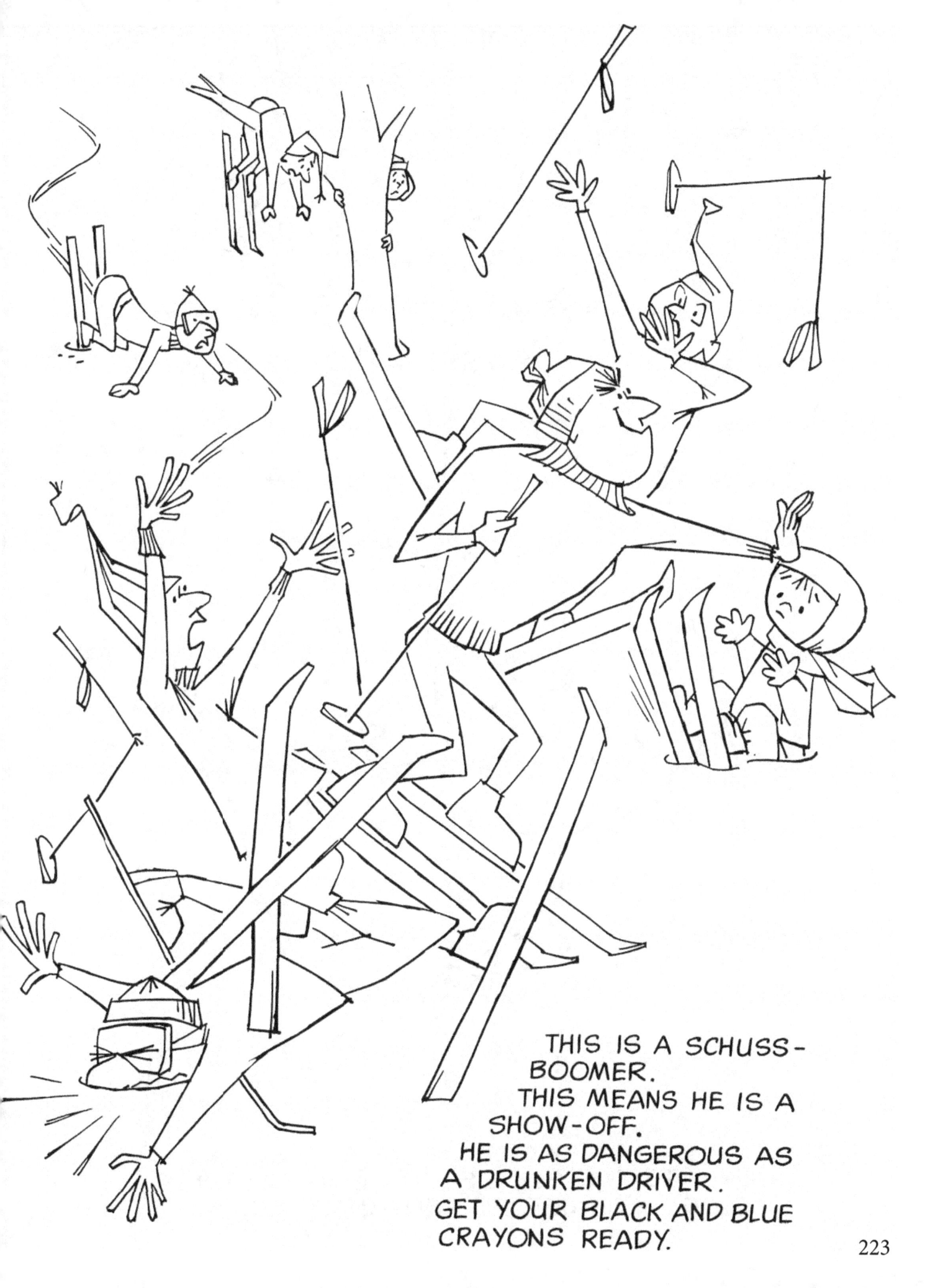

THIS IS A SCHUSS-
BOOMER.
THIS MEANS HE IS A
SHOW-OFF.
HE IS AS DANGEROUS AS
A DRUNKEN DRIVER.
GET YOUR BLACK AND BLUE
CRAYONS READY.

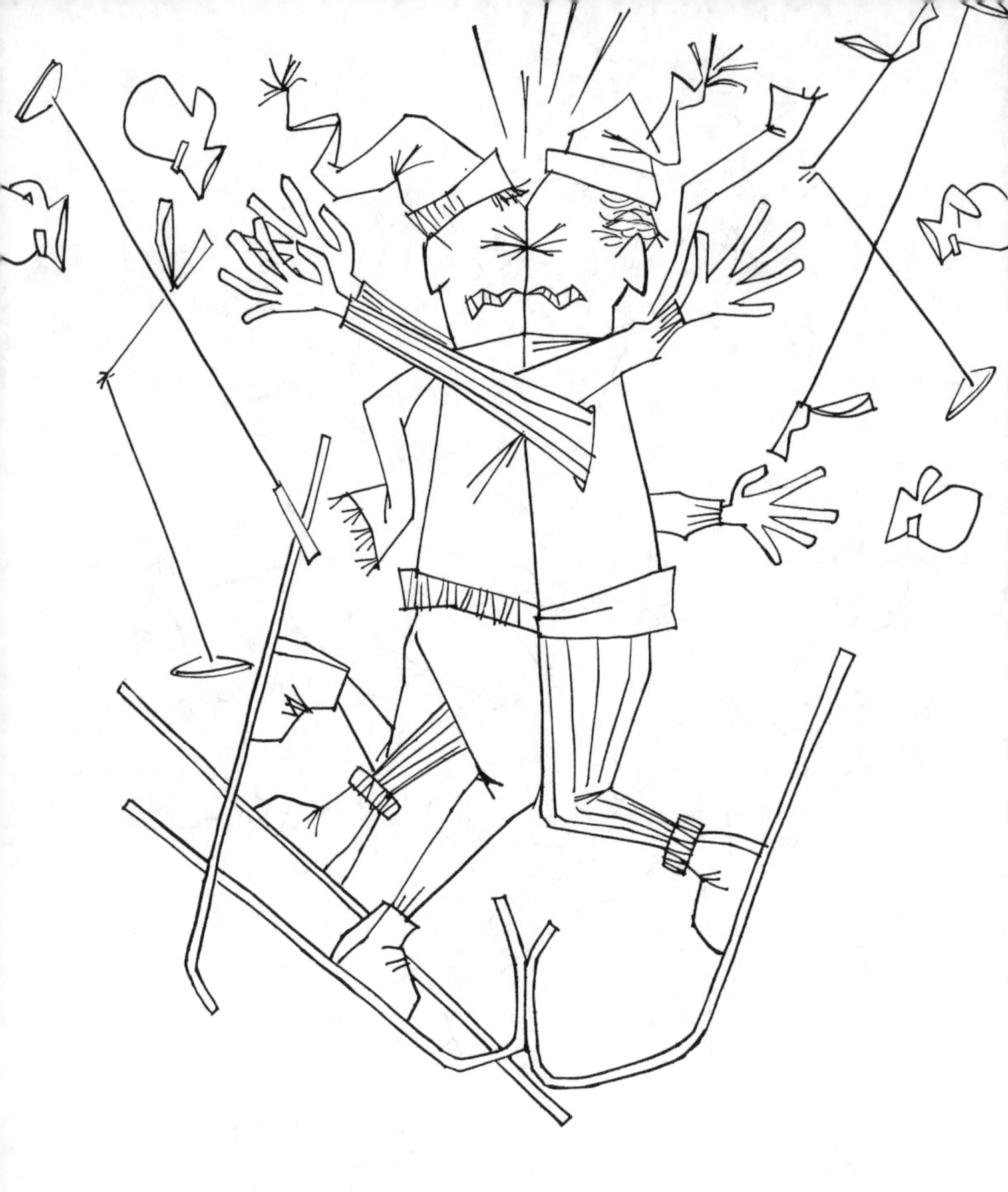

HERE ARE TWO SCHUSS-BOOMERS MEETING.
COLOR THESE HEROES RED-BLOODIED.

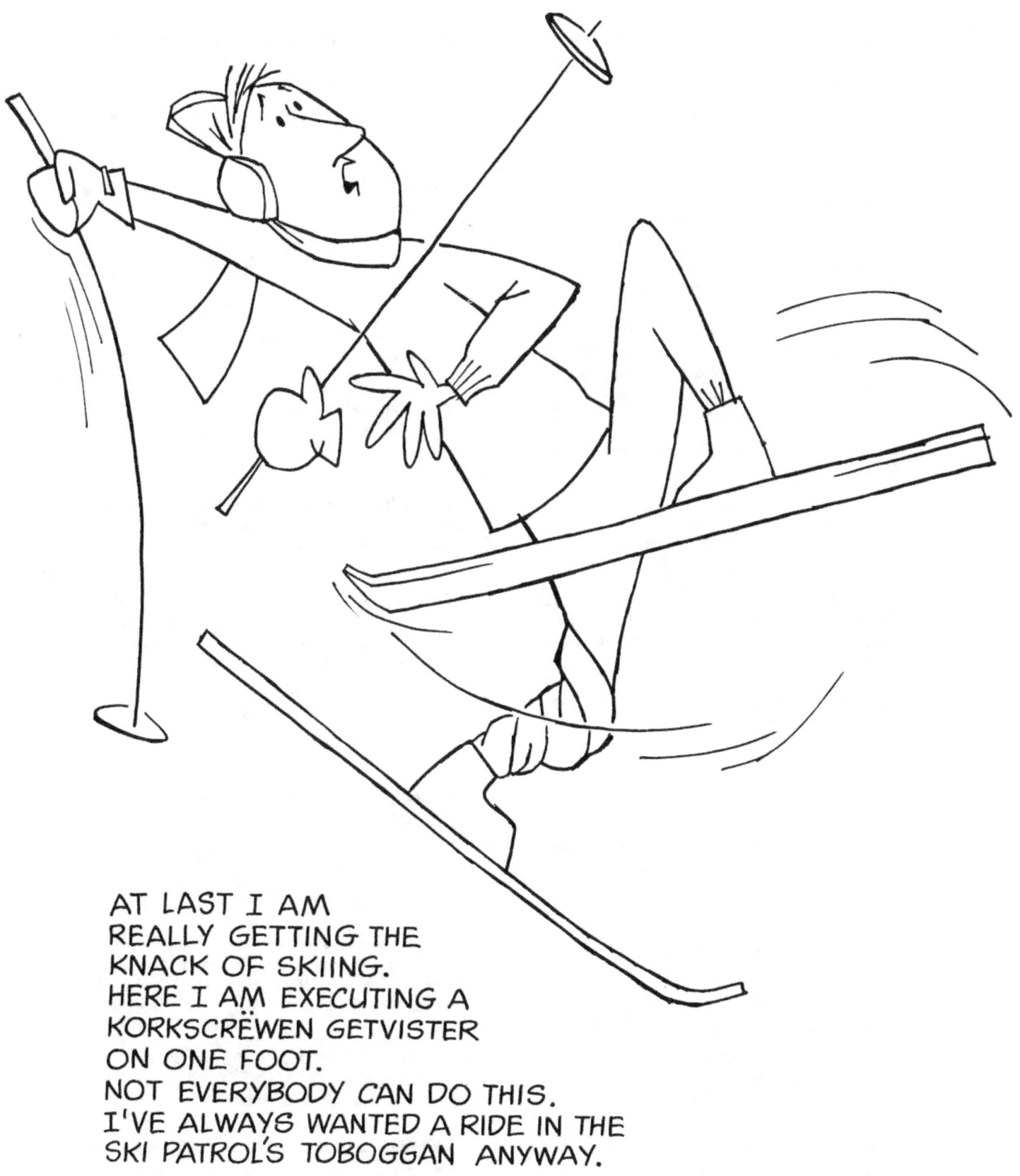

AT LAST I AM
REALLY GETTING THE
KNACK OF SKIING.
HERE I AM EXECUTING A
KORKSCRËWEN GETVISTER
ON ONE FOOT.
NOT EVERYBODY CAN DO THIS.
I'VE ALWAYS WANTED A RIDE IN THE
SKI PATROL'S TOBOGGAN ANYWAY.

GLOSSARY OF *Way-out* SKI TERMS

Aprés Ski: Generalized adjective covering a multitude of sins, most of them expensive, fattening or immoral.

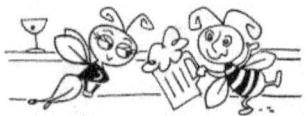

Bar-Flies: As in the case of the mosquito, the female's diet requires some fresh blood whereas the male subsists largely on sugarous liquids usually derived from malt, sugar cane, rye, etc. The female may be distinguished by a greater amount of hair on the cranium and lumps on the sweater, usually two in number. Although largely of nocturnal habits, some sub-species may venture forth by mid-morning, thus evincing atypical activity, and may occasionally be seen at the foot of ski slopes. There is no clearly defined mating season.

Cornice: If you run out of ice for drinks, there are usually icicles at the corner of the lodge.

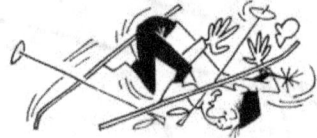

Egg-Beater: Head-over-teakettle spill at high speed. Results in skier (not the egg) feeling well beaten-up. Excellent means of returning home early (in a toboggan).

Expert: Skier who has learned how to make a parallel turn to the right at the end of the lift line.

Glug: Hot spiced wine; useful in case of a leak in your car's cooling system.

Goggles: Apparatus worn on forehead or around neck. Origin of this custom is obscure but it appears to have symbolism of ability as skier.

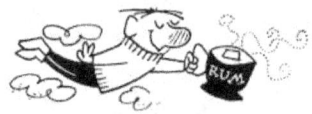

Hot Buttered Rum: The road to Euphoria after a long, cold day of skiing. Handle with care.

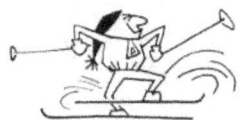

Kick Turn: Ingenious method of maneuvering skis into opposing directions. A favorite of indecisive skiers.

Mambo, Wedlen: Early forerunners of The Twist.

Mogul: Skier who arrives in sports car with glamorous blonde of opposite sex; also refers to hump in the trail.

Reverse Shoulder: Popular method of reaching crowded bar.

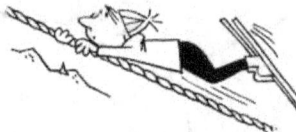

Rope Tow: Medieval torture machine adapted to ski slopes.

Schuss-Boomer: Frustrated Kamikazi pilot. Dangerous as a rattlesnake. Usually ends run in egg-beater.

Scissorbill: Beginning skier with crossed skis and all the other abnormal problems which make normal people wonder why we ski.

Sitzmark: Depression in snow caused by a sit-down fall in which that portion of the anatomy sometimes referred to as "so firm, so round, so fully packed" does the main portion of the excavating.

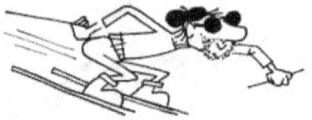

Ski Bum: Beatnik with super-active thyroid.

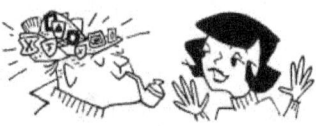

Ski Emblems (and Headwear): Status symbols, particularly when worn on a HAT. (Ski caps are bourgeois; a few special types of lightweight IMPORTED stocking caps with proper tassels are acceptable.)

Ski Train and/or Ski Bus: Lonely Hearts Club on wheels. Also used on return trip for transporting bodies, broken skis, etc.

Skiing Conditions Report:
Excellent: We have plenty of unrented rooms.
Fair: Not many rocks protruding through the ice.
Poor: It may snow; OK if you have other things in mind.

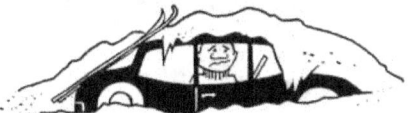

Snow Bunny: Attractive female beginner; most easily approached by offering a helping hand after a tumble. WARNING! When stopping to help, make a graceful turn so that you are face to face. If closer inspection in this position reveals that it is your wife or is not a bona fide Bunny, the ski patrol will probably be along soon anyway.

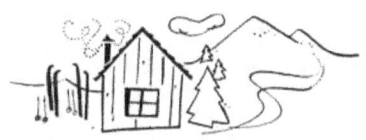

Snow Plow: Devilish device which prevents your being delayed in returning home; also useful in covering over sports cars parked along the road.

Stretch Pants: Proof that the credit for the growing popularity of skiing belongs to the women, God Bless Them!

T-Bar: Mechanized Social Hostess, if your timing is good.

Tea Dance: Serves similar function as warming house but in a much more intimate and crowded manner. Propriety suggests that couples dancing move their feet occasionally, if possible.

Track! FORE!

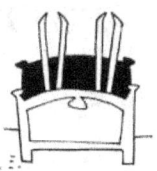

Warming House: A good location for admiring the scenery and making surveys for those who really dislike skiing but have nothing better to do until the bar opens.

SOME VERY SPECIAL TIPS FOR THE BEGINNER

1. Carrying a wine skin is smart appearing. By a slight alteration it will hold your lunch, thus postponing the necessity of starting the downhill run.

2. A camera case may be slung over the other shoulder but be sure to leave the camera home to avoid damage to it and yourself.

3. To avoid excessive tiring, make frequent stops along the trail in a strategic spot where you can be admired, and enjoy the scenery. This also allows the snow to melt off your clothes.

4. Be prepared with some witty sayings for autographing casts on broken legs. Be sure to include your office phone number.

5. Crampons and an ice-axe attached to the *outside* of a well-worn rucksack give an impressive atmosphere to your arrival, which should be timed so that the lobby is well-populated. The rucksack may be filled with telephone books and dark pancake make-up (in case you don't have a sun lamp at home).

6. Ski wax of a number of varieties should always be conspicuously carried. It is useful in fixing squeaky doors.

DON'T EVER...
Wear socks outside ski pants.
Kick tea dancers on the shins while wearing ski boots.
Wear baggy pants.
Use a ski class as a slalom course.
Bring your mother-in-law.
Wear skis to bed.

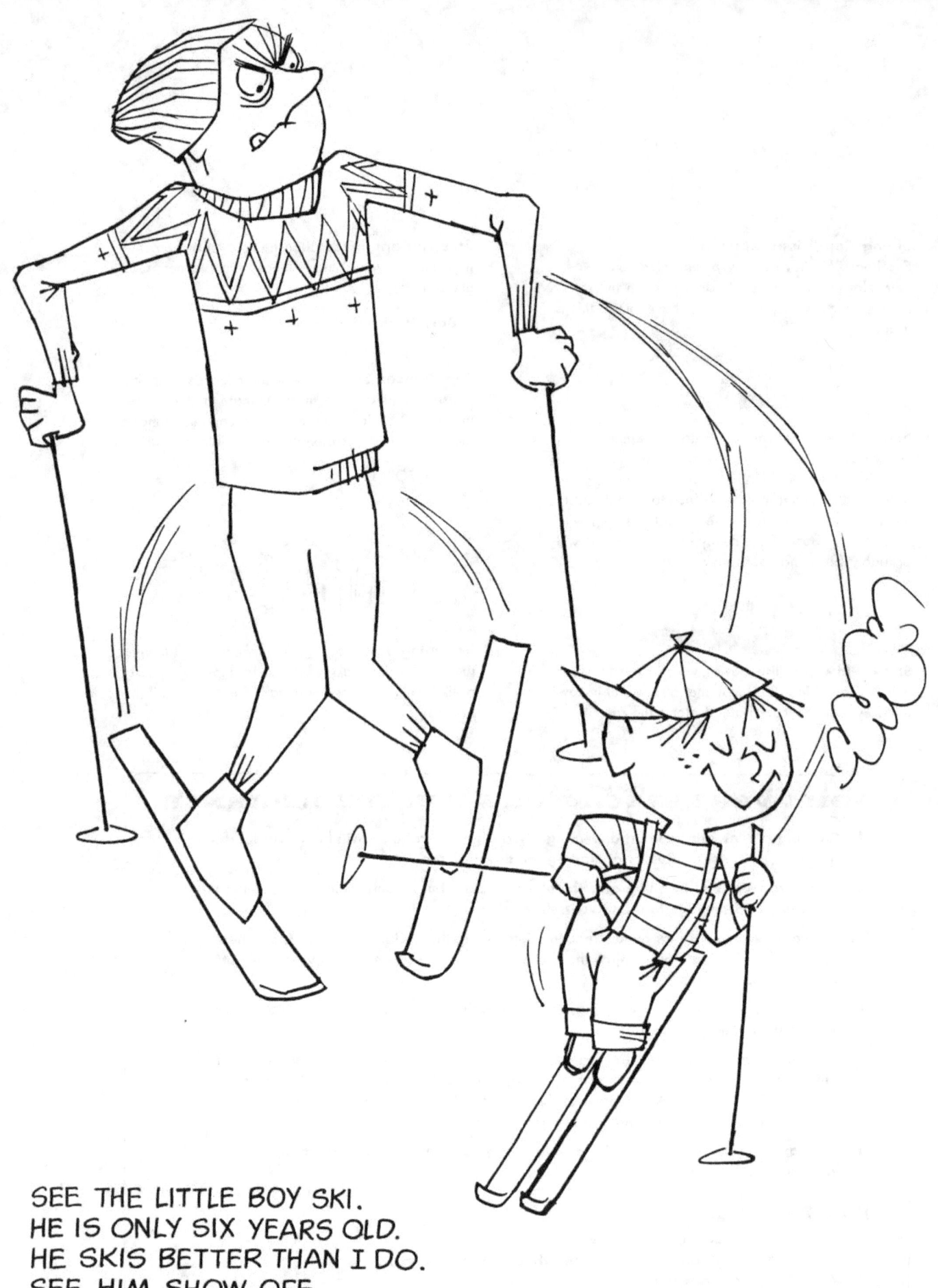

SEE THE LITTLE BOY SKI.
HE IS ONLY SIX YEARS OLD.
HE SKIS BETTER THAN I DO.
SEE HIM SHOW OFF.
HE'S A ROTTEN KID.

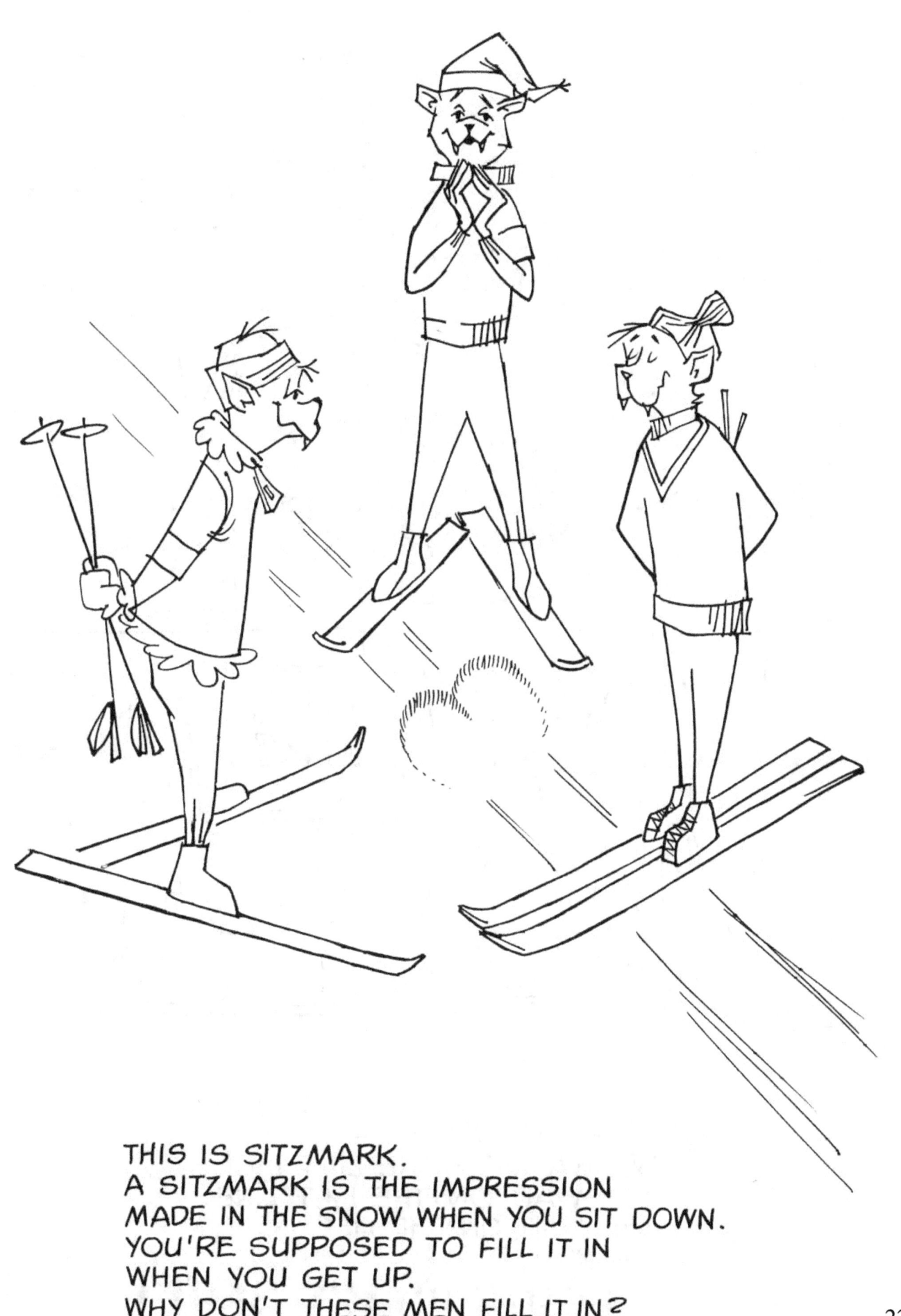

THIS IS SITZMARK.
A SITZMARK IS THE IMPRESSION
MADE IN THE SNOW WHEN YOU SIT DOWN.
YOU'RE SUPPOSED TO FILL IT IN
WHEN YOU GET UP.
WHY DON'T THESE MEN FILL IT IN?

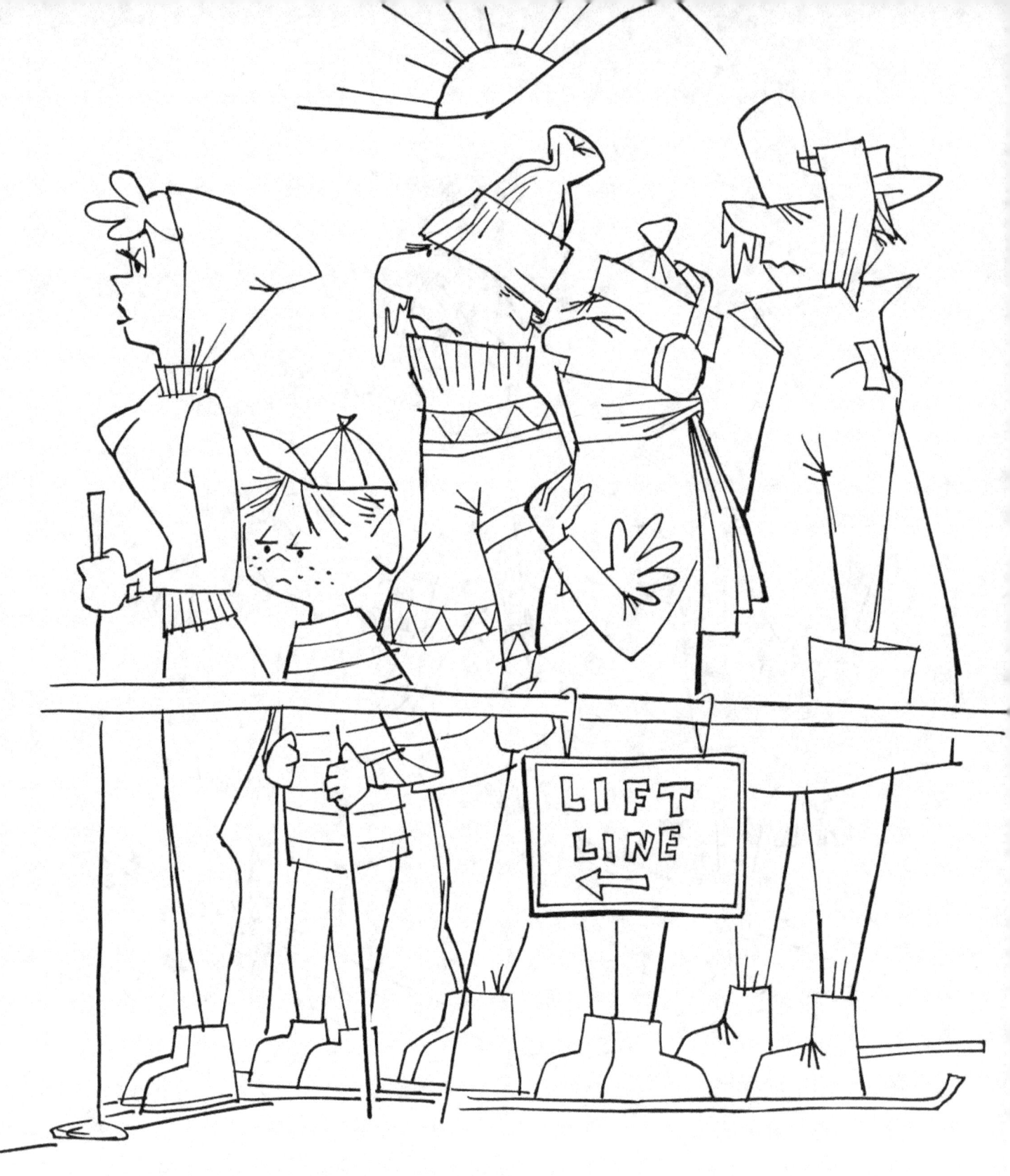

THIS IS A LIFT LINE.
WE WAIT ON THE LIFT LINE.
WE WAIT ON THE LIFT LINE.
WE WAIT ON THE LIFT LINE.
WE WAIT ON THE LIFT LINE.

COLOR US ICY BLUE!

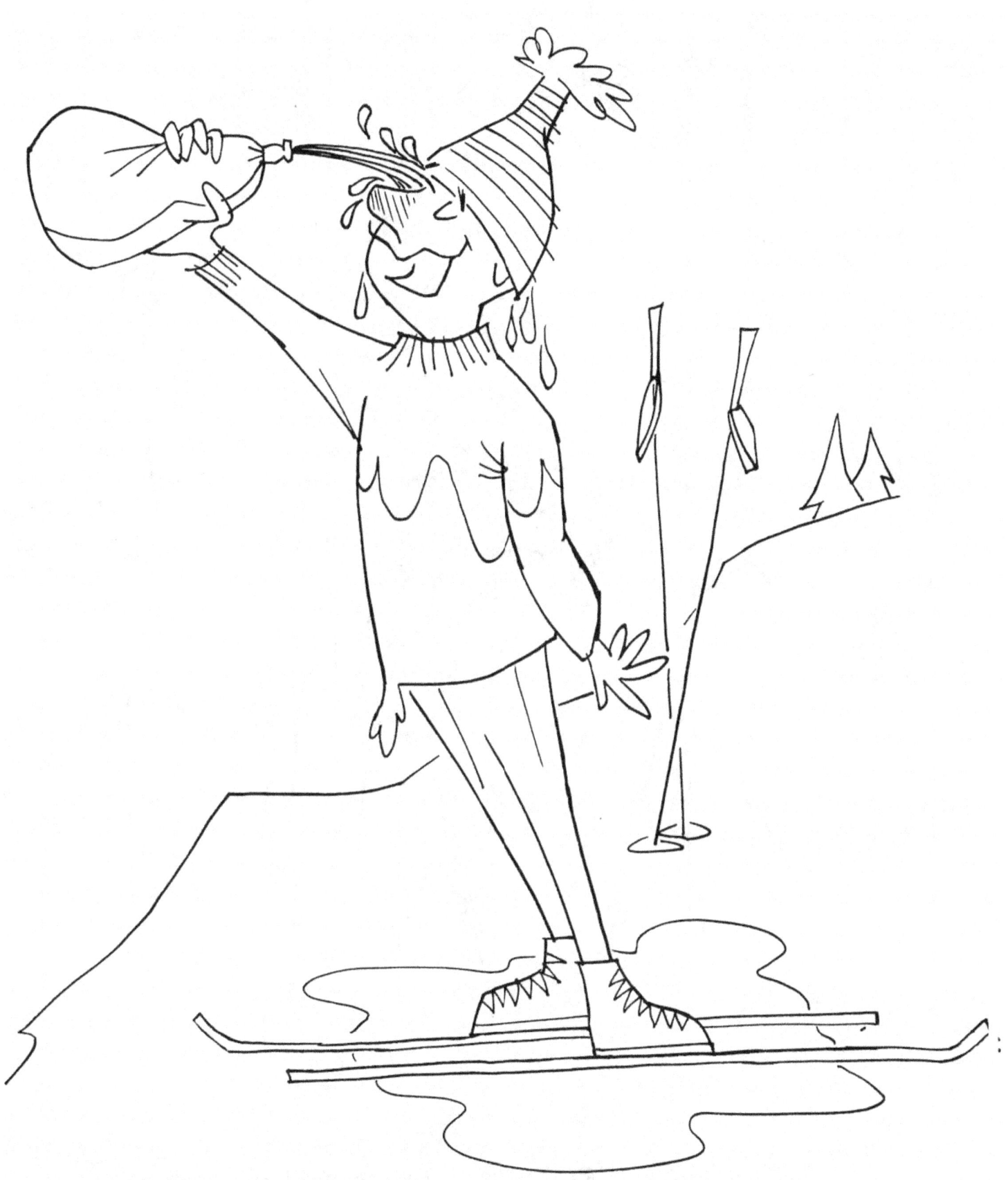

THIS IS A WINESKIN.
ALL GOOD SKIERS KNOW
HOW TO DRINK FROM A WINESKIN.
IT IS EASHY TO DRINK FROM A WINESHKIN.
COLOR MY FACE SHPOTTED BURGUNDY.

231

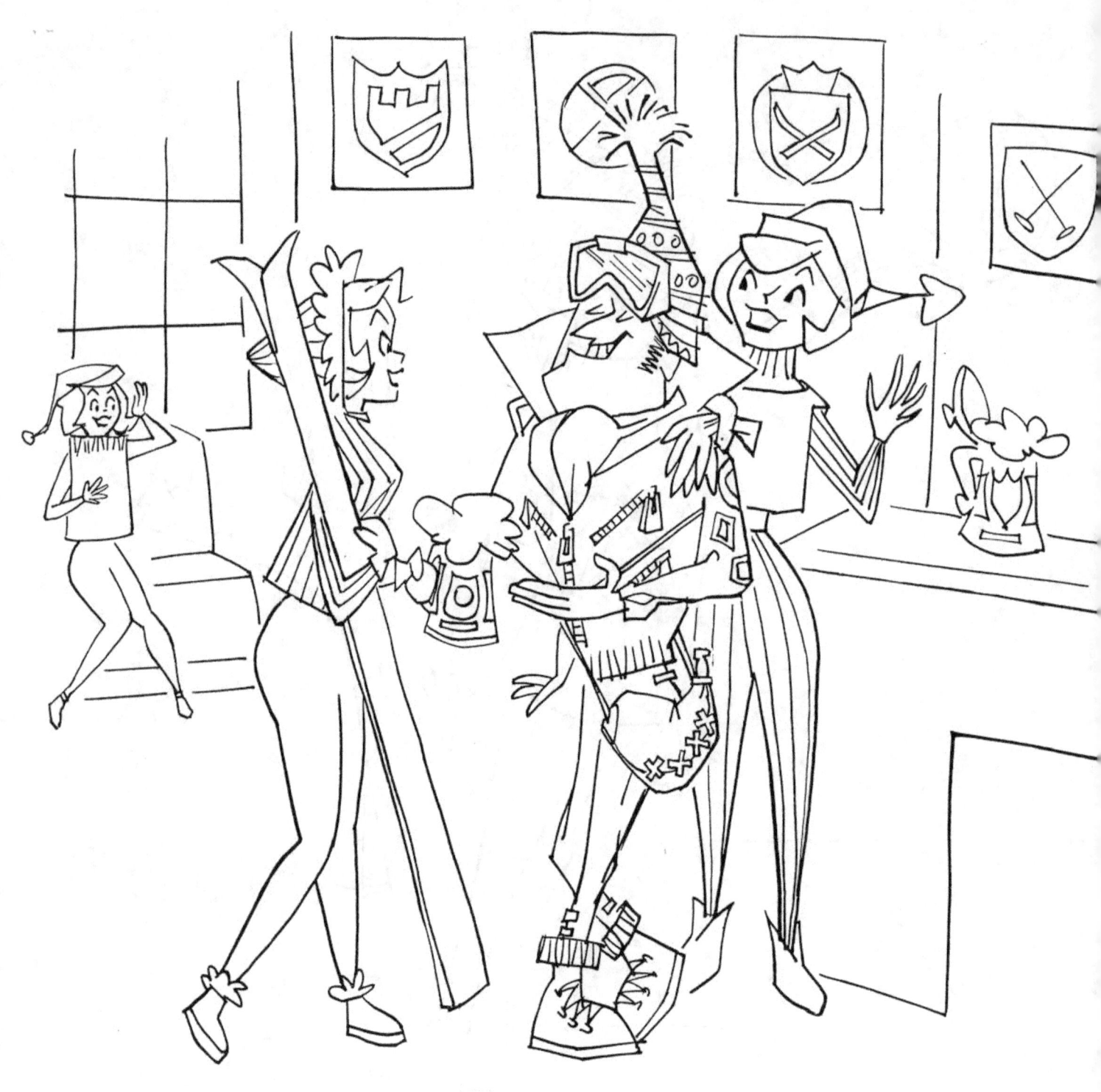

THIS SKIER IS PRACTICING SKIMANSHIP.
HE TALKS MUCH AND SKIS LITTLE.
HE ALSO DRESSES IN THE LATEST FASHIONS.
COLOR HIM PEACOCK.
DO NOT COLOR HIS SKIS.
HE DOES NOT OWN ANY.

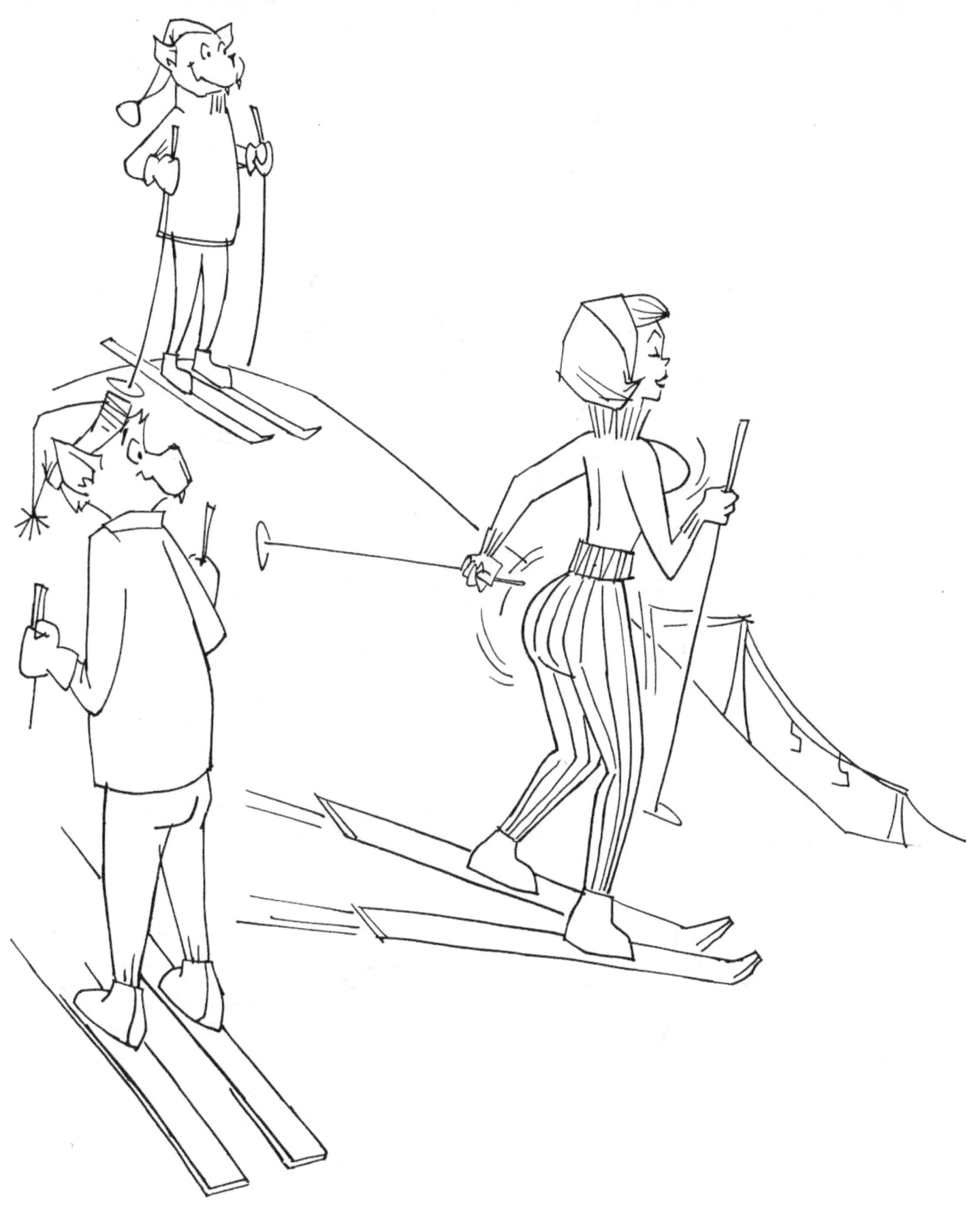

A FAVORITE SKI TECHNIQUE IS WEDELN.
TO WEDELN MEANS TO WIGGLE.
HERE IS A REAL EXPERT.
I WONDER IF SHE'D GIVE ME A LESSON?

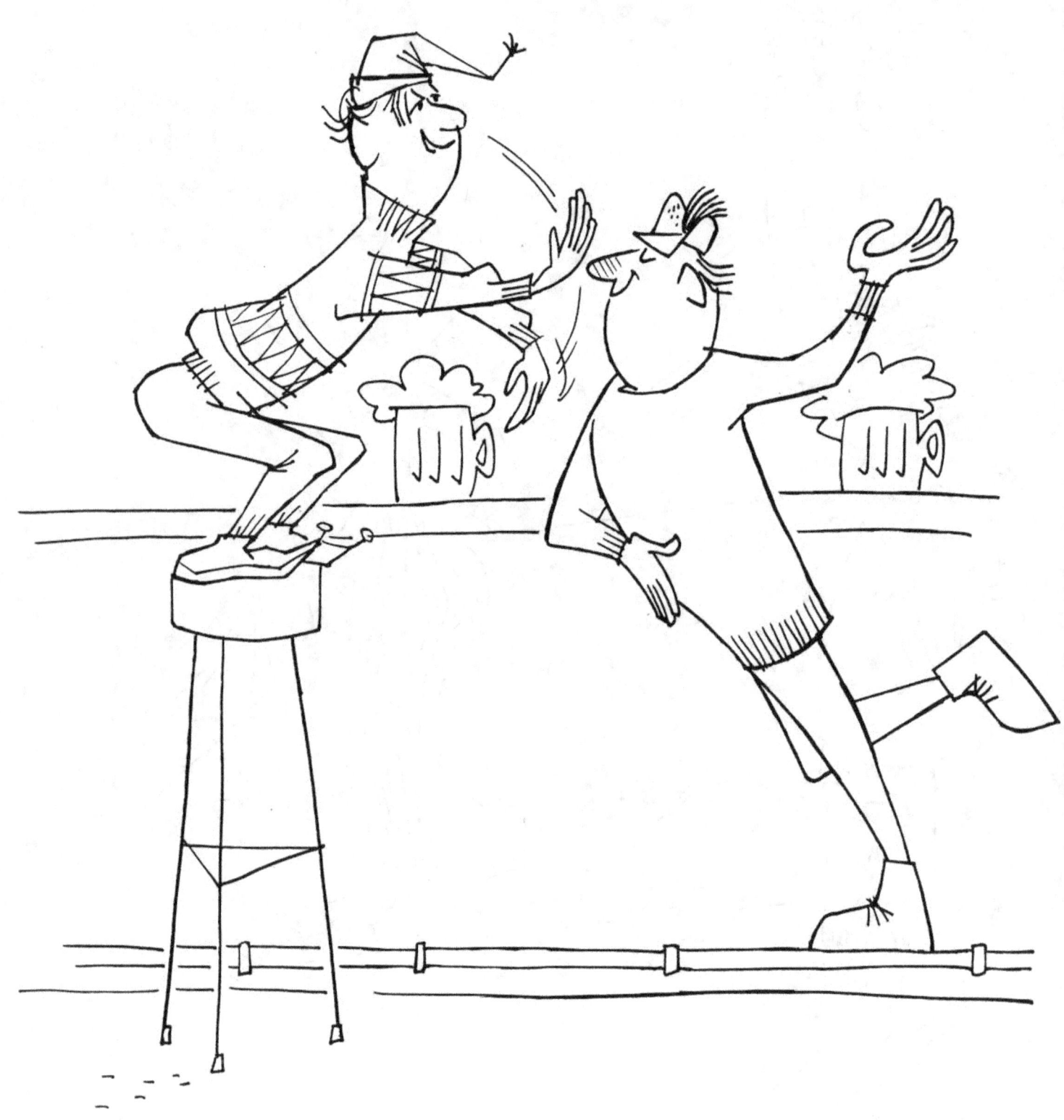

SEE THE SKIERS DRINKING AT THE BAR.
SEE THE SKIERS TALKING.
THEY ARE TALKING ABOUT SKIING.
THE MORE THEY DRINK, THE BETTER THEY SKI.

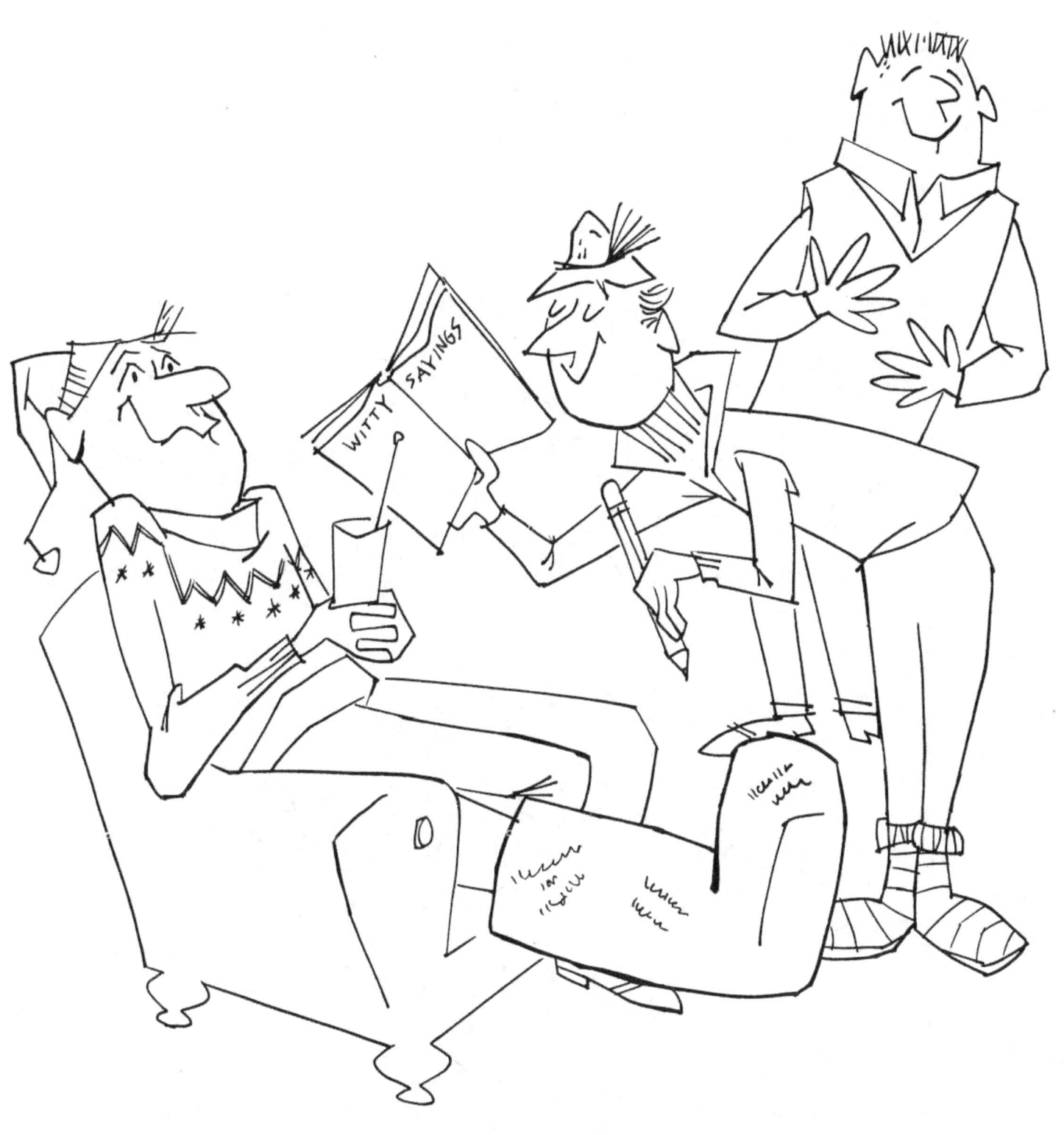

THIS IS MY CAST.
MY WITTY FRIENDS WROTE
WITTY SAYINGS ON MY CAST.
COLOR IT OFF-COLOR.

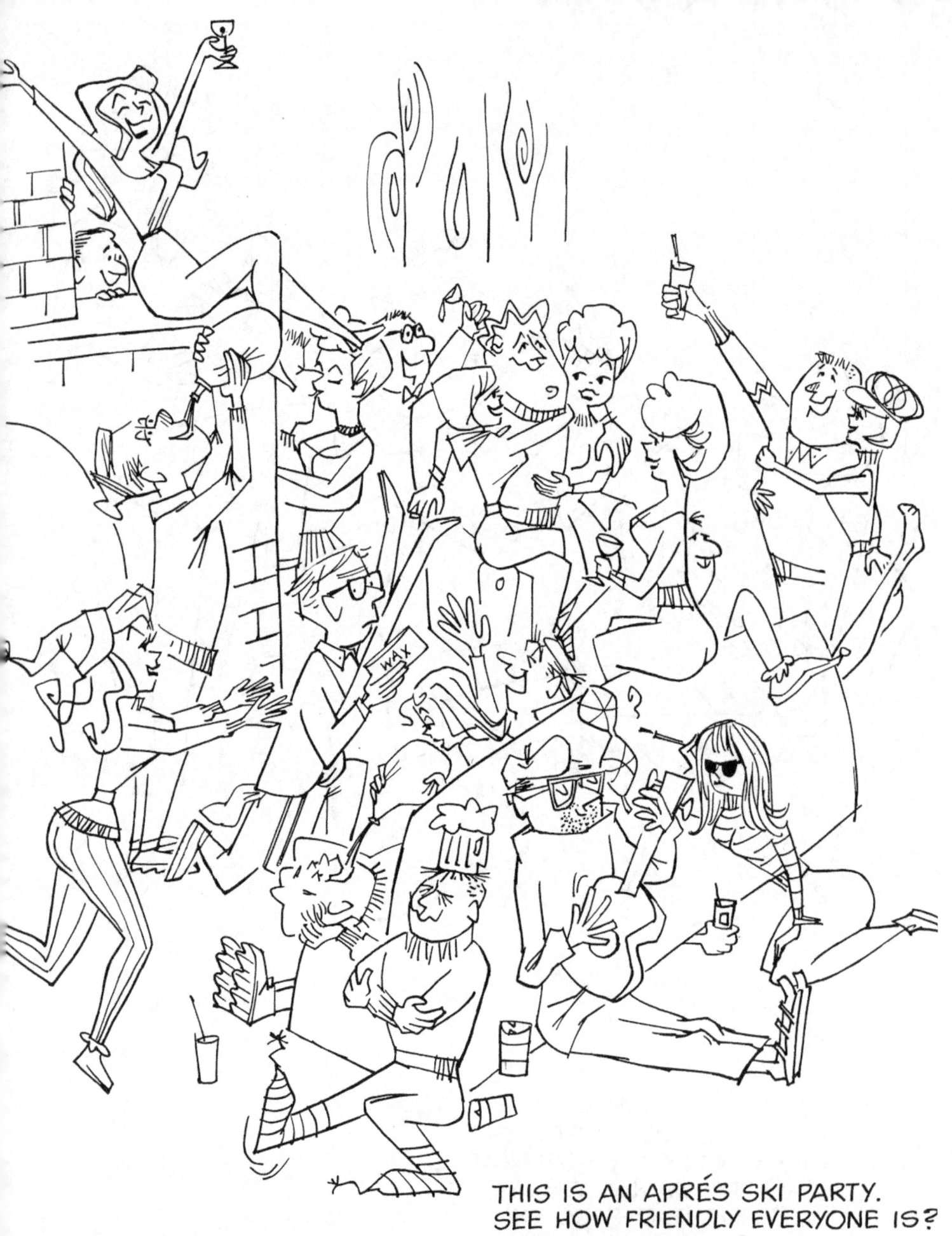

THIS IS AN APRÉS SKI PARTY.
SEE HOW FRIENDLY EVERYONE IS?
COLOR US PICKLED.

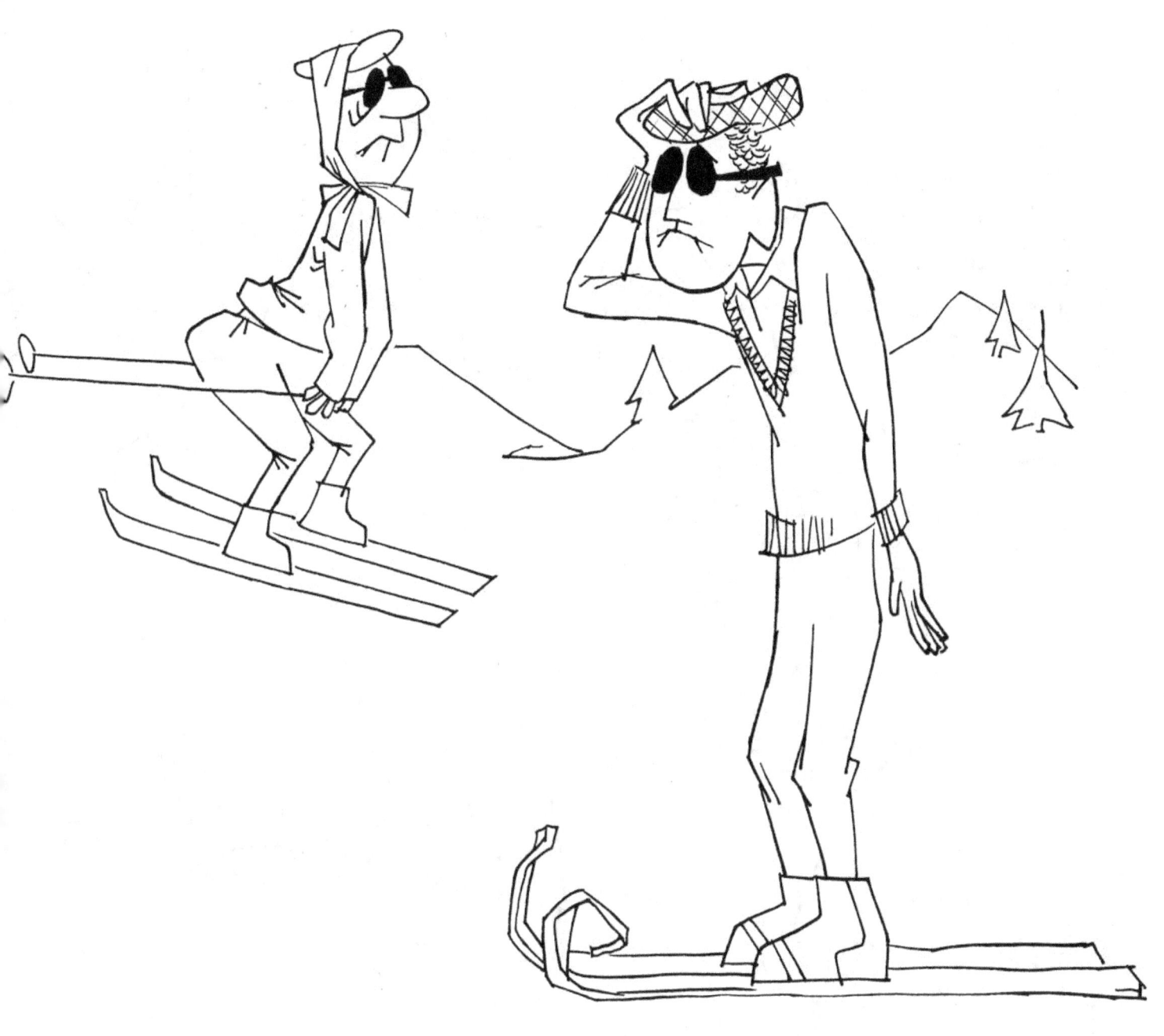

THIS IS THE MORNING AFTER APRÉS SKI.
NOBODY IS SPEAKING TO ANYBODY.
COLOR THEIR SUNGLASSES BLOODSHOT.

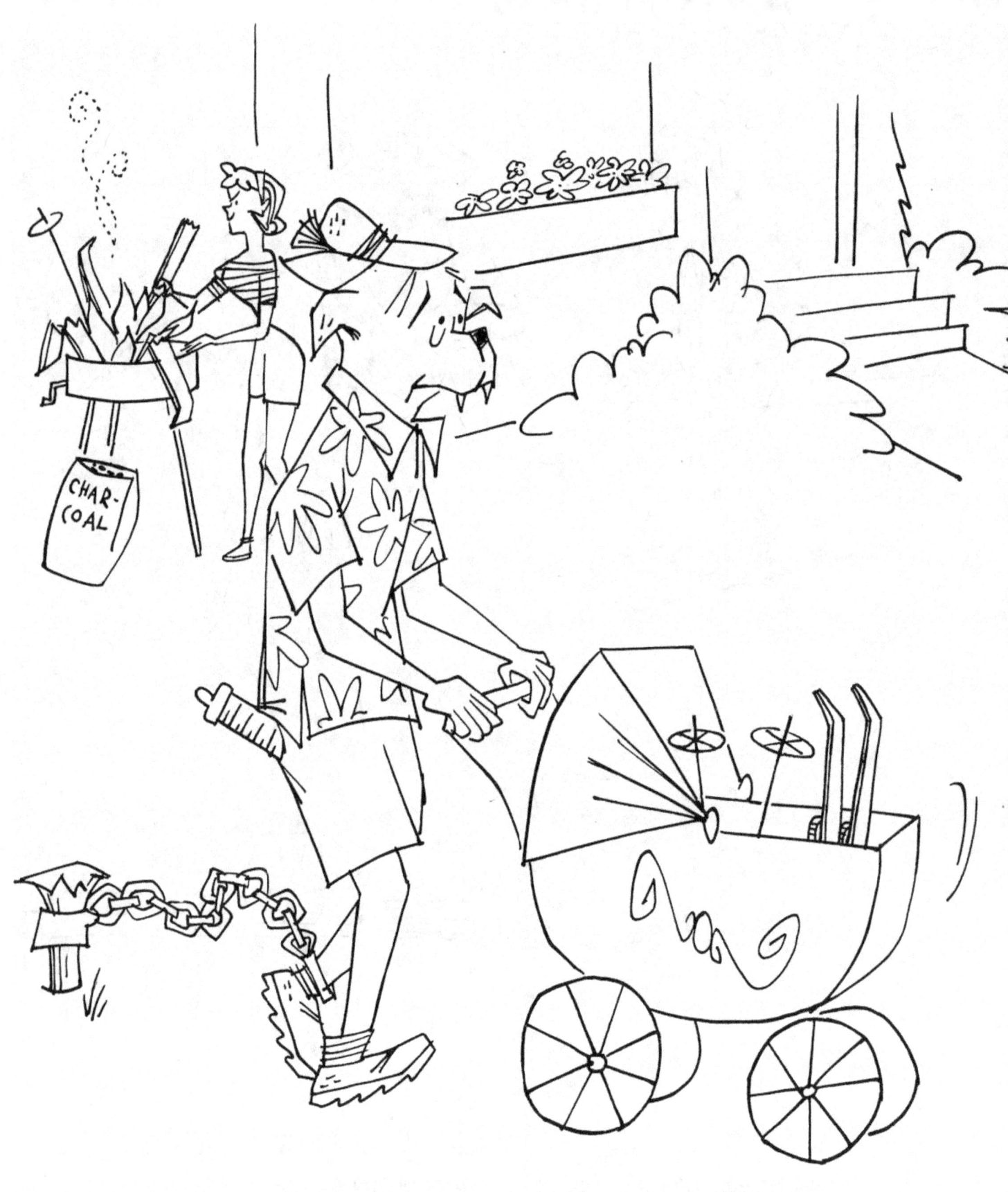

DAMN THAT APRÉS SKI PARTY!

Orville Fenderlob's

Mother Goose is Loose!

Goose Juice

A Coloring book for juiced up Adults...

THIS IS <u>MY</u> PROPERTY

My name is _____

My favorite booze is _____

My capacity is _____

When stoned, deliver body to _____

Mother Goose is Loose! was published by Kanrom, who also published the best-selling *JFK Coloring Book* and *The Therapy Coloring Book*. Author "Orville Fenderlob" is also credited with the brief text in Kanrom's *A Guest Book for the John*.

Old Mother Goose was on the loose
For many years my friend
Sometimes we thought her tales too short
But questioned not their end.

Now times have changed and re-arranged
The characters we knew
They're not so sweet or so petite
You'll know the truth now too.

They've gone astray I'm sad to say
Those little story folk
Let us retract and then look back
You'll see it is no joke.

Just crack this book and take a look
We're turning on the juice
And now you Mother, we're all set
For cooking Mother's Goose.

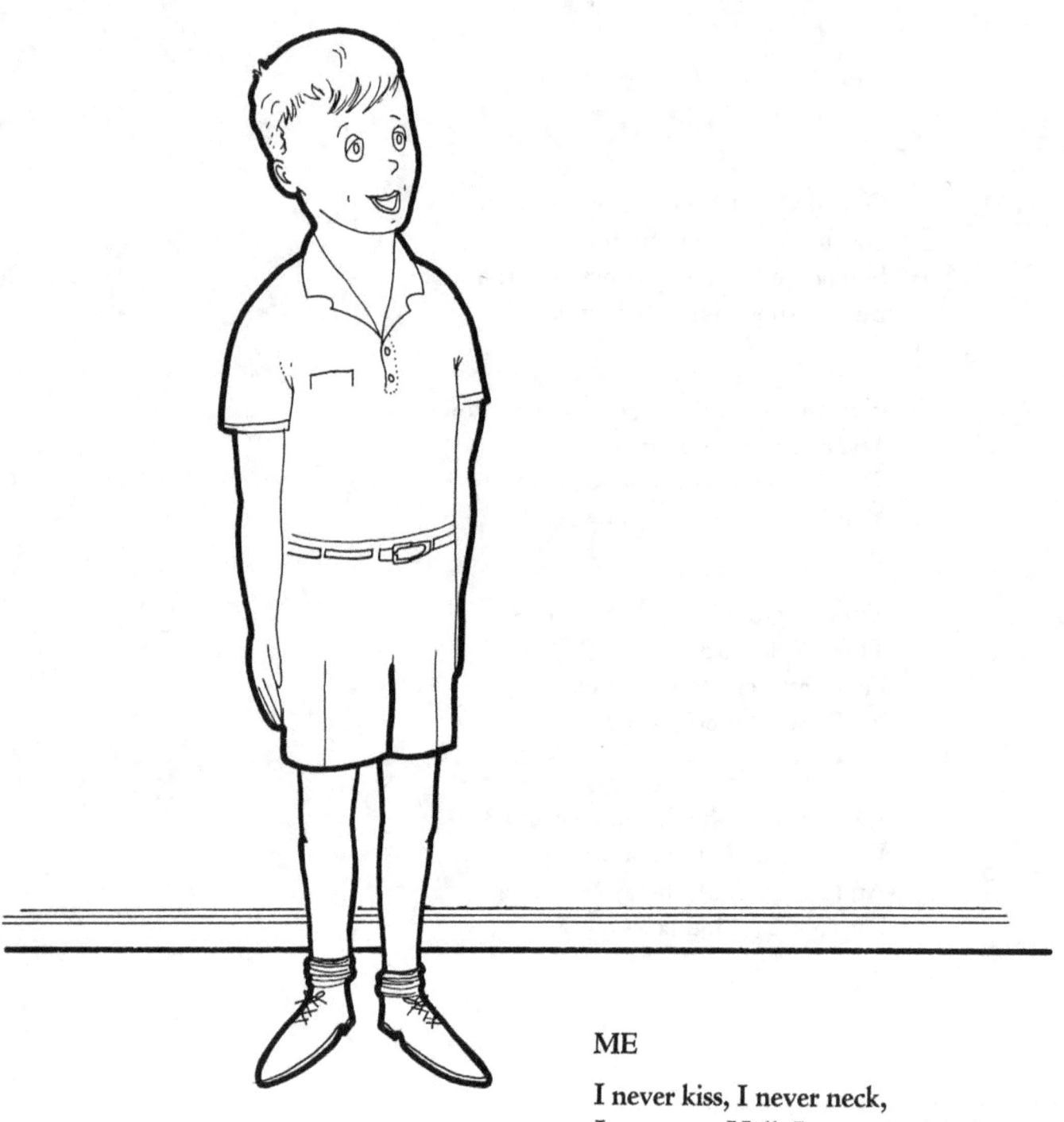

ME

I never kiss, I never neck,
I never say Hell, I never say Heck,
I'm always good, I'm always nice,
I don't play poker, I shake no dice,
I never drink, I never flirt,
I never gossip or spread the dirt,
I have no sex, no funny tricks,
But what the Hell, I'M ONLY SIX!

242

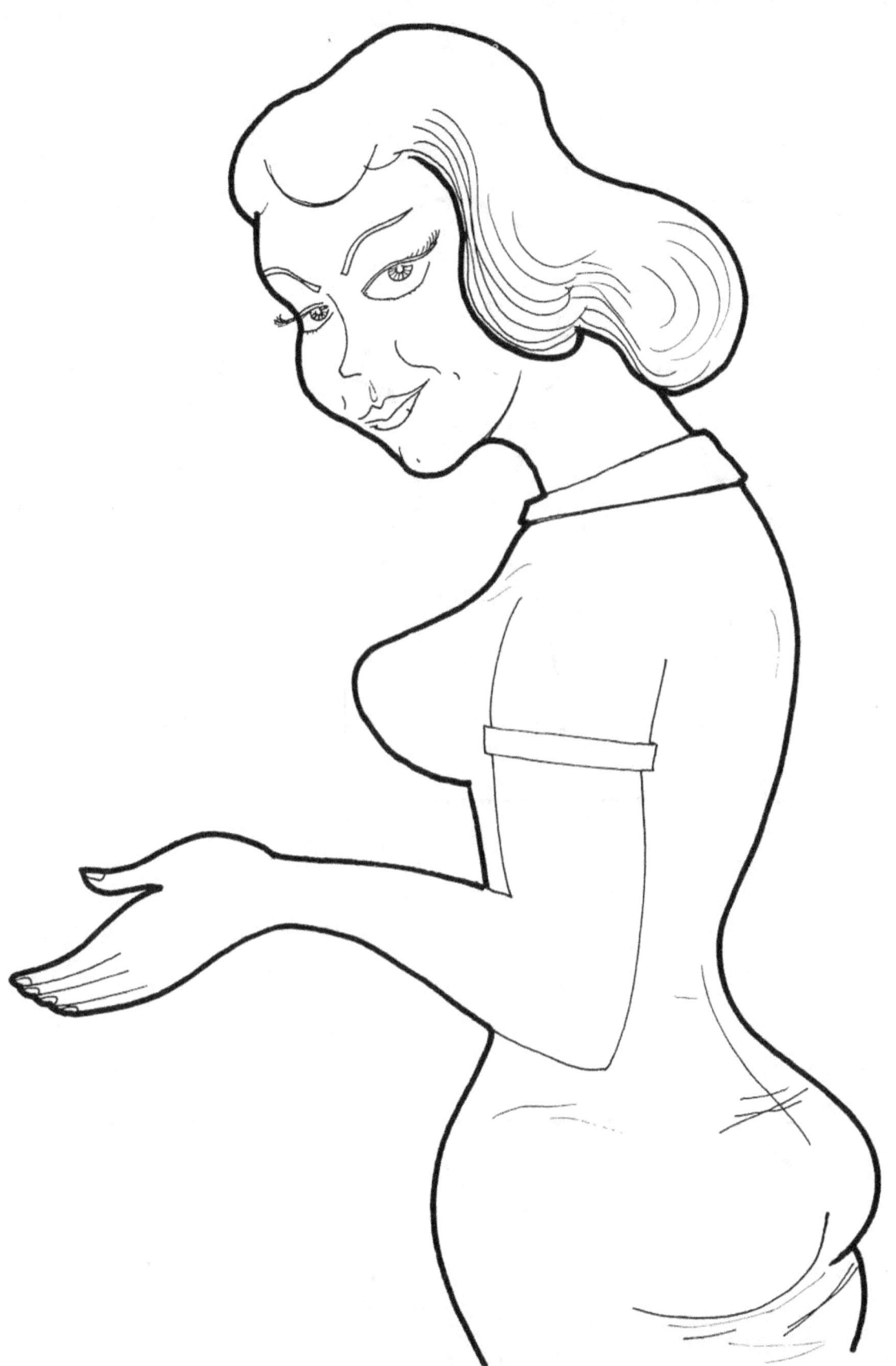

MY TEACHER

My teacher is so very nice
I always take her good advice;
She's just as soft as bunny fur—
—I think I'd like to sleep with her.

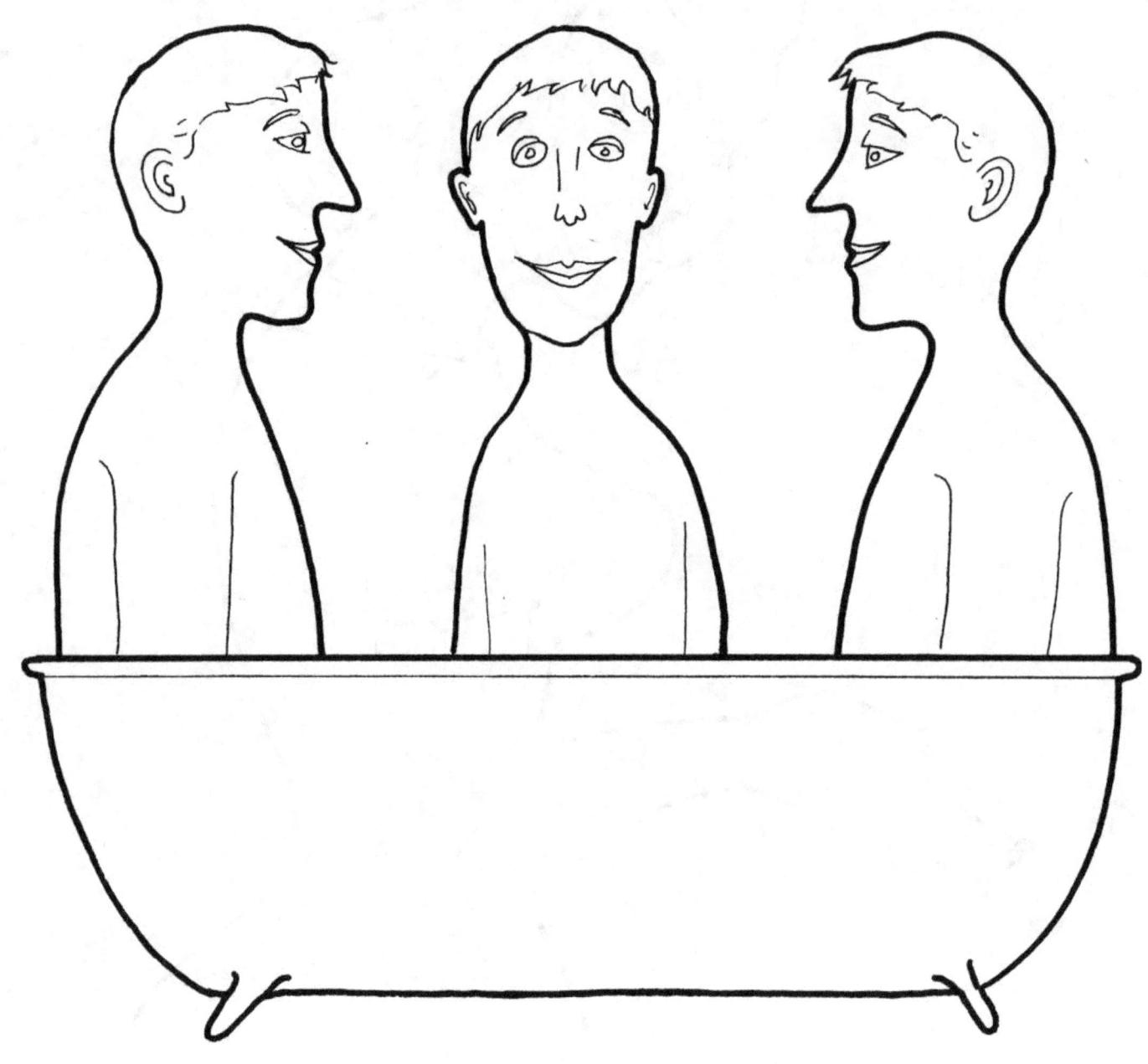

MY UNCLES

Rub-a-dub-dub,
Three men in a tub—
They all got arrested.

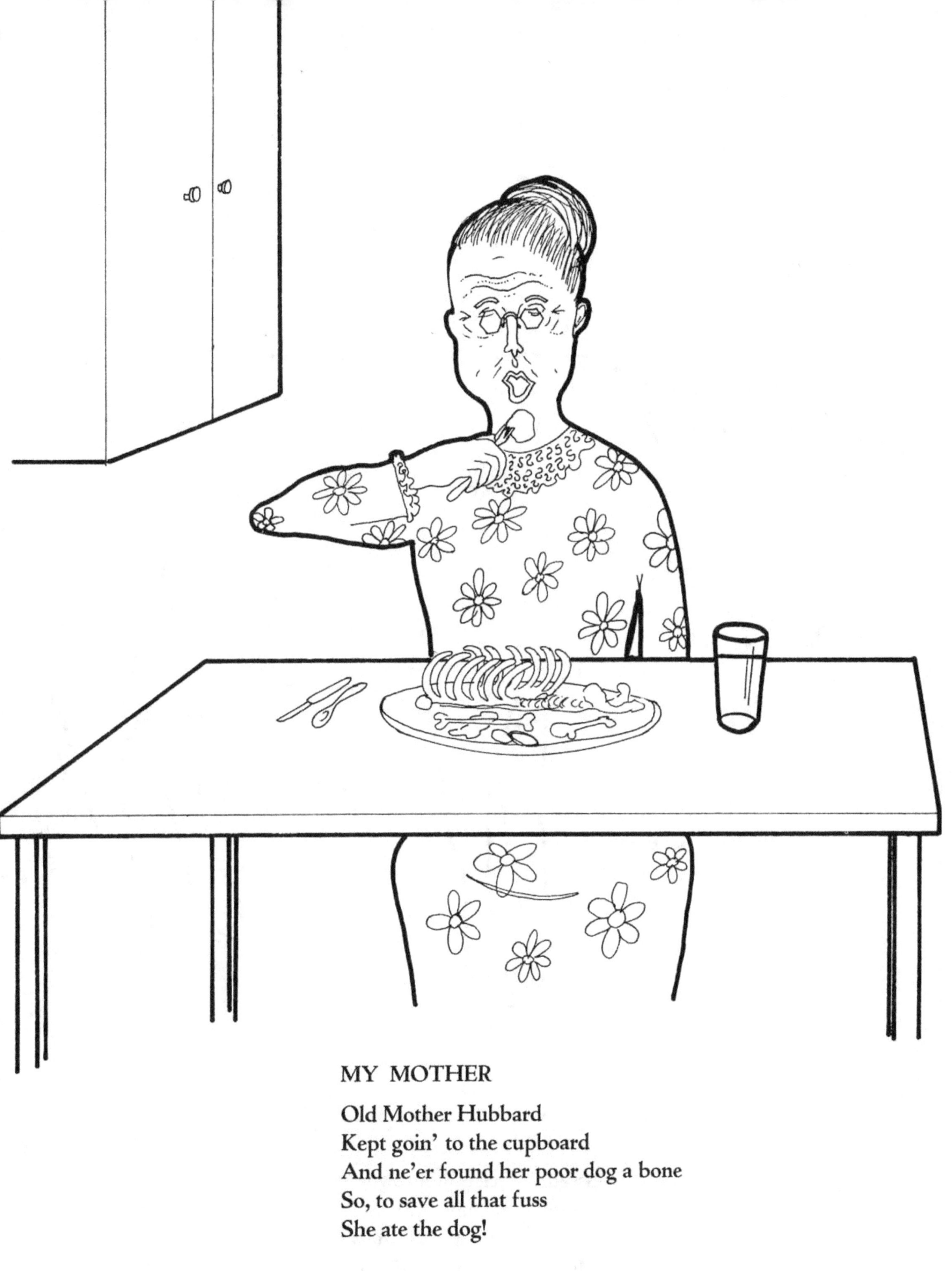

MY MOTHER

Old Mother Hubbard
Kept goin' to the cupboard
And ne'er found her poor dog a bone
So, to save all that fuss
She ate the dog!

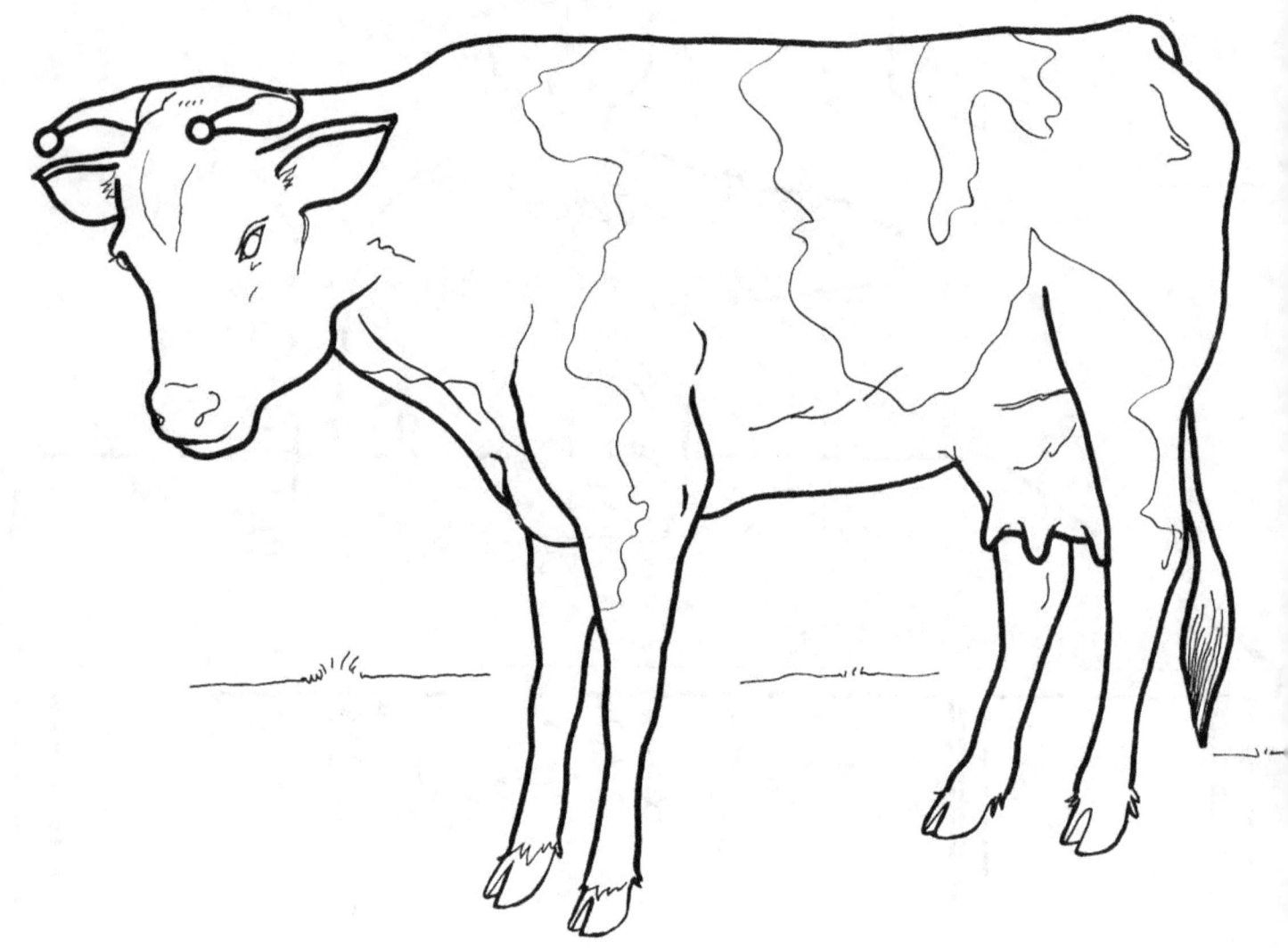

MY COW

I kissed the friendly brown-eyed cow,
Who gives me milk and cheese,
I'm lying in my nursery now,
With hoof and mouth disease.

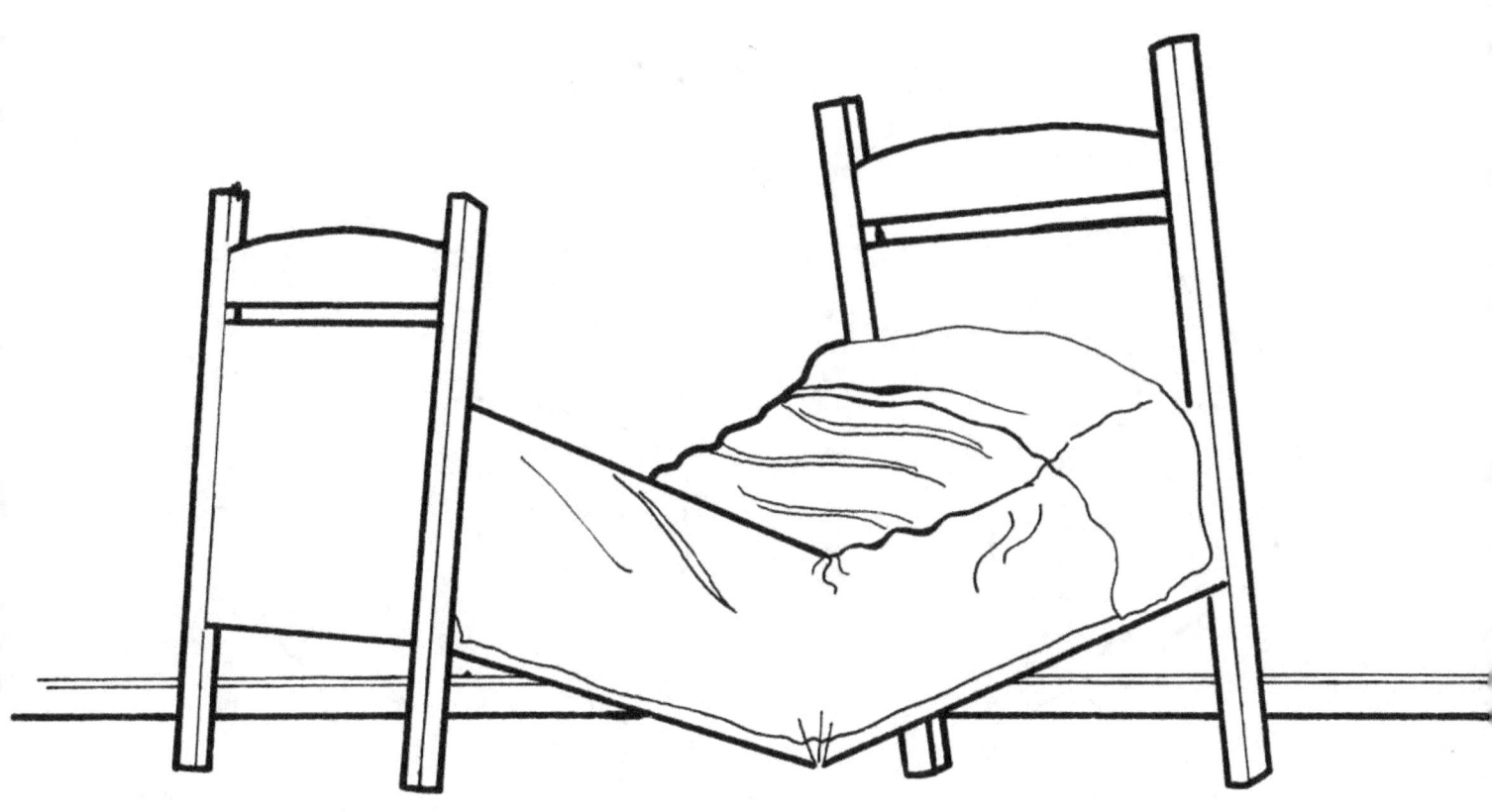

MY BED

Girls and Boys come out to play
You're too grown up inside to stay
The time has come for you to wed
Cause after all, you broke the bed.

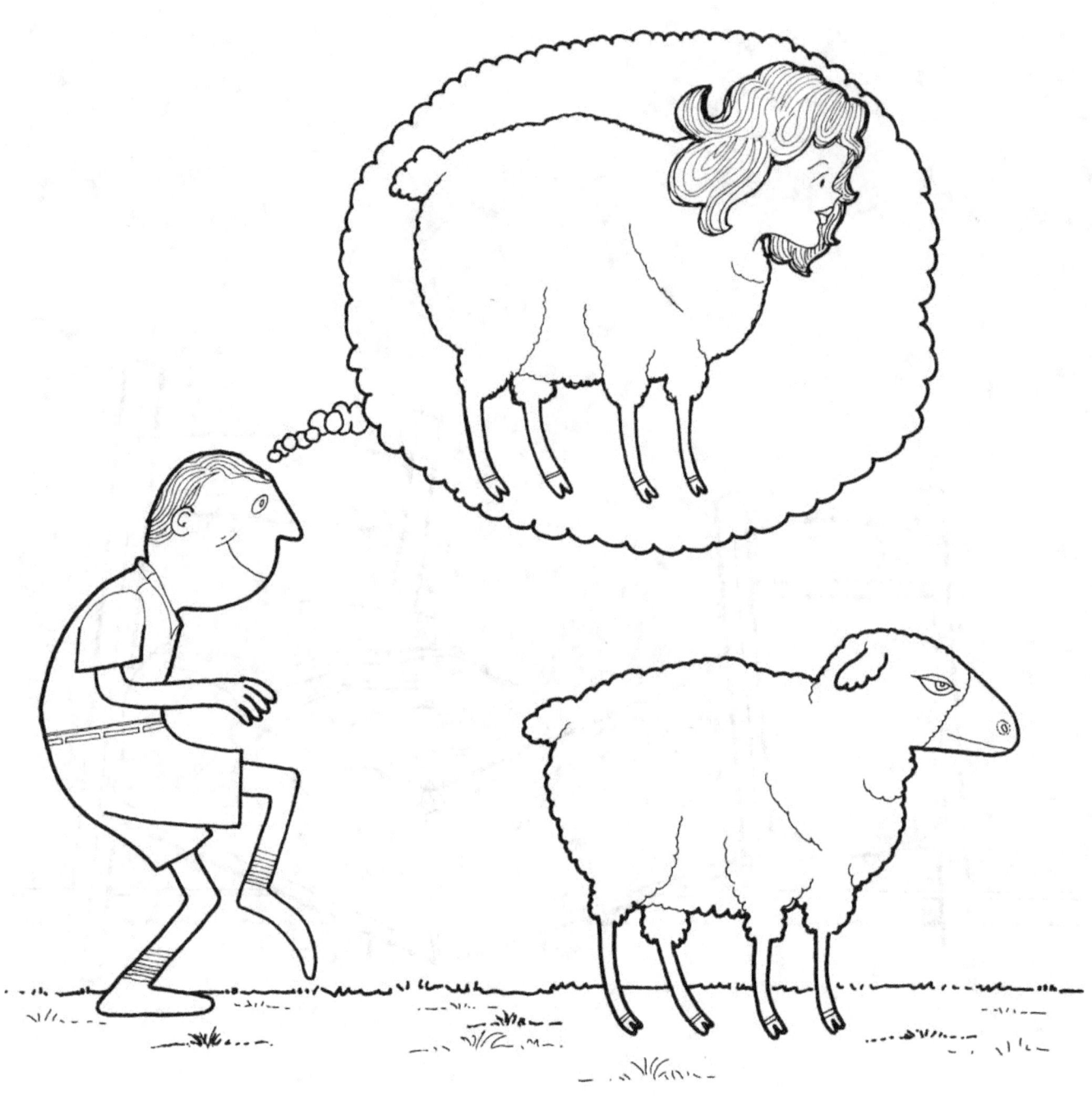

MY LITTLE BOY BLUE

Little Boy Blue, come blow your horn!
The sheep's in the meadow, the cow's in the corn.
Where's the boy who looks after the sheep?
He's after the sheep, the dirty creep.
Will you stop him? No, siree—
Better the lousy sheep than me.

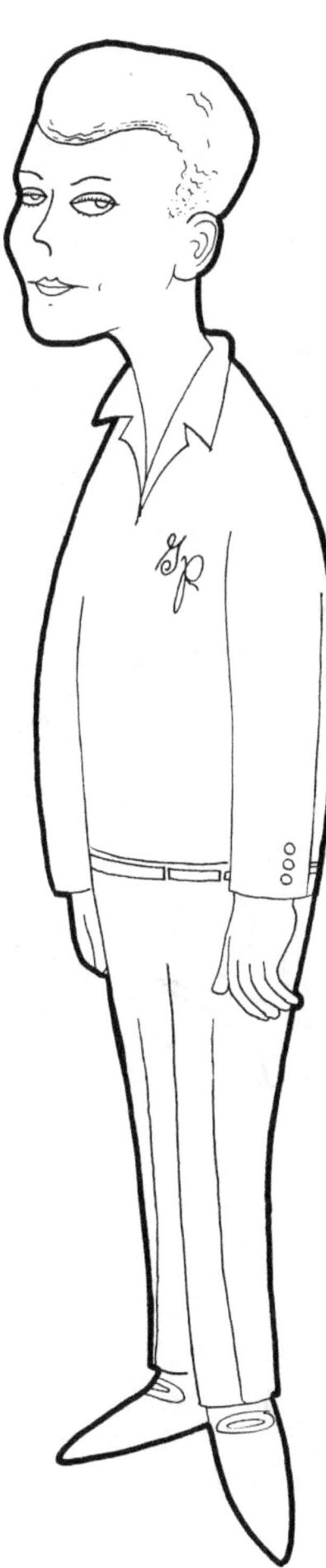

MY FRIEND

Georgie Porgie, pudding and pie
Once kissed the girls and made them cry
And now because he can't stand noise
Georgie Porgie's kissing boys.

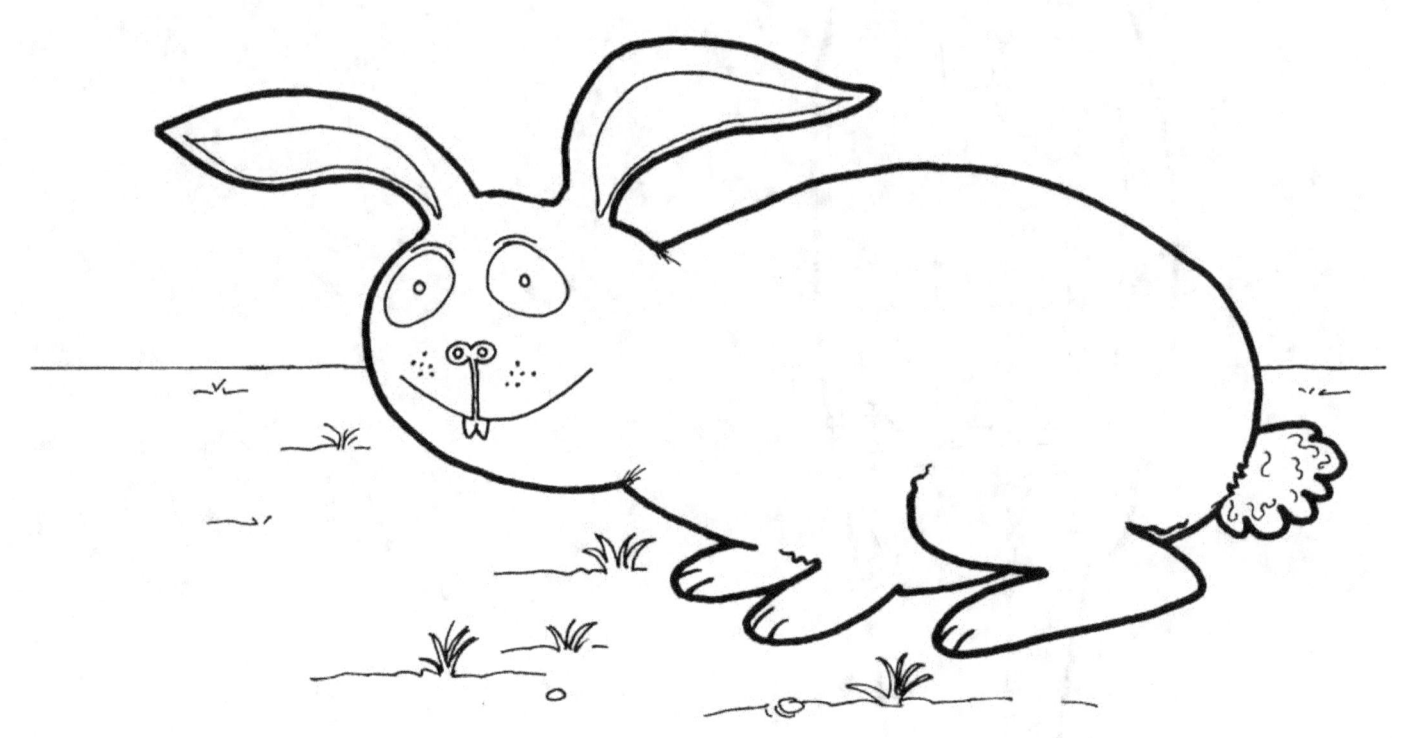

MY WABBIT

The wabbits are an awful wace,
The things they do is a dis-gwace.
You'd be surpwised if you but knew,
Those awful things that wabbits do—
AND OFTEN, TOO!

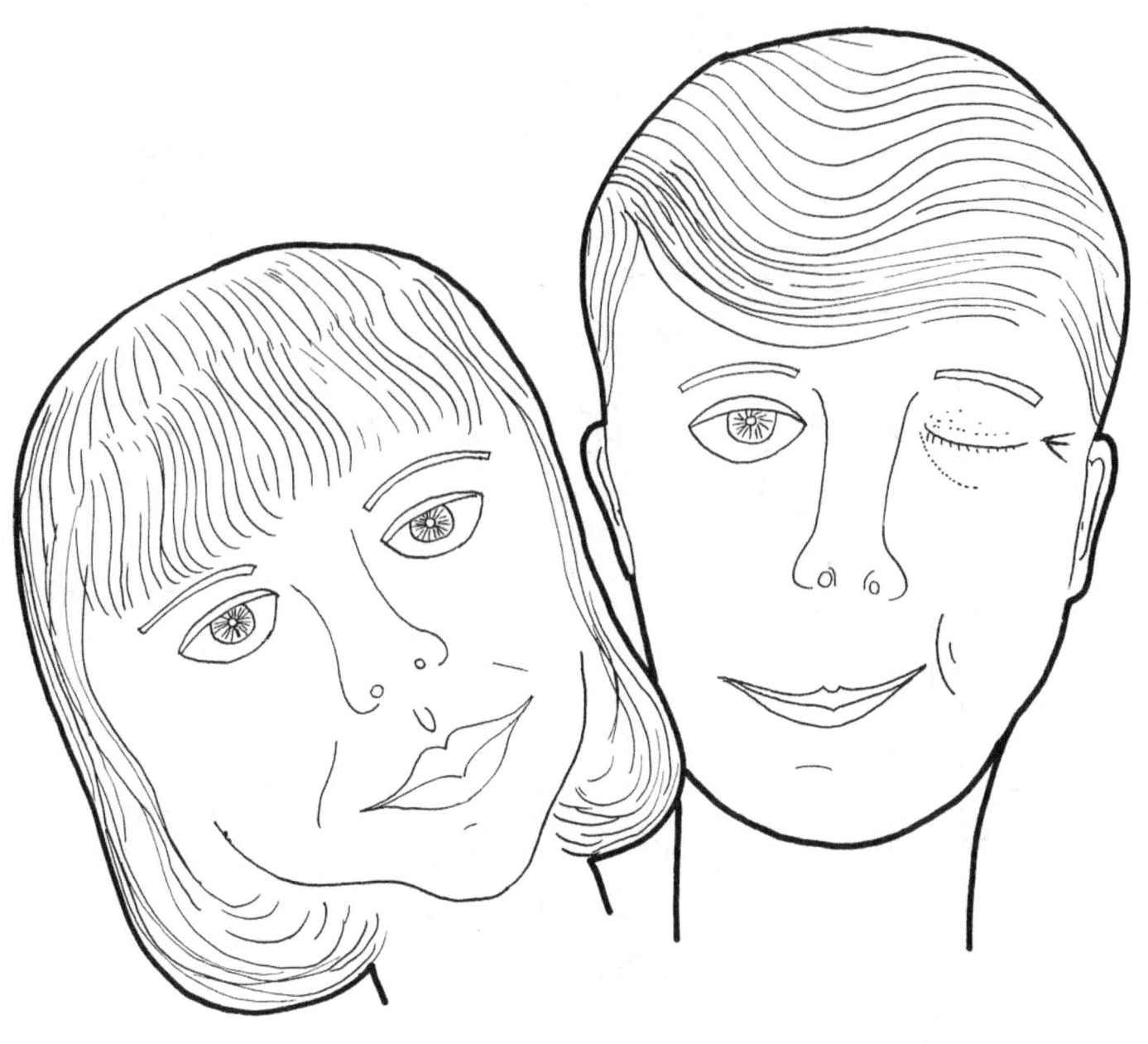

MY JACK AND JILL

Jack and Jill
They opened a Still
And mixed it most with water
Jack got thin from bootleg gin
And Jill got pregnant.

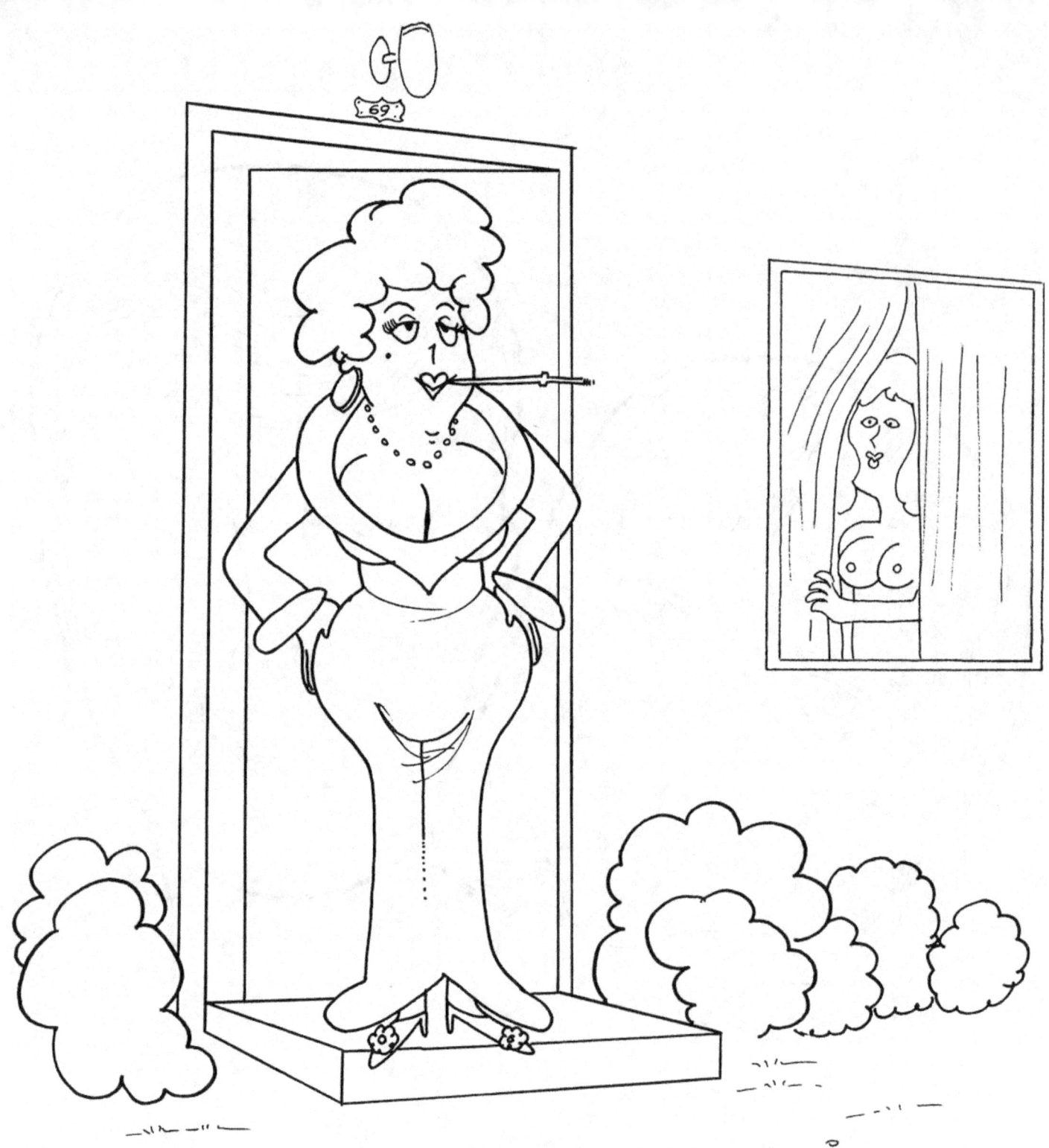

MY SLEIGH RIDE

Over the hills and through the woods,
To grandmother's house we go.
Our sleigh bells ring so merrily,
As we jog along through the snow.

Aha...there's granny on the porch,
The old gal's quite a battler,
We love the fun at granny's house,
For she is Polly Adler.

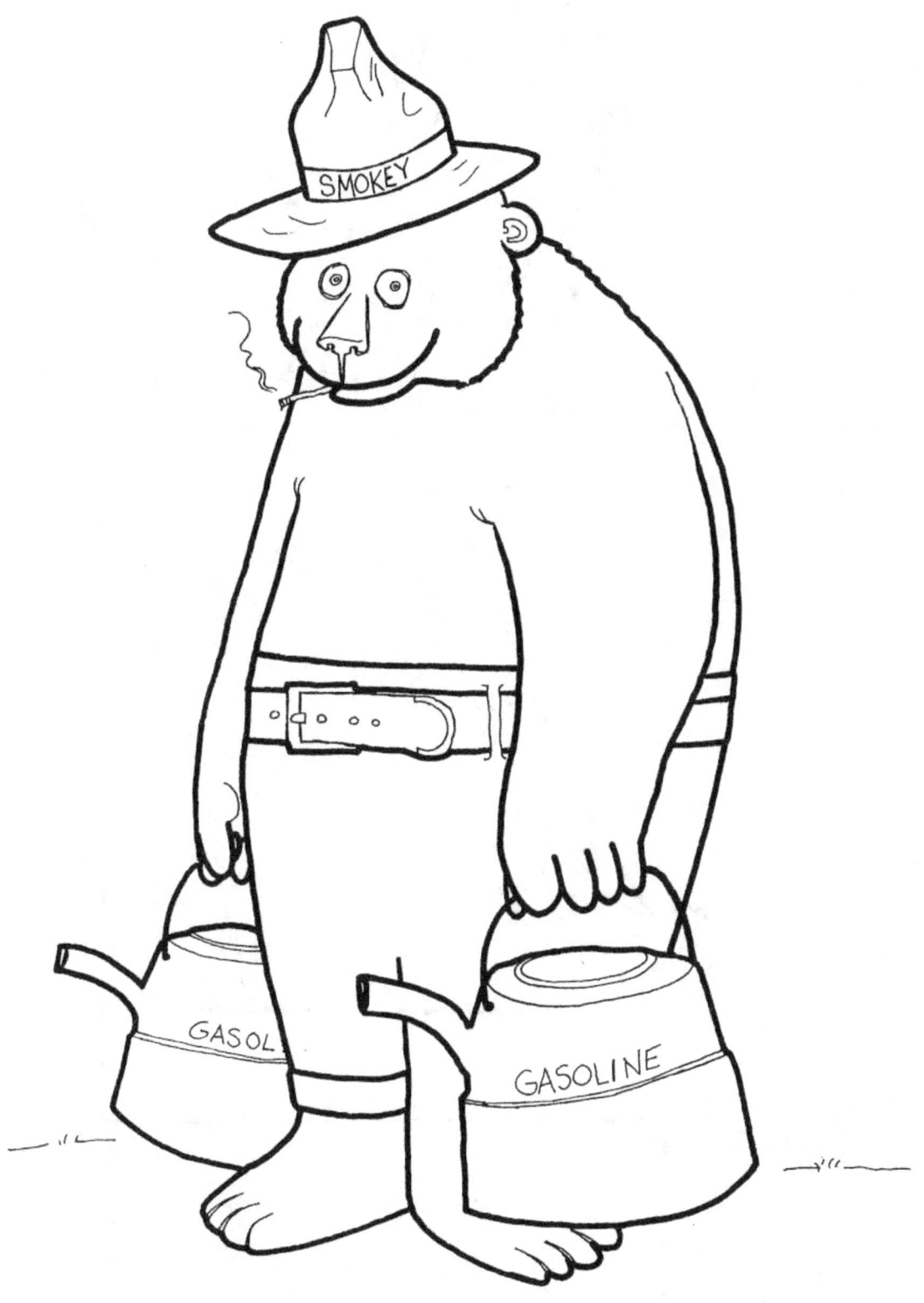

MY BEAR

The forest is burned to a cinder,
Charred stumps can be seen everywhere.
Guess WHO was arrested for arson?
That's right...it was Smokey the Bear.

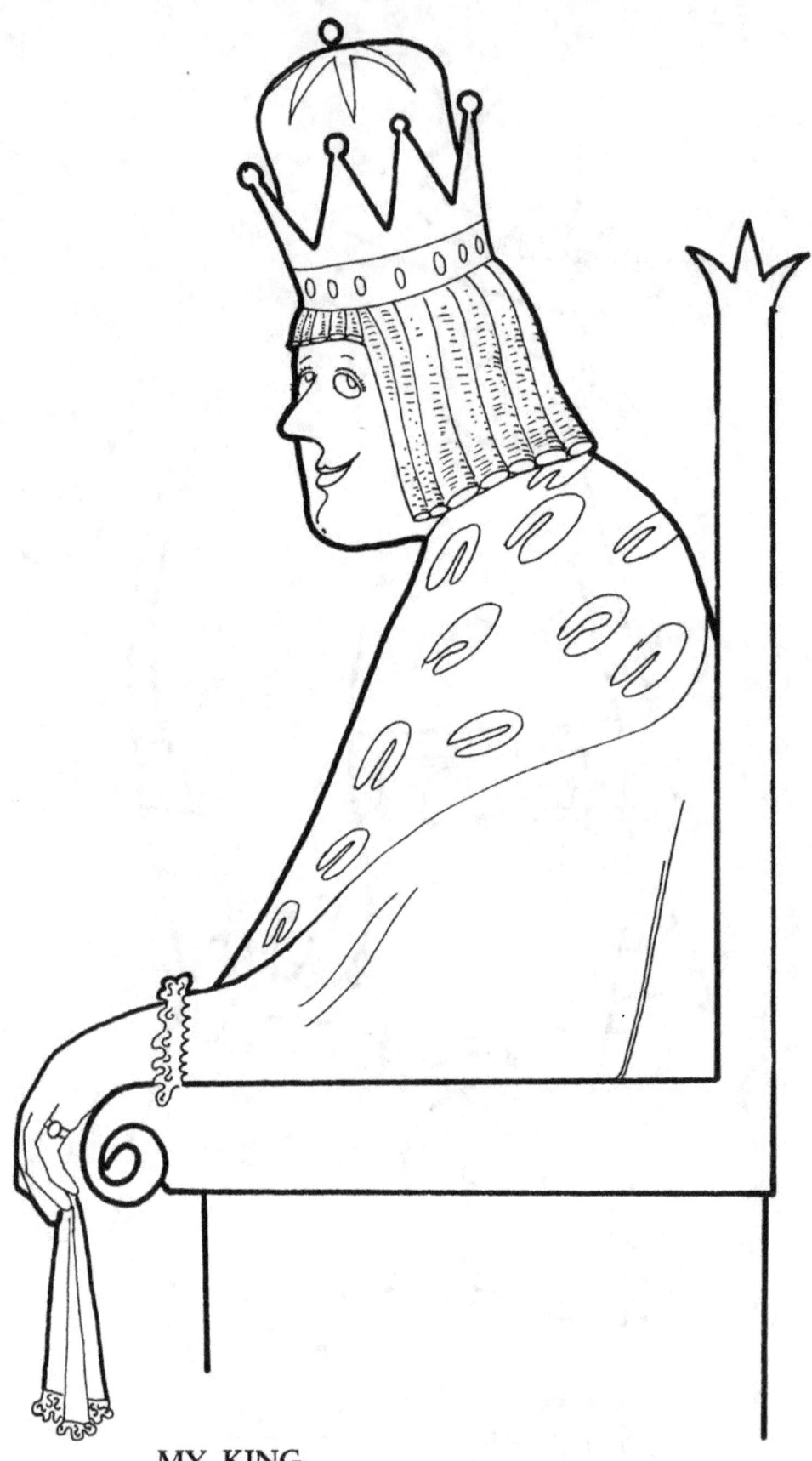

MY KING

Old King Cole was a very old soul,
A very old soul was he;
He called for his gown and his new mink stole,
Then picked up an ad executive on Madison Avenue.

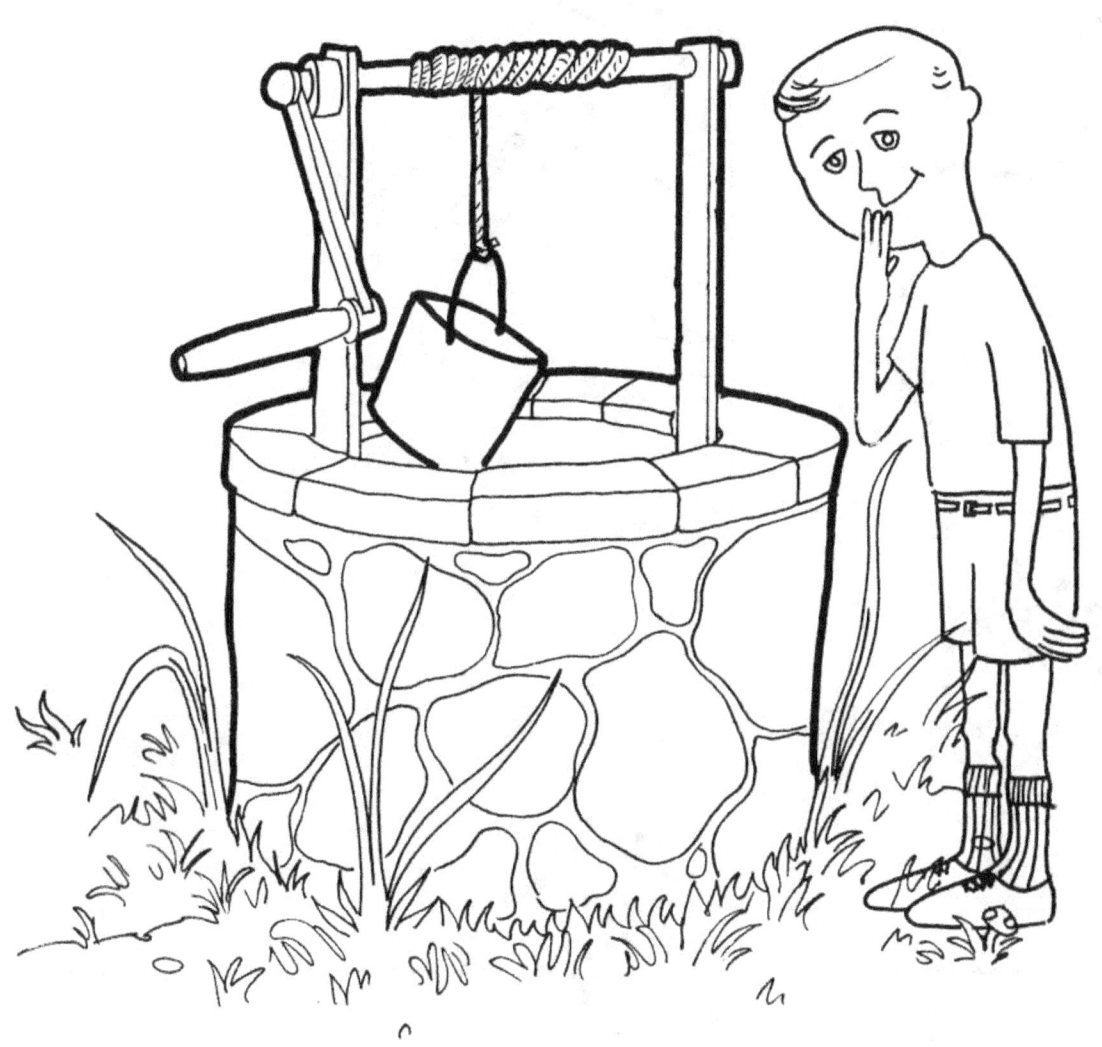

MY WELL

Ding Dong Bell
Pussy's in the Well
Let's all look down
And watch the poor thing drown.

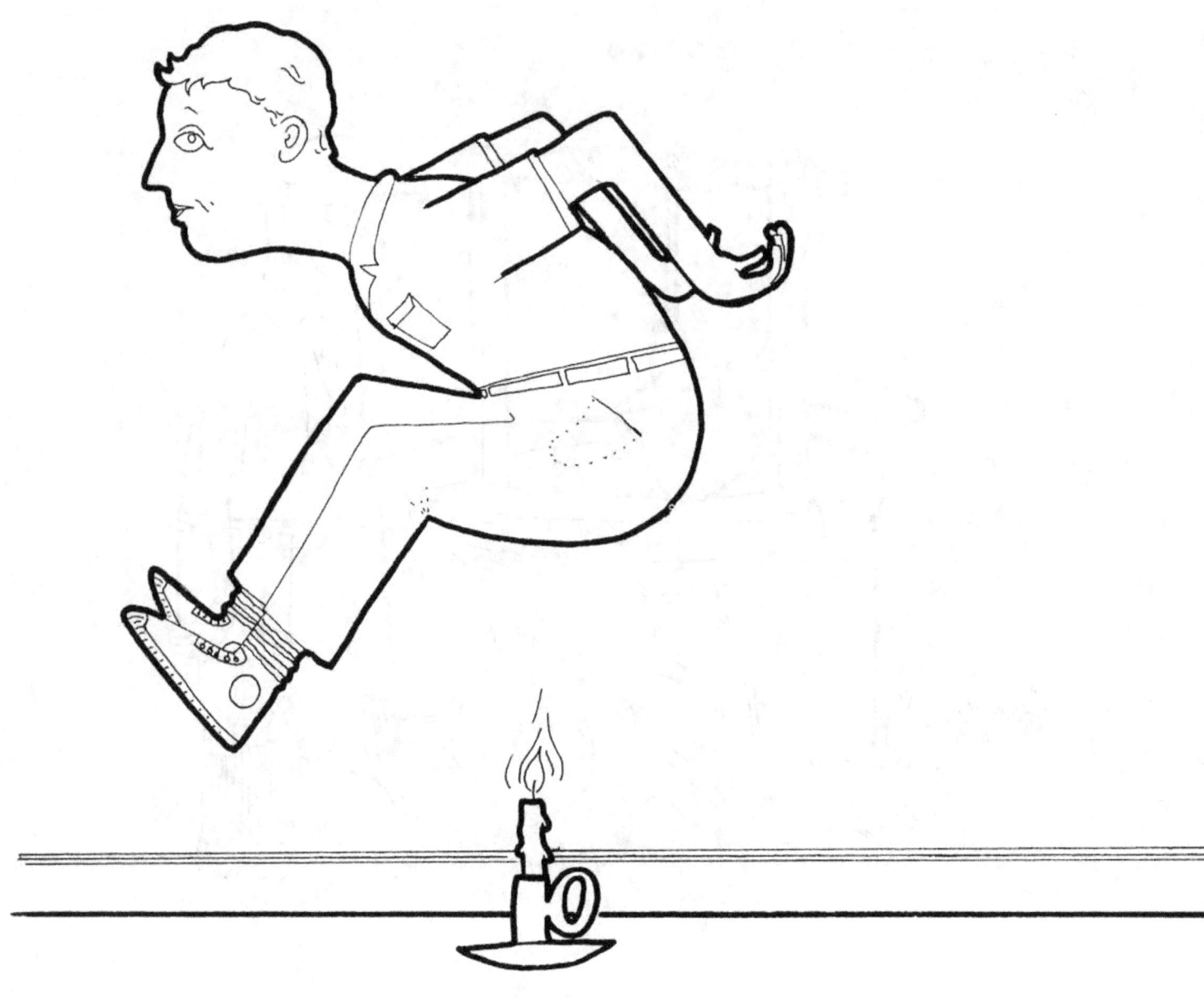

MY CANDLE

Jack be nimble
Jack be quick
Jack jumped over the candle-stick
Jack realized he took a chance
And till this day, Jack's got Hot Pants.

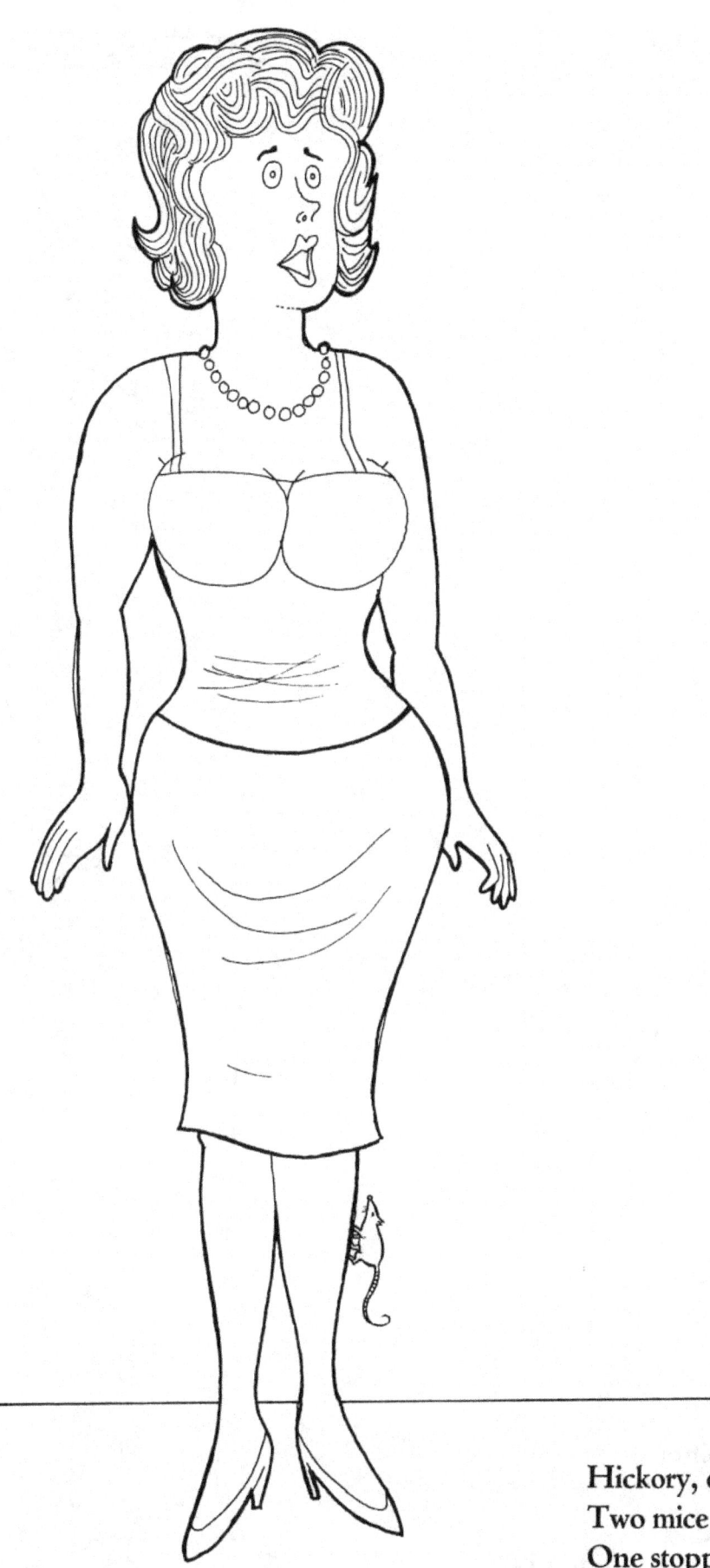

Hickory, dickory, dock,
Two mice ran up her sock.
One stopped at the garter,
The other was smarter,
Hickory, dickory, dock.

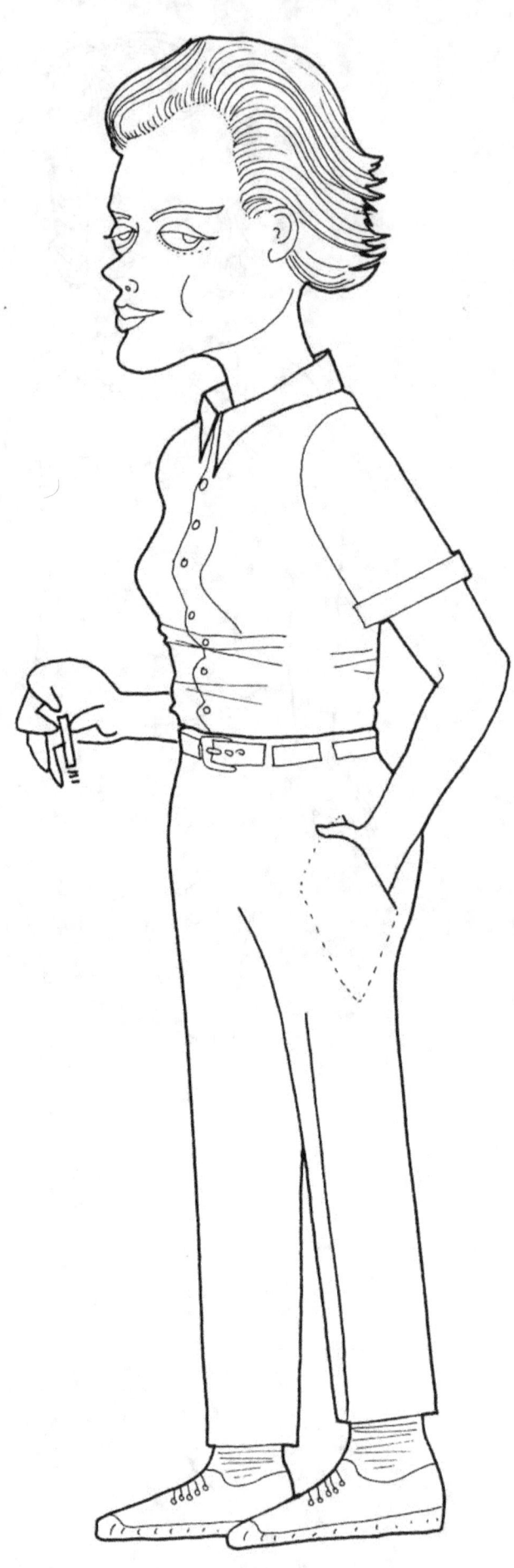

MY TOM BOY

She's thirty-six
And goes for chicks,
That's Tom Boy.
She'll pull a knife
And rape your wife,
That's Tom Boy.

No silk and lace,
No made-up face,
No frilly pink chiffon.
She's hard as rock
And wears a jock,
She even stands up in the JOHN,
That's Tom Boy!

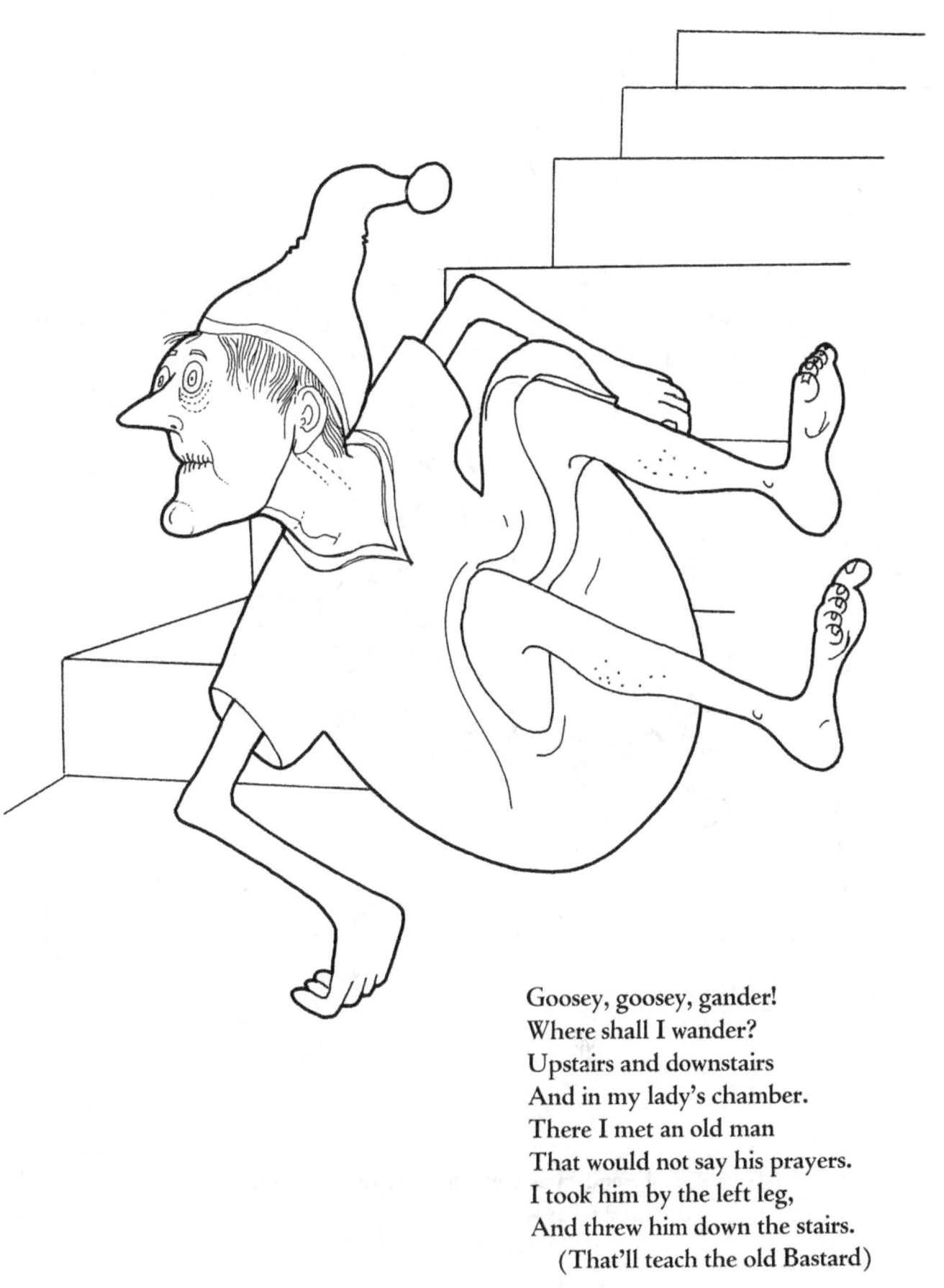

Goosey, goosey, gander!
Where shall I wander?
Upstairs and downstairs
And in my lady's chamber.
There I met an old man
That would not say his prayers.
I took him by the left leg,
And threw him down the stairs.
    (That'll teach the old Bastard)

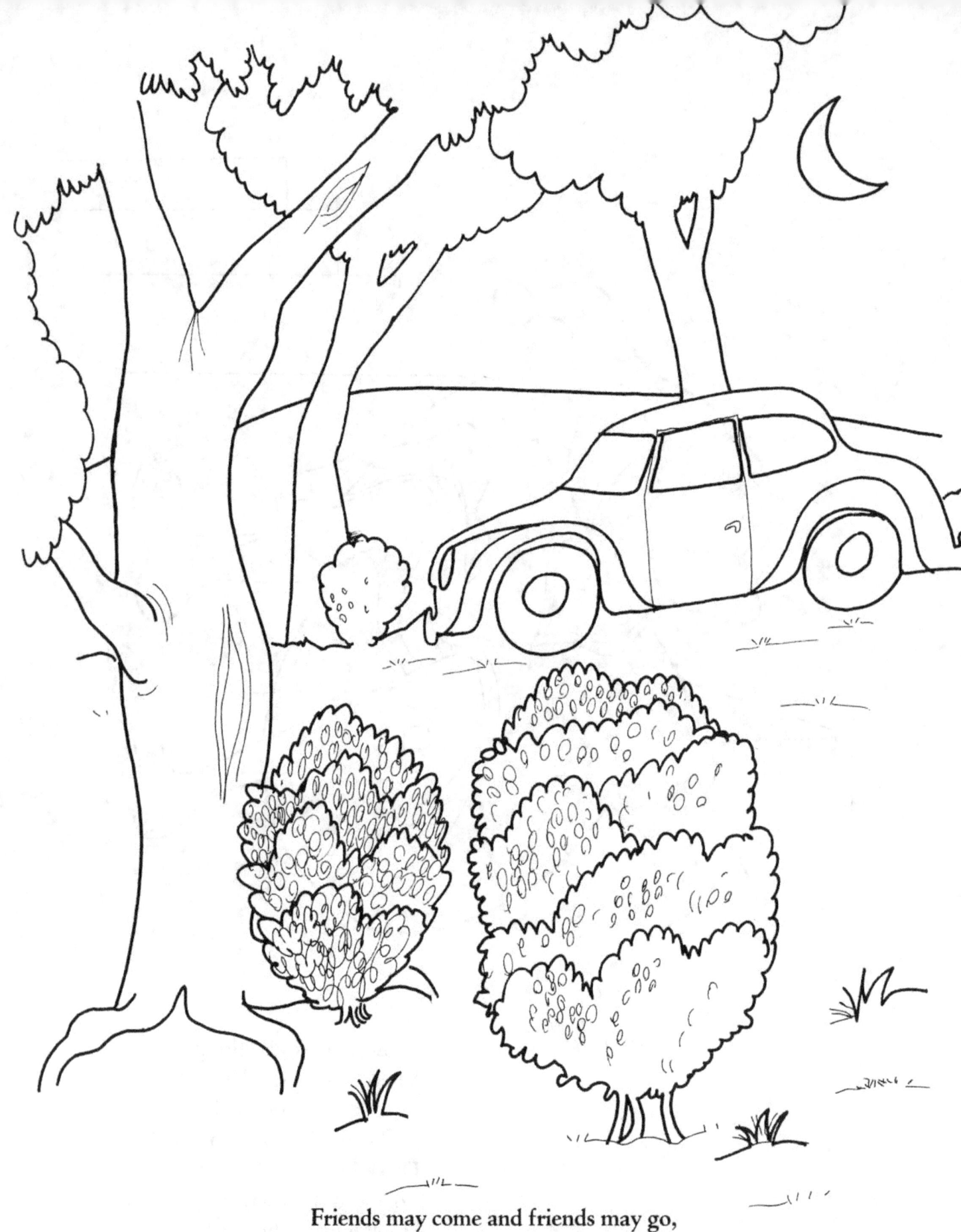

Friends may come and friends may go,
And friends may peter out, you know,
But we'll be friends through thick and thin,
Peter out or peter in.

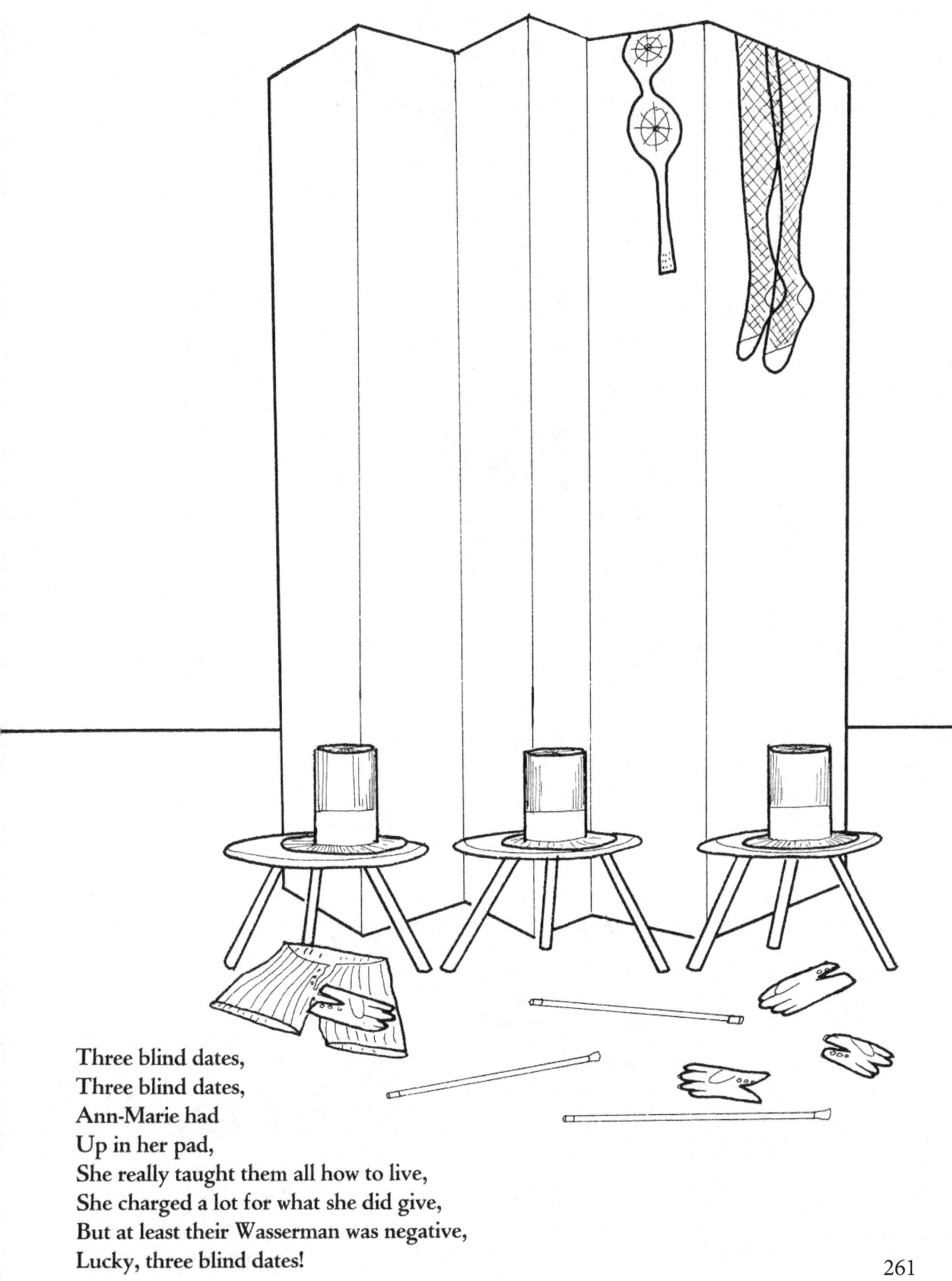

Three blind dates,
Three blind dates,
Ann-Marie had
Up in her pad,
She really taught them all how to live,
She charged a lot for what she did give,
But at least their Wasserman was negative,
Lucky, three blind dates!

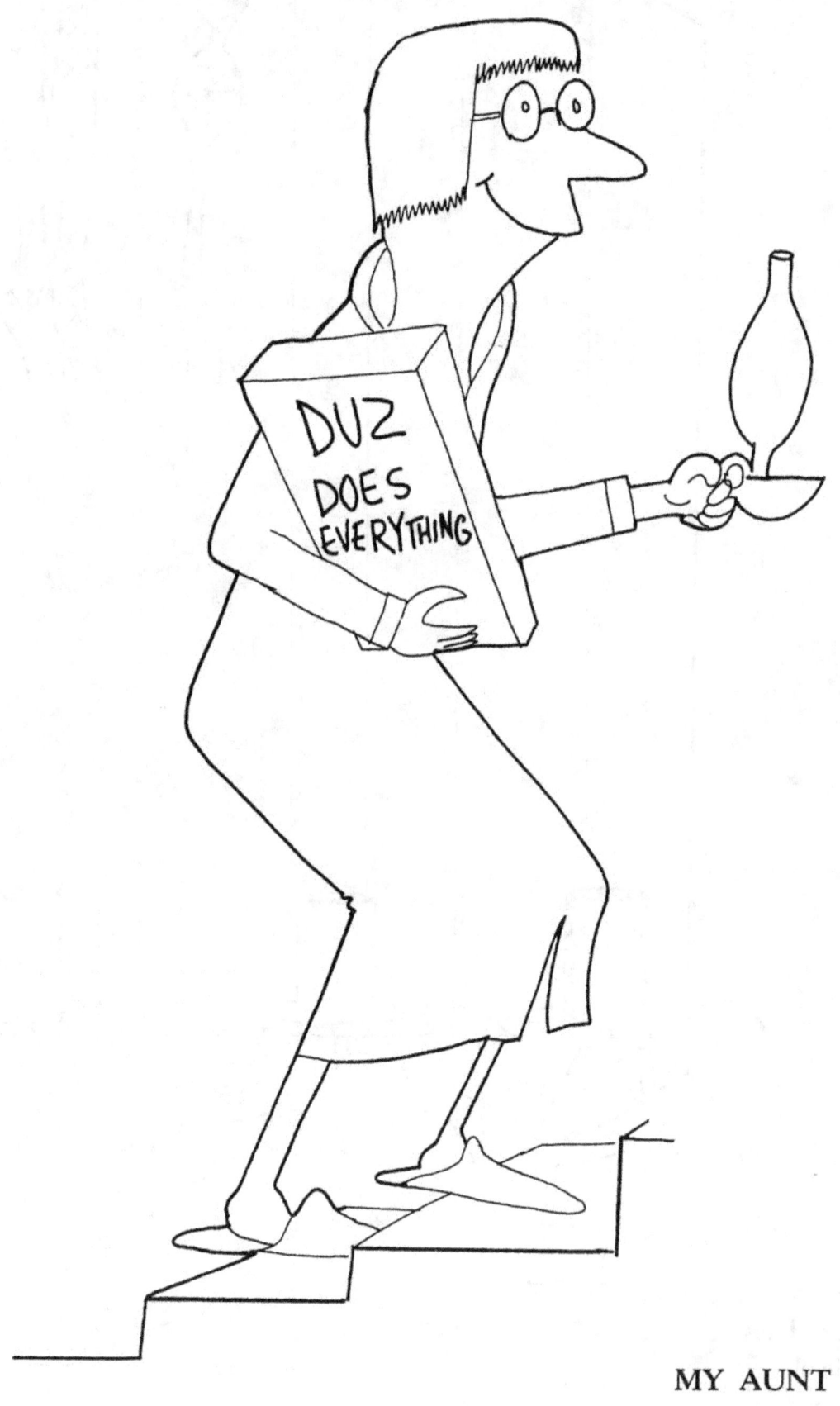

MY AUNT

Rings on her fingers,
Bells on her toes.
She shall have music,
Wherever she goes.

THE THERAPY COLORING BOOK

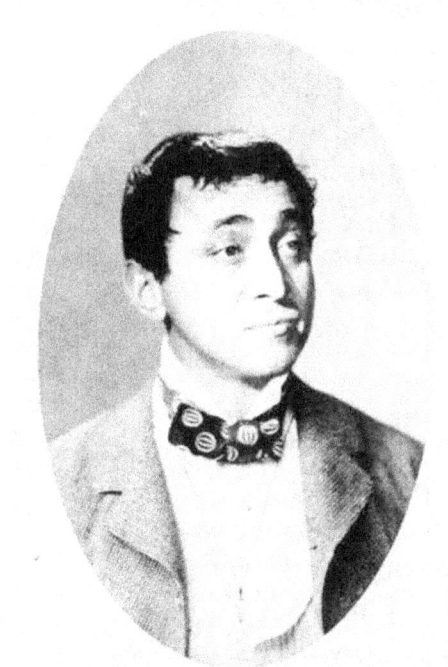

Dr. J. K. Kannon
ON
HEALTH AND HAPPINESS

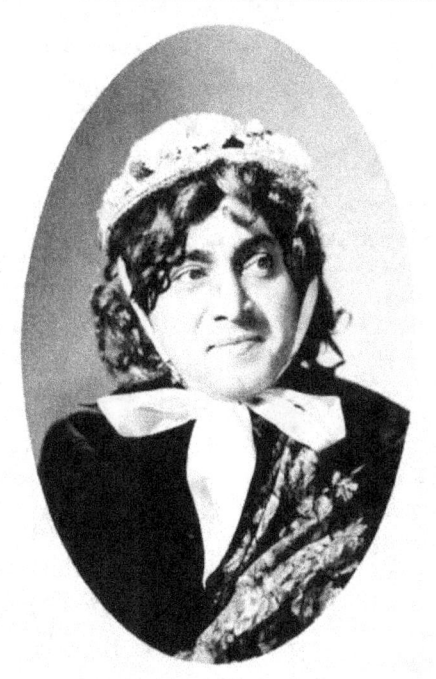

Mother Kannon
ON
Manners Morals & Decorum

LEARNING ...the simple fun way!

PREFACE

Coloring has come to be recognized today as a form of therapy for young and old. Some, who have found it to be a relaxing hobby, have also developed this pastime into a highly artistic career.

After learning of the success of Grandma Moses, Mother Kannon and her son, the doctor, J. K. Kannon, decided that they might invade the field of coloring to pass on to the public for therapeutic value, the benefit of Ma's knowledge of manners, morals and decorum and Dr. J. K's helpful hints to health and happiness.

The text matter in these pages has been taken verbatim from Godey's Lady's Book, published in the 19th century.

What stands as today's humor is often based upon the disinterred skeletons of yesterday's serious viewpoint. The leading U.S. magazine, from 1830 to 1898, GODEY'S LADY'S BOOK, had, what was considered in its day, the most moral and uplifting viewpoint. In the words of Mr. Godey, "the magazine never printed an immoral thought or a profane word; it is the guiding star of female education, the beacon light of refined taste, pure morals and practical wisdom."

Although GODEY'S was famous as a fashion magazine, it contained departments pertaining to manners, morals and medical advice to housewives. These bits of advice found in the pages of the magazine would, today, require a district attorney and a physician to handle the effects of the advice and remedies prescribed by the editors and doctor on the staff of GODEY'S LADY'S BOOK.

It has occurred to us that Mr. Godey might be flattered by the reprinting of material, which was contained in the sixty-eight years of publication of his magazine, but he would cringe at the possibility that this coloring book might fall into the hands of an old letcher who'd suggest to a young innocent that she go to his quarters to see his colored etchings.

The material found in these pages was compiled and edited by Jay Garon and Morgan Wilson.

Mother Kannon
ON
Manners Morals & Decorum

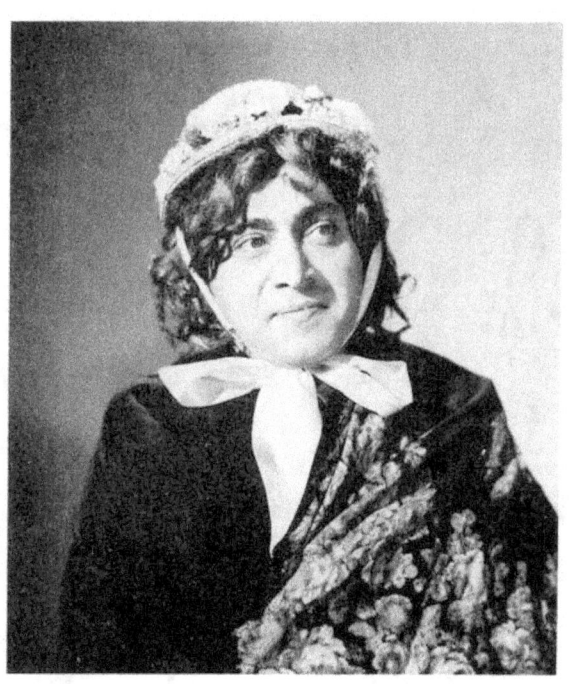

Jackie Kannon was a New York-based stand-up comedian with a vicious style, as well as the "Kan" in Kanrom Inc., the company that published not only this coloring book but also the *Mother Goose is Loose* book in this volume and the *JFK Coloring Book* seen in *Cold War Coloring*. This section is based on a pamphlet that Kanrom had issued, *Mother Kannon Advises on Manners Morals & Decorum*, which had the photographs that the following outline drawings are based on.

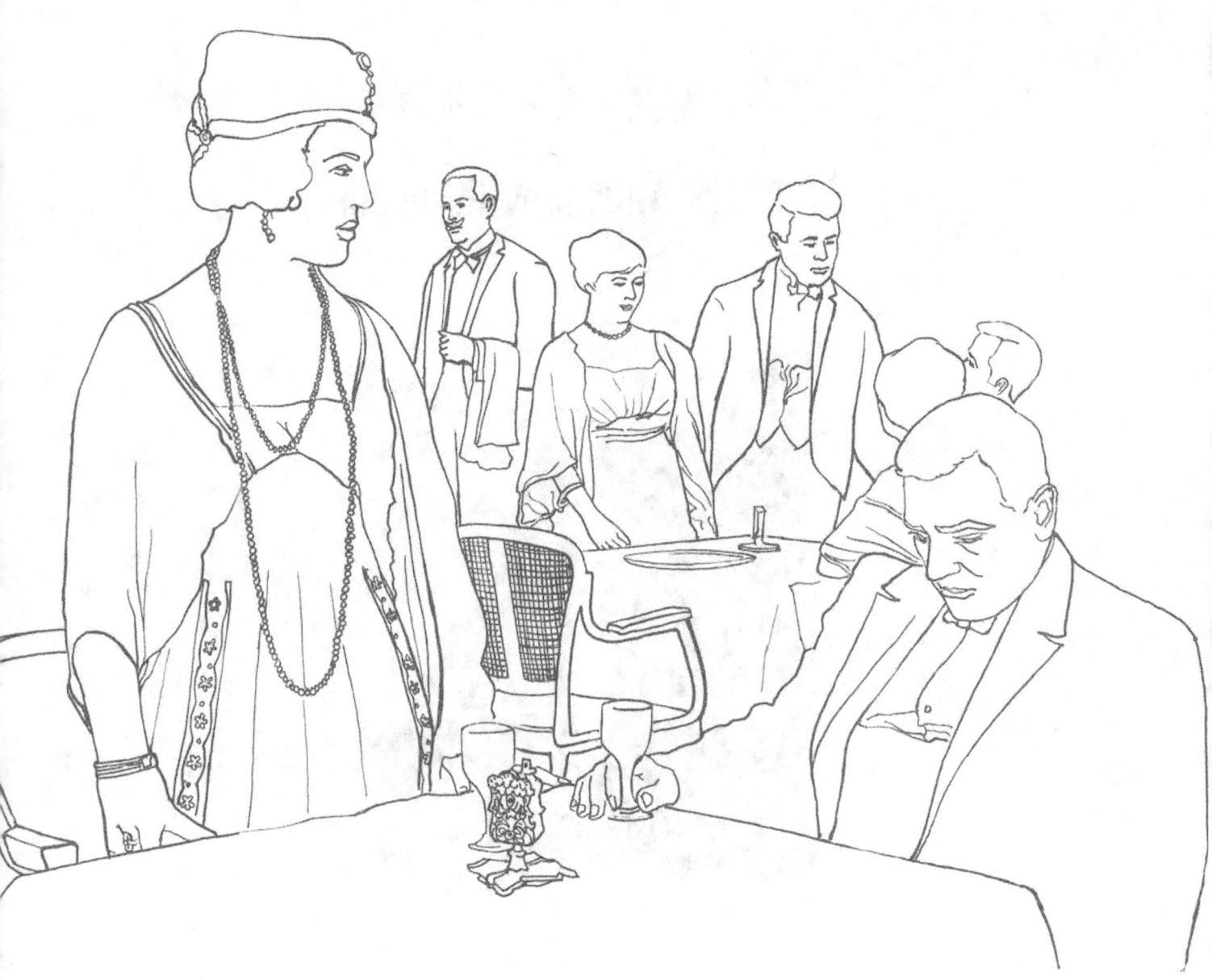

Never expect any assistance or consolation in thy necessities from drinking companions.

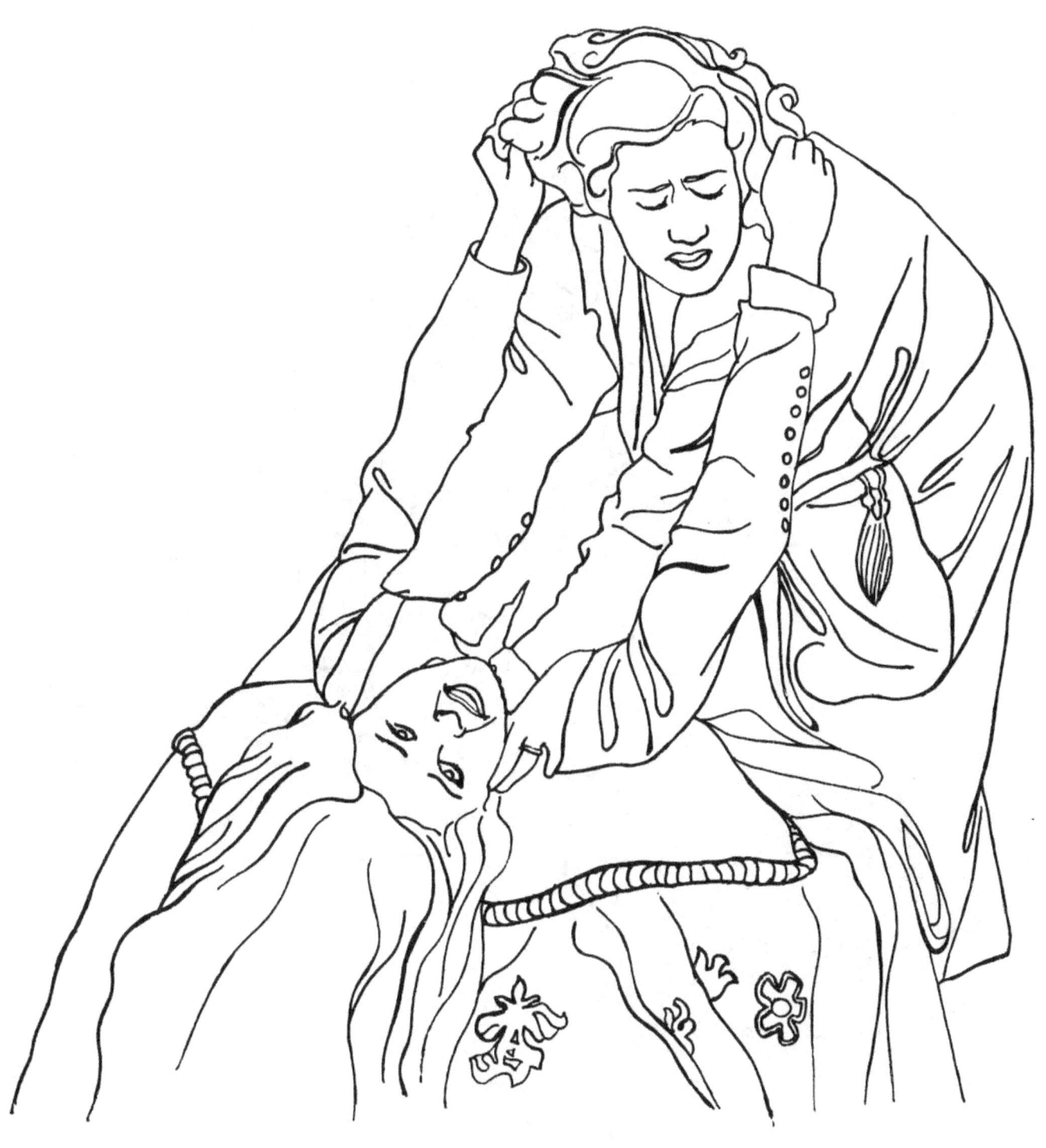

Be not provoked when opinions differ from your own.

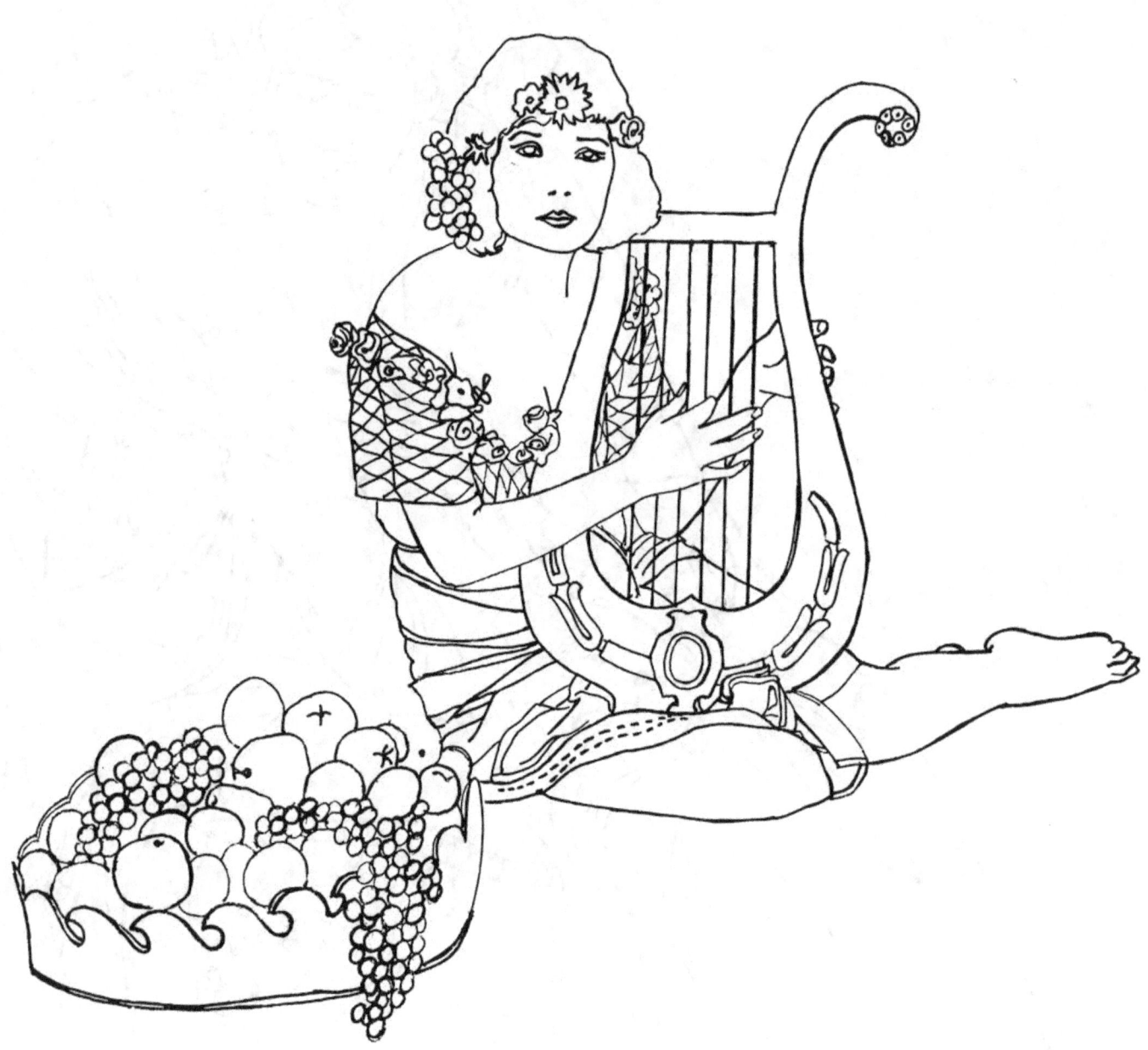

When asked to sing make no apology, but unobtrusively consent, considering it rather a compliment to be asked than not.

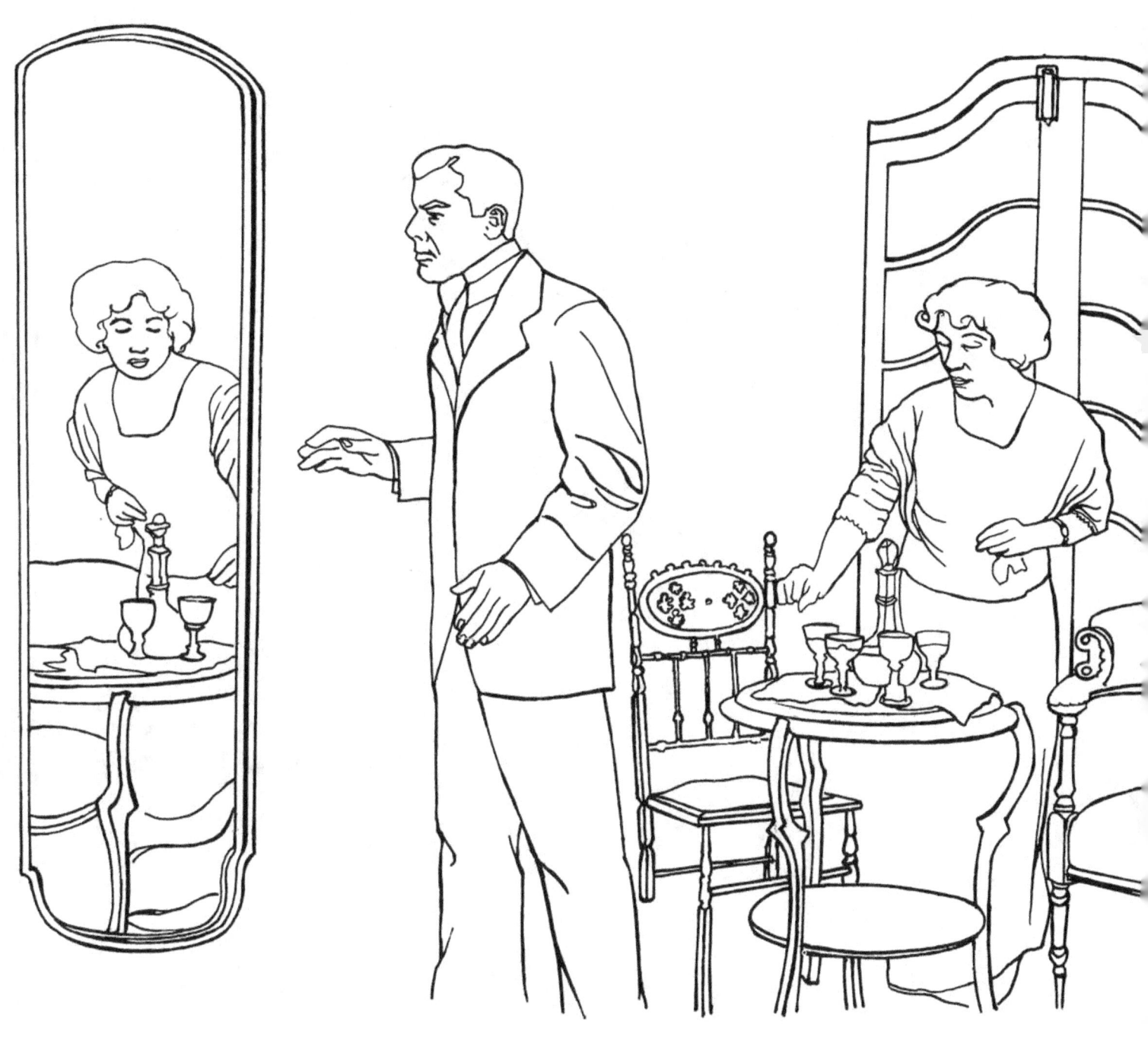

It is dreadful as well as dishonest to marry a man for his wealth, in hopes of his death.

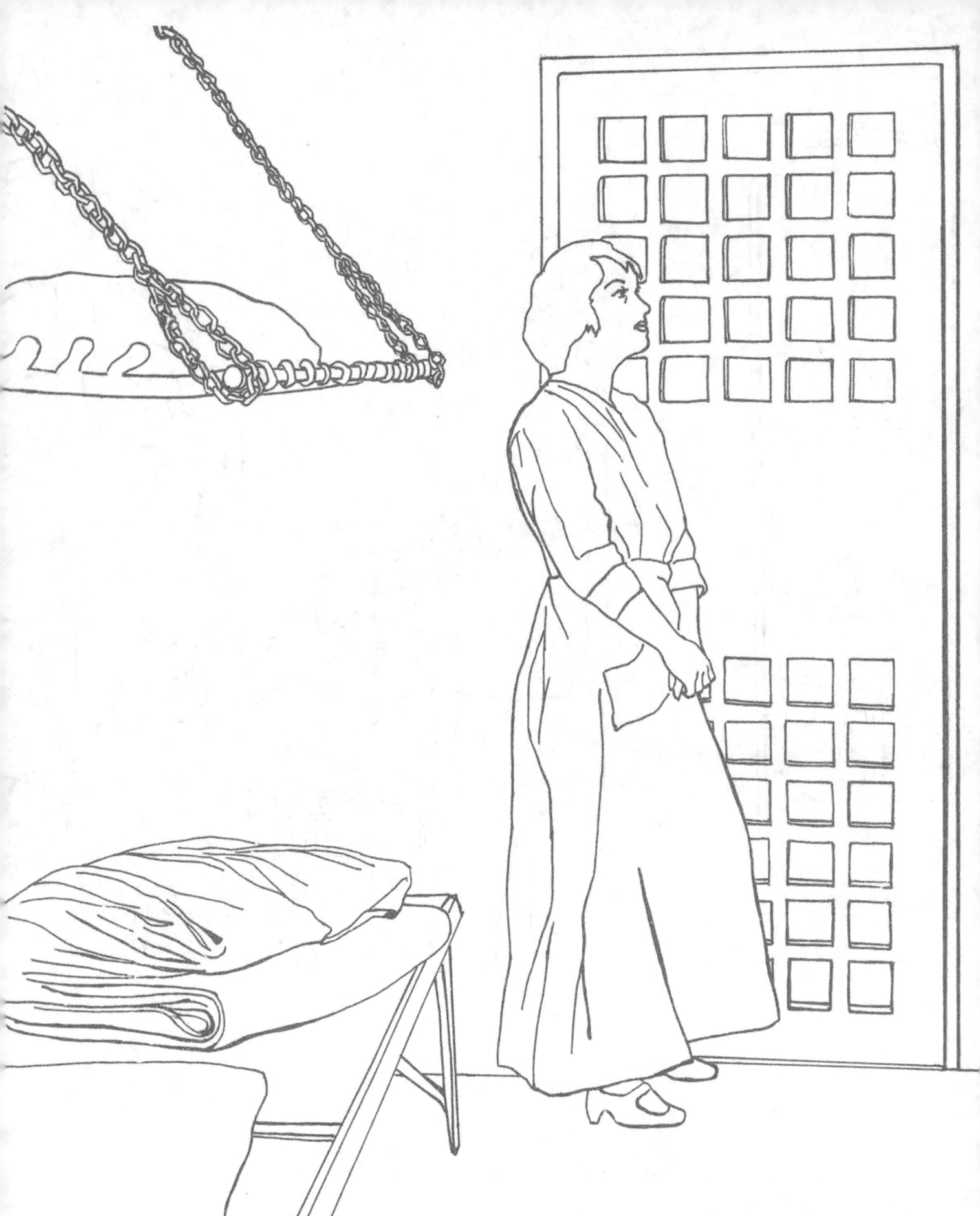

Ladies, beware of your eyebrows; use them discreetly, since very frequently they are either treacherous or imprudent.

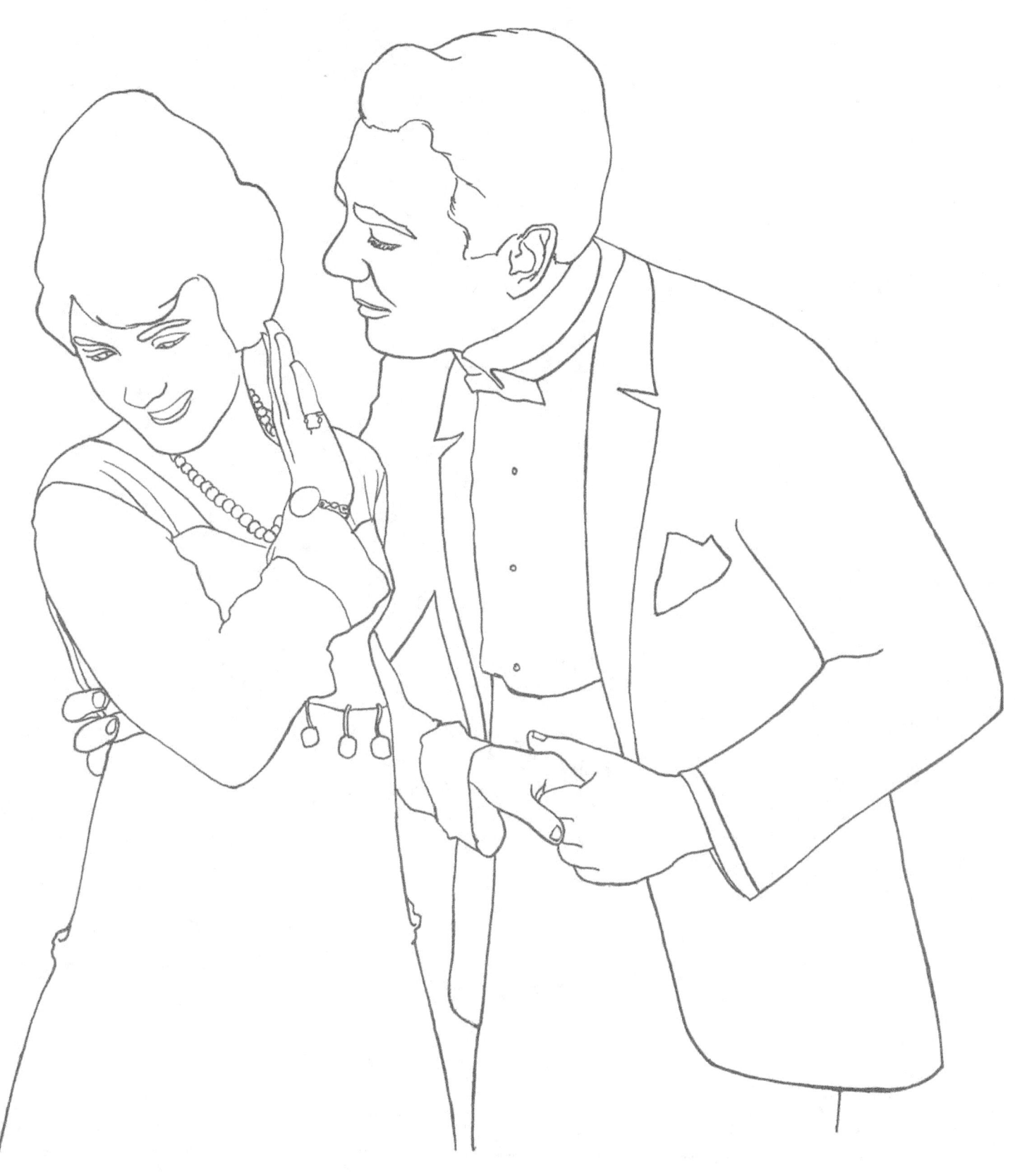

If you yield a little to flattery, you have placed yourself on a dangerous ground
...if you continue to yield, you are probably undone.

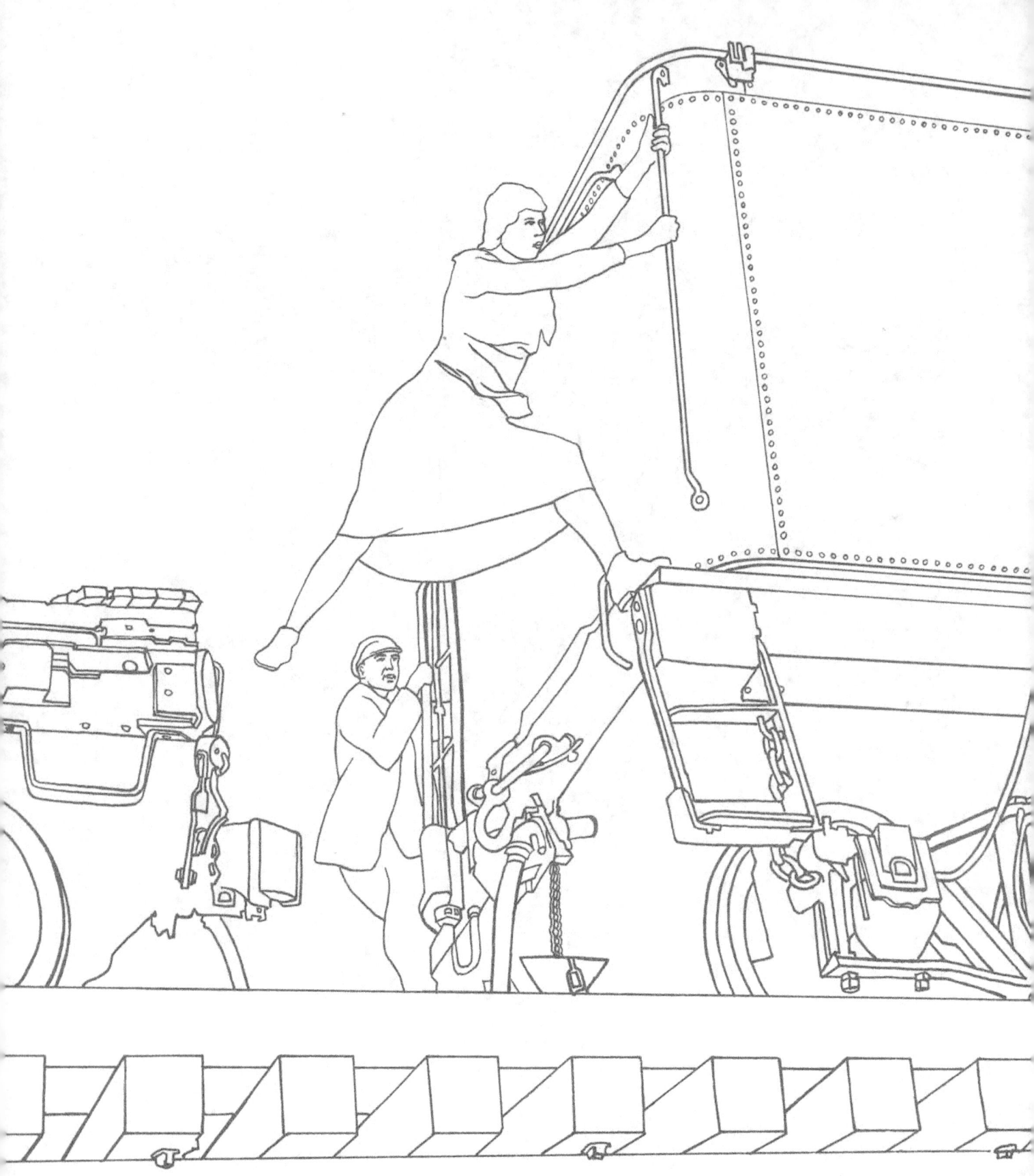

The only way to learn to do a thing is to do it...

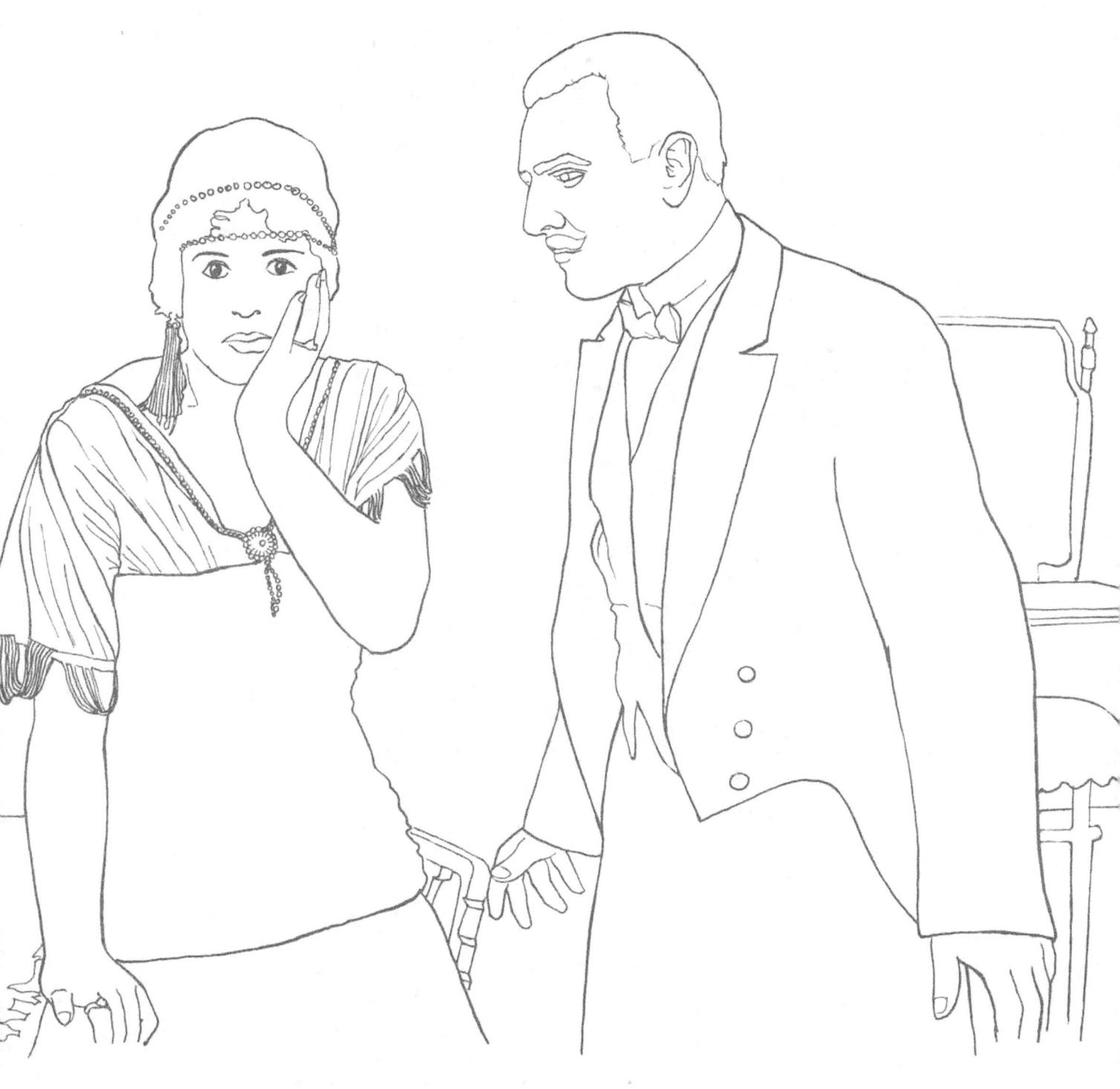

Ladies should never put pins in their mouths. Their lips should be roses without thorns.

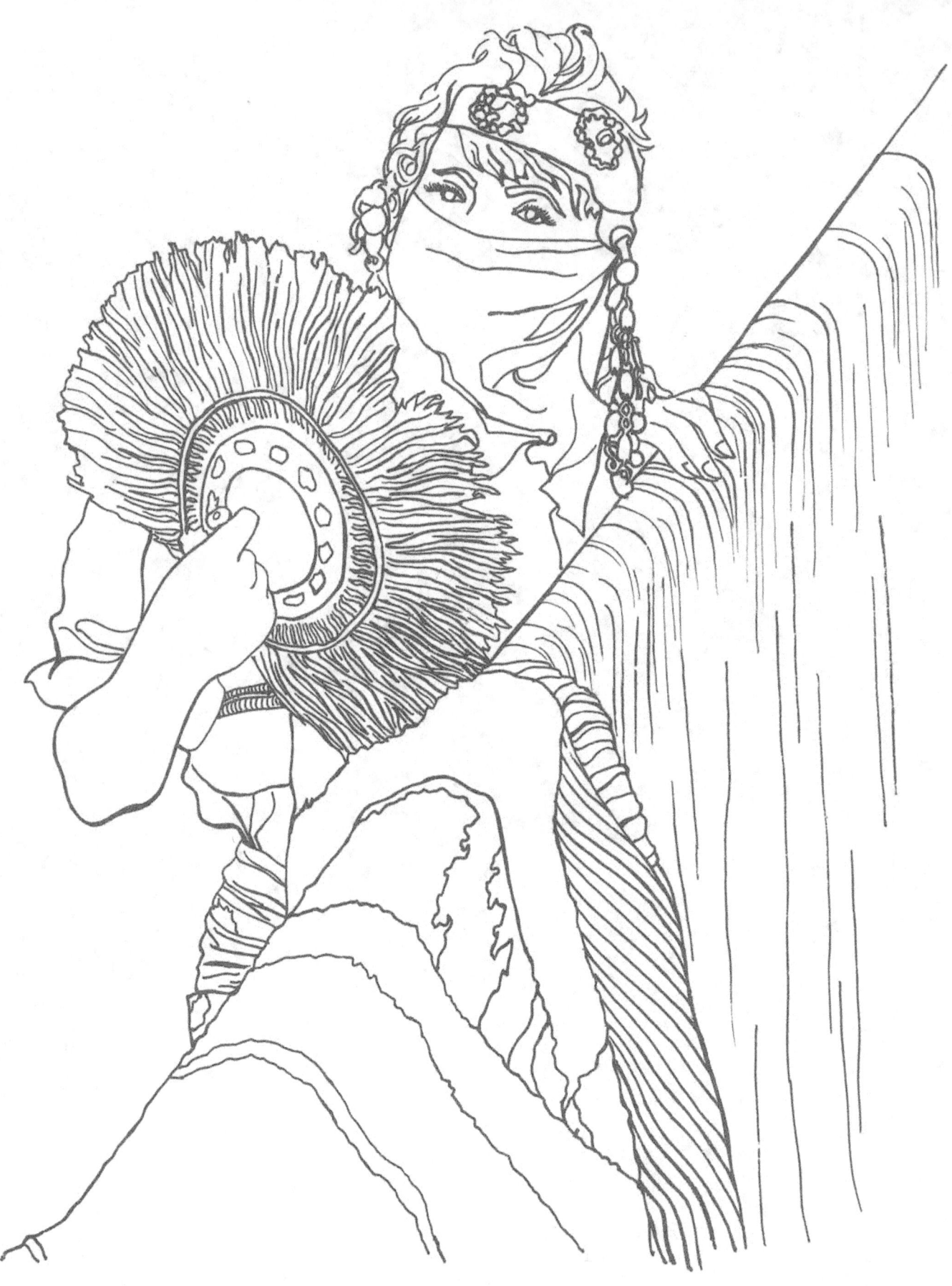

Where secrecy begins, vice is not far off.

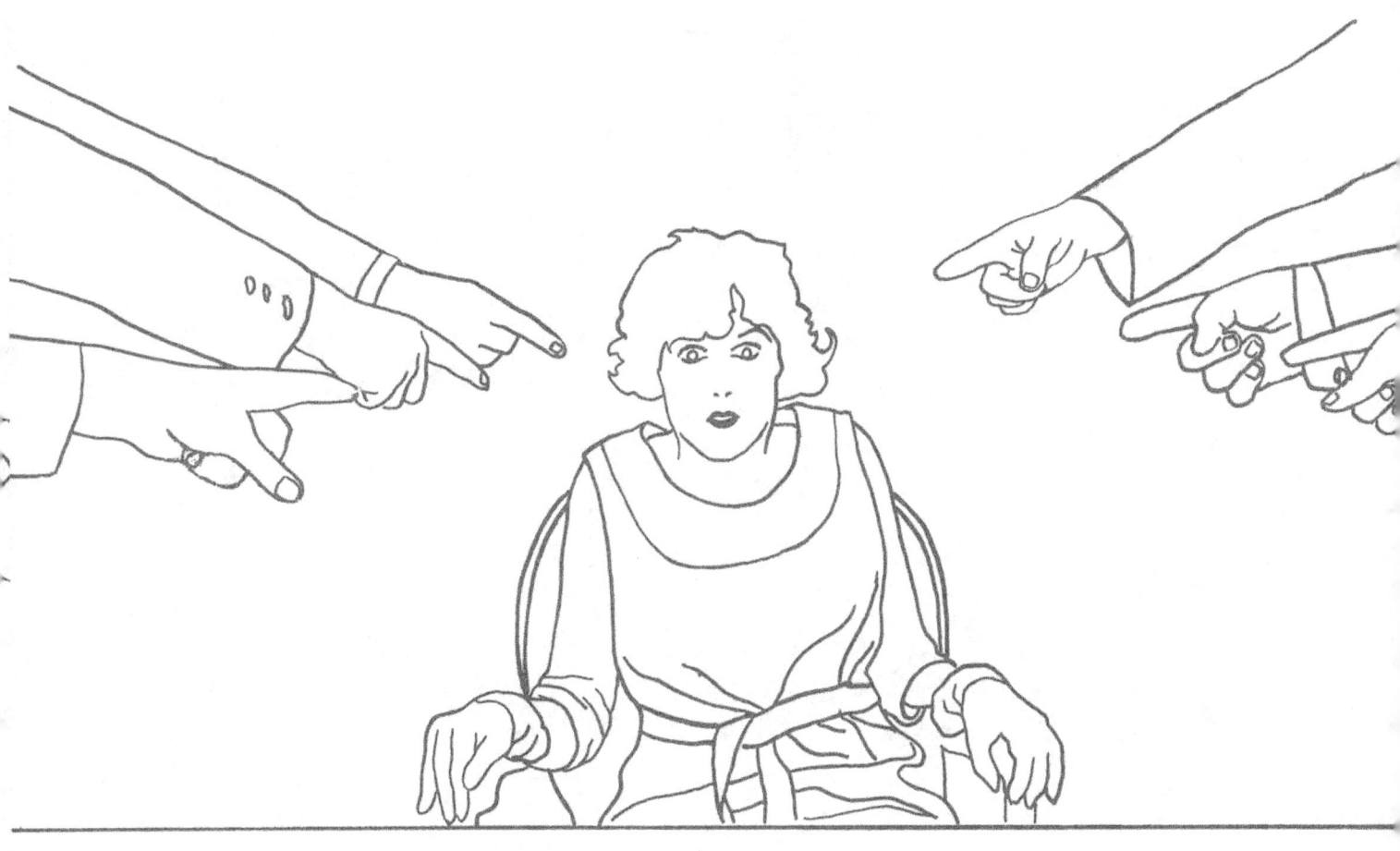

A flirting girl is indeed bad enough, but a flirting married woman should be an object of contempt wherever she appears.

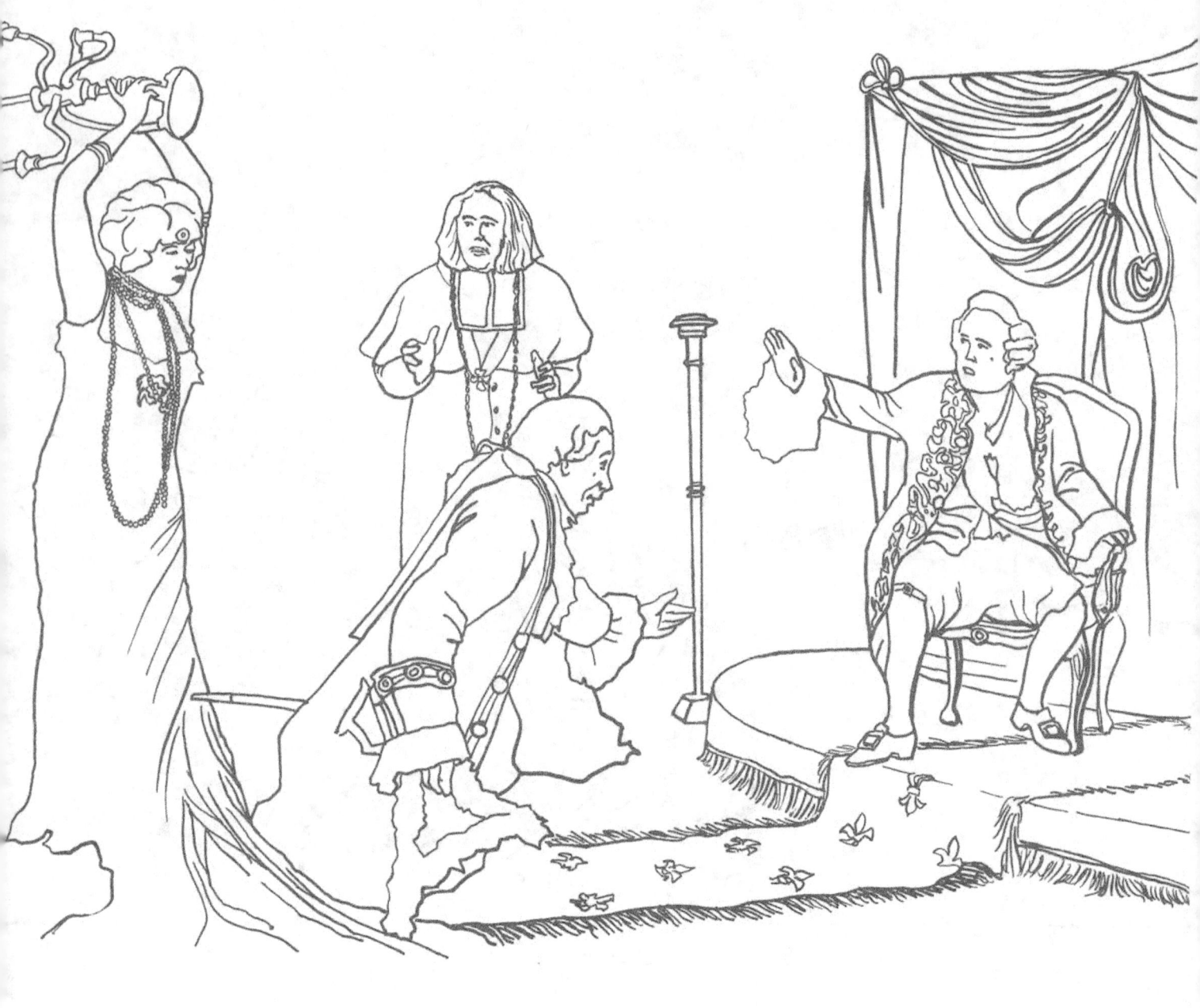

DECORUM! Women do not transgress the bounds of decorum so often as men; but when they do, they go greater lengths.

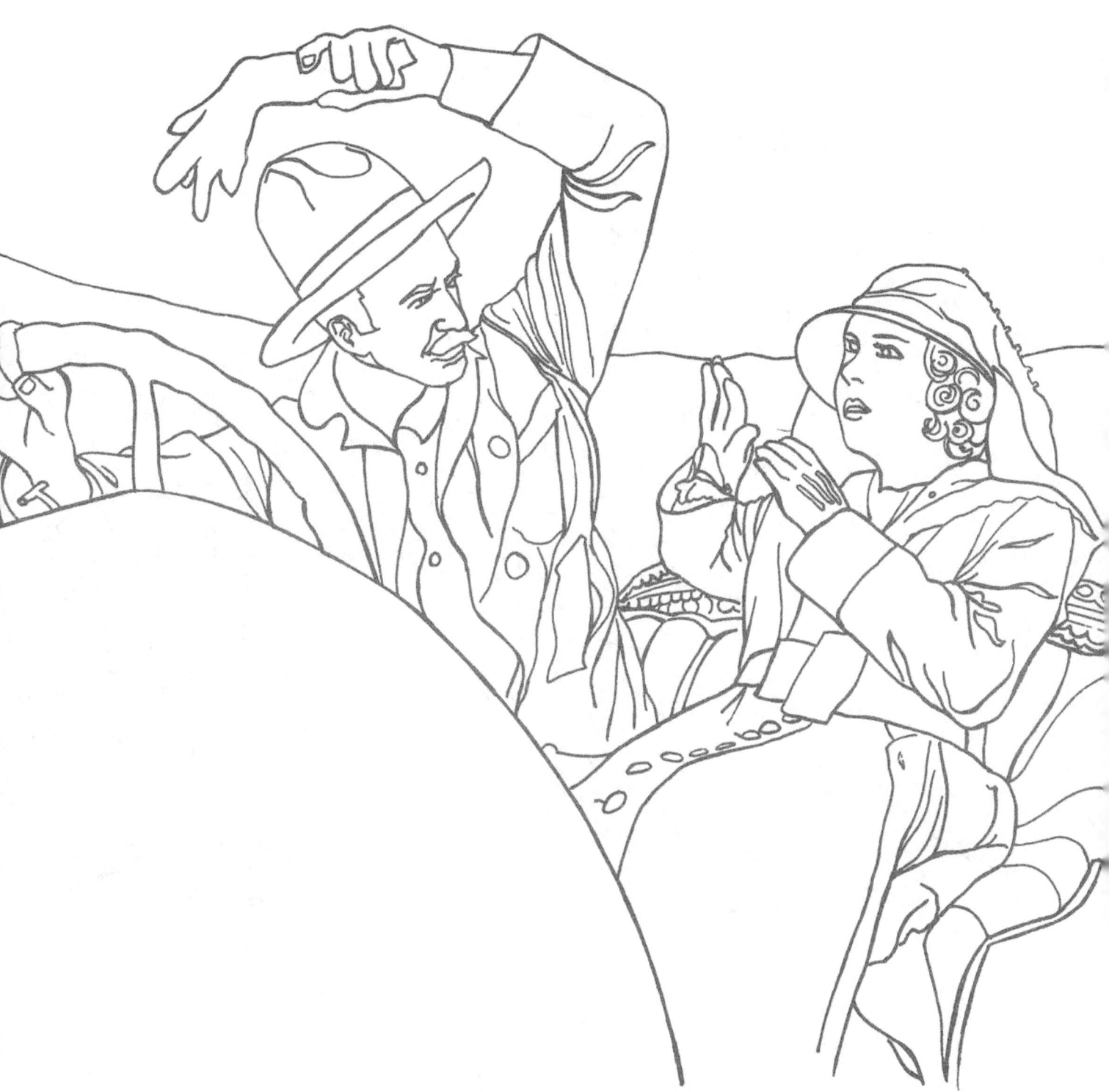

LOUD TALKING WOMEN...Persons desirous to be thought ladies sometimes converse screamingly in public vehicles, apparently for the purpose of attracting attention. They succeed, but the attention they elicit is not of a complimentary nature. Their gentler sisters are sorry and ashamed for them, and men are disgusted at such conduct.

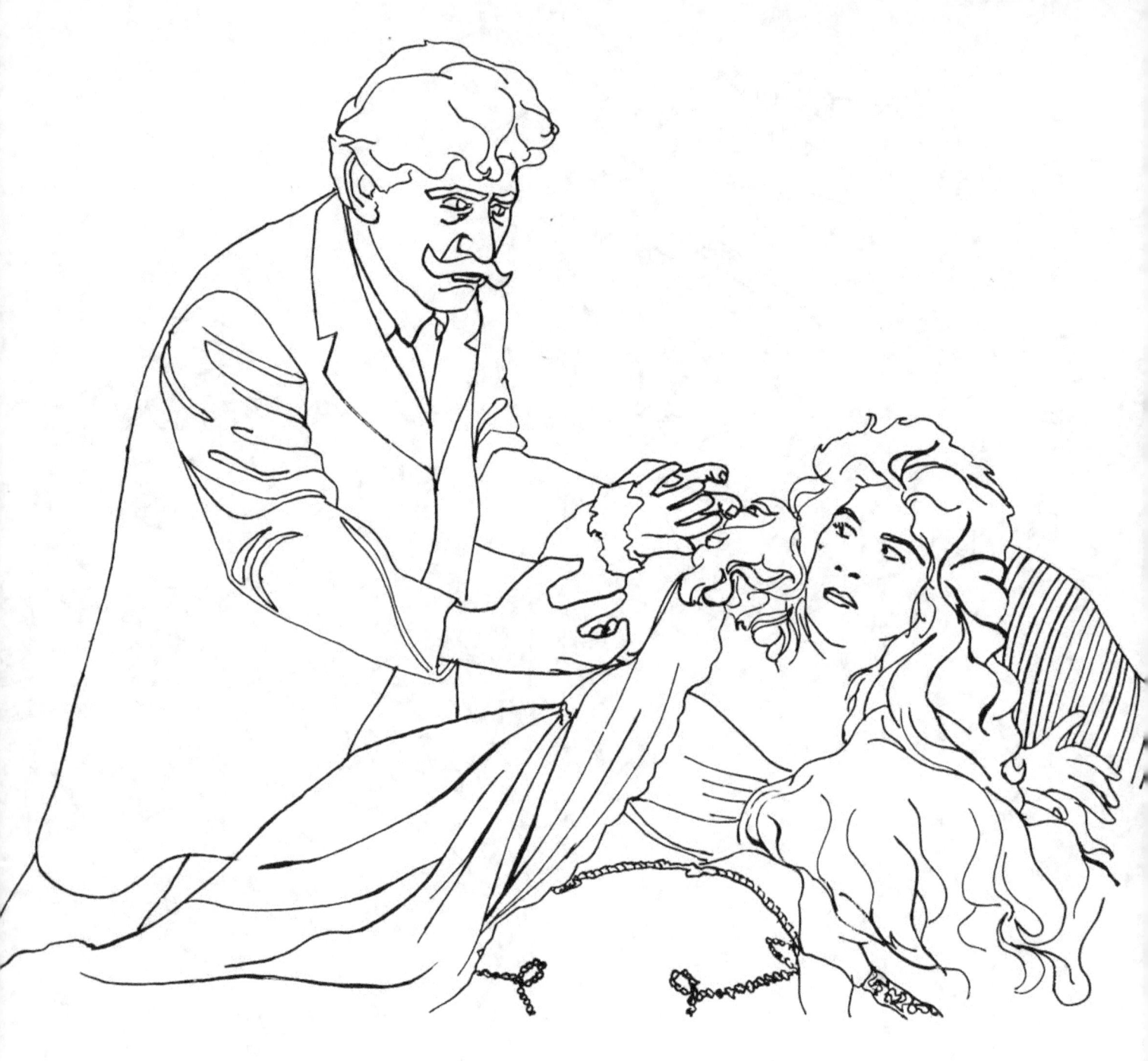

Love is an alliance of friendship and of lust; if the former predominate, it is a passion exalted and refined, but if the latter, gross and sensual.

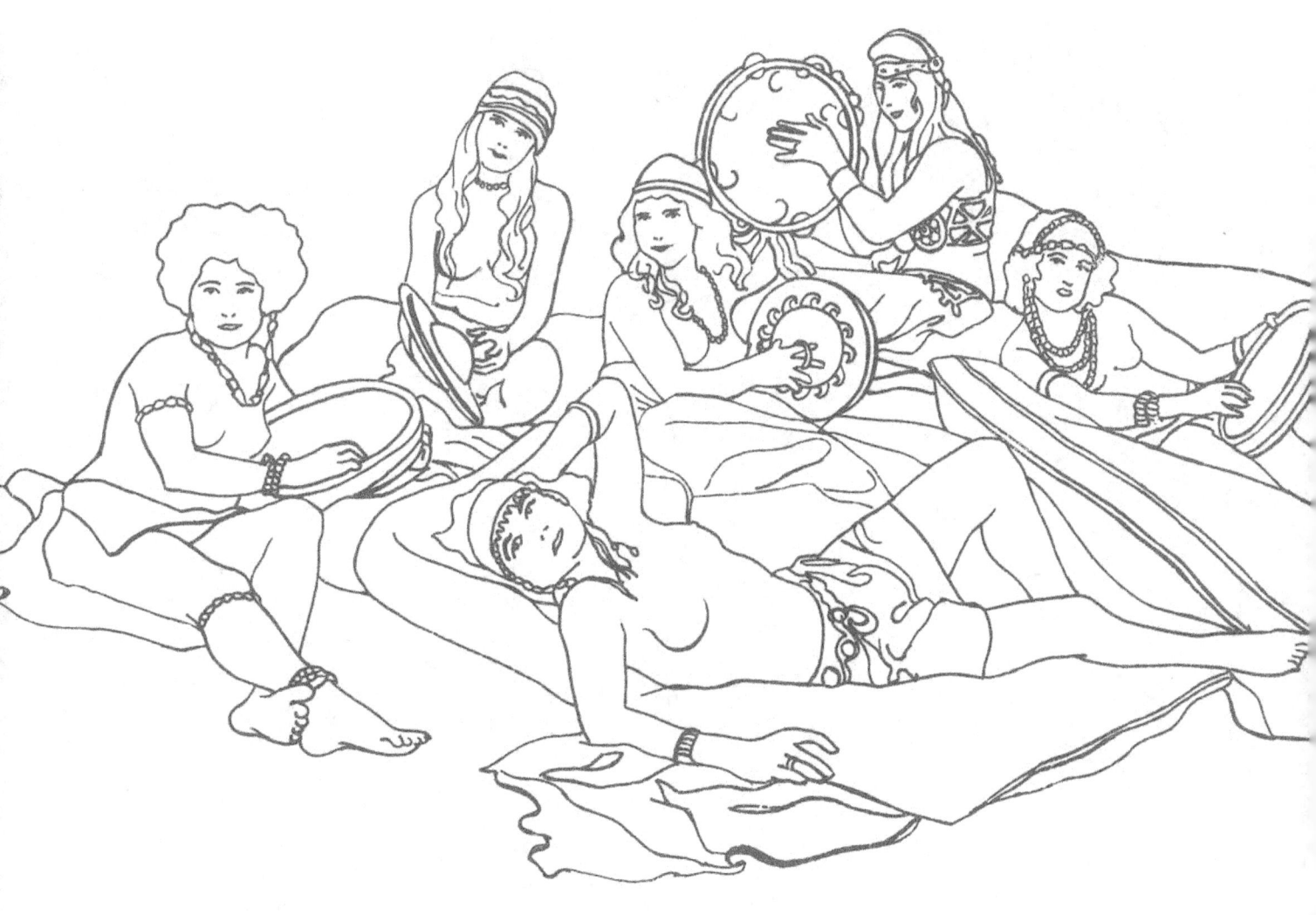

Be not ambitious to be considered a belle.... It is the fate of most belles that they become foolishly vain; think of nothing beyond personal display; and not infrequently sacrifice themselves in a mad bargain, which involves their destinies for life.

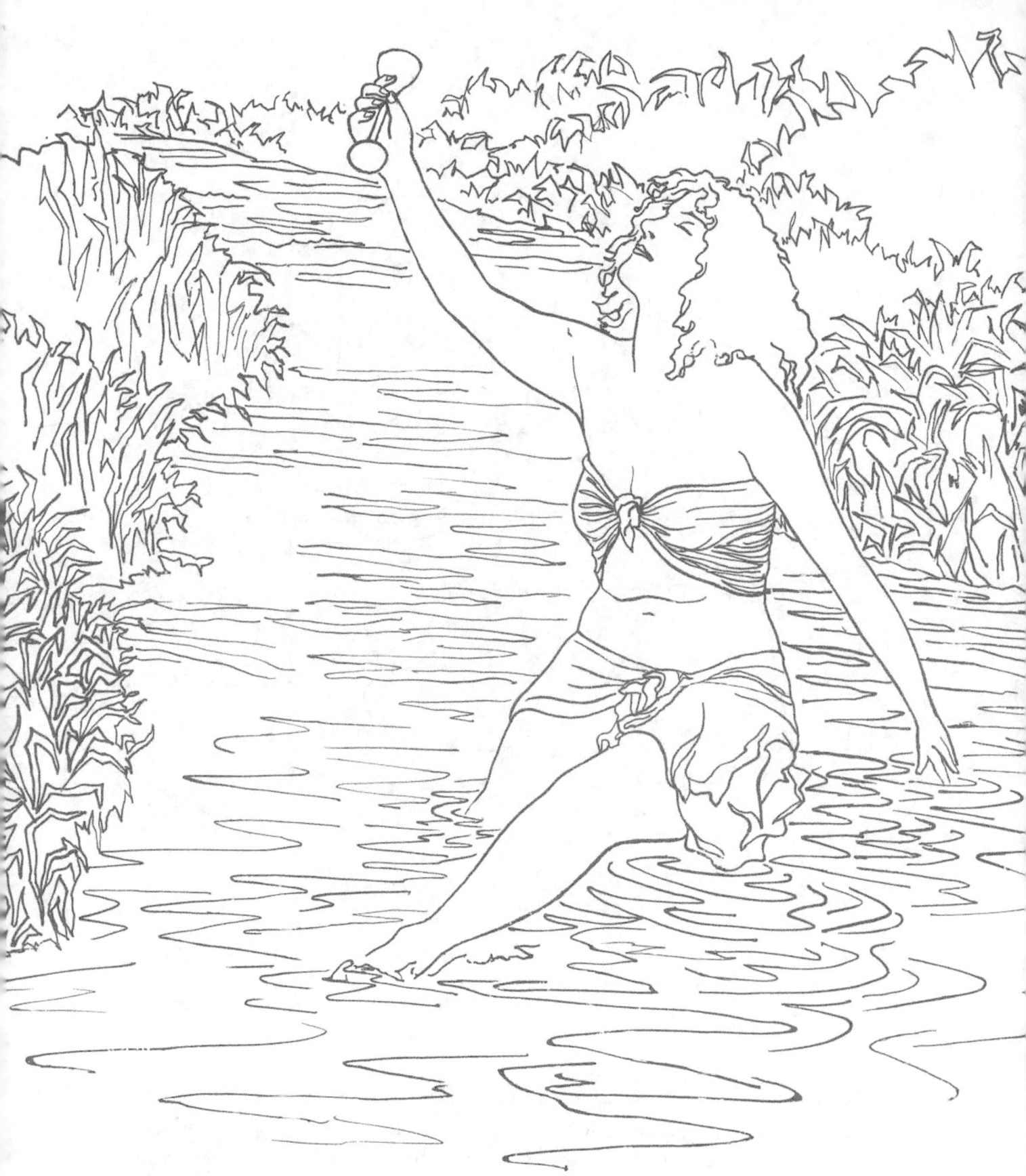

If you cannot be a great river, bearing great vessels of blessings to the world, you can be a little spring by the dusty wayside of life, singing merrily all day and night, and giving a cup of cold water to every weary, thirsty one who passes by.

Dr. J. K. Kannon
ON
Health and Happiness

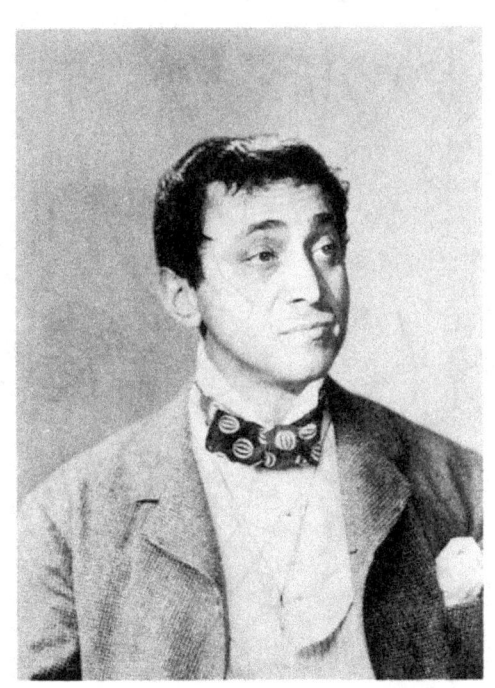

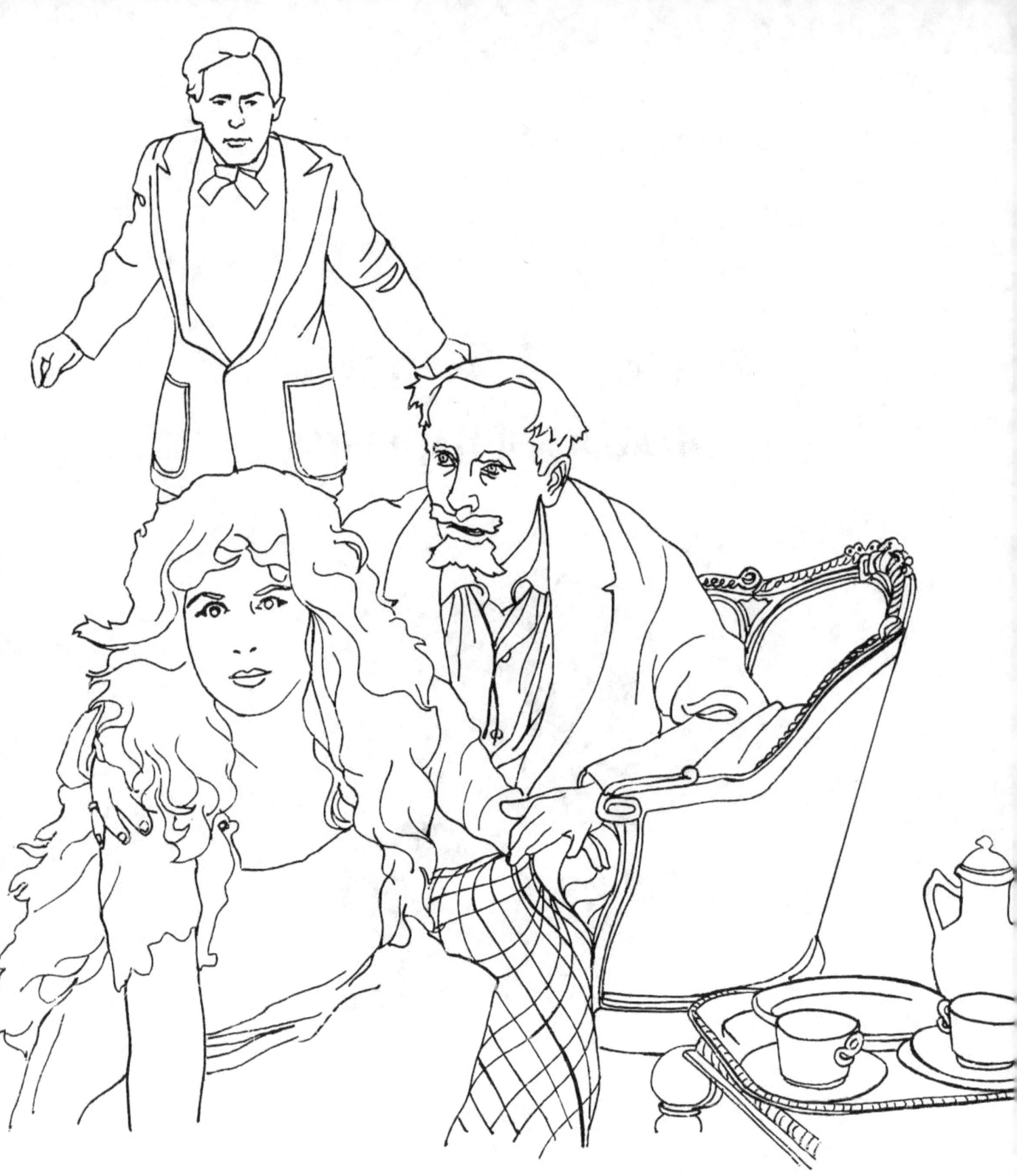

POISON! When you have reason to suppose that you have accidentally swallowed a poisonous substance, and proper medical advice is not at hand, take an emetic.

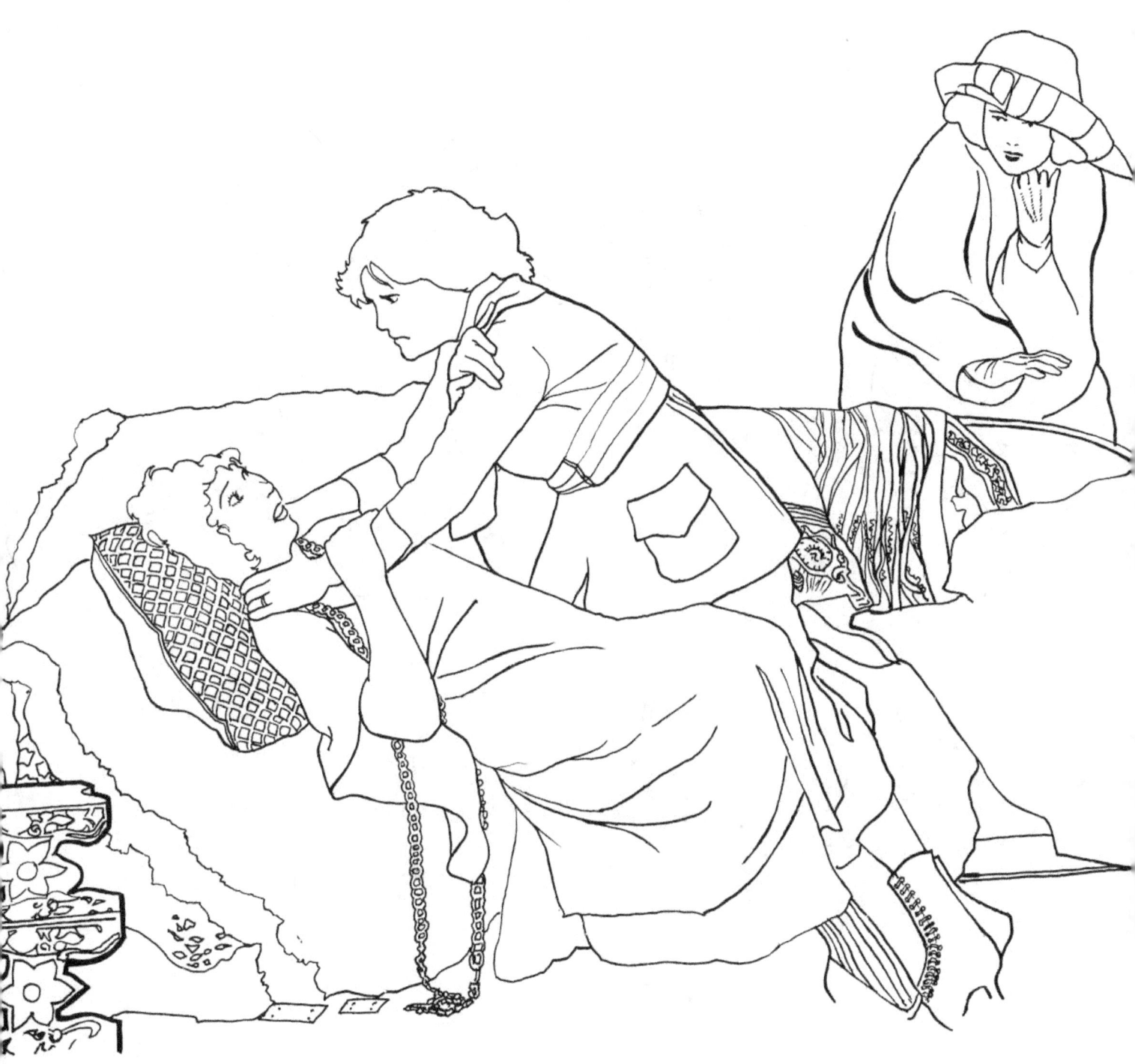

BENEFITS OF MASSAGE...A massage can be very stimulating, especially if administered by a competent practitioner. Results from manipulation of the joints can be most exhilarating.

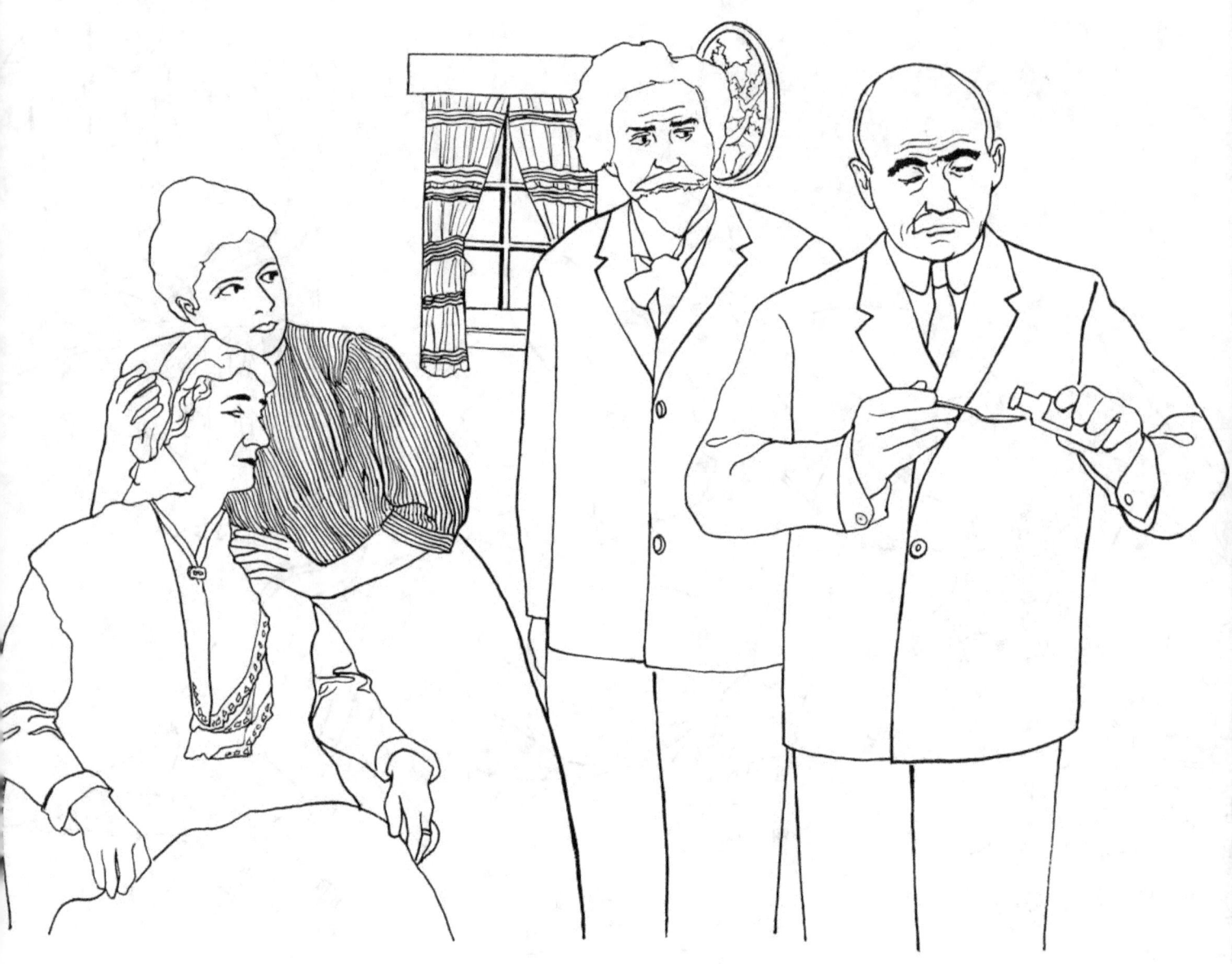

It is better to have recourse to a quack, if he can cure our disease, although he cannot explain it, than to a physician, if he can explain our disorder, but cannot cure it.

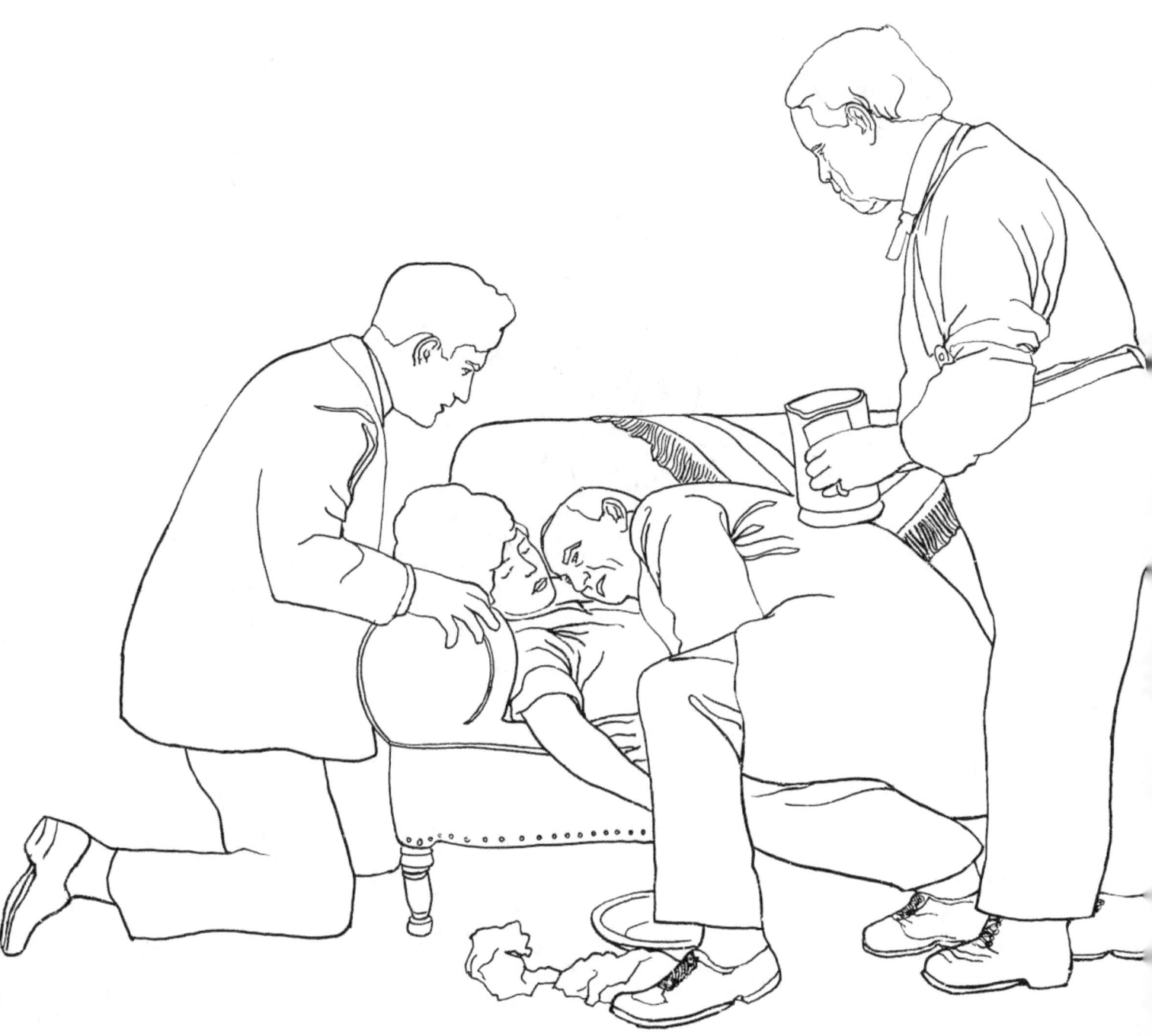

COLD AFFUSION... In diseases termed "inflammatory," what measure so ready or so efficacious as to dash a pitcher or two of cold water over the patient ... Cold Affusion, as it is called?

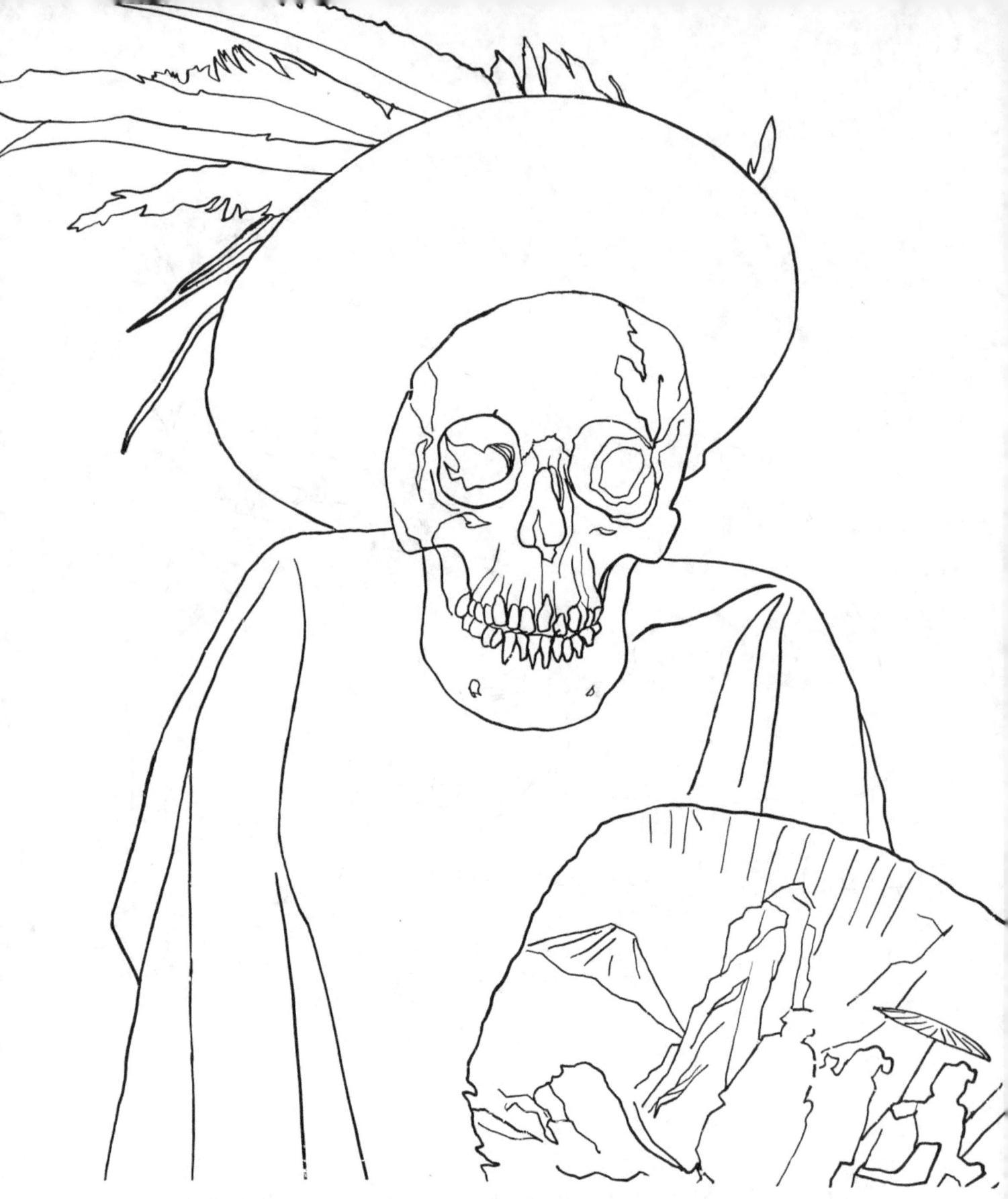

FRECKLES may be removed by the following ingredients, made into a wash:
One ounce of rectified spirits of wine, a teaspoonful of muriatic acid, applied
with a camel's hair pencil two or three time a day.

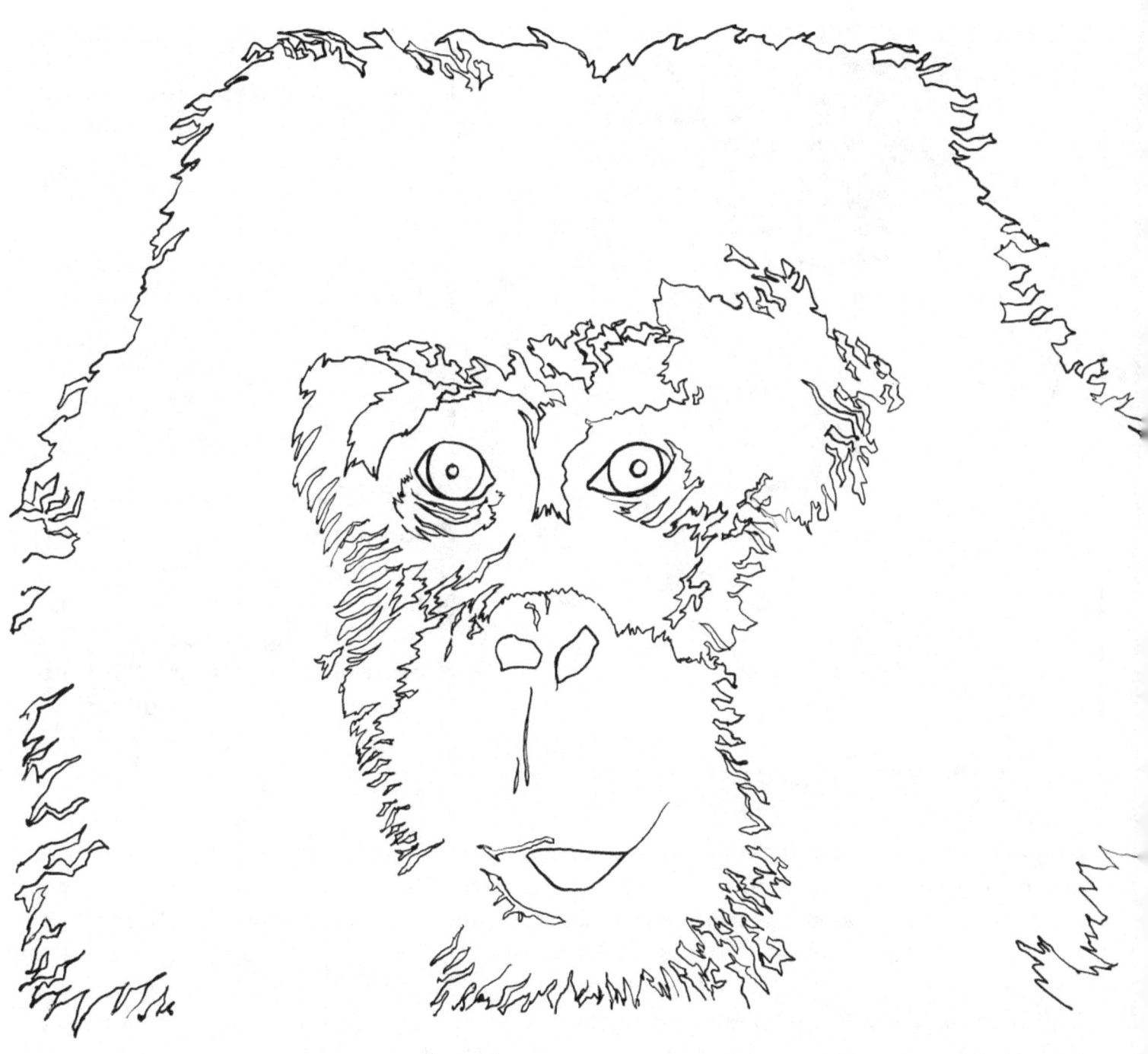

SCURF IN THE HEAD...A simple and effectual remedy. Into a pint of water drop a lump of fresh quick lime, the size of a walnut; let it stand all night, then pour the water off clear from sediment or deposit, add a quarter of a pint of the best vinegar, and wash the head with the mixture. Perfectly harmless; only wet the roots of the hair.

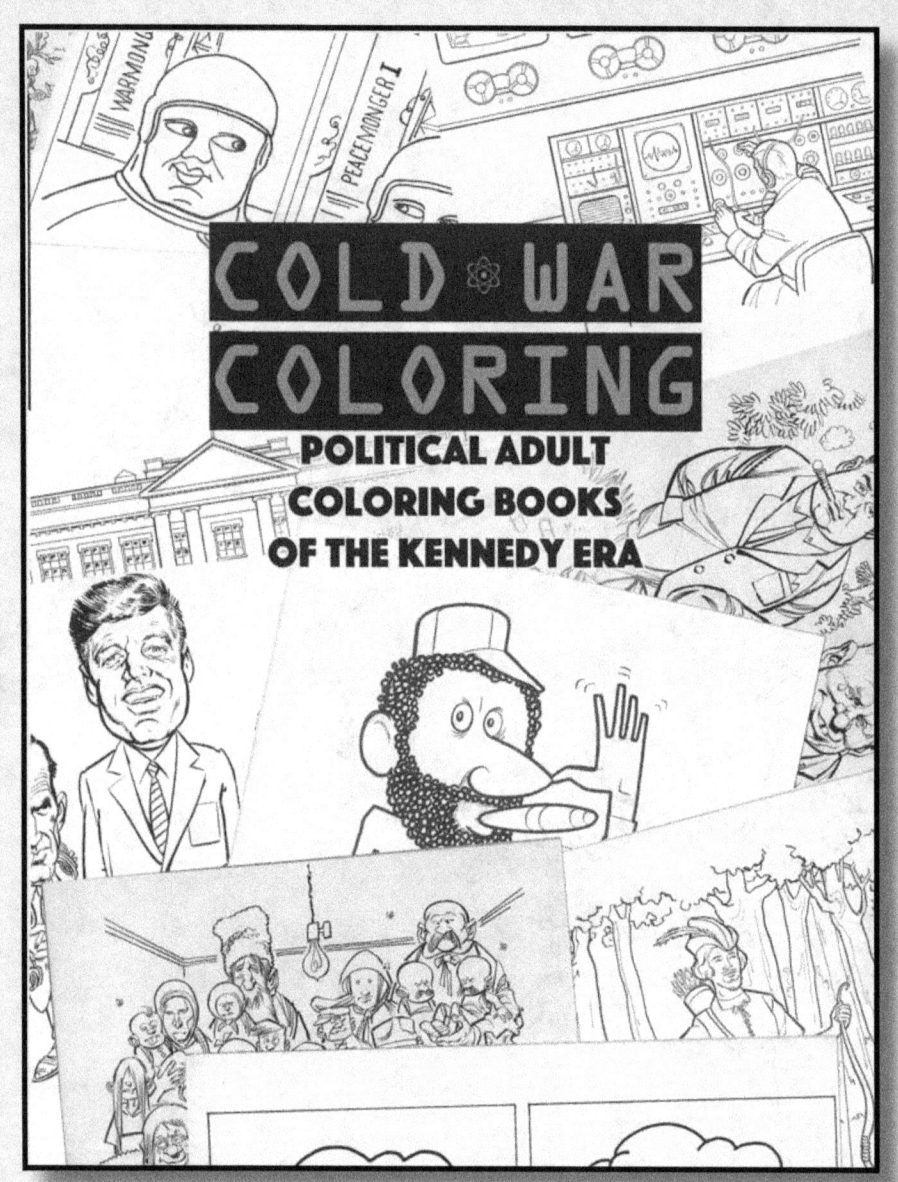

The first time adult coloring books swept America, they weren't therapeutic... they were satiric.

In the early 1960s, the first wave of parody coloring books used the form to mock the culture of the day. Here are five prime examples that took on the politic conflicts of that era. Most of these have been out of print for half a century.

JFK Coloring Book - a genuine *New York Times*-certified best seller, this look at the Kennedy White House, the Kennedy friends, and especially the Kennedy family contains beautiful art by Mort Drucker, master caricaturist from *Mad*.

New Frontier Comic Coloring Book - an all-out attack on the Kennedy administration, produced by Arthur J. Weaver, grandson of a Republican congressman, son of a Republican governor, brother of a Republican congressman and Republican gubernatorial candidate himself, and thus a personal expert on political dynasties.

Nikita Sergeyevich Khrushchev Coloring Book - a look at the notorious but colorful Soviet leader, written by Amram Ducovny, father of actor David Duchovny.

Khrushchev's Top Secret Coloring Book - with Gene Shalit on the writing and Jack Davis of *Mad* fame handling the art, the communists take it on the chin.

The John Birch Coloring Book – a poke at the right-wing John Birch Society, who were concerned about communists abroad and communists (real and perceived) at home.

COLD WAR COLORING
Published by About Comics.
Ask for it where you got this book!

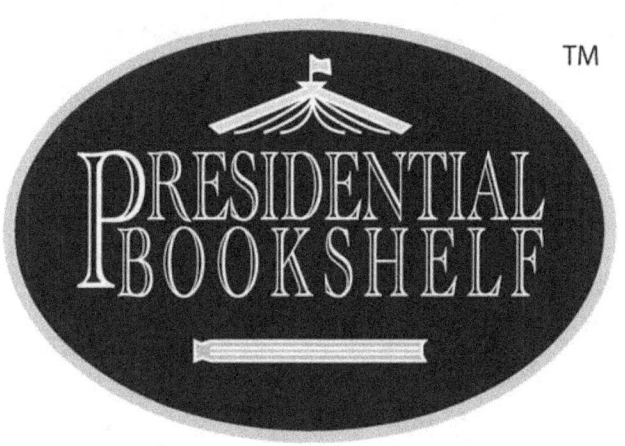

The **Presidential Bookshelf** project is designed to reflect on the American presidency from a wide variety of angles, whether ithrough the eyes of children, from the sharp pen of satirists, or from the words of the Presidents themselves. Books in this project are available at museum, presidential library, and national park gift shops, as well as online.

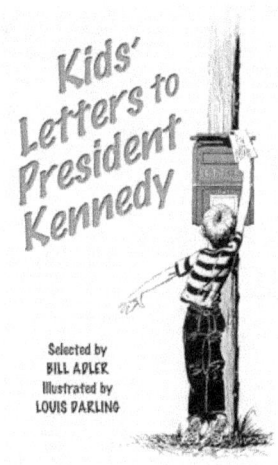

Kid's Letters to President Kennedy

From the early days of the JFK administration comes this collection of letters from the youth of America, edited by Bill Adler (creator of the *New York Times* best=seller *The Kennedy Wit*, profusely illustrated by Silent Spring artist Louis Darling.
ISBN 978-1936404-61-2

Dear President Johnson reveals children's letters to LBJ, edited by *New York Times* best-seller Bill Adler, illustrated by Peanuts creator Charles M. Schulz.
ISBN 978-1936404-56-8

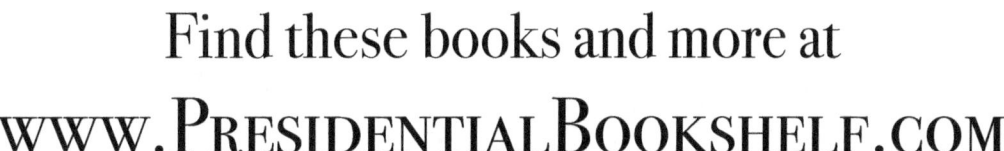

Find these books and more at
www.PRESIDENTIALBOOKSHELF.COM

www.ingramcontent.com/pod-product-compliance
Lightning Source LLC
Chambersburg PA
CBHW081716220526
45468CB00008B/1866